D0912888

The Grand Scribe's Records

VOLUME X

The Memoirs of Han China, Part III

The Grand Scribe's Records

VOLUME X

The Memoirs of Han China, Part III

by Ssu-ma Ch'ien

William H. Nienhauser, Jr.

Editor

Chiu Ming Chan, Hans van Ess, William H. Nienhauser, Jr.,
Thomas D. Noel, Marc Nürnberger, Jakob Pöllath,
Andreas Siegl, and Lianlian Wu

Translators

INDIANA UNIVERSITY PRESS

NANJING UNIVERSITY PRESS

This book is a copublication of

Indiana University Press
Office of Scholarly Publishin
Herman B Wells Library 350
1320 East 10th Street
Bloomington, Indiana 47405 USA
iupress.indiana.edu

and

Nanjing University Press
22 Hankou Road
Nanjing, Jiangsu, China

© 2016 by William H. Nienhauser, Jr.
© 2020 by William H. Nienhauser, Jr.

All rights reserved
No part of this book may be reproduced or utilized in any form or by any means, electronic or mechanical, including photocopying and recording, or by any information storage and retrieval system, without permission in writing from the publisher. The paper used in this publication meets the minimum requirements of the American National Standard for Information Sciences—Permanence of Paper for Printed Library Materials, ANSI Z39.48-1992.

Manufactured in the United States of America

Originally cataloged by the Library of Congress (and revised for volume 7 [1994]) as

Ssu-ma Ch'ien, ca. 145–ca. 86 B.C.
The grand scribe's records.

Includes bibliographical references and index.
Contents: v. 1. The basic annals of pre-Han China — v. 2. The basic annals
    of Han China v. 7. The memoirs of pre-Han China.
1. China—History—To 221 B.C. 2. China—History—Ch'in dynasty, 221-
    207 B.C. 3. China—History—Han dynasty 202 B.C.-220 A.D.
I. Nienhauser, William H. II. Cheng, Tsai Fa. III. Title.
DS741.3.S6813 1994
931—dc20   094-18408
ISBN 0-253-34021-7 (v. 1)
ISBN 0-253-34027-6 (v. 7)

ISBN 978-0-253-01931-8 (hdbk.)
ISBN 978-0-253-02069-7 (web PDF)

1 2 3 4 5   25 24 23 22 21 20

**DEDICATED TO
THREE OF MY FIRST TEACHERS**

Lillian Stolle Nienhauser,

Julie Harding Brown,

and Nancy Brown Nienhauser

CONTENTS

Acknowledgments

In the past nearly twenty-five years I've been reading the *Shih chi* with some regularity, often with large groups of other students of the *Shih chi*. It has been a memorable experience which has allowed me to meet with a number of scholars with similar interests around the world. Strangely, as I read more of the text carefully, I become less sure of things. This transformation made poignant recent comments by the centarian M. H. Abrams:

> The world of the prophet is a hot, intense world of total assurance that you have the humanistic truth that you know what we must do to be saved—and as such, it has great contemporary appeal. In comparison with the hot world of prophecy, the world of the liberal humanist is a cool world. What we need to get our students to recognize is that the stance of the liberal humanist is a very difficult one, which takes poise and courage to maintain."[1]

The title for our translations could have been changed to *Grand Scribes' Records* [from *Grand Scribe's Records*] to reflect evolving ideas about the authorship of the *Shih chi*. This current assumption might be best summed up by citing Hans van Ess:

> I am fully aware that his father Sima Tan must have written large parts of the *Shiji* . . . There are good reasons to believe that some chapters of the *Shiji* as we have them today go back to Sima Tan. . . .Yet I do not believe that is it possible to divide the *Shiji* into one part that was written by Sima Qian and one that derives from the hand of Sima Tan . . . I share Zhang Dake's view (*Shiji yanjiu*) . . . that the *Shiji* in the end was finished by Sima Qian and that, should there really have been major differences between his father's views and his own, we cannot say very much about them for sure today . . . For these reasons, whenever Sima Qian is mentioned . . . he is seen as the final editor of the *Shiji* whose ideas we can analyze today."[2]

The chapters in this volume have been produced and revised in various venues by a host of scholars. I am grateful to all for their effort, their knowledge, and their

---

[1] Cited from Vidyan Ravinthiran's review of Abrams *The Fourth Dimension of a Poem* (New York: Norton, 2012), *Times Literary Supplement* 24 May 2013: 12.

[2] See van Ess, "Cosmological Speculations and the Notions of the Power of Heaven and the Cyclical Movements of History in the Historiography of the *Shiji*," *BMFEA* 78 (2006). 79 [79–107], n. 2. See also my own statements on the authorship question in *Grand Scribes' Records*, 5.1 (Bloomington: Indiana University Press, 2006), xviii–xix), *Grand Scribes' Records*, 8 (2008), p. ix and n. 3, and especially "Sima Qian and the *Shiji*," *Oxford History of Historical Writing, Volume I: Beginnings to AD 600*. Grant Hardy and Andrew Feldherr, eds. (Oxford: Oxford University Press, 2011), p. 474.

patience. Chapters 114 and 115 were done in Singapore during my stay at Nanyang Technical University in Spring 2011. Our reading group there consisted of Chiu Ming Chan, Jia Li, Jifen Liu, So Jeong Park, Michael Puett, Jingyi Qu, Winnie Song, and Shoucheng Yan. Chapters 113 and 116 were prepared and thoroughly discussed in the summer of 2011 in Munich. Thanks to the Alexander von Humboldt Foundation Thomas D. Noel and I were able to work at the University of Munich for two months. Han van Ess' reading group was then made up of Vera Dorofeeva-Lichtmann, Maria Khayutina, Marc Nürnberger, Jakob Pöllath, Andreas Siegl and Anna Stecher. Chapters 117, 118 and 120 were first presented in June 2012 in Munich and then were the focus of discussion at the Sixth International Workshop on the *Shih chi* held in Madison in October 2012; the participants were Zhi Chen, Hans van Ess, Bernhard Führer, Rania Huntington, Bruce Knickerbocker, Zongli Lu, Hans-Georg Moeller, Mark Meulenbeld, Julia Murray, Marc Nürnberger, Jakob Pöllath, Michael Puett, Andreas Siegl, Jingyi Qu, Jia Li, Aaron Reich, Dewei Shen, and Yiwen Shen. Two subsequent smaller meetings on Chapter 117 were held at Hong Kong Baptist University (17–18 January 2013), hosted by Zhi Chen, and at Bernhard Führer's invitation in St. Julien de Lampon, France (11–14 September 2013).

Much gratitude is also owed the Center for Advanced Study (CAS), Ludwig Maximilian University of Munich, which has supported my research in Munich the past three summers. During my tenure at CAS in June 2013 and June 2014, Chapters 115, 119 and 121 were completed and discussed by an expanded Munich *Shih chi* group including Maddalena Barenghi, Panlam Chuen, Sebastian Eitel, Guje Kroh, Clara Luhn, Kathrin Messing, Marc Nürnberger, Jakob Poellath, Florian Shirk, Andreas Siegl, Anna Stecher, and Katrin Weiss. All of these chapters have at one time or another been read by the ever evolving *Shih chi* reading group here in Madison which over the past three years has included Min An, Aaron Balivet, Yaping Cai, Yang Gu, Maria Kobzeva, Hai Liu, Lu Lu, Xiang Lü, Ning Luo, Nan Ma, Thomas D. Noel, Youyong Qian, Ying Qin, Dewei Shen, Yiwen Shen, Henghua Su, Chen Wu, Lianliang Wu, Yinyin Xue, Fang Yan, Hong Yan, Shuxiang You, and Xin Zou.

Following this long list of scholars who have contributed to our project, a word is needed about momentum. Over the past several years I admit to having felt that perhaps I had done all I could with the *Shih chi*. However, Hans van Ess has encouraged me to continue the work. His contributions to the project in recent years have been immense and inspiring. In June 2013, while walking through several rooms devoted to an exhibition of Jan Brueghel the Elder at the Alte Pinakothek in Munich, I was struck by Brueghel's method of cooperating with a number of painters.[3] Brueghel worked most closely with Hendrick van Balen, often skillfully brushing landscapes himself while depending on van Balen's skills provided the vitally important staffage. Brueghel and

---

[3] Including his friend Peter Paul Rubens and Hans Rottenhammer among others. Ruben's Madonna Ringed in Flowers, Rottenhammer's figure of the saint added to Brughel's *Waldschafter mit dem hl. Hieronymus*.

van Balen both lived on Lange Nieuwstratt in Antwerp and scholars believe that some paintings were shipped back between the ateliers of these two artists and composed in several stages. This cooperation suggests the relationship between Hans van Ess and myself for nearly a decade.

Receiving a signed copy of the new edition of the *Shih chi* from Professor Chao Sheng-ch'ün 趙生群 and his fellow editors was a special gift. Although we have not been able to use this new edition extensively in translations for this volume, it promises to be a basic text for future renditions (see also the Introduction below).

I am particularly grateful to Maria Kobzeva who has produced the maps, done the indexing, and generally helped bring this volume into shape, and to David Miller of Indiana University Press, whose careful eye helped avoid a number of formatting slips. As in previous volumes, thanks are also due to Teresa Nealon who skillfully managed the finances here in Madison. On the home front my wife Judith remains patient and supportive throughout the paper storms that this new volume has brought.

William H. Nienhauser, Jr.
October 2014

Introduction

"The time has come," the Walrus said

This past year has seen the publication of two important works on the *Shih chi* 史記. The first is Hans van Ess's two volume *Politik und Geschichtsschreibung im alten China, Pan-Ma i-t'ung* 班馬異同 (2v.; Wiesbaden: Harrassowitz, 2014), the result of over a decade of van Ess's careful readings of the *Shih chi* and *Han shu* 漢書. The second is the newly edited edition of the *Shih chi*,[1] completed over a similar period by a team of eight scholars at Nan-ching Shih-fan Ta-hsüeh 南京師範大學 under the leadership of Chao Sheng-ch'ün 趙生群.

Professor van Ess' study deserves a more thorough reading than could be provided here. Suffice it to say that over the last eleven years I have been reading and translating the *Shih chi* with Hans van Ess and that his ideas have found their way into many of the translations and translator's notes in this volume.

Although the new *Shih chi* edition has not been consulted for most of the chapters included in this tenth volume of the *Grand Scribe's Records* (it was published in September 2013 after most of the translations herein were completed), it deserves a brief introduction. The new edition begins with a "Tien-chiao pen erh-shih-ssu chi Ch'ing shih kao hsiu-ting yüan-ch'i" 點校本二十四史及清史稿修訂緣起 (On the Origins of the Revisions of the Collated Edition of the Twenty-four Histories and the History of the Ch'ing) which explains the reasons for undertaking a new critical edition for these twenty-five histories. This is followed by Professor Chao's "Hsiu-ting ch'ien-yen" 修訂前言 (Preface to the Revision) which incorporates some material from the "Ch'u-pan shuo-ming" 出版說明 in the 1959 edition of the Chung-hua *Shih chi* and offers more details concerning the evolution of the 1959 edition. That first edition was based on a draft prepared by Ku Chieh-kang 顧頡剛 (1893–1980) and Ho Tz'u-chün 賀次君 (1914–1988) which Sung Yün-pin 宋雲彬 (1897–1979) worked into a draft text. This draft was final edited by Nieh Ch'ung-ch'i 聶崇歧 (1903–1962).[2]

---

[1] Newly edited versions of the *Shih chi jen-ming so-yin* 史記人名索引, *Shih chi ti-ming so-yin* 史記地名索引, and *Shih chi "San-chia chu" yin shu so-yin* 史記三家注引書索引 are all forthcoming.

[2] See also the present author's "Historians of China," *CLEAR* 17 (1995) 207-16 and the

The new 2013 edition of the *Shih chi* is—as was the 1959 edition—based on the Chin-ling Shu-chü 金陵書局 text, but it has been collated with over a dozen other early texts and manuscripts; the textual notes by Liang Yü-sheng 梁玉繩 (1745–1819), Ch'ien Ta-hsin 錢大昕 (1728–1804), Wang Nien-sun 王念孫 (1744–1832), Chang Wen-hu 張文虎 (1808–1885), Takigawa Kametarô 瀧川龜太郎 (1865–1946), Mizusawa Toshitada 水澤利忠 and others, as well as parallel passages in the *Han shu* 漢書, are also cited regularly (see pp. x–xii in the Preface).

A recent communication from Su P'eng 蘇芃, one of the eight editors, explains that the editorial responsibilities were divided among the team with Fang Hsiang-tung 方向東 responsible for collating the Chin-ling Shu-chü edition, Wu Hsin-chiang 吳新江 comparing the Yüan dynasty P'eng Yin-weng 彭寅翁 edition, Wang Yung-chi 王永吉 examining Mao Chin's *Ku-ko tan So-yin* 毛晉汲古閣單索隱 edition, Su P'eng collating the Huang Shang-fu 黃善夫 edition along with some old manuscript editions, and Chao Sheng-ch'ün studying the Northern Sung-dynasty Ching-yu 景祐 edition together with other old manuscripts. Professor Chao then wrote the introductory materials.[3]

Volume 10 contains the original "Tien-chiao hou-chi" 點校後記 (now retitled "*Shih chi* tien-chiao hou-chi" 史記點校後記, pp. 4055–4077), but includes a new section, "Chu-yao ts'an-k'ao wen-hsien" 主要參考文獻 (Selected Bibliography of Important Texts), which again provides details on the texts that have been collated (including Tun-huang materials and Japanese manuscript editions) and consulted (primarily newly published critical editions of about 150 classical works published since 1959).

A comparison of the 1959 rendition of chapter 115, "Ch'ao-hsien lieh-chuan" 朝鮮列傳 (Memoir of Ch'ao-hsien), to that of the new edition version revealed few differences. The pagination differs greatly (pp. 2985–90 in the 1959 edition vs. 3593–3600 of the new version). The chapter concludes with a page of collational notes, but most of the increase in size is due to a slightly larger type size employed in the new edition. Professor Chao and his team have made two changes in the text: the correction of a typographical error (*ch'i* 期 replaced the erroneous *chao* 朝 on p. 3597, line 1) and Lieh-k'ou 洌口 became Lieh-k'ou 列口 in the final paragraph of the new text (p. 3598, line 1). There were also two or three changes in punctuation and several places where, although text-critical notes indicated a change was needed, none was made (for example, text-critical note 6 on p. 3599 reads: 韓陰，疑當作「韓陶」, where the text remains 韓陰). These text-critical notes (there are nine for the "Ch'ao-hsien

biographical sketches for Ho and Sung in *Grand Scribe's Records,* 9:401-7.

[3] The other participating editors were Wang Hua-pao 王華寶, Wang O 王锷, and Ts'ao Hung-chün 曹紅軍.

lieh-chuan") are numbered and placed within the text. But they overlap with the original 1959 notes to the "San-chia chu" 三家注 and are somewhat difficult to discern (although they are highlighted in a light-grey color). Thus on p. 3598 following the phrase 樓船將軍亦坐兵至洌口 there are two footnote numbers, "9" (highlighted) and "1" (not highlighted). Note 9 is found on p. 3600 and explains that because the Ching-yu 景祐 edition and other texts read Lieh 洌 for Lieh 列 the text has been changed accordingly. Note 1 is to the original "So-yin" footnote which cites Su Lin 蘇林 as follows: "[Lieh-k'ou] is the name of a county. When he [Yang P'u] crossed the sea, he first took it" 縣名. 度海先得之.

Despite these peccadilloes, this new text marks an important improvement on the original Chung-hua edition and will now surely become the standard edition. All readers of the *Shih chi* will benefit greatly from the diligence of Chao Sheng-ch'ün and his team.

William H. Nienhauser, Jr.

On Using This Book

Most **Texts** are cited by chapter and page in a particular edition–*Shih chi,* 62.2185 indicates *chüan* 卷 62, page 2135 of the Chung-hua edition (see **List of Abbreviations**)–but references to the *Lun yü* 論語 (Analects of Confucius) and *Meng Tzu* 孟子 (Mencius) are according to chapter and verse (學而時習之 is thus *Lun yü* 1.1) and to *Lao Tzu* 老子 (Lao Tzu) by section. When comments in a modern critical edition are relevant, however, we cite it. All dynastic history references are to the modern punctuated editions from Chung-hua Shu-chü 中華書局. For many other citations we have referred to the ***Ssu-pu pei-yao*** 四部備要 or ***Ssu-pu ts'ung-kan*** 四部叢刊 **Editions** to allow the reader to more easily locate the passage. Other abbreviated titles can be found in the **List of Abbreviations.**

For **Official Titles** we have for the most part employed the translations of Hans Bielenstein in his *The Bureaucracy of Han China* (Cambridge: Cambridge University Press, 1980), often making reference to Lu Zongli [Lü Zongli] 呂宗立, ed. *Chung-kuo ku-tai chih-kuan ta tz'u-tien* 中國古代職官大辭典 (Chengchow: Ho-nan Jen-min Ch'u-pan-she, 1990), and on occasion also to Charles O. Hucker, *A Dictionary of Official Titles in Imperial China* (Stanford: Stanford University Press, 1965), as well as to other texts and to the traditional commentators.

Locations of **Place Names** are based on T'an Ch'i-hsiang 譚其驤, ed. *Chung-kuo li-shih ti-t'u chi* 中國歷史地圖集, *Vol. II: Ch'in, Hsi Han, Tung Han shih-ch'i* 秦， 西漢， 東漢時期 (Shanghai: Ti-t'u Ch'u-pan-she, 1982). T'an's identifications are not without problems, but they have been adopted by a number of large projects in China (such as the *Chung-kuo ta pai-k'o ch'üan-shu* 中國大百科全書) and provide the only practical means to attempt to identify the great number of place names in the *Shih chi*. On occasion we have added information from Ch'ien Mu's 錢穆 *Shih chi ti-ming k'ao* 史記地名考 (Rpt. Taipei: San-min Shu-chü, 1984).

Han 漢 is distinguished from Hann 韓 and Wei 魏 from Wey 衛 by means of romanization. We have found it difficult to decide when to translate a place name. Our basic principle has been to translate names which seem to still have meaning in the *Records* and to leave untranslated those which were understood by Ssu-ma Ch'ien primarily as toponyms. Words like *yi* 邑, *ch'eng* 城 or *chün* 郡 (in two-syllable compounds) are treated as suffixes and usually transliterated rather than translated. For example, place names like An-yi 安邑, Tung-ch'eng 東城, and Nan-chün 南郡, in

xvii

which *yi, ch'eng* and *chün* are similar to the "-ton" in Washington or "-ville" in Nashville, are transliterated as An-yi, Tung-ch'eng, and Nan-chün, rather than translated as An Town, East City or Southern Commandery. For modern cities and provinces we have used the postal-system romanization (Peking, Szechwan, etc.). In the notes we have tried whenever possible to refer both to the distance from some well-known location as well as to a local identification.

Weights and Measures are generally given in romanization only. More information is often provided in the notes and especially in the "Weights and Measures" section below.

Although there has been extensive discussion of ***chiu*** 酒 (traditionally translated as **"wine"**), according to H. T. (Hsing-tsung) Huang, *Science and Civilization in China,* Joseph Needham, ed. in chief. v. 6: *Biology and Biological Technology. Part V: Fermentations and Food Science* (Cambridge: Cambridge University Press, 2000), there were two ways the ancient Chinese made wine (p. 162). One from the mould ferment *ch'ü* 麴, and the other, *chiu* 酒, from steamed millet or other grains and rice. Huang notes that this second process is "fairly similar" (p. 163) to the method of making Shao-hsing wine today. Thus, although *chiu* during Han times may be quite different from the wine drunk in the West today, we follow Huang (see his lengthy discussion of how to translate *chiu* on pp. 149–50 and his depiction of Han wines on 165–66) and translate *chiu* consistently as "wine."

Dates given according to the sexagenary cycle have been romanized: *chia-tzu jih* 甲子日 becomes "the *chia-tzu* 甲子 day." These dates whenever possible have been converted to the Western calendar using Hsü Hsi-ch'i 徐錫祺. *Hsi Chou (Kung-ho) chih Hsi Han li-p'u* 西周（共和）至西漢歷譜 (2v. Peking: Pei-ching K'o-hsüeh Chi-shu, 1997).

We have used a slightly modified version of Wade-Giles' **Romanization** in which *i* is written throughout as *yi* to avoid the confusion between the English first-person pronoun and Chinese proper names. For Chinese passages over four characters in length, romanization is usually not provided.

Our **Base Edition** has been that edited by Ku Chieh-kang 顧頡剛 (1893–1980) *et al.* and published by Chung-hua Shu-chü in 1959; see the "Introduction" in the current volume). It was based on the Chin-ling Shu-chü 金陵書局 edition and published originally in six hardbound volumes; subsequently it was issues in a paperback version in ten volumes. References to this edition are given by chapter and page (69.2250) in the notes and by page numbers in emboldened brackets in the translation itself **[2250]** (or as **[*2250*]** intertextually).

In citing the standard three **Commentaries**–"Chi-chieh" 集解, "Cheng-yi" 正義, and "So-yin" 索隱, page numbers are given only if the reference is to a chapter other than that being translated. In other words, in the translation of 61.2124 no page number is provided for a citation from the "Cheng-yi" if that citation occurs on 61.2124 or

61.2125, since the reader should easily be able to locate it. If a "Cheng-yi" comment is provided from another section or chapter of the *Shih chi,* the reader is referred to the appropriate chapter/page. A brief introduction to these commentaries can be found in the Introduction to Volume 1. Also appended here is a list of **Frequently Mentioned Commentators**.

Our **Annotation** has attempted to identify major textual problems, place names, book titles, rituals, unusual customs, individuals and groups of people. **Chinese Characters** are normally given only at their first occurrence.

The translation of each chapter is followed by a **Translators' Note** and a short **Bibliography**. The former may provide a summary of analyses from traditional commentators, point out problems in the text, or discuss its relations to other chapters. The latter includes the major studies and translations. A list of **Selected Recent Works** is appended.

Weights and Measures

Throughout the text we have given words indicating weights and measures in their romanized form. The approximate values and original Chinese characters are given on the following pages.

Generally speaking, the basic unit of length, the *ch'ih* 尺, was the most stable. It varied from 23.1 cm in Warring States to about 23.2 cm in the Western Han. In terms of volume, one *sheng* 升 was roughly equal to 200 cc throughout the period. The greatest variance can be seen in weights, but even there we can assume that one *chin* 斤 remained equal to approximately 250 g through the era.

Our understanding of these units of measurement is based on the arguments presented by Sung Hsü-wu 宋敍五 in *his Liang Han huo-pi shih kao* 兩漢貨幣史稿 (Taipei: Wen-hai, 1978). Although 24 *chu* 銖 are equivalent to 1 *liang* 兩, 20 *liang* equal 1 *yi* 鎰, and 1 *chin* 斤 contains 16 *liang*, there is no set relationship between copper coins and gold until the Hsin 新 dynasty (Sung, pp. 139 and 145). The price of gold fluctuated under the Han, but it can be argued that under Emperor Wu 1 *chin* of gold varied from 1000–2500 copper coins (p. 142). The larger *wu-chu* 五銖 coins exchanged at about 2000 to the *chin* of gold and the *pan-liang* 半兩 coins at about 2500 to the *chin* (pp. 146–47). There are eight designations used for coins during the Former Han, but they actually designate only three basic types: (1) *pa-chu ch'ien* 八銖錢 (introduced in 186 B.C. and also called *pan-liang ch'ien* 半兩錢 or *san-fen ch'ien* 三分錢 after 136 B.C.), (2) *san-chu ch'ien* 三銖錢 (introduced in 140 B.C.) and (3) *wu-chu ch'ien* 五銖錢 (introduced in 118 B.C. and later known in slight variations as *ch'ih-tse ch'ien* 赤仄錢 and *ch'ih-tse ch'ien* 赤側錢). On other types of coin denominations (which are not referred to in the *Shih chi*), see Sung, pp. 112–13. Moreover, *chin* 金 is often used interchangeably with *huang chin* 黃金 (Sung, pp. 144–45) and refers to gold. Finally, the term *pai chin* 百金 (cf. *Shih chi*, 30.1417 and the comments in "So-yin" to that passage) refers to *pai chin* 百斤 (one hundred *chin*) of *huang-chin* 黃金 (gold).

On the romanization of the measure word 石, we follow the general usage of *shih* instead of *tan*. *Tan* did at some time become the colloquial pronunciation for 石, but may not have started in the Han dynasty (cf. Michael Loewe, "The Measurement of Grain during the Han Period," *TP* 49 (1961), p. 76.

The following list is arranged by category (Length, Capacity, etc.) and under each category by the importance of the term. Variances are listed with the most ancient value first. A selected list of sources (along with a key to the abbreviated sources cited in the list) is appended.

Length

Unit Name	Western Equivalent (Era)	Source (see appended Bibliography)
ch'ih 尺	23–23.7 cm (Western Han)	*K'ao-ku hsüeh*
ts'un 寸	1/10th *ch'ih*	
chang 丈	10 *ch'ih*	
li 里	415 m 416 m = 300 *pu* or 180 *chang*) often stands for x-*li on a side* i.e., x by x *li*)	"Han Weights and Measures" *Ku-tai wen-hua*

Capacity

Unit Name	Western Equivalent (Era)	Source (see appended Bibliography)
sheng 升	from 194–216 cc (Ch'in)	*K'ao-ku hsüeh*
tou 斗	10 *sheng* = 1900 cc (Ch'in dynasty)	Ch'en Meng-chia

Weights

chin 斤	244–268 g (Western Han) 245 g (Western Han)	Ch'en Meng-chia "Han Weights and Measures"
liang 兩	1/16 *chin* (ca. 15.625 g–15.36 g)	"Han Weights and Measures"
chu 銖	1/24 *liang* (ca. 0.651 g–0.64 g)	"Han Weights and Measures"
yi 溢	20 *liang*	See previous page
Shih 石	120 *chin* = (ca. 30 kg–29.5 kg)	"Han Weights and Measures"
chin 金 =	yi (of copper or bronze) 1 *chin* = 1 *ts'un*^{3} of gold = 238–251	See previous page (Ch'in-Han)

Key to Abbreviated Sources

Ch'en Meng-chia

Ch'en Meng-chia 陳夢家. "Chan-kuo tu-liang heng shih-lüeh shuo" 戰國度量衡史略說, *K'ao-ku,* 6.6 (1964): 312–14.

"Han Weights"

"Han Weights and Measures," in *The Cambridge History of China, Volume 1, The Ch'in and Han Empires.* Denis Twitchett and Michael Loewe, eds. Cambridge: Cambridge University Press, 1986, p. xxxviii.

K'ao-ku hsüeh

Chung-kuo ta pai-k'o ch'üan shu, K'ao-ku hsüeh 中國大百科全書, 考古學. Peking and Shanghai: Chung-kuo Ta Pai-k'o Ch'üan Shu Chu-pan-she, 1986.

Ku-tai wen-hua

Ku-tai wen-hua ch'ang-chih 古代文化常識. Yang Tien-k'uei 楊殿奎 et al., eds. Tsinan: Shan-tung Chiao-yü Ch'u-pan-she, 1984, pp. 271–92.

Selected Bibliography

Ch'ien Chien-fu 錢劍夫. *Ch'in Han huo-pi shih kao* 秦漢貨幣史稿. Wuhan: Hu-pei Jen-min, 1986.

Ch'iu Kuang-min 丘光明 et al. *Chung-kuo k'o-hsüeh chi-shu shih, Tu-liang-heng chüan* 中國科學技術史. Peking: K'o-hsüeh Chu-pan-she, 2001.

Hulsewé, A. F. P. "Ch'in-Han Weights and Measures," in Hulsewé, *Remnants of Ch'in Law.* Leiden: E. J. Brill, 1985, p. 19.

Kuo-chia Chi-liang Tsung-chü 國家計量總局. *Chung-kuo ku-tai tu-liang-heng t'u-chi* 中國古代度量衡圖集. Peking: Wen-wu 文物, 1981.

Loewe, Michael. "The Measurement of Grain during the Han Period," *TP,* 49 (1961): 64–95.

Sung Chieh 宋傑. *Chung-kuo huo-pi fa-chan shih* 中國貨幣發展史. Peking: Shou-tu Shih-fan Ta-hsüeh Ch'u-pan-she, 1999.

Sung Hsü-wu 宋敍五 in *his Liang Han huo-pi shih kao* 兩漢貨幣史稿. Taipei: Wen-hai, 1978.

Lu Zongli

Abbreviations

I. Books

Ancient China — Michael Loewe and Edward L. Shaughnessy, eds. *The Cambridge History of Ancient China from the Origins of Civilization to 221 B.C.* Cambridge: Cambridge University Press, 1999.

Aoki — Aoki Gorō 清木五郎. *Shiki* 史記. V. 12. Tokyo: Meiji Shoten, 2007. *Shinaku Kanbun taikei* 新釈漢文大系, 92. Contains translations of chapters 111–121.

Bielenstein — Hans Bielenstein. *The Bureaucracy of Han Times.* Cambridge: Cambridge U. Press, 1980.

Chang Lieh, *Han shu* — Chang Lieh 張烈, ed. *Han shu chu yi* 漢書注譯. 4v. Haikow: Han-nan Kuo-chi Hsin-wen Chu-pan Chung-hsin Ch'u-pan Fa-hsing 海南國際新聞出版中心出版發行, 1997.

Chang Wen-hu — Chang Wen-hu 張文虎 (1808–1885). *Chiao-k'an Shih chi "Chi-chieh," "So-yin," "Cheng-yi," cha-chi* 校刊 史記集解索引正義札記. 2v. Rpt. Peking: Chung-hua, 1977.

Chavannes — Édouard Chavannes, trans. *Les Mémoires historiques de Se-ma Ts'ien.* 5v. Paris, 1895–1905; rpt. Leiden: E. J. Brill, 1967. V. 6. Paris: Adrien Maisonneuve, 1969.

"Cheng-yi" — Chang Shou-chieh 張守節 (fl. 730). "*Shih chi cheng-yi*" 史記正義, as found in the *Shih chi.*

Ch'eng Shu-te	—	Ch'eng Shu-te 程樹德 (1877–1944). *Lun-yü chi-shih* 論語集釋. 4v. Peking: Chung-hua, 1990.
"Chi-chieh"	—	P'ei Yin 裴駰 "*Shih chi* chi-chieh" 史記集解, as found in the *Shih chi*.
Ch'ien Mu, *Ti-ming k'ao*	—	Ch'ien Mu 錢穆. *Shih chi ti-ming k'ao* 史記地名考. Rpt. Taipei: San-min Shu-chü, 1984.
De Crespigny, *Dictionary*	—	Rafe de Crespigny. *A Biographical Dictionary of Later Han to the Three Kingdoms (23–220 AD)*. Leiden: E. J. Brill, 2007.
Giele, *Imperial-Decision*	—	Enno Giele. *Imperial-Decision Making and Communication in Early China: A Study of Cai Yong's Dudan*. Wiesbaden: Harrassowitz, 2006.
Grand Scribe's Records	—	*Grand Scribe's Records, Volumes 1, 2, 5.1, 7, 8 and 9*. William H. Nienhauser, Jr., ed. Bloomington: Indiana University Press, 1994, 2002, 2006 and 2010.
Han Chao-ch'i	—	Han Chao-ch'i 韓兆琦, ed. *Shih chi chien-cheng* 史記箋證. 9v. 2nd printing. Nanchang: Chiang-hsi Jen-min Ch'u-pan-she, 2005 [2004].
Han shu	—	*Han shu* 漢書. Edited by Chen Chih 陳直 *et al.* 12v. Peking: Chung-hua, 1962.
Han shu pu-chu	—	*Han shu pu-chu* 漢書補注. Wang Hsien-ch'ien 王先謙 (1842–1918). Lü Chien 呂健, ed. 10v. Shanghai: Shang-hai Ku-chi Ch'u-pan-she, 2008.
Hawkes	—	David Hawkes. *Ch'u Tz'u, the Songs of the South*. Oxford: Oxford University Press, 1959.
Hervouet, *Le chapitre 117*	—	Yves Hervouet. *Le chapitre 117 du Che-ki (Biographie de Sseu-ma Siang-jou)*. Paris: Paris: Presses Universitaires de France, 1972.

Hervouet, *Un poète*	—	Yves- Hervouet. *Un poète de cour sous le Han: Sseu-ma Siang-jou*, Paris: Presses Universitaires de France, 1964.
Hucker	—	Charles O. Hucker. *A Dictionary of Official Titles in Imperial China.* Stanford: Stanford University Press, 1985.
Hulsewé, *Han Law*	—	A. F. P. Hulsewé. *Remnants of Han Law, Volume 1.* Leiden: E. J. Brill, 1955.
Ikeda	—	Ikeda Shirōjirō 池田四郎次郎 and Ikeda Hideo 池田英雄. *Shiki kenkyū shomoku kaidai (kōhon)* 史記研究書目解題 (稿本). 2v. Tokyo: Meitoku Shuppansha, 1978.
Knechtges, *Wen xuan*	—	David R. Knechtges. *Wen xuan or Selections of Refined Literature.* 3v. Princeton: Princeton University Press, 1982, 1987, 1996.
Lau, *Analects*	—	D. C. Lau, trans. *Confucius, the Analects.* Harmondsworth, England: Penguin, 1979.
Legge	—	James Legge (1815–1897), trans. *The Chinese Classics.* 5v. 2nd rev. ed. Taipei: Southern Materials Center, 1985.
Li Jen-chien	—	Li Jen-chien 李人鑑. *T'ai-shih kung shu chiao tu chi* 太史公書校讀記. Lanchow: Kan-su Jen-min, 1998.
Liang Yü-sheng	—	Liang Yü-sheng 梁玉繩 (1745–1819). *Shih chi chih-yi* 史記志疑. 3v. Peking: Chung-hua, 1981.
Loewe, *Dictionary*	—	Michael Loewe. *A Biographical Dictionary of the Qin, Former Han, and Xin Periods (221 BC–AD 24).* Leiden: Brill, 2000.
Lu Zongli	—	Lu Zongli 呂宗力 [Lü Zongli], ed. *Chung-kuo li-tai kuan-chih ta tz'u-tien* 中國歷代官制大辭典. Peking: Pei-ching Ch'u-pan-she, 1994.

Mizusawa	—	Mizusawa Toshitada 水澤利忠. *Shiki kaichū koshō fu kōhō* 史記會注考證附校補. Reprinted with Tokyo, 1934 ed. of *Shiki kaichū koshō* 史記會注考證. 2v. Shanghai: Shang-hai Ku-chi, 1986.
Ogawa, *Retsuden*	—	Ogawa Tamaki 小川環樹, Imataka Makoto 今鷹真, and Fukushima Yoshihiko 福島吉彥, trans. *Shiki retsuden* 史記列傳. 5v. 1975; 2nd ed., Tokyo: Iwanami, 1989.
Palace edition	—	*Wu Ying-tien k'an-pen Shih chi* 武英殿刊本史記. Rpt. Taipei: Wen-hsiang 文馨 Ch'u-pan-she, 1978.
Po-na	—	*Po-na pen Erh-shih-ssu shih* 百衲本二十四史. Rpt. Taipei: Shang-wu Yin-shu Kuan, 1968.
Shih chi	—	*Shih chi* 史記. 10v. Peking: Chung-hua shu-chü, 1963.
Shih chi p'ing-lin	—	*Shih chi p'ing-lin* 史記評林. Ling Chih-lung 凌稚隆 (fl. 1576), comp. 5v. Rpt. Taipei: Ti-ch'iu 地球 Ch'u-pan-she, 1992.
Shih chi tz'u-tien	—	Ts'ang Hsiu-liang 倉修良, ed. *Shih chi tz'u-tien* 史記辭典. Tsinan: Shan-tung Chiao-yü, 1991.
Shih chi yen-chiu	—	*Shih chi yen-chiu chi-ch'eng* 史記研究集成. Chang Ta-k'o 張大可, An P'ing-ch'iu 安平秋, and Yü Chang-hua 俞樟華, eds. 14v. Peking: Hua-wen Ch'u- pan-she, 2005.
SKCS	—	*Ssu-k'u ch'üan-shu*. 四庫全書.
"So-yin"	—	Ssu-ma Chen 司馬貞 (fl. 730). *"Shih chi* So-yin" 史記索隱, as found in the *Shih chi*.
SKCS	—	*Ssu-k'u ch'üan-shu* 四庫全書.

SPPY   —   *Ssu-pu pei-yao* 四部備要.

SPTK   —   *Ssu-pu ts'ung-k'an* 四部叢刊.

T'ai-p'ing yü-lan   —   *T'ai-p'ing yü-lan* 太平御覽. Wang Yün-wu 王雲五,
                                    ed. 7v. Rpt. Taipei: T'ai-wan Shang-wu, 1968.

Takigawa   —   Takigawa Kametarō 瀧川龜太郎 (1865–1946).
                                    Shiki kaichû koshō fu kōhō 史記會注考證附校補. 2
                                    volumes. Reprint; collation notes by Mizusawa
                                    Toshitada 水澤利忠. Shanghai: Shang-hai Ku-chi,
                                    1986.

T'an Ch'i-hsiang   —   T'an Ch'i-hsiang 譚其驤, ed. *Chung-kuo li-shih
                                    ti-t'u chi* 中國歷地圖集. 9v. Shanghai: Ti-t'u, 1982.

van Ess, *Politik*   —   Hans van Ess. *Politik und Geschichtsschreibung im
                                    alten China: Pan Ma i-t'ung* 班馬異同. 2v.
                                    Wiesbaden: Harrassowitz, 2014.

Wang Li-ch'i   —   Wang Li-ch'i 王利器 (1912–1998), ed. *Shih chi
                                    chu-i* 史記注譯. 4v. Sian: San Ch'in, 1988.

Wang Li-ch'i, *Jen-piao*   —   Wang Li-ch'i and Wang Chen-min 王貞玟, editors.
                                    Han shu ku-chin jen-piao shu-cheng 漢書古今人表
                                    疏證. Tsinan: Ch'i Lu Shu-she, 1988.

Wang Nien-sun   —   Wang Nien-sun 王念孫 (1744–1832). "*Shih chi
                                    tsa-chih* 史記雜志," in Volume 1 of Wang's *Tu-shu
                                    tsa-chih* 讀書雜志. Rpt.; Taipei: Shih-chieh, 1963.

Wang Shu-min   —   Wang Shu-min 王叔岷. *Shih chi chiao-cheng* 史記
                                    斠證. 10v. Taipei: Chung-yang Yen-chiu Yüan,
                                    Li-shih Yü-yen Yen-chiu So, 1982.

Watson   —   Burton Watson, trans. *Records of the Grand
                                    Historian.* 2v. Rev. edition. Hong Kong and New
                                    York: Chinese U. of Hong Kong and Columbia
                                    University Press, 1993.

Watson, *Qin*	—	Watson, trans. *Records of the Grand Historian: Qin Dynasty.* V. 3. Hong Kong and New York: Chinese U. of Hong Kong and Columbia U. Press, 1993.
Watson, *Ssu-ma Ch'ien*	—	Burton Watson. *Ssu-ma Ch'ien, Grand Historian of China.* New York: Columbia University Press, 1958.
Wu and Lu	—	Wu Shu-p'ing 吳樹平 and Lu Zong-li 呂宗力 [Lü Zongli], eds. and trans., in *Ch'üan-chu ch'üan-yi Shih chi* 全注全譯史記. 3v. Tientsin: T'ien-chin Ku-chi, 1995.
Yang, *Li-tai*	—	Yang Yen-ch'i 楊燕起 *et al.*, eds. *Li-tai ming-chia p'ing Shih chi* 歷代名家評史記. Peking: Pei-ching Shih-fan Ta-hsüeh, 1986.
Yang, *Lun-yü*	—	Yang Po-chün 楊伯峻 (1909–1992). *Lun-yü yi-chu* 論語譯注. Peking: Chung-hua, 1980.
Yang, *Tso-chuan*	—	Yang Po-chün 楊伯峻. *Ch'un-ch'iu Tso-chuan chu* 春秋左傳注. 4v. Peking: Chung-hua, 1982.
Yang Yen-ch'i	—	Yang Yen-ch'i 楊燕起. *Shih chi ch'üan-yi* 史記全譯. 9v. Kweiyang: Kuei-chou Jen-min, 2001.
Yangs	—	Yang Hsien-yi and Gladys Yang. *Records of the Historian.* Rpt. Hong Kong: The Commercial Press, 1985.
von Zach, *Anthologie*	—	Erwin Ritter von Zach. *Die chinesische Anthologie; Übersetzungen aus dem Wen hsüan.* 2v. Cambridge: Harvard University Press, 1958.

II. Journals

AM	—	*Asia Major*
BIHP	—	*Bulletin of the Institute of History and Philology* (Academia Sinica, Taiwan)

BMFEA	—	*Bulletin of the Museum of Far Eastern Antiquities*
BSOAS	—	*Bulletin of the School of Oriental and African Studies*
CLEAR	—	*Chinese Literature: Essays, Articles, Reviews*
EC	—	*Early China*
HJAS	—	*Harvard Journal of Asiatic Studies*
JAOS	—	*Journal of the American Oriental Society*
JAS	—	*Journal of Asian Studies*
MS	—	*Monumenta Serica*
OE	—	*Oriens Extremus*
TP	—	*T'oung Pao*
ZDMG	—	*Zeitschrift der Deutschen Morgenländischen Gesellschaft*

III. Other

ed.	—	editor
mss.	—	manuscript
n.	—	note
nn.	—	notes
no.	—	number
rev. ed.	—	revised edition
rpt.	—	reprint

transl. — translator

v. — volume

The Grand Scribe's Records

VOLUME X

The Memoirs of Han China, Part III

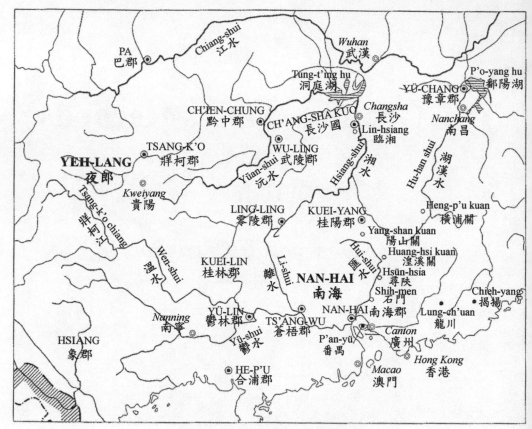

Nan Yüeh 南越 (Southern Yüeh)

⊙ Han Commandery Seats   ◎ *Modern Cities*

○ Han Places   • Han Counties

The Southern Yüeh,[1] Memoir 53

translated by William H. Nienhauser, Jr.

[113.2967] The King of Southern Yüeh 南越王,[2] [formerly] Commandant-Governor[3] [Chao] T'o [趙]尉佗 (230–137 BC, r. ca. 204–137 BC) was a native of Chen-ting 真定.[4] He had the *cognomen* Chao 趙. During the time of Ch'in, when [Ch'in] had already unified the empire,[5] it overran and stabilized Yang Yüeh 楊越,[6]

[1] As the new 2013 Chung-hua edition of the *Shih chi* notes (113.2581), a number of early editions title this chapter "Nan Yüeh T'o Wei lieh-chuan" 南越佗尉列傳 (The Memoir of Commandant–Governor [Chao] T'o of Southern Yüeh).

[2] According to the "Cheng-yi," the capital of Southern Yüeh was located near modern Canton. Chinese commentators, ancient and modern, refer to the Southern Yüeh as one of the one hundred Yüeh 百越 tribes, but modern scholarship has shown that there were several indentifiable political entities in this area for several hundred years before, including Tung Ou 東甌 (Eastern Ou), centered about modern Wenchow 溫州 and stretching across southern and eastern Chekiang, Min Yüeh 閩越, to the south of Eastern Ou in modern Fukien (both introduced in more detail in the following chapter 114), Hsi Ou 西甌 (Western Ou) stretching from Kwangsi south into the Red River Delta of modern Vietnam, and Nan-hai 南海 (cf. *Han shu*, 1B.77–78, 44.2141 and 64A.2780). The text of the current chapter below argues that Chao T'o was able to bring together a coalition of these states through bribes (*Shih chi*, 113.2979). At the start of the Han dynasty, Southern Yüeh was bordered to the north by the kingdom of Ch'ang-sha 長沙, a descendant of Ch'u, which had conquered some of the Yüeh peoples under Wu Ch'i's 吳起 leadership in the late fourth century BC (cf. *Shih chi*, 65.2168). See also the map at the start of this chapter.

[3] *Wei* 尉 (Commandant–Governor) was the designation for the official who governed a smaller commandery; *Shou* 守 (Governors or Administrators) were in charge the larger commandaries (cf. the citation from the *Shih-san chou-chi* 十三州記 in "So-yin").

[4] Chen-ting was a Ch'in county a few miles northeast of modern Shih-chia-chuang 石家莊 in Hopei (T'an Ch'i-hsiang, 2:26).

[5] The *Han shu* parallel account is contained in chapter 95, "Hsi-nan Yi, Liang Yüeh, Ch'ao-hsien chuan" 西南夷兩粵朝鮮傳 (Memoir of the Southwestern Yi, the Two Yüeh, and Ch'ao-hsien; *Han shu*, 95.3847–58). It begins in the slightly simpler fashion of the *Han shu* memoirs, uses the variant 粵 for 越 throughout, and includes a text that is often in simpler

1

setting up the commandaries of Kuei-lin 桂林, Nan-hai 南海, and Hsiang-chün 象郡[7]; by means of banishment it moved common people [there], where they resided mixed together with Yüeh [people] for thirteen years.[8]

[Chao] T'o, during the time of Ch'in, had been employed as the Magistrate of Lung-ch'uan 龍川[9] in Nan-hai 南海.[10] When it came to the time of the Second

syntax than the *Shih chi* (thus the *Shih chi* opens "During the time of Ch'in, when [Ch'in] had already unified the empire" 秦時已并天下 whereas in the *Han shu* we read "when Ch'in had for some time unified the empire" 秦并天下).

[6] The interpretations of Yang-Yüeh 楊越 (also written 揚越) are manifold; Han Chao-ch'i indicates it refers to areas south of the Ling-nan Mountains and north of modern Vietnam (see his lengthy explanation in Han Chao-ch'i, 9:5664, n. 2). Chang Lieh 張烈 (95.3761n.) explains that the name came from the fact that Yang-chou 揚州, one of the nine ancient "provinces" (Chiu chou 九州) oversaw all areas to the south; following this line or reasoning, Ch'en Tseng-fang 陳增芳 takes it to refer to the lands south of classical Yang-chou 揚州 and approximating the location and area of Eastern Ou ("'Lüeh-ting Yang Yüeh, chih Kuei-lin, Nan-hai, Hsiang-chün' pien" "略定揚越，置桂林，南海，象郡" 辨, *Min-tsu yen-chiu* 民族研究, 1994.2, p. 100). Vera Dorofeeva–Lichtmann in a personal communication argues that Yang refers to the lower Yangtse Valley and Yüeh to the regions south of the Ling-nan, as early Chinese maps indicate. Cf. T'an Ch'i-hsiang, 1:46 for a map of the area in pre–Ch'in times; and T'an, 2:11–12 as well as Francis Allard (see bibliography below), p. 13, for Ch'in and Han maps. The Ch'in campaign to subdue Yüeh began in 221 BC under the commandant T'u Sui 屠睢 (Loewe, *Dictionary*, p. 514). T'u was killed in 220 and Ch'in followed this up with two other expeditions, both under Chao T'o's command. By 214 the area was pacified and three commandaries set up. For an alternative chronology, see Han Chao-ch'i (ibid.) and *Shih chi*, 7.253.

[7] These three commanderies stretched from Nan-hai, which was furthest east and approximated modern Kwangtung, to Kuei-lin just to its west and occupying much of modern Kwangsi, to Hsiang-chün, which curled around Kuei-lin, stretching southwest through modern Kweichow then bending east to the southernmost Chinese coasts just northeast of modern Vietnam (see the maps on T'an Ch'i-hsiang, 2:11–12 and at the end of this chapter). All three commandaries were set up in 214 BC; Kuei-lin Commandery had its seat to the southwest of modern Kuei-p'ing 桂平 in Kwangsi; Nan-hai's seat was P'an-yü 番禺 (modern Canton); various locations have been suggested for the seat of Hsiang-chün, Lin-ch'en 臨塵, but Wu and Lu (113.2972) place it near modern Ch'ung-tso 崇左 in Kwangsi.

[8] The translation here is tentative and presumes an implied *jen* 人, reading of *yü Yüeh jen* 與越人 (cf. Wu and Lu, 113.2980).

Hsü Kuang ("Chi-chieh") notes that Ch'in took eight years to finish uniting the empire in 209 BC (the first year of the Second Emperor) and another six years to pacify Yüeh.

[9] *Ling* 令 was the Ch'in designation for the head of a county of ten thousand households or more; counties with fewer than ten thousand households were headed by *chang* 長.

Emperor 二世 ([of Ch'in] r. 210–207 BC), Jen Hsiao 任囂,[11] the Commandant of Nan-hai, fell ill and was on the point of dying; he summoned Chao T'o, the Magistrate of Lung-ch'uan and said to him: "I have heard that Ch'en Sheng 陳勝[12] and others have made rebellion, that Ch'in has acted against all that is moral, that the world has suffered under it, that Hsiang Yü 項羽, Liu Chi 劉季, Ch'en Sheng, Wu Kuang 吳廣,[13] and other prefectural and commanderial [leaders] have together each together raised troops[14] and gathered armies to struggle like tigers for the empire, that the central states are troubled by rebellion, no one yet knowing by what means peace can be achieved, and that the powerful local magnates have turned against Ch'in and set themselves up.[15] [Although] Nan-hai is remote and far away, I fear that bandit troops[16] in invading [Ch'in's] territory would reach [even] this place. I hoped to raise troops to cut off the new road,[17] to prepare ourselves, and to await changes in the

Lung-ch'uan was located northwest of the eponymous modern county in Kwangtung about 105 miles northeast of the seat of Nan-hai at P'an-yü 番禺 (Wu and Lu, 113.2972n. and T'an Ch'i-hsiang, 2:36.).

[10] This sentence, which may be seen as redundant since Chao T'o's position is given again just below, does not appear in the *Han shu* parallel (95.3847).

[11] Otherwise unknown. Chung Hsing 鍾惺 (1574–1624) notes that since we know the times and the location, we can imagine that Jen Hsiao was a heroic figure (*chün-chieh* 俊傑; *Shih chi p'ing-lin,* 113.1b).

[12] See his biography in *Shih chi* chapter 48.

[13] Accounts of Hsiang Yü and Liu Chi's rebellions can be found in their annals (*Shih chi* chapters 7 and 8); Wu Kuang's activities are found in Ch'en Sheng's biography (*Shih chi,* 48.1949ff.).

[14] The phrase *ko kung hsing-chün* 各共興軍 is troubling. It suggests that the various rebels somehow acting in concert (*kung* 共). The expression *ko kung* 各共 is found only once in the *Shih chi* and is uncommon in other texts. The *Han shu* omits this line (see the following note).

[15] Takigawa (113.3) notes that this first part of Jen Hsiao's summons is repetitive. The forty–nine graphs in the opening lines of the *Shih chi* version of this summons have been simplified in the *Han shu* account (*Han shu,* 95.3847) to twelve and read: "I have heard that Ch'en Sheng and others have made rebellion, and the powerful local magnates have turned against Ch'in and set themselves up" 聞陳勝等作亂，豪傑畔秦相立. These rebellions began in 209 BC.

[16] The label *tao ping* 盜兵 also occurs in describing these troops on *Shih chi,* 8.367 (*Grand Scribe's Records,* 2:44).

[17] Su Lin 蘇林 notes ("So-yin") that this was the road the Ch'in had built as a link to the South. There is no record of this road elsewhere in the *Shih chi,* but it ran north from P'an-yü 番禺 through modern Shao-kuan 韶關 and through the Heng-p'u Pass (see text below).

situation among the feudal lords.[18] [However,] just at this time my illness has become grave. Furthermore, P'an-yü 番禺[19] backs up to mountainous defiles, is blocked by the Nan-hai 南海 (Southern Sea),[20] which from east to west is several thousand *li*; there are quite a few people from the central states [here] who would provide support. In addition, [P'an-yü] can be regarded as the master of an entire region and it could be used to set up a state. There are no senior officials in the commandery worth talking to; therefore I summoned you, sir, to inform you of this." He then immediately gave T'o a document causing him to handle the affairs of Commandant of Nan-hai.[21] When Hsiao died, T'o immediately sent a dispatch informing the Heng-p'u 橫浦, Yang-shan 陽山, and Huang-hsi 湟谿 border passes[22] that: "The bandit troops are about to arrive, quickly cut off the roads and gather troops to defend yourselves!" He took advantage of this situation to gradually execute, according to the law, senior officials who had been installed by the Ch'in, taking men from his own faction to serve as acting chief administrators.[23] After the Ch'in had been defeated and wiped out, T'o attacked and annexed Kuei-lin and Hsiang commandaries, enthroning himself as King Wu of Southern Yüeh 南越武王.[24]

After Emperor Kao 高帝 (of the Han; r. 206–195 BC) had already stabilized the empire, as the central states had toiled and suffered, he therefore absolved T'o and did not cause him to be punished.

In the eleventh year of the Han (196 BC), he sent Lu Chia 陸賈 (ca. 228–ca. 140 BC),[25] to take advantage [of the situation that Chao T'o had already declared himself

---

[18] That is, to wait to see which of the rebels comes out victorious.

[19] That is, modern Canton; it was the commandery seat of Nan-hai (T'an Ch'i-hsiang, 2:12).

[20] The punctuation in the Chung-hua *Han shu* (95.3847) makes much better sense here: "Furthermore, P'an-yü backs up to mountains, defiles, and redoubts and Nanhai stretches several thousand *li* from east to west" 且番禺負山險阻, 南海東西數千里.

[21] Fu Ch'ien 服虔 (cited in "So-yin") says that Jen Hsiao forged an imperial edict causing him [Chao T'o] to become the Commandant of Nan-hai.

[22] These three passes are located (respectively) about 40 miles northeast of modern Shao-kuan 韶關 (and 175 miles north–northeast of P'an-yü), just northwest of modern Yang-shan 陽山 (120 miles northwest of P'an-yü), and about 10 miles southwest of modern Ying-te 英德 (75 miles north–northwest of P'an-yü), all in Kwangtung (Han Chao-ch'i, 113.5066, n. 13 and T'an Ch'i-hsiang, 2:35–36). These passes form an arc above P'an-yü and were the only three ways through the mountains north of P'an-yü.

[23] *Chia shou* 假守 may mean "false chief administrators" or "governors," i.e., those not appointed by the Han. *Han shu* (95.3847) reads *shou chia* 守假.

[24] Adding to his chutzpah by giving himself a title that is normally a posthumous honor.

[25] Lu Chia's biography is in *Shih chi* chapter 97 (see *Grand Scribe's Records*, 8:251–5). More than half of the biography is devoted to a detailed account of Lu Chia's meetings with Chao T'o. Lu was a native of Ch'u and an early follower of Han Kao-tsu who was known for

king] to enthrone T'o as King of Southern Yüeh, splitting a tally and exchange envoys [with T'o], and to harmonize and gather the Pai Yüeh 百越 (One Hundred Yüeh Tribes),[26] preventing him from causing any distress [*2968*] on the southern frontier, and allowing him to share a border with [the Han state of] Ch'ang-sha 長沙.[27]

[2969] During the time of Empress Kao 高后 (r. 195–180 BC), the authorities in charge requested to ban iron implements from the markets at the border passes to the Southern Yüeh. T'o said, "When Emperor Kao enthroned me, he opened up the exchange of envoys and goods. Now Empress Kao listens to a slanderous vassal, who singles out the Man Yi 蠻夷 [non-Han peoples of the South] as different, and breaks off the trade in implements and goods. This certainly is a plan of the King of Ch'ang-sha 長沙王![28] Relying on the central states, he wants to attack and wipe out Southern Yüeh, to annex and rule over it also as king, claiming this as his own merit."[29] Only at

his ability to negotiate and persuade. He was also the author of the *Hsin yü* 新語 (New Orations).

[26] Pai Yüeh 百越 is a term used extensively first in the *Shih chi* to refer to all the states and tribes south of the territory the early Han controlled. The term itself may result from the diaspora of the nobles of the state of Yüeh throughout the south after Yüeh was conquered by Ch'u in 333 BC (see Erica Brindley, "Representations and Uses of Yue Identity along the Southern Frontier of the Han, ca. 200–111 B.C.E.," *Early China*, 33/34 (2010–2011): 7; see also Brindley, "Barbarians or Not?", p. 11.

The syntax between the phrases 與剖符通使 and 和集百越 seems problematic. The *Han shu* parallel (95.3847) adjusts the text to read "splitting the tallies and exchanging envoys [with him], and causing him to make peace among the Pai Yüeh" 與剖符通使，使和輯百越. Compare also the parallel passage in Lu Chia's biography (*Shih chi*, 97.2697) and our translation (*Grand Scribe's Records*, 8:252).

[27] One of the states set up on the founding of the Han with its seat near modern Changsha in Hunan. On the northern border of Nan Yüeh at this time see Liang Kuo-chao 梁國昭, "Han ch'u Nan Yüeh kuo pei-chieh chi yu-kuan wen-t'i" 漢初南越國北界及有關問題, *Je-tai ti-li* 熱帶地理 15.4 (December 1995): 369–75.

[28] Chao T'o had taken Kuei-lin 桂林 and Hsiang 象 commandaries from the King of Ch'ang-sha's control, fomenting the bad blood between them.

[29] Although Watson (2:208) identifies this king as Wu Jui 吳芮, he errs. Wu Jui was enfeoffed as King of Ch'ang-sha in 202 BC but died in a campaign against the Min 閩 the following year. He was succeeded by his son Wu Ch'en 吳臣, who died in 193 BC; his son Wu Hui 吳回 ruled until his death in 186 BC. Thus the King of Ch'ang-sha at this time was Wu Jui's great-grandson, Wu Yu 吳右 or Wu Jo 吳若 (r. 186–178 BC), posthumously titled King Kung 恭 (or 共; Loewe, *Dictionary*, p. 586).

this point did T'o on his own authority honor himself in his title[30] as Emperor Wu of the Southern Yüeh 南越武帝 and send out troops to attack the border towns of Ch'ang-sha, defeating several counties and [then] leaving them. Empress Kao sent [Chou] Tsao [周]竃 (d. 162),[31] a general and Marquis of Lung-lü 隆慮侯,[32] to go to attack him. [But] he encountered such heat and humidity, that many of his officers and men fell to infectious diseases and his troops were not able to cross the mountain range [into Southern Yüeh].[33]

After more than a year, Empress Kao passed away (180 BC), and the troops were immediately dismissed. T'o took advantage of this to display his military might in the border regions, and to give bribes, gifts of money and goods to the Min Yüeh 閩越, Hsi Ou 西甌, and Lo 駱,[34] causing them to serve as subordinates, so that from east to west [he ruled over] more than ten thousand *li* on a side.[35] Only then did he ride in a carriage with a yellow baldachin with a pheasant feather on his left, claim his orders to be imperial decrees[36] and believe himself equal with [the ruler of] the central states.

[30] Echoing the elevation in titles (*tsun hao* 尊號) under the First Emperor of the Ch'in (*Shih chi*, 6.236: "We subjects risk a capital offense to offer the most honored designations: the king is to be called 'The Majestic Deified One'" 臣等昧死上尊號，王為『泰皇』.

[31] Chou Tsao was originally a conscript who joined the rebellion against Ch'in and was enfeoffed in 201 BC with Lung-lü as a reward for leading an attack on Hsiang Yü (Loewe, *Dictionary*, p. 736).

[32] Lung-lü was a county located near modern Lin 林 County in Honan.

[33] Ssu-ma Chen argues ("So-yin") that this was the Yang-shan 陽山 mountain range.

[34] Min Yüeh was established in 197 BC and included the area around the Min River in modern Fukien. The Western Ou were located in modern Kwangsi extending into what is now northern Vietnam. Lo (also Ou Lo 甌駱) very likely refers to the kingdom of Au Lac in the Red River delta (modern Vietnam). As Brindley ("Barbarians or Not?," p. 14) points out, the term Ou (originating apparently from the river of the same name in the southern part of modern Chekiang) would imply a tie to Eastern Ou, one of the regions ruled by descendants of the last King of Yüeh, Kou-chien (compare *Shih chi*, 41.1751), and may have been used by the Lo (and the Eastern and Western Ou) to add to their pedigree.

Hsieh Ch'ung-an 謝崇安 locates the Western Ou in early Han times in Kuei-lin 桂林 Commandery and the Lo in Hsiang-chün 象郡, pointing out that their proximity west of Southern Yüeh has led some scholars to believe they were the same state/people (see Hsieh's "Kuan-yü Lo-Yüeh tsu de kao-pien" 關於駱越族的考辨, *Kuang-hsi Min-tsu Shih-fan Hsüeh-yüan hsüeh-pao* 廣西民族師範學院學報, 2011.4: 8[6–11].

[35] Erica Brindley argues that Southern Yüeh was "was quite massive, covering a distance roughly from Canton Province through the northern reaches of contemporary Vietnam" ("Representations and Uses of Yue Identity," p. 5).

[36] Ch'eng chih 稱制, "to claim (or cause) one's orders to be imperial decrees," is used several times to depict Empress Lü's usurpation (see *Shih chi*, 9:400 and *Grand Scribe's Records*, 2:115–16, n. 63, for example).

[2970] When it came to the first year of Emperor Hsiao Wen 孝文帝 (179 BC), as he [the Emperor] had just brought order to and insured peace in the empire,[37] he sent envoys to the feudal lords and the four barbarians to announce his intention in coming from Tai 代 [38]to take the throne, causing them to understand the flourishing virtue in this. Only then did he on behalf of the graves of T'o's parents in Chen-ting establish a town to take care of them and to offer sacrifices at the proper times of the year. He summoned his [T'o's] cousins [to court], raising them to high office and generously conferring [gifts] and favor on them. When he issued a decree that the Chancellor Ch'en P'ing 陳平[39] and his group recommend someone who could be sent as envoy to Southern Yüeh, P'ing suggested Lu Chia of Hao-chih 好畤,[40] who had at the time of the previous emperor had the experience of being sent as envoy to Southern Yüeh.[41] Only then did [the Emperor] summon [Lu] Chia, make him a Grand Palace Grandee,[42] and send him as envoy.[43] Through him he reprimanded T'o for on his own authority enthroning [himself] as emperor and for never having sent as envoy even a single person to report [this].[44] When Lu Chia arrived in Southern Yüeh, the King was greatly afraid[45] and wrote a letter apologizing in which he stated: "Your Vassal the Old Gent Who is Grand Headman of the Man Yi, T'o, when in earlier days Empress Kao cut off and treated Southern Yüeh as alien, was secretly suspicious of

[37] Referring to the eradication of "the Lüs" and the restoration of rule to the legitimate Liu line (see *Shih chi* chapters 9 and 10 for details).

[38] Where he had been serving as king.

[39] See his biography in *Shih chi* chapter 56 and Loewe, *Dictionary*, p. 35–37.

[40] Hao-chih was a county northeast of modern Ch'ien County 乾縣 in Shansi (*Grand Scribe's Records*, 1:93, n. 71); during Empress Lü's reign, Lu Chia bought some land there and retired from court (compare *Shih chi*, 97.2699 and *Grand Scribe's Records*, 8:254, n. 47).

[41] The *Han shu* parallel (95.3849) omits reference to Hao-chih, says Lu Chia had been sent to Yüeh (not Nan Yüeh), and deletes *hsi* 習, "had the experience of" or "was familiar with."

[42] Wu and Lu (113.2973n.) point out that this position, under the Lang-chou Ling with a salary of one–thousand *shih*, was a kind of personal attendant to the emperor who often discussed matters with the sovereign and was sent out as envoy.

[43] Lu Chia's biography (*Shih chi*, 97.2701) does not give details of this but instead refers the reader to this chapter.

[44] Liang Yü-sheng, 53.1405 notes that the *Shih chi* does not include the letter Emperor Wen wrote to Chao T'o, which is provided in the *Han shu* parallel.

[45] The *Han shu* has moved a long passage (about fifty characters), depicting how supplicating Chao T'o was in receiving Lu Chia and recording an order he issued to his subjects renouncing the imperial title and the associated accoutrements, from the end of this paragraph to the beginning. There is a more detailed account of Lu Chia's visit in his biography in the *Shih chi* (97.2697; *Grand Scribe's Records*, 8:252).

the slanderous vassal, the King of Ch'ang-sha.[46] I also heard rumors that Empress Kao had executed all of my class and dug up my ancestors' graves, burning [their corpses]. For these reasons I despaired and violated the borders of Ch'ang-sha.[47] Moreover, the southern regions are low-lying and wet[48] and lie among the Man Yi 蠻 夷 [tribes][49]; to its east [the ruler of] Min Yüeh 閩越 with a populace of a thousand people has declared himself a king; to its west is [Hsi-]Ou [西]甌 and the Lo Lo 駱裸 (Naked Lo), [whose rulers] also declared themselves kings. Your old servant recklessly ventured to call himself an emperor, merely to amuse myself by it. How could I dare to make this known to the King of Heaven?!" Only then did he knock his forehead on the ground, expressing the wish to eternally serve as a vassal protecting [the marches] and offering up tribute and labor services. Only at this point did he issue an order to throughout his state reading: "I have heard that two heroes cannot stand next to each other, two worthies cannot share the same age.[50] The August Emperor is a worthy Son of Heaven. From this time forth, I will do away with the imperial edicts, the yellow canopy and the pheasant feathers on the left [of my chariot]." When Lu Chia returned [to the capital] and reported, Emperor Hsiao Wen was greatly pleased. From this time until the end of [Emperor] Hsiao Ching's time he called himself a vassal and sent men as envoys to the court in the spring and fall. However, Southern Yüeh within its own state secretly [kept] as before the [imperial] titles and names, [but] in his sending of envoys to the Son of Heaven, he called himself "king" and [sent envoys] to court in the spring and fall as if he were a feudal lord. Finally in the fourth year of the Chien-yüan era (137 BC), he passed away.[51]

---

[46] This was Wu Jo 吳若, King Kung of Ch'ang-sha 長沙恭王 (r. 186–178 BC), who Chao T'o believed was responsible for advising Empress Lü to ban the sale of iron produced to Nan Yüeh (*Shih chi*, 17.817f.).

[47] This sentence "I also heard . . ." is omitted from the *Han shu* parallel account.

[48] The same topical depiction of the southern regions occurs in *Shih chi* chapters 101 and 118.

[49] Man Yi was a general Han Chinese term for southern non–Han peoples.

[50] Compare the comment made by the Household Prefect of Kao-tsu's father to remind the old man that he should pay respect to his son, the newly crowned emperor: "Heaven does not have two suns, earth cannot have two kings" (*Shih chi*, 8.382 and *Grand Scribe's Records*, 2:69).

[51] Chao T'o was active ca. 220 BC (see text above); thus if he died in 137 BC, he would have been over 100 years old (Chang Lieh, 95.3766n. argues over 110). Wu and Lu (113.2974n.) point out that some scholars believe *tsu* 卒 here to be an interpolation. The text would then read "When it came to the fourth year of Chien-yüan era, T'o's grandson Hu became the King of Southern Yüeh." Yet the *Shih chi* text suggests that T'o lived a long time through the word *chih* 至, "finally": "finally in the fourth year of Chien-yüan he passed away."

T'o's grandson,[52] [Chao] Hu 胡,[53] became King of Southern Yüeh. At this time (138 BC),[54] when [Tsou] Ying [騶]郢, the King of Min Yüeh 閩越,[55] raised troops and attacked the border towns of Southern Yüeh,[56] Hu sent someone to present a letter to the emperor which read: "The two Yüehs are both vassals protecting [the marches] and should not be allowed on their own authority to raise troops and attack one another. Now when Min Yüeh has raised troops and invaded Your Servant'[s state],[57] Your Servant does not dare to raise troops, but only to [request] that the Son of Heaven issue a decree on this [situation]." At this, the Son of Heaven held [the King] of Southern Yüeh's sense of duty and his adherence to [*2971*] official duties or obligations and treaties in high esteem, raising an army for him and sending two generals to punish Min Yüeh.[58] The troops had not yet crossed the mountain range when Yü-shan 餘善, the younger brother of the King of Min Yüeh, killed Ying and thereby surrendered.[59] At this the troops were dismissed.

The Son of Heaven sent Chuang Chu 莊助[60] to go and explain his intent to the

[52] Various commentators have speculated on why there is no mention of Chao T'o's son. Ch'i Chao-nan 齊召南 (1703–1768; cited in *Han shu pu-chu*, 95.11b), for example, believes that T'o's heir must have died at a young age. But if T'o actually lived to be one hundred years old, it is quite possible that the heir died at quite an advanced age. Loewe (*Dictionary*, p. 707), citing "other finds," suggests that Hu was one of Chao T'o's younger grandsons and that he died "between the ages of 35 and 45."

[53] This the man identified by archaeologists as Chao Mo 趙眜 (see Hermann–Josef Röllike, "Nan Yue in der Überlieferung des Hofschreibers Sima Qian," in Margarete Prüch, ed. *Schätze für König Zhao Mo: Das Grab von Nan Yue* [Heidelberg: Umschau/Braus Verlag, 1998], p. 33).

[54] The *Han shu* parallel (94.3852) reads *li san nien* 立三年, "three years after he had been enthroned," i.e., 138 BC.

[55] He was said to be a distant descendant of the King of Yüeh, Kou-chien 越王勾踐.

[56] The current *Han shu* (94.3853) text is garbled here, reading 興兵南擊遍邑 (compare Wang Nien-sun's comments cited in *Han shu pu-chu*, 95.11b).

[57] "Now Eastern Yüeh has on its own authority raised troops to and invaded Your Servant['s state] 今東越擅興兵侵臣 is the *Han shu* reading.

[58] The generals were Wang Hui 王恢 and Han An-kuo 韓安國.

[59] Compare the parallel passage on *Shih chi*, 2981–2. These events took place in 135 BC.

[60] Chuang Chu (i.e., Yen Chu 嚴助) was a native of K'uai-chi 會稽 (near modern Soochow) and the son or a close relative of Chuang Chi 莊忌 (see the opening of Chu's lengthy biography, *Han shu*, 64A.2775–91; he and his father had their surnames changed to Yen 嚴 in the Later Han to avoid the taboo of the given name of Emperor Ming 漢明帝, r. 43–57). Chuang Chu was one of Emperor Wu's favorite courtiers. He had, in opposition to T'ien Fen 田蚡, argued that the Han should come to Tung Ou's 東甌 aid when it was in 138 BC

King of Southern Yüeh. [Chao] Hu knocked his forehead against the ground and said, "The Son of Heaven has actually for Your Servant raised troops to suppress Min Yüeh. Were I to die [in his service] I have no means to repay my indebtedness." He sent his heir [Chao] Ying-ch'i 嬰齊 (d. 114 BC)[61] to enter [court] as an imperial bodyguard.[62] He spoke to [Chuang] Chu: "Our state has recently been plundered, and the envoy has already set out [for Ch'ang-an]. I am just now night and day outfitting myself to enter [court] and seek audience with the Son of Heaven." After Chu had left, his grand ministers admonished Hu saying: "When Han raised troops to punish [Tsou] Ying, they also moved so that they alarmed and provoked Southern Yüeh. Moreover, the late king [Chao T'o] long ago explained that in serving the Son of Heaven one should hope not to err in ritual. The essential thing is that it is not permissible because you are pleased with some pleasant words to go in [to court] for an audience. If you were to go to court for an audience, then you would not be able to return again and this would be a situation in which the state would be lost!" At this point Hu claimed to be ill and did not after all go to court for an audience. More than ten years later, Hu really became very ill and the heir, Ying-ch'i, asked to be allowed to return. When Hu passed away, he was posthumously titled as King Wen 文王 [The Civil].

Ying-ch'i was enthroned in his place, and immediately hid away the imperial seal of the former "Emperor Wu" [that is, Chao T'o].[63] It was indeed when Ying-ch'i had gone in [to court] as an imperial bodyguard that he took in marriage a daughter of the Chiu 樛 Clan from Han-tan 邯鄲.[64] She bore him a son, Hsing 興.[65] When [Ying-ch'i] ascended the throne, he submitted a letter requesting that the daughter of the Chiu Clan be made queen and Hsing be made successor [to the throne]. Han several times sent envoys to persuade and instruct Ying-ch'i, [but] Ying-ch'i still took pleasure in arrogating the power to kill or let live and to act with reckless abandon. He feared that

---

under attack from Min Yüeh and was picked to lead the troops. Min Yüeh withdrew, however, and Chuang's forces were disbanded, much as in the present case (see also Loewe, *Dictionary*, p. 748).

[61] Compare Loewe (*Dictionary*, p. 715); Loewe also notes (p. 656) a "Ying-ch'i" 嬰齊 listed in the bibliographic treatise of the *Han shu* (30.1731 and 1749) who was a Palace Attendant during the reign of Emperor Wu who also wrote a Taoist work and a number of *fu*.

[62] *Su wei* 宿衛 (not in Bielenstein); this position also rendered him a virtual hostage against Nan Yüeh.

[63] The *Han shu* parallel reads "imperial seals of the former emperors Wu and Wen." Liang Yü-sheng (54.1406) speculates that both Chao T'o and his unknown son both called themselves emperors internally, denigrating their postions to "kings" only in correspondence with the Han.

[64] The *Han shu* parallel (95.2454) reads simply: "When Ying-ch'i was in Ch'ang-an . . ." 嬰齊在長安時.

[65] Loewe, *Dictionary*, p. 711–12.

if he were to go to court for an audience, he certainly would be made to use Han laws and be considered on the same level as those feudal lords of the interior, so he remained firm in claiming to be ill and in the end did not go in for an audience. He sent his son [Chao] Tz'u-kung 次公 to [court] as an imperial bodyguard. When Ying-ch'i passed away, [the Han] posthumously titled him King Ming 明王 [The Enlightened].

[2972] The heir Hsing was enthroned in his place. His mother became the [Queen] Dowager. The Dowager before when she had not yet become Ying-ch'i's concubine had once had an affair with An-kuo Shao-chi 安國少季, a man of Pa-ling 霸陵.[66] After Ying-ch'i had passed away, in the fourth year of Yüan-ting 元鼎 (113 BC), Han sent An-kuo Shao-chi to go to instruct the King and the Queen Dowager, and by that means have them go to court and be considered on the same level as the feudal lords of the interior; [the Sovereign] ordered the rhetorician, Chung Chün 終軍,[67] the Grandee Remonstrant, and his people to transmit his message, the courageous warrior, Wei Ch'en 魏臣, and his men to assist where help was needed, and Lu Po-te 路博德,[68] the Commandant of the Guards, to lead his troops and station them at Kuei-yang 桂陽,[69] to await [the return of] the envoys. The King was [still] young and the Dowager was a person from the central states who had once had an affair with An-kuo Shao-chi; when he [An-kuo Shao-chi] came as envoy, she again had sexual relations with him.[70] The people of the state generally knew about it, and many of them felt no attachment to the Dowager. The Dowager was afraid that a rebellion would break out, and she also wanted to rely on the prestige of the Han, so she several times urged the King and his assembled ministers to seek to come under the internal jurisdiction [of the Han]. She quickly submitted a letter [to the Emperor] by means of the envoys, asking that [Southern Yüeh] be considered on the same level as the feudal lords of the interior, to come to court once every three years, and to abolish the border

[66] The mausoleum town for Emperor Wen located about 10 miles northeast of Ch'ang-an (T'an Ch'i-hsiang, 2:14–15).

[67] A young, but notable, presence at Emperor Wu's court, during the decade between 122 and 112 BC. He seems to have died shortly thereafter (compare Loewe, *Dictionary*, pp. 727–8).

[68] A senior military man who had been served under Huo Ch'ü-ping 霍去病 in 119 BC (Loewe, *Dictionary*, pp. 413–14).

[69] The seat of Kuei-yang County about 150 miles south of modern Changsha in Hunan (T'an Ch'i-hsiang, 2:23).

[70] The rather prolix syntax of the *Shih chi* line 王年少，太后中國人也，嘗與安國少季通, 其使復私焉 is simplified in the *Han shu* (85.3854) version 王年少, 太后中國人也，安國少季往，復與私通.

frontier crossings. Thereupon the Son of Heaven approved it and conferred on Lü Chia 呂嘉,[71] its [Southern Yüeh's] Chancellor, a silver seal, and the seals for the Clerk of the Capital, Commander of the Capital, and the Grand Tutor; the remaining [positions][the King] was able to establish himself. [The Emperor] abolished their old punishments of tattooing and cutting off the nose,[72] and caused Han laws to be used, treated [Southern Yüeh] as one of the [states of the] feudal lords in the interior. The [Han] envoys all lingered [in Southern Yüeh] to settle and soothe [the situation]. The King and the Queen Dowager made ready; they prepared their baggage for the trip and valuable gifts, as utensils for their court audience.

Their Chancellor, Lü Chia, was indeed aged and had served three kings as minister. Those people in his clan who held positions as high officials were more than seventy. The sons had all been allowed to marry the king's daughters and his daughters all married to cousins of the King or [members of] the royal household. He even had a connection [through marriage] to [Chao Kuang 趙光], King Ch'in of Ts'ang-wu 蒼梧秦王.[73] His position within the state was exceedingly important and the Yüeh people put their trust in him and many served for him as eyes and ears, [so that] he won the hearts of the populace more than the King. In the matter of the King's submitting a letter [to the Emperor], he several times admonished and tried to stop the King, but the King would not listen to him. [Lü Chia] had a heart filled with rebellion and several times claimed sickness so as not to receive the Han envoys. The envoys all paid close attention to Chia, but the situation had not yet [reached the point] that they were able to execute him. Only when the King and the Queen Dowager also feared that Chia and the others would cause trouble first did they set out wine and a feast[74] and, relying on the opportunity of having the Han envoys [present], to plot to execute [Lü] Chia and the others. The envoys were all [seated] facing east,[75] the

[71] Otherwise unknown (compare Loewe, *Dictionary*, p. 422). On the state of Ts'ang-wu see chapter 116 below.

[72] Emperor Wen had abolished these punishments (compare *Shih chi*, 10.427–28).

[73] He was one of the local Yüeh leaders with his base at Kuang-hsin 廣信 (modern Wu-chou 梧州 in Kwangsi). Other than this chapter and that in the *Han shu* parallel, he is unknown (Loewe, *Dictionary*, p. 706). The "Chi-chieh" based on the *Han shu yin-yi* 漢書音義 claims he was called "the Ch'in King of Ts'ang-wu" because he was related to the Ch'in by marriage, but Wu and Lu (113.2975n.) note that the title Ch'in Wang was one he gave himself and should thus be understood as King Ch'in of Ts'ang-wu.

[74] The *Han shu* (95.3855) text is quite different here: "When the King and the Queen Dowager also feared that Chia and the others would cause trouble first they wanted to rely on the might of the Han envoys to plot to execute Chia and the others. They set out wine and a feast and invited the envoys and the great ministers to sit in attendance and drink"; 王、王太后亦恐嘉等先事發，介漢使者權，謀誅嘉等。置酒請使者，大臣侍坐飲.

[75] The seats facing east were the most honored for guests (the ruler usually faced south and his ministers north; less important guests faced west). Yü Ying-shih in his "The Seating

Dowager facing south, the King facing north; [*2973*] Chancellor Chia and the great ministers were all facing west, sitting in attendance and drinking[76]; Chia's younger brother was a commander and commanded his troops to occupy the [area] outside the palace. After the wine toasting had begun, to arouse anger in the envoys, the Dowager said to Chia, "If Southern Yüeh were submit to being within [the Han empire], it would benefit the state, yet the Lord Chancellor is troubled and finds this inconvenient. Why is this?" By this she wanted to provoke anger in the envoys. The envoys looked to each other for support, and in the end none dared to make the first move. Chia perceiving with his eyes and ears that something was not right, immediately rose and went out.[77] The Dowager was angered and wanted to stab him with a spear, but the King stopped the Dowager. In the end Chia came out [of the palace] and, dividing up[78] some of his younger brother's troops [as an escort], went to his residence. He claimed to be ill and was not willing to see the King or the envoys. Only then did he secretly [plot] with the great ministers to make a rebellion.[79] The King had never had the intention to execute Chia, and Chia knew this. For this reason for several months he [Chia] did not make a move. As for the Dowager, with her immoral behavior and the people of the state not feeling any attachment to her, though she only wanted to execute Chia and his people, her strength was still not up to it.[80]

Order at the Hong Men Banquet" (translated by T. C. Tang in *The Translation of Things Past,* [Hong Kong: Chinese University Press, 1982], pp. 57–58) comments on the current passage: "the seating arrangements this time also contained a delicate political meaning... The Empress Dowager strongly favored the pledging of Southern Yüeh's allegeance to the Han Court. For this reason, she invited the Han envoys ... to take the honored seats facing east. She herself was Southern Yüeh's supreme ruler. So she occupied the next highest seat facing south. The King of Southern Yüeh sat facing north so as to signify his submission to Han... Prime Minister Lü Chia and other ministers then 'faced west, attended, (and then) sat drinking.'... Her idea then was to put on an appearance of submission to the Han Court... Lü Chia was the leader of the group that most resolutely opposed the policy of Southern Yüeh become Han's vassal state. Quite obviously, at this banqueting scene where 'internal submission' was the main theme and where a bloodthirsty spirit lurked, the order of seating had the effect of deciding the basic atmosphere of the entire occasion."

[76] *Shih tso yin* 侍坐飲 could be read "sitting in attendance and causing them to drink."

[77] The *Han shu* parallel (95.3855) reads *chi ch'ü ch'u* 即趨出 "he immediately rushed out" (where 趨 is probably a scribal error for 起而).

[78] *Fen ch'i* 分其 is *chieh* 介, "to use as a shield" in the *Han shu* parallel.

[79] The *Han shu* makes explicit the plotting: "Only then did he secretly plot to make rebellion" 乃陰謀作亂.

[80] The *Han shu* text is more straightforward: "The Dowager alone wanted to execute Chia and the others, [but] her strength was still not up to it" 太后獨欲誅嘉等，力又不能。

The Son of Heaven heard that Chia was not obeying the King, that the King and the Queen Dowager were weak and alone, unable to control [the situation], and that the envoys had acted cowardly in not coming to a decision.[81] Moreover, he considered that as the King and the Queen Dowager had already submitted to Han and that only Lü Chia was making rebellion, it was not necessary to raise troops. He wanted to send Chuang Ts'an 莊參 to take two thousand men and go as an envoy. Ts'an said, "If we go as allies, a few men would indeed be sufficient; if we go as combatants, two thousand men will not be sufficient to manage it." When he refused because it was not possible,[82] the Son of Heaven dismissed Ts'an.[83] [At this] Han Ch'ien-ch'iu 韓千秋, a young hearty from Hao 郟 who was the former Chancellor of Chi-pei 濟北,[84] cried out, "This is tiny, insignificant Yüeh and moreover [*2974*] there is the King and the Dowager to rely on,[85] with only the Chancellor Lü Chia to cause harm. I should like to obtain two hundred[86] courageous warriors and I will certainly cut off Chia's head and report back with it." At this the Son of Heaven sent Ch'ien-ch'iu and Chiu Yüeh 樛樂,[87] the Queen Dowager's younger brother, to command two thousand men and go, and enter the borders of Yüeh.[88] Only then did Lü Chia and the others finally rebel, issuing an order to those in the state which read: "The King is young. The Dowager is a native of the Central States and moreover has acted promiscuously with the envoy. She solely desires to make [Nan Yüeh] accept subordinate status [to Han], to take all of the late king's treasures and present them to the Son of Heaven in order to curry favor; her numerous attendants, once she has traveled to Ch'ang-an, will be sold as captives to be become slaves. To grasp temporary advantage of extricating herself [from Southern Yüeh], she pays no attention to the altars of soil and grain of the Chao clan nor does she consider and plan for the ten thousand

[81] The *Han shu* reads simply: 天子聞之，罪使者怯無決, "When the Son of Heaven heard this, he judged the envoys guilty for acting cowardly in not coming to a decision."
[82] Or "when he made the excuse that it was not permissible."
[83] This becomes "the Son of Heaven dismissed Ts'an's troops" 天子罷參兵 in the *Han shu* parallel.
[84] According to Li Ling's 李陵 biography in the *Han shu* (54.2454), Han Ch'ien-ch'iu had formerly been Chancellor to the King of Chi-nan 濟南.
[85] The *Han shu* does not mention "the Queen Dowager" here.
[86] The *Han shu* (95.3856) reads "three hundred." This leads to an interesting discussion among modern scholars. Takigawa (113.13) notes that the Mao [Chin] edition "makes it three hundred men, which is the same as the Han shu" 毛本二百人作三百人與漢書合. Shih Chih-mien 施之勉, who is wont to deride Takigawa, notes that the Ching-yu 景祐 edition also reads "three hundred" (see Wang Shu-min, 113.3041–42). But as Wang Shu-min points out, Shih erred and the Ching-yu edition in fact also reads "two hundred."
[87] Loewe, *Dictionary*, p. 202, reads Chiu Le.
[88] Takigawa (113.13) cites a "Chi-chieh" note which is not in the Chung-hua edition citing Hsü Kuang that Han Ch'ien-ch'iu's position was colonel (*hsiao-wei* 校尉).

generations [of successors]." Only then did he and his younger brother command troops to attack and kill the King, the Dowager, and even the Han envoys.[89] He sent someone to report to King Ch'in of Ts'ang-wu and to his various commandaries and counties, and enthroned as king [Chao] Chien-te 建德, Marquis of Shu-yang 術陽,[90] and King Ming's 明 [Chao Ying-ch'i's] eldest boy, the son of a Yüeh wife.[91] At the same time Han Ch'ien-ch'iu's troops entered [Nan Yüeh] and defeated several small towns. Thereafter, Yüeh straightaway opened up roads and gave [them] food. When they were still forty *li* from reaching P'an-yü, Yüeh attacked Ch'ien-ch'iu and the others with troops and finally wiped them out. He sent men to encase and seal up the tallies of the Han envoys and have them placed at frontier forts, easily coming up with some disingenuous phrases to apologize for his offenses, and sent out troops to guard the strategic points. At this point the Son of Heaven said, "Although Han Ch'ien-ch'iu was not successful, he still was the crown of the vanguard." He enfeoffed his son, [Han] Yen-nien 延年, as Marquis of Ch'eng-an 成安.[92] As for Chiu Yüeh, because his elder sister had been the Queen Dowager, and first of all wanted to submit to the Han, he enfeoffed his son, Kuang-te 廣德 as Marquis of Lung-k'ang 龍亢.[93]

[89] The *Han shu* parallel (95.3856) reads: "Only then did he and his younger brother command troops to attack and kill the Dowager and the King, killing every one of the Han envoys" 乃與其弟將卒攻殺太后、王，盡殺漢使者.

[90] As the elder brother of Chao Hsing 趙興 he had been made Marquis of Shu-yang in 111 BC.

The seat of Shu-yang County was Hsia-p'ei 下沛 County in Tung-hai 東海 Commandery (modern Sui-ning 睢寧 county in Kiangsu (Wang Li-ch'i, 113.2977n.). Hsü Kuang (cited in "Chi-chieh") says that in 113 BC. Chao Yüeh 趙越, the elder brother of the King of Nan Yüeh, was enfeoffed as Marquis of Kao-ch'ang 高昌. See also Kung Liu-chu 龔留柱, "Nan Yüeh Wang Chien-te k'ao-pien" 南越王建德考辨, in *Nan Yüeh kuo shih-chi yen-chiu t'ao-lun hui lun-wen hsüan-chi* 南越國史跡研究討論會論文選集, Chung-kuo Ch'in Han shih yen-chiu hui 中國秦漢史研究會 et al., ed. (Peking: Wen-wu Ch'u-pan-she, 2005), pp. 42–46.

[91] In support of this reading, "the son of a Yüeh wife," see Sun Chih-tsu 孫志祖 (1737–1801) cited in Wang Shu-min (113.3042).

[92] The Chung-hua editors of the *Han shu* read this sentence as part of the Emperor's statement: "Let his son Yen-nien be enfeoffed as Marquis of Ch'eng-an!"

Ch'eng-an is located southeast of modern Lin-ju 臨汝 county in Honan (Wang Li-ch'i, 113.2977n.).

[93] The *Han shu* (95.3857) reads "Marquis of Hsi" (Hsi Hou 襲侯), but commentators are quick to point out that Hsi was the old graph for Lung 龍 (see "So-yin"). Wang Shu-min (113.3042) goes a step further to cite various commentators and other editions of this passage only to conclude that a scribe must have erred in reading a handwritten *lung k'ang* 龍亢 as a single character *hsi* 襲.

Only then did he issue an amnesty, which read: "When the Son of Heaven is in decline, and the feudal lords by means of force administer [the state], [the *Ch'un-ch'iu*⁹⁴] criticized the ministers who did not suppress bandits. Now that Lü Chia, Chien-te, and the others have revolted, calmly and coolly enthroned themselves, I have ordered convicts [freed by this amnesty] and an army of 100,000 [sailors] from the towering ships⁹⁵ south of the Chiang 江 and Huai 淮 [rivers] to go and suppress them."

[2975] In the autumn of the fifth year of Yüan-ting (112 BC), Lu Po-te, the Commandant of the Guards was made the Fu-po Chiang-chün 伏波將軍 (Wave-calming General) and set out from Kuei-yang 桂陽, descending the Huai 匯 River⁹⁶; Yang P'u 楊僕,⁹⁷ the Chief Commandant over the Nobility, was made Lou-ch'uan Chiang-chün 樓船將軍 (General of the Towering Ships) and set out from Yü-chang 豫章,⁹⁸ descending the Heng-p'u 橫浦 [Pass]. Two men of Yüeh who had formerly turned their allegiance [to Han] and been made marquises were made Ko-ch'uan Chiang-chün 戈船將軍 (General of the Pole-ax Ships)⁹⁹ and Hsia-li Chiang-chün 下

---

⁹⁴ Watson (2:215) believes this refers to Confucius's criticism in the *Ch'un ch'iu*.

⁹⁵ This was the Han navy (Wu and Lu, 115.2977n.). Estimates suggest that each towering ship (*lou-ch'uan* 樓船) could hold up to 3,000 sailors, so the figure 100,000 may seem improbable. Yet the "P'ing-chün shu" 平準書 (Treatise on the Balanced Standards, *Shih chi*, 30.1436) notes that already in 116 BC *lou-ch'uan* more than ten *chang* tall were built on Lake K'un-ming in the palace as part of the preparations for a campaign in the south because "at that time Yüeh was intending to use ships against the Han to give battle and drive them out" 是時越欲與漢用船戰逐. Later in the same chapter (*Shih chi*, 30.1438) the Emperor pardoned prisoners so that "in the south more than 200,000 sailors on towering ships assaulted Southern Yüeh" 南方樓船卒二十餘萬人擊南越. Another reckoning of Yang P'u's strength in the text below (*Shih chi*, 115.2976) says he had "several tens of thousands." The towering ships themselves were already employed by the Ch'in in their campaigns against the Pai Yüeh 百越 (compare *Shih chi*, 112.2958). See also Sun Chan-min 孫占民 and Ch'eng Lin 程林, "Ch'in, Han lou-ch'uan k'ao" 秦漢樓船靠, *Kun-ming Hsüeh-yüan hsüeh-pao*, 32 (2010.2): 72–74.

⁹⁶ The *Han shu* reads Huang 湟 for Huai 匯. This is the modern Lien 連 River in Kwangtung which flows southeastward from Kuei-yang into the Hsia River 狹水, which drains into P'an-yü (T'an Ch'i-hsiang, 2:36).

⁹⁷ Yang P'u's biography can be found on *Shih chi* 122.3149, in the "K'u-li lieh-chuan" 酷吏列傳 (Biographies of the Harsh Officials). See also *Shih chi* chapter 115 where Ssu-ma Ch'ien depicts his lackluster performance in the campaign against Ch'ao-hsien resulted in his dismissal (*Shih chi*, 115.2987ff.) and the translator's note at the end of this chapter.

⁹⁸ Yü-chang was a Han commandery with its seat at modern Nanchang in Kiangsi.

⁹⁹ Chang Yen ("Chi-chieh") says that the pole–axes were affixed to the bottom of the boats to ward off *Alligator sinensis*.

厲將軍 (General Who Brings Down Severity)[100] [respectively] and set out from Ling-ling 零陵,[101] one descending the Li River 離水[102] and the other reaching Ts'ang-wu 蒼梧.[103] The Ch'ih-yi Hou 馳義侯 (Marquis Who Gallops to Duty)[104] relying on convicts from Pa and Shu sent forth [these] troops from Yeh-lang 夜郎,[105] and descended the Tsang-k'o River 牂柯江.[106] They all met at P'an-yü.

In the winter of the sixth year of Yüan-ting (111 BC), the General of the Towering Ships [Yang P'u] led crack troops to first cause Hsün-hsia 尋陝[107] to surrender, broke through at Shih-men 石門,[108] captured grain from Yüeh ships and, relying on it, drove back the vanguard of the Yüeh; [*2976*] he then waited with his several tens of thousands of men for the Wave-calming [General]. The Wave-calming General [Lu Po-te] was commanding convicts and the way was long, so he came too late to the point [they were] to meet. When he finally met up with the [General of the] Towering Ships, he had only a little over one thousand men. Finally they advanced together. With [the General of the] Towering Ships at the front they reached P'an-yü. [Chao] Chien-te and [Lü] Chia were both guarding the city walls. [The General of the] Towering Ships personally selected an advantageous place and took up position facing the southeast [corner of the wall]. The Wave-calming General took up position

---

[100] *Ko-ch'uan Chiang-chün* 戈船將軍 and *Hsia-li Chiang-chün* 下厲將軍. Hsü Kuang ("Chi-chieh") notes a variant *Hsia-lai Chiang-chün* 下瀨將軍, General for Descending the Rapids which is also the reading in the *Han shu*.

According to Liang T'ing-nan's 梁廷楠, *Nan Yüeh Wu-chu zhuan* 南越五主傳 (Biographies of Five Rulers of Southern Yüeh [Canton: Kuang-tung Jen-min, 1982], cited in Wang Li-ch'i, 113.2977n.), these generals were Cheng Yen 鄭嚴 and T'ian Chia 田甲, respectively.

[101] A Han county with its seat found to the southwest of modern Ch'üan-chou 全州 in Kwangsi (Wang Li-ch'i, 113.2977n.).

[102] The modern Li 漓 River (Wu and Lu, 113.29877n.). These troops approached Nan Yüeh from the northwest.

[103] Modern Wuzhou City 梧州市 (T'an Ch'i-hsiang, 2:36).

[104] Again based on Liang T'ing-nan (op. cit.), this was Ho Yi 何遺.

[105] A state or ethnic region, the largest of the Nan Yi (compare *Shih chi*, 116.2991).

[106] This river flows southeast from modern Kweichow, then bends east into Canton (T'an Ch'i-hsiang, 2:36).

[107] According to "So-yin" this was near Lien-k'ou 連口, which is the place where the Lien River flows into the Pei 北 River in Kwangtung.

[108] Northwest of modern Canton (T'an Ch'i-hsiang, 2:36). This seems is probably the "strong position" that Yang P'u "caused to fall" (*hsien jian* 陷堅, see text below, *Shih chi*, 113.2977).

facing the northwest [corner]. When darkness fell, [the General of the] Towering Ships attacked and defeated the men of Yüeh, setting fire to the city wall. Yüeh had long heard the name of [the General of] Towering Ships and as the day had turned dark they did not know how many troops he had. Only then did [the General of the] Towering Ships set up camp and send an envoy to entice those who would surrender, conferring on them the seal [of a marquis], and letting them loose again with orders to entice others. [The General of the] Towering Ships with all his force attacked and burned the enemy [positions], which on the contrary drove them to enter the camp of the Wave-calming [General]. When it began to get light, those within the city walls had all surrendered to the Wave-calming [General]. [Lü] Chia, [Chao] Chien-te, and several hundred of their followers had by night already[109] escaped onto the sea; they left heading west by boat.[110] The Wave-calming [General] also took advantage to question a nobleman who had surrendered and thereby learned where Lü Chia had gone[111]; he sent men to pursue him. By means of this, Su Hung 蘇弘 (d. 104), Master of the Horse [for the Wave-calming General] and a former colonel,[112] captured [Chao] Chien-te and was enfeoffed as Marquis of Hai-ch'ang 海常侯.[113] Tu Chi 都稽,[114] a palace attendant of Yüeh, captured [Lü] Chia and was made Marquis of Lin-ts'ai 臨蔡侯.[115]

[2977] When this Chao Kuang 趙光, the King of Ts'ang-wu,[116] who had the same *cognomen* as the King of Yüeh, heard that the Han troops had arrived, along with [Shih] Ting [史]定, the Prefect of Yüeh's Chieh-yang 揭陽,[117] they arranged for themselves to submit to Han.[118] Chü Weng 居翁, the Inspector of Kuei-lin 桂林,[119]

---

[109] *Han shu* (95.3858) reads "by means of night" (*yi yeh* 以夜 for 已夜).

[110] The *Han shu* parallel omits *yi ch'uan hsi ch'ü* 以船西去.

[111] The *Han shu* parallel of this rather prolix syntax of the *Shih chi* reads simply: "The Wave-calming [General] also asked one who had surrendered and learned where Lü Chia had gone" 伏波又問降者，知呂嘉所之.

[112] The translation follows the exegesis provided in Wang Li-ch'i (113.2978n.). Although Bielenstein gives "major" for *ssu-ma*, here it refers to a high ranking lieutenant of Lu Po-te (compare Loewe, *Dictionary*, pp. 491–92).

[113] According to Hsü Kuang ("Chi-chieh") his fief was located in Tung-lai 東萊 Commandery, which had its seat at modern Yeh 掖 county in Shantung.

[114] Also known as Sun Tu 孫都.

[115] Located southwest of modern Wu-chih 武陟 County in Honan.

[116] This is the King Ch'in of Ts'ang-wu mentioned above (*Shih chi*, 113.2972).

[117] A county about 25 miles northwest of modern Shan-t'ou 汕頭 near the modern county of the same name in Kwangtong (T'an Ch'i-hsiang, 2:36).

[118] Shih Ting's name is provided by the *Han shu* parallel. Without going into a detailed comparison, suffice it to say that the *Han shu* adds information on the appointment of Chao Kuang as well as several other men who surrendered at this time.

also convinced the [Hsi] Ou [西]甌 and the Lo [Yüeh] 駱[越] to submit to the Han; all were able to become marquises.[120] The troops which the generals of the Pole-ax Ships and Who Brings Down Severity together with the Marquis Who Gallops to Duty sent out from Yeh-lang had not yet descended [the rivers], when Southern Yüeh was already pacified. In the end it was made into nine commandaries.[121] The Wave-calming General had his fief increased. As the troops of the Pole-ax Ship General caused a strong position to fall, he was made Marquis of Chiang-liang 將梁侯.[122]

Five generations[123] and ninety-three years after the time when Commandant-Governor T'o was first made king the state perished.[124]

[*2978*] His Honor the Grand Scribe says:
Commandant-Governor [Chao] T'o's becoming king was originated
    from Jen Hsiao['s 任嚣 advice].
When it so happened that Han first stabilized [the empire],
he was ranked as a feudal lord.
The [Marquis of] Lung-lü 隆慮 [Chou Tsao 周竈] encountered the
    heat and infectious diseases [of Southern Yüeh]
and T'o was able because of this to become increasingly arrogant.

[119] Modern Hsiang-chou 象州 in Kwangtung (T'an Ch'i-hsiang, 2:35).

[120] The *Han shu* parallel says Chao Kuang was made Marquis of Sui-t'ao 隧桃侯, Shih Ting became Marquis of An-tao 安道侯, and Chü Weng was made Marquis of Hsiang-ch'eng 湘城侯.

The "So-yin" cites to *Han shu* to read: "More than 300,000 of the Ou and Lo promised to surrender to the Han" 甌駱三十餘萬口降漢, but the received text of the *Han shu* (95.3858) reads "more than 400,000" 四十餘萬.

[121] The nine counties are listed by Hsü Kuang in the "Chi-chieh." Ssu-ma Chen ("So-yin") believes that this list was based on the *Han shu* (95.3858). The ordering of the nine commandaries in the *Han shu* differs from that Hsü provides, however.

[122] According to the chronological tables, Yang P'u, not the otherwise unknown Pole–ax Ship General, was enfeoffed as Marquis of Chiang-liang in 116 BC (*Shih chi*, 20.1050). Ch'ien Mu, *Ti-ming k'ao*, p. 782, says the village of Chiang-liang is northwest of modern Ch'ing-yüan 清苑 County southeast of Pao-ting 保定 in Hopei.

[123] Liang Yü-sheng (54.1407) notes that a certain Chih 織, Marquis of Nan-wu 南武 侯 and a descendant of the ancient Yüeh state, was made King of Nan-hai 南海 by Kao-tsu in 195 BC (see "Kao-tsu pen-chi" in *Han shu*, 1B:77), so he should be considered a sixth generation or at least be included in this biography.

[124] The *Han shu* parallel (95.3859) reads simply "In all five generations and ninety–three years from when Commandant-Governor T'o became king the state perished" 自尉佗王五世, 九十三歲而亡.

When Ou and Lo attacked each other,[125]
Southern Yüeh was shaken.
When the Han troops approached the border,
[Chao] Ying-ch'i [趙]嬰齊 went in to court.[126]
Thereafter the loss of the state was presaged by the daughter of the
    Chiu 樛 [family][127];
Lü Chia's diminishing loyalty,
caused T'o to have no descendants.
The [General of the] Pole-ax Ships gave in to his desires [for
    merit],[128]
and his negligence and haughtiness led to loss and confusion;
the Wave-calming [General, Lu Po-te], though in difficult straits,
[showed] his intelligence and planning was more developed,
and based on this made disaster into fortune.
The twists of success and failure[129]
may be compared to the many strands of a rope.[130]

---

[125] Liang Yü-sheng (54.1407) notes that Ou and Lo did not attack each other and that the text should probably read "When Eastern Min raised troops, Southern Yüeh was shaken" 東閩興兵, 南越動搖. Wang Shu-min (113.3045) agrees with Liang that the original text does not make sense but suggests an alternate revision: "When Min and [Southern] Yüeh attacked each other, Southern Yüeh was shaken" 閩越相攻, 南越動搖.

[126] Ch'en Jen-hsi 陳仁錫 (1581–1636, cited on Takigawa, 113.19) points out that this entire passage, like the Grand Scribe's comments in "Chao-hsien lieh-chuan," is rhymed; the rhyme scheme is xaxa xaxa xaxb xbxb xbxb (侯 is pronounced here as 號). This, Ch'en believes, was the basis for the rhymed commentaries Pan Ku appended to chapters in the *Han shu*. In his comments to chapter 115 (cited on Takigawa, 115.10), "Chao-hsien lieh-chuan," which is also rhymed, Ch'en argues that the historian's comments to both this chapter and chapter 115 are interpolations provided by a later poetic hand.

[127] Nakai Sekitoku 中井積德 (cited on Takigawa, 113.19) argues that to keep the rhyme pattern "daughter of the Chiu" 樛女 should read "Queen Chiu" 樛后.

[128] By seizing the best position in the battle at P'an-yü.

[129] The language here is reminiscent of that in Kuan Chung's 管仲 biography to depict his skills: "As for his political strategies, he excelled in creating blessings from disasters and turning failures into success" 其為政也，善因禍而為福 (*Shih chi*, 62.2133; translation from *Grand Scribe's Records*, 7:12).

[130] Compare the passage in the "Owl Fu" by Chia Yi 賈誼 (*Shih chi*, 84.2498; translation *Grand Scribe's Records*, 7:305): Disaster is that on which fortune is based, / Fortune is that in which disaster hides. / Sorrow and joy live within the same gate, / Good luck and bad come from the same domain. / Though Wu was mighty and great / Fu-ch'ai was defeated because of it. / When Yüeh took refuge on K'uai-chi, / Kou Chien held sway over all the world. / Li Ssu traveled abroad and achieved success / But finally suffered the

*   *   *   *   *

After the Han pacified the Central States, and [Chao] T'o was able to create harmony [among the peoples of] Yang-Yüeh 楊越 [131] in order to protect the southern marches, he submitted taxes and labor services. [Thus] I composed the "Memoir of Southern Yüeh, Number Fifty-three." [132]

Five Punishments. / After Fu Yüeh had been in bonds, / He served Wu-ting as minister. / Disaster and fortune / Are no different than two strands of a rope. 禍兮福所倚，福兮禍所伏；憂喜聚門兮，吉凶同域。彼吳彊大兮，夫差以敗；越棲會稽兮，句踐霸世。斯游遂成兮，卒被五刑；傅說胥靡兮，乃相武丁。夫禍之與福兮，何異糾纆。命不可說兮，孰知其極？

[131] Referring the Chao T'o's initial charge from Kao-tsu (delivered by Lu Chia in 196 BC) "to cause him to unite the One Hundred Yüeh" 和集百越 (*Shih chi*, 113.2967).

Yang-Yüeh refers to all the Yüeh peoples south of Yang-chou 楊州, i.e., the region south of the Huai River (compare Chang Yen's 張宴 comment cited in "Chi-chieh" [Han Chao-ch'i, 130.6420–21, n. 186]).

[132] These are the Grand Scribe's reasons for compiling this chapter, given in his postface (*Shih chi*, 130.3317: 漢既平中國，而佗能集楊越以保南藩，納貢職。作南越列傳第五十三).

Translator's Note

The term Yüeh 越 (or 粵 in parallel accounts in the *Han shu*) was probably an attempt to reproduce the name that the people called themselves, but it also reflects one of the basic meanings of the term: "to cross over, beyond," since these peoples lived beyond the pale of Han Chinese influence (even in pre-Ch'in times). The "Cheng-yi" (*Shih chi*, 41.1739) explains Yüeh, citing Ho Hsün's 賀循 *K'uai-chi ji* 會稽記, as originating from the name of the youngest son of the mythical Shao-k'ang Emperor 帝少康 of the Hsia dynasty, Yü-yüeh 於越. Erica Brindley cites two other possible origins of the term ("Barbarians or Not? Ethnicity and Changing Conceptions of the Ancient Yue (Viet) Peoples, ca. 400–50 ," *Asia Major*, 16 [2003]: p. 4, n. 10). Yüeh may also refer to the area in which these people lived.

Whatever the etymology of the term, the reader of this chapter is left with few impressions of what the people of Southern Yüeh were like. This in constrast to the detail provided in the first account of a foreign people, that of the Hsiung-nu 匈奴 in chapter 110, which provides so much ethnographic information and reads in part:

> The Hsiung-nu . . . move around in search of water and grass. They do not have inner and outer city walls or permanent residences and do not engage in tilling fields. Nevertheless, each [group or leader] has land allotted [to him for use]. They do not have written documents [but] make agreements and bonds by means of the spoken words. The children are able to ride on sheep and to draw the bow to shoot birds and rodents. When they grow a little older, they shoot foxes and hares to use as food. As men their strength is sufficient to draw the bow fully, and all become armored horsemen. It is their custom that, when they have ample [resources], they make a living by following the livestock and hunt with their bows wild birds and beasts (*Shih chi*, 112.2958; *Grand Scribe's Records*, 9:382).

This omission may result from the lack of source material. Or perhaps Ssu-ma Ch'ien thought that the following brief description of the people in the Warring States era state of Yüeh in his "Yüeh-wang Kou-chien shih-chia" 越王句踐世家 (Hereditary House of Kou-chien, the King of Yüeh, *Shih chi*, 41.1739) suffices to portray their descendants in Southern Yüeh during the Han dynasty:

> [The descendants of Yü] were enfeoffed at K'uai-chi 會稽 so as to maintain the offering of sacrifices to Yü. They tattooed their bodies and cut their hair short, cleared the plants and the weeds, and established settlements there.

A third, more likely possibility is related to the motivation behind the chapter. Whereas the Hsiung-nu campaign, which stretched out over several decades, was the major foreign policy issue of Emperor Wu's reign, the war with Southern Yüeh, which resulted in Southern Yüeh's submission to the Han, ended quickly. Following this line of thinking, some scholars have suggested that the process of converting Southern Yüeh from a rival state to a "border vassal" *fan ch'en* 藩臣 (and in the subsequent three chapters, converting Tung Yüeh 東越, Ch'ao-hsien 朝鮮, and the Hsi-nan Yi 西南夷) provided the link between these chapters and was the leitmotif for this section of the *Shih chi*.[133] Ssu-ma Ch'ien's comments in chapter 130 explaining his motives in compiling the account of the Southern Yüeh seem to support this view:

> After the Han pacified the Central States, and [Chao] T'o was able to create harmony [among the peoples of] Yang–Yüeh in order to protect the southern marches, he submitted taxes and labor services. [Thus] I composed the "Memoir of Southern Yüeh, Number Fifty–three.

Regardless of the motives behind this account of Southern Yüeh and those of Eastern Yüeh, Ch'ao-hsien, and the Barbarians of the Southwest which follow, these four chapters beg the question of the overall order of the chapters in the *Shih chi*. The placing of this chapter, following the biographies of generals and officials who were most involved with the Hsiung-nu question, rather than after the chapter on the Hsiung-nu itself (chapters 108–112), has at least raised the possibility that there was originally a different order.[134] On the other hand, Yen An's memorial (cited in Chu-fu Yen's 主父偃 biography, *Shih chi*, 112.2958, *Grand Scribe's Records*, 9:382–3) may be considered a segue between the current chapters 112 and 113. It speaks to the suffering brought to the common people by the Ch'in dynasty's campaign against Southern Yüeh and uses this suffering as one of the examples to argue against foreign expansion. Yet this account of Southern Yüeh in chapter 113 shows no suffering among the Han people or even its troops. There is a link between the biography of Ssu-ma Hsiang-ju 司馬相如 (179–117 BC) in chapter 117, which deals with Ssu-ma's role in establishing relations with the people of the southwest, and the preceding chapter 116, "Hsi-nan Yi lieh-chuan" 西南夷列傳 (Memoir of the Barbarians of the Southwest). A meaningful tie between chapters 113 through 116, however, is more elusive, and we can only echo the overall conclusion of Chao Yi 趙異 who questions the logic of the arrangement of these four chapters: "As their sequence [of chapters

---

[133] Cf. for example, Ch'en Jen-hsi's 陳仁錫 (1581–1636) argument (*Shih chi p'ing-lin*, 113.1a, *margine scriptus superior*).

[134] Chang Shou-chieh in his "Cheng-yi" (*Shih chi*, 110.2779) notes that in some early editions the "Hsiung-nu lieh-chuan" follows the biography of Kung-sun Hung 公孫弘 and Chu-fu Yen (now chapter 112), but then gives several reasons to discount this claim.

113–123] is all without significance, it is obvious that they were completed and compiled randomly" 其次第皆無意義，可知其隨得隨編.[135]

Finally, the account of Yang P'u's 楊僕 role in the climatic battle at P'an-yü here differs greatly from the *Han shu* parallel. Here the *Shih chi* version:

The Wave-calming General [Lu Po-te] took up position facing the northwest [corner]. When darkness fell, [the General of the] Towering Ships [Yang P'u] attacked and defeated the men of Yüeh, setting fire to the city wall. Yüeh had long heard the name of [the General of] Towering Ships and as the day had turned dark they did not know how many troops he had. Only then did [the General of the] Towering Ships set up camp and send an envoy to entice those who would surrender, conferring on them the seal [of a marquis], and letting them loose again with orders to entice others. [The General of the] Towering Ships with all his force attacked and burned the enemy [positions], which on the contrary drove them to enter the camp of the Wave-calming [General]. When it began to get light, those within the city walls had all surrendered to the Wave-calming [General]. [Lü] Chia, [Chao] Chien-te, and several hundred of their followers had by night already escaped onto the sea; they left heading west by boat. The Wave-calming [General] also took advantage to question a nobleman who had surrendered and thereby learned where Lü Chia had gone; he sent men to pursue him. By means of this, Su Hung 蘇弘 (d. 104), Master of the Horse [for the Wave-calming General] and a former colonel, captured [Chao] Chien-te and was enfeoffed as Marquis of Hai-ch'ang 海常侯. Tu Chi 都稽, a palace attendant of Yüeh, captured [Lü] Chia and was made Marquis of Lin-ts'ai 臨蔡侯.

Yang P'u's role is key to Ssu-ma Ch'ien's version. He maneuvers his troops and drives the enemy into the hands of Lu Po-te who by chance is able to accept their surrender and subsequently capture some of the officers who fled. The *Han shu*, on the contrary, depicts Yang P'u's actions as full of blunders, recording, in Yang P'u's biography, the Emperor's own comments cataloguing five errors Yang committed in this campaign (*Han shu*, 90.3659). The *Shih chi* biography of Yang, though included

[135] Chao Yi, "*Shih chi* pien-tz'u" 史記編次 (The Sequence of Compilation in the *Grand Scribe's Records*; [rpt. Taipei: Hua-shih Ch'u-pan-she, 1977], p. 8).

On the ordering of the chapters see also van Ess's arguments (*Politik*, pp. 717–25); he concludes that chapter 105 on the medical practioners should be seen as introducing the era of Emperors Ching and Wu and of presenting the maladies that beset states because of the lifestyles of their rulers. Chapters 106–117 mark the depiction of what Ssu-ma Ch'ien saw as the aggravation of the illnesses of Emperor Wu's reign, beginning with the revolt by Liu P'i 劉濞, the King of Wu 吳王, and ending with the expansionist politics in the southwest which caused many internal problems and which Ssu-ma Hsiang-ju 司馬相如 (in chapter 117) clearly sought to oppose.

in the chapter on "K'u-li lieh-chuan" 酷吏列傳 (Biographies of the Harsh Officials, *Shih chi*, 122.3140), is a brief life which describes his role in the campaign against Nan Yüeh as follows:

> When Southern Yüeh rebelled, he was appointed General of the Towered Ships, had merit, and was enfeoffed as Marquis of Chiang-ling.
>
> 南越反，拜為樓船將軍，有功，封將梁候.

The contradiction in treatments is explained by the modern scholar Han Chaoch'i 韓兆琦 (114.5685) as an attempt not to praise Yang P'u but rather to demean the contribution of Lu Po-te 路博德, the Wave-calming General, to the battle. This because Lu had been instrumental in slandering Li Ling 李陵 (cf. Li Ling's biography, *Han shu*, 54.2451), the general whom Ssu-ma Ch'ien had defended so courageously.

Bibliography

Translations:
Aoki, *Shiki*, 12:147–80.
Watson, *Han*, 2:207–18.

Studies
Allard, Francis. "Lingnan and Chu during the First Millennium BC: A Reassessment of the Core-Periphery Model," in *Guangdong, Archaeology and Early Texts, Archäologie und frühe Texts (Zhou-Tang)*. Shing Müller, Thomas O. Höllmann, Putao Gui, eds. Wiesbaden: Harrassowitz, 2004, pp. 1–21.
___. "Panyu: Die südliche Pforte nach China während der Han-Zeit," in Margarete Prüch, ed. *Schätze für König Zhao Mo: Das Grab von Nan Yue*. Heidelberg: Umschau/Braus Verlag, 1998, pp. 109–113.
Brindley, Erica. "Barbarians or Not? Ethnicity and Changing Conceptions of the Ancient Yue (Viet) Peoples, ca. 400–50 ," *Asia Major*, 16 (2003): 1–32.
___. "Representations and Uses of Yue Identity along the Southern Frontier of the Han, ca. 200–111 B.C.E," *Early China*, 33/34 (2010–2011): 1–35.
Chang Jung-fang 張榮芳 and Huang Miao-chang 黃淼章. *Nan Yüeh kuo-shih* 南越國史. Guangzhou: Kuang-tung Jen-min, 1995.
Chen Kuo-chiang 陳國強 et al. *Pai Yüeh min-tsu shih* 百越民族史. Peking: Chung-kuo She-hui K'o-hsüeh, 1988.
Eberhard, Wolfram. *Lokalkulturen im alten China*. Vol. 1. Leiden: E. J. Brill, 1942.
Hu Shouwei 胡守衛. *Nan Yüeh k'ai-t'o hsieh-ch'ü: Chao T'o* 南越開拓先驅: 趙. Guangzhou: Kuang-tung Jen-min, 2005.
Huang Miao-chang 黃淼章. *Nan Yüeh kuo* 南越國. Canton: Kuang-tung Jen-min, 2004.
Hu Shou-wei 胡守爲. *Ling-nan ku-shih* 嶺南古史. Canton: Kuang-tung Jen-min, 1999.
Jao Tsung-i 饒宗頤. "Wu Yüeh wen-hua" 吳越文化, *BIHP* 41 (1969): 609–36.
Lary, Diana. "The Tomb of the King of Nanyue: The Contemporary Agenda of History: Scholarship and Identity," *Modern China* 22.1 (1996): 3–27.
Liang T'ing-nan 梁廷楠 (1796–1861). *Nan Han shu* 南漢書. Canton: Kuang-tung Jen-min, 1981.

___. *Nan Yüeh wu-chu chuan chi ch'i-t'a ch'i chung* 南越五主傳及其他七種. Canton: Hsin-hua Shu-tien, 1982.

Liang Yün-lin 梁允麟. *Ling-nan ku-shih shang-ch'üeh* 嶺南古史商榷. Canton: Ling-nan Mei-shu Ch'u-pan-she, 1997.

Loewe, Michael. "Guangzhou: The Evidence of the Standard Histories from the *Shiji* to the *Chen shu*, A Preliminary Study," in *Guangdong, Archaeology and Early Texts, Archäologie und frühe Texts (Zhou–Tang)*. Shing Müller, Thomas O. Höllmann, Putao Gui, eds. Wiesbaden: Harrassowitz, 2004, pp. 51–80.

Milburn, Olivia. "The Bai Yue during the Han Dynasty" and "Changing Studies of the Bai Yue," in Milburn, *The Glory of Yue, An Annotated Translation of the Yuejue shu*. Leiden: Brill, 2010, pp. 23–29 and 29–34, respectively.

Nan Yüeh-kuo shih-chi yan-t'ao hui 南越國史跡研討會. Zhongshan Daxue Lishixi 中山大學歷史系, ed. Peking: Wenwu, 2005.

Peters, Heather. "Tattoed Faces and Stilt Houses: Who Were the Ancient Yue," *Sino-Platonic Papers* 17 (April 1990), p. 7.

Röllike, Herrmann–Josef. "Nan Yue in der Uberlieferung des Hofschreibers Sima Qian," in *Schätze für König Zhao Mo: Das Grab von Nan Yue*. Heidelberg: Umschau/Braus Verlag, 1998, pp. 109–113.

Wiens, Herold J. *China's March Towards the South*. Hamden: Shoestring Press, 1954.

Wu Ling-yün 吳淩雲. *Chao T'o* 趙佗. Guangzhou: Kuang-tung Jen-min, 2010.

Yü T'ien-ch'ih 余天熾. *Ku Nan Yüeh kuo-shih* 古南越國史. Nanning: Kuang-hsi Jen-min, 1988.

___. "*Shih chi* Nan Yüeh Wei T'o lieh-chuan chien-cheng" 史記南越尉佗列傳箋証. *Hua-nan Shih-fan Ta-hsüeh hsüeh-pao* 華南師範大學學報, 1982.1: 126–130.

Yü, Ying-shih. "Han Foreign Relations," in *The Cambridge History of China, vol. 1: The Ch'in and Han Empires, 221 B.C.–A.D. 220*. Denis Twitchett and Michael Loewe, eds. Cambridge: Cambridge University Press, 1986, pp. 453–7.

___. "Surrendered Barbarians and Their Treatment," *Trade and Expansion in Han China: A Study in the Structuve of Sino–barbarian Economic Relations*. Berkeley and Los Angeles: University of California Press, 1967, pp. 65–91.

Tung Yüeh 東越 (Eastern Yüeh)

⊙ Han Commandery Seats   ◎ *Modern Cities*

○ Han Places   • Han Counties

NAN-YANG
南陽郡

JU-NAN
汝南郡

Huai-shui
淮水

LIN-HUAI
臨淮郡

Tung-ch'eng
東成

KUANG-LING KUO
廣陵國

Nanking
南京

Tan-t'u
丹徒

Wu-hsi
無錫

K'UAI-CHI 會稽郡

CHIANG-HUAI CHIEN
江淮間

Wuhan
武漢

Chiang-shui
江水

TAN-YANG
丹陽郡

WU 吳

Jo-yeh
若邪

Shanghai
上海

Hangchow
杭州

Yü-erh
標兒

Ch'ien-t'ang
錢唐

Kou-chang
句章

Ningpo
寧波

Tung-t'ing hu
洞庭湖

P'o-yang hu
鄱陽湖

Che-chiang
浙

Changsha
長沙

YÜ-CHANG
豫章郡

Nanchang
南昌

P'o-yang
鄱陽

TUNG-HAI
(TUNG YÜEH)
東海(東越)

Tung-ou
東甌

CH'ANG-SHA KUO
長沙國

Chien-ch'eng
建成

Pai-sha
白沙

Wu-lin
武林

Hsiang-shui
湘水

Hu-han shui
湖漢水

Mei-ling
梅嶺

MIN YÜEH
閩越

Tung-yeh
東冶

KUEI-YANG
桂陽郡

Foochow
福州

TS'ANG-WU
蒼梧郡

Chieh-yang
揭揚

Canton
廣州

P'an-yü
番禺

Hong Kong
香港

Macao
澳門

The Eastern Yüeh,[1] Memoir 54

translated by William H. Nienhauser, Jr.

[114.2979] As for Wu-chu 無諸,[2] the King of Min Yüeh 閩越王,[3] and Yao 搖, the King of Tung-hai 東海王 in [the region of] Yüeh, their ancestors were both descendants of Kou-chien 句踐,[4] the King of Yüeh, and had the *cognomen* Tsou 騶.[5]

---

[1] In this chapter Eastern Yüeh refers alternately to those Yüeh people who traced their ancestry to the pre-Ch'in state of Yüeh and lived in the area that is now southern Chekiang and northern Fukien, to the state of Min Yüeh, and to the region itself. The translation of the title as "the Eastern Yüeh" attempts to bring out that pluresignation. See also the discussion of Yüeh and its usages in the *Shih chi* in the translator's note.

[2] The *Han shu* parallel narrative runs from 95.3859–3863; it uses the graph Yüeh 粵 for the *Shih chi*'s 越.

[3] Under the Ch'in dynasty, this region had been part of Min-chung Commandery 閩中郡 with the commandery seat at Tung-chih 東治 (modern Foochow–see text below); at the start of the Han dynasty, Wu-chu had been enfeoffed as King of Min Yüeh and, under Emperor Hui 惠帝, Yao had been made King of Tung-hai with his capital at Tung-ou near modern Wenchow on the Ou 甌 River (see Ying Shao's comments on *Han shu*, 6.158: 應劭曰：高祖五年立無諸為閩越王。惠帝立搖為東海王，都東甌，故號東甌, the map at the start of this chapter, and T'an Ch'i-hsiang, 2:12).

[4] The attempt to link the various ancestors of neighboring peoples to Han Chinese relatives is made in many of the chapters depicting them. On the history of Yüeh see "Yüeh-wang Kou-chien shih-chia" 越王勾踐世家, *Shih chi* chapter 41 (41.1751): "Seven generations later [after King Wu-ch'iang 無疆 (r. 343–323 BC)], there was Lord Yao 搖 of Min 閩, who assisted the Feudal Lords in pacifying Ch'in. The Exalted Emperor of Han (r. 206–195 BC) again considered Yao the King of Yüeh in order to carry on the succession of Yüeh. The lords of Eastern Yüeh and Min were all his descendants"; 后七世，至閩君搖，佐諸侯平秦。漢高帝復以搖為越王，以奉越后。東越，閩君，皆其后也.

[5] Hsü Kuang ("Chi-chieh") notes that one text read Lo 駱 for Tsou. Wu and Lu note that Chen Chih 陳直 in his *Shih chi hsin-cheng* 史記新證 argues that Tsou was a major clan in the state of Ch'i 齊 and it unknown as a Yüeh *cognomen*; Lo, Ch'en argues, must be correct. Wang Shu-min (114.3047) cites a poem by Chang Ching-yang 張景陽 (from the *Wen-hsüan*) in which the *cognomen* is given as Lo. He also points out that both the "So-yin" commentary

29

After [First Emperor of] Ch'in had already united all under Heaven,[6] he deposed them both and made them lords and chieftains, taking their territory to make Min-chung Commandery 閩中郡.[7] When the feudal lords rebelled against Ch'in, Wu-chu and Yao led the Yüeh, turning their loyalty to Wu Jui 吳芮 (d. 201 BC), the Magistrate of Po-yang 鄱陽令, he who was styled "the Lord of Po" 鄱君,[8] and followed the feudal lords to annihilate Ch'in. In the meantime, Hsiang Chi 項籍 [Hsiang Yü 項羽] who was in charge of issuing orders [to the various leaders], did not make them kings[9] and for this reason they did not attach themselves to [the King of] Ch'u 楚 [Hsiang Yü].[10]

in both the Huang Shan-fu 黃善夫 (Po-na edition) and the Palace edition (Tien-pen 殿本, 114.1a) differ from that which appears in the Chung-hua edition or Takigawa and reads: "Hsü Kuang's explanation is correct. The preceding [chapter] reads "Ou and Lo"; here it refers separately to Min and they do not have the *cognomen* Tsou" 徐廣說是。上云甌駱，此別云閩，不姓騶也. *Shang* 上 points to the preceding chapter, "Nan Yüeh lieh-chuan" (*Shih chi*, 113.2969) which reads: "[Chao] T'o took advantage of this to display his military strength in the border regions and to give bribes and gifts of money and goods to the Min Yüeh, Hsi Ou, and Lo" (see also n. 34 and the translation on p. 6 above).

To go a step beyond Wang Shu-min to point out that "So-yin" in the Chung-hua edition seems flawed. It reads: "Hsü Kuang says in one edition it is written "Lo." This in the preceding [chapter] reads "Ou Lo" and [they] do not have the *cognomen* Tsou" 徐廣云一作「駱」，是上云「甌駱」，不姓騶. To this reader the syntax of this note seems distorted and it seems likely that the Chung-hua version (and the original Chin-ling edition it is based on, 14.1a) is the result of a scribal error or an attempt to simplify the note by later editors.

Takigawa (114.2) cites Chang Chao 張照 and others and questions the whole narrative depicting the descent from Kou-chien.

[6] The *Han shu* parallel (95.3859) omits *yi* 已 and *chieh* 皆 to read "When the Ch'in united all under Heaven, they were deposed as kings . . ." 秦并天下，廢為君長.

[7] Takigawa (114.2) cites Wang Ming-sheng's 王鳴盛 (1722–1797) argument that the *Han shu* "Ti-li chih" 地理志 does not mention Min-chung as one of Ch'in's thirty-six commanderies but thinks it may have been created late in the First Emperor's reign. Wang Shu-min (114.3048) says it was in the twenty-sixth year of Ch'in Shih-huang (231 BC). Yen Shih-ku (*Han shu*, 95.3859n.) locates this in Chien-an 建安 in Ch'üan-chou 泉州.

[8] For details on Wu Jui's role in the interregnum between Ch'in and Han, see Loewe, Dictionary, p. 586. Liu Pang made him King of Ch'ang-sha in 202 BC and on his death his son succeeded him, but he died the following year.

[9] The *Shih chi* uses the composite negative *fu* 弗 here (不+之) but the *Han shu* simplifies this to *pu* 不 ("did not king them" 不王).

[10] Although these events are not mentioned in Hsiang Yü's biography in chapter 7 of the *Shih chi*, they suggest that both Wu-chu and Yao were kings before as does the text below.

When [the King of] Han assaulted[11] Hsiang Chi, Wu-chu and Yao led the men of Yüeh to assist Han.

In the fifth year of Han (202 BC), [Han] reinstalled Wu-chu as the King of Min Yüeh, to be king over his former territory of Min-chung, and set the capital at Tung-yeh 東冶 (Eastern Yeh).[12]

In the third year of [Emperor] Hsiao Hui 孝惠 (192 BC), only when someone raised the issue of Yüeh's meritorious service during Emperor Kao's time and said: "The merits of Yao, the Lord of Min, were numerous and his people easily allied themselves to him [to Emperor Kao]," did [the Emperor] install Yao as King of Tung-hai, with his capital at Tung Ou 東甌 (Eastern Ou)[13]; the world commonly calls him "King of Tung Ou" 東甌王.[14]

[2980] Several reigns later,[15] when it came to[16] the third year of [Emperor] Hsiao Ching 孝景 (154 BC), [Liu] P'i [劉]濞, the King of Wu,[17] revolted, and wanted to cause [the King of] Min Yüeh to follow him but Min Yüeh was still unwilling to set out and only [the King of] Tung Ou followed Wu. At the time Wu was defeated, Tung Ou accepted a bribe from Han and killed the King of Wu [at] Tan-t'u 丹徒.[18]

---

[11] "Assault" is *chi* 擊. We have tried to distinguish *kung* 攻 and *chi* 擊 throughout our translation; *kung* is certainly the most common term used to depict attacks in the *Shih chi* but in this chapter Ssu-ma Ch'ien's employs *chi* 擊.

[12] Near modern Foochow in Fukien (Wu and Lu, 114.2987n.).

[13] Near modern Wenchow in Chekiang (see n. 3 above).

[14] The *Han shu* parallel omits *su* 俗 to read simply "the world calls him the King of Eastern Ou."

[15] *Hou shu shih* 後數世 "several reigns later" refers to the reigns of Empress Lü and the young boys she set up as emperors in addition to that of Emperor Wen. This ellipsis may imply some subtle criticism of the former child rulers.

[16] The *Shih chi* text reads *chih Hsiao ching san nien* 至孝景三年 but the *Han shu* parallel (95.3860) here (and *passim*) omits this *chih* 至.

[17] See his biography in *Shih chi* chapter 106.

[18] Tan-t'u was the name of a county northeast of modern Chen-chiang 鎮江 City in Kiangsu (Wu and Lu, 114.2987n.).

A parallel and more detailed account can be found in Liu P'i's biography (*Shih chi*, 106:2834; translation revised from *Grand Scribe's Records*, 9:25): "Wu was crushed, officers and men mostly died of starvation, and only then did they desert and scatter. At this the King of Wu then joined several thousand of the stalwart fellows under his banner to flee at night and leave, they crossed the Chiang, fled to Tan-t'u, and took refuge with the Tung-Yüeh. Only when the troops of the Tung-Yüeh were surely more than ten thousand men, did they send men to retake and gather the fleeing soldiers. The Han sent a man to entice the Tung-Yüeh by [offering] rewards, and the Tung-Yüeh then tricked the King of Wu; when the King of Wu left [his refuge] to reward his army, [the Tung-Yüeh] immediately sent a man to stab and kill the King of Wu, put his head into a box, and send it by fast carriage [to the Han] to make it known

Therefore, they both were able to avoid being executed and returned to their states.

[Liu] Tzu-chü [劉]子駒,[19] the son of the King of Wu, escaped and fled to Min Yüeh; as he felt resentment towards the [King of] Tung Ou for killing his father, he constantly urged Min Yüeh to attack Tung Ou 東甌.

When it came to the third year of *chien-yüan* 建元 (138 BC), Min Yüeh sent out troops to besiege Tung Ou. Only when Tung Ou's provisions were exhausted, when they were in straightened circumstances and about to surrender,[20] did they send someone to report their dire situation to the Son of Heaven. The Son of Heaven put the question to the Grand Commandant T'ien Fen 田蚡[21] and T'ien Fen answered: "For the men of Yüeh to attack and assault each other is after all their norm. Moreover, they have several times changed loyalties,[22] so it is not worth troubling the Central States to go and rescue them. [As for the men of Yüeh], since Ch'in times we have abandoned them and not considered them to be subordinate [to us]."[23] At this the Palace Grandee Chuang Chu 莊助[24] called Fen to account[25]: "The only thing that should concern us is whether our strength would not be able to rescue them, our

[to them]. The Sons of the King of Wu [Liu] Tzu-hua [劉]子華 and [Liu] Tzu-chü 子駒 escaped and fled to the Min-Yüeh. As the King of Wu had abandoned his army to flee, the army consequently fell apart"; 吳大敗，士卒多飢死，乃畔散。於是吳王乃與其麾下壯士數千人夜亡去，度江走丹徒，保東越。東越兵可萬餘人，乃使人收聚亡卒。漢使人以利啗東越，東越即給吳王，吳王出勞軍，即使人鏦殺吳王，盛其頭，馳傳以聞。吳王子子華、子駒亡走閩越。吳王之棄其軍亡也，軍遂潰, As Wang Shu-min (114.3048) points out, the "Wu-ti chuan" 吳地傳 in the *Yüeh chüeh wai-chuan chi* 越絕外傳記 reports that King Wu's assassin was the younger brother of the King of Yüeh, the Yi-wu General 夷烏將軍.

The *Han shu* parallel (95.3860) omits *kuei kuo* 歸國, "returned to their states."

[19] Little is known of Liu Tzu-chü aside from the mention in his father, Liu P'i's biography (see the preceding note), and this passage (Loewe, *Dictionary*, p. 410).

[20] The *Han shu* parallel (95.3860) omits six graphs here (食盡，困，且降，乃) and reads simply "to besiege Tung Ou. Tung-Ou sent someone to report . . ."

[21] See his biography in *Shih chi* chapter 107 (2841–45; *Grand Scribe's Records*, 9:141–48). Wang Shu-min (114.3048) argues T'ien was not Grand Commandant at this time.

[22] The *Han shu* parallel omits four graphs here (*yu shu fan-fu* 又數反覆: "moreover, they have several times changed their loyalties") and reads simply "For the men of Yüeh to attack and attack each other is after all their norm, so there is no good reason to trouble the Central States to go and rescue them."

[23] The *Han shu* parallel omits eight graphs here: 自秦時棄弗屬。於是 "Since Ch'in times [the court] has abandoned then and not considered them a [people] under its command. At this . . . ."

[24] Chuang Chu was a native of K'uai-chi was mentioned above (*Shih chi*, 113.2971) and was an envoy to Southern Yüeh (see also Loewe, *Dictionary*, pp. 748–49).

[25] This entire speech is omitted from the *Han shu* parallel. In its place the *Han shu* reads: *yen tang chiu* 言當救 "He explained [or "argued"] that they should go to [Yüeh's] rescue."

virtuous power not be able to provide them shelter. If we truly are able in strength and virtuous power [to do so], why would we abandon them? Moreover, the Ch'in raised up Hsien-yang 咸陽 yet abandoned it,[26] so what need is there to mention Yüeh! Now that a small state in distress and straitened circumstances has come to report its crisis to the Son of Heaven, if the Son of Heaven does not go to its rescue, where can it turn to report its plaint? Further, on what basis can he be considered to treat the myriad states as his sons?" The Sovereign said, "The Grand Commandant [T'ien Fen] is not worth including in Our planning. I have just taken the throne and do not desire to send out the tiger tallies and send out troops of the commanderies and states."[27] Only then did he send Chuang Chu with a caduceus to send out the troops of K'uai-chi 會稽.[28] The Grand Administrator of K'uai-chi intended to defend [his borders] and not send out troops for this; only then did [Chuang] Chu cut off the head of one of the majors,[29] to make clear the [Sovereign's] intent; in the end [the Grand Administrator] sent out troops, transporting them by sea to rescue Tung Ou.[30] Before they arrived, [the King of] Min Yüeh departed at the head of his troops. Tung Ou[31] requested to take up his state[32] and move it to within the Central States, and only then did all his people come,[33] settling between the Chiang 江 and Huai 淮 [rivers].

[26] The Ch'in capital; by extension this suggests Ch'in's losing the empire to Liu Pang and the Han.

[27] There seems to be a contradiction between what Emperor Wu (who refers to himself as *wu* 吾) says here and his subsequent actions. Perhaps for this reason the *Han shu* parallel omits this imperial statement. For a discussion of these events and the parallel account in the *Han shu*, see van Ess, *Politik*, 1:339–40.

[28] A Han commandery stretching along the coast through modern Kiangsu and Chekiang from Yang-chou in the north to Ningpo in the south (T'an Ch'i-hsiang, 2:12).

[29] Takigawa (114.4) cites Shen Ch'in-han 沈欽韓 (1775–1831) who argues that following the *Tang liu-tien* 唐六典 regulations sending out someone with a *chieh* 節 authorized him to kill (as opposed to *ching* 旌, which under which rewards were dispensed).

[30] The *Han shu* (95.3860) again provides a synopsis of these lines, reading: "The Son of Heaven sent [Chuang] Chu to send out the troops of K'uai-chi Commandery transporting them by sea to rescue them [Tung Ou]" 天子遣助發會稽郡兵浮海救之.

[31] Here the *Han shu* reads Tung Yüeh (Eastern Yüeh) 東粵 for Tung-ou (Eastern Ou) 東甌 (*Han shu*, 95.3860).

[32] On *chü-kuo* 舉國 compare *Shih chi*, 69.2266: 寡人舉國委子; "We shall take up our state and entrust it to you" (*Grand Scribe's Records*, 7:112).

[33] The *Han shu* account omits *lai* 來 "come" here. *Shih chi*, 22.1134 reads: "Wang, the King of Eastern Ou and The Marquis of Kuang-wu, led his host of more than 40,000 to come and surrender; they were settled in Lu-chiang Commandery" 東甌王, 廣武侯望, 率其眾四萬餘人來降, 處廬江郡. This king is otherwise unknown.

[2981] When it came to the sixth year of Chien-yüan (135 BC), Min Yüeh assaulted Southern Yüeh. Southern Yüeh held to the agreement with the Son of Heaven and did not venture to presume on his own authority to send out troops to assault but reported this [to the court]. The Sovereign sent the Grand Usher Wang Hui 王恢[34] to set out from Yü-chang 豫章 [Commandery],[35] the Grand [Prefect] of Agriculture Han An-kuo 韓安國[36] to set out from K'uai-chi, and made both generals. Before the troops had crossed the [mountainous] divide [and entered the lands of the Yüeh], [Tsou] Ying [騶]郢, the King of Min Yüeh, sent out troops to hold and defend from redoubts. Only then did his younger brother, [Tsou] Yü-shan [騶]餘善 (d. 110 BC),[37] plot with the prime minister and with members of his house and his clan: "The King has on his own authority sent out troops to assault Southern Yüeh; he did not make a request [to the Han], and therefore the troops of the Son of Heaven have come to punish him. Now, the Han troops are multitudinous and mighty. Now,[38] should we be fortunate to defeat them, later more and more will come, until in the end they will wipe out our state. Now, if we were to kill the king[39] as a means to apologize to the Son of Heaven, and should the Son of Heaven listen to this and dismiss the troops, this would certainly keep us intact as one state. Should he would not listen, then we can strongly give battle. If we do not defeat them, we can escape into the sea." All [present] saying "Well put!" he immediately stabbed the king with a spear and sent an envoy to present his head to the Grand Usher [Wang Hui]. The Grand Usher said, "The reason for my coming was to punish the king. Now that the king's head has arrived, the problem has been weeded out without giving battle; nothing could be of greater advantage."[40] Only then did he inform the Grand Prefect of Agriculture's army that, as befit the situation, he was retraining his troops and sending an envoy bearing the king's head to hasten and report to the Son of Heaven. [The Son of

---

[34] See the brief parallel passage in Han An-kuo's biography (*Shih chi*, 108.2860) and Loewe's entry (*Dictionary*, p. 526).

[35] Approximating modern Kiangsi with its seat at Nanchang 南昌 (T'an Ch'i-hsiang, 2:24–25).

Han An-kuo's biography (ibid.) says he was Grand Prefect of Agriculture; on *Shih chi*, 22.1134 it notes that Han became Grandee Secretary in 135 BC, apparently following his return from this southern expedition.

[37] See Loewe, *Dictionary*, pp. 667–68.

[38] Here is the first of four usages of *chin* 今 in this speech, suggests a colloquial, rhetorical pattern that can also be seen in other *Shih chi* harangues (see Wu Tsu Hsü's oration on *Shih chi*, 31.1469). Pan Ku excises all but the last of these *chin* from his parallel account (*Han shu*, 95.3860).

[39] An alternate reading might be "Now, let us kill the king as a means . . . !"

[40] My reading of this text is that *yün* 耘 is the main verb here and that *erh yün* 而耘 suggests that the preceding verb phrases are adverbial. The subject is the unexpressed *so wei lai che* 所為來者.

Heaven] issued an edict dismissing the troops of the two generals which read: "Ying and his band at the head of this evil. Wu-chu's grandson, Ch'ou, the Lord of Yao 繇君丑, alone did not take part in the plotting with them."[41] Then he sent one of the generals of the Gentlemen of the Palace to enthrone Ch'ou as the King of Yao in Yüeh 越繇王 to serve the ancestors[42] of Min Yüeh through sacrifices.

Having killed Ying, Yü-shan's prestige spread through the state and most of the people of the state gave their support to him, [so] he secretly enthroned himself as king. The King of Yao was not able to constrain his people and maintain the proper [rule]. When the Son of Heaven heard this, he decided it was not worth again raising an army on account of Yü-shan and declared: "Yü-shan plotted rebellion several times with Ying but later he headed the execution of Ying so that our armies were able to avoid suffering." Accordingly he enthroned Yü-shan as the King of Eastern Yüeh placed next to the [*2982*] King of Yao.[43]

When it came to the fifth year of Yüan-ting 元鼎 (112 BC), Southern Yüeh revolted; Yü-shan, the King of Eastern Yüeh, sent in a memorial requesting to take eight thousand foot soldiers to follow [Yang P'u 楊僕], the Lou-ch'uan Chiang-chün 樓船將軍 (General of the Towering Ships) and attack Lü Chia 呂嘉 and his band. When the troops reached Chieh-yang 揭揚, using the excuse of high waves from ocean winds, he went no further, and intending to hold to ties to both sides, secretly sent an envoy to Southern Yüeh. When the Han defeated [the Southern Yüeh troops] at P'an-yü 番禺,[44] he had not arrived. At this time the General of the Towering Ships, Yang P'u, sent an envoy to submit a memorial, wishing to take advantage [of the situation] to lead troops to assault Eastern Yüeh. The Sovereign said[45] that the officers and men were suffering from fatigue and did not allow this, dismissing the troops and ordering the various officers to garrison Mei-ling 梅嶺 (Plum Ridge)[46] in Yü-chang and await his command.

[41] "So-yin" says Yao was a fief in Min Yüeh. Takigawa (114.6) cites Ting Ch'ien 丁謙 (1843-1919) who points out that the location is unknown. It seems also possible that this was the name of the tribe or clan that Ch'ou headed.

[42] *Han shu* (ibid.) omits the *hsien* 先, "ancestors."

[43] This passage, 與繇王並處, is problematic (the parallel in the *Han shu*, 95.3861, is identical). Wu and Lu (114.2991) read it as 與繇王同時並存, "co-existing at the same time as the King of Yao." Watson's (2:222) "ruling side by side with Zou Chou, the king of Yao" seems closer.

[44] That is, modern Canton; it was the commandery seat of Nan-hai (T'an Ch'i-hsiang, 2:12).

[45] *Han shu* reads *yi* 以 "considered" for *yüeh* 曰 "said" making this indirect speech. Pan Ku seems to have sought some text in support of the *Shih chi* reading and not found it.

[46] Mei-ling is a range of mountains located a few miles northwest of modern Kuangchang 廣昌 in Kiangsi (T'an Ch'i-hsiang, 2:25).

Only in the autumn of the sixth year of Yüan-ting (111 BC), when Yü-shan heard that the [General of the] Towering Ships had requested to punish him and the Han troops had approached the border and were about to move, did he finally revolt[47] and send out troops to defend the roads from the Han. Designating General Tsou Li 騶力[48] and his group T'un Han Chiang-chün 吞漢將軍 (Swallow Up the Han Generals), he entered Pai-sha 白沙, Wu-lin 武林,[49] and Mei-ling and killed three of the Han colonels. At this time, the Han sent the Grand [Prefect] of Agriculture, Chang Ch'eng 張成,[50] and the former Marquis of Shan-chou 山州侯,[51] [Liu] Ch'ih [劉]齒,[52] to command the garrison but they did not dare to assault him, [Tsou Li] instead going to a more advantageous place; both were tried for cowardice and executed.

Yü-shan had a "Martial Emperor" 武帝 seal carved and he installed himself [as Emperor], deceiving his people and making false statements.[53] The Son of Heaven sent Han Yüeh 韓說,[54] the Heng-hai Chiang-chün 橫海將軍 (General Who Crosses the Seas), to set out from Kou-chang 句章[55] and sail the sea to approach from the east [*2983*], Yang P'u, the General of the Towering Ships, to set out from Wu-lin, and Wang Wen-shu 王溫舒,[56] the Commandant of the Capital, to set out from Mei-ling; and two marquises of Yüeh who became the Ko-ch'uan 戈船 (Pole-ax) and Hsia-lai 下瀨 (Descending the Torrents) generals,[57] to set out from Jo-yeh 若邪[58] and Pai-sha.

[47] *Han shu* (ibid.) omits *fan* 反 and reads simply: "sent out troops."

[48] Otherwise unknown.

[49] Both places have been located by T'an Ch'i-hsiang (2:24) about 50 miles northeast and east-northeast (respectively) of modern Nanchang in Kiangsi. According to Ssu-ma Chen ("So-yin") both places were on the route from Min to the capital.

[50] Otherwise unknown.

[51] The exact location of Shan-chou is unknown.

[52] Liu Ch'ih was the son of Liu Hsi 劉喜, King of Ch'eng-yang 城陽 from 175–168 and 164–143 BC. He was enfeoffed in 125 BC but deprived of his holdings in 111 because of financial irregularities. Thus this campaign marked the end of his undistinguished career (compare Loewe, *Dictionary*, p. 283).

[53] They were "false pronouncements" (*wang yen* 妄言) because he had not be formally installed by the Han (compare the use of *wang yen* on *Shih chi*, 7.296; *Grand Scribe's Records*, 1:18: 項梁掩其口曰：毋妄言，族矣; "[Hsiang] Liang covered his mouth with his hand and said, 'Don't talk nonsense or our entire clan will be executed'").

[54] Another favorite courtier of Emperor Wu; he was ennobled as Marquis of An-tao 案道侯 for his role in this campaign (see text just below).

[55] On the pronunciation "Kou-chang" see "So-yin."

[56] He was one of the "harsh officials"; see his biography in *Shih chi* chapter 122 (see also Loewe, *Dictionary*, pp. 554–55).

[57] Wu and Lu (114.2988n.) cite Liang Ting-nan's 梁廷楠 *Nan Yüeh Wu-chu chuan* 南越五主傳 which claims that the Spear-boat General was a certain Cheng Yen 鄭嚴 and the

In the winter of the first year of Yüan-feng 元封 (late 111 BC) they all entered Eastern Yüeh. Eastern Yüeh which earlier had sent out troops to defend the redoubts, sent the Hsün-pei Chiang-chün 徇北將軍 (General Who Patrols the North) to defend Wu-lin, and defeated several of the Lou-ch'uan General's colonels, killing the subordinate officials [of the area]. Yüan Chung-ku 轅終古 (d. 104 BC) of Ch'ien-t'ang 錢唐,[59] who was under the leadership of the General of the Towering Ships, cut down the General Who Patrols the North and was made Marquis of Yü-erh 禦兒侯.[60] Those troops of [the General] himself did not go forward.

Wu Yang 吳陽 (d. 101 BC), the former Marquis of Yüeh-yen 越衍侯,[61] before had been among the Han. The Han sent him to return to exhort Yü-shan [to submit] but Yü-shan did not listen to him. When the General Who Crosses the Seas [Han Yüeh], arrived, Wu Yang, Marquis of Yüeh-yen together with his fief of seven hundred men, revolted [against Yü-shan], attacking the Yüeh army at Han-yang 漢陽.[62] He followed Ao 敖, the Marquis of Chien-ch'eng 建成侯,[63] and together with [the troops] he led, followed Chü-ku, the King of Yao 居股繇王.[64] He made a plot [for the King, saying]: "Yü-shan is the primary evil one, and coerced all those entrusted to us. Now when the Han troops arrive, their host will be mighty. If we make a plan to kill Yü-shan, and return the loyalties of all our commanders [to the Han],[65] perhaps we shall be fortunate enough to be able to escape [death]." Only then did they finally act together and kill Yü-shan, and with their armies surrender to the Heng-hai General. For this reason Chü-ku, the King of Yao, was enfeoffed as

---

Descending the Torrents General a man named T'ien Chia 田甲. Nothing further is known of them.

[58] Located south of modern Shaohsing in Chekiang (Wu and Lu, 114.2988n.)

[59] A Han county near modern Hangchow in Chekiang (Aoki, p. 194n.)

[60] A county southwest of modern T'ung-hsiang 桐鄉 County in Chekiang (Aoki, p. 194n.).

[61] On Wu Yang see also Loewe, *Dictionary*, p. 587. Yüeh-yen must be a place in Yüeh.

[62] A place in modern P'u-ch'eng 浦城 County in the northern tip of Fukien about 135 miles north-northwest of Foochow (Aoki, p. 196n.).

[63] Ao is otherwise unknown. The *Han shu* parallel (95.3862) reads "When the former Marquis of Chien-ch'eng, Ao, plotted together with Chü-ku, the King of Yao" . . . 及故粵建成侯敖與繇王居股謀.

[64] Chü-ku was the son of Ch'ou 丑, King of Yao. His name is given as Chü-fu 居服 on *Shih chi*, 20.1051. The *Han shu* (95.3862) reads Chü-ku.

[65] Two other alternate readings of this passage: (1) parse it six-six, "If we make a plan to kill Yü-shan and on our own return our loyalty [to the Han], all of you commanders will perhaps be fortunate enough to escape [death]"; "if we make a plan to kill Yü-shan and return our loyalties to the various [Han] commanders, we may perhaps be fortunate enough to escape [death]."

Marquis of Tung-ch'eng 東成侯[66] with ten thousand households; Ao, the Marquis of Chien-ch'eng was enfeoffed as the Marquis of K'ai-ling 開陵侯[67]; Wu Yang, Marquis of Yen-yüeh, was enfeoffed as Marquis of Pei-shih 北石侯[68]; [Han] Yüeh, the General Who Crosses the Seas, was enfeoffed as Marquis of An-tao 案道侯[69]; and [Liu] Fu [劉]福, the Colonel Who Crosses the Seas 橫海校尉, was enfeoffed as Marquis of Liao-ying 繚嫈侯.[70] This Fu was the son of King Kung of Ch'eng-yang 成陽共王.[71] Formerly he had been Marquis of Hai-ch'ang 海常侯,[72] was tried before the law and lost his marquisate. For a long time he was in the army without achieving merit and had been made a marquis because he was of the royal house. None of the various other commanders [of the Han armies] achieved merit and were not enfeoffed. When the Han troops arrived, To-chün 多軍,[73] an Eastern Yüeh commander, abandoned his troops and surrendered and was enfeoffed as Marquis of Wu-hsi[74] 無錫侯.[75]

[2984] At this the Son of Heaven said, "Eastern Yüeh is narrow and has many

---

[66] A county southeast of modern Ting-yüan 定遠 County in Anhwei about 75 miles northwest of Nanking (Aoki, p. 196n.).

[67] Located in the Han commandery of Lin-huai 臨淮 southeast of the modern county of Ssu-hung 泗洪 in Kiangsu about 100 miles north-northwest of Nanking (Chang Lieh, *Han shu*, 95.3775n.).

[68] The *Han shu* parallel reads Mao-shih 卯石 and there seems no way to determine the original reading.

[69] Written 按道 in the *Han shu* parallel but the exact location of An-tao in either writing remains unknown.

[70] Another unknown location.

[71] Liu Fu was another son of Liu Hsi 劉喜 (see n. 52 above and Loewe, *Dictionary*, p. 297). Ch'eng-yang was an early Han commandery, made into a state under Emperor Wen (r. 180-156 BC). Its seat was near modern Chü 莒 County in Shantung (Chang Lieh, *Han shu*, 95.3774n.).

[72] Liu Fu was enfeoffed with Hai-t'ang in 125 BC. He was deprived of his nobility in 112 BC because of annual tribute violations, enfeoffed again here, only to be reduced to the status of a commoner in 108 BC for unknown crimes.

[73] His *cognomen* is not known.

[74] Wu-hsi was a Han county located near the city of the same name in modern Chekiang (Chang Lieh, 95.2775n.).

[75] The *Han shu* parallel (95.2863) has an additional line here that reads: The Huang T'ung, the former General of the Left of Ou-lo, beheaded the King of Hsi-yü [ruler of a statelet within Tung Ou], and was enfeoffed with Hsia-fu" 故甌駱左將黃同斬西于王, 封為下郦侯." Hsia-fu is also given as Hsia-li 下酈 in the chronological tables (Hsia-li was located nouth of Nan-chao 南召 County in modern Honan; Chang Lieh, *Han shu*, 95.3775n.). On Huang T'ung see Loewe, *Dictionary*, p. 166).

[mountainous] defiles. Min Yüeh is fierce and has often turned against [Us]." He issued an edict that the army officials should all take command of their peoples and move them to reside between the Chiang and Huai rivers. The territory of Eastern Yüeh was in the end emptied.

His Honor the Grand Scribe says: Although the Yüeh are Man Yi 蠻夷 [barbarians], did not their ancestors have great merit and virtue with their people? How long they [reigned]! Through many eras they have always been lords and kings and Kou-chien was once declared Hegemon. But Yü-shan brought about high treason, caused his state to be wiped out and his populace to be moved. [Yet] descendants of their ancestors, Chü-ku, King of Yao, and others, still were enfeoffed as marquises of ten thousand households. From this we can understand that the Yüeh generation after generation have been lords and leaders. This is no doubt due to the brilliant legacy of Yü 禹.

*   *   *   *   *

When Wu [Liu P'i 劉濞] rebelled and turned against [Han], the men of [Eastern] Ou executed P'i, [when attacked by Min Yüeh], they protected and guarded Feng and Yü 封禺[76] as loyal subjects. [For this reason] I composed "The Memoir of the Eastern Yüeh, Number 54."[77]

---

[76] Two mountains east of modern Wu-k'ang County in Chekiang where the Yüeh peoples have since early times worshipped Yü 禹 (see *Shih chi*, 130.3309 and 41.1739).

[77] 吳之叛逆，甌人斬濞，葆守封禺為臣。作東越列傳第五十四. These are the reasons given in the concluding chapter of the *Shih chi* for compiling this memoir (see *Shih chi*, 130.3317).

Translator's Note

Reference to Tung Yüeh 越東 (Eastern Yüeh) in the *Shih chi*, as in this chapter, usually designates the Han-era states of Min Yüeh 閩越 and Tung Ou 東甌 (sometimes referred to as Tung-hai 東海). Yet even in the opening sentence of this chapter Yüeh can take on a more general meaning, as when the ruler Yao 搖 is called "King of Tung-hai in [the region of] Yüeh" 越東海王.

The text of this chapter picks up where Ssu-ma Ch'ien's account of the state of Yüeh in the Warring States era, chapter 41, "Yüeh-wang Kou-chien shih-chia" 越王 句踐世家 (The Hereditary House of Kou-chien, King of Yüeh), left off:

> Seven generations later there was Lord Yao of Min, who assisted the Feudal Lords in pacifying Ch'in. The Exalted Emperor of Han again considered Yao the King of Yüeh in order to carry on the succession of Yüeh. The lords of Tung-yüeh (East Yüeh) and Min were all his descendants (*Shih chi*, 41.1751).[78] 後七世，至閩君搖，佐諸侯平秦。漢高帝復以搖為越王，以 奉越後。東越，閩君，皆其後也。

Here Yao is perhaps anachronistically termed the "King of Yüeh." Yüeh was still used in the late second century BC as a general reference to residents of the Southeast, as in "Wu-ti pen-chi" 五帝本紀 (*Shih chi*, 12,478, translation revised from *Grand Scribe's Records*, 2:248):

> At this time [109 BC], after having annihilated Southern Yüeh, a native of Yüeh, Yung Chih, said, "It is customary among the people of Yüeh to believe in ghosts and at their sacrifices they always saw ghosts; of this there are numerous proofs. Formerly, the King of Tung-ou was reverential towards the ghosts and lived to be 160 years old. But the subsequent generations became negligent and indifferent and so they declined and died."
> 是既滅南越，越人勇之乃言「越人俗信鬼，而其祠皆見鬼，數有效。昔 東甌王敬鬼，壽至百六十歲。後世謾怠，故衰耗」.

The pregnant nature of the term can best be seen in the final paragraph of this chapter which reads:

---

[78] Chao T'o also stressed the ties between his state of Southern Yüeh and old Yüeh and built a Yüeh-wang T'ai 越王臺 (Terrace of the King of Yüeh), dedicated to the memory of Kou-chien 句踐 at Chao's capital P'an-yü (see Olivia Milburn, "The Bai Yue during the Han Dynasty," p. 25).

41

At this the Son of Heaven said, "Eastern Yüeh is narrow and has many [mountainous] defiles; the Min Yüeh are fierce and have often turned against [Us]." He issued an edict that the army officials should all take command of their peoples and move them to reside between the Chiang and Huai rivers. The territory of Eastern Yüeh was in the end emptied.

於是天子曰東越狹多阻，閩越悍，數反覆，詔軍吏皆將其民徙處江淮閒。東越地遂虛。

The Emperor is apparently referring to the topography and the people of the same state, Min Yüeh or Eastern Yüeh. Eastern Yüeh is the location, Min Yüeh the people.[79] But Wu Shu-p'ing and Lu Zongli note that the second Eastern Yüeh refers to "the whole state of Min Yüeh" unlike the first reference to Eastern Yüeh.[80] Chang Lieh 張烈 (Chang Lieh, *Han shu*, 95.3775n.) cites three explanations of this passage and prefers that of Nakai Sekitoku who suggests that the first Eastern Yüeh refers to Min Yüeh and the second to Tung Ou, whose people had already been moved in 138 BC (*Shih chi*, 114.2980) to the lands between the Chiang and Huai rivers.

Like the preceding account of early Yüeh, this chapter is written in an annalistic style. Whereas chapter 41 focused on the relationship between Wu and Yüeh, here we have an account of the contacts between the Han and the various states of Eastern Yüeh (Min Yüeh, Tung Ou, and Yao). The chapter ignores some cultural information on Eastern Yüeh that is found in other chapters of the *Shih chi*,[81] perhaps because it was more concerned with the conversion of Eastern Yüeh to a Han state (see translator's note to chapter 113). The result is a narrative in a mundane style that has caught the attention of scholars; Yang Ch'i-kuang's 楊琪光 (Qing dynasty) assessment seems apt:

> In this chapter Pan [Ku] retains the text of the Grand Scribe without many additions or changes. But the *Records* is without any excellent passages—considering Min Yüeh, how could there be nothing unusual which would be brought together here! Similarly in moving their people to the region between the Chiang and Huai [rivers], why would there at that time even be empty territory in such an expanse, how could the populace of Min not show an increase of a huge number? One just cannot get a detailed account [here]"; 次傳班[固]仍史文，無多增易。然史亦無佳文，豈以閩越無奇足采耶？然遷徙其眾江淮間，何是時尚為虛土如是之廣，豈閩眾亦無億兆之繁衍乎？不可得詳矣.[82]

---

[79] This is also the reading given in the translation by Wu and Lu (114.2992) as well as that by Watson (2:224).

[80] "東月底"，指整個閩越國控制區，與前述"東越"，含義不同 (Wu and Lu, 114.2989n.).

[81] See the example quoted just above from the "Wu-ti pen-chi."

[82] Cited from his *Shih chi ch'iu shih* 史記求是 as found in Chang Hsin-k'o 張新科 et al.,

The historian's comments at the end of this chapter, by mentioning Yü the Great again ("From this we can understand that in Yüeh for generation after generation there have been lords and leaders. This is no doubt due to overabundant brilliant [legacy] of Yü" 由此知越世世為公侯矣。蓋禹之餘烈也) also continue the remarks found at the end of "Yüeh-wang Kou-chien shih-chia" 越王句踐世家 (The Hereditary House of Kou-chien, King of Yüeh, *Shih chi*, 41.1756):

> His Honor the Grand Scribe says: Yü's meritorious service was great! In extending the Nine Rivers and stabilizing the nine lands, up until now all of Hsia 夏 is still at peace. When it came to the time of his remote descendant, Kou-chien, he suffered his body and wearied his mind, in the end destroyed the mighty Wu. He went north to display his armies to the Central States in honor of the Chou House, which proclaimed him Hegemon King. Could Kou-chien not be called worthy? This was because of the brilliant legacy of Yü that was handed down to him.
>
> 禹之功大矣，漸九川，定九州，至于今諸夏艾安。及苗裔句踐，苦身焦思，終滅彊吳，北觀兵中國，以尊周室，號稱霸王。句踐可不謂賢哉！蓋有禹之遺烈焉。

These textual ties are further evidence that Ssu-ma Ch'ien believed Eastern Yüeh to be ruled by descendants of earlier Yüeh and to continue the history of that state.

While most of this chapter depicts events in the far south of the Han empire and beyond, there is one interesting record of an exchange at court in Ch'ang-an, between Chuang Chu 莊助[83] and T'ien Fen 田蚡, over whether the Han should become involved in the internecine war between the two Yüeh states. Chuang Chu argues for intercession concluding: "If the Son of Heaven does not go to its rescue, where can it turn to report its plaint? Further, on what basis can he be considered to treat the myriad states as his sons?" 天子弗振，彼當安所告愬？又何以子萬國乎? Ssu-ma Ch'ien seems to agree with this approach, perhaps because of the age-old ties between Yü and Yüeh (his reasons for composing chapter 41 include the fact that the Yüeh state had consistenly protected and maintained Feng 封 and Yü 禹 mountains where sacrifices to Yü were performed). T'ien Fen here, as in his biography (chapter 107), is not someone the Grand Scribe admired. Yet the result of this policy of intervention

---

eds., *Shih chi yen-chiu tzu-liao ts'ui-pien* 史記研究資料萃編 (Sian: San Ch'in Ch'u-pan-she, 2011), 2:650.

[83] Also referred to as Yen Chu 嚴助 (Chuang was the *praenomen* of Emperor Ming of the Later Han 漢明帝 [r. 57-75] and thus taboo after his reign; see van Ess, *Politik und Geschichtsschreibung*, 1:298, n. 145).

It is notable that Ssu-ma Ch'ien showed little interest in Chuang Chu and men like him–literary men such as Chu Mai-ch'en 朱買臣 and Yü-ch'iu Shou-wang 吾丘壽王–who were among Emperor Wu's favorites. Recognizing this, Pan Ku gave them full biographies in *Han shu* chapter 64.

was that people were moved to the region between the Yangtze and Huai rivers, a move that Ssu-ma Ch'ien in the "P'ing-chun shu" 平準書 (Treatise on the Balanced Standard) clearly blames for having caused suffering to the people already living there:

> From this time on, Yen Chu, Chu Mai-ch'en and their group summoned [the people] of Tung Ou to come, causing trouble between the two Yüehs, so that between the Chiang and Huai rivers [the people living there] were put to great trouble and expense; 自是之後，嚴助、朱買臣等招來東甌，事兩越，江淮之閒蕭然煩費矣.

Bibliography

anslations

ki, *Shiki*, 12:181–200.

tson, *Han*, 2:219–24.

dies

lenstein, Hans. "The Chinese Colonization of Fukien until the End of T'ang," in *Studia Serica Bernhard Karlgren Dedicata.* Søren Egerod and Else Glahn, eds. Copenhagen: E. Munksgaard, 1959, pp. 98–122.

'en Ming-shih 陳名實. "Min Yüeh kuo chu-wang shih-shih t'an-hsi" 閩越國諸王史事探析, *Fu-chien shih-chih* 福建史志, 2001.3: 37–40.

Hsüeh-kang 胡雪岡. "Ou Yüeh yü Pai Yüeh chi ch'i-t'a" 甌越與百越及其他, *Wen-chou Shih-fan Hsüeh-yüan hsüeh-pao (Che-hsüeh she-hui k'o hsüeh-pao)*, 26.6 (Dec. 2005): 19–21.

Po 李勃. "Yang-yüeh chi Nan Yüeh erh fei Tung Yüeh pien" 楊越即南越而非東越辨, *Min-tsu yen-chiu*, 1995.6: 99–104.

Hua-tung 林華東. "Tung Ou kuo-tu ti-wang ch'u-t'an" 東甌國都地望初探, *Che-chiang she-hui k'o-hsüeh*, 2012.7: 111–18.

lburn, Olivia. "The Bai Yue during the Han Dynasty" and "Changing Studies of the Bai Yue," in Milburn, *The Glory of Yue, An Annotated Translation of the Yuejue shu.* Leiden: Brill, 2010, pp. 23–29 and 29–34 respectively.

Ess, "Yüeh," in *Politik und Geschichtesschreibung*, pp. 338–40.

ng Ts'ung 楊琮. "Min Yüeh kuo shih-hsi k'ao" 閩越國世系考, *Fu-chien lun-t'an* 福建論壇, 1995.1: 44–48 and 58.

Liao-shui
遼水

LIAO-TUNG
遼東郡

鴨綠江 Ya-lu chiang

浿水 P'ei-shui

列水 Lieh-shui

HSÜAN-T'U
玄菟郡

CH'AO-HSIEN
朝鮮

LIN-T'UN
臨屯郡

Pyongyang
平壤

LO-LANG
樂浪郡

Wang-hsien
王險

CHEN-P'AN
真番郡

Lieh-k'ou
列口

Han-ch'eng
漢城

Po-hai
渤海

CH'EN-HAN
辰韓

MA-HAN
馬韓

PIEN-HAN
弁韓

Ch'ao-hsien 朝鮮

⊙ Han Commandery Seats   ◎ *Modern Cities*

Ch'ao-hsien, Memoir 55[1]

translated by Chiu Ming Chan and William H. Nienhauser, Jr.

[115.2985] [Wei] Man [衛]滿 (ca. 220-ca. 130 BC),[2] the King of Ch'ao-hsien 朝鮮,[3] was a native of old Yen 燕.[4] Starting from the time when Yen was at its height, it overran and took control of Chen-fan 真番 and Ch'ao-hsien, it set up officials and

---

[1] The parallel version of this chapter can be found on *Han shu*, 95.3863–67.

Eun-jung Choi and Jimi Kim drafted a translation of the first half of this chapter several years ago. Chiu Ming Chan more recently undertook a revision of the text and notes. The translator's note and a final revision was completed by the editor.

[2] Wei Man's full name is given in the account of Ch'ao-hsien found in the "Tung-yi lieh-chuan" 東夷列傳 of the *Hou Han shu* (not the *Han shu* as "So-yin" argues; *Hou Han shu* 85.2817; see also the translator's note). Accounts of Wei Man (Wiman in Korean) can also be found in various Korean historical records. Some historians believe Wei Man was Korean, not a Han Chinese and this has skewed modern scholarship on the question along nationalistic lines. Chien Chiang-tso 簡江作 provides a summary of the controversy in his *Han-kuo li-shih yü hsien-tai Han-kuo* 韓國歷史與現代韓國 (Taipei: Commercial Press, 2005), pp. 4–8.

[3] Ch'ao-hsien under Wei Man included most of modern North Korea and the eastern half of modern Liao-ning (see the map at the start of this chapter). The same name was given to the fief King Wu of the Chou gave to Chi-tzu 箕子 ("Sung Wei-tzu shih-chia" 宋微子世家, *Shih chi*, 38.1620). The "So-yin" (ibid.) says Ch'ao-hsien was the name of a river and the "Cheng-yi" (not in the Chung-hua edition but Takigawa, 38.21) places this fief at modern Pyongyang. Takigawa (115.2), citing Nakai Sekitoku 中井積德, points out that other pre-Han references to Ch'ao-hsien do not necessarily relate to a state but merely a location assumed to be the same as that early fief.

[4] The *Han shu* account (95.3863) omits *ku* 故: "Man, King of Ch'ao-hsien, was a native of Yen" 朝鮮王滿, 燕人. The *Shih chi* text distinguishes "old Yen" (or "former Yen"), that is, the state of Yen during the Warring States period, from the Kingdom of Yen during the Han dynasty. A similar case can be found in a few sentences later, where we have reference to "old states of Yen and Ch'i" 故燕齊. This distinction is also used to refer to Tsang T'u 臧荼, the King of Old Yen 故燕王 (*Shih chi*, 8.366, 49.1975 and 93.2638). On the former state of Yen see *Shih chi*, 34.1549–62.

47

built up border fortifications.[5] After Ch'in annihilated Yen,[6] it took control of the Liao-tung Commandery 遼東[7] and its outermost regions.[8] After the Han [dynasty] rose, [the Han court], considering it [the region] was far away and difficult to guard, rebuilt the old Liao-tung border fortifications up to the P'ei 浿 River[9] as a [new] boundary, and put it under the control of the [Kingdom of] Yen.[10] When Lu Wan 盧

[5] Yen was at its height around 285 BC (see Han Chao-ch'i, 115.5711, n. 3).

According to Aoki (115.203n.), Chen-fan was a small state located between the Li-ch'eng 禮成 and Han 漢 rivers in what is now North Korea a few miles to the northwest of modern Seoul (see map at the start of this chapter).

[6] 222 BC.

[7] In the "Hsiung-nu lieh-chuan" 匈奴列傳 of (*Shih chi* 110.2885–86), it is recorded that some time after the reign of King Wu-ling of Chao 趙武靈王 (r. 325–298 BC), the state of Yen, following the example of the state of Chao, built its own section of the great wall and set up a Liao-tung Commandery to guard against the Hsiung-nu. Han Chao-ch'i (115.5711, n. 3) argues that this took place during the time of King Chao of Yen 燕趙王 (r. 312–279 BC), probably around 280 BC, after the Yen general Yüeh Yi 樂毅 attacked the state of Ch'i. The "Ti-li Chih" 地理志 of *Han shu* (28.1625) notes that the Liao-tung Commandery was set up by the Ch'in dynasty. Apparently, Ch'in retained the commandery after it had occupied Yen. The Liao-tung Commandery of the Ch'in had its headquarters at Hsiang-p'ing 襄平, modern Liao-yang city 遼陽市, covering the area from the east of the Ta-ling River 大凌河 in modern Liao-ning Province in China, and extending west to the estuary of the Ch'ong-ch'on River 清川江 of North Korea.

[8] There are several interpretations of the term *wai-chiao* 外徼. Chang Po-ch'üan 張博泉 (1926–2000) observes in his *Tung-pei ti-fang shih-kao* 東北地方史稿 (Ch'ang-ch'un: Chih-lin Ta-hsüeh Ch'u-pan-she, 1980, p.46) that Liao-tung wai-chiao refers to the outer regions of Liao-tung Commandery. Sun Chin-yi 孫進已 (*Tung-pei li-shih ti-li* 東北歷史地理 [Harbin: Hei-lung-chiang Jen-min Ch'u-pan-she, 1989], pp. 236–40) suggests that *wai-chiao* refers to other dependant states who submitted to the Han court. Liu Tsu-min's 劉子敏, in his "Liao-tung wai-chiao k'ao-shih" "遼東外徼" 考釋, *Yen-pien Ta-hsüeh hsüeh-pao*, 1996.2:45) is of the view that *wai-chiao* might be the buffer zone between Ch'in 秦 and other barbarians. In this context, it seems to simply refer to the regions lying beyond the boundary of the Liao-tung Commandery but still under its control. This is what Han Chao-ch'i suggests, whose notes explains the term "Liao-tung wai-chiao" as "the controlled area lying beyond the boundary of Liao-tung" 遼東郡的界外管區 (Han Chao-ch'i, 115.5711, n. 3)

[9] Backed by archeological finding of Yen artifacts in the Ch'ong-ch'on River area, modern scholars are generally believe that the P'ei River refers to the Ch'ong-ch'on River, which also lies to the northwest of Pyongyang (compare, for example, Tan Ch'i-hsiang, 1.42; 2.28).

[10] Yen here refers to the kingdom established after the Han unified China, and is not the same as the former state of old Yen mentioned above. The Han-dynasty kingdom of Yen had its eastern boundary at the P'ei River and did not include Chen-fan or Ch'ao-hsien.

綰 (256–194 BC), King of Yen (r. 202–195 BC), revolted and joined the Hsiung-nu,[11] Wei Man fled from his local registry,[12] gathered together a band of more than one thousand followers, and in a mallet-style hairdo[13] and barbarian clothing, escaped east over the fortifications. After crossing the P'ei River, he occupied the lands formerly vacant under the Ch'in,[14] and moving up and down the fortifications he gradually, subjugated and took control over the barbarians in Chen-fan and Ch'ao-hsien, as well as those who had fled from their local registries of old Yen and Ch'i 齊, made himself king,[15] and established his capital at Wang-hsien 王險.[16]

[11] Lu Wan and Liu Pang 劉邦 (later Emperor Kao-tsu, r. 206–195 BC) were close friends who came from the same village (see Lu's biography in *Shih chi* Chapter 93 and Loewe, Dictionary, pp. 417–18). Lu was a most trusted official until Kao-tsu in his last years became suspicious of his generals including Lu Wan. Lu fled to the region near the Han Great Wall. When Kao-tsu died in 195 BC, Lu rebelled and eventually crossed over to Hsiung-nu territory, to became King Lu of Eastern Hu 東胡盧王 under the Hsiung-nu.

[12] Li Shan 李善 (d. 689) explains *wang ming* 亡命 as 犯罪名已定而逃亡避之 "to flee and avoid the name one has already established as a criminal" (see *Liu ch'en chu Wen hsüan* 六臣注文選, 37.30b–31a, *SPTK*), suggesting the idea of fugitives." See the long note on *wang ming* on *Grand Scribe's Records*, 8:1, n.5) and Chang Kung 張功, *Ch'in Han t'ao-wang fan-tsui yen-chiu* 秦漢逃亡犯罪研究 (Wuhan: Hu-pei Jen-min Ch'u-pan-she, 2006).

[13] What we have translated as "mallet-style hairdo" is *chui-chieh* 魋結 in Chinese. Also written as 椎結 and 椎髻, it consisted of a topknot shaped like a mallet. See P'eng Nien 彭年, "Shu-fa chui-chi fei Nan Yüeh chih su-chien lun shu-fa chih su te ch'i-yüan chi ch'i-t'a" 束髮魋結非南越之俗–兼論束髮之俗的起源及其他, *Chung-yang Min-tsu Ta-hsüeh hsüeh-pao* 中央民族大學學報會 (2001.6).

[14] "So-yin," citing the "Ti-li chih" of the *Han-shu*, notes that there was a county named Yün-chang 雲障 in Lo-lang 樂浪 Commandery during the Han dynasty. Some scholars argue that Shang-hsia Chang 上下障 is a place name and refers to Yün-chang, which lay to the southeast of modern Pyongyang. We follow the Chung-hua editors who do not believe this is a place name. Our punctuation, with a full stop after *ku k'ung ti* 故空地, however, differs from the Chung-hua edition.

[15] Wei Man usurped the throne of Ch'ao-hsien in the first year of the reign of the Han Emperor Hui 漢惠帝 (194 BC). The *Hou Han-shu* (85.2820) gives more details: "Formerly, King Wu [of the Chou Dynasty] enfeoffed Chi-tzu at Ch'ao-hsien . . . . More than forty generations later, Chun, Marquis of Ch'ao-hsien, declared himself king. During the disorder at the beginning of the Han dynasty, those people from Yen, Ch'i and Chao who fled to [Ch'ao-hsien] amounted to tens of thousands, and a native of Yen, Wei Man, attacked and crushed King Chun, making himself King of Ch'ao-hsien." 昔武王封箕子于朝鮮……其後四十余世，至朝鮮侯準自稱王。漢初大亂，燕、齊、趙人往避地者數萬口，而燕人衛滿擊破準，而自王朝鮮. Chun then fled with several thousand supporters onto the sea; he eventually attacked Ma-Han, defeated it, and became for a time king of Ma-Han 馬韓 (*Hou Han shu*, 85.2820).

[2986] It happened that during the time of Emperor Hsiao-hui 孝惠 (r. 194–188 BC) and Empress Dowager Lü (241–180 BC, r. 187–180 BC) when the empire had just been stabilized, the Grand Administrator of Liao-tung quickly made an agreement with [Wei] Man to become a foreign vassal [of the Han],[17] to protect the barbarian tribes living beyond the [boundary] fortifications but not let them plunder the [Han] frontier; and if various chieftains of the barbarian tribes wanted to go in and pay homage to the Son of Heaven, Man was not allowed to obstruct them. [When this] was reported, the Sovereign approved it. For this reason, Man, obtaining [from Han] military might, property and goods, was able to invade and subjugate his neighboring statelets.[18] Ch'en-fan and Lin-t'un 臨屯[19] came under his control, [his borders] stretching several thousand *li* on a side.[20]

[16] Wang-hsien (Korean: Wanggeom), also written 王儉, is generally considered to have been just south of modern Pyongyang (see the map at the start of this chapter). Another theory places it northwest of modern An-shan City 鞍山市 in Liao-ning (Aoki, p. 204n.).

[17] "Foreign vassals" *wai-ch'en* 外臣, were entitled to have political autonomy, though were required to pay tribute to the Han court. See Liu Jui 劉瑞, "Ch'in, Hsi-Han te nei-ch'en ho wai-ch'en," 秦西漢的內臣和外臣, *Min-tsu yen-chiu*, 2003.3: 69–79.

[18] Wang Li-ch'i (115.2427n.) believes Wei Man may have controlled parts of the three proto-Korean states of Ch'en-Han 辰韓, Ma-Han 馬韓, and Pien-Han 弁韓 which controlled much of the Korean peninsula south of Ch'ao-hsien (see the map at the start of this chapter).

[19] "So-yin" says that Lin-t'un was a small state of the eastern Yi-tribe, which later became a commandery 東夷小國, 後以為郡. Han Chao-ch'i (115.5713, n. 12) notes that Lin-t'un was the name of the tribe whose state came to be called Lin-t'un approximating the area in modern South Hamkyeong Province 咸镜南道 and the northern part of Kangweon Province 江原道 in North Korea.

[20] Although the reference here may be a hyperbolic depiction of a large empire, it would seem that Ch'ao-hsien was about twelve hundred miles from its extreme southeastern point to its northwest border (T'an Ch'i-hsiang, 2:27–28). *Fang shu ch'ien li* 方數千里 appears several times in the *Shih chi* (compare, for example, *Shih chi*, 100.2732: "Ch'u had thousands of *li* of territory and a million halberd-bearing troops" 楚地方數千里，持戟百萬). See also Yang Po-chun's 楊伯俊 reading of *fang liu ch'i shih* 方六七十 in the Chapter "Hsien chin" 先進篇 as "sixty to seventy *li* horizontally and vertically" 縱橫各六七十里, i.e. "sixty to seventy *li* on a side" and his note explaining the usage (*Lun-yü yi-chu* 論語譯注 [Peking: Chung-hua, 1984], p. 120 and 121, n. 4) as well as the translation of a parallel passage in the *Samguk yusa* 三國遺事 as "extending several thousand *li* in the four directions" (Ilyon 一然 [fl. 1280], *Samguk yusa, Legends and History of the Three Kingdoms of Ancient Korean*, Tae-Hung Ha and Grafton K. Mintz, translators [Seoul: Honsei University Press, 1972], p. 34).

Chapter 30 of the *San-kuo chih* 三國志 (30.848) says that after Emperor Wu wiped out Ch'ao-hsien in 108 BC he "divided its territory into four commanderies" 分其地為四郡; i.that is, Liao-hsi 遼西, Liao-tung 遼東, Hsüan-t'u 玄菟, and Lo-lang 樂浪. See also the translator's note below.

When [Ch'ao-hsien] was handed down to his [Wei Man's] son and to his grandson [Wei] Yu-ch'ü 右渠,[21] those fugitives from the Han who were enticed [to come to Ch'ao-hsien] increased greatly in number and [Yu-ch'ü] did not go to [the Han court] again to pay homage. [All the while] Chen-fan and its neighboring states[22] had wanted to submit memorials [expressing the wish] to pay homage to the Son of Heaven but he also blocked the way and would not let them through.[23]

In the second year of Yüan-feng 元封 (109 BC), the Han dispatched She Ho 涉何[24] to reprimand and instruct Yu-ch'ü but to the end [Yu-ch'ü] was not willing to accept the imperial edict. [She] Ho left and when he arrived at the border overlooking the P'ei River, he had his driver stab to death Chang 長, a subordinate King of Ch'ao-hsien,[25] who was sent to see him off. Ho quickly crossed [the river] and hastened into the Han fortifications,[26] finally returning [to court] and reporting to the Son of Heaven: "I killed a Ch'ao-hsien commander." The Sovereign made a good name for him [as the killer of an enemy commander][27] then did not investigate [the matter] [*2987*] [but] appointed Ho Commandant of the eastern part of Liao-tung 遼東東部.[28] [The King of] Ch'ao-hsien bore a grudge against Ho and dispatched troops to attack by surprise, assault, and kill [She] Ho.[29]

---

[21] Ugŏ in Korean.

[22] The *Han shu* parallel (95.3864) reads "Ch'en-kuo" 辰國 (the state of Ch'en) for *pang chung kuo* 旁眾國 (neighboring states). Yen Shih-ku's annotation to the *Han shu* says this Ch'en-kuo refers to Ch'en-Han 辰韓, a state located in what is now the southeastern part of the Korea Peninsula (see map at the start of this chapter). The *Hou Han shu* (85.2817) says that the people of Ch'en-Han claimed to be refugees from the Ch'in dynasty, and their language was similar to that of Ch'in. Their state was thus also called Ch'in-Han 秦韓. Chang Wen-hu (115.673) notes that Sung-dynasty editions also read "Ch'en-kuo."

[23] It seems that already under Emperor Wen Wei Man was inhibiting access to court for peoples on the Korean Peninsula (compare Ch'en Wu's 陳武 comments on *Shih chi*, 25.1242).

[24] She Ho is unknown other than for the mention here and in the parallel text in *Han shu*, 95.3824.

[25] Probably one of the rulers of the statelets which Wei Man had invaded and subjugated (see text above).

[26] "Cheng-yi" notes that the "border" here refers to P'ing-chou 平州, where the Yü-lin Pass 榆林關 was located, near modern Chang-chia-k'ou 張家口, Hopei.

[27] An alternate reading (see Wang Li-ch'i, 115.2427n. and Wu and Lu, 115.2997) would be "the Sovereign, because She Ho had made a good name [by killing an enemy commander], . . ."

[28] Eastern Liao-tung had its seat at Wu-tz'u 武次 County, near modern Shenyang in Liao-ning (Wang Li-ch'i, 115.2427n.).

[29] Han Chao-ch'i (115.5716, n. 7) observes that the use of the three verbs *hsi* 襲, *kung* 攻, *sha* 殺 (attack by surprise, assault and kill) in succession indicates the strength and speed of Ch'ao-hsien's reaction.

The Son of Heaven [then] recruited convicts to attack Ch'ao-hsien.[30] That autumn (109 BC), [the Son of Heaven] dispatched the Lou-ch'uan Chiang-chün 樓船將軍 (General of the Towering Ships),[31] Yang P'u 楊僕,[32] to sail out from Ch'i on the sea of Po-hai 渤海 with a force of fifty thousand soldiers, and Hsün Chih 荀彘 (d. 108 BC),[33] Tso Chiang-chün 左將軍 (General of the Left),[34] to set out from Liao-tung, to suppress Yu-ch'ü. Yu-ch'ü sent out troops to defend the redoubts. To 多, a Company Commander[35] under the General of the Left, led the Liao-t'ung troops to launch the first attack, [but] they were defeated and scattered. To turned and ran, was tried before the [military] law, and beheaded. The General of the Towering Ships commanded seven thousand troops of Ch'i and arrived at Wang-hsien first. Yu-ch'ü defended the city walls. When he learned through spies that the army of [the General of] the Towering Ships was few in number, he quickly came out from the city walls and attacked the troops of the Towering Ships. The troops of the Towering Ships were defeated, scattered, and fled. General Yang P'u, having lost his host, fled and hid in the mountains for more than ten days. Gradually he sought to gather his scattered soldiers and regroup them. The General of the Left assaulted the Ch'ao-hsien troops west of the P'ei River,[36] but still could not defeat [them] and advance on his own.

Only when the two commanders were still without victory, did the Son of Heaven send Wei Shan 衛山,[37] to rely on [Han] military might and go to instruct Yu-

---

[30] Compare the use of convicts in the campaign against Southern Yüeh (*Shih chi*, 113.2974) and against the Barbarians of the Southwest (*Shih chi*, 116.2996). As Han Chao-ch'i (115.5716, n. 8) points out, these men would be forgiven their crimes by enlisting, a practice that still exists in many countries today.

[31] On Yang P'u's appointment, see Michael Loewe, "Military Titles and the Armed Forces," in Loewe, *Companion*, pp. 186–87.

[32] Yang P'u was a native of Yi-yang 宜陽, in modern Honan 河南; he was appointed Lou-ch'uan General in the fifth year of Yüan-ting 元鼎 (112 BC). See *Shih chi*, 113.2975, our translation above (especially n. 97 to Chapter 113), and the translator's note for chapter 113.

[33] Hsün Chih was a native of Kuang-wu 廣武 in T'ai-yüan 太原 commandery. He is given a short biography in the list of a dozen generals appended to the biographies of Wei Ch'ing 衛青 and Huo Ch'ü-ping 霍去病 (*Shih chi*, 111.2941–46; *Grand Scribe's Records*, 9:345–53).

[34] *Tso chiang-chün* was a title given *ad hoc* to commanders of special expeditions or campaigns ranking above the Nine Ministers (compare Bielenstein, p. 116).

[35] Han Chao-ch'i (115.5717, n. 12) notes that *tsu* was a military unit of one hundred soldiers and *tsu-cheng* was a leader of such a unit.

[36] These troops were Yu-ch'ü's advance guard; Wang-hsien was located just east of the Lieh-shui 列水 across from modern Pyongyang (see T'an Ch'i-hsiang, 2:28 and the map at the start of the chapter).

[37] The *Han shu* (55.2478) lists a Wei Shan but in the parallel passage in the *Shih chi*

ch'ü. Yu-ch'ü met the envoy, touched his head to the ground, and apologized, "I had wanted to surrender but I was afraid that the two commanders would kill your subject through deceit.[38] Now that I have seen the tally and caduceus [of the imperial envoy], I ask to submit and surrender." [Yu-ch'ü] sent his heir [to court] to apologize, to present five thousand horses, and to offer military provisions.[39] The host of people [accompanying the heir] were more than ten thousand. Carrying [their] weapons, they were about to cross the P'ei River when the envoy and the General of the Left, suspecting they would change [their allegiance],[40] said that since the heir had already submitted and surrendered, it would be appropriate to order [his] people not to carry weapons. The heir also suspected that the envoy and the General of the Left were trying to kill him through deceit; [*2988*] in the end he did not cross the P'ei River, [but] instead led [his people] to return [to Wang-hsien]. [Wei] Shan went back [to the Han court] and reported to the Son of Heaven. The Son of Heaven had [Wei] Shan executed.

Only when the General of the Left [Hsün Chih] defeated the troops [of Ch'ao-hsien] on the banks of the P'ei River did he advance reaching the base of the city walls [of Wang-hsien], surrounding its northwest. The General of Towering Ships [Yang P'u] also went to meet [Hsün Chih], stationing [his troops] to the south of the city walls. Yu-ch'ü in the end resolutely defended the city walls, and after several months [the Han troops] were not able to cause it to submit.

The General of the Left had been a courtier[41] for a long time and was favored. The troops from Yen and Tai that he commanded were ferocious, and, riding on the victory [on the banks of the P'ei River], they were mostly haughty. The General of Towering Ships commanded the Ch'i troops, who came across the sea, and as a matter of course had already had many losses. Previously, when battling with [Wei] Yu-ch'ü, [Yang P'u] was hard pressed, humiliated, and lost [many] troops. His [remaining] troops were all frightened and the General himself felt ashamed. Though besieging Yu-ch'ü, he always carried a flag of truce. Only when the General of the

(111.2936) his name is given as Hsing Shan 邢山 (compare *Grand Scribe's Records*, 9:338 and n. 187). Liang Yü-sheng (34.1410), points out that this must be a different Wei Shan.

[38] Compare *Shih chi*, 38.1630 (*Grand Scribe's Records*, 5.1:288): "In the tenth year (522 BC), Duke Yüan was unfaithful; he killed the Noble Scions through deceit" 十年，元公毋信，詐殺諸公子.

[39] Han Chao-ch'i (115.5717, n. 17) argues that these foodstuffs were intended for Yang P'u and Hsün Chih.

[40] Alternatively *pien* 變 could be read as "cause an emergency" or even "rebel."

[41] Wang Li-ch'i (115.2428n.) points out that *shih chung* 侍中 refers to those generations, chancellors, grandees, and other high officials who had access to the sovereign, usually only a few dozen at a time.

Left fiercely attacked [Yu-ch'ü], did the great ministers of Ch'ao-hsien secretly send people to make a private agreement of surrender to [the General of] the Towering Ships, coming and going with messages; but they were not yet willing to make a decision. The General of the Left had several times fixed a time to go to battle with [the General] of the Towering Ships but [the General of] the Towering Ships, desiring to rashly reach [a peace] agreement, did not join with him [the General of the Left]. The General of the Left also sent someone to find an opportunity [to persuade] [the King of] Ch'ao-hsien to surrender but [the King of] Ch'ao-hsien was unwilling, because at heart he wanted to submit to [the General of] the Towering Ships.[42] For this reason, the two generals were not able to be on good terms. The General of the Left, who at heart thought that [the General of] the Towering Ships was previously guilty of losing an army[43] and at present was secretly on good terms with [the King of] Ch'ao-hsien so that [the King] would not even surrender, had suspected [the General of] the Towering Ships of planning rebellion but had not yet ventured to set it in motion. The Son of Heaven said[44] that the two generals had not been able to advance and when he had [previously] sent Wei Shan to instruct Yu-ch'ü to surrender, Yu-ch'ü had sent his heir [to court]. [Wei] Shan had not been able to make a decision on his own and had made plans with the General of the Left, [but] they had miscalculated and in the end had put a stop to the [peace] agreement. Now the two generals had besieged the city but were again at odds with each other; for this reason [the affair] has for a long time not been resolved. [The Son of Heaven] therefore sent Kung-sun Sui 公孫遂,[45] the Grand Administrator of Chi-nan Commandery 濟南郡,[46] to go and rectify this [their mistakes],[47] and, were he to come upon an advantageous situation, to take action on his own [without requesting imperial approval]. When Sui arrived, the General of the Left said, "Ch'ao-hsien should have fallen long ago; as for why it has not fallen, there seems to be some reason." He spoke of how [the General of] the

---

[42] In the *Han shu* (95.3866) version, this line reads, "The General of the Left also sent someone to find an opportunity to persuade [the King of] Ch'ao-hsien to surrender. He was not willing, in his heart being attached to [the General of] the Towering Ships" 左將軍亦使人求間隙降下朝鮮. 不肯, 心附樓船.

[43] Referring to the losses Yang P'u took at Wang-hsien.

[44] This indirect speech is accorded the status of direct speech in the *Han shu* (95.3866) parallel.

[45] Otherwise unknown.

[46] The seat of its central administration was at Tung-p'ing Ling 東平陵, northwest of modern Chang-ch'iu 章丘 in Shantung (Wang Li-ch'i, 115.2429n.).

[47] Or "to straighten things out." A number of *Shih chi* editions read "to go and campaign against [Ch'ao-hsien]" 公孫遂往征之 but the text was changed–reading 正 for 征–by the Chung-hua editors based on the *Han shu* parallel and Liang Yü-sheng's comments.

Towering Ships had several times not joined with him as arranged[48] and told Sui in detail what he had all along been thinking [about Yang P'u]: "Now with things like they are, if we do not take hold of [Yang P'u], I am afraid there will be a great disaster. It is not [a matter of the General of] the Towering Ships alone but that he may in addition together with Ch'ao-hsien wipe out my army." Sui also thought that things were like this and with his caduceus he summoned [the General of] the Towering Ships to the camp of the General of the Left to plan affairs. [Upon his arrival] Sui immediately ordered soldiers under the flag of the General of the Left to arrest [the General of] the Towering Ships and combine his army [with their own]. This he reported to the Son of Heaven. The Son of Heaven had [Kung-sun] Sui executed.[49]

The General of the Left, having combined the two armies, immediately attacked Ch'ao-hsien fiercely. Lu Jen 路人 and Han Yin 韓陰, ministers of Ch'ao-hsien, Ts'an 參, a minister of Ni-hsi 尼谿, and Wang Chia 王唊, a general [of Ni-hsi],[50] met and plotted together, [*2989*] saying, "Earlier we had wanted to surrender to [the General of] the Towering Ships. Towering Ships is has now been seized and the General of the Left on his own has combined his command [over the two armies of Han]. The battles are increasingly fierce. We are afraid we could no longer oppose him,[51] but the king is still not willing to surrender." [Han] Yin, [Wang] Chia and Lu Jen fled to surrender to Han. Lu Jen died on the way.

In the summer of third year of the Yüan-feng era (108 BC), Ts'an, the minister of Ni-hsi, sent someone to kill Yu-ch'ü, the King of Ch'ao-hsien, and came [to the Han camp] to surrender. The city walls of Wang-hsien had not yet been subdued, [moreover], Ch'eng-ssu 成巳, a former high official of Yu-ch'ü, rebelled and also

---

[48] The Chung-hua edition reads *shu ch'ao pu hui* 數朝不會 but this is apparently a typographical error for *shu ch'i pu hui* 數期不會, as corrected in the new Chung-hua edition (115.3597) and born out by the texts in Takigawa (115.7) and the Chin-ling edition (115.3a).

[49] Liang Yü-sheng (34.1410) who notes all editions of the *Han shu* here read *hsü Sui* 許遂 (approved of Sui?). Wang Hsien-ch'ien 王先謙 points out that the historian's comments at the end of the chapter clearly that that Kung-sun Sui and Hsün Chih "both were executed" 皆誅; on this basis, the Chung-hua edition of the *Han shu* has been revised to read the same as the *Shih chi* text (compare *Han shu*, 95.3866 and the textual note on 3869).

[50] These men are otherwise unknown. Ni-hsi is probably a statelet or region subordinate to Ch'ao-hsien. The meaning of *hsiang* 相 here is also unclear (compare contrasting opinions in "So-yin"). Ying Shao (*ibid.*) identifies Lu Jen as a man from Yü-yang 漁陽 County (southwest of modern Mi-yün 密雲 County in metropolitan Peking).

[51] *Pu neng yü* 不能與 could also be read as "are not able to match him" or "measure up to him," as Yen Shih-ku's gloss *pu ru* 不如 suggests (*Han shu*, 95.3866).

attacked the [Ch'ao-hsien] officials.[52] The General of the Left dispatched [Wei] Ch'ang-chiang [衛]長降,[53] Yu-ch'ü's son, and [Lu] Tsui [路]最, son of the minister Lu Jen, to instruct its [Wang-hsien's] people [to surrender] and to execute Ch'eng-ssu. For these reasons, [the Han] finally stabilized Ch'ao-hsien and made it into four commanderies.[54] [The Sovereign] enfeoffed Ts'an as the Marquis of Hua-ch'ing 澅清侯, [Han] Yin as the Marquis of Ti-chi 狄苴侯,[55] [Wang] Chia as the Marquis of P'ing-chou 平州侯,[56] and Ch'ang[-chiang] as the Marquis of Chi 幾侯.[57] Tsui, having some merit by means of his father's death, was made the Marquis of Wen-yang 溫陽侯.[58]

The General of the Left was summoned [to the capital]. He was sentenced for contending for merit, for jealousy [of Yang P'u], and for acting contrary to [military] plans, was executed, and had his corpse was exposed in the marketplace.[59] [The General of] the Towering Ships was also found guilty: when his troops reached Lieh-k'ou 洌口,[60] he should have waited for the General of the Left. [Instead] on his own initiative he first **[*2990*]** launched [his troops], so that those lost and missing were numerous. He was sentenced to be executed but redeemed himself and became a commoner.

His Honor the Grand Scribe says:
    Yu-ch'ü relied on redoubts[61]
    and the sacrifices of his state were cut off [i.e., the state came to an end].
    She Ho was falsely considered to have merit [by Emperor Wu]

[52] Ch'eng-ssu, apparently no longer in office under Yu-ch'ü, attacked those Ch'ao-hsien officials (*fu kung li* 復功吏) who were hoping to surrender to Han (see Wang Li-ch'i, 115.2429n. and Aoki, 115.216n.). There was already a revolt against Yu-ch'ü in 128 BC suggesting that Ch'ao-hsien was a fissiparous and factional realm in the late second century BC (see the discussion in the translator's note below).

[53] Wang Shu-min, 115.3060 lists several alternate graphs for his name.

[54] The four commanderies thus set up were: Chen-fan 真番 Commandery, Lin-t'un 臨屯 Commandery, Hsüan-t'u 玄菟 Commandery and Lo-lang 樂浪 Commandery (see Han Chao-ch'i, 115.5719-20, n. 44 and T'an Ch'i-hsiang, 2:29).

[55] Both of these marquisates are otherwise unknown.

[56] Compare *Shih chi*, 20.1054.

[57] Compare *Shih chi*, 20.1057.

[58] Ibid.

[59] Loewe, *Companion*, p. 186 feels that the "reasons are not clear" behind Hsün Chih's execution. Kung-sun Sui's death seems even more unexplained (see n. 49 above).

[60] Ch'ien Mu points out that Lieh-k'ou was located southeast of modern Seoul (see *Shih chi ti-ming k'ao*, 34.1480).

[61] These comments are, like those in chapter 113, presented in four-character rhymed lines.

and [this] was the reason [troops] were sent out [to Ch'ao-hsien].
[The General of] the Towering Ships commanding a limited force[62]
met with calamity and encountered blame.
Regretting his errors at P'an-yü 番禺[63]
but on the contrary came under suspicion [of planning to rebel].
Hsün Chih contended for rewards for his service,
[but] he and [Kung-sun] Sui were both executed.
The two armies [of Yang P'u and Hsün Chih] both suffered humiliation;
of their generals and commanders none was made a marquis.[64]

*   *   *   *   *

When [Heir] Tan of Yan 燕丹[子] fled wildly into Liao 遼,[65] [Wei] Man collected his people who had fled [there], then he assembled [all] east of the [Yellow] Sea,[66] thereby gathering in Chen-fan 真藩,[67] and protecting the [border] fortifications as an outer vassal; [thus] I have composed the "Memoir of Ch'ao-hsien," number fifty-five.[68]

[62] Wang Li-ch'i (115.2430n.) cites Nakai Sekitoku's 中井積德 reading (from Takigawa) of *chiang* 將 as "to act independently" and *hsia* 狹 "to be narrow minded" which Wang prefers.

[63] See note 43 above.

[64] These comments, like those of "Nan Yüeh lieh-chuan" (Chapter 113), are rhymed.

[65] After sending Ching K'o 荊軻 to assassinate the First Emperor of Ch'in, Ch'in conquered Yen (226 BC) and Tan fled into Liao-tung 遼東 (a Ch'in commandery, see T'an Ch'i-hsiang, 1:42) where he was beheaded by his own father Hsi, King of Yen 燕王喜, who hoped thereby to prevent Ch'in from wiping out Yen. In 222 BC, however, Ch'in captured Hsi and destroyed his state (see *Shih chi*, 86.2536 and *Grand Scribe's Records*, 7:332–33).

[66] Although there are several places named Tung-hai 東海 mentioned elsewhere in the *Shih chi*, this refers to the lands east of the Huang-hai 黃海, that is, those on the Korean peninsula.

[67] Referred to in text above as Chen-fan 真番 (see n. 5 above).

[68] These are the reasons given on *Shih chi*, 130.3317, for the composition of this chapter: 燕丹散亂遼閒，滿收其亡民，厥聚海東，以集真藩，葆塞為外臣。作朝鮮列傳第五十五.

Translator's Note

This chapter is not a history of Korea but rather a depiction of the military campaign against Wei Yu-ch'ü 衛右渠 which took place from late 109 to 108 BC.[69] Preceding the main section, Ssu-ma Ch'ien provides a backstory which relates how Wei Yu-ch'ü's grandfather, Wei Man 衛滿, fled the chaos in the northeast at the start of the Han dynasty and set himself up as king ruling over a large part of what is today eastern Liaoning province and North Korea (see map at the start of this chapter). More detailed Chinese accounts of the early history of Ch'ao-hsien can be found in the "Tung Yi lieh-chuan" 東夷列傳 chapters of both the *Hou Han shu* 後漢書 (85.2817) and the *San-kuo chih* 三國志 (30.848 and 850).[70] These accounts relate how in the third century BC Ch'ao-hsien under a King Fou 否 lost much of its territory to the state of Yen. Under the reign of Fou's successor, Chun 準, the Ch'in dynasty fell and refugees number in the tens of thousands fled to Ch'ao-hsien from Yen, Chao and Ch'i. Among them was Wei Man who overthrew Chun and became king. Although it is not known how long Wei Man ruled, the *Hou Han shu* (ibid.) relates that the Lord of Wei 濊[71] along with the the Nan Lü 南閭, revolted against Wei Yu-ch'ü in 128 BC. It is said they took 280,000 people with them and that out of their territory Emperor Wu had Ts'ang-hai Commandery 蒼海郡 set up for them.[72]

[69] *Shih chi*, 12.479 says 108 BC; but *Shih chi*, 22.1140 dates the campaign as beginning in the fall of 109.

[70] See also the translation of this passage in Gardinier, "Ancient Korea," p. 10.

[71] The state of Wei-mo was located north of Ch'en-Han 辰韓 and south of Kao-chü-li 高句麗 on the eastern seacoast of the Korean peninsula (see *Han shu*, 6.169).

[72] The commandery, probably located on the east coast of the Korean peninsula (T'an Ch'i-hsiang, ed. *Chung-kuo li-shih ti-t'u chi shih-wen hui-pien, Tung-pai chüan* 中國歷史地圖集釋文彙編，東北卷 [Peking: Chung-kuo Min-tsu Hsüeh-yüan Ch'u-pan she, 1988], pp. 49-50), was dissolved in 126 BC (*Han shu*, 6.169). See Mark E. Byington's comments on Ts'ang-hai Commandery and these events in his "Historical Geography of the Han Commanderies," in Byington, ed., *The Han Commanderies in Early Korean History* (Cambridge, Mass.: Early Korea Project, Korea Institute, Harvard University, 2013, pp. 287–91).

See *Shih chi*, 30.1420: "P'eng Wu opened a trade route to wipe out Ch'ao-hsien and established a commandery at Ts'ang-hai" 彭吳賈滅朝鮮，置滄海之郡. The *Han shu* parallel

59

According to the "P'ing-chun shu" 平準書 (*Shih chi*, 30.1421), a certain P'eng Wu by setting up a road for trade with Ch'ao-hsien fostered the establishment of this commandery.[73]

Ssu-ma Ch'ien thus seems to have had more information about Wei Man and events in Ch'ao-hsien during the second century BC but chose to focus on the role played by Emperor Wu and his generals here. As the origin of the hostilities, Emperor Wu's handling of She Ho after he had his driver murder the Subordinate King Chang 長 is crucial to the larger meaning of this chapter. By failing to investigate the circumstances of Chang's death and instead rewarding She Ho through appointment as Commander of Eastern Liao-tung, Emperor Wu's actions led to Yu-ch'ü's reaction and the subsequent disastrous campaign against him. The Ming commentator Chung Hsing 鐘惺 (1574–1624) summarizes this reading:

> When the Sovereign made a good name for him [She Ho] and did not investigate the matter], it would seem he understood the offense and yet intentionally overlooked it. He himself was deceiving a deceiver,[74] actually "making a good name [for him]," he erred and was the one who brought about this calamity. 上為其名美即不詰, 蓋知而故縱之, 自欺欺人, 實名美二字誤之, 此大病痛也.[75]

Ssu-ma Ch'ien reiterates the importance of the emperor's actions in his closing comments on this chapter: "She Ho was falsely considered [by the emperor] to have merit and this was the reason troops were sent out to Ch'ao-hsien" 涉何誣功, 為兵發首.

Ssu-ma Ch'ien also condemned the entire campaign indirectly through the interpretation of Kung-sun Ch'ing 公孫卿, a man from Ch'i who was favored by the emperor between 113 and 108 BC. Kung-sun claimed to be able to help the sovereign achieve immortality through the performance of the *Feng* and *Shan* sacrifices. His interpretations of events are recorded in the annals for Emperor Wu. He cautioned the emperor regarding the Ch'ao-hsien hostilities as follows:

> The following year [108 BC] there was a campaign against Ch'ao-hsien; in summer there was a drought. Kung-sun Ch'ing said, "In the Yellow Emperor's time, when the *Feng* Sacrifice was performed there was a drought

---

(24B.1157) reads "P'eng Wu penetrated Wei-mo (Yemack) and Ch'ao-hsien (Joseon) and set up Ts'ang-hai Commandery" 彭吳穿穢貊、朝鮮, 置滄海郡.

[73] By allowing the Han armies access. The original text reads 彭吳賈滅朝鮮, 置滄海之郡. "So-yin" argues that this meant "P'eng Wu first opened up a road and wiped it [Ch'ao-hsien] out" 彭吳始開其道而滅之也.

[74] The King of Ch'ao-hsien refers twice to his fear that he might be *cha sha* 詐殺 (killed by deceit) in this chapter (*Shih chi*, 113.2987). This view of the Han generals may resonate with She Ho's behavior and Emperor Wu's reaction to it.

[75] Cited by Han Chao-ch'i (115.5723).

that dried the earthen altar mound [*feng*] for three years." 其明年，伐朝鮮。
夏，旱。公孫卿曰：「黃帝時封則天旱，乾封三年」.[76]

A further criticque of Emperor Wu's foreign policy of *ch'iung ping* 窮兵 "exhausting military means" can be read from the awards recorded at the end of this chapter: five men of Ch'ao-hsien were enfeoffed, whereas both of the Chinese generals were sentenced to die.

Aside from a critique of Emperor Wu's aggression towards neighboring peoples, the chapter also provides an opportunity for Ssu-ma Ch'ien to portray Yang P'u's inept military leadership, something he covered up in "The Memoir on Southern Yüeh" (see the translator's note to chapter 113).

---

[76] *Shih chi*, 12.479 (*Grand Scribe's Records*, 1:249).

Bibliography

Translations:
Aoki, 12:201–18.
Watson, 2:225–30.

Studies:
Barnes, Gina L. "Early Korean States: A Review of Historical Interpretation," in Barnes, *State Formation in Korea, Historical and Archaeological Perspectives.* Richmond: Curzon Press, 2001, pp. 1–19.

Byington, Mark, ed. *The Han Commanderies in Early Korean History.* Cambridge, Mass.: Early Korea Project, Occasional Series, 2013.

Chiang Wei-kung 姜維公. "Kuan-yü Wei Man te kuo-chi wen-t'i" 關於衛滿的國籍問題, in *Tung-pei Ya li-shih wen-t'i yen-chiu* 東北亞歷史問題研究. Chao Li-hsing 趙立興 et al., eds. Chi-lin: Chi-lin Wen-shih Ch'u-pan she, 2001, pp. 95–102.

Gardinier, K. H. J. "Ancient Korea," in in Gardiner, *The Early History of Korea.* Canberra: Center of Oriental Studies, Australian National University, 1969, pp. 3–17.

Ikeuchi Hiroshi. "A Study on Lo-lang and Tai-fang, Ancient Chinese Prefectures in Korea," *Memoirs of the Toyo Bunko* 5 (1931): 79–95

___. "The Fu-yü in the Former and Later Han Period," *Memoirs of the Toyo Bunko* 6 (1932): 23–60.

Komai Kazuchika 駒井和愛 (1905–1971). "*Shiki* "Chōsen restsuden" yakuho oyobi chū—Ōmachi Kenji Kyōju ni sasagu" 史記朝鮮列伝訳補及び註—故大間知教授にささぐ, *Minkan denshō* 民間伝承 35 (1971): 142–45 (not seen).

Mikami Tsugio 三上次男. "Eishi Chōsenkoku no seiji shakaiteki seikaku" 衛氏朝鮮國の政治社會的性格, in *Chūgoku kodaishi no shomondai* 中國古代史の諸問題. Tokyo: University of Tokyo Press, 1954 (not seen).

Wang Ch'eng-kuo 王成國. "Kuan-yü ku Ch'ao-hsien yen-chiu te chi-ko wen-t'i" 關於古朝鮮研究的幾個問題, *She-hui k'o-hsüeh chi-k'an*, 2004.3: 94–98.

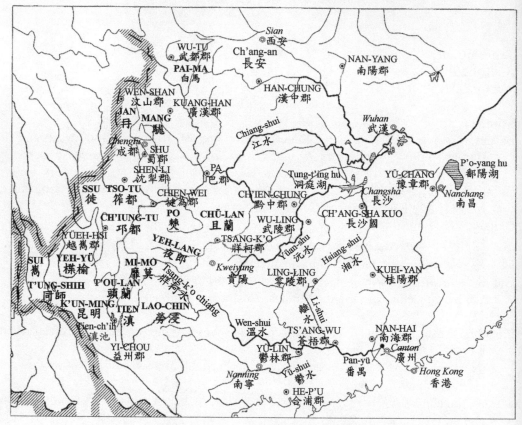

Hsi Nan Yi 西南夷 **(Southwestern Barbarians)**

⊙ Han Commandery Seats ⊚ *Modern Cities*

The Barbarians[1] of the Southwest, Memoir 56

translated by Thomas D. Noel and Lianlian Wu

[116.2991] The lords of the Barbarians of the Southwest number in the tens,[2] and the greatest is Yeh-lang 夜郎.[3] To its [Yeh-lang's] west, the clans of the Mi-mo 靡莫

---

[1] The term *yi* 夷 (barbarian) is problematic and Nicola Di Cosmo's assertion that there is no direct equivalent for "barbarian" in the Chinese lexicon it well taken (see Di Cosmo, *Ancient China and its Enemies: The Rise of Nomadic Power in East Asian History*, [Cambridge: Cambridge University Press, 2002], p. 95). However, we have retained this translation in order to follow convention established in other studies of the era (see, for example, Yuri Pines, "Beasts or Humans: Pre-Imperial Origins of Sino-Barbarian Dichotomy," in Reuven Amitai and Michal Biran, eds., *Mongols, Turks and Others: Eurasian Nomads and the Sedentary World* [Leiden: Brill, 2005], p. 61, n. 8). It has been suggested that this term's use in the *Han shu* is more closely related to specific ethnic groups than it is in the *Shih chi* (Fang T'ieh 放鉄. "*Shih chi, Han shu* shih-tsai Hsi-nan Yi jo-kan shih-shih k'ao-pien," 史記 漢書失載西南夷若干史實考辨, *Chung-yang Min-tsu Ta-hsüeh hsüeh-pao,* 3 [2004]: 65–72). See also the translator's note below.

[2] According to "Cheng-yi" (*Shih chi*, 116.2991), the Barbarians of the Southwest were to the south of Shu 蜀. Takigawa (116.1) cites Ting Ch'ien 丁謙's comment that the Barbarians of the Southwest cover the south of Szechwan, the southwest of Kweichow and the whole of Yunnan province.

Hanshu 漢書 (95.3837) has no *hsi* 西 in the opening line. Takigawa (116.2) cites Nakai Sekitoku's 中井積德 (1732–1817) argument that *hsi* is an interpolation. This seems unlikely, however, as the *Shih chi* text frequently makes use of both graphs in unison to differentiate this specific regions and its peoples from those residing in what is now modern Szechuan to the north and the non-Chinese peoples of Yüeh to the East.

[3] The "So-yin" cites Hsün Yüeh 荀悅 (148–209) on Yeh-lang: "this was a subordinate state of Ch'ien-wei" 犍為屬國也; Ch'ien-wei was a stock term (see T'an Ch'i-hsiang, 2:55–56) referring to the states and minor statelets that fell under the adminstrative control of the Ch'ien-wei Commandery formed by Han conquest of the region as recorded at the conclusion of this chapter. "So-yin" also cites Wei Chao 韋昭 (204–273), who says "During the Han [dynasty,] it became a county that belonged to Tsang-k'o 牂柯 Commandery" 漢為縣, 屬牂柯, which also seems to reference the commandery adjacent to Ch'ien-wei that was also formed

number in the tens, and the greatest is Tien 滇.[4] From Tien northward the lords and chieftains number in the tens, and the greatest is Ch'iung-tu 邛都.[5] These all tie [their hair in] hammer topknots,[6] cultivate fields, and possess towns. Beyond them to the

after the Han Empire's subdugation of the southwest. *Hou Han shu* 後漢書 also records that "To the east, Yeh-lang was adjacent to Chiao-chih Commandery 交阯 (located in northeastern Vietnam). Its land was to the south of the Hu 胡; its lords and chieftans originally grew forth out from bamboo, [and so] they took *Chu* [bamboo] as their *cognomen*." 夜郎東接交阯, 其地在胡南, 其君長本出於竹, 以竹為姓也. Yeh-lang was an ancient state which, at its height, encompassed parts of modern-day southwestern Kweichow, southern Szechwan, and eastern Yunnan Provinces and perhaps parts of modern Kwangsi 廣西 Province. Its chief settlement was situated at what is now modern day Kuan-ling 關嶺 in Kweichow (T'an Ch'i-hsiang, 2:11–12, 2:31–32, and 2:55–56). See the map at the start of this chapter.

    [4] According to "So-yin," Mi-mo was "the name of a barbarian town," which shared a *cognomen* with the peoples of Tien, the "Cheng-yi" notes that the Mi-mo controlled a region southward of Tien and extending into the west, and that the Mi-fei 靡非 were situated to the north of the T'ang 唐 dynasty (618–907) prefecture of Yao-chou 姚州 (present-day 姚安 Yao-an County in the Ch'u-hsiung 楚雄 Yi 彝 Nationality Autonomous Prefecture). From this it can be inferred that the term Mi-mo refers to a larger confederation of peoples who resided in what is now central and northeastern Yunnan Province, controlling a region which may have stretched from modern Ch'ü-ching 曲靖 Municipality (compare both T'an Ch'i-hsiang 2:11, and Wu and Lu, 116.3001n.), to present-day Ch'u-hsiung Prefecture, with their largest settlement located at Tien (near the site of modern-day K'un-ming 昆明). According to the "Cheng-yi," K'un-chou 昆州 and Lang-chou 朗州 counties originally comprised the state of Tien.

    Takigawa (116.2) cites Ting Ch'ien 丁謙 (1843–1919) that "the State of Tien was named after the Lake Tien 滇池, which was today's K'un-ming county in Yunnan;" 滇國以滇池名, 今雲南昆明縣. This now defunct state, from which the postal abbreviation for Yunnan Province is derived, controlled much of modern-day eastern and central Yunnan, and its capital was located at the southern end of what is now Lake Tien. See T'an Ch'i-hsiang, 1:31–32, 2:11–12, 2:55–56 and the map at the start of this chapter. For a more detailed account of the history of Tien, see the translator's note below.

    [5] Or the "Main Settlement of the Ch'iung," a people who controlled much of what is now northern Yunnan and southern Szechwan in the region of Hsi-ch'ang 西昌 Municipality (T'an Ch'i-hsiang, 2:11). It is possible that *tu* 都 may refer to the chief city of a state rather than the chief settlement of a people who held sway over the surrounding territory (see also n. 10 below).

    [6] *Han shu* (95.3837) writes *ch'ui* 椎 for *ch'ui* 魋. Yen Shih-ku's 顏師古 (581–645) commentary to *Han shu* confirms that "the topknot was in the shape of mallet" 為髻如椎之形也. This term however seems to function not as an actual description of custom's common to the peoples of this region but rather as a leitmotif employed by the Grand Scribe to signify

west, from T'ung-shih 同師 eastward,[7] north to Yeh-yü 楪榆,[8] are those named Sui 嶲 and K'un-ming 昆明[9]; all braid their hair, follow their herds, move from one place to another, are without any permanent residence, and are without lords or chieftains; their lands could [extend] some several thousand *li* on a side. From Sui northeastward, the lords and chieftains number in the tens, and the greatest are Ssu 徙 and the City of Tso-tu 筰都.[10] From the Tso northeastward, the lords and chieftains number in the tens, the greatest are Jan 冄 and Mang 駹.[11] Their custom is that some had fixed aboves,[12] some move about from place to place in the west of Shu 蜀.[13] From Jan and

peoples of "Non-Chinese" origin. See the translator's note for more on this term's appearance in the *Shih chi*.

[7] "Chi-chieh" (*Shih chi*, 116.2992) cites Yen Shih-ku that T'ung-shih was a town. The *Han shu* (95.3837) writes T'ung-shih 桐師 for T'ung-shih 同師 but Yen Shih-ku's comment does not appear there. According to Wang Shu-min (116.3065), *Han chi* 漢紀 [Records of Han] and *Hua yang kuo chih* 華陽國志 [Records of the States South of Mount Hua] also read T'ung-shih 桐師. Takigawa (116.2) cites Shen Ch'in-han 沈欽韓 (1775–1831) that T'ung-shih was to the north of Ch'ü-ching and Ting Ch'ien locates T'ung-shih on the southwestern boundary of Tien. Wu and Lu (116.3001n.) locate T'ung-shih near the modern counties of Lung-ling 龍陵 and Pao-shan 保山 in Yunnan province.

[8] A town on what is modern Erh-hai 餌海 Lake about thirty miles north of Modern Hsia-kuan 下關 city. T'an Ch'i-hsiang (2:55–56). Wang Shu-min (116.3065) notes that *Han shu* and *Hou Han shu* both all write *yeh* 葉 for *yeh* 楪.

[9] A people who inhabited large parts of modern Ta-li 大理, Ch'u-hsiung 楚雄, and Pao-shan 保山 municipalities in Yunnan (T'an Ch'i-hsiang, 2:11).

[10] Yen Shih-ku's comments (*Han shu*, 95.3838n.) that 徙 should be pronounced *si* 斯. T'an Ch'i-hsiang (2:11) locates both the Ssu and the Tso in southern Szechwan and northern Yunnan just to the northwest of the Ch'iung-tu. We follow Wu and Lu (116.3002n.) in their interpretation of *tu* 都 as meaning "main settlement" or "city," a convention we have adapted and discussed in regard to Ch'iung-tu above.

[11] Some modern scholars argue that the Man-mang were Tibetan tribes and were located between modern Mao-wen 茂汶 county and Sung-p'an 松潘 county in Szechwan, about one hundred miles north of modern Chengtu (see also T'an Ch'i-hsiang, 2:11).

The *Han shu* (95.3837) reads *jan* 冉 for *jan* 冄, as does the *Shih chi p'ing-lin* (116.2a). Yen Shih-ku notes that many people living in K'ai-chou 開州 and K'uei-chou 夔州 during his lifetime had the surname Jan and were likely descendants of the Jan.

[12] The 1959 Chung-hua edition has the typographical error *shih* 士 for *t'u* 土. Most other editions have *t'u* (and the 2013 edition [116.3601] has corrected this).

[13] Shu was a Han commandery located in what is modern western Szechwan with its seat at modern Chengtu (T'an Ch'i-hsiang, 2:11).

Mang northeastward,[14] the lords and chieftains number in the tens, and the greatest is that of Pai-ma 白馬[15]; all are of Ti 氐 stock.[16] These are all Man barbarians[17] beyond Pa 巴 [18] and Shu to the southwest.

[2993] At the beginning in the time of King Wei 威 of Ch'u (r. 340–329 BC), [the King] sent General Chuang Chüeh 莊蹻[19] to command troops patrolling the upper reaches of the Chiang 江, overrunning Pa, Shu, Ch'ien-chung 黔中 and [lands] westward.[20] This Chuang Chüeh was a distant descendant of the former King Chuang

[14] *Han shu* (95.3837) reads simiply "from Mang northeastward," apparently the result of a scribal error as the previous clause preserves both graphs from the *Shih chi* account and Yen Shih-ku explicity discusses the frequent use of this graph as a surname (see note 11 above).

[15] The Pai-ma people lived in the northern Szechwan and southern Kansu (T'an Ch'i-hsiang, 2:11).

[16] On the Ti 氐 peoples see "So-yin," *Shih chi*, 110.2981 and *Grand Scribe's Records*, 9:262, n. 165.

[17] Here the word *man* does not seem to be used in reference to a specific ethnicity or confederation of peoples but rather as a more general term designating foreign or "non-Chinese peoples" living on the southern frontiers of the Han Empire.

[18] Pa was a Han commandery located in what is modern eastern Szechwan with its seat at modern Chungking (T'an Ch'i-hsiang, 2:11).

[19] "So-yin" notes that Chuang Chüeh was the younger brother of King Chuang 莊 of Ch'u (r. 613–591 BC), while also mentioning that Chuang was a *tao* 盜 (bandit), no doubt referring to his rebellion against Ch'u. Liang Yü-sheng (34.1411–12) therefore notes that the main texts of the *Shih chi* and the *Han shu* are both in error, arguing that in the reign of King Ch'ing-hsing of Ch'u 楚頃襄王 (r. 298–263 BC) a man named Chuang Hao 莊浩 ruled as King of Tien, concluding that the invasion by Ch'in occurred fifty-two years after the reign of King Wei of Ch'u, and that the *Hou Han shu* and *T'ung tien* must be correct in their accounts. However this Chuang Hao could have simply been a descendant of the original Chuang Chüeh ruling as King of Tien.

Wang Shu-min (116.3066), citing Shen Chin-han from the *Han shu pu chu* 漢書補註, notes that the *Hua-yang kuo chih* 華陽國志 [Records of the States South of Mount Hua] records that in the time of King Ch'ing-hsing of Ch'u, Ch'in took Ch'ien-chung Commandery from the state of Ch'u. While extant editions of *Hua yang kuo chih* state that these events occurred during reign of King Wei of Ch'u, commentary to the extant edition of the "Ti-li chih" 地理志 [Treatise on Geography] in the *Han shu* records these events as having occurred during the reign of King Ch'ing-hsiang. Takigawa's (116.4) arguments corroborate those of Wang this, and he goes on to point out that according to the *Han Fei-tzu* 韓非子 [Master Han Fei] there was a Chuang Chüeh related to King Chuang who served as a *Hsiao ssu-ma* 小司馬 [Minor Master of the Horse]; thus, Wang argues, the claim that Chüeh lived during the time of King Wei is erroneous.

[20] The extent of Ch'in control over these regions remains a subject of debate.

莊 of Ch'u (r. 613–591 BC).[21] Ch'iao reached Tien-ch'ih 滇池 [The Lake of Expansive Waters],[22] three hundred *li* on side, flanked by flatlands rich and bountiful for many thousand *li*; by his strength of arms he stabilized [that region] annexing it for Ch'u. Just as he was about to return to report this, Ch'in 秦 was attacking and taking Ch'u's Pa and Ch'ien-chung commanderies.[23] The road being blocked and impassible, [Ch'iao] accordingly turned back; relying on his host he ruled as king of the Tien, changing [his] clothing, following their customs, and thereby acting as their chieftain. In the time of the Ch'in (221–206 BC), Ch'ang An 常頞 overran [this area],[24] opening the Five-foot Road,[25] [so that Ch'in] in most of these various states [mentioned above] set up officials in them.[26] More than ten years later (206 BC), Ch'in was wiped out. When the Han 漢 arose (202 BC), it abandoned all of these states and opened the old Shu border stations.[27] Among the peoples of Pa and Shu

[21] See note 19 above.

[22] A large freshwater, endorheic lake whose northern shores reach the southwest of the Hsi-shan 西山 District of modern-day Kunming city proper, it still bears this name. "So-yin" (*Shih-chi*, 116.2993) cites the *Hou Han shu*, which records that the lake waters at their source were both deep and wide, [but] became shallow and narrow, appearing as if they flowed backwards, and thus it was named Tien-chih, or the "Pool of Tien." An alternative gloss offered by Wang Li (*Tz'u-tien*, p. 617) renders *tien* as: "a broad expanse of water," therefore partially concurring with "So-yin" in that both seem to take the graph as descriptive of the lake's considerable breadth from north to south, an axis along the which it flanked a sizable area of arable land. Another possibility is that *tien* is merely a transliteration of the name of the state (and also perhaps the people) controlling the region.

[23] Chien-chung Commandery was located in modern southeastern Szechwan and northwestern Kweichow (T'an Ch'i-hsiang, 2:11, 2:31–32).

[24] The existence of Ch'ang An is not widely supported by other texts. Takigawa (116.5) and Wang Shu-min (116.3066) both note that the *Han shu* (95.3838) records his name as Ch'ang P'o 常頗. All other sources record his name as An 頞, with the "Chi chieh" (*Shih chi*, 116.2993) moreover glossing the graph's pronunciation.

[25] According to "So-yin" the Five-foot Road was made of planks built onto a cliff-face and was so named due to its breath.

[26] Takigawa (116.5) cites Nakai Riken's argument that the text should read: *tz'u chu kuo* 此諸國 "these many states," in according with the text below which reads: *ch'ieh ch'i tz'u kuo* 皆棄此國 "all of these states were abandoned." Wang Shu-min (116.3067) notes that the *Han chi* 漢紀 reads: 此諸國 "these many states," thus corroborating Nakai's suggestion. However, Wang also argues that in the *Shih chi* the use of the character *chu* 諸 could be here synonymous with the character *fan* 凡, as the two are often used interchangeably in the *Shih chi*.

[27] The *Han shu* reads *kuan* 關 "closed" for *k'ai* 開 "opened," which drastically alters the meaning of the text. While *Han shu* suggests that all relations with these states were cut-off, the *Shih chi* account offers a more nuanced image of Han policy aimed at controlling relations and especially the flow of people across the borders of Shu and Pa. Wang Hsien-ch'ien (95.2a

some would secretly go out to engage in trade, obtaining their Tso horses, Po 僰 slaves,[28] and yaks; by this Pa and Shu were enriched.

In the sixth year of the Chien-yüan era 建元 (135 BC)[29] Wang Hui 王恢,[30] The Grand Usher, assaulted Eastern Yüeh. Eastern Yüeh killed Ying 郢, the King, and reported this.[31] Hui, relying on strength in arms, sent T'ang Meng 唐蒙,[32] the Prefect of P'o-yang 番陽,[33] to point out through gentle persuasion and make clear [the Sovereign's will] to Southern Yüeh 南越. [*2994*] [The Lord of] Southern Yüeh served Shu Betel sauce to [T'ang] Meng,[34] Meng asked where it came from and he [the Lord] said: "By way of the northwest is Tsang-k'o 牂柯[35]; the Tsang-k'o River is

---

[2625]) cites Yen Shih-ku, claiming that there must have been fortifications in Shu similar to those along the northern borders of the Han, while mentioning several extant editions of the *Han shu* and *Shih chi* deviate from their current texts.

[28] According to the "So-yin" the P'o were subservient to the Ch'ien-wei, and there were P'o slave-girls in the capital city. T'an Ch'i-hsiang (2:11) locates the P'o near modern Yi-pin 宜賓 City in southern Szechwan one hundred miles south-southeast of Chengtu.

[29] The Chien-yüan, lasting from 140 to 135 BC, was the first era of the reign of Emperor Wu 武 of Han (156–87 BC, r. 141–87 BC).

[30] Wang Hui was appointed Prefect Grand Usher in 136, and, sharing command with Han An-kuo 韓安國, was sent on a punitive expedition against Eastern Yüeh (*Shih chi*, 114.2981). He later failed in an expedition against the Hsiung-nu, and upon his return he was sentenced to die. As a result he committed suicide in prison. See Loewe, *Dictionary*, p. 526 and *Shih chi*, 108.2860.

[31] Wang was sent to diffuse a crisis which began with Min Yüeh's 閩越 illegal military incursions against its neighbor, Southern Yüeh. For a account of the circumstances surrounding Ying's regicide, see both *Shih chi*, 114.2981, and our translation "The Eastern Yüeh, Memoir 54" in this volume.

[32] T'ang Meng, though remembered for his role in these events, is otherwise unknown. See parallel accounts of these events in *Han shu*, 95.3839.

[33] Takigawa cites the "Ti-li chih," which records that P'o-yang was the name of a county during the Han dynasty, using the graph *p'o* 鄱 in place of *p'o* 番.

[34] The "Chi-chieh" claims that one edition (unnamed) uses the graph *chü* 蒟 and describes the plant which bears this fruit as a *kou* 枸 tree, whose leaves resemble those of the mulberry and are used to make this sauce in Szechuan. However the "So-yin" cites Liu Te 劉德, who claims that it is a vine that grows up trees; this points to *Piper betel* (betel pepper), a creeping vine whose leaves and fruit are indeed used to make a famously stimulating sauce known as *chü-chiang* 蒟醬. Yen Shih-ku (*Han shu*, 95.3840) and Wang Shu-min (116.3068) give similar explanations.

[35] Confusion has arisen as to the nature of this Tsang-k'o, with a number of editions presenting it as the name of a place or settlement, while others including the *Han shu* (95.3839) record it only as the name of a river, marking it with the graph *chiang* 江, as Ssu-ma Ch'ien does in the following sentences. However, it appears that, given its listing as the name

several *li* wide, and it flows past the walls of P'an-yü 番禺.[36] Meng went back and reached Ch'ang-an; he asked a Shu merchant, and the merchant said: "Only Shu produces Betel sauce, most is taken out secretly and sold on the markets of Yeh-lang. This Yeh-lang is overlooks the Tsang-k'o River, and there the river is over one-hundred paces across, enough to move [goods by] boat. Southern Yüeh using its wealth and goods has subordinated Yeh-lang, to the west as far as the T'ung-shih, but as of yet it is unable to cause it [Yeh-lang] to act as a vassal." Only then did Meng submit a memorial, stating: "The King of Southern Yüeh [rides in a chariot with] a yellow canopy and a yak's tail on his left, his territory from east to west is over one-hundred thousand *li*; he is called a march-vassal, in truth he is ruler of an entire region. If [one were] to go by Ch'ang-sha 長沙 and Yü-chang 豫章, the waterways would often be impassable[37] and they would difficult to travel. I have privately heard that of Yeh-lang's crack troops, we could recruit more than ten thousand; drifting them down the Tsang-k'o River, leaving while they are unaware—with this one spectacular strategy [it would be easy to] restrain Yüeh! Indeed through the might of Han and the richness of Pa and Shu, connecting a road through Yeh-lang and establishing officials [therein] would be quite easy." The Sovereign consented to this. Only then did he appoint Meng the Commander of the Palace Attendants,[38] to command a thousand men, and with supply wagons for more than ten thousand, to enter [the region of Yeh-lang] through the Tso Pass 筰關 of Pa and Shu, and in the end to meet To-t'ung 多同, the Marquis of Yeh-lang.[39] Meng presented him with lavish gifts, instructing him of the majesty and virtue [of Han], making an agreement to set up [Han] officials, and

of a region in both the *Han shu* ("Ti li chih") and appended commentary as well as the *Hua-yang kuo chih*, this place has taken its name from the river or vice versa, and editions which record Tsang-k'o only as the name of a river have been erroneously revised by later editors. See Han Chao-ch'i, 116.5734, n. 9.

The river itself is most likely the Pei-p'an 北盘, but we can only conclude with certainty that it was a tributary of the Pearl River 珠江 (Wang Shu-min, 116.3068)

[36] Situated at the site of present-day Kwangchow 廣州 Canton, one main districts of the city proper which lies on the estuary of the Pearl River continues to bear this name.

[37] Ch'ang-sha, a commandery with its seat located near the modern city which bears the same name in present-day Hunan. Yü-chang was a commandery with its seat situated near modern Nan-ch'ang 南昌 municipality (T'an Ch'i-hsiang, 2:11–12, 2:31–32).

[38] Liang Yü-sheng (34.1412), Wang Shu-min (116.3068), and Takigawa (116.7) all note that the graphs *Lang-chung ch'iang* 郎中將 should read 中郎將, citing the *Hua yang kuo-chih*. However, it appears that such terms, including the phrase *Lang-chung ling* 郎中令 (Prefect of the Palace Attendants) and its variant 郎中令 were used interchangeably.

[39] Shih Ku's commentary to the *Han shu* (95.3840) says that this was the name of the regions' enfeoffed lord. Moreover, in the *Han shu* (95.3839) parallel to this passage, "Shu" 蜀 is omitted. Takigawa (116.7) explores several later sources including which all state this pass was located the region of Tso 筰 county, which was of old the region of the Pa barbarians.

having his son made Prefect. The small townships around Yeh-lang all coveted Han silk; [but] thinking the road to Han dangerous and in the end never having obtained this [silk], they temporarily assented to Meng's agreement. [Meng] returned to report, only then was [Yeh-lang] made Ch'ien-wei 犍為 Commandery.[40] Foot soldiers from Pa and Shu were sent to put the roads in order; from Po 僰 built a road to Tsang-k'o River.[41] Ssu-ma Hsiang-ju 司馬相如 (179–117 BC),[42] a native of Shu, also said that western barbarian [regions of] Ch'iung and Tso could be established as commanderies. Sending Hsiang-ju as Commander of the Palace Attendants to go there and inform them, and all were, like the barbarians of the south, established under a single Chief Commandant in more than ten counties attached to Shu.

[2995] In the meantime, in the four commanderies of Pa and Shu,[43] in order to connect a road to the Barbarians of the Southwest, [troops] were defending the caravans to provide rations [for the workmen].[44] After several years the road was [still]

[40] During the Han, Ch'ien-wei Commandery comprised swaths of northern Yun-nan, southern Szechwan, and western Kweichow (T'an Ch'i-hsiang 2:31–32). However based on the information provided in this chapter, this does not comprise the entirety of area controlled by the state Yeh-lang. It is unclear if Ch'ien-wei at first comprised a much larger territory which was later ceded to other Han administrative divisions, or if this annexation was initially more nominal than the text suggests.

[41] Takigawa (116.8) believes that Po-tao 僰道 refers to a Han-dynasty county. "So-yin" (*Shih chi*, 116.1995) glosses *tao* 道 here as being similar to *tsung* 從 (to follow). Han Chao-ch'i (116.5735, n. 18) cites a *Shui-ching chu* 水經注 passage which depicts how T'ang Meng completed a road through the mountains to Yeh-lang. We therefore read *tao* 道 here as "to build a road."

[42] Arguably the pre-eminent poet of the Han dynasty and the greatest practitioner of the *fu* 賦 poetic form, Ssu-ma Hsiang-ju (*cognomen* Ch'ang-ch'ing 長卿) played an important role in the establishment of Han hegemony over the the peoples of the southwest, however sources disagree on the exact role he played. Later in this chapter, it is recorded that the Emperor ordered other men to go forth and seek the road to India. However, his biographies claim (*Shih chi*, 117.3046 and *Han shu*, 57.2851) that Hsiang-ju first led these men on an expedition to the southwest, and his role in the search for a way India remains unclear as the commentaries are silent on this matter. See his biographies in *Han shu* chapter 57, *Shih chi* chapter 117, and the translation of that chapter in this volume.

[43] "Chi-chieh" claims that these were the commanderies of Han-chung 漢中, Kuang-han 廣漢, Pa 巴, and Shu 屬; which roughly corresponds to an area stretching from the upper reaches of the Yangtze to the mountains dividing the Szechuan Basin from the plains of modern Shensi 陝西. See *Shih chi*, 116.2995 and Tan Ch'i-hsiang, 2:31–32.

[44] An alternative punctuation for this line has been suggested by Takigawa Kametaro, whose edition reads: "During this time, the four commanderies of Pa and Shu were connecting the road to the Barbarians of the Southwest, guarding the caravans and providing supplies for

not completed; soldiers were exhausted by starvation and suffering from the damp, and the dead were extremely numerous. The Barbarians of the Southwest rebelled repeatedly; troops were sent out to counter their attacks, and losses were suffered without merit.[45] The Sovereign was distressed by this, sending Kung-sun Hung 公孫弘 (ca. 200–121 BC) to observe and ask about [this].[46] He returned to respond [to the Sovereign], explaining that [the project] was not expedient. When Hung was made a Grand Master of the Imperial Secretariat, at that time [Han was] in the midst of building Shuo-fang 朔方 fortifications in order to defend the Ho 河 (Yellow River) and drive out the Tatars. Hung accordingly explained many times of the dangers of Barbarians of the Southwest, that they could be temporarily abandoned, and that all force should [be focused] on the Hsiung-nu 匈奴. The Sovereign abandoned the Western Barbarians, only establishing the two counties of Nan-yi 南夷 and Yeh-lang under a single Capital Commandant, gradually allowing Ch'ien-wei to protect itself.[47]

By the first year of the Yüan-shou 元狩 era (122 BC), Chang Ch'ien 張騫 (d. 113),[48] the Marquis of Po-wang 博望侯, came from his embassy to Ta-hsia 大夏,[49] saying that during the time he lived in Ta-hsia he had seen Shu fabrics and bamboo staffs from [Mount] Ch'iung[-lai] 邛[崍].[50] He caused inquires to be made about where they came from, and it was said: "By way of the southeast some several

many years; the road was not completed." 當是時巴蜀四郡通西南夷道，戍轉相饟數歲，道不通.

[45] Yen Shih-ku (*Han shu*, 95.3840) glosses *hao* 耗 as *sun* 損 (to lose, decrease).

[46] Kung-sun Hung, *cognomen* Chi 季, was a man of Po 薛 in the state of Ch'i 齊. He enjoyed the favor of Han Emperor Wu, first serving as an academician, then made Grandee Secretary in 126 BC, and Chancellor in 124 BC and was the Confucian whom Ssu-ma Ch'ien most disliked. This inspection trip was taken in 130 BC as a result of which Emperor Wu disregarded Kung-sun Hung's denunciation of the project. See *Shih chi*, 112.2949, the translation on *Grand Scribe's Records*, 9:364, and Loewe, *Dictionary*, pp. 125–128.

[47] "Cheng yi" (*Shih chi*, 116.1995) notes that by "protect itself" it is meant that Ch'ien-wei was instructed to both be responsible for its own defenses as well as the ordering of its administration.

On the road project in general, see *Grand Scribe's Records*, 112.365, n. 10.

[48] Takigawa (116.9) notes that Liang Yü-sheng (34.1412) believes that Chang could not have returned in this year. For further information concerning Chang Ch'ien's odyssey though Central Asia see *Shih chi*, 123.3157–3180, and *Han shu*, 61.2687–2698.

[49] Ta-hsia is commonly known in the west as Bactria, region located between the Hindu Kush and the Amu Darya mountain ranges, and was at the time of Chang Ch'ien's arrival under the aegis of the Greco-Bactrian Kings.

[50] Located in the central part of modern Szechwan, southeast of modern Hsi-ch'ang City 西昌市 (Wu and Lu, 116.3006n. and Han Chao-ch'i, 116.5738, n. 2).

thousand *li* is the state of Chüan-tu 身毒,[51] [there] they are found in the markets of the Shu merchants." It had also been heard that two thousand *li* the west of Ch'iung there was a state [called] Chüan-tu. Therefore Ch'ien on the basis of this spoke with conviction that Ta-hsia was to the southwest of Han, that it admired the Central States, and were dismayed that the Hsiung-nu had cut-off the road; that if Shu really could be connected to Chüan-tu, the road would be shortened, an advantage without harm. Only then did the Son of Heaven order [*2996*] Wang Jan-yü 王然于, Pai Shih-chang 柏始昌, Lü Yüeh-jen 呂越人, and others out as envoys west from Hsi-yi 西夷,[52] with the goal of seeking the state of Chüan-tu. When they reached Tien, Ch'ang Ch'iang 嘗羌, the King of Tien 滇王, retained then and for them looked for a way [to Chüan-tu]. He sent more than ten teams to the west. After more than a year,[53] all had been harried by the K'un-ming, and none were able to pass on to the state of Chüan-tu.

The King of Tien spoke with the envoys from Han, saying: "Han or my [own], which state is greater?"[54] When it came to the Marquis of Yeh-lang, he also asked in this way.[62] It was for the reason that the roads were impassable, each thought himself the master of an entire region, unaware of the great expanse of Han. When those sent on envoy returned, they spoke with conviction of the greatness of the state of Tien, and that it deserved to be treated with closer ties. The Son of Heaven gave his close attention to this.

When it came to the rebellion of Southern Yüeh (112 BC),[55] the Sovereign sent the Ch'ih-yi Marquis 馳義侯[56] to Ch'ien-wei as a base in order to raise troops from Nan-yi 南夷.[57] The Lord of the Chü-lan 且蘭[58] feared that if they travelled far neighbor-ing states would take captive their elderly and youth, and so with his host he rebelled, killing the envoys and the Grand Administrator of Ch'ien-wei. Only then did

[51] Chüan-tu was one of the more common names used for India during Han times.

[52] Whether or not the text is here referring directly to the peoples of the southwest, or using the term metonymically to denote the region they inhabit, remains ambiguous, though we have however chosen the latter possibility in this translation. See the translator's note below for a continued discussion of this issue.

[53] The *Han shu* parallel (95.3841) reads "after more than four years" 四歲.

[54] This could also be read "the Emperor of Han or myself, who is greater" 漢孰與我大.

[55] On Southern Yüeh's see the *Shih chi*, 113.2973 and the translation of this text above.

[56] Based on Liang T'ing-nan's 梁廷楠 *Nan Yüeh Wu-chu zhuan* 南越五主傳 (Biographies of Five Rulers of Southern Yüeh [Canton: Kuang-tung Jen-min, 1982], cited in Wang Li-ch'i, 113.2977n.), this was Ho Yi 何遺.

[57] Again, we have understood this term as referring to a region, in this particular case Yeh-lang, as it does not appear that Tien was directly involved in this military action. See note above as well as our translator's note below.

[58] According to Wu and Lu (116.3755n.) Chü-lan was a barbarian state located near Huang-p'ing 黃平 county in Kueichow.

Han raise eight colonels and [a force comprised of] criminals from Pa and Shu to assault Southern Yüeh, assaulting and crushing it. When Yüeh had already been destroyed, Han's eight commanders did not go down [the river], [instead they] immediately led their troops back, traveling to punish the T'ou-lan 頭蘭 [i.e., Chu-lan].[59] The T'ou-lan were those who had often cut off the road to Tien. After subduing the T'ou-lan, in the end they subdued Nan-yi and it was made Tsang-k'o 牂柯 Commandery.[60] The Marquis of Yeh-lang in the beginning relied upon Southern Yüeh, [however with] Southern Yüeh already being wiped out, [he] met those returning and punished rebels, [and The Lord of] Yeh-lang in the end went to court. The Sovereign thereby made him King of Yeh-lang 夜郎王.

[2997] After Southern Yüeh was destroyed, Han executed the lords of Chu-lan and Ch'iung, killed the Marquis of Tso, and all in Jan and Mang trembled in fear; all became [vassals] and were established as officials. Only then[61] was the seat of the Ch'iung was made Yüeh-hsi 越巂 Commandery,[62] the city of the Tso was made Ch'en-li 沈犂 Commandery,[63] the Nan and Mang [region] was made into Wen-shan 汶山 Commandery,[64] and the Pai-ma [region] to the west of Kuang-han 廣漢 was made into Wu-tu 武都 Commandery.[65]

---

[59] The "So-yin" glosses T'ou-lan as Chu-lan. This perhaps follows the *Han shu* parallel which here has a much different reading: "Only then did Han send out the criminals from Pa and Shu and those eight colonels who were to attack Nan-Yüeh to attack them. When it happened that Yüeh was already defeated, the eight Han colonels did not descend [the Tsang-k'o River] but the Palace Attendant Commanders Kuo Ch'ang [see the entry in Loewe, *Dictionary*, p. 138] and Wei Kuang [see the entry in Loewe, *Dictionary*, p. 570] led the troops to return and moved to punish Chu-lan which had cut off the road to Tien, cutting off several ten thousands of heads, and in the end pacifying Tsang-k'o Commandery of the South[western] Barbarians" 漢乃發巴蜀罪人當擊南粵者八校尉擊之. 會越已破，漢八校尉不下，中郎將郭昌、衛廣引兵還，行誅隔滇道者且蘭，斬首數萬，遂平南夷為牂柯郡. The thrust of these texts is that although what actually happened is difficult to determine without further references, the *Han shu* text seems to make better sense (as Han Chao-ch'i, 116.5741, n. 18 argues). It would seem that all three mentions of T'ou-lan should be read Chu-lan.

[60] Compare T'an Ch'i-hsiang (2:28–29).

[61] In 111 BC (see Wu and Lu, 116.3007n.)

[62] With its seat southeast of modern Hsi-ch'ang City about 230 miles southwest of Chengtu in Szechwan (Han Chao-ch'i, 116.5742, n. 24).

[63] With its seat at Tso-tu about northeast of modern Han-yüan 漢源 County about forty miles west-southwest of O-mei Shan and ninety miles southwest of modern Chengtu (ibid.).

[64] With its seat at Wen-shan 汶山 north of modern Mao County 茂縣 about ten miles west of modern Chengdu in Szechwan (ibid.).

[65] The commandery seat was at Wu-tu, modern Ch'eng County in Kansu, some 260 miles west of modern Sian (Han Chao-ch'i, 116.5742, n. 24, and T'an Ch'i-hsiang, 2:28–29).

The Sovereign sent Wang Jan-yü to tell of the strength of arms that destroyed Yüeh and executed the Southern Barbarians so that the King of Tien might come to court. The King of Tien, [with] his host numbering in the several tens of thousands, [and with] his neighbors to the northeast being the Lao-chin 勞浸[66] and Mi-mo who all shared the same *cognomen* and aided one another, was not yet willing to obey. The Lao-chin and Mi-mo had many times harried those sent on envoy, officials, and soldiers. In the second year of the Yüan-feng 元封 era (109 BC), the Son of Heaven raised troops from Shu and Pa to assault and wipe out the Lao-chin and Mi-mo, and taking [these] soldiers to approach Tien. The King of Tien in the beginning had been among the most friendly, and for this reason they did not execute him. The King of Tien distanced himself from the Southwestern Barbarians,[67] took his state and surrendered, requesting the establishment of [Han] officials and to come to court. At that point [his lands] were made into Yi-chou 益州 Commandery,[68] the sovereign conferred a king's seal upon the King of Tien, and he was restored as chieftain of his people.[69]

The chieftains of the Barbarians of the Southwest number in the hundreds, [yet] only those of Yeh-lang and Tien have received the seals of kings. Although Tien was just a small city-state, it because of this enjoyed the highest favor.

---

[66] Otherwise unknown.

[67] Takigawa (116.12) believes "Li-nan" 離難 to be name of the then King of Tien but the graph *nan* 難 is absent from the *Han shu* (95.3840) edition. Thus the *Han shu* reads "the King of Tien separated himself from the Southwestern Barbarians." This suggests more Pan Ku's struggle with the original. The "San ch'ia chu" (*Shih chi*, 116.2997) are silent on this matter, and all modern editions, including Chung-hua text which this volume uses as a base edition, does not mark the graphs *li nan* 離難 as a proper name. Watson also translates "Li-nan" as a proper name but notes that "The text of the first part of the sentence appears to be corrupt and the translation is highly tentative" (2:296, n. 3). If Takigawa and Watson are followed, the following Hsi-nan Yi is a problem. Wu and Lu (116.3011) read *li nan* 離難 as *fu li* 附麗, "to attach oneself to." Han Chao-ch'i (116.5742–43, n. 30) has a lengthy discussion of the possibilities and concludes that *li nan* means *t'uo li* 脫離, "to isolate or distance oneself," from the other states in the region (Lao-chin, Mi-mo and others) who were in opposition to the Han. We have followed this reading but recognize that the passage is problematic.

[68] Modern Chin-ning County 晉寧縣 on the southwestern short of Lake Tien about thirty miles south of Kunming in Yunnan (Han Chao-ch'i, 116.5743, n. 31).

[69] It is now widely accepted that this very seal was unearthed at Tomb No. 6 at Shih-chai-shan 石寨山 in 1956 with the inscription: "Tien Wang chih yin" 滇王之印 (The Seal of the King of Tien." For a use comparative discussion of this and other contemporaneous seals recovered see Li K'un-sheng 李昆声, "'Tien Wang zhi yin' yü 'Han Wei Nu kuo-wang' yin chih pi-chiao yen-chiu" 滇王之印與漢委奴國王印之比較研究, *Ssu-hsiang chan-tien*, 1986.3: 78–81.

His Honor the Grand Scribe says: Have not the ancestors of Ch'u had Heaven's blessings? During the Chou one served as tutor to King Wen 文 and was enfeoffed at Ch'u.[70] When it came to Chou's decline, their territory corresponded to five thousand *li* [on a side]. Ch'in wiped out all the feudal lords, and among Ch'u's distant descendants there still were only Kings of Tien. When Han executed the Barbarians of the Southwest, most states were wiped out; only Tien continued as a favored King.[71] Yet the beginning of the affairs with the Southwest was the sighting of the [Shu] berry sauce in P'an-yü, and in Ta-hsia staffs made of Ch'iung bamboo. The Western Barbarians were later split, divided up into two parts, and finally made into seven commanderies.[72]

*   *   *   *   *

T'ang Meng was sent to seize and open [the way to] Yeh-lang, and the lords of Ch'iung and Tso requested to be made ministers of the State and receive [Han] officials; [thus] I composed the "Memoir of the Barbarians of the Southwest."[73]

[70] "Hereditary House of Ch'u" records that a member of what would become the Royal House of Ch'u, Yü Hsiung 鬻熊, indeed served King Wen of Chou but it was however his great-grandson, Hsiung Yi 熊繹, who was enfeoffed by King Ch'eng 成 of Chou (r. ca. 1115–1077 BC) See *Shih chi*, 40.1691–92 and *Grand Scribe's Records*, 5.1:383–84.

While Takigawa (116.12) agrees with this, Liang Yü-sheng (22.1006) seems to favor this chapter's account, noting that based on evidence contained in the *Mo tzu* 墨子, it is possible that this enfeofment may have occured as earlier in the time of Yü Hsiung's son Hsiung Li 熊麗. However this rests wholly upon the fact that Hsiung Li is refrred to as Hsiung Li of Ch'u (Chu Hsiung Li) 楚熊麗, and makes no mention of who he served nor of any enfeoffment.

[71] Takigawa (116.12) argues that the lords of Tien were able to retain the title of "King" due to reverence held for their noble ancestry, an act which he sees a similar to the treatment of Fu 福, who was enfeoffed as the Marquis of Liao-ying 繚嫈侯 largely because of his regal heritage. (*SC*, 114.2983) See our translation of the same chapter, "The Eastern Yüeh, Memoir 54" in this volume.

[72] "Chi-chieh" (*Shih chi*, 116.2998) notes that these commanderies were Ch'ien-wei 犍為, Tsang-k'o 牂柯, Yüeh-hsi 越雟, Yi-chou 益州, Wu-tu 武都, Shen-li 沈犁, and Wen-shan 汶山.

[73] These are Ssu-ma Ch'ien's reasons behind the composition of this chapter (see *Shih chi*, 130.3317: 唐蒙使略通夜郎，而邛笮之君請為內臣受更。作西南夷列傳第五十六).

Translator's Note

A full account of who "The Barbarians of the Southwest" were in the time of Ssu-ma Chien, the nature of their societies, the structures of their political organization, the nature of their economic systems, and the realities of their everyday lives are issues that remain much contested and which lay far beyond the scope and goal of our concern here.[74] We instead have focused on the present text and what insights it may offer in respect to contemporary Han frontier policies.

Ssu-ma Ch'ien descriptions of foreign peoples have been described as examples of "Chinese resistance to the kind of ubiquitous ethnographic tradition that either commemorates political domination or facilitates conquest."[75] However, despite the growing number of scholars who have described his work as ethnographic or anthropological, this chapter seems to offer little in the way description of the actual customs and habits of peoples of the southwestern frontiers. This issue is particularly problematic since the Grand Scribe himself travelled to many of the regions described in this chapter and must have therefore had direct knowledge of their inhabitants.[76] Indeed, of the few terms used specifically to describe the people's in question, most seem to be taken from a common lexicon of stock tropes and motifs employed not to provide an actual descriptions of foreign cultures but rather to provide a sufficient foreign color to the account. A particularly striking example from this chapter is the hammer topknots ascribed to the people of Ch'iung-tu, a hairstyle which is also attributed throughout the text of *Shih chi* to various populations of frontier groups including the King of Southern Yüeh 南越 and the people of Ch'ao-hsien 朝鮮 in the

---

[74] The answers to many of these questions await the of ongoing archeological research in the region.

[75] Tamara T. Chin, "Defamiliarizing the Foreigner Sima Qian's Ethnography and Han-Xiongnu Marriage Diplomacy," *HJAS*, 70.2 (2010): 313.

[76] See *Shih chi,* 130.3293–94; *Han shu,* 62.2714–45. An excellent discussion of his early travels in the south is Fang T'ieh 放鉄, "*Shih chi, Han shu* shih-tai Hsi-nan Yi jo-kan shih-shih k'ao-pien," 史記漢書失載西南夷若干史實考辨, *Chung-yang Min-tsu Ta-hsüeh hsüeh-pao* 2004.3: 65–72.

northeast.[77] Moreover recent archeological discoveries in the region of bronzes dating from this era suggest a wide variety of hairstyles which again, the Grand Scribe must have seen himself.[78]

This ambiguity in nomenclature is not purely restricted to the identification of specific tribes or their customs but more general markers of ethnicity or foreignness in reference to regions as well. Nicola Di Cosmo has argued that terms employed in Han sources like Hsiung-nu, Yüeh, or Yi should be taken as "ethno-political divisions" rather than purely ethnographic signifiers, or even geographical referents.[79] While this issue seems to merit a case by case examination for specific sections of the *Shih chi*, it offers a feasible explanation for many of the peculiarities in this chapter. The first two such instances act as a conclusion to the brief catalogue of the peoples living "beyond Pa and Shu to the southwest," in which Ssu-ma Ch'ien describes many of these people as being of "Ti stock," despite the fact that this phrase is used almost exclusively for people's living on the western and northwestern frontiers elsewhere in the *Shih chi*. More troublesome is the following conclusion made at the conclusion of the passage, in which the author asserts that tribes and states previous described: are all Man Yi 蠻夷 (Man Barbarians).[80] This, along with the vague use of "Hsi-yi" 西夷 three times in this chapter as well as elsewhere in the *Shih chi* to refer to an "ethno-political geography,"[81] all seem to suggest that the Grand Scribe is not attempting to provide a detailed account of foreign people's but rather convincing, recognizable accounts of foreignness within a greater political intrigue of his times.

---

[77] *Shih chi*, 97.2697; 115.2985. The "So-yin" (97.2698) is particularly reflective of this trend, as it notes that King of Southern Yüeh was adopting a hairstyle common among *yi* (barbarian) peoples.

[78] Hairstyle seems to have played a significant role in ethnic identification among southwestern peoples, not only in terms of distinguishing themselves from Han interlopers, but also among themselves. See Francis Allard, "Stirrings at the Periphery: History, Archaeology, and the Study of Dian," *International Journal of Historical Archaeology*, 2.4 (1998): 321–341; Wang Ningsheng (1930–2014), "Ancient Ethnic Groups as Represented on Bronzes from Yunnan, China," in Stephen Shennan, ed. *Archaeological Approaches to Cultural Identity*, (London: Unwin Hyman, 1989), pp.195–206.

[79] Di Cosmo, "Han Frontiers," (2009): 201, n. 7; see also his discussion in: "Ethnography of the Nomads and 'Barbarian' History in Han China." in *Intentional History: Spinning Time in Ancient Greece*, Lin Foxhall et al., eds. (Stuttgart: Franz Steiner Verlag, 2010), pp. 229–325.

[80] *Shih chi*, 116.2991.

[81] Compare the descriptions of Hsi Yi peoples and territory cited from various early texts in "Cheng-yi," *Shih chi*, 2.49.

Bibliography

Translations:
Aoki, pp. 219–38.
Watson, pp. 253–8.

Studies:
Allard, Francis. "Stirrings at the Periphery: History, Archaeology, and the Study of Dian." *International Journal of Historical Archaeology*. 2.4 (1998): 321–341;

Chin, Tamara T. "Defamiliarizing the Foreigner Sima Qian's Ethnography and Han-Xiongnu Marriage Diplomacy." *HJAS*, 70.2 (2010): 311–354.

Chou Ch'un-yüan 周春元 et al. *Kui-chou chin-tai shih* 貴州近代史 [A Recent History of Kui-chou]. Kweiyang: Kui-chou Jen-min Ch'u-pan-she, 1987.

Di Cosmo, Nicola. "Han Frontiers: Toward an Integrated View." *JAOS* 129.2 (2009): 199–214

Fang T'ieh 放鉄. "*Shih chi, Han shu* shih-tsai Hsi-nan Yi jo-kan shih-shih k'ao-pien," 史記漢書失載西南夷若干史實考辨, *Chung-yang Min-tsu Ta-hsüeh hsüeh-pao*, 3 (2004): 65–72.

Nylan, Michael. "The Legacies of the Chengdu Plain," in *Ancient Sichuan, Treasures from a Lost Civilization*. Robert Bagley, ed. Seattle: Seattle Art Museum, 2001, pp. 309–25.

Pines, Yuri. "Beasts or Humans: Pre-Imperial Origins of Sino-Barbarian Dichotomy," in Reuven Amitai and Michal Biran, eds., *Mongols, Turks and Others: Eurasian Nomads and the Sedentary World*. Leiden: Brill, 2005. pp. 59–102.

Shih Shuo 石碩 "Han tai Hsi-nan Yi chih "Yi" te yü-ching chi pien-hua" 漢代西南夷之夷的語境及變化, *Kuei-chou min-tsu yen-jiu* (2005): 124–31.

Wang Ningsheng, "Ancient ethnic groups as represented on bronzes from Yunnan, China." *Archaeological Approaches to Cultural Identity*. Stephen Shennan, ed. London: Unwin Hyman, 1989, pp. 195–206.

Ssu-ma Hsiang-ju, Memoir 57

translated by Hans van Ess

[2999] Ssu-ma Hsiang-ju 司馬相如 (179–117 BC) was a man from Ch'eng-tu 成都 in the commandery of Shu 蜀.[1] His *agnomen* was Chang-ch'ing 長卿. In his youth he loved reading and studied swordplay.[2] Therefore his parents gave him the *praenomen* "Puppy" 犬子.[3] Since Hsiang-ju had studied, he admired how Lin Hsiang-ju 藺相如 had been as a man[4] and he changed his *praenomen* to Hsiang-ju. By

---

[1] Ch'eng-tu was located roughly in the same area where modern Chengtu lies today. Shu was and is an old name for the central region of what today is the province of Szechwan.

[2] The same depiction is given to Ching K'o on *Shih chi,* 86.2527: 荊卿好讀書擊劍 See *Grand Scribe's Records,* 7:325. Note that Ssu-ma Ch'ien says that there were three branches of the family ancestors, one in Wey, one in Chao and another one in Ch'in. The branch in Chao was famous for its swordsmanship. Ching K'o came from Wey. Maybe there was a tradition in the Ssu-ma family that was linked to the art of swordsmanship.

[3] Meng K'ang 孟康 (ca. 180–260) explains that the parents gave him the *praenomen* "Puppy" because they loved him. If *ku* 故 here is understood as "therefore," it leaves the problem that a *praenomen* is normally given at birth. Nakai Riken 中井履軒 (1732–1817) quoted on Takigawa, 117.2, suggests that the words for the "puppy" (*ch'üan* 犬) and for the sword (*chien* 劍) were phonetically close. Cf. Pulleyblank, *Lexicon of Reconstructed Pronunciation in Early Middle Chinese, Late Middle Chinese, and Early Mandarin*, EMC *kʰwɛn* for *ch'üan* and *kiamʰ* for *chien*. I am not sure whether this is indeed a plausible explanation. Yen Shih-ku 顏師古 (581–645) on *Han shu,* 57.2529 says that the parents loved him and did not want to scold him. Therefore they chose this name. This would suggest that the name was chosen because a puppy is strong and nimble and that the name was not meant to be an apotropaic insult. It could also be that *ku* here means "formerly," which would mean the parents chose the name because they loved Ssu-ma Hsiang-ju like a puppy and his *praenomen* is unrelated to his studies.

[4] Lin Hsiang-ju's biography is contained in *Shih chi* chapter 81. He was the man from Chao–where some members of the Ssu-ma family had settled down (see on *Shih chi,* 130.3286) who were good at swordsmanship–who had been so audacious as to travel to Ch'in in order to bring the famous Ho jade for which the King of Ch'in had offered to cede fifteen

handing in wealth he became an gentleman [of the palace],[5] served Emperor Hsiao Ching 孝景帝 (r. 157–141 BC) and became an Armed Mounted Horseman in Regular Attendance[6] which was not to his liking. It so happened that Emperor Ching did not like *tz'u* 辭 and *fu* 賦 poems. When at this time King Hsiao 孝 of Liang 梁 (r. 168–144 BC)[7] came to court for an audience, he was followed by such men as the wandering rhetoricians Tsou Yang 鄒陽 from Ch'i 齊, Mei Sheng 枚乘[8] from Huai-yin 懷陰, and "Master"[9] Chuang Chi 莊忌 from Wu 吳.[10] [Ssu-ma] Hsiang-ju met

cities to Chao. Everybody in Chao knew that he would never cede these cities but had probably looked for a reason to attack Chao. Lin Hsiang-ju promised to travel to Ch'in and then return the jade to Chao again. By making a courageous speech in Ch'in he actually managed to bring the jade back. See on *Shih chi*, 81.2439–41.
    Hsiang-ju means "to be like...," or "to be as [predicted] by a physiognomist."
    [5] Takigawa adds a "Cheng-yi" comment here that is not in the Chung-hua *Shih chi*: it says that Ssu-ma Hsiang-ju became a Gentleman of the Palace because of the wealth of his family. Takigawa (117.2) says that this is correct, referring the reader to the text in Chang Shih-chih's 張釋之 biography, *Shih chi*, 102.2751 (compare *Grand Scribe's Records*, 8:357): "Through his family's wealth he became a Cavalry Gentleman and served Emperor Hsiao Wen." "So-yin" says there that to amount wealth means *tzu* 訾. Wu and Lu, 117.3013, n. 5, quote an edict contained in *Han shu*, 5.152, according to which Emperor Ching decreed that he lowered the ten poll-taxes (explained by Ying Shao 應劭 (ca. 140–203/204) as 100,000 cash, 1 *suan* being 10,000 cash, that one had to pay in order to become an attendant, *huan* 宦) to only four poll-taxes. The reason for this measure is explained by the fact that poor officials would be greedy and corrupt. See on this Dubs, *History of the Former Han Dynasty*, 1:329–31.
    [6] Chang Yi 張揖 (3rd century) (cited in "So-yin") notes that this position, *Wu-ch'i ch'ang-shih* 武騎常侍, involved controlling fierce animals, something that may be linked to his study of swordsmanship. Controlling fierce animals comes up again later in the biography when Ssu-ma Hsiang-ju warns the emperor against attacking such beasts himself. Takigawa (117.2) points out that this was the same title that Li Kuang 李廣 and Li Ts'ai 李蔡, both generals, also held (see on *Shih chi*, 109.2867).
    [7] King Hsiao of Liang was the younger brother of Emperor Ching from the same mother, Empress Tou 竇后. See his biography on *Shih chi*, 58.2081–86.
    [8] Most Western authors read Mei Sheng, although Mei Ch'eng seems to make more sense. See Victor Mair, *Mei Cherng's "Seven Stimuli" and Wang Bor's "Pavilion of King Terng." Chinese Poems for Princes* (Lewiston/Queenston: The Edwin Mellen Press, 1988, p. 3).
    [9] Both "Chi-chieh" and "So-yin" say that "Fu-tzu" was the *cognomen*.
    [10] See the biographies of Tsou Yang and Mei Sheng in *Han shu*, 51.2338–58 and 2359–65. There is no biography for Chuang Chi, but he is mentioned on *Han shu*, 51.2338, together with the other two men, as a retainer and literary scholar at the court of Liu P'i 劉濞, King of Wu. On *Han shu* Chuang Chi's surname is spelled Yen in order to avoid the taboo of the first name of Emperor Ming 明 of the Latter Han (r. 58–75 A.D.).

and rejoiced in them. Accordingly he retired on account of an illness and travelled to Liang to become a retainer. King Hsiao of Liang ordered him to lodge together with these scholars, and only when Hsiang-ju had managed to live together with the scholars and the itinerant rhetoricians for several years did he write the "Tzu-hsü fu" 子虛賦 (*Fu* on Master Empty).

[3000] It so happened that King Hsiao of Liang died[11] and [Ssu-ma] Hsiang-ju returned. Yet, since his household was impoverished, he had no means to sustain his goals. He had always been friends with Wang Chi 王吉,[12] the Prefect of Lin-ch'iung 臨邛.[13] [Wang] Chi said: "In former times you have travelled around to serve as an official. As this did not work out,[14] come and stop by my [county]!" Thereupon [Ssu-ma] Hsiang-ju went to him and lodged in a precinct of the city. The Prefect of Lin-ch'iung pretended to be awestruck and respectful and went daily to call upon [Ssu-ma] Hsiang-ju. In the beginning Hsiang-ju still received him, but later he claimed to be ill and ordered his followers to apologize for him to [Wang] Chi. [Wang] Chi respected him even more.[15]

In Lin-ch'iung there were many rich people, yet in the household of Cho Wang-sun 卓王孫[16] there were eight hundred bond servants, and [in the one] of Ch'eng Cheng 程鄭[17] there also were several hundred men. So these two people said to each other: "Our prefect has a noble guest, so we should prepare something and invite him." They also invited the prefect. When the prefect arrived, the guests in [the home of] the Cho family could be numbered in the hundreds. At noon someone went to invite Ssu-ma Chang-ch'ing, [yet] Chang-ch'ing claimed that he could not come

---

[11] In the year 144 BC, see on *Shih chi*, 58.2086. *Shih chi*, 117.3000, just as on 58.2086, uses the word *tsu* 卒 which Pan Ku on *Han shu*, 57A.2530 has changed to *hung* 薨, the more correct expression–a clear improvement of the text that suggests that *Han shu* was in this case the later text.

[12] Nothing is known about Wang Chi. See Hervouet, *Poète de cour*, pp. 36f.

[13] Lin-ch'iung lay about fifty miles southwest of Ch'eng-tu.

[14] *Han shu*, 57A.2530 has added the words *erh k'un* 而困 "and you have been in dire straits."

[15] Takigawa (117.3) cites Hsü Fu-yüan 徐孚遠 (1599–1665), presumably from *Shih chi p'ing-lin*, who says that there were many rich people in Lin-ch'iung and that Wang Chi wanted to give Ssu-ma Hsiang-ju face by his behavior.

[16] A Cho-family from Chao which became rich by iron-mining and iron-casting is mentioned on *Shih chi*, 129.3277. They had been driven away when Ch'in had destroyed Chao and sent them to Shu.

[17] On Ch'eng Cheng who also had cast iron see *Shih chi*, 129.3278. He had originally lived East of the Mount and had also been transferred after having been taken prisoner of war by the Ch'in.

because of an illness. The Prefect of Lin-ch'iung did not dare to taste the food and went in person to receive [Ssu-ma] Hsiang-ju. Hsiang-ju could not do otherwise than let himself be forced to proceed, and all those seated were spellbound by him. When everybody was in their cups, the Prefect of Lin-ch'iung came forward to play a zither and said: "I have privately heard that you, Chang-ch'ing, like this [instrument]. I would like you to take it and enjoy yourself." [Ssu-ma] Hsiang-ju made some excuses to decline but then strummed one or two pieces. At that time Cho Wang-sun had a daughter called Wen-chün 文君 who had recently become a widow. She liked music. Therefore, [Ssu-ma] Hsiang-ju pretended to pay close attention to the prefect, but [in reality] aroused her fervor[18] with his zither's spirit.

When [Ssu-ma] Hsiang-ju had come to Lin-ch'iung with chariots and riders as his entourage, he had been peaceful and mild, relaxed and elegant, very handsome. Now that he was drinking [at the house] of the Cho family and played the harp, Wen-chün privately peeked through the door at him. She rejoiced in her heart and wanted him so that she only feared that she would not be able to match him. Yet, only when the [drinking] was over did [Ssu-ma] Hsiang-ju send someone to give lavish presents to the attendants of Wen-chün and to convey his highest appreciation. At night Wen-chün escaped and eloped with [Ssu-ma] Hsiang-ju, and Hsiang-ju galloped back with her to Ch'eng-tu.

In their dwelling there was nothing else but the four bare walls standing. Greatly enraged Cho Wang-sun said: "My daughter really is without any capacity. I cannot bear to kill her but I will not give her a single copper-coin!" Some people spoke [on behalf of her] to [Cho] Wang-sun but he never listened. After a long time Wen-chün became unhappy and said: "Chang-ch'ing, let us just go together to Lin-ch'iung. If we borrow money from my cousins, this would still be enough for a living. Why should we let ourselves come to such bitterness?" [Ssu-ma] Hsiang-ju went with her to Lin-ch'iung, sold all his carriages and horses, and bought a wine-house instead where they sold wine. He let Wen-chün stay at the wine-booth while Hsiang-ju himself wore short wraps [that looked like] a calf's snout[19] and, standing together with the bond servants, washed dishes in the marketplace. When Cho Wang-sun heard of this, he was ashamed of it, and because of this he barred his gates and did not go out anymore. His cousins and uncles said one after the other to [Cho] Wang-sun: "You

[18] Kuo P'u 郭璞 (276–324) quoted by "Chi-chieh" explains that he incited her by the sounds coming from the zither. Kuo P'u thus seems to understand that he incited her with the heart of the zither. Yet, it seems more plausible to me that Ssu-ma Ch'ien wants to say that Ssu-ma Hsiang used the zither in order to make her heart resonate.

[19] See on these trousers Hervouet, *Le chapitre 117*, p. 7, n. 2. Wei Chao 韋昭 (204–273) explains that in his time there was a three-foot long cloth that looked like a calf's snout and adds that the meaning of this passage is that Ssu-ma Hsiang-ju was not ashamed. Apparently there were holes in the trousers so that parts of the legs were visible. This was probably something that poor people wore to avoid the heat.

have one son and two daughters, and what you are lacking is not money. Now Wen-chün is already lost to Ssu-ma Chang-ch'ing. Chang-ch'ing formerly has tired himself by wandering about [to be a rhetorician at the court of a King]. Although he is poor, you can rely on his human abilities. Moreover, he was the guest of the prefect, why [*3001*] do you have to humiliate him so much?" Cho Wang-sun could not but hand over a hundred servants to Wen-chün and a million cash as well as the clothing, bedding and wealth that she would have [received as a dowry] at her marriage. Wen-chün only then returned with [Ssu-ma] Hsiang-ju to Ch'eng-tu, bought land and a house and [they thus] became rich people.

[3002] After some time, Yang Te-yi 楊得意, a man from Shu, became Master of the Hounds,[20] serving the sovereign. The sovereign read the "Fu on Master Empty" and liked it [so much] that he said: "Why couldn't We have lived at the same time as this man!" [Yang] Te-yi said: "Ssu-ma Hsiang-ju who is a man from your servant's city has said that he himself made this Fu!" The Sovereign was startled. Only then did he summon Hsiang-ju to question him.[21] [Ssu-ma] Hsiang-ju said: "This is true. But these are affairs of the feudal lords which do not deserve to be looked at. I beg to make a hunting-Fu for the Son of Heaven. When the Fu is completed, I will present it." The Sovereign allowed this and ordered the secretaries to give him brush and wooden tablets. [Ssu-ma] Hsiang-ju used "Master Empty," meaning "empty talk," to praise Ch'u; Master Nonexistent, meaning that this thing does not exist, to argue for Ch'i; and "Lord There Is No Such Thing," meaning that there is no such man, was to make clear the righteousness of the Son of Heaven. Therefore he emptily listed these three people to make a statement and took the occasion to make an analogy on the parks and gardens of the Son of Heaven and the feudal lords. In his final stanza he let [the poem] turn to principles and parsimony. By this he wanted to criticize indirectly. He presented this to the Son of Heaven, and the Son of Heaven was greatly pleased. The text ran:

> Ch'u sent Tzu-hsü on envoy to Ch'i, whereupon the King of Ch'i raised all the men within his borders and prepared a host of [men in] chariots and riders in order to

[20] *Kou chien* 狗監.
[21] Compare the story about how the First Emperor met with Han Fei on *Shih chi,* 63.2155, translated in *Grand Scribe's Records,* 7:29: "Someone brought Han Fei's work to Ch'in. When the King of Ch'in had seen the works "Pent-up Emotions of a Solitary Man" and "Five Parasites," he said, "Alas, If We could only see this man and make his acquaintance, We would not regret it even if it meant death." Li Ssu said, "These are the writings of Han Fei." The King of Ch'in thus vigorously attacked Han. The King of Han at first had not employed Fei, but when things grew dire, he at last sent Fei as an emissary to Ch'in...."

go on a hunting excursion with the envoy. When the hunt was over, Master Empty exceedingly bragged in front of Master Nonexistent while Lord There Is No Such Thing was present. After the seating arrangement had been made, Master Nonexistent asked: "Have you had fun during our hunt today?" Master Empty answered: "Yes, I had fun." [*3003*] "Was the catch plenty?" "Little." "But why did you then have fun?" "Your slave had fun when the King of Ch'i wanted to impress your slave with the host of chariots and riders, while your slave could answer him with the services [we render] at Yün-meng."[22] "Is it possible to hear about that?"

"Yes," said Master Empty: "The King led a thousand chariots,[23]
selected as his followers ten thousand riders,
To hunt at the shore of the sea.
His arrayed soldiers filling the marshes,
Fully spread their nets[24] over the mountain.
They snared hares, and they rolled over the deer,
shooting the roebuck, they caught the unicorn at its feet.
Racing along the salt banks,
The slaughtered game stained their wheels.
Their shots hit, their catch plenty,
Proudly he praised his achievements.

He turned to your slave and said: "Are there in Ch'u also level plains and broad marches to enjoy hunting and to have such great fun as here? How does the hunt of the King of Ch'u compare to mine, the lonely one's?" Your slave descended from his chariot and answered: "As a rustic fellow from Ch'u your servant has been lucky enough to serve in the palace guards for more than ten years. At times he has been [allowed] to be in the entourage when [the King] went on a hunting excursion. So he went to the rear garden and looked to inspect what was there, but it seems that he has not yet been able to see all of it. How should he be able to talk about [his king's] outer marshes?" The King of Ch'i said: "Even if it is so, please tell me roughly what you have heard and seen."

Your slave answered: "Yes, yes. Your servant has heard that Ch'u has seven marshes of which I once saw one. I have not yet had a look at the others. What your servant has seen seems just to have been the smallest one, [*3004*] the name of which is Yün-meng. Yün-meng covers nine hundred miles on a side, and in it there

[22] Yün-meng (literally: "The Cloud-Dream") is already mentioned as two different marshes (Yün and Meng) in modern Hopei in the Yü-kung chapter of the *Book of Documents* (Legge, 3:115), quoted on *Shih chi*, 2.60–61 (see *Grand Scribe's Records*, 1:26).

[23] Which is the number of chariots a feudal lord should have.

[24] It is unclear what *fu* 罘 actually means although T'ang commentaries associate it with the nets of a chariot of a baldachin 幡車罦 or 幡車罔. See "Cheng-yi" on *Shih chi*, 117.3003 and Yen Shih-ku on *Han shu*, 57A.2534.

is a mountain.[25] This mountain
winds twisting up, its curves lush with vegetation,
Eminently lofty, rocky and dangerous,
Steep and majestic its uneven heights,
Hide fully or partly the sun and the moon;
Connected in manifold ways,
It attacks above the blue clouds;[26]
Sliding slopes
Extending down as far as the Yang-tse and the Yellow River.[27]
Its soil with[28]
Cinnabar and blue, red earth and clay,
Female ochre, white quartz,
Tin, jade, gold and silver,
A crowd of colors sparkling and shining,
Reflecting the scales of the dragon.[29]
Its stones are
Red jade and rose stones[30],

[25] Hervouet, *Poète de cour*, p. 253–54, has pointed out that there is actually no mountain in the plain of Yün-meng. He tries to explain this by saying that Ssu-ma Hsiang-ju never went to Yün-meng in person and that the following enumeration is just phantasy.

[26] See *Huai-nan tzu chi-chieh*, 8.592, *The Huai-nan tzu, A Guide to the Theory and Practice of Government in Early Han China*. Translated by John Major, Sarah Queen, Andrew Meyer, and Harold Roth (New York 2010), p. 281, where buildings that rise up to the blue clouds (there translated as "ascend to the clouds and blue [sky]" are clearly seen as a sign of usurpation.

[27] The commentaries are divided over the question whether the text is speaking of the two big rivers, as Yen Shih-ku says, or just of some rivers. I think that Yen Shih-ku is right, as *chiang* and *ho* are almost always specific terms in Han China. The envoy from Ch'u is thus exaggerating the size of his home country.

[28] From this passage on Ssu-ma Hsiang-ju mentions a great number of realia that are in fact partly not translatable. Although Western scholars such as Yves Hervouet and David Knechtges have looked for French and English equivalents to what some of the commentators starting with the 2nd or 3rd centuries A.D. have said on these objects, the reader should be aware that there are usually at least two different, often very contradictory ideas present in the commentaries which shows that commentators themselves quite often did not know what to do with them. For this, the reader is referred to Hervouet's copious notes in *Le chapitre 117*. The Modern Chinese translations of *Shih chi* 117 are of no help at all since they just quote the commentaries and leave the difficult names simply untranslated.

[29] The scales of the dragon are compared on *Han-fei Tzu*, "Shuo-nan" 說難, *Han-fei Tzu so-yin*, Peking 1982, p. 750, to the dangerous scales of the ruler. The text is quoted on *Shih chi*, 63.2155.

[30] Following the translation of David R. Knechtges (see Bibliography).

Marble from K'un-wu.[31]
All Forced[32] and dark whetstone,
Quartz and Warrior Rock.
In the east
Lies a basil garden with asarum and orchid,
Angelica and tiger lily,[33]
Hemlock parsley and sweet flag,
Fragrant Separation[34] and rotting of the elaphures,[35]
sugar cane and ginger.
In its south lie
level plains, broad marshes,
Rising and falling slopes and hollows,
Meandering, smoothly, vast and wide.
Their border, the Great Yang-tse,
Their frontier, the Magical Mountain.[36]
High and dry grow
Indigo, oats, and iris,
Artemisia and green sedge.
Low and humid grow
fountain grass, reeds and rushes,

[31] The grammar would suggest that it is "marble and K'un-wu" 琨珸 (*Han shu* 昆吾). "So-yin" quotes Ssu-ma Piao 司馬彪 (243–306) who says that K'un-wu is an inferior form of jade 次玉 which might justify the translation "alabaster" that Hervouet has for "lin-min" 琳瑉 (*Han shu*: 琳珉), translated here as "marble" (Knechtges: "Orbed Jades"). Chang Yi thinks that 琳 is a pearl while 瑉 is an inferior jade. He explains K'un-wu as the name of a mountain that produces excellent gold. Yet, K'un-wu 昆吾 is also the name of an ancestor of the ruling house of Ch'u (*Shih chi*, 40.1690 and 1705), and it is also the name of a a fief of one of the last lords who remained loyal to the Hsia dynasty (*Shih chi*, 3.95), so I think that this probably is a place name that is placed after the name of the stone because of its rhyme.

[32] Hervouet, *Le chapitre 117*, p. 18 has chosen not to translate the name 瑊玏 because the commentaries apparently also do not know what it is. Chang Yi again says that it is an inferior kind of jade. As many stones in this passage seem to have names that transport the meaning of the characters without the jade or stone radical I have decided to translate this as "all force"

[33] *Yeh-kan* 射干 (tiger lily) is not mentioned on *Han shu*, 57A.2535 and *Wen-hsüan (Li Shan chu Wen-hsüan* (Shanghai: Shang-hai Ku-chi, 1986), 7.350. Li Shan 李善 (d. 689) says that *Shih chi* is wrong in having it.

[34] *Chiang-li* 江離 is the first herb that Ch'ü Yüan puts at his girdle after he has been banned to the south (see "Li-sao," in *Ch'u-tz'u pu-chu* 楚辭補註 (Kyoto: Chūbun Shuppansha, 1979), p. 11.

[35] *Mi-wu* 蘪蕪 occurs several times in *Ch'u-tz'u* as a fragrant herb (p. 499, Hawkes 157.19): "parsley and pollia," p. 121: "Deer-Parsley."

[36] *Wu-shan* 巫山 (Magic Mountain) lies at the border between Szechwan and Hopei.

Eastern mallow, wild rice,
Lotus root, gourds,
Southernwood and stink grass.
The host of beings that live there cannot fully be depicted.
In its west lie
Bubbling spring, a clear pond,
its gushing waters whirling.
Around it grow water lotus, water chestnut
Below, hidden boulders, white sands.
In it the divine turtle and the sweet water crocodile,
The Tai-mao and the gigantic tortoise.
In its north lies a shadowy forest with gigantic trees,
Elm, plane and camphor,
cinnabar, pepper and magnolia,
Cork, wild pear and red willow,
Hawthorn, pear, persimmon, chestnut,
Tangerine and pomelo, fragrant scents.

Above
[Red monkeys and Ch'ü-nao 蠷蝚,][37]
Roc, peacock and phoenix,
Longjumper and squirrel.[38]
Below there are the
White tiger, dark panther
Long fox and the jackal,
[Female rhinoceros, elephant and wild rhinoceros,
Exhausting Wonders,[39] Wolves.][40]

[37] This line is missing in *Han shu* and *Wen-hsüan* and it seems to be redundant since the text speaks of monkeys later on and should speak here about birds rather than monkeys (see Hervouet, *Le chapitre* 117, p. 29).

[38] There is complete disagreement about the "longjumper" although some later authors want to understand it as a monkey. Meng K'ang thinks it is a bird, Ssu-ma Piao and Kuo P'u a snake. The "yeh-kan" is described as resembling a fox but being able to climb trees. We have a problem here since the *Shih chi* text above speaks of *yeh-kan* as a plant, translated here as "tiger-lily." This may be the reason why Li Shan, quoted in n. 31, says that the line in *Shih chi* is displaced.

[39] See *Tso-chuan*, Wen 18, where the so-called "four evils" 四凶 are listed. One of them is Ch'iung-ch'i 窮奇, son of Shao-hao shih 少皞氏.

[40] The two lines in brackets are missing in *Han shu* and *Wen-hsüan*. Moreover, there are no commentaries on the last line. Takigawa quotes the Ch'ing scholar Ch'ien Ta-hsin 錢大昕 (1728–1804) who says that both lines were added by a later person, and Ch'ien T'ai-chi adds that the "wolf" 獌狿 is simply a duplication of the "long fox" 蟃蜒 mentioned two lines

[3009] Thereupon he sent men like Chuan Chu[41]
To [bare] handedly attack these animals.
Only then did the King of Ch'u drive in a carriage with four tamed bestiephages,[42]
Mount a carriage made of carved jade,
Haul down the flabby standard with its baleen plates,[43]
Unfold the flag with the pearl called bright moon.[44]
He established the male halberd of Kan-chiang 干將,[45]

above. As there is no commentary, one could also imagine that the last line is not listing animals anymore but that it says something like: "All kinds of strange animals are wandering about in this park." It may also be a commentary that crept into the text.

[41] Chuan Chu 專諸 was an assassin from the state of Wu who was hired to killed King Liao 僚 and was then killed himself. The new King, Ho-lü 闔閭 of Wu, rewarded his son by giving him a fief and making him one of his senior ministers (see on *Shih chi,* 86.2516–18, *Grand Scribe's Records,* 7:320–21).

[42] For the horselike unicorn *po* 駁 which I have translated as bestiephages; see the *Book of Odes,* Mao #132, where Mao explains it as an animal "like a white horse with a black tail, and strong teeth like a saw, which eats tigers and leopards." James Legge (Legge, 4:201) thinks that an animal is out of the place there and translates *po* as "elm," but Ssu-ma Hsiang-ju obviously took it as an animal as Mao. Chang Yi refers to this in his commentary to *Han shu,* 57A.2538, quoted on *Shih chi,* 117.3009 from the *Han shu yin-yi.* Interestingly enough, Mao #132 speaks of a northern forest just as our poem does.

[43] Hervouet suggests that the king flies this flag, yet the word *mi* 靡 in combination with flag means to "haul down" (See on *Tso-chuan,* Chuang 10: "I looked after their flags, and they were all drooping" 望其旗靡; Legge, 5:85) The reason that the King hauls this flag down is probably that the baleen plates at it were, according to *Li-chi,* "Yü-tsao" 玉藻 (*Shih-san ching chu-shu* 1480B), the sign of dignitaries. Interestingly, according to the same text, the son of Heaven had a flag with a jade-pearl while the feudal lords embroidered their flags with elephants.

[44] Compare *Ch'u-tz'u,* "Chiu-t'an," *Ch'u-tz'u pu-chu,* p. 504; Hawkes, p. 158.11: "At my waist hangs the dusky Moon-bright Pearl," *Li Shan chu Wen-hsüan,* 39.1757 and *Shih chi,* 85.2543, where Li Ssu says that the First Emperor wore this pearl. Compare also *Huai-nan tzu,* 13.966, 16.1146 and 17.1224, *Shih chi,* 83.2476 (= *Han shu,* 51.2350) and 128.3227, 3232.

[45] *Wu Yüeh ch'un-ch'iu* contains the story about the sword smith Kan-chiang who had promised the King of Ch'u two swords. Since it took him three years to produce the swords the King was angry. Therefore Kan-chiang hid the male sword and gave only the female one to the king. The king put him to death. Years later the son of Kan-chiang fetched the sword and killed the King of Ch'u. Chang Yi says that Kan-chiang was the sword master of the King of Han while Ying Shao means that it is the name of a good caster from Wu. However, Ju Ch'un 如淳 (fl. 230) thinks that Kan-chiang is a place were iron is exported and Chin Cho 晉灼 (fl. 275) that Ho-lü had a sword named Kan-chiang. Hervouet thinks that all these traditions are too late and that the text actually just speaks of a sword with a small hook.

At his left the carved bow "Call of the Raven,"
At his right the hard arrows from the quiver of [the Lord of] Hsia.[46]
Master Yang the third man on the chariot,
Hsieh-o the charioteer.[47]
He held up his caduceus, the [horses] not yet racing,
They quickly jumped at the crafty animals,
Trampled the Ch'iung-ch'iung 邛邛,[48]
Rolled down mules,
Overtook wild horses,
Passed by T'ao-t'u 駒駼.[49]
Mounted horses that leave the wind behind,[50]
They shot at the running piebalds.
Fast and swift, smart and relentless,
Like the thunder they moved, like the whirling wind they came
Comets falling, lightning striking.
The bow was not drawn in vain,
Always hitting the eye,
Piercing the breast and hitting the side,
Cutting through the heart muscle.
Their catch rained animals,
Flattening the grass, covering the ground.

Only at this moment did the King of Ch'u
lower his caduceus, go back and forth,
Looking pleased with himself.
Gazing into the dark forest,

[46] The bow "Call of the Raven" is also mentioned in *Huai-nan tzu chi-chieh*, 1.26. *Shih chi*, 12.468 and 28.1394 say that this bow was owned by the Yellow Emperor. There are numerous other places where it is mentioned. Both verses are to be found in the poem "Seven Stimuli" by Mei Sheng–an envoy from Wu suggests to the King of Ch'u to take up these weapons. The Lord of Hsia is Emperor Yü.

[47] Master Yang 陽子 is identified by Chang Yi as Sun Yang 孫陽, style Po-lo 伯樂, a servant of Duke Mu 穆 of Ch'in. Fu Ch'ien 服虔 (fl. 188) says that Hsien-o 纖阿 is the charioteer of the moon or a beautiful woman. Yüeh Ch'an 樂產 (8th c. or earlier), quoted on *Shih chi*, 117.3010, interprets Hsien-o as the name of a mountain. A girl lived in a cave there. When the moon came to this place she jumped onto it. Therefore she is called charioteer of the moon. However, Kuo P'u, quoted on *Han shu*, 57A.2540, says that Hsien-o is a good charioteer of old. He is mentioned in the *Ch'u-tz'u*, "Chiu-t'an," *Ch'u-tz'u pu-chu*, 533.

[48] Explained as an animal that looks like a horse but is greenish.

[49] According to Chang Yi an animal that looks like a horse and lives in the Northern Sea.

[50] "So-yin" quotes *Ku-chin chu* 古今注 claiming this was the horse of the First Emperor.

He watched the fierce anger of his stout men,
And the fright of the wild beasts,
Stirring up the exhausted, taking the wearied,
Surveying all the creatures' transformation.
[3011] At this the daughters of Cheng, fairest maidens,
Draped in finest silk,
Drawing white crepes,
Blending finest gauze,
Their misty nettings floating,
Their clothing pleated, trimmed to finest fit,
Winding, twisting, turning, sweeping,
Thick and yet delicate, like ravines and valleys,
Waving, floating,
Their long sleeves cut fine,
Flying tufts descending down like long hair.
Turning quickly, nimbly,[51]
Robes rustling
Brushing orchids and basil below,
Above touching the feathered baldachin.
Tangled in majestic bushels of kingfisher feathers,
Entwined with jaded bands.[52]
Misty, lightly and blurred,
They resembled fairies.[53]

[3012] Then, and only then, he hunted with them in basil garden,
Crawling through the thickets,
They climbed the Metal Dike,
Catching kingfishers,
Shooting golden pheasants,

---

[51] Kuo P'u, quoted on *Shih chi*, 117.3012, claims that this sentence 扶與猗靡 is the same as one in *Huai-nan tzu chi-chieh*, 19.1367 which describes the movements of dancers (曾撓摩地，扶旋猗那; Kuo P'u has 曾折摩地，扶與猗委). *Han shu*, 57A.2541 and *Li Shan chu Wen-hsüan*, 7.353 as well as *Shih chi*, "Chi-chieh," have 興 instead of 與 which leads "Cheng-yi" as well as Yen Shih-ku and Li Shan to the interpretation that the girls either support the chariot of the king or are themselves supported in their chariots by servants. With Hervouet I think that the *Shih chi* text fits actually better with the fact that the robes brush the flowers below. I therefore rely on the translation by Sarah Queen and John Major in J. Major, ed., *The Huai-nan-tzu* (New York: Columbia University Press, 2010), p. 787.

[52] Kuo P'u here says that the bands are actually bands that are needed to mount a chariot while Yen Shih-ku says that the bands belong to the hairstyle of the maiden from Cheng.

[53] Kuo P'u refers to a parallel in *Chan-kuo ts'e* (Shanghai: Shang-hai Ku-chi, 1978), 16.540.

Their small arrows came out,
Fine threads spread,
Netting white swans,
Nabbing wild geese,
A pair of herons fell,
A dark crane added.
Exhausted they set out, amused themselves in the clear pond
Floated in a [*3013*] sea-bird prow,[54]
Raised the oars of cinnamon wood,
Unfolded the kingfisher's sail,
Erected the feathered baldachin,
Netted the Tai-mao 瑇瑁 tortoise,
Fished purple clams,
Struck bells and drums,
Blew the singing flutes;
The boatman sang,
His voice floated melancholically,
Water creatures were frightened,
Waves billowed,
Bubbling springs gushed up,
Running waters extended and met again,
Rocky stones stopped them,
Clanging, clashing,
Like the sounds of a thunderbolt,
Heard hundreds of miles afar.

[3014] Now that he wanted to give rest to the hunters,
He hit the sacred drum,
Raised the beacon fires,
The chariots moved slowly,
The riders went to their battalions,
Attached like a streaming river,
Arranged in lines in their formations.
Then, and only then, the King of Ch'u ascended the Tower of the Sunny Clouds,[55]
Remained calm and did not act,[56]

[54] Chang Yi refers to *Huai-nan tzu,* 8.592, Major, *The Huai-nan tzu,* p. 281, and says that
this is a boat reserved for the Son of Heaven.
[55] Hsü Kuang 徐廣 (352–425) says that this is the tower about which Sung Yü 宋玉
wrote his poem on the meeting of King Huai of Ch'u 楚懷王 with the goddess.
[56] This is an allusion to *Lao Tzu* 20: "As though they ascend to the spring terrace. I alone
remain calm . . . ."

Took leisure, controlled himself,[57]
Only after the peony was added to the sauce,
Was it served.[58]

He is not like you, My Great King, who races around all day long without descending from your chariot, with game cut down and wheels stained, thinking that you are enjoying yourself in this. Your subject has dared to watch this: Ch'i probably does not equal Ch'u!"

Thereupon the king remained silent and did not know how to respond to your slave."

Master Nonexistent said: "How exaggerated are these words! You did not consider a thousand miles far away and came to pay a visit to the state of Ch'i. The king raised all the knights within his borders, mobilized a host of chariots and riders and went out hunting with them. By this he wanted to exert himself to bring a catch in order to please your entourage. How can you call this an exaggeration? When he

---

[57] Compare also *Ch'u-tz'u, Ch'u-tz'u pu-chu*, p. 269, "Yüan-yu."

[58] On the *Shao-yao* 勺藥 (or *Chüeh-yüeh*; see on *Wen-hsüan,* 4.155) sauce see David Knechtges, "Sir Vacuous," in *Wenxuan* 2, p. 66, n. to line 195. *Shao-yao* is mentioned in the "Nan-tu fu" 南都賦 by Chang Heng 張衡 (78–139) on *Wen-hsüan,* 4.155, and by Mei Sheng in his "Ch'i-fa" 七發 in *Wen-hsüan,* 34.1563. Both texts speak of a well-done dish composed of several ingredients. In the "Nan-tu fu" Chang Heng mentions the delicacies of the kitchen and several ingredients such as the returning goose, yellow rice, or a special fish out of which the Chüeh-yüeh is made. Wen Ying 文穎 (fl. 196–200) there comments that *Chüeh-yüeh* is just a kind of potpourri of the five different tastes. This is interpretation taken up on *Han shu,* 57A.2544. It could thus be that the *Shao-yao* or *Chüeh-yüeh* is just a mix of the meats of the game that was shot by the hunters before. Similarly, Mei Sheng mentions several delicacies and the continues to say that one orders Yi Yin to roast this and Yi Ya to harmonize its taste. He then speaks of bears meat and of the "sauce of Chüeh-yüeh."

Yet Fu Ch'ien in a commentary on *Wen-hsüan,* 7.355 says that some think that one takes *Chüeh-yüeh* in order to harmonize the food. He obviously thinks that this is a kind of spice or ingredient that has to be added. On *Han shu,* 57B.2544 we find a similar explanation by a certain Fu Yen 伏儼 who says that "the *Chüeh-yüeh* harmonizes the food by means of orchids and cinnamon" 勺藥以蘭桂調食. Of course, in the *Book of Odes* we find one poem, #95 (Legge, 4:148), in which *Shao-yao*, translated by Legge as "little peony," are given as presents. The topic of Mao #95 is sex, and one might see an allusion to this topic in Ssu-ma Hsiang-ju's poem, too, since the text uses the word "yü" 御, translated here as "served" because of a parallel on *Wen-hsüan,* 4.155 where the sentence is quoted in the commentary with "chin" 進 instead of "yü." "Yü" is quite regularly used for sexual intercourse (see on this Hans van Ess, "The Blended Sauce or the *Shao-yüeh* Herb?" unpublished paper presented at the Edinburgh European Association of Chinese Studies Conference, September 1998). Wang Hsien-ch'ien 王先謙 (1842–1918), however, in *Han shu* 57A rejects the idea that Ssu-ma Hsiang-ju could have had Mao #95 in mind. I do not find Wang Hsien-ch'ien's argument very convincing.

asked what exists in the territory of Ch'u he wanted to hear about your great kingdom's spirit and glory and the discussions of its former men that have come down to us.[59] Now you have not praised the greatness of the virtue of the King of Ch'u but instead in plentiful words marketed Yün-meng as superior [to Ch'i], spoke excessively about the licentious [*3015*] pleasures, and displayed the luxuriant extravagances. I venture to say that in your place I would not choose that. If it really is like you said, it then would really not be a good side of the state of Ch'u. If it is such and you say it, then you make the evil of your lord known, and if it is not and you say it, then you do damage to your own trustworthiness. To make the evil of one's lord known or to wound your own righteousness are both things that are not permissible, but you, Master, have done it, which means that you certainly take Ch'i lightly and lay a burden on Ch'u. Moreover, Ch'i

In the east builds a peninsula in the huge sea

And has to its south Lang-yeh 琅邪.

It looks upon Mount Ch'eng 成山,

We shoot on [Mount] Chih-fu 之罘,

Float in [the gulf] of Po-hsieh 勃澥,

Roam in Meng-chu 孟諸.[60]

To the left the Su-shen 肅慎 are our neighbors,[61]

To the right we have Soup Valley 湯谷 as our border.[62]

Our autumn hunt takes place at Blue Hill 青丘,[63]

We range beyond the sea,

And could [with this territory] swallow eight or nine of your Yün-meng,

And in our breast it would not even be a sliver or a stalk.

As far as all is concerned that is

Bizarre and weird,

[59] Li Shan on *Wen-hsüan*, 7.355 and Yen Shih-ku on *Han shu*, 57A.2546 think that the meaning of the last sentence 先生之餘論 is: "What you yourself have to say." Hervouet, *Le chapitre 117*, p. 49 follows them with the translation: "et écouter les considérations que vous pouviez développer." However, von Zach, *Anthologie*, p. 107, has chosen to adopt the interpretation of Chang Yen 張晏: 願聞先賢之遺談美論 and translated: "über die Sitten und hervorragenden Männer Eures Landes," which I find more plausible, because otherwise the character "yü" 餘 is difficult to understand.

[60] According to Kuo P'u a marsh in Sung.

[61] The commentaries explain that "to the left" means northeast.

[62] "Cheng-yi" explains T'ang valley as a place where in mythical times the ten suns took a bath. Chang Yi and Ssu-ma Piao add that the sun comes out of this place. Hsü Shen 許慎 (ca. 58–147), also cited in "Cheng-yi," says that "T'ang" means that the sea there was as hot as a soup.

[63] According to Kuo P'u a mountain where foxes with nine tails originate.

From different regions all kinds of
Precious and wondrous, birds and beasts,
Myriad kinds, like scales, gathered,
Fill our lands,
In numbers innumerable.
Yü 禹 could not name them,
Hsieh 契 not count them.

But as someone with the position of only a feudal lord, one does not dare to talk about the pleasures derived from having fun and playing around or from the greatness of one's gardens and parks. Moreover, you, master, have been received here as a guest, so the king excused himself and did not answer. How could it be that he did not have anything to respond?"

[3016] Lord There Is No Such Thing laughed with a smile: "Ch'u has already missed it but Ch'i also has not yet got it. Now the reason why [the ruler] lets the feudal lords bring their tribute is not that he wants goods or money, but that they thereby can report on their duties. That he has enfeoffed them and drawn up borders is not to protect oneself or to control them, but that by this one calls a halt to their licentiousness. Now Ch'i is ranked as an eastern hedge but it has secretly [taken up relations with] the Su-shen; it has abandoned its state by going beyond its bounds, has crossed the sea, and hunted there. This is certainly something that has never been accepted as righteous. Moreover, the discussions of both of you two lords have not taken it as your endeavor to clarify what is the right of a lord and a servant, to correct the proper behavior of a feudal lord. You have only tried to compete over the pleasures derived from having fun and playing around and the greatness of your gardens and parks, wanting to outdo each other in extravagances and luxury, to excel each other at filthy licentiousness. With this one should not make one's name known and propagate one's glory, but it just serves to reprimand your lords and to diminish themselves. Moreover, the affairs of Ch'i and Ch'u really are not worth talking about! Sirs, have you not yet seen real greatness and beauty, have you alone not heard of the Forest of the Sovereign 上林?

[3017] To its left there is Ts'ang-wu 蒼梧, to its right the Western Limit,
The Cinnabar River measures its South,
The Purple Abyss crosses its North;[64]

---

[64] Ts'ang-wu was the place where Emperor Shun was buried. In Han times it was one of the southern provinces of the empire. The Western Limit is mentioned on *Ch'u-tz'u,* "Li-sao," p. 72, and on *Han shu,* 6.202, 22.1060, 61.2694 and *Shih chi,* 24.1178 and 123.3170 as the ultimate western point of the empire, the place, where the best horses of the world come from. Kuo P'u, however, explains that according to the *Erh-ya* 9 (*Shih-san ching chu-shu,* 2616B), the region to the West from Ch'ang-an is the state of Pin 豳—to which a section of the *Odes* is devoted. Ying Shao and Wen Ying also have explanations for the Cinnabar river and the Purple Abyss.

From source to end, the [rivers] Pa 霸 and Ch'an 滻,
Going in and out, the Ching 涇 and the Wei 渭,
Feng 酆 and Hao 鄗 stream forth,[65]
Meander and twist[66]
Ordering and fortifying its interior.[67]
Vastly majestic[68]
The eight rivers float in various directions,
Showing the back to each other and taking on different stances.
East, West, South, and North,
They race and gallop back and forth,
Coming out of the gap at Pepper Hill,
Running over the banks of isles and holms,
They pass through the cinnamon forest,
And leave behind the wilderness of vast deserts.[69]

[65] Kuo P'u and Ying Shao both explain the last two words "lao-chüeh" 潦溔 as describing the flowing of water. Other commentators think that Lao and Chüeh are also names of rivers. There is a basis for this in P'an Yüeh's 潘岳 (247–300) "Kuan-chung chi" 關中記, but I still believe that it is useful to follow the idea of Ying Shao and Kuo P'u who believe that the number of eight rivers mentioned below is reached by adding the Cinnabar river and the Purple Abyss. Feng and Hao are, as is well-known, also the names of the ancient capitals of the Chou, and it seems to me that this is what Ssu-ma Hsiang-ju was hinting at when he mentioned these two names. It would be strange if these significant rivers were coupled with the names of completely insignificant ones.

[66] On wei-she 委蛇 compare Mao #18 (Legge 4:28): "easy are they and self-possessed." Closer is Mao #47 (Legge, 4:76): "The husband's to their old age; / In her headdress, and the cross-pins, with their six jewels; / Easy and elegant in her movements/[Stately] as a mountain, [majestic] as a river." The poem is according to Mao directed against Hsüan-chiang 宣姜 and the criticism can be seen in the last lines of the first stanza: "[But] with your want of virtue, O lady, / What have you to do with these things?"

[67] On the term "ordering and fortifying" (ching-ying 經營) see Mao #262. The title of the poem is "The rivers Chiang and Han." The floods of these rivers are taken here as a metaphor for the mighty troops of the Duke of Shao who marched against the tribes living at the Huai river. Legge translates (Legge, 4:552): "Large flowed the Keang and the Han,/And grandly martial looked the troops. The whole country had been "reduced to order" (ching-ying),/And an announcement of our success had been made to the king."

[68] On tang-tang 蕩蕩 see Mao #262, quoted in the preceding footnote. The binomial is used in many other classical context among which Shu, "Yao-tien" (Legge, 3:24), is important: "Destructive in their overflow are the waters of the inundation. In their vast extent they embrace the mountains and overtop the hills, threatening the heavens with their floods, so that the inferior people groan and murmur."

Fast they gush forth,
Obeying the slopes they go down,
Racing through the mouths of narrow straights,
They hit lofty rocks,
And agitate rising embankments.
Bubbling up in sheer anger,
Sweeping up and surging, boiling and roaring,
Flagging high they wander in haste,
Pressing and urging each other,
Revolting against the stream,
Spinning over they run down.
Growling, rumbling, with wretched noises,
Majestic, eminent, surrounded by clouds,
Playing and tossing, viciously revolting[70]
Jumping waves hastening to the chasm,
Crushing down the precipices,
Hitting caves, rushing against dikes,
Racing gushingly down,
Coming close to moats and flushing through ditches,
Splashing, spuming, falling down,
Deeply and hidden,
p'ing-p'ang, rattling,
Whirling, swirling,
Twirling and flowing over,
Running waves jump and disappear,
Swooshing wildly downwards.
Into the long widths, beholding it longingly,
Calmly, vastly without a sound,
It unfolds forever.
Thereafter,
it grandly floats,
in peace and at ease slowly downwards,
Glittering and glimmering,
Eastwards flowing to the Great Lake,[71]

[69] The parallelism of pepper and cinnamon is important: Both trees are important metaphors for virtuous persons.

[70] See commentary 19 on *Shih chi,* 117.3019 by Ssu-ma Piao who thinks that 膠戾 is a hint at wrong moral behavior 邪屈. Hervouet, *Le chapitre 117,* p. 63, n. 9 believes that Ssu-ma Piao is wrong when he gives a moral meaning to a word that describes waters. Yet, maybe this is how the movements of the water were understood by the commentators.

Where they spread along the slopes and marshes.
Thereupon
Scaly dragons[72] and red lindworms,
Sturgeons slowly take their leave.[73]
Striped fish, tench, eel, and golden catfish,
Fish-ox,[74] flounders,
Raising their dorsal fins, shaking their tails,
Spreading their scales, kicking up their fins,
They hide in deep caves.
Fish and turtles, clamoring sounds,
Ten thousand creatures, a plentiful crowd.
The shining moon pearl[75]
Glimmers and glitters at the banks of the River.
Stones from Shu, yellow quartz,
Water jades heaped up,

[71] On the various identifications of the Great Lake see Hervouet, *Le chapitre 117,* p. 67, n. 10. One possibility is the T'ai-hu near modern Hang-chou but other commentators have tried to identify it as the Yellow River while Hervouet thinks it is actually the ocean.

[72] Scaly dragons are also mentioned on *Ch'u-tz'u,* "Chiu-chang," "Pei-hui-feng" 悲回風, p. 256, and Ai Shih-ming 哀時命, a poem mourning Ch'ü Yüan who did not encounter a good ruler. Ai Shih-ming was composed by Master Yen 嚴夫子, a poet who "together with Ssu-ma Hsiang-ju liked *tz'u* and *fu* poetry and sojourned as a guest in Liang where King Hsiao of Liang held him in high esteem." (*Ch'u-tz'u,* p. 441). The poem says that the scaly dragons hid in whirling abysses in order not to be caught by nets (*Ch'u-tz'u,* p. 453). Wang Yi 王逸 (ca. 89–158) explains that this means that the worthy ones also should hide away in order to escape the net of the law. This is interesting since Ssu-ma Hsiang-ju's scaly dragon is also hiding away. The lindworm, too, is mentioned in the *Ch'u-tz'u* (p. 129 and 209). In the second passage Wang Yi explains it again as a symbol for the worthy man.

[73] I am following the identifications of these dragons and fish by Hervouet and Knechtges. *Han shu,* 57A.2548 and *Wen-hsüan,* 8.364 both have 漸離 meaning "to depart slowly" as the fourth binomial. *Shih chi,* 117.3017 has 斬離, and Ssu-ma Piao on *Wen-hsüan,* 8.364 says that it is a fish too, hence Knechtges translates it tentatively as "crayfish" while Hervouet, *Le chapitre* 117, p. 68 simply leaves it untranslated as "tsien-li." However, Li Ch'i on *Han shu,* 57A.2551, com. 38, remarks that he has never heard of it. Chang Yi says that he has not heard of its appearance. I therefore prefer to take the binomial at face value. Li Ch'i 李奇 (fl. *ca.* 200) also says that the *keng-meng* 鮪鱨, translated by Hervouet and Knechtges as "sturgeon" comes from a cave at Kung-shan 鞏山 and reaches after three months the Yellow River. If it is able to pass through the passage at Lung-men it obtains the form of a dragon.

[74] On the fish-ox see on *Ch'u-tz'u pu-chu,* "Ta-chao" 大招, p. 364. They are one of the dangers that the soul of Ch'ü Yüan according to the poet himself will encounter in the south.

[75] See n. 44 above.

Clearly showing their splendor,
Their colors glistening and flashing,[76]
A great variety assembled in it.
Wild geese, kingfishers, swans, bustards,[77]
Wild ducks, geese and egrets,
Squacco herons and the rolling eye bird,[78]
Fan[79]-duck and grey water-chicken,
Needle picker and cormorant,
Flocking float on its [*3018*] surface.
Drifting, billowing,
Swimming with the winds,
Dandling with the waves,
Resting on water islets, covering them
They swallow river grasses,
And chew water chestnut and lotus.
[*3022*] Thereupon,
A lofty mountain, mantled by clouds,[80]
A majestic peak with uneven jags,
With deep forests and huge trees,
Rises steeply high, in uneven heights.[81]

[76] On *lin-lin* 磷磷 Li Shan on *Wen-hsüan*, 23.1115 (*tseng ts'ung-ti san shou* 贈從弟三首) refers to Mao #116 "Yang chih shui" (Legge, 4:178): "Amidst the fretted waters / The white rocks clearly show (in *Mao Shih* written 鄰鄰)." On *lan* 爛 as "splendor" see Mao #261 (Legge, 4:549). *Hao* 澔 also occurs on Mao #116 (Legge, 4:178): "Amidst the fretted waters / The white rocks stand glistening." The Mao/Cheng explanation takes the stones as a metaphor for the people and the water as one for the transforming influence of a good ruler who washes away evils from them. I have taken the translation "flashing" from Hawkes, *Ch'u-tz'u*, p. 158.9, to "Chiu-t'an" 九歎, *Ch'u-tz'u pu-chu*, p. 504 (there 皓旰 for 澔汗).

[77] I am following the translation of David Knechtges. Compare *Ch'u-tz'u pu-chu*, p. 374 and 401 where the wild geese and swans are interpreted by Wang Yi as symbols for worthy people.

[78] "Rolling eye" (*huan-mu* 睘目 or *hsüan-mu* 旋目) is a bird, the early commentators do not know what to do with.

[79] I do not know what this character means here. It seems to be part of a name of a duck-like bird.

[80] Although Kuo P'u on *Han shu*, 57.2553 says that this is just a description of the height of a mountain, I follow the "Five Servants" (*Wu-ch'en* 五臣) who in *Ch'u-tz'u*, "Chao yin-shih" 招隱士, p. 392, say that *lung-tsung* 巃嵷 refers to the appearance of clouds at a mountain. It is interesting to note that without the mountain radical the binomial means "followers of the dragon."

[81] *Han shu*, 57A.2553 and *Li Shan chu Wen-hsüan*, 8.364 have two characters more after the words for "lofty mountain." Consequently, they have to drop one binomial for "uneven

Nine Peaks, steep and high,[82]
Southern Mountain, stately,
Cliffs and slopes, craters and funnels,
Wild landslips, rugged, brusque,
Trembling gorges, penetrating valleys,
Long and winded gulleys and channels,
Open widely, hollow sluices,
Hillocks and separate islets,
Majestic, intimidating, awe inspiring,
Hills, holes, harsh, and hefty,
Hidden, rolling, like protecting demons,[83]
Rising and descending, far away,
Slopes and ponds linking up.[84]
Streaming through the gorges, flooding,
The waters submerge the flat land.
Stations[85] in the marshes over a thousand miles,
Built in all places.
Covered with green basil,
Protected by Fragrant Separation[86]
Spread out deer-parsley[87]

jags." Because the two characters that make up this binomial occur in two neighboring lines the *Han shu* version seems to be preferable, at least at to the reader accustomed to the rules of later Chinese poetry.

[82] Yen Shih-ku and *Han shu yin-i* take "steep and high" as the name of another mountain. Yet Kuo P'u on *Wen-hsüan* thinks that it is parallel to the attributes that follow Southern Mountain in the next line.

[83] Compare *Lun-heng chiao-shih* 論衡校釋, Peking 1990, 47 "Luan lung 亂龍," p. 699 and 65 "Ding gui 訂鬼," p. 939, on this meaning of *yü-lei* 鬱壘.

[84] Slopes and ponds are understood by commentators and translators as descriptive adjectives rather than nouns. Yet, the text also works the way we translate here, so I do not see any reason why to change the first meaning.

[85] Knechtges, n. to line 126–127, quotes Wang Hsien-ch'ien, *Han shu pu-chu*, 57A.27a, who suggests that "t'ing" 亭 means "level" here. Yet, all ancient commentaries including Yen Shih-ku think that it means "postal station" or "watch post" 亭候. On this *Han-yü ta tz'u-tien* 2.365 quotes *Hou Han shu*, 89.2940, that at the borders there were built watch towers and fire places for signals. There are several other occurrences of the term in *Hou Han shu* (1B.60 and 75; 22.777; 47.1592; 77.2881 etc.) all of which point to the same meaning. The passage is important since it shows that the place where the hunt is being conducted also has a military significance, and this is a most relevant aspect of this poem.

[86] On *chiang-li* see n. 34 above.

[87] See n. 35 above.

Mingled with the floating-in-the-plain.[88]
Bundled with tied-locks,
Garlanded with twisted sedges.
Chariot-stopper,[89] horizontal orchid,
Nothosmyrnium,[90] blackberry lily,[91]
Purple ginger, *jang-ho* 蘘荷,[92]
Winter cherry, iris,[93]
Fresh twig, yellow gravel,[94]
Water bamboo and green sedge,
Spread out over vast marshes,
Stretching widely through the great plain,
Lush and dense in broad abundance,
Bending with the winds,
Emitting fragrance, unfolding brilliance,[95]
Completely and elegantly[96] smelling sweetly,[97]

[88] *Ch'u-tz'u pu-chu,* "Li-sao," p. 20, Wang Yi: a fragrant herb. The name "liu-yi" 流夷 is explained as "xin yi" 新夷 (new plain) by the early commentators. *Han shu* and *Wen-hsüan* have 留夷 (stay in the plain). Yen Shih-ku says that it is a tree (magnolia) but that here it must mean a plant. Hervouet and Knechtges translate it as the name of a plant, the peony. This may be true. However, it seems to me that the name was similar to "forget me not" in English: it is a speaking name.

[89] Compare "Li-sao," p. 20.

[90] See Knechtges, probably taken from Hawkes, p. 157, l. 19. The plant occurs several times in *Ch'u-tz'u* (p. 499) and is always positively connoted.

[91] On *Yeh-kan* 射干 see *Ch'u-tz'u,* p. 525, a fragrant herb (Wang Yi). Also *Hsün-tzu* 1 and 27 where it is compared to a superior person.

[92] I follow Hervouet in not translating this last plant, since the commentators do not agree on the meaning. Knechtges has "mioga ginger."

[93] It is not clear whether there are two or four plants mentioned in this line. Iris is the translation that Hawkes gives for *sun* 蓀 mentioned on *Ch'u-tz'u pu-chu,* p. 106, 114, 122, 223, 225. See Hawkes, p. 107, l. 12.

[94] Cf. the commentaries by Kuo P'u and Chang Yi that both admit not to know what this is. Ssu-ma Piao explains the *hsien-chih* 鮮枝 (or *shih*) as a *chih-tzu* 支子 that Knechtges identifies as Gardenia florida. But Ssu-ma Piao also says that there is the opinion that this, too, is a fragrant herb. He rejects Yen Shih-ku's opinion that *huang-li* 黃礫 (yellow gravel) might be a shrub. So there is in fact no way to decide what these plants are. Therefore I have chosen to translate as far as possible the literal meaning of the characters.

[95] On *yang-lieh* 揚烈 see *Shang shu,* chapter "Li-cheng" 立政, Legge, 3:521: "So shall you display the bright glory of king Wen and *render more illustrious the great achievements of king Woo.*" This plant obviously helped to increase the prestige of the ruler.

[96] See on this expression *Lun-yü,* 3.14., Legge, 1:160: "Chou had the advantage of viewing the two past dynasties. How *complete and elegant* are its regulations! I follow Chou."

Numerous perfumes rising and flying,
Like swarming insects spreading and scattering,
Fragrant, sweet, diffusing.

[*3025*] Thereupon,
He gazes around and looks into the distance,
Obscure, vast,
Huge the schemes,[98]
He sees them without a beginning,
Examines them without an end.
The sun rises in the Eastern Pond,
And descends at the Western Slope.
To its south,
Life and growth in deepest winter,
Bubbling waters, gushing waves;
Animals,
Zebu, yak, tapir, ox,
Water buffalo, elaphure,
Red Head, roundhoof,
Exhausting wonder, elephant, rhinoceros.
To its north,
In mid-summer hoarfrost splits the earth,[99]
One lifts the shirt to traverse the ice.[100]
Its animals,
Unicorn, horn-top,
T'ao-t'u 駒騟, camel,
Ch'iung-ch'iung 跫跫, *tien-hsi* 騨騱,
Huge ass, donkey, mule.[101]

[97] "Li-sao," pp. 32, 68, 99, 122, 527.

[98] *Mang mang* 芒芒 occurs, for example in Mao #303 (Legge, 4:636) and #304 (Legge, 4:638), with the meaning of "great." For *huang-hu* 恍忽 see for example *Lao-tzu* 21.

[99] See the "Ch'ing-chung" 輕重 chapter of the *Yen-t'ieh lun* (*chiao-chu*, Peking 1992, 14.180) where this sentence is used as an argument against expansionist politics in the north.

[100] Compare Mao #34 (Legge, 4:53–54): "... and the crossing at the ford is deep. If deep, I will go through with my clothes on; If shallow, I will do so, holding them up... The wild goose... By the gentleman, who wishes to bring home his bride, [Is presented] before the ice is melted. The boatman keeps beckoning; And others cross with him, but I do not. Others cross with him, but I do not..." The poem contains a warning against crossing the ford. If it is alluded to here, then Ssu-ma Hsiang-ju does not like the idea of the hunters crossing the river.

[*3026*] Thereupon,
Detached palaces, separate belvederes,
Fill up mountains, straddle valleys,
High porches stretch out in the four directions,
Several floors, winded [paths to] pavilions,
Jade discs as endings of flowery rafters,
Carriage roads linking [these places],
Covered-walk paths drifting around,
So long the ways that one has to stay overnight in between.
On leveled peaks built halls,
Multi-layered towers rising higher and higher,[102]
Cliffs and caverns, rooms in grottoes.[103]
Looking down all obscure, nothing to be seen,
Looking up, clutching the rafters one touches the sky,[104]
Shooting stars pass by the gates of the harem,
Rainbows stretched over the balustrades and balconies.
A green dragon coiling at the eastern chamber,
Elephant drawn chariots stagger in western clarity,
Ling Yü 靈圉 plays at the leisure belvedere,[105]
Such fellows as Wo Ch'üan 偓佺 expose themselves to the sun under the eaves,
Sweet springs bubble at the clear rooms,
Traversing streams flow through the middle court.
Strong boulders heaped at the riverside,
Steeply hanging, supporting each other,[106]
Unevenly rising, collected for the grand work,[107]

[101] Again it is very difficult to decide what the untranslated animals actually are. What is important, however, is that with the exception of the unicorn, horn-top and ch'iung-ch'iung all these animals are listed as animals of the Hsiung-nu on *Han shu*, 94A.3743.

[102] On 增成 see *Han shu*, 97B.3983. Pan Chieh-yü used to live in a multi-layered building. Ying Shao says that in the harem there were eight areas and that the one of the multi-layered building was the third one of them.

[103] Grotto-rooms are mentioned on *Ch'u-tz'u pu-chu*, "Chao-hun" 招魂, p. 345; Hawkes, p. 227, l. 79: "inner chambers" where beautiful women live–just as in the line before.

[104] Compare *Ch'u-tz'u pu-chu*, "Chiu-chang," "Pei hui-feng," p. 262, Hawkes, p. 182, l. 74: "On I rushed until I touched the heavens, deep and dim the distance..." This describes the estrangement of Ch'ü Yüan from the world.

[105] Kuo P'u says that Ling Yü 靈圉 (The Divine Stable Warden) is an immortal, Chang Yi thinks this is a group of immortals. *Wen-hsüan*, 8.367 has Ling Yü 靈圉, The Divine Prison Warden. Compare *Ch'u-tz'u pu-chu*, p. 535.

[106] Compare *Ch'u-tz'u pu-chu*, p. 394.

Cut and reduced the stones that strive for glory.[108]
Rose stone, green and dark jades,
corals growing thickly,
Marble strong and full,
Striped and streaked, patterned scales,[109]
Red jade, motley, brindle,
Are stuck in between,
Like hanging straps,[110] the jades *wan* 琬 and *yen* 琰,[111]
[The jade of] Master Ho comes forth.[112]
[*3028*] Thereupon,
The blood orange that ripens in summer,
Yellow and sweet[113] the orange and the mandarin,
Loquats, Jujubes,
Mountain Pears with thick bark,[114]
Persimmons, sloes,
Cherries, grapes,
[Like] hermits[115] dense plums,
Mountain plums, lychee,
Arranged in the rear palaces,
Arrayed in the northern garden,

[107] *Chi-yeh* 礋礏 is a binomial that the commentators do not mention. Without the stone radical it means "to be collected for the grand work," which is an interesting association. The stones may be metaphors for living beings after all.

[108] "Stones that strive for glory" are again stones read without their radicals: 爭榮. For "Cut and reduced" see on *Shih chi*, 11.449: "Ch'ao Ts'o cut and reduced the feudal lords" 晁錯刻削諸侯.

[109] *Shih chi*, 117.3026 and *Wen-hsüan*, 8.368 have the fish-radical, *Han shu* the stone radical for "scales."

[110] For *sui* 綏 (straps) *Wen-hsüan*, 8.368 and *Han shu*, 57A.2557 have *ts'ai* 采 "colors," for hanging they have *ch'ao* 晁 that is explained as "morning" 朝 by the commentaries to *Han shu* and *Wen-hsüan*.

[111] Explained by Kuo P'u according to the *Bamboo Annals* as two concubines that Chieh, the last ruler of the Hsia, loved so much that he engraved their names on jade.

[112] See on the famous jade of Pien Ho 卞和, *Shih chi*, 83.2471 and 87.2543.

[113] Kuo P'u says on *Han shu*, 57A.2559 and on *Wen-hsüan*, 8.368 that "Yellow and sweet" is also an orange, yet I think that it can also be an attribute to the following trees.

[114] Thick bark is explained by Ssu-ma Piao on *Shih chi* and Chang Yi as the name of a herb, and Knechtges writes "magnolias." Yen Shih-ku explains that this herb has a thick bark. One could just translate this as a tree called "thick bark."

[115] Chang Yi and Yen Shih-ku say that they do not know what this is. Yet, 隱夫 simply means "hidden man."

Stretching over hills and slopes,
Coming down into the plain,
Spreading blue-green leaves,
Swaying purple stalks
Unfolding red blossoms,
Flourishing vermilion splendor,
Glistening, glimmering,
Brightly shining in the wide wilderness.
Apples and oaks,
Birch, red gum, gingko, smoke tree,
Pomegranate and coconut,[116]
Betel, windmill palm,
Sandalwood, magnolia,
Camphors, wax trees,
High ten thousand feet,
A large group jointly spanning them,
Stretching out their branches, straightly erected,
Fruits and leaves flourishing, lush,
Standing in thickets, next to each other,
Joint, latched, leaning,
Blocking horizontally, interlocking,
Hanging branches, expanding far,
Falling petals fluttering **[*3029*]**,
whirling slowly, grandly,
swaying with the wind,
Sighing faintly over the grass,
Indeed, this resembles
The sound of bells and chimes,
The tones of pipes and flutes.
Their height uneven,
They surround the rear palaces,
Covering each other, layers intertwined,
Blanketing the mountains and linking valleys,
Following slopes, descending into the lowlands,
Watching them there is not beginning,
Examining them there is no end.
[*3031*] Thereupon,
Dark monkeys, white females,
Long-nosed monkeys, grand gibbons, flying squirrels,

---

[116] While Chin Cho acknowledges frankly that he does not know what the meaning of *Liu-lo* 留落 actually is (we follow Knechtges who admits that his identification is tentative), coconut seems to fit very well the commentary by Ssu-ma Piao.

Four-winged monkeys,[117] gibbons,
Hairy gibbons, foxes, white foxes, kuei 蜼 apes,[118]
Live and rest among [the trees].
Long are they howling, sadly singing,
Coming and going, changing places with each other,[119]
Exercising, raging on tips of twigs,
Crouching, hanging on tree tops,
Thereupon,[120]
They jump over cut bridges,
Spring in to extreme thickets,
Cling on hanging branches,
Climb to rare spaces,
Run and fall to the ground and disperse[121];
Tumultuously they depart into the distance.
[*3033*] From this sort,
There are hundreds and thousands of places.
Playing and sporting here and there,
Staying in palaces and taking rest in belvederes,
Kitchens do not have to be displaced,
Rear palaces[122] not to be removed,
The hundred officers were all present.
Thereupon,
Turning the back on autumn and passing into winter,
The Son of Heaven goes hunting with his divisions.[123]

[117] The *Shan-hai ching* (Yüan K'o 袁珂 ed., *Shan-hai ching chiao-chu* 山海經校注, [Shanghai: Shang-hai Ku-chi, 1980], 17.421) says that on Pu-hsien 不咸 mountain their is a flying gibbon with four wings.

[118] There is no consensus in the commentaries whether there are two animals mentioned here or four. I have taken the most neutral translations, knowing that we cannot give a better one than the commentators. Kuo P'u says that he has never heard of a "kuei," although there is a *kuei* that resembles a turtle with a white body and a red head that is mentioned in the *Shan-hai ching* (5.177).

[119] Compare on *p'ien-fan* 翩幡 Mao #200 (Legge, 4:347), "With babbling mouths you go about, scheming and wishing to slander others... Clever you are, and ever changing, In your schemes and wishes to slander." 緝緝翩翩、謀欲譖人。捷捷幡幡、謀欲譖言.

[120] Missing on *Wen-hsüan*, 8.370 and *Han shu*, 57A.2562.

[121] See the note by Hervouet, *Le chapitre 117*, p. 108, n. 10: All the four characters in this line start with an "l," and this is what was apparently most important for Ssu-ma Hsiang-ju. I have tried to imitate the meaning of some of the characters itself rather than to give tentative meaning for the binomials that is difficult to get.

[122] Meaning the harem. The women stayed there all the time.

He mounts his carriage of carved ivory,
With six jade dragons,[124]
Dragging rainbow banners,
Flying[125] cloud flags,
In front a leather-covered chariot,
Behind the road and the excursion carriage.[126]
Uncle Sun holds the reigns,
His Excellency Wei is the third man on the chariot.[127]

---

[123] Hervouet, *Le chapitre 117*, p. 111, and Knechtges, l. 269, both decide to translate *chiao-lieh* 校獵 as "barricade." Li Ch'i 李奇 on *Wen-hsüan* 8.370 and *Han shu,* 57A.2536 says that it means to go out hunting with the five different divisions (*wu-hsiao* 五校) of the army. These five divisions are explained, for example in Li Hsien's 李賢 (654–684) commentary to *Hou Han shu,* 6.253 as those of the commandant of the marine, infantry, arrow-shooters, cavalry and chariots. However, Yen Shih-ku bluntly says that the explanation by Li Ch'i is wrong and interprets the word "hsiao" as "to hunt with three barricades." However, although this may sound attractive, it is only one way of explanation. Yen apparently disliked the idea that the Son of Heaven did not go out hunting just for fun but out of other reasons. Yet, the military aspect becomes clear in many more early commentaries to different passages of the *fu.* Therefore, I have chosen to follow Li Ch'i.

[124] Chang Yi on *Han shu,* 57A.2564 and *Wen-hsüan* 8.370f explains that the six dragons were actually six horses that were embroidered with jade so that they looked like dragons. Kuo P'u, however, quotes *Han-fei tzu* 10, "The ten evils," that when the Yellow Emperor had unified the spirits on Mount T'ai he rode in an elephant carriage drawn by six dragons. While Chang tries to make the content of the *fu* as plausible as possible, Kuo alludes to the spiritual travels known from the Taoist tradition.

[125] *Mi* 靡. Interestingly, in *Tso,* Chuang 10.1, we find the sentence: "He saw that the flags were taken down, therefore he pursued them." 望其旗靡，故逐之. Could it be that in the *fu,* too, the "cloud flag" is being taken down while the rainbow banner flies? In *Ch'u-tz'u pu-chu,* "Li-sao," p. 55, Wang Yi explains the cloud flag as: "His own virtue was like a cloud, enabling him to moisten the ten thousand things and exert his influence on them." The cloud flag is a positive image for civil influence while the rainbow traditionally is associated with disaster. On *Li-chi,* "Ch'ü-li A" (*Shih-san ching chu-shu* 1250A), it is said that the flag of a chariot in peace is kept folded round the pole.

[126] The road and the excursion carriages are mentioned on *Chou-li, Shih-san ching chu-shu* 826B in the context of the great inspection. A leather covered chariot 革車 is mentioned on *Chou-li, Shih-san ching chu-shu* 826A. Cheng Hsüan 鄭玄 (127–200) comments on this passage that the five war chariots all are like this. Instead of a 革車 Ssu-ma Hsiang-ju's *fu* speaks of a 皮軒 which, however by Kuo P'u is equated with the leather covered chariot of the *Chou-li.* Kuo adds that another explanation is that this chariot is the same that is mentioned on *Li-chi,* "Ch'ü-li A," *Shih-san ching chu-shu* 1250A, 前有士師，則載虎皮: "For a body of troops in the front [the flag on the chariot] with a tiger's skin [should be] displayed."

[127] Cheng Hsüan (On *Han shu,* 57A.2564 just a master Cheng, but on *Liu-ch'en chu Wen-hsüan* 8.11b identified by Li Shan as Cheng Hsüan) identifies Uncle Sun with Kung-sun

Recalcitrant[128] [the troops] are marching,
Leaving the four divisions.[129]
Drumming solemnly in the imperial escort,
The hunters are unleashed.
The Great Stream and the Yellow River their pen,
Mount T'ai their lookout tower,
Chariots and riders rise like thunder,
Hiding Heaven, shaking earth,
Front and rear spreading out, dispersing,
Leaving the ranks, pursuing separately,
Streaming, marching,
Along the slopes, running into marshes,
Like rain that falls when clouds have spread.
[3034] Catching leopards[130] and panthers alive,

Ho 公孫賀 (see on Shih chi, 111.2941–42 and Han shu, 66.2877–78) and His Excellency Wei with Wei Ch'ing 衛青 (Shih chi 111), both generals who fought during the Hsiung-nu wars for Han Wu-ti. This explanation was accepted unanimously until the Ch'ing when some scholars began to question whether Ssu-ma Hsiang-ju really would have mentioned contemporaries. See on this Takigawa, 117.45, Hervouet, Le chapitre 117, p. 112, n. 8 and 9, and Knechtges commentary to ll. 276–77. We assume that the authority of the ancient commentators is too strong to go against them and, as Hervouet believes, that Ssu-ma Hsiang-ju did, indeed, think about Kung-sun Ho and Wei Ch'ing. On Shih chi, 117.3043 Ssu-ma Ch'ien says that Ssu-ma Hsiang-ju was made a courtier after having presented his fu; and on p. 3044 he adds that after Ssu-ma Ch'ien had been a courtier for several years it so happened that T'ang Meng opened up a road to the west of Yeh-lang. These events are described on Shih chi, 116.2994 as having started in 135 BC. Wei Ch'ing and Kung-sun Ho apparently at that time rose at court (see on Shih chi, 111.2922). Wei Ch'ing became general only in 129 BC. If the poem were composed around 135 BC, then the chronology would still fit. Yet, it seems that Ssu-ma Ch'ien with his fu was already alluding to the might of Emperor Wu, a power that rose to its absolute height after 130 BC during the wars against the Hsiung-nu. Therefore, it is plausible that the fu in its actual form was written at a later point. Ssu-ma Ch'ien probably ascribed it to the early years of Ssu-ma Hsiang-ju for literary reasons.

[128] Kuo P'u and Chang Yi unanimously say that "hu" 扈 means "pa-hu" 跋扈, "recalcitrant." No ancient commentator has contradicted this, so we should follow this explanation although there are Ch'ing commentaries who want to see here an ordered kingly excursion as Hervouet and Knechtges translate. Kuo and Chang also explain that the troops do not stick to their battalions.

[129] Wen Ying refers to the five divisions (see n. 123 above) that Li Ch'i mentioned and explains that one division is the entourage of the chariot of the Son of Heaven.

[130] On the p'i 貔 see Mao #261 (Legge, 4:551), there translated as "white fox" according to an entry in the Erh-ya, section "explanation of Animals," and Lu Te-ming 陸德明 (556–

They fight jackals and wolves,[131]
Bare-handedly they go against black and brown bears,[132]
Run after chamois,
On their heads pheasant-feather caps,[133]
Pants of the white tiger,[134]
Wearing striped embroideries,
Straddling wild horses,[135]
They gallop down risky paths on Three Peaks,[136]
Descend to Rocky Islands,[137]

627) says that another name for it is "catcher of barbarians" (*chih yi* 執夷; see *Shih-san ching chu-shu* 572B). Lu quotes Lu Chi 陸機 (261–303) who says that the *p'i* resembles a tiger or a bear (ibid.). "Cheng-yi" quotes Kuo P'u that the "catcher of barbarians" belongs to the category of tigers and leopards (*Shih-san ching chu-shu* 573A) while on *Shih chi,* 117.3034, *Han shu,* 57A.2565 and *Wen-hsüan,* 8.371 he is just quoted as saying that the *p'i* belongs to the category of tigers. Compare also *Shu,* Legge, 3:304, "Be like tigers and panthers!" The K'ung An-kuo commentary (*Shih-san ching chu-shu* 183C) also says that the *p'i* is a "barbarian catcher," but adds that it belongs to the tigers. The first commentator to say that *sheng* 生 means "to catch alive" is Wei Chao, quoted on *Wen-hsüan* 8.371. On *Han shu,* 57A.2565. Yen Shih-ku accepts Wei's opinion which is followed by all major translators. However, one could also understand that "sheng" is used to describe the animal-like soldiers or hunters: "Like living leopards and panthers." Then the animals mentioned in the next three verses could also be metaphors for qualities of the soldiers themselves, not their game.

[131] On a metaphorical level, jackals and wolves are in many ancient Chinese texts just evil-doers. See for example *Meng-tzu* 4A17, Legge, 2:307. *Shih chi,* 25.1241 says that Chieh of Hsia and Chow of Yin attacked jackals and wolves with bare hands, adding that their valor was not small.

[132] On these bears see for example, Mao #189, *Shih-san ching chu-shu* p. 437C, Legge, 3:306. On *Han shu,* 51.2328 Chia Shan 賈善 says that the Ch'in with the strength of black and brown bears swallowed up all within the seas but disregarded rites and righteousness.

[133] On the pheasant cap see *Hou Han shu chih,* 30.3670 and the commentary by Ssu-ma Piao on *Hou Han shu chih,* 30.3670. The pheasant fights to the death without giving up, hence this was used as a cap for warriors.

[134] On *Hou Han shu chih,* 30.3670 it is said right after the description of the pheasant cap that the general of the gentlemen who run like tigers wears such pants.

[135] *Erh-ya* (*Shih-san ching chu-shu* 2652B) explains that this horse comes from beyond the passes.

[136] Kuo P'u on *Wen-hsüan,* 8.372 says that this is a place name near Wen-hsi 聞喜 in modern Yün-ch'ung in Shansi north of the Yellow River (T'an Ch'i-hsiang, 3:35). Yen Shih-ku, however, thinks that this is just the description of the shape of a mountain. However, there is also a San-tsung on *Shih chi,* 3.96 (*Grand Scribe's Records,* 1:44, see n. 48) in Western Shantung. This is the place where Ch'eng T'ang 成湯 defeated Chieh 桀 of Hsia.

[137] Again Kuo P'u on *Han shu,* 57A.2565 explains this as a place name without giving the exact location. Yen Shih-ku thinks again that it is just some stony slope.

Take steep shortcuts and race through narrow passes,
Pass over channels and wade through waters.
They push the dragon sparrow[138]
And tease the unicorn,
Hunt down the *Hsia-ko* 瑕蛤
And spear Sir Fierce,
Rope the ten thousand mile horse,
Shoot the wild boar.
Arrows do not do wantonly harm,
They cut the neck and smash the brain,
The bow is not taken up in vain,
in response to the sound [the animal] falls.
Thereupon,
the Son of Heaven on his chariot
Lowers his caduceus, going back and forth,
Roaming he wanders about,[139]
Watches how his companies and battalions push forth and withdraw,
Gazes at the changing state of his generals and leaders.
Afterwards he
Gradually progresses, hurrying with his caduceus,
Swiftly moving into the distance.
Scattering like light birds,[140]
Trampling wild animals,
Crushing white deer,
Catching wild hares,
Taking over the red lightning,
Pursuing strange beings,
Leaving the universe,
Bending the *fan-jo* 繁弱 bow,[141]
[Arrows] full with white feathers,

[138] *Fei-lien* is written 飛廉 or 蜚廉. Knechtges, *Wenxuan* l. 303: "flying dragon bird," referring to the "Hsi-ching fu," Knechtges, *Wen-hsüan* 1, p. 68: "The emperor goes on a festive excursion in order to threaten the Jung and Ti." In *Ch'u-tz'u pu-chu* ("Li-sao," p. 47, "Yüan-yu," p. 280 and "Chiu-pien," p. 328, *Fei-lien* is a companion of Ch'ü Yüan. On *Han shu,* 6.193 a *fei-lien* lodge is mentioned which is in Ch'ang-an. *Meng-tzu* 3B9, Legge, 2:281, and *Shih chi,* 5.174 say that this is a minister of the last ruler Chou 紂 of Shang 商.

[139] Compare on *Shih chi,* 117.3009.

[140] On *liu-li* 流離 see *Shih,* Mao No. 37, *Shih-san ching chu-shu* 306A, where Mao explains this as the name of a bird.

[141] According to several commentaries the name of an excellent bow of Emperor Yü 禹.

Shooting the roaming Man-eater[142],
Hitting the flying chimera,
Selecting the meat, they strike,
Aiming first, determining the goal,
String and arrow separate,
The victim immediately collapses.
[*3036*] Thereupon he
Raises his caduceus and rises high,
Storming down with startling winds,
Passing through terrifying tempests,
Riding on emptiness and non-existence,
Unifying with the gods,
Rolling over dark cranes,
Disturbing a bunch of chickens,
Chasing peacock and phoenix,
Pressing gold pheasants,
Striking the five-colored bird,
Seizing male and female phoenix,
Catching roc,
Grabbing firebirds.[143]
[*3037*] Where the streets end, the roads are finished,
He turns around his carriage and travels back.
Roaming and wandering,
They come down to gather at the northern bounds.[144]
Leading straight ahead,
He suddenly turns the direction.
Entering Stony Pass,
Passing by Sealed Peak,
Traveling past Jaybird,
Watching out at Dew Frost,[145]

---

[142] Kuo P'u says that this animal resembles a man but eats men.

[143] What I following Knechtges tentatively translate as "firebird" is mentioned on *Ch'u-tz'u pu-chu,* p. 537 ("Chiu-t'an" 九歎, "Yüan-yu" 遠遊). Hawkes, p. 301, l. 30, leaves it untranslated. What is important is that as many other birds in the list given by Ssu-ma Hsiang-ju, this bird is explained as a pure official by the *Ch'u-tz'u* commentator Wang Yi. Most of the birds that are hunted here are most precious, whatever that may mean in our context.

[144] According to *Huai-nan-tzu chi chieh,* 4.334–36 the most distant regions of the world in the eight directions are called "bounds."

[145] According to *San-fu huang-t'u chiao-shih* 三輔黃圖校釋 (Peking: Chuan-hua Shu-chü, 2005), 143, 18. Stony Pass, Sealed Peak and Jaybird are pavilions situated within the precincts of Kan-ch'üan (Sweet Springs) palace to the northwest of Ch'ang-an while "Dew Frost" was a pavilion in Yün-yang slightly to the west of Kan-ch'üan. On these places see T'an Ch'i-hsiang, 2:15. All four pavilions were according to *San-fu huang-t'u* and Chang Yi,

Riding down to Pear Belvedere,[146]
Resting at Let It Be Spring! 宜春[147]
To the west galloping to Hsüan-ch'ü 宣曲,[148]
Rowing the heron-prow at Ox Head,[149]
Climbing the Dragon Terrace,[150]
Concluding at Thin Willows.[151]
He oversees the painstaking captures of his officers and dignitaries,
Measures the catch of the hunters,
What has been trampled and rolled over by soldiers and chariots,
What cars and riders have crunched and squashed,
The people trod upon,
And what has been driven to extremes and fatigued,
What in fright and fear cowers down,[152]
Having died without encountering a blade,
Lying all over the place,
Clogging ditches, filling valleys,
Leveling plains, covering marshes.
[*3038*] And then,
He joyfully plays, relaxes and takes rest,
Sets out drinks at the Terrace of Vast Heaven,
Suspends music in his broad realm,
Beats a bell of thousand piculs,
Erects bell racks of ten thousand piculs,[153]

quoted on *Han shu,* 57A.2568, built by Emperor Wu shortly after he ascended the throne in 140 BC.

[146] Chang Yi says that T'ang-li 棠梨 was about ten miles southeast of Yün-yang, *San-fu huang-t'u*, ibid., that it is south of the park at Kan-ch'üan.

[147] According to *K'uo-ti chih* thirty miles southwest of Wan-nien 萬年 district in Yung-chou 雍州. Yen Shih-ku says it is close to Tu 杜 district, and T'an Ch'i-hsiang, 2:15, accordingly locates it to the southeast of Ch'ang-an.

[148] According to Chang Yi a belvedere to the west of Lake K'un-ming, located southwest of Ch'ang-an (see T'an Ch'i-hsiang, 2:15).

[149] A lake at Western end of the Shang-lin park (according to Chang Yi).

[150] According to Chang Yi a belvedere northwest of Feng 豐 River, close to the Wei 渭 River.

[151] Kuo P'u says that this is a belvedere to the south of lake K'un-ming, but T'an Ch'i-hsiang, 2:15 locates it north of Wei River which makes more sense. See the discussion of the location on *Han shu,* 4.130 and 94A.3764. See also on *Shih chi,* 10.432 (*Grand Scribe's Records,* 2:178, n. 239), 57.2074. *Hsi-liu* 細柳 was apparently an important camp for the northern bound armies.

[152] Cf. *Han shu,* 31.1797 where this is said of the men of Hsiang Yü.

Establishes a flag with turquoise flowers,
Plants a drum decorated with a divine alligator.[154]
He performs the music to the dance of Sir T'ao-t'ang 陶唐,
Listens to the songs of Sir Ko-t'ien 葛天,
A thousand people sing,
ten thousand people join in,
Mountains and slopes quake because they are moved by this,
Streams and valleys billow, shaken by it.
[Musicians] from Pa 巴, Yü 俞,[155] Sung 宋[156] and Ts'ai 蔡,
Kan-che 干遮 from Huai-nan,[157]
Songs from Wen-ch'eng 文成 and from Tien 顛,[158]
Are presented in groups, performed in alternation,
Bells and drums come forth here and then,
Cling-clang, *tang-ta,*
Piercing the heart, they startle the ears.
Sounds from Ching 荆, Wu 吳, Cheng 鄭, and Wei 衛,[159] music of Succession, Salvation, Martial Prowess, and the Elephants,[160] tones of hidden licentiousness, slow and exuberant, a potpourri from Yen-ying 鄢郢,[161] the turbulent melody called "Aroused Ch'u,"[162] jesters and dwarfs, singers from Ti-ti 狄鞮.[163] All that gives

---

[153] Cf. *Chan-kuo ts'e,* 11.408 where this is said to have been the display of power by King Hsüan of Ch'i 齊宣王 who is portrayed in a negative way on *Shih chi,* 46.1893.

[154] See on *Shih chi,* 87.2543, *Grand Scribe's Records,* 7.338.

[155] On the musicians from Pa and Yü see on *Han shu,* 22.1073 and 96B.3928, *Yen-t'ieh lun* 10 criticizes the expenditures for music from Pa and Yü, the two *Han shu* passages point into the same direction.

[156] *Li-chi,* "Yüeh-chi," *Shih-san ching chu-shu* 1540C, criticizes the music from Sung in one breath with the one from Cheng, Wei, and Ch'i.

[157] Nothing is known about the *Kan-che,* a melody according to Kuo P'u. It is written *yü-che* 于遮 in *Shih chi.*

[158] Kuo P'u says that he has never heard of these places but Wen Ying says that Wen-ch'eng is a district in Liao-hsi in North-Eastern China where people were good at singing, while Tien is a district in Yi-chou where the inhabitants were able to sing the songs of the southwesterns barbarians.

[159] One wonders whether Cheng and Wei are mentioned here just as states where good music came for or whether the traditional bias against this music is intentionally alluded to.

[160] The music of Emperor Shun, King Ch'eng of the Shang, King Wu of the Chou and the Duke of Chou. The three last ones are devoted to military successes.

[161] The ancient capital of Ch'u.

[162] Kuo P'u points to the fact that this music is mentioned on *Lieh-nü chuan.* Today the sentence is not to be found in *Lieh-nü chuan* but in *Huai-nan-tzu chi-chieh,* 1.75 and 12.831. There it is compared to the music from Cheng and Wei that disturbs just the common people, not the sage.

pleasure to ear and eye and pleases the heart and its intentions is beautifully and splendiferously displayed in front of him while lasciviousness and eros lure behind.[164]

[*3039*] Such consorts as Blue Zither and Concubine Fu 宓,[165]
Extraordinarily apart from the common,
Seductive, enticing, refined, elegant,
Powdered nicely, hair cut and adorned,
Sleek and supple, meek and modest,
Limp and [*3040*] limber, soft and stately,
Pleasant and pliant, weak and slender,
They trail hemps and sleeves of pure silk,
Subtly displaying their robes, tailored like paintings,
Whirling and fluttering,
Clothing different from those of our generation.
Of fragrant perfumes profusely soaked,
Aggressive and ardent, pure and strong,
Their white teeth shine and glisten,
With decent smiles they glimmer and glitter.
Long eyebrows roundly curved,
Secretly they cast glances afar;
When they offer their eros, our soul gives in,
Our heart is attracted to their side.[166]

[3041] And then, in the midst of drinking while the music is at its height, the Son of Heaven turns melancholic and starts to think, and it seems to him as though he had lost something.[167] "Alas!" he exclaims, "this is too extravagant and luxurious! Because we have spare time from overseeing and listening [to government affairs] and because we might waste our days without doing anything, we have obeyed to the

[163] According to Wei Chao a place in Ho-nei.

[164] The two characters for "behind" are missing on *Liu ch'en chu Wen-hsüan*, 8.375 where Li Shan comments that all that has been described is lascivious and erotic and that "behind" is not needed, therefore.

[165] Nothing is known about Blue Zither whom Fu Yen calls a goddess of old. Concubine Fu was according to Ju Ch'un a daughter of Fu-hsi who drowned in Lo River and then became the spirit of the Lo.

[166] Chang Yi explains: "When their eros comes and is given [to us], [our] soul goes and joins with them." "So-yin" adds that "yü" 愉 written with the heart radical has the tone of "to go over" 踰 and means "to go to them." But Ssu-ma Chen 司馬貞 (fl. 745) also says that "yu" with the heart radical means "to rejoice" and says that this meaning which is preferred by Yen Shih-ku is possible, too: "Our heart rejoices to be at their side."

[167] Compare on this the expression 芒然自失, used on *Chuang-tzu chi-shih* 莊子集釋, 30.1021 and *Lieh-tzu chi-shih* 列子集釋, 4.117.

course of Heaven and killed and attacked and from time to time taken a rest in this place. [Yet], we fear that later generations will find this so beautiful that they will proceed with it without reconsideration. This is not the way to create a legacy for one's heirs and establish a line of succession.[168] Thereupon he finally let the alcohol go, disbanded his hunters, and ordered his officials: "The land should be cultivated, opened up and completely turned into farming space, in order to be given to people and public servants. Overthrow the walls, level the channels, and enable the people from mountains and marshes to go there. Fill the slopes and ponds and do not spell out prohibitions [for the common people], empty the palaces and belvederes and do not staff them. Open the granaries and storehouses in order

to help the poor and distressed,
add where there is not enough,
pity widowers and widows,
let orphans and childless survive.
Issue appellations of virtue,
Diminish punishments and penalties,
Reform measures and regulations,
Alter the color of the uniforms,
Change [the beginning of the year] to the new moon of the first month,
And give the empire a [new] start.

Thereupon he calculates an auspicious day at which he fasts and respects commandments,

Wears his court robes,
Mounts the proscribed equipage,
Erects a flowery flag,
Lets the jade peacock sing,[169]
And travels in the garden of the Six Arts,[170]
Gallops over the road of humanity and righteousness,
Gazes and reads in the forest of the *Spring and Autumn Annals*,
Shoots to the "Head of the Wildcat,"
And also to the "Tsou-yü" 騶虞,[171]

---

[168] Compare on this line *Meng-tzu*, 1B14. *T'ung* 統 may well be translated as "dynasty" here.

[169] C.f. *Ch'u-tz'u pu-chu*, "Li-sao," p. 71, Hawkes, p. 77, l. 343, 44: "The cloud-embroidered banner flapped its great shade above us; And the jingling jade yoke-bells tinkled merrily."

[170] I.e. the six canonical disciplines songs, documents, rites, music, changes and annals.

[171] Both, the "Head of the Wildcat" and the "Tsou-yü" seem to be names for pieces of music that where played at ritual archery competitions. While "Tsou-yü" is known to us as the 25th piece of the *Shih-ching* (Mao explains on *Shih-san ching chu-shu* 294A that Tsou-yü is the name of a righteous animal), we can only assume that "Li-shou" (Head of the Wildcat) also was a piece of music from its being mentioned on *Li-chi*, "She-yi," *Shih-san ching chu-shu* 1686C–1687A. The Tsou-yü was the rhythm to which the Son of Heaven had to shoot, the

Hits with corded arrows the dark crane,
Establishes the shields and axes,[172]
Carries the Cloud Nets,
Catches the group of accomplishment,[173]
Feels sorrow at "Cutting Sandalwood,"
Rejoices at "Rejoicing them all,"[174]
Cultivates his appearance in the garden of the Rites,
Flies and roams in the park of the Documents,
Transmits the way of the Changes,
Bans the strange animals,[175]
Ascends the Bright Hall,
Sits in the Clear Temple,[176]
Gives a sequence to the crowd of vassals,
Lets them memorialize their achievements and failures,
So that within the four seas there is nobody who is not received.
At this point the empire is [*3042*] greatly pleased and obeys following the general tendency, reforms itself according to the current, spontaneously practices the way and becomes righteous. Punishments are put to rest and are not used anymore, His virtue is more eminent than the one of the Three Sovereigns, His achievements more

---

Li-shou the one of the feudal lords. On *Shih chi,* 28.1364 it is said that the word "wildcat" (*li* 貍) was also pronounced as "pu-lai" 不來, suggesting that there was an ancient pronunciation of "mrai" for the animal. "Pu-lai" means "did not come," and the *Li-chi* text says that "Li-shou was about the joy of meeting on time." Thus, the shooting at "pu-lai" probably meant that one was shooting at those who did not come on time for the arranged meeting. *Shih chi,* 24.1229 says that shooting to the left on Li-shou and to the right on Tsou-yü was done when the empire knew that King Wu of Chou did not want to make use of arms anymore. Thus, these seem to be songs played for the beginning of a period of peace. Tsou-yü and Li-shu are also mentioned on *Chou-li,* Yüeh-shih 樂師, *Shih-san ching chu-shu* 793C, 800C and 845A–B. Probably there were songs or dances named after the animals or named targets that were shot during the ceremony.

[172] Both, the "dark crane" and the "shields and axes" are explained as dances by Li Shan on *Liu-ch'en chu Wen-hsüan* 8.377.

[173] Chang Yi explains that these are the performers of the Lesser and Greater Elegantiae of the *Shih-ching.*

[174] "Cutting Sandalwood" is the title of Mao #112 that according to the traditional interpretation criticizes evildoers, while "rejoicing them all" is a quotation from Mao #215 (Legge, 4:386) that is also traditionally understood as a critical poem but includes a praise of the feudal lords who protect the state.

[175] According to Chang Yi, the Son of Heaven does not hunt strange animals (= those from foreign countries described above) in his park anymore.

[176] The place where the Son of Heaven receives the feudal lords for his audience.

admired that those of the Five Emperors. Only when everything is like this, can hunting finally be enjoyed.

[3043] Yet, if you all day long
Exposing yourself to the dew and galloping about,
Tire your spirit and fatigue your body,
Spending resources for chariots and horses,
Exhaust the skills of officers and soldiers,
Wasting the wealth of your treasuries and granaries
Not have the mercy to be virtuous and generous,
Only concentrating on pleasure,
You do not care for the common people,
While forgetting about the politics of the state,
You covet the catch of pheasants and hares,
Then this is a path a benevolent man does not follow.

Looking at it from this perspective, are not the affairs of Ch'i and Ch'u deplorable? Their territories do not exceed a thousand miles, but their parks occupy nine hundreds of them. This means that grass and trees cannot be cultivated and opened up and that the people have nothing to feed on. Now with the insignificant position of a feudal lord to enjoy the luxury of the [lord] over ten thousand chariots, this is something from which your slave thinks the hundred kindred will suffer harm.

Thereupon the two sirs were startled and changed countenance, looked depressed as troubled, hurried back from their mats and said: "We rustic fellows are really mean that we did not know the taboos. Only today did we receive instruction and have respectfully heard your command!"

When the *Fu* had been presented, the Son of Heaven made him a gentleman. The words of Lord There Is No Such Thing about the space and vastness of the Shang-lin Park of the Son of Heaven and about its mountains, valleys, waters, springs and all the things in it as well those of Sir Empty about the many things that the Yün-meng Park of Ch'u [possessed] were excessive and exaggerated their reality. Moreover this went against what was righteously allowed and by normal reason to understand. Therefore, he [the Son of Heaven] by way of abridgement took [only] its essentials and discussed it as [a text] that belonged to the right way.[177]

---

[177] Yen Shih-ku on *Han shu*, 57A.2576 says that those are wrong who think that the word "shan" 刪 (abridgement) that Ssu-ma Ch'ien uses here means that the historian (Ssu-ma Ch'ien) shortened the poem. According to Yen, the historian says that only the exhortation to parsimony expressed at the end of the poem was accepted as essential. Wang Hsien-ch'ien on *Han shu pu-chu*, 57A.51a, quotes Liu Feng-shih 劉奉世 (1041–1113) as an example for someone who thought that the poem had actually been shortened. But he explains "shan" as "ting" 定, "to establish the meaning." Interestingly, "So-yin" ascribes half of Yen Shih-ku's explanation to the Elder Yen and the other half to the Younger Yen. Commentaries of Yen Shih-ku have been made to the *Han shu*, not to the *Shih chi*, which suggests that Ssu-ma Chen

[3044] After [Ssu-ma] Hsiang-ju had been a gentleman for several years, it so happened that T'ang Meng 唐蒙 had as an envoy overrun and connected by road the territory west of Yeh-lang 夜郎 until within Po 僰[178] and had called out a thousand officers and soldiers from Pa 巴 and Shu 蜀. The commanderies had in addition to this several times called out more than ten thousand men for him to make land and water transport. He used martial law[179] to execute their chieftains, and the population of Pa and Shu was greatly startled and in fear. Only when the sovereign heard this, did he send [Ssu-ma] Hsiang-ju to reproach T'ang Meng and to take the occasion to make a proclamation with allusions[180] to the population of Pa and Shu that [all this had] not been the intention of the sovereign. The mobilization order read:[181]

had a *Han shu* in front of him that was different from our's today. Takigawa (117.59) explains that Ssu-ma Hsiang-ju "reduced and established the words of Master No Such and Sir Empty" 司馬相如刪定無是子虛之語. He also quotes the opinion of Wang Wei-chen 王維楨 (1507–1556) who said that this was the judgement by Ssu-ma Ch'ien which also proved that Ssu-ma Hsiang-ju had not written this chapter as an autobiography (as Knechtges assumes for Yang Hsiung's biography in *Han shu* 87). It is interesting to note that in *Han shu* the comment constitutes the end of the A section of the 57th chapter. This may be the reason why some have read this passage as a kind of final comment by Ssu-ma Ch'ien, not as the judgement by the Son of Heaven.

[178] According to T'an Ch'i-hsiang, 2:29, Po lay about 120 miles to the south of Ch'eng-tu in what today is Yi-pin 宜賓 city while Yeh-lang was according to T'an Ch'i-hsiang, 2:32 another 250 miles to the southeast. Thus, the road was built into the direction of the Southern Barbarians in the east, not to the west.

[179] It seems that the texts says here that there was in fact a martial law that allowed the killing of people without the normal legal procedure. *Shih chi* has *hsing-fa* 興法, while *Han shu*, 57B.2577 has *chün-hsing fa* 軍興法. Below at the end of p. 3044 the text speaks of a *fa chün hsing chih* 發軍興制 which Chang Yi explains as "to call out the multitudes of the three armies. Martial regulations are law and regulations [for the time] when troops are raised." 發三軍之眾也。興制，謂起軍法制也. Ssu-ma Chen adds that when T'ang Meng went on envoy he "used the law and orders [for the time] when troops are called out." 用軍興法制 He thus understands that the verb "fa" here does not mean "to call out troops" as Chang Yi understands but "to issue regulations." This understanding probably goes back to Yen Shih-ku who on *Han shu*, 57B.2578, n. 7, says that [T'ang Meng] according to the law for [the time when] troops are called out made regulations for mobilizing the multitudes" 以發軍之法為興眾之制也.

[180] *Yü-kao* 喻告. As will be seen, Ssu-ma Hsiang-ju is speaking about the war against Min-Yüeh in order to let the people of Pa and Shu know that their territory can become part of the Han empire in a peaceful way just as of Min-Yüeh did.

[181] For this text see also on *Li Shan chu Wen-hsüan*, 44.1963–65.

Proclamation to the Grand Administrators of Pa and Shu: Long are the days that the Man and Yi have not been punished for acting arrogantly. From time to time they have invaded the frontiers, troubling our officers and dignitaries. When His Majesty acceded to the throne, he preserved All Under Heaven and cherished it, harmonizing and bringing peace to the central states. Afterwards he raised armies and let the troops march out in order to campaign against the Hsiung-nu in the north. The Ch'an-yü[182] trembling with fear folded his hands and accepted servitude, bent his knee and begged for peace. K'ang-chü in the Western Territories, rendering [its request] from one language into the other several times [until it finally was rendered into Chinese], has asked to come to a court audience,[183] to knock their heads to the ground and present gifts. We dispatched an army to march eastward but the Min-Yüeh killed each other.[184] To their right[185] we condoled at P'an-yü 番禺, and their heir apparent came to our audience.[186] The lord of the southern

[182] For "shan" 禪 *Kuang-yün* gives the reading 市連切. The *K'ang-hsi tzu-tien* (Shanghai: Shang-hai Tz'u-shu, 1985), p. 212, adds that for the word 單于 the *Chi-yün* has the reading 時連切 and the pronunciation 蟬 *ch'an*. Both 市 and 時 in middle Chinese point to "ch'" as initial.

[183] Chang Ch'ien 張騫 in his report about his travels to the Western Territories also talks about K'ang-chü 康居 which lay to the north of Bactria (Ta-hsia 大夏) and Parthia (An-hsi 安息). He said that people in this country were greedy and that one could therefore bring them to court by offering bribes and advantages. If one in this way attached K'ang-chü and the Yüeh-chih the territory could be broadened to ten thousand miles square and translators would have to render the languages from all these regions. The sentence "ch'ung chiu yi" 重九譯 is explained by Chang Shou-chieh 張守節 (fl. 725) as meaning "This means that they came one after another with translated words from all places" 言重重九遍譯語而致 (*Shih chi*, 123.3166). It does not seem, however, that at this time there were already envoys from K'ang-chü who came to Ch'ang-an. Ssu-ma Hsiang-ju is exaggerating here as in his sentences about the Hsiung-nu begging for peace. The wars against them had not yet started in 135 BC when he was sent out to the southwest. Instead of "has asked to come to the court audience" *Han shu*, 57A.2577 reads "brings tribute" 納貢. The compound "ch'ung-yi" occurs twice more in *Shih chi*. On *Shih chi*, 60.2109 there is no commentary on its meaning, but on *Shih chi*, 130.3299 Chang Shou-chieh repeats his interpretation that there had to be several translators. Yen Shih-ku on *Han shu*, 12.348 comments that "to translate means to transmit words" 譯謂 傳言也. On *San-kuo chih*, 47.1126 there is a text from the "Wei-lüeh" that writes 重驛累使 apparently meaning "to take several postal carriages and numerous envoys."

[184] See on *Shih chi*, 114.2981. The Han army in the end did not have to proceed to the Min-Yüeh because they killed their king and surrendered.

[185] Meaning west of them.

[186] The events that are mentioned here must have taken place shortly before T'ang Meng came to the Southwestern regions in 135 BC. Already at the time when Emperor Wen ascended the throne Lu Chia 陸賈 had been sent to Southern Yüeh for the second time. Wei

barbarians and the chieftains of Western Po 西僰 constantly have brought tributes and presents not daring to be lax or remiss. They crane their necks and stand on tiptoe, with their mouths open they compete with each other to turn to righteousness, wanting to become servants and handmaidens. Yet, the way is far and mountains and rivers are steep and deep so that they are not able to come on their own. Thus, while those who were not obedient have already been punished, those who did good have not yet been rewarded. Therefore [the Emperor] has sent the Commander of the Gentlemen of the Palace to go and treat them as honored clients. He has sent out five hundred people each from Pa and from Shu in order to carry the silken gifts and to guard those who had been sent against unforeseen events.[187] There has been no case of warfare and there was no anxiety that fighting may break out. Now we have heard that [T'ang Meng] has gone so far as to issue a call to arms and [*3045*] has frightened the young and troubled the elderly. The commandery has moreover arrogated to itself the authority to transport grain and bring other supplies. This all was not the intention of His Majesty. Some of those who had to go on campaign have fled and wantonly murdered. This is also not

T'o 尉佗, the Han-Chinese ruler of that state, later declared himself to be a vassal and sent envoys to the court although he did not really submit. His envoys were treated at the court just as the feudal lords were. After Wei T'o had died in 137 BC, the King of Min-Yüeh in 135 BC attacked Southern Yüeh. Southern Yüeh asked the Han for help. Emperor Wu sent out an army which, however, had not yet reached the mountain ranges that apparently served as a border when the brother of the King of Min-Yüeh killed the king, sent his head to Ch'ang-an and established himself as ruler. An envoy from the Han came to P'an-yü (Canton) and returned with the heir apparent of Southern Yüeh who afterwards served in the palace guard at Ch'ang-an. See on *Shih chi,* 113.2970 and *Shih chi,* 114.2981. Min-Yüeh was thus pacified in a peaceful way, and this is what Ssu-ma Hsiang-ju wants to allude to here.

The commentaries discuss the meaning of "tiao" 弔, "to condole." Wen Ying says that it actually means "to arrive at." After their attack against Min-Yüeh, he adds, an envoy arrived at P'an-yü. Ssu-ma Chen, however says, that "tiao" should be read with its original meaning, "to condole." Yen Shih-ku says that when both states waged war on each other the Han sent troops to rescue [Southern Yüeh] and ordered them to condole at P'an-yü. Therefore they sent their heir-apparent to court. He adds that "tiao" does not just mean "to arrive at." Thus, Yen Shih-ku thinks that after the war an envoy of the Han who is not mentioned in the text must have come to Southern Yüeh in order to condole the relatives of the fallen soldiers or the family of the ruler. It could, however, also be possible that Ssu-ma Hsiang-ju thinks of the death of Wei T'o when the Han who received envoys from Yüeh on a regular basis certainly sent someone to condole.

[187] The sentence is strange. I follow the explanation by Chang Yi on *Han shu,* 57B.2576 who explains 不然 as 不然之變. See on this Wu and Lu, 121.3077, and Watson, *Records* 2:323.

the proper behavior of a servant of somebody else.

Thus, when servicemen who live in the commanderies at the borders hear that beacon fires are being raised and that the brushwood is burning, they take up bows and hurry, seize weapons and run, sweat streaming they catch up with one another, only fearing they might be the last. They rush into the bare blades and are covered by streams of arrows. In a just cause[188] they do not look back, a plan once made, they do not turn about on their heels. Each of them harbors anger in his heart as if taking his private revenge. Do you think they rejoice in death and hate life, are no [ordinary] registered people and have a different ruler than [you, the people of] Pa and Shu?[189] [No], they calculate profoundly and think far, and taking the difficulties of the state seriously, they rejoice in fulfilling the way of a vassal servant of others. Therefore, there are enfeoffments with tallies split [for them], noble titles with carved jade scepters. Their positions reach those of proper marquises[190] and they live in mansions to the east [of the palace]. If they die, they leave behind an illustrious name for later generations, they transmit their lands to their sons and grandsons. They carry out their duties with utmost loyalty and respect and in their positions they are most relaxed and at ease. Their name and fame spread without an end, their merits and bravery are so eminent that they cannot be obliterated. Therefore, worthy and superior men do not decline [to serve] even though their liver and guts may smear the [ground] of the central plain or the juices of their heart's blood may soak the grassland. Now those who received gifts for service among the Southern Barbarians and yet instead became robbers and murderers or were executed because they fled will not enjoy fame when their bodies have died.[191] Their posthumous title will be

---

[188] *Han shu* and *Wen-hsüan* both read *yi* 議 instead of *yi* 義. At first sight this also fits better the word *chi* 計 (strategy) in the next line ("when they have deliberated they do not look back, when they have made a plan they do not turn aside...") but at a second glance the *Shih chi* reading makes perfect sense, too.

[189] The whole paragraph is a general statement, clearly speaking about all kinds of servicemen at the borders of the Han. The rhetorical question asks whether the rulers of those who fight so brave for the Han are different than those of Pa and Shu—and the answer is that they are not. Everybody knows how good it is to fight for the Han.

[190] On *t'ung-hou* 通侯 see *Shih chi,* 8.381, *Grand Scribe's Records* 2:69, n. 462.

[191] *Shih chi,* 116.2994 says that Ssu-ma Hsiang-ju was sent out after T'ang Meng's campaign and had to make "allusions" 喻 that all should be "just as in the case of the Southern Barbarians" 皆如南夷. Above, on *Shih chi,* 117.3044, the text said that Ssu-ma Hsiang-ju made a "proclamation with allusions" 喻告 to the people of Pa and Shu in order to make the intentions of the sovereign understood. Thus, it seems that he is referring here to problems of discipline in the Han army during the campaign against Min-Yüeh which had attacked Southern Yüeh (see on *Shih chi,* 113.2970–71 and 114.2981), not to the campaign of T'ang Meng to the Southwestern Barbarians 西南夷.

"utmost stupidity,"[192] their disgrace will reach their parents, and they will become the laughing stock for All-Under-Heaven. Do not the standards and capacities of [some] men really by far surpass those of others? But this is not just the fault of those who did this. If the teaching of fathers and elder brothers does not precede, then the obedience of sons and younger brothers will not be sincere; and it also was due to the fact that there was little modesty and almost no shame, and that the customs were not noble and generous. Is it not appropriate that they also suffered from corporal punishment and mutilation?[193]

[3046] His Majesty is distressed that the envoy [T'ang Meng] and the authorities have acted like this; he bemoans that the unworthy and the stupid people are like that.[194] Therefore, he has dispatched [me], his trusted envoy, in order to make the hundred kindred understand why he has sent out foot soldiers. Having taken this opportunity to enumerate to them what the crime of disloyalty for which one deserves the death penalty is,[195] I reprimand the

---

[192] The lowest of the categories of nine people mentioned on *Han shu,* 20.863ff, "Table of Men from Ancient and Modern Times" is called "stupid people."

[193] Watson, *Records* 2:323–24, takes this as an accusation against the elders of Pa and Shu: They did not fulfill their duties, and thus there were people killing and robbing among their own population. Wu and Lü, 117:3077–78, think that all this refers to the campaign against the Southern Barbarians. We think that Ssu-ma Hsiang-ju refers to border troops from the South who during the campaign against Min-Yüeh committed crimes. Ssu-ma Hsiang-ju wants to tell the people from Pa and Shu that if they cooperate with the Han and educate their soldiers to be loyal than only the best things will happen to them. In the case of the other campaign, also the elders justly had to be punished. Compare Hervouet, *Le chapitre 117*, p. 152.

[194] Meaning that T'ang Meng has gone as far as to issue a call to arms and decapitating chieftains on the one hand and that there have been stupid servicemen from the border just as in the case described above.

[195] The sentence about the 不忠死亡之罪 is difficult. Hervouet, *Le chapitre 117*, p. 153, translates it as "pour expliquer au peuple... et en même temps lui reprocher les crimes des suicides et des fuites par déloyauté." This is also the understanding of Wang Li-ch'i, 117:2489, who translates that the emperor sent Ssu-ma Hsiang-ju to reproach the people who have fled or committed suicide for their crime of disloyalty. Watson, *Records* 2:324, translates: "to explain to the common people... and at the same time to reprimand those who have proved themselves disloyal in the face of death." Wu and Lü, 117.3078, also think that the sentence means that the people were disloyal because they were not able to die for the cause of the state. However, I neither see that a 死亡之罪 could be a crime that consists in not having been able to die for a cause nor that it could mean that people killed themselves. There is a clear parallelism with the following sentence. Therefore, I think that *pu-chung* 不忠, being disloyal, is a crime which is punished by death and extinction of the whole clan. Another solution would be to translate that they committed the crime of being disloyal by fleeing when

Three Elders[196] and the filial sons for their failure to teach and instruct.[197]

Just at the moment is the season for husbandry. We have repeatedly annoyed the people and I have already visited the neighboring counties, fearing lest people living in distant places like valleys, mountains or marshes might not all hear this. Now that the mobilization order arrived, send it down immediately to the districts and marches in order to let everybody know the intention of His Majesty. I just beg you do not ignore this!

When [Ssu-ma] Hsiang-ju returned to report, T'ang Meng had already overrun and penetrated Yeh-lang, and he took the opportunity to construct a road through [the territory] of the Southwestern barbarians. He called out foot soldiers from Pa 巴, Shu 蜀 and Kuang-Han 廣漢, and those who worked on it were tens of thousands. When they had been constructing for two years, the road was still not completed. Many officers and soldiers had died and the costs could be figured in the millions. Among the people from Shu as well as among those in charge of the matter for the Han, many said that this was not suitable. At that time many of the rulers and chieftains of Ch'iung 邛 and Tso 筰 who had heard that the Southern Barbarians had through their contact with the Han received many rewards and presents wanted to become servants and handmaidens of the interior and asked for functionaries to the same extent as in the case of the Southern Barbarians.[198]

When the Son of Heaven asked [Ssu-ma] Hsiang-ju about this, Hsiang-ju said: "Ch'iung, Tso, Jan 冄, and Mang 駹 are close to Shu,[199] and a road to them would be easy to open. At the time of the Ch'in [roads] had already been opened and commanderies and counties been made. When the Han arose this was abolished. If we now really could open it up again and for them establish commanderies and counties, there would be even more than in the case of the Southern Barbarians." Only when the Son of Heaven deemed this to be correct, did he appoint Hsiang-ju as Commander

the faced death. Another solution would be translate this as "a crime for being disloyal and not dying [for the state] but fleeing." Compare *Han-fei tzu chi-chieh*, Peking 1998, 45:410: "Corporal punishment and mutilation are that by which one monopolizes authority, but our generation calls those who take the law lightly and do not try to escape crimes that deserve corporal punishment, mutilation, death and extinction men of courage." 刑戮所以擅威也，而輕法、不避刑戮死亡之罪者，世謂之勇夫.

[196] On the title of the Thrice Elder see *Grand Scribe's Records,* 2:48, n. 327, to "Kao-tsu pen-chi."

[197] This reprimand has been made by way of "allusion" to what happened during the campaign against the Southern Barbarians.

[198] The road that connected Ch'eng-tu with the Southern Barbarians had been successfully constructed. Now the Han had turned west and went into the direction of what are today the Tibetan parts of Szechwan.

[199] On these states see on *Shih chi,* 116.2991.

of the Gentlemen of the Palace, let him carry a caduceus and go there as an envoy. The vice-envoys Wang Jan-yü 王然于, Hu Ch'ung-kuo 壺充國 [*3047*] and Lü Yüeh-jen 呂越人 rode in a postal convoy of four carriages and relied on the gift items of the functionaries from Pa and Shu in order to bribe the Western Barbarians. When they arrived in Shu, everybody from the Grand Administrator of Shu on downwards came to the suburbs to greet them, and the prefects of the counties rode in front of them, carrying a quiver with arrows in it.[200] The people from Shu thought this to be an honor.[201] Thereafter Cho Wang-sun and the notables from Lin-ch'iung all through their gate attendants[202] presented beef and alcoholic drinks in order to make friends with them. Cho Wang-sun sighed deeply and thinking that he too late had been able to have his daughter marry Ssu-ma Chang-ch'ing, he generously gave his daughter a share of his wealth, an amount that was the same as that [he had given] to his sons. Ssu-ma Chang-ch'ing used the favorable situation in order to overrun and pacify the Western barbarians, and the rulers of Ch'iung, Tso, Jan, Mang and Ssu-yü 斯榆[203] all begged to become interior[204] vassals. He removed the [old] frontier passes, and expaned the passes outward to the west reaching the Mo 沫 and Jo 若 rivers, to the

---

[200] "So-yin" explains that normally speaking in a t'ing 亭 there are two functionaries and that the quiver and the arrows should be carried by the head of the t'ing. Now if the prefect of the district himself carries the arrows then the head of the t'ing should carry the quiver. The commentary then adds that there is no determined way who should carry the quiver and that maybe one handled that according to the weight which probably means that these objects were sometimes very heavy and could not be carried by just one person. Wang Hsien-ch'ien criticizes Ssu-ma Chen for this commentary because he thinks that one cannot on the one hand argue that the quiver should be carried by the ting chang and on the other hand say that this was determined according to the weight.

[201] The meaning here is either that the mission of Ssu-ma Hsiang-ju fully achieved its goal and that the people of Shu felt honored although they had been annexed peacefully, or that the people of Shu in this way did him honor.

[202] Wu and Lu, p. 3048, n. 23, think that Ssu-ma Ch'ien is speaking of the attendants of Ssu-ma Hsiang-ju, not those of Cho Wang-sun et al.

[203] Ssu-yü is only mentioned by Ssu-ma Hsiang-ju, and we do not know where it lay. However, as the other places form according to T'an Ch'i-hsiang, 2:12, a group of people stretching from northwest to southwest of Ch'eng-tu where the mountains start, we can guess that Ssu-yü was located even further down to the south. Near the northern border of modern Yünnan.

[204] There were "outer vassals" (wai-ch'en 外臣), too. Shih chi, 110.2911 and 123.3168 speak of the hope that the Hsiung-nu and the Central Asian countries could become "outer vassals," as was the case already for Korea and Southern Yüeh (Shih chi, 115.2986 and 116.2994). Ssu-ma Ch'ien here obviously wants to show how successful Ssu-ma Hsiang-ju was.

south the Tsang-k'o as the [new] frontier,[205] establishing a road through the Ling 零 Pass and building a bridge over the Sun 孫 River in order to connect [Shu] with the main settlement[206] of Ch'iung. When he returned to report to the Son of Heaven, the Son of Heaven was greatly pleased.

[3048] At the time [Ssu-ma] Hsiang-ju was an envoy, the majority of the elders of Shu explained that to establish relations with the Southwestern barbarians would not be of use for him, and even[207] high servants [at court] were of this opinion.[208] [Ssu-ma] Hsiang-ju wanted to remonstrate, but as he had already established the enterprise, he did not dare to and after all [did write a document] listing the arguments of the fathers and elders from Shu, criticizing them himself. With this he indirectly gave a hint to the Son of Heaven. Moreover, by this he propagated his mission as an envoy and let the hundred kindred know the intentions of the Son of Heaven. The words of this [document] ran:[209]

[3049] The Han arose eight and seventy years ago[210] and the blossoms of their virtue have persisted until the sixth generation. Their majestic military might has spread gloriously and their blessing and mercy deeply soaks [the country]. All living beings are moistened by it, and it [even] is flooding beyond our regions. Only in this situation has [the emperor] ordered an envoy to go west, following the stream to press back [those living there]. Whatever the wind covers would bend down to it.[211] Accordingly he made Jan to come to the audience and Mang to obey, stabilized Tso and preserved Ch'iung, overran Ssu-yü and uprooted Pao-man 苞滿.[212] Ending the rush forward and turning the chariot around, [the envoy] headed east in order to make his report. So he came to the capital of Shu.

---

[205] On the Tsang-k'o see *Shih chi*, 116.2994.

[206] See n. 5 of the translation of *Shih chi* chapter 116 above.

[207] The text says "only" (*wei* 唯) which makes no sense. Takigawa, 117.67 says that *wei* hear means *sui* 雖 (even) and he adds that the high servant was Kung-sun Hung 公孫弘.

[208] One such high servant was Kung-sun Hung, see on *Shih chi*, 112.2950 where it is explicitly said that Kung-sun Hung remonstrated against the expedition.

[209] This text is also contained in *Wen-hsüan*. See on *Li Shan chu Wen-hsüan*, 44.1992-5.

[210] Hsü Kuang says that hence this letter must have been written in the sixth year of *yüan-kuang* (129 BC). However, according to *Shih chi*, 112.2950, Kung-sun Hung rejected the plan to built a road to the southwestern barbarians in 126 BC. Hsü Kuang obviously takes 207 to be the year when the Han were founded. There is, however, also the year 202, when Liu Pang had defeated Hsiang Yü. Therefore, the letter could also have been sent in 124 BC.

[211] See on *Lun-yü*, 12.19: 君子之德風，小人之德草。草上之風，必偃. "The superior man has the virtue of wind, the inferior man the virtue of grass. Under the wind above it the grass necessarily bows."

[212] Pao-man is called Pao-p'u 苞蒲 on *Han shu*, 57B.2583 and *Wen-hsüan*, 44.1992. On *Wen-hsüan* Fu Ch'ien comments that it is a tribe of the Yi-Barbarians.

There were seven and twenty white haired elderly people, dignitaries, and gentlemen wearing official girdles who sternly approached him. When he had made his statement, they accordingly stepped forward and said: "We have heard that the Son of Heaven in his treatment of the Yi- and Ti-barbarians should rightfully do nothing more than to halter and yoke them and not allow them to break loose. Now it has been three years that the men of three commanderies have been exhausted by constructing a road through to Yeh-lang. Yet the effort has not come to an end, the officers and soldiers are tired and worn out, the ten-thousand fold people have no means to depend on, and now you will also create a connection to the Western barbarians. The force of the hundred kindred will then be broken, and we fear that they will not bring the enterprise to an end. That should also be a concern for you, the envoy. We dare to be afraid for your entourage. Moreover Ch'iung, Tso and Western Po have been connected to the Middle States for so many years that they cannot be completely recorded.[213] The benevolent have not been able to cause them to come with their virtue, the strong have not been able to annex them to [the middle states] by force. Couldn't the intention perhaps be an impossible task? Now you harm common people in order to attach the Yi- and Ti-barbarians, and you exhaust those whom you rely on in order to just make them serve a useless cause. We rustic people are really stupid and do not know what we are saying."

[3050] The envoy answered: "How can you say such things? If it is really as you say then Shu would not have changed clothes and Pa would not have altered its customs [but remained barbarian].[214] How shall I continue to listen to your persuasions? This affair is in fact of so great scope that it really cannot by chance be perceived by onlookers. I have to set out soon, so that I cannot let you know all the details, but I beg of you to be allowed to unfold its rough outline."[215]

"In this world you need extraordinary men in order to have extraordinary events. Only if you have extraordinary events will you achieve extraordinary results. The extraordinary is really something that is different from the

---

[213] Li Shan in his commentary to *Wen-hsüan*, 44.1993 points out that a similar sentence is used by *Meng-tzu*, 5A6. There it is said that the mythic emperor Yü had served Shun for so many years.

[214] Takigawa, 117.69 here records a "Cheng-yi" commentary that is not to be found in the Chung-hua edition. It says that Pa and Shu had been barbarian but had changed to the customs of the middle states, and the same applied to the Southwestern Barbarians.

[215] Li Shan in his commentary to *Wen-hsüan*, 44.1993 points out that a similar sentence is used by *Meng-tzu*, 5B2.

ordinary.[216] Therefore it is said that the common black-haired people fear the origins of something extraordinary. But if it then is completed, all under Heaven is happy.

In former times when the great floods poured out, bubbling forth and swelling vastly so that the people had to climb mountains and descend the slopes in order to change their settlements, they had to go on rough roads but did not find peace. Lord Hsia-hou 夏侯氏[217] pitied them and began to stem the floods, channeling the Chiang and setting the Yellow River apart, dividing and deepening them in order to smooth the effects of disasters. He led [the floods] to the east into the sea and all under Heaven was peaceful for ageless times. Such care was certainly not accomplished by just the [common] people! His heart was troubled by thoughts and he personally toiled exerting his own person. His body was covered by callouses[218] and on his skin there grew no hair. Therefore, his achievements shine gloriously for eternity and his name has been praised until today.

[3051] Moreover, when a worthy ruler accedes to the throne, he will surely not just concentrate on trifles and petty things, stick to the letter of the law and cling to vulgar manners, follow that which is sung [by everybody] and practice that which has been transmitted or merely seek pleasure in his own times.[219] He will certainly take exalted discussions and lofty proposals, create a legacy that can be left for future generations[220] and become a standard for ten thousand generations. Therefore, he will hurry to add generosity and include patience, earnestly thinking about forming a trinity with heaven and duality with earth. Does not a Song say:

Under the wide heaven,
All is the king's land.
Within the sea-boundaries of the land,
All are the king's servants.[221]

Therefore within the six joints and beyond the eight directions[222]

---

[216] Or, if we accept the emendation made by the Chung-hua editors: "The extraordinary is something that ordinary people 常人 find strange."

[217] Hsia-hou was the name of the state of Emperor Yü (see *Shih chi*, 2.82 and *Grand Scribe's Records*, 1:36).

[218] The sentence is difficult, and the commentaries give various explanations. Moreover, *Han shu*, 57B.2585 and *Wen-hsüan* 44.1993 add characters to it, in order to make it better understandable. With my reading I follow Hervouet, *Le chapitre 117*, p. 165. See also Hervouet's commentary 6.

[219] This is the understanding of Yen Shih-ku on *Han shu*, 57B.2568.

[220] *Meng-tzu*, 1B.14.

[221] Mao #205 (Legge, 4:360).

[222] The six joints (Heaven, Earth and the four directions) are mentioned in *Chuang-tzu* 2, *Chuang-tzu chi-shih* (Peking: Chung-hua Shu-chü, 1961 and 1997), p. 83. Yen Shih-ku

wherever [his virtue] streams and overflows, among every single living being, if there is one that is not moistened and enriched by his favor, the worthy ruler is ashamed. Now within the borders of our territory all people wearing caps and belts have received the auspicious blessings and none has been left out. Yet the Yi- and Ti-barbarians and the states of different customs living in territories that are distant, cut off and where other parties live, where those boats and carriages cannot go to, where the traces of [our] people rarely reach, regions that are as yet unaffected by corrective instruction, where the flowing winds [of our sovereign] are still weak.[223] If we take them in, then they will rebel against what is righteous and will undermine our rites at the borders, if we keep them out, then they will do evil and act against us, driving off and killing their superiors. Ruler and subject have changed places, honored and lowly have lost the proper sequence, fathers and elder brothers suffer innocently, while the young and orphaned become slaves, are bound, weep and cry, turn to the interior and say angrily: "We have heard that in the central states there is someone who has the utmost benevolence. His virtue is vast and his grace far-reaching, there is not one being that has not found its place. Why now have only we been left out?"[224] They stand on tiptoe, and admire him longingly, as the withered and thirsty look for rain. A cruel man would shed tears for them, how much less would the supreme sage be able to stop doing so! Therefore, we have sent out troops in the north in order to punish the mighty Hu barbarians and in the south we have swiftly dispatched envoys in order to reprimand the vigorous Yüeh, in all four directions there is [royal] influence and virtue. The rulers of these two regions, like scales aligning themselves in the direction of the flow, who want to receive titles, number in the millions. Therefore, only now did we make a pass at the Mo and the Jo, a barricade at Tsang-k'o, a watch-tower at Mount Ling and a bridge at the source of the Sun [River]. We have created a road of way and virtue, we have established a line of benevolence and righteousness.[225] We want to broaden grace and to widen its effects, to cherish those afar and to travel wide with our carriages in order to make those who are distant not be shut off and those places that are blocked in deep darkness and obscurity obtain our sparkling

explains that the eight directions are the four directions plus those directions lying between them.

[223] *Meng-tzu*, 2A1 speaks of "flowing wind and good government."

[224] Compare *Meng-tzu*, 1B11, 3B5 and 7B4 where Meng K'o says that at the time of King T'ang of Shang the barbarians that had not yet been integrated into his realm all complained that he had not yet led war against them.

[225] Compare on *Meng-tzu*, 1B14 quoted above.

light.[226] By this we want to give the armored troops a rest here and stop our punishing attacks there. Far and near will be just the same body, inner and outer will receive fortune. Would that not be prosperous? Now to deliver the people from drowning and to raise them to the highest favor, to turn around the downward swing of a degenerating age and to rescue the legacy that had been cut off after the house of Chou, this, then, is the most urgent task of the Son of Heaven. Although the hundred kindred have to toil, how could he put a stop to this?

[3052] Moreover, there really has never been a kingly enterprise that did not begin with sorrow and pain but end in ease and joy.[227] But this means that the tallies that testify that [the king] has received the mandate are attached to this fact. He just started to add the *feng*-sacrifices at Mount T'ai 泰 and the services at Mount Liang-fu 梁父 [to the existing cults],[228] he will cause the *luan* 鸞-bells sound harmoniously [on his carriage] and the joyous songs of praise be raised. Above he comes close to the Five [Emperors of old], below he mounts to the heights of the Three [Dynasties]. The onlookers have never seen such a direction and the listeners never heard such tones. He is soaring like the phoenix to the vast vault of the universe,[229] while those who want to catch him with their net are still looking for him down in the marshes and swamps! How sad!"

[3053] Thereupon the dignitaries in confusion forgot what they had brought in their hearts and lost why they had stepped forward, sighing and all calling out: "How just wonderful is the virtue of the Han, this is what we rustic people wanted to hear. Although the people are lazy, we request to lead with our persons the way for them." Disheartened they stumbled back and accordingly withdrew, taking their leave.

Afterwards someone presented a memorial saying that [Ssu-ma] Hsiang-ju had

---

[226] On this "sparkling light" compare on *Shih chi*, 12.477 (*Grand Scribe's Records*, 2:246–47) in a song devoted to the goddess T'ai-yi.

[227] See on *Shih chi*, 61.2125 for "ease and joy." Ssu-ma Ch'ien there speaks of the great injustice that those who did no good deeds nevertheless ended their life in ease and joy. Compare, however, Mao #170, *Shih-san-ching chu-shu*, p. 417, where Mao's preface to the ode says that the works of Kings Wen and Wu began with sorrow and pain but ended with ease and joy.

[228] As is well-known Emperor Wu performed the *feng*-sacrifice at Mount T'ai and the service at Mount Liang-fu for the first time in 110 BC (see on *Grand Scribe's Records*, 2:242–43), so Ssu-ma Hsiang-ju is talking here of something that was still to happen.

[229] See the end of the "Far Journey" of the *Ch'u-tz'u*, *Ch'u-tz'u pu-chu*, p. 287 where the poet rises to the vast vault of Heaven.

accepted money when he was on envoy, so he lost his office.[230] After more than a year living in privacy he was again summoned to become an gentleman.

[Ssu-ma] Hsiang-ju was a stutterer but he was excellent at composing texts.[231] He suffered constantly from diabetes.[232] Since he was married to a woman from the Cho family, he was abundantly wealthy. When he advanced in office, he was never willing to participate in the affairs of state of the excellencies and ministers, but claimed to be ill and lived idly without yearning either for office or title. Once he followed the sovereign on his hunting excursions at the Ch'ang-yang 長楊 (Tall Poplar [Palace]). Just at that time the Son of Heaven liked to attack in person bears and boars and to race in pursuit of wild animals. Hsiang-ju handed in a memorial in which he remonstrated against this. His words read:[233]

> Your servant has heard that there are beings that are of the same species but have different abilities. Therefore, as far as strength is concerned we praise Wu Huo 烏獲, for agility we speak of [Wang] Ch'ing-chi [王]慶忌, as far courage we expect it from [Meng] Pen [孟]賁 and [Hsia] Yü [夏]育.[234] Your servant in his stupidity dares to think that if this is true for men it will certainly also be so for animals. Now Your Majesty likes to race down narrow mountain slopes and to shoot wild animals. If you all of a sudden encounter an animal with extraordinary capabilities or are startled [by an animal that springs out] of a place where you did not expect it and attacks out of the pure

---

[230] The interesting question here is whether Ssu-ma Hsiang-ju actually wanted to persuade the emperor to continue the project or to abandon it. It would seem that he was in favor of the project, and that this was the reason why those who were against it tried to get rid of him.

[231] Compare on *Shih chi*, 63.2146 where the same is said about Han Fei.

[232] *Han shu pu-chu*, 57B.10a quotes Ch'ien Ta-hsin who refers to a parallel in the second chüan of the *Hsi-ching tsa-chi* 西京雜記 (Peking: Chung-hua Shu-chü 1985), p. 11, where it is said that Ssu-ma Hsiang-ju because of his illness returned to Ch'eng-tu in order to rejoice in the beauty of his wife. Then he got a disease called "ku-chi" because of which he composed the *fu* on the beautiful woman. By this he wanted to criticize himself but was not able to change his conduct. Finally he died from this illness.

[233] See on this text also *Wen-hsüan* 39, *Li Shan chu Wen-hsüan*, 39.1777–78.

[234] On Wu Huo see *Shih chi*, 5.209 (*Grand Scribe's Records*, 1:114) and *Shih chi*, 70.134 (*Grand Scribe's Records*, 7:134), on Wang Ch'ing-chi, Meng Pen and Hsia Yü *Shih chi*, 79.2407 (*Grand Scribe's Records*, 7:237) where a similar catalogue to this is given.

dust[235] of one of the vehicles in your entourage, then the carriage will not be able to turn around and the others will not have the time to display their skills. Although they might have the skill of a Wu Huo or a P'eng Meng 逢蒙,[236] they will not be able to use their strength. Rotten wood and decayed stumps all could cause disaster. This would be the same as [Northern] Hu and [Southern] Yüeh rising at your wheel-hubs or [Western] Ch'iang and [Eastern] Yi grabbing the yoke of your horses. Is this not dangerous? And even if it is absolutely safe and you do not need to worry, this still is not something the Son of Heaven should approach.

[3054] Moreover, even if you go only after the way has been cleared and start to race only after you are on the middle-road,[237] there are still at times emergencies with the bit of [your horses] or the axle. How much more so if you cross the reeds and grasses, race over hills and slopes, if in front you just feel the pleasure of stabbing the animal without keeping in mind the possibility of a sudden emergency. If this were to cause an accident, wouldn't it be a really difficult situation? Now to take the importance of ten thousand carriages[238] lightly, not caring about safety, and instead to rejoice in taking pleasure in going out on a road where there is a chance of one in ten thousand that there be a danger, that is an option that your servant would in the place of your Majesty not take.[239]

Now the enlightened one sees something from afar before it germinates and the knowledgeable one avoids danger before it yet takes shape.[240] A disaster is often hidden in obscure and small things and breaks out in situations that one has not paid attention to. Therefore a rustic proverb says: "If in your family the one thousand cash strings pile up, your seat should not

---

[235] Yen Shih-ku on *Han shu*, 57B.2590 explains that this is the dust of the Emperor which by its nature cannot be dirty. Compare Wang Li-ch'i, 117.2470, who says that Ssu-ma Hsiang-ju does not dare to speak openly about the emperor.

[236] P'eng Meng was a famous archer who studied with the archer Yi who had according to legend shot down the nine suns that had made the earth too hot. P'eng Meng killed Yi because he thought that Yi alone was his superior. See *Meng Tzu*, 4B.24, Legge, 2:328–30.

[237] See on *Shih chi*, 6.241 and 242, n. 6. *Grand Scribe's Records*, 1:138 translates the relevant sentence as: "He built the Speedway." On this see ibid., n. 155. Ying Shao says that the "Speedway" is the same as the "middle-ways" of his times.

[238] I.e. the empire.

[239] I follow the punctuation of *Han shu*, 57B.2590, *Wen-hsüan*, 39.1778 and Takigawa, 117.77 instead of *Shih chi* which rather suggests that the emperor takes pleasure in not being safe itself (不以為安而樂).

[240] Compare for this common wisdom also *Shih chi*, 118.3085: "The one who is good at hearing hears before there is a sound, the one who is clear at sight sees before there is a shape." See also on *Shih chi*, 68.2229.

be at the edge of the hall."[241] This saying may be small but with it we can hint
at something that is big. Your servant hopes that Your Majesty considers this
and gives it favorable thought!"

The sovereign appreciated this. When on his way back he passed by the Yi-ch'un
宜春宮 [Let It Be Spring!] Palace,[242] [Ssu-ma] Hsiang-ju presented a *fu* in order to
lament the mistakes in the behavior of the Second Emperor [of Ch'in]. Its words ran:

[3055] I climb the uneven long slope of the rising bank,
And enter the lofty, looming, storied-palace.
Near the long islet midst the winding stream,
I gaze at the rocky silhouette of Southern Mountain.
Majestic the cliffs in the deep Mountain,
Cut through by the yawning openings of ravines.
Its waters speeding downwards used to depart in eternity,[243]
channelled into the wide spaces of the flat plain.
Observing groups of trees in wind and shadow,
I overlook the thicket of the bamboo forests.
In the east I race over soil and mountains,
in the north I wade through the stony rapids.
Putting my caduceus aside in relaxed composure,
I proceed to condole the Second Emperor.
In establishing himself he lacked carefulness,
ruined his state and lost his power.
Believing in slanderers without awakening,
his ancestral temple was extinguished and his line cut off.
Alack and alas!
That he did not reach a refined behavior,
On his grave mound weeds grow and it is not kept up,
His soul has nowhere to turn and is not fed.
It remains far removed, feeling transitory,
The longer and farther, the more it decays.

[241] Chang Yi says in a commentary quoted by "So-yin" that the person should fear that a
tile could fall down on him, while Yüeh Ch'an says that he fears he could fall down from the
hall. Compare on *Shih chi*, 101.2740, Takigawa, 117.78. Apparently the text wants to say that
those who can afford it do not have to take risks anymore. Compare *Meng-tzu*, 7A2 which
says that those who understand fate will not stand beneath a precipitous wall.
[242] *Shih chi*, 6.275 and 6.290 says that the Second Emperor was buried in the Garden at
Yi-ch'un which probably got it's name for this reason—one apparently wished the Second
Emperor Eternal Spring. See also above, n. 147.
[243] Compare *Lun-yü*, 9.17.

His essence like a ghost flies upwards,
Touching the Nine Heavens and departing forever.
Alack and alas![244]

[3056] [Ssu-ma] Hsiang-ju was appointed as Prefect of the Grave Garden of Emperor Wen. As the Son of Heaven had admired the story of "Master Empty," when [Ssu-ma] Hsiang-ju saw that the sovereign liked [to study] the way to become an immortal, he accordingly said: "The story of the Shang-lin Park does not deserve to be admired because there still is something more beautiful. Your servant once made a "Ta-jen Fu" 大人賦 (*Fu* on the Great Man) that he has not finished. I beg to be allowed to complete and then submit it." [Ssu-ma] Hsiang-ju remarked that the traditions[245] of the various immortals [said] that they lived in mountains and marshes, that in their appearance they were most emaciated, and that this was not what an emperor or king had in mind for becoming an immortal. Only then did he finish his "*Fu* on the Great Man."[246] Its words ran:

In our age there is a great man,
In the Middle Region.
His dwelling[247] measures ten thousand miles,
Yet it is never enough for him to remain a while.
Grieved by the oppressing narrowness of the vulgarities of our age,
he went and rose lightly to travel far away.[248]

[244] The last five verses are missing from the parallel text in *Han shu*, 57.2591.

[245] *Han shu*, 57B.2592 has "ju" 儒 instead of "chuan" 傳 and Yen Shih-ku in a note writes that "ju" means "jou" 弱, weak, which according to him is a name for any scholar mastering a technique. "All those who have a method or a technique are called *ju*." He adds that some popular editions of the book write *chuan* instead of *ju*–just as the received *Shih chi* version does. This he thinks is wrong and a change by later persons. So Yen Shih-ku thinks the expression means "the specialists for the immortals" which matches well with the fact that in the "Feng-shan shu" the "ju" are frequently mentioned together with the *fang-shih*. On this subject see already Ku Chieh-kang 顧頡剛 (1893–1980), *Ch'in Han te fang-shih yü ju-sheng* 秦漢的方士與儒生 (Shanghai: Ch'un-lian Ch'u-pan-she, 1935).

[246] A much more positive account of how Ssu-ma Hsiang-ju came to write this text is to be found in *Hsi-ching tsa-chi*, *chüan* 2, p. 21 where it is said that he dreamt of an old man in a yellow robe who told him that he should write the "*Fu* on the Great Man."

[247] The term "dwelling" is with reference to several canonical passages translated as "place where the people lives" in *Ssu-ma Hsiang-ju chi chiao-chu*, Shanghai 1993: 93.

[248] 悲世俗之迫隘兮, 揭輕舉而遠遊. There is a close parallel to this in the first two lines of the "Yüan-yu" poem of the *Ch'u-tz'u* (*Ch'u-tz'u pu-chu*, p. 268): "Grieved by the parlous state of this world's ways, I wanted to float up and away from it." 悲時俗之迫阨兮, 願輕舉而遠遊 (Hawkes, p. 193). There the "oppressive narrowness" is explained by the commentator Wang Yi as the jealousness of the ministers at the Ch'u court. Ju Ch'un quoted

Mounting[249] a plain rainbow with its red sails,[250]
He rides the cloud airs and drifts up.[251]
Establishing a long pole out of the Ho-to 格澤 star,[252]
He puts together the multi-colored flag of its radiant brilliance.[253]
Flying the pennants of the Hsün-shih 旬始 constellation,[254]
He drags a comet to make of it his tail.[255]

by "So-yin" says however that Emperor Wu complains about other constraints. He quotes the sentence from the Annals of Emperor Wu who said to one of the *fang-shih* who promised immortality to him: "Ah! If We could truly be like the Huang-ti, leaving Our wives and children would be like doffing a slipper!" (see on *Shih chi*, 12.468, *Grand Scribe's Records*, 2:237, and 28.1394).

[249] I follow *Han shu*, 57B.2592 in reading "to mount" 乘 instead of "to hang down" 垂. The characters resemble each other, but Takigawa (117.80) rightly points out that "to hang down" does not fit here because four verses later a line starts with another "to hang down" (there translated as "flying"). One of them must be wrong, and Wang Hsien-ch'ien quoted ibid. and on *Han shu pu-chu* 57B.12b says that it must be this one.

[250] Red is the color which usually is to be seen either on the upper or on the lower side of the rainbow. I think that the text is here thinking of a rainbow on the lower side of which there is a strong red.

[251] 垂絳幡之素蜺兮，載雲氣而上浮. Compare "Yüan-yu" ll. 3–4 (*Ch'u-tz'u pu-chu*, p. 268): 質菲薄而無因兮，焉托乘而上浮? And below, l. 86, Hawkes, p. 196: "I clung to a floating cloud to ride aloft on" (*Ch'u-tz'u pu-chu*, p. 278).

[252] On the *Ho-to* constellation (pronunciation given by Yen Shih-ku on *Han shu*, 57B.2593) see on *Shih chi*, 27.1335 where this pronunciation is given. It looks "like fire," is yellow and white and rises from the earth—whatever that may mean. Interestingly, the text says that if it is seen there will be a harvest without that one has to sow, but also that one should not start earth works because there will certainly be great harm.

[253] 建格澤之長竿兮，總光耀之采旄. *Ch'u-tz'u*, "Yüan-yu," verses 99–100: "The standards we carried bore rainbow devices: Five contrasting colors, dazzling to behold" 建雄虹之採旄兮，五色雜而炫耀.

[254] 垂旬始以為幓兮. This constellation is mentioned on *Shih chi*, 27.1336. It looks like a rooster. If it is enraged it turns bluish-black and resembles a crouching turtle. Li Ch'i and Chin Cho in their commentaries to this passage say that "enraged" could also mean "hen." The text would thus say that the hen of the rooster is bluish-black. Yet, Chin Cho adds that there is also the explanation that the star is "angry" as translated above. In both cases it is hard to imagine how this should work with a star constellation. Compare also "Yüan-yu" (*Ch'u-tz'u pu-chu*, p. 278), verse 92: 造旬始而觀清都, Hawkes, p. 196, "Visited the Week Star and gazed on the Pure City." Wang Yi explains *Hsün-shih* as a name for August Heaven but adds that there is also the explanation that it is a constellation. He also says that *Hsün-shih* is Venus (*T'ai-pai* 太白). Hung Hsing-tsu in the end says that according to *Shih chi* 27 whenever *Hsün-shih* shows up there will be war.

Drifting with the wind the flag now sinks and bends,[256]
then flutters shaking in the air.
Grabbing the Ch'an 欃- and Ch'iang 槍-stars he uses them as his guidon,[257]
[*3057*] Turning a broken rainbow into his scabbard.
Red, the sun sets, blurred and obscure at the horizon,
whirling, the wind blows clouds floating [past the sun].[258]
He drives the winged dragons[259] on his ivory carriage, inching along and
    meandering,
with red lindworms and the green horned dragon snaking sinuously.
Tossing their heads they undulate and prance,
zigging and zagging up and down.[260]
Their necks held high they hesitate,
[then] giving way they gallop away.
Quickly they advance on their winding way,

[255] 拽彗星而為髾. "Yüan-yu" verse 116 (*Ch'u-tz'u pu-chu*, p. 281): "I took the Broom Star to use it as a banner" 攬慧星以為旍兮.

[256] 掉指橋以偃蹇兮 Literally: "Shaking the fluttering flag" 掉指橋. Chang Yi says that 指矯 means "to point the flag in the direction of the wind": 指矯，隨風指靡. 偃蹇, too, is a problem: Chang Yi simply says that it means "the appearance of being tall" 高皃 but Ying Shao says it means that "the flag is wound and bent" 旌旗屈撓之皃.

[257] "Cheng-yi" here refers to the "T'ien-kuan shu" *Shih chi*, 27.1316 in which these two stars are said to be emanations of the Jupiter. "Cheng-yi" explains that "if the essence of the Jupiter disperses" it becomes several other stars or probably comets, among them the heavenly *ts'ang* and the heavenly *ch'an*. In his commentaries on *Shih chi*, 27.1317 "Cheng-yi" furthermore explains that "Ch'an" and "Ch'iang" are associated with war. On Heavenly Ch'an he quotes the Han scholar Ching Fang 京方 (77–37 BC) that "Heavenly Ch'an means troops. There are a thousand miles of red soil [from the blood of the dead soldiers] and rotten bones all over." "Cheng-yi" also refers to *Han shu*, 26.1280 where the Ch'iang and the Ch'an are related to "destroyed states and chaotic rulers" with death as the severest consequence. But there are also droughts, disasters, hunger, cruelties and illnesses." On *Han shu*, 26.1303 an appearance of the heavenly Ch'an in the second year of the later reign period of Emperor Wen is related to war. As a consequence four years later the Hsiung-nu invaded two provinces in the north. The Han had to raise three armies in order to guard the capital.

[258] As is well-known, Wang Yi deciphered the whirling wind in the *Ch'u-tz'u* as a metaphor for turmoil "small men" (*Ch'u-tz'u pu-chu*, preface, p. 9. On the floating clouds, also interpreted by Wang Yi as a metaphor for small men see *Lun-yü*, 7.16 and *Ch'u-tz'u pu-chu*, p. 322, 325 ("Chiu-pien" 九辯), 406, 424 ("Ch'i-chien" 七諫). There are many more passages in the *Ch'u-tz'u* that mention the "drifting clouds," but the commentary does not refer to them as a metaphor for the "small men." The first occurrence of "floating clouds" is in the "Chiu-chang," where Wang Yi explains them as a metaphor for the fickle ruler.

[259] On the winged dragon and various other fabulous animals mentioned here see also *Huai-nan tzu chi-shih*, 6.483–84.

[260] *Ch'u-tz'u pu-chu*, "Yüan-yu," p. 279, Hawkes, p. 196.

close bound[261] they storm forward in narrow formation.

Vying for the lead and neighing loudly, they trample all reaching the road,

almost flying they spring and rush madly.

In their whirling flight they overtake the lightning,

through mists that flame and disappear,

clouds that all of a sudden vanish.

[3058] Having left the pole of Lesser Yang [in the east] behind, he ascends to
    the Utmost Yin [in the north],

Searching out the true men.[262]

He wheels to the right in the remote secludedness,[263]

Crosses the "Flying Springs" to move straight east again.[264]

Summons all the spirits from the Magic Garden[265] and selects from them,

And forms a battalion of riders from the various ghosts at the Yao-kuang 瑤
    光 star.[266]

He orders the Five Emperors[267] to be in the front,

Returning to the Great Unity and leaving Ling-yang 陵陽 behind.[268]

To his left is Hsüan-ming 玄冥, the Dark Obscurity,

and to his right Han-lei 含靁, the Bearer of Thunder,[269]

In front is Lu-li 陸離,[270] behind is Yü-huang 潏湟.[271]

---

[261] Ch'ou-mou 綢繆 is the title of Mao #118 (Legge, 4:179): "Round and round [ch'ou-mou] the firewood is bound; And the Three Stars appear in the sky. This evening is what evening, That I see this good man?" The preface says that the poem criticizes disorder in the state of Chin, but it would probably go to far to see an allusion here. Yet, It is interesting that the text speaks of this "good man" which could be taken as an allusion to the Ta-jen.

[262] The "true men" are obviously Taoist immortals. In his attempt to gain immortality Ch'in Shih-huang tried to make the "true men" come. See on Shih chi, 6.257.

[263] "Remote darkness" is "yao-tiao," the word describing the modest, retiring lady in Mao #1. "Wheeling to the right" see Ch'u-tz'u, "Yüan-yu," p. 280, Hawkes p. 197, l. 107.

[264] On the Flying Springs see Ch'u-tz'u pu-chu, "Yüan-yu," p. 276, Hawkes, p. 196, l. 75. Chang Yi locates them near K'un-lun (in the west).

[265] Cf. the "Yüan-yu" poem ascribed to Liu Hsiang in Ch'u-tz'u pu-chu, Chiu-t'an, p. 535.

[266] Which according to Chang Yi is to be found in the handle of the big dipper.

[267] The Five Emperors can either be the five mythical emperors to whom the first chapter of the Shih chi is devoted, or the five powers on high who are associated to the five cardinal colors and for whom the Han erected shrines. See on them Shih chi, 28.1378.

[268] On Ling-yang see Hervouet, Poète de cour, pp. 314–15.

[269] See on these gods Ch'u-tz'u pu-chu, "Yüan-yu," p. 286–87, Hawkes p. 198.

[270] Called Ch'ang-li 長離 on Han shu, 57B.2595 and by Yen Shih-ku, ibid., associated with ch'ang-li 長麗, the magic bird 靈鳥, on Han shu, 22.1058.

[271] Nothing is known about Yü-huang.

He enslaves Cheng Po-ch'iao 征伯僑, and indentures Hsien-men 羨門.[272]

[*3059*] He attaches Ch'i-po 岐伯 to himself and lets him prepare recipes.[273]
Chu-jung 祝融 clears the road for him, shouting "attention!"
Clearing the foul vapors, and then going ahead.
He stations his carriages, numbering ten thousand,
Displaying their cloud canopies and posting the multi-colored flags.
He orders Kou-mang 句芒 to lead the march:[274]
"I want to proceed to the south to amuse myself."[275]

[3060] He crosses by Emperor Yao of T'ang's [grave] at Mount Sung 嵩,[276]
And passes by the one of Emperor Shun of Yü at the Nine Peaks.[277]
Spread in massive array [the chariots] advance in big waves,
In big rows they gallop at a rush.[278]
In swift movements they press each other forward,
Gushing forth and swooping, like a forest [in the wind].
Like a thicket of bushes kept together, they roll by,
Mightily streaming through the plain.
He crosses through the stony vegetation of the House of Thunder,
Arrives through a canyon at the cliffs and crags of the Demon Valley.[279]
He gazes at all the eight cardinal points and looks at the deserts of the four
    directions [at the outskirts of the known world],
Fords the Nine Streams and goes beyond the Five Rivers.[280]

---

[272] See on these immortals Hervouet, *Le chapitre 117*, p. 193, n. 11: Cheng Po-ch'iao is either the famous immortal Wang Tzu-ch'iao or a magician at the court of Ch'in Shih-huang ti. The latter makes much more sense since on *Shih chi* 28.1368 Cheng Po-ch'iao is mentioned together with Hsien-men as a magician of the First Emperor.

[273] On Ch'i-po as the doctor of the Yellow Emperor see *Shih chi* "Cheng-yi" quoting Chang Yi on *Shih chi,* 12.484.

[274] On Kou-mang see *Ch'u-tz'u pu-chu*, Yüan-yu, p. 279, Hawkes, p. 197.

[275] *Han shu,* 57B.2597 reads "he wants to travel to the southern coast." Hervouet, *Le chapitre 117*, p. 193, follows this text, Watson, *Records* 2, p. 334, the version of the *Shih chi*. Compare *Ch'u-tz'u pu-chu*, "Yüan-yu," p. 283, Hawkes, p. 198: "I wished to journey onwards to the world's southern shore."

[276] In modern Honan.

[277] South of Modern Hunan.

[278] "Rushing forward" (*chiao-ko* 膠葛) is to be found in *Ch'u-tz'u pu-chu*, "Yüan-yu," p. 279.

[279] *Kuei-ku* 鬼谷 evokes the place of origin of Kuei-ku tzu, the Master of the Demon Valley, who is according to the *Shih chi,* 70.2241 the teacher of Chang Yi and Su Ch'in.

[280] On the different explanations for these streams and rivers see Hervouet, *Le chapitre 117,* p. 196, n. 4. For the Nine Streams see *Shang shu*, Yü-kung, Legge, 3:130.

He tours Flaming Mountain and sails on Jo 弱-water,
Embarks to the floating islands and wades through the Moving Sands.[281]
Resting at the peak of the Ts'ung-[ling] 總領 range he sets out to take
    pleasure in its pouring waters,
Making the divine [Nü]-wa 女媧 strike the zither and the River-god P'ing-yi
    馮夷 dance.[282]
When at dawn everything becomes obscure,
He calls Ping-yi 屏翳, the Thunder Master, to kill the Earl of the Wind[283] and
    to execute the Rain Master.[284]
To the west he looks at the blurred schemes of K'un-lun 崑崙 Mountain,
Racing directly to the Three Summits.[285]
He pushes open the gate of Heaven and enters the palace of the God-Emperor,
Letting the Jade Maidens mount his chariots, he returns with them.[286]
They rest at Lang-feng 閬風 Mountain[287] and assemble far away,

---

[281] The Moving Sands are to be found in the Yü-kung chapter of the *Shu-ching*. See Legge, 3:132, where also Jo-water is mentioned. At the same time they may be read as the place at which Ch'ü Yüan committed suicide. See on *Ch'u-tz'u pu-chu*, "Li-sao," p. 73, but also in "Chao-hun," p. 336, and "Ta-chao," p. 364.

[282] The "Chi-chieh" commentary explains that Feng-yi is the *agnomen* of the River God Ho-po 河伯. Nü-wa, of course, is the goddess at the origin of the world.

[283] Chang Shou-chieh says that the *agnomen* of the Earl of the Wind is Fei-lien 飛廉, a common name in ancient China.

[284] According to *Shan-hai ching*, when the Yellow Emperor wanted to campaign against Ch'ih-yu, the latter sent the Earl of the Wind and the Rain Master to create a great tempest. Both were apparently followers of Ch'ih-yu, the later god of war. So the great man here assumes the position of the Yellow Emperor. However, it is also said that the Rain Master is also called Ping-yi which is the name of the Thunder Master who here is asked to kill the Earl of the Wind and the Rain Master. See on this Yüan K'o 袁珂, *Chung-kuo shen-hua ch'uan-shuo tz'u-tien* 中國神話傳說詞典 (Shanghai: Shang-hai Tz'u-shu Ch'u-pan-she, 1985), p. 225, and Lü Tsung-li 呂宗力 and Luan Pao-qun 欒保群, *Chung-kuo min-chien chu-shen* 中國民間諸神 (Taipei: T'ai-wan Hsüeh-sheng, 1991), pp. 138–44.

[285] See Hervouet, *Le chapitre 117*, 199, n. 6, who explains that this is a mountain range in Kan-su but at the same time also the seat of the three white birds, messengers of the Queen Mother of the West.

[286] Jade Maiden is a polite term for beautiful girls. Cf. *Li-chi*, "Chi-t'ung," *Shih-san ching chu-shu* 1603A, where it is prescribed that a ruler asks his future father in law for his "jade maiden." Otherwise jade maiden is a term for female immortals. In many later Taoist texts Jade Maidens are said to be in the entourage of the Jade Emperor.

[287] Mentioned in the "Li-sao" (*Ch'u-tz'u pu-chu*, p. 50). Wang Yi says that it is a mountain at K'un-lun.

Flying high like crows, they hold on together.
He returns to Shadowy Mountain, hovering through the winding crags,
"Today I finally behold the glimmering white hair of the Queen Mother of the
    West![288]
It is full of jewels and yet she is living in a cave.
Fortunately there is the three-legged crow who acts as her envoy.[289]

She will surely live long in such a state and not die,
Though she passes ten thousand generations it will not be reason for joy.[290]

[3062] So he turns his chariot around and leaves to come back,
Stopping at Mount Pu-Chou 不周,
Gathering to dine at Secluded City.[291]
Inhaling nightly vapors, swallowing the morning mists,
Chewing blossoms of wild arum and sipping petals of the hortensia.[292]
Elegantly they soar up to the heights,
In great array they fly to the zenith.
He passes through the setting sun's lightning fissure[293],
And traverses the pouring showers of the [Cloud Master] Feng-lung 豐隆.[294]

[288] The Queen Mother of the West is mentioned on *Shih chi,* 123.3164. The elders from Parthia said that she lived to the west but that they had never seen her. Compare also on *Shih chi,* 43.1779 where the famous story of King Mu of Chou is told who saw the Queen Mother of the West.

[289] In Han mythology the three-legged crow was said to live in the sun. It is often to be found in Han tomb reliefs. K'un-lun where the Queen Mother of the West lives is also the place where the sun sets.

[290] Yen Shih-ku, *Han shu,* 57B.2598, explains that the Queen Mother of the West was said to be the apex of the immortals, but that the Great Man after his own journey looks down upon her and thinks that no envy is needed.

[291] See Hervouet, *Le chapitre* 117, p. 201, n. 2, on the various identifications of Mount Pu-chou and the Secluded City to the southeast or northwest of K'un-lun.

[292] Ying Shao quoted on *Han shu,* 57A.2599 cites the biography of Ling Yang-tzu 陵陽子 in the *Lieh-hsien chuan* 列仙傳 that says that one eats morning mists in spring. Morning mist is the reddish yellow light of the sun when it first comes out. In summer one eats the vapors of the night. These vapors are the pneuma of midnight in the north.

The hortensia is according to Chang Yi on *Han shu,* 57A.2599 a huge tree that grows in the moving sands at K'un-lun. Eating its petals ensures long life. However, a "Ch'iung-hua" 瓊華, here translated as petals of the hortensia, is already mentioned in Mao #98 (Legge, 4:152). Mao explains it as a stone or precious gem.

[293] On this place where the light comes down from the gates of Heaven see *Ch'u-tz'u pu-chu,* p. 287, "Yüan-yu," Hawkes, p. 198, l. 165.

[294] The cloud master Feng-lung is also mentioned, among many other places, on *Ch'u-tz'u pu-chu,* "Yüan-yu," p. 277.

He races along his journey path, long descending,
Drives through the remaining mists far into the distance.
Pressing through the narrow straits of the universe,
Holding out his caduceus [to order a race], he comes out at the northern
    boundary.
He leaves riders behind in a garrison at the Dark Pass,
And as the first one drives his chariot through the Cold Gate.[295]
"In the sheer depths below, the earth was invisible;
In the vastness above, the sky could not be seen.
When I looked, my obscured eyes saw nothing,
When I listened, no sound met my amazed ear."[296]
He rode the emptiness and ascended high,
Transcended the world of companions and stayed alone.

[3063] When Ssu-ma Hsiang-ju had presented the "Ta-jen chih song" 大人之頌 (Eulogy on the Great Man),[297] the Son of Heaven was greatly pleased; he had the air of whirling on pure clouds, and it seemed that he wanted to roam between Heaven and Earth.

After [Ssu-ma] Hsiang-ju had retired because of illness, he lived privately at Mao-ling 茂陵.[298] The Son of Heaven said: "Since Ssu-ma Hsiang-ju is gravely ill, we should go and take all his writings. If we do not do this [now], later they will already be lost."[299] He sent So Chung 所忠 to proceed. But [when he arrived, Ssu-ma]

---

[295] See on these northern most places *Ch'u-tz'u pu-chu*, "Yüan-yu," p. 286, Hawkes, p. 198. The Cold Gate is also mentioned on *Shih chi*, 12.468 and 28.1394. There, Kung-sun Ch'ing explained to Emperor Wu that the Yellow Emperor after having studied for over a hundred years was able to communicate with the spirits and and received the ten thousand spirits. See the translation on *Grand Scribe's Records*, 2:237.

[296] These four verses are also to be found at the end of the "Yüan-yu" poem in *Ch'u-tz'u pu-chu*, p. 287. The translation is with a small change in line 3 where the text runs lightly differently in Ssu-ma Hsiang-ju's poem, by David Hawkes, *The Songs of the South*, p. 199.

[297] In later times *fu* and *sung* (eulogy) became different literary genres. Here, however, it seems that *sung* is just used as a description of what the *fu* did, namely praise the great man.

[298] This means that Ssu-ma Hsiang-ju had moved out of the capital city to Mao-ling, Emperor Wu's mausoleum town.

[299] The sentence 可往後悉取其書；若不然，後失之矣 as on *Shih chi,* 117.3063 is difficult. *Han shu,* 57B.3600 instead writes 可往從悉取其書，若後之矣. Takigawa, 117.90 and Hervouet, *Le chapitre 117*, both have 可往從 as in *Han shu* instead of 可往後 in the early versions of the Chung-hua shu-chü edition. These editions have been changed recently to have the same wording as *Han shu* and Takigawa. Yen Shih-ku thinks that 若 means "you" and

Hsiang-ju had already died and in his home there were no writings. When he asked his wife, she answered: "Chang-ch'ing really never had any writings. From time to time he wrote things, but then others took them away so that he lived in a [house] that was empty [of writings]. Shortly before his death, Chang-ch'ing produced one written roll and said: 'If an envoy comes and asks about my writings, submit it.' There are no other writings." The writing on wooden tablets[300] that he had left behind dealt with the affairs of the *feng*- and *shan*-sacrifices. It was submitted[301] to So Chung. When So Chung submitted this writing, the Son of Heaven found it extraordinary. His writing read:

> From the first beginning of highest antiquity when vast Heaven created man
> There have been numerous bright rulers until the Ch'in.
> Following those who were close in time one can tread in the path of their martial achievements,[302] while for listening to those who were distant there are the sounds of melodies.[303] [*3064*] In the disorder and abundance those majestic fellows[304] who

adds: "If you go now, you are already behind others." 言汝今去已在他人後也. Takigawa rejects this reading.

[300] Compare on this writings on wooden tablets *Shih chi*, 12.466. Yen Shih-ku on *Han shu*, 57B.2600 says that this was written on a wooden tablet (*cha* 札) and kept behind 書於札而留之. However, this contradicts the text before which states that the writing was a "roll" (*chüan* 卷). Takigawa, 117.91 and Hervouet, *Le chapitre 117*, 205a, have a "Cheng-yi" commentary missing in the Chung-hua shu-chü edition that says: "The *feng*- and *shan*-sacrifices are the most important rituals of the state. Therefore it is said that this was a *cha-shu*. I fear that Yen is wrong when he says that the text is called a left-over tablet because it was written on a wooden tablet and kept." 封禪國之大禮。故曰札書。顏云「書於札而留之，故云遺札」,恐非. "Cheng-yi" obviously wants to explain "cha-shu" as a term for "official writings," not as "wooden tablets." The passage ten times speaks of "writings," obviously ascribing great importance to the text involved.

[301] There again is a problem with the text here. Ssu-ma Hsiang-ju's wife first says that her husband had told her to hand this writing in. The term he uses is "tsou chih" 奏之 which actually means "to memorialize." Now *Shih chi*, 117.3063 says that it was "memorialized to So Chung" 奏所忠 which is awkward, and then that So Chung submitted it at court 所忠奏其書. *Han shu*, 57B.2600 has cut several redundant passages. First the wife does not say that "there are no other writings." Then Pan Ku simply added that the text dealt with the *feng*- and *shan*-sacrifices and that So Chung submitted it at court: 其遺札書言封禪事, 所忠奏焉.

[302] Both Hsü Kuang quoted in the "Chi-chieh" commentary on *Shih chi*, 117.3064 and Wen Ying on *Han shu*, 57B.3601 have read "wu" 武 (martial) as "chi" 迹 (footsteps), but I do not see why this should be necessary.

[303] Wen Ying on *Han shu*, 57B.3601 says that these sounds are the sounds of the Elegantiae and the Hymns [of the *Book of Odes*]. Ssu-ma Chen on *Shih chi*, 117.3064 thinks that these sounds are those of the first sections of the *Book of Odes*. Yen Shih-ku rejects this idea. For him the songs are unspecified.

have sunk into oblivion so that their names are not mentioned anymore were innumerable.

Following the Bright and Majestic music [of Shun and Yü][305] among those who have been honored by an appellation and a posthumous name

There were seventy-two lords who are probably worth talking about.[306]

None obedient and pure who did not prosper.

Who ran counter to and lost [reason], and yet was able to persist?

What was before Hsien-yüan 軒轅[307]

is remote and far removed,

And there is no way to know about details.

About the Five [Emperors] and the Three Dynasties:

By the traditions in the records of the six scriptures

We see that they are worth examining.

A Document says: "When the head is bright

The limbs are good."[308]

Basing myself on this to start my discussion,

There was no ruler more brilliant than Yao from T'ang and no servant more worthy than Hou-chi 后稷.[309] Hou-chi founded his legacy in T'ang while Kung Liu 公劉 began to make his mark among the Western Jung 戎.[310]

King Wen changed all the rules, the Chou through this arrived at eminence.

By their great deeds they neared perfection,

And when later they declined and faded away,

[304] The commentaries on *Shih chi* and *Han shu* (ibid.) think that the whole expression "fen-lun wei-jui" 紛輪威蕤 (text in *Han shu*; *Shih chi* reads 紛綸葳蕤) means "confusion." This reading follows the *Shih chi* version of the text. See Hervouet, *Le chapitre 117*, p. 40, n. 13, where following Li Shan's commentary to the "Tzu-hsü fu" Hervouet understands "wei-jui" 威蕤 as a certain hairstyle, possibly because the compound is also used on 117.3011 to describe the dancers of Cheng. Still I think that "wei" 威 may mean "majestic" while "jui" 蕤 gives the idea of a thick group or bundle of something.

[305] Hervouet, *Le chapitre 117*, p. 206 follows the ancient commentaries and reads this just as "l'éclat et la grandeur," while Watson says "Shun and Yü" (*Records* 2: 336). See on the *chao-hsia* music *Chou-li, Shih-san ching chu-shu*, 790C and 800B.

[306] See on this number on *Shih chi*, 28.1361 and Hervouet, *Le chapitre 117*, p. 206, n. 5.

[307] That is, the Yellow Emperor.

[308] "Yü shu" 虞書, *Shang shu*, Yi and Chi, Legge, 3:90. Compare on *Shih-chi*, 2.81 and 24.1175. In the latter passage, the treatise on music, the historian himself says that he has to cry when he thinks of the possibility that the "limbs"–i.e. the officials–are not good.

[309] The founder of the Chou dynasty.

[310] On Kung Liu see Mao #250, an ode that is devoted to this ancestor of the Chou, and *Shih chi*, 4.112, 5.206 and 13.490.

After a thousand years there was no sound of them.[311]

Did they not begin well and end well?

But they did not have any special initiatives of their own: They were just careful about the way they had come in the beginning and were diligent to leave a teaching behind for posterity. Therefore the traces of their rule were plain and easy, easy to follow. Their mercy had been overflowing, and so it was easy for them to be abundant. Their laws and standards were obvious and clear, and so to take them as a model was easy. The succession that they had handed down was reasonable so to continue it was easy. Therefore the legacy was eminent [even when a ruler still] was in his swaddling clothes, and **[*3065*]** his might topped the two [first] rulers' [King Wen and Wu].[312] Examining where all this began and how it finished in the end there are no extraordinarily remarkable traces that can be looked into today. But they still ascended Mount Liang-fu and climbed Mount T'ai, establishing an illustrious appellation and displaying an honorable reputation.

The virtue of the great Han

A mighty gush at the source of a spring,

Bubbling and spreading about,

on all sides it covered the passes in the four directions,

Like clouds that cover [the sky] and mists that spread.

Above it reaches the nine levels of [Heaven],

Below it extends to the eight end points [of the earth].

All species that embrace life,

Are moistened, nourished and enriched by it;

Harmonious vapors revolting,

Its martial standards whirl in far remote areas.

In nearby narrows one plays at their source,

In the far away vastness one swims in its waves,

Leaders in evil sink and drown,

The dull and stupid [barbarians] are illuminated,

Even insects and reptiles rejoice,

turning their heads to the interior [of our land].

After this

[311] Hsü Kuang understands this as meaning that after a thousand years the sounds of their reforms ceased. P'ei Yin 裴駰 (fl. 438) (followed) by Watson, *Records* 2:337, says that their was no "bad sound" at the end–contrary to the rules of the Hsia and the Shang whose last rulers had a very bad reputation.

[312] That the "two rulers" are King Wen and Wu is the opinion of Meng K'ang on *Han shu,* 57B.2602. See also *Shih-chi,* 117.3066. I could not find a basis for Watson's (*Records* 2: 337) idea that the Hsia and the Shang are meant although this is not impossible. The ruler who was in swaddling clothes was King Ch'eng, son of King Wu.

He [the Great Man] brought into his garden the precious herd of white tigers,[313]
And brought to the park such strange animals as the Mi 麋-deer,
Selects stalks with six heads for the kitchen,
And sacrifices animals with a pronged horn,[314]
He obtains the remnant treasure of the Chou[315] and receives a turtle on the Ch'i.[316]
Calls forth from the pond a green and yellow dragon horse.[317]
His demons and spirits contact the gods of old
And lodge in the pleasure pavilion,[318]
Extraordinary beings in strange transformations,
exhaust with their movements all possible changes.
How admirable it is,
That the auspicies have arrived here,
Yet, he still believes them to be few
And does not dare to speak about the *feng-* and *shan*-sacrifices.
Under the Chou, a leaping fish fell into a boat and [King Wu] found it so excellent

[313] See on the *tsou-yü* 騶虞 *Shih ching*, Mao #25, *Shih-san ching chu*-shu 294A-C: The poem entitled "The White Tiger" is said to have been written at a point when the relations among men were correct and the government at court in order. All under Heaven profited from the reforms of King Wen. At this point even a humane (*jen* 仁) animal as the white tiger appeared. Mao explains the animal as a "righteous" one, a white tiger with black stripes that does not eat living beings. "Only when one has the virtue of the highest trustworthiness it appears."

[314] Fu Ch'ien (*Han shu*, 57B.2603) here sees an allusion to the fact that Emperor Wu captured a white unicorn after which one of his reign periods was named.

[315] This is interpreted by Wen Ying (Takigawa, 117.95) as the tripod of the Chou after which also a reign period was named.

[316] We are following *Han shu* (57B.2602) that reads *fang* 放 for *shou* 收, a textual variant noted by Hsü Kuang in "Chi-chieh" (*Shih chi,* 117.3066, n. 16). Wen Ying commens on the Han shu passage that the Chou released turtles into the Chao Pond 沼池 who lived one thousand years before the Han obtained them.

[317] Here the opinions are very different: Chang Yi says that we are dealing with a quadriga of horses. Meng K'ang thinks that this is a manlike dragon like the one that the Yellow Emperor rode. He points to the treatise on Music in which the famous divine horse is mentioned that came from a marsh and thinks that Ssu-ma Hsiang-ju is actually talking about this horse. Yen Shih-ku rejects these ideas saying that the text just speaks about ordinary dragons.

[318] Wen Ying says that at that time Emperor Wu was looking for immortals and got a female magician from Shang-chün who was able to get into contact with ghosts and spirits. She could also cure illnesses. He set her up in the Shang-lin park and called her "Divine Lady." She resembled the Ling-yü 靈圉 [i.e. the gods] of old, and he treated her with respect in his leisure palaces und let her live there.

that he burned it in sacrifice.[319] Small was this as an omen, and yet he ascended this high mountain. Was this not shameful? How great is the difference between [their] tackling the task and our modesty?[320]

[3067] Thereupon the Grand Marshal[321] stepped forward and said:

"Your Majesty's humanness nourishes the multitude of living beings.

Your righteousness campaigns against those who were not obedient.

All the people of Hsia joyfully offer tribute,

The hundred barbarian tribes bring their presents,

In virtue you equal the [rulers] at the beginning,

In merit you come second to none.

Brilliantly your harmony spreads everywhere,

A multitude of auspicious omens in variations,

Timely responding and coming continuously,

They have not just been created for this occasion.

I have been thinking that an altar at Mount T'ai and at [Mount] Liang-fu should be erected where one waits for your visit. It should perhaps be named: "May glory be given!"[322] The powers on high have shown their grace and multiplied their blessings, intending that the offerings may be complete. [Yet] Your Majesty has been too modest and has not set out [for Mount T'ai]. You cut off the joyful [expectations] of the three spirits[323] and you are lacking the standards of the royal way. Therefore the multitude of your servants of state is ashamed. Some say that Heaven is by nature obscure. Hence when it does show precious omens, one really is not allowed to reject them. Had one still rejected them, then Mount T'ai would not have got an inscription and at Liang-fu nothing would have taken place. And would they both

---

[319] *Shih chi*, 4.120, *Grand Scribe's Records* 1:59, says that a white fish lept into the king's boat. His followers thought that this was the sign that King Wu could attack the last ruler of the Shang but he himself thought that it was still too early.

[320] The text on *Shih chi*, 4.120 does not say that the founders of the Chou ascended Mount T'ai. Yet, the commentaries on *Shih chi*, 117.3067 and *Han shu*, 57A.2604 think that they did. According to them there is even the idea that the Chou should not have ascended Mount T'ai while the Han should have.

[321] The Grand Marshal who is mentioned here should be Huo Ch'ü-ping 霍去病 who died at about the same time as Ssu-ma Hsiang-ju in 117 BC.

[322] Wen Ying explains that the names of previous rulers should be combined in order to confer glory.

[323] According to Ju Ch'un on *Han shu*, 57B.2605, these are the ghosts of earth, the gods of Heaven and the Mountains. Ssu-ma Chen on *Shih chi*, 117.3068 quotes Wei Chao who says that the three spirits are the powers on high, the T'ai-shan and the Liang-fu. The "powers on high" are sometimes translated as "God on High" but in Ch'in and Han times they apparently actually were the group of celestial emperors associated with the five directions and the five colors.

have flourished at one time and then been neglected for many generations,[324] how would it come that rhetoricians still praisingly talk about seventy-two rulers [who performed the sacrifices long] after this [took place]?[325]

Thus, to cultivate one's virtue and to get the gift of signs, to take up these signs in order to proceed to perform [the sacrifice] does not constitute a presumptuous transgression.

Therefore,

The sage kings did not abolish this,

But instead cultivated rituals for the spirits of the earth.

They approached the gods in Heaven with sincerity,

And had their merits inscribed at the Central Peak,[326]

In order to display the utmost reverence.

They promulgated flourishing virtue,

Made known their names and glory,

Received ample blessings,

And with this benefitted the black-headed people.

How magnificent are these services, [*3068*] a splendid spectacle for All under Heaven in one's strongest position. They are the ultimate legacy of a true king and are not to be disregarded. We wish that Your Majesty complete them [the sacrifices]. Thereafter you can take advantage of the various arts of the masters with red girdles, letting them grasp even the last rays and the blaze of the dazzling sun and moon in order to do their duty and fulfill the affair.[327] Then they should all correctly lay out

---

[324] Compare the introductory section of the treatise on the *feng*- and *shan*-rites (*Shih chi,* 28.1355) in which Ssu-ma Ch'ien says that there were always long periods during which the sacrifices were actually not performed. The last of these periods lasted since the beginning of the Chou.

[325] Cf. *Shih chi,* 28.1363 where Ssu-ma Ch'ien says that according to tradition there were over seventy kings who after a new clan had taken over the rule, became kings and sacrificed at the two mountains.

[326] Under the Han Central Peak was Mount Sung. Yet, there were no inscriptions there so one may wonder whether this peak is not actually Mount T'ai.

[327] This complicated sentence is explained by Wen Ying on *Han shu,* 57B.2606, quoted by P'ei Yin on *Shih chi,* 57.3069, as "You should let the scholars write down your merits and describe your work and let them look the extraordinary brightness of the last rays of sun and moon, in order to display their official duties and to perform their affairs." I think that Ssu-ma Hsiang-ju wants to say that the emperor should profit from the fact that he has good scholars at court who after the ceremony can write about it. He should give them the chance to work so hard that they make use of even the last rays of the sun. So they can show what they are able to do and arrange everything that has to do with this sacrifice. Maybe the point is that they have to care about what takes place at the sites after the actual performance by the emperor. See for the men with "red girdles" also the passage on *Shih chi,* 28.1398 where the ceremonies at Mount T'ai are described in detail.

the meaning [of the sacrifice], edit and embellish the relevant texts, create a chronicle [of matters related to *feng*- and *shan*-rituals] as one new discipline,[328] in order to add to the old [canon] of six [disciplines] a seventh one. It should be propagated forever in order to let ten thousand generations get the chance to be submerged in this pure stream, to drift in its subtle waves, to let blossoms of its repute fly and to make the fruits leap forth in profusion. The former sages forever preserved a name of fame and are always praised first, precisely because of this. You should order the authorities on ancient matters to memorialize all the relevant meanings of [this ceremony] and read them.

[3070] Thereupon the Son of Heaven in a preoccupied way changed his expression and said: "Ah! We will try it." Only then did he shift his thoughts [to the subject] and consider it again. Only after he had combined the advice of the excellencies and ministers and looked into the matters of the *feng*- and *shan*-sacrifices, had songs sung on the vastness of the great nourishing influence and thereby elaborating the richness of the auspicies, did he compose a praise song which ran:

Since Heaven covered Us,
Clouds have drifted,
Sweet dew came and timely rain,
So that one could freely roam in this territory,
Enriching liquids seep into the earth.
Which living being is not nourished by this?
Splendid stalks [of grain] with six heads,
Where shall We store our harvest?

It does not just rain on it [the territory],
But it also moistens and enriches it;
It does not just soak it,
But diffuses everywhere.[329]
All the ten thousand beings rejoice,
Cherish and admire it.
Illustrious places like famous mountains
Wait for the lord to come.
Oh lord, oh lord,
Why do you not come for an inspection tour?

[3071]

---

[328] Meng K'ang quoted on *Han shu*, 57B.2606 says that the *Spring and Autumn Annals* (here translated as "chronicle") correct the Heavenly seasons and arrange the affairs of men. The scholars should do the same in their new discipline.

[329] This is the understanding of Hu Kuang 胡廣 (91–172), quoted in the "So-yin."

The striped animal,[330]
Enjoys our lord's park,
White its complexion, black the ornament,
Its manner fills one with joy;
Gentle and reverent,
The capability of a superior man.
We had heard of its fame
Now we see that it came.
The way it took can not be followed,
Proof, it's a portent from Heaven.
This also was with Shun,
And the "[White] Tiger"[331] clan rose from it.

The stout unicorn,
Roamed about at this spiritual altar.
In early winter, the tenth moon,
The lord set up the sacrifices in the suburb,[332]
It is racing with our lord's chariot,
Celebrated and blessed by the powers.
Since before the Three Eras,[333]
Surely this has never happened.

Sporting, the yellow dragon-horse,
Reared up at His virtue,[334]
Its colors sparkle,
Glimmering, glittering, shine like fire.
The rightest light is to be seen in its brilliance,[335]

---

[330] Hu Kuang quoted ("So-yin") explains that this is the "white tiger" mentioned above.

[331] The word for the "white tiger" is "tsou-yü" 騶虞. The character for "yü" 虞 is also the character used for the clan name of Emperor Shun.

[332] On *Shih chi*, 12.457 (*Grand Scribe's Records*, 2:226) and 28.1387 a suburban sacrifice (*chiao* 郊) is mentioned when a one-horned animal appeared. On *Shih chi*, 28.1387 Ssu-ma Ch'ien speaks of a suburban sacrifice to Heaven at which Hou-chi, the founder of the Chou lineage, received offerings. In late Western Han times the yearly suburban sacrifices to Heaven and Earth became a major part of the state cult (see Michael Loewe, *Crisis and Conflict in Han China* [London: George Allen and Unwin, 1974], pp. 167ff. and Marianne Bujard, *Le sacrifice au ciel dans la Chine ancienne* [Paris: École Française d'Extrême-Orient, 2000]).

[333] Obviously the time of Yao, Shun, and Yü.

[334] See on the horses that the Han got in Central Asia on *Shih chi*, 24.1178.

Awakening and enlightening the black-headed people.
In a record it is written,
This is the one who carries the mandate.[336]

[3072]
This is supported by clear evidence,
It is unnecessary to drone on.
Through simile and metaphor,
It instructs Us to offer the *feng*-sacrifice at the mountain.

If we open the scriptures and look at them, [we find] that the realms of Heaven and man already interact,[337] and that above and below inspire each other in concert. By the virtue of the sage kings there was respect and good order.[338] Therefore it is said: "When you have risen think about decline, when you are secure think about danger."[339] Therefore, although T'ang and Wu were most revered and stern, they did not neglect to be reverent to the earth spirits; Shun, as can be observed in the old statutes, reflected on whether he had left out something.[340] This is what it meant [by the above saying].

In the fifth year after Ssu-ma Hsiang-ju had died, the Son-of-Heaven for the first time sacrificed at the Altar of the Earth (113 BC). In the eighth year (110 BC) he

---

[335] Wen Ying explains "light" (*yang* 陽) as "brilliance" and adds that this means the sovereign turns south and holds an audience." The stana seems to allude to the *Book of Changes*, first hexagram: the first line speaks of a hidden dragon, doing nothing which means that "*yang* (the light) is still below." The second line says that the "dragon appears in the field" and that this means that "it is advantageous to appear in front of the great man." The same is said about the fifth line of the hexagram, traditionally associated with the ruler: "A flying dragon in the sky: It is advantageous to appear in front of the great man."

[336] Ju Ch'un on *Shih chi*, 117.3072 points to the fact that since the Han had the element "earth," a "yellow" dragon came in response. This could be seen when under Emperor Wen a yellow dragon came to Ch'eng-chi 成紀, a district in northwestern Lung-hsi 隴西 (see *Shih chi*, 10. 429–30, 28.1381 and *Han shu*, 4.127 and 25A.1212). Yen Shih-ku on *Han shu*, 57.2608 refers to the *Yi-ching*: "At times he rides six dragons in order to govern Heaven." See the T'uan commentary to the first hexagram.

[337] The famous "realms of Heaven and man" are also mentioned by Ssu-ma Ch'ien in his postface to the *Shih chi* (*Shih chi*, 130.3319) and in his letter to Jen An on *Han shu*, 62.2735. One of his main goals is to find out about these realms.

[338] "Respect" 兢兢 and "good order" 翼翼 are both to be found often in the *Odes*.

[339] Compare *Yi Chou-shu hui-chiao chi-chu* 逸周書彙校集注 (Shanghai: Shang-hai Ku-chi, 1995), 12.193: "When you are secure think about peril, at the beginning think about the end."

[340] Following the interpretation of Yen Shih-ku on *Han shu* 57B.2609.

finally paid respect to the Central Peak for the first time, brought a *feng*-sacrifice to Mount T'ai and proceeded to Mount Liang-fu in order to give a *shan*-sacrifice at the Su-jan 肅然.[341]

[3073] I have not included in this chapter other writings by [Ssu-ma] Hsiang-ju, such as the "Yi P'ing-ling Hou shu" 遺平陵侯書 (Letter left for the Marquis of P'ing-ling),[342] "Yü Wu-kung-tzu hsiang-nan" 與五公子相難 (Critique of the Five Princes), and the "Ts'ao-mu shu" 草木書 (Writing on Herbs and Trees). I just included those that are most well known among the excellencies and ministers.

His Honor the Grand Scribe says: "The *Spring and Autumn Annals* let one deduce the most hidden things. The *Changes* are rooted[343] in hiding them so as to make them obvious. Although the *Greater Elegantiae* speak about Kings, Dukes and great men, the virtue of this reaches down to the black-headed commoners. The *Lesser Elegantiae* criticizes the mistakes of the small self, but it reaches those above. Although what they speak about may externally be very different, in their accord with virtue they are one. Although [Ssu-ma] Hsiang-ju used many empty expressions and superfluous speeches, his main aim was to draw [the ruler] to moderation and frugality.[344] Where in this should there be a difference to the indirect admonishments of the *Odes*?

Yang Hsiung was of the opinion that a beautifully worded *Fu* encouraged a hundred times but indirectly criticized only once. He thought that this was like racing

---

[341] On these places see Chavannes, 3:474–76, and 500–501; Dubs, *History of the Former Han Dynasty* 2, pp. 86–88, and Hervouet, *Poète de cour*, pp. 198–209. The dates are slightly confused since the sacrifice to Hou-t'u took place in 114 while the *feng*-sacrifice was in 110, four, not three years after the sacrifice to Hou-t'u as one should think when reading that this took place in the 8th year after the death of Ssu-ma Hsiang-ju. Hervouet has calculated that Ssu-ma Hsiang-ju must have died in 117 BC which fits well the eighth year, but not the fifth year for the sacrifice to Hou-t'u. See *Le chapitre 117*, p. 227, n.1.

[342] Hsü Kuang ("Chi-chieh") says that this was Su Chien 蘇建, on whom see *Han shu*, 54.2459.

[343] The editors of *Han shu*, 57B.2609, obviously because the *Spring and Autumn Annals*, the *Greater* and the *Lesser Elegantiae* all are titles with two characters, think that Yi pen 易本 also should be a text, maybe the "*Basic Text of the Changes*." However, I think it is more logical to take "pen" as a verb here.

[344] Compare the biography of Tsou Yen 鄒衍, *Grand Scribe's Records* 7:181, n. 25, which shows that Ssu-ma Ch'ien thought of Tsou in a similar way as of Ssu-ma Hsiang-ju.

through the sounds from Cheng and Wei[345] and then when the melody was over to intone an elegant piece. Is that not benighted?[346]

I have collected those of his words that are worthy of discussion and have written them down in this chapter.

*   *   *   *   *

The affairs of Master Empty and the persuasions of the great man were so beautiful that they were often exaggerated. Yet, their intent was to criticize and admonish [the sovereign] to turn to non-action. Thus I made the memoir of Ssu-ma Hsiang-ju.[347]

---

[345] Ssu-ma Ch'ien several times talks about the tones or notes from Cheng and Wei 鄭衛之音 (see especially on *Shih chi,* 130.3305, in his preface to the treatise on music, but also on *Shih chi,* 24.1176, 1182 and 1221, *Shih chi,* 87.2544). Famously, under Emperor Ai of the Han, the Bureau of Music was abolished with the argument that one had played the music of Cheng and Wei there. See on *Han shu,* 22.1073–74.

[346] Unless this chapter was written by Pan Ku, not by Ssu-ma Ch'ien, which we do not assume (see the translator's note), this last paragraph was added by a later hand. Maybe it was a commentary that crept into the main text. We do not know whether the sentence "Is that not benighted" is Yang Hsiung's final comment on those who make Fu or whether it is a comment by someone who criticized Yang Hsiung. Yang Hsiung's famous critical remarks on the Fu are to be found in the first and second paragraph of the second chapter "My master" of the *Fa-yen*.

[347] These are the reasons offered for the composition of this chapter on *Shih chi,* 130.3318:子虛之事，大人賦說，靡麗多誇，然其指風諫，歸於無為。作司馬相如列傳第五十七.

Translator's Note

Chapter 117, the biography of Ssu-ma Hsiang-ju, stands at a crucial position in Ssu-ma Ch'ien's *Shih chi*. With the exception of the chapter on *Ta-yüan* (*Shih chi* 123), it marks the end of the chapters concerned with the expansion of the Han empire. Ssu-ma Hsiang-ju was a protagonist of the expansion in the Southwest, which is described in chapter 116 just before his biography. After the chapter on Ssu-ma Hsiang-ju there follow the biographies of the kings of Huai-nan and Heng-shan and their rebellions (*Shih chi* 118) and then, starting with the "Reasonable Officials" (*Shih chi* 119), the so-called collective biographies (although chapter 120 on Chi An and Cheng Tang-shih exceptionally is devoted to two individuals). So Ssu-ma Hsiang-ju's biography marks a sharp division in the entire book. Pan Ku seems to have imitated Ssu-ma Ch'ien's sequence when he wrote his *Han shu* in which he gave the biography of Ssu-ma Hsiang-ju number 57 and the biography of Yang Hsiung, his countryman from Shu who like Ssu-ma Hsiang-ju was a famous *Fu* poet, number 87, before his collective biographies and the chapters on the expansion start.[348]

The format of the chapter itself is quite unusual. Although it is the longest of all chapters in the *lieh-chuan* section, contrary to most other chapters in the *Shih chi* its narrative is rather limited: We learn that Ssu-ma Hsiang-ju came from Shu but we do not hear anything about his ancestry. After a brief account of his career as a poet at the court of King Hsiao of Liang, Emperor Wen's younger brother, there follows the romantic story of his affair and marriage with Cho Wen-chün, the daughter of Cho Wang-sun, a rich merchant from Shu. Most of the first half of the chapter is then made up of two *fu*-poems, the *Fu* on Master Empty and the one on the Imperial Hunting Park. A few sentences follow on Ssu-ma Hsiang-ju's mission to Szechuan where he had to reprimand the imperial envoy for his harshness, but where he also took the opportunity to issue a long "mobilization order" addressed to the people from Pa and Shu in which he both apologized for damage that was done while also basically justifing the Han expedition. Upon his return Ssu-ma Hsiang-ju endorsed further expansion into the territory of the Southwestern tribes and was sent there again. As there were protests against this move in Shu and at court, Ssu-ma Hsiang-ju had to write a long text in which he again justified his opinion. For this purpose he constructed a ficticious dialogue between the elders from Pa and Shu and himself. Only a few sentences after this text we again find a literary text, namely Ssu-ma

---

[348] On this see van Ess, *Politik*, pp. 726–728.

Hsiang-ju's admonishment against hunting.

All the texts just mentioned are also to be found in China's most important anthology of early literary writings, the *Wen-hsüan*. This is not true for the next two pieces to be found in the biography, namely Ssu-ma Hsiang-ju's *Fu* "Lamenting the Mistakes of the Second Emperor" and the "*Fu* on the Great Man," a satirical piece on Emperor Wu of the Han that relies heavily on the language of the "Yüan-yu" poem from the *Songs of the South*. Although Emperor Wu took it seriously, the reader will notice that the text is full of exaggerations which suggest that it was not meant to praise. The chapter ends with yet another text, Ssu-ma Hsiang-ju's suggestion to conduct the *feng-* and *shan*-sacrifices.

This last text that is said to have been discovered postumously in Ssu-ma Hsiang-ju's house links the poet to the other two Ssu-ma, T'an and Ch'ien, both of whom also strongly argued in favor of the *feng-* and *shan*-sacrifices that Emperor Wu was to perform for the first time in 110 BC, seven years after Ssu-ma Hsiang-ju's death. The unusual lack of a genealogy in Ssu-ma Hsiang-ju's biography, too, may be seen as an indicator that Ssu-ma Ch'ien was telling here the story of a distant member of the family, and the fact that Ssu-ma Hsiang-ju in his youth studied swordmanship is a further hint that he may have been related to the Ssu-ma branch in Chao that was also known for its expertise in this profession.[349] So Ssu-ma Ch'ien actually may have placed the biography of a relative at a crucial juncture where something new begins in his book.

However, some scholars have raised doubts about the authenticity of the Ssu-ma Hsiang-ju chapter. They have suggested that it may have actually been written by Pan Ku and recopied into the *Shih chi* by a later hand. One of the reasons for this is the eulogy at the end of the text which contains a comment by Yang Hsiung who, as is well-known, lived long after Ssu-ma Hsiang-ju. In addition, Yves Hervouet has shown that many characters especially of the *Fu* in Ssu-ma Hsiang-ju's biography look older in the *Han shu* version.[350] Moreover, it has been argued that to compose a biography basically out of literary texts was something very unusual for the *Shih chi* but very common for the *Han shu.* On the other hand, the Yang Hsiung comment may just have been a commentary that has crept into the text. This is what the otherwise extremely critical Ts'ui Shih 崔適 (1852–1924) thought[351] who after all was the man

---

[349] See on *Shih chi* 130.3286.

[350] Hervouet, "La valeur relative."

[351] Ts'ui Shih, *Shih chi t'an-yüan* 史記探源 (Peking: Chung-hua Shu-chü, 1986), pp. 210f. See also the opinion of Wang Ming-sheng 王鳴盛 (1722–1797) on Yang Yen-ch'i 楊燕起, Ch'en K'o-ch'ing 陳可青 and Lai Chang-yang 賴長揚, *Shih chi chi-p'ing* 史記集評 (Peking 2005; repr. of *Li-tai ming-chia p'ing Shih chi* 歷代名家評史記 [Peking: Pei-ching Shih-fan Ta-hsüeh Ch'u-pan-she, 1986]), p. 517, who thought that the comment by Yang Hsiung came from the hand of Pan Ku and was inserted into Ssu-ma Ch'ien's text by an unknown person.

who brought up the theory that *Shih chi* may have borrowed from *Han shu*, not the other way round. While saying that in many cases the *Han shu* version looks older than the one preserved in *Shih chi*, Hervouet has also shown that there are instances where *Shih chi* chapter 117 seems to have the earlier version of the text.[352] This suggests that textual differences were caused by different ways of transmission of *Shih chi* and *Han shu* and do not go back directly to their authors. Finally, there are actually many more memoirs in *Shih chi* that draw heavily on literary writings—examples are the memoir of Han Fei in chapter 63, the one of Yüeh Yi in chapter 80, and to some extent also the one on Li Ssu in chapter 87. Thus, the arguments against Ssu-ma Ch'ien as the author of this chapter are not very conclusive. So we suggest accepting the chapter as authentic.

Another important question is related to Ssu-ma Hsiang-ju's *Fu*: Were they written to praise? Are they panegyrical?[353] Or is the traditional claim true that they were actually critical? Attached to these questions is a larger problem: Why were these texts included in a book on history? Ssu-ma Ch'ien usually included in his book texts that were related to history. This seems also to have been true for the texts of Ssu-ma Hsiang-ju, which have a deeper political sense attached to them. Both *Fu* on hunting parks were written in periods when military adventures loomed large in the states of their respective addressees. Not only in China, but in all ancient cultures, hunting has been a metaphor for war; moreover, as ritual texts say and later nomadic empires show, in China hunting was used as a training for war. So there may be good reason to take the concluding paragraph of the *Fu* on the Imperial Hunting park, which warns against extravagant hunting expeditions, at face value. Here, Ssu-ma Hsiang-ju tells his emperor that after all his splendid wars he should return to civil government. The same may be true for the *Fu* on the Great Man which may well be a hyperbolic comment on journeys that the emperor embarked on with the help of his armies, campaigns that ventured deep into hitherto unknown territories, or the aide of his magicians and specialists who were in search of immortality for him.

There are some small hints at the end of Ssu-ma Hsiang-ju's biography which indicate that he may have had problems with his emperor just as Ssu-ma Ch'ien did.[354] On p. 3063 Ssu-ma Ch'ien says that Ssu-ma Hsiang-ju, after having written the *Fu* on the Great Man, retired because of an illness. This was one of the usual excuses for those who did not want to serve any longer. His family moved to Mao-ling, the place where Emperor Wu erected his mausoleum. At the same time, this was also the place where following a proposal made by Chu-fu Yen all the troublemakers in the

---

[352] Hervouet, "La valeur relative".

[353] This is Martin Kern's position (see his "Western Han Aesthetics" in Bibliography).

[354] The following interpretations follow an email received from William Nienhauser on October 2, 2014.

empire were transferred.[355] Thus, it seems plausible that Emperor Wu, after having been so pleased with the *Fu* on the Great Man at first, had realized that Ssu-ma Hsiang-ju had actually criticized him.

The passage on the search for writings in Ssu-ma Hsiang-ju's house that follows is also ambiguous. At first sight one may think that the Son of Heaven liked Ssu-ma Hsiang-ju's works so much that he desperately wanted to get more of them before Ssu-ma Hsiang-ju's death. On the other hand, it is also possible that the emperor wanted to find out whether there was any proof of Ssu-ma Hsiang-ju's disloyalty. He sent a person called "The One to whom one is Loyal" (So Chung 所忠)[356] to make a search, but no writings were found. The name of the envoy is more than strange, and although later commentators plausibly suggest that So was a *cognomen* and Chung a *praenomen*,[357] it remains possible that the historian chose this name for a person whose real name he did not know or wanted to conceal because he may have been a relative.[358] In the end, So Chung found only the text that Ssu-ma Hsiang-ju had written on the *feng*- and *shan*-sacrifices and that conveyed by and large ideas that Ssu-ma T'an and Ch'ien themselves shared. So it might be that the Emperor sent a trusted servant who was at the same time related to the Ssu-ma in order to find evidence for Ssu-ma Hsiang-ju's being loyal or disloyal. Yet the only evidence the servant then produced was a writing on a subject the Ssu-ma preferred.

The remaining important question is, of course, what Ssu-ma Ch'ien thought of Ssu-ma Hsiang-ju. Several Ch'ing era literai have noted that Ssu-ma Ch'ien in his treatise of the economy was openly critical of Ssu-ma Hsiang-ju's advice to open a road through the lands of the Southwestern barbarians.[359] On the other hand, it is obvious that Ssu-ma Ch'ien must have liked Ssu-ma Hsiang-ju's text on the *feng*- and *shan*-sacrifices. It seems that to the historian Ssu-ma Hsiang-ju was in fact a controversial figure who combined good and bad characteristics.

---

[355] See on *Shih chi* 112.2961. Compare also on *Shih chi* 122.3138 and 124.3187. According to a commentary to *Shih chi* 130.3287, Ssu-ma T'an also was in Mao-ling when he was promoted to become Grand Scribe.

[356] Compare on *Shih chi* 87.2560. On So Chung see the remarks by Dorothee Schaab-Hanke, "The Power of an Alleged Tradition,"in *Der Geschichtsschreiber als Exeget* (first in *BMEFA* 74 [2002], 243-290), (Gossenberg 2010), pp. 303 and 329.

[357] See on *Shih chi* 30.1437, 59.2101.

[358] On *Shih chi* 12.468 and 28.1393 Ssu-ma Ch'ien mentions that So Chung told the emperor that he should not rely on the words of a *fang-shih* on immortality, which suggests that he shared the convictions of the Ssu-ma who were also opposed to *fang-shih*.

[359] See *Shih chi* 30.1420. Compare *Shih chi chi-p'ing*, pp. 571-72. Wu Ju-lun 吳汝綸 (1840–1903), ibid., p. 573, thinks that Ssu-ma Hsiang-ju was not in favor of the expedition and that he had to perform it only because he had been asked to do so by the emperor.

Bibliography

Translations

Aoki, 12:240–375.

Hervouet, Yves. *Le chapitre 117 du Che-ki (Biographie de Sseu-ma Siang-jou)*. Paris: Paris: Presses Universitaires de France, 1972.

Knechtges, David R. *Wenxuan or Selections of Refined Literature. Volume 2: Rhapsodies on Sacrifices, Hunting, Travel, Sightseeing, Palaces and Halls, Rivers and Seas*. Princeton: Princeton University Press, 1987, 2:53–114. The *Fu*.

Noguchi Sadao 野口定男. *Shiki retsuden* 史記列伝. Tokyo, 2011, pp. 142–188.

Ogawa Tamaki 小川環樹 *et al. Shiki retsuden* 史記列伝. Tokyo: Iwanami Bunko, 1975, pp. 154–227.

Watson, *Records* 2:297–342

von Zach, Erwin Ritter. *Die chinesische Anthologie*. Cambridge: Harvard University Press, 1958.

Studies

Hervouet, Yves. *Un poète de cour sous le Han: Sseu-ma Siang-jou*, Paris: Presses Universitaires de France, 1964.

___, "La valeur relative des textes du *Che Ki* et du *Han Chou*," in *Mélanges de Sinologie offerts a Monsieur Paul Demieville*, Vol. II, Paris: Paris: Presses Universitaires de France, 1974, pp. 55–76.

Kern, Martin. "The 'Biography of Sima Xiangru' and the Question of the *Fu* in Sima Qian's *Shiji*." *Journal of the American Oriental Society* 123.2 (2003): 303–316.

___, "Western Han Aesthetics and the Genesis of the *Fu*." *Harvard Journal of Asiatic Studies* 63.2 (2003): 383–437.

[The Kings of] Huai-nan and Heng-shan, Memoir 58

translated by Marc Nürnberger

Liu Ch'ang

[118.3075] [Liu] Ch'ang [劉]長 (d. 174 BC, r. 196–174 BC), King Li 厲 of Huai-nan 淮南, was a younger son of Kao-tsu 高祖.[1] His mother was formerly a Beautiful Lady 美人 of Chang Ao 張敖, the King of Chao 趙王 (d. 182 BC, r. 202–198 BC).

In the eighth year of Kao-tsu (199 BC), when [Kao-tsu] passed Chao 趙 coming from Tung-yüan 東垣,[2] the King of Chao presented him with Beautiful Ladies.[3] [After] the mother of King Li was favored by him, she was with child. [Chang] Ao, the King of Chao, did not dare to take her inside the palace [again]; he build an outer palace for her and housed her there. When it came to Kuan Kao 貫高 and others' plotting a rebellion and the incident at Po-jen 柏人 was discovered,[4] and the King was

---

[1] Liu Ch'ang 劉長 was the seventh son of Liu Pang 劉邦. Wang Shu-min (118.3199) refers to the taboo practice of the *Huai-nan Tzu* that replaced all 長 characters with a *hsiu* 修 whenever it was used in the sense of "long" and not "mature" to show that his *praenomen* should be accordingly pronounced: "Ch'ang." See also the *Han shu* parallel (44.2135-45) and his entry in Loewe, *Dictionary*, pp. 271–73, and the parallel account of the life and death of the King of Huai–nan, on *Shih chi*, 101.2738–39 (*Grand Scribe's Records*, 8:328–30).

[2] Tung-yüan is located five miles northwest of modern Shih-chia-chuang 石家庄 in Hopeh (Tan Ch'i-hsiang, 2:26). Liu Pang went there to fight against the "remaining rebels" of Han Hsin 韓信. Later on, Liu Pang changed the name of the place to Chen-ting 真定 [Truly Stabilized]. According to "So-yin" (118.3075), Chen-ting, former Tung-yüan, was also the hometown of Liu Ch'ang's mother, who was buried there after her suicide.

[3] As the following anecdote reveals, one of these Beautiful Ladies would probably have come from the Chao 趙 family of Tung-yüan.

[4] The King apparently still treated the Emperor with greatest honors and remained grateful, while Kuan Kao 貫高, an old companion of Chang Erh and Chancellor to his son, felt deeply insulted by the way Liu Pang had treated Chang Ao on his visit in 200 BC (see *Shih chi*,

also captured and tried, the King's mother, brothers, and Beautiful Ladies were all taken into custody, and detained in Ho-nei 河內.[5] When the mother of King Li was also detained, she informed the official saying: "I was favored by the Sovereign, I am with child." The official made this known to the Sovereign and the Sovereign just at this time became angry with the King of Chao, but he had not yet settled [the case of] the mother of King Li. Chao Chien 趙兼, the younger brother of the mother of King Li,[6] relied on the Marquis of Pi-yang 辟陽[7] [Shen Yi-chi 審食其] to speak of this to

89.2583). At the age of over sixty years, he wanted to murder the Emperor in order to restore the dignity of his King together with his colleague Chao Wu 趙午. Ignoring the King's explicit interdiction, they laid an ambush at Po-jen 柏人 (located about fifty miles south of modern Shih-chia-chuang 石家庄 in Hopeh; see T'an Ch'i-hsiang, 2:26), hiding an assassin within the side walls of the local post station in 199 BC. But Liu Pang had a premonition to avoid this stop and chose another route. One year later, the failed scheme was made known to the Sovereign by an old enemy of Kuan Kao and led to the subsequent arrest of all parties involved. As opposed to his collaborators, Kuan Kao chose imprisonment over suicide in order to convince the Emperor that his King was not involved in their plotting. Only when he had accomplished Chang Ao's release, and despite the Emperor's pardon, did he end his own life, deeming himself no longer fit to serve his King. See also *Shih chi*, 89.2583–5 (*Grand Scribe's Records*, 7:20–23) and his entry in Loewe, *Dictionary*, p. 135.

Chou Shou-ch'ang 周壽昌 (1814–1884; cited in Takigawa, 118.2) calculates that if Liu Pang passed Chao in the winter of the eighth year (199 BC) and the assassination plot of Kuan Kao was discovered in the twelfth month of the ninth year (198 B.C; according to *Han shu*, 1B.67), the child would have been already born by then.

[5] Ho-nei is the name of a commandery situated north of the bow of the Huang Ho, established in 205 BC on the former grounds of the short-lived state of Yin 殷, a fief awarded to the Chao General Ssu-ma Ang 司馬卬 (d. 205) by Hsiang Yü 項羽.

[6] Chao Chien 趙兼 was enfeoffed as Marquis of Chou-yang 周陽侯 in 179 BC (see *Shih chi*, 8.421), but lost his title again in 174 BC, being accused of an unspecified crime. His son Yu 由 adopted the name of Chou-yang as his *cognomen* and became one of the most feared cruel officials under Wu-ti (see *Shih chi*, 122.3135–6). Wang Shu-min (118.3199) notes that his name is recorded as Chao Lien 趙廉 in the *Han chi* 漢紀, 7.7b, SPTK. See also Loewe, *Dictionary*, p. 708.

[7] Shen Yi-chi 審食其, a man of P'ei 沛, served originally in the entourage of the future Empress Lü (*Shih chi*, 18.926), when they became hostages of Hsiang Yü's 項羽 troops (*Shih chi*, 7.322). He was enfeoffed as Marquis of Pi-yang 辟陽 in 201 B.C, and rose to great power in his service as the Chancellor to the Left when Empress Lü took control of the empire (*Shih chi*, 22.1123). According to his entry on *Shih chi*, 18.926, his posthumous name was the rather unflattering title Yu-hou 幽侯 [The Obscuring Marquis] remeniscent of the dubitable role he played during the reign of Empress Lü. See also Loewe, *Dictionary*, pp. 470–71.

Lü Hou 呂后 (Empress Lü, r. 188–180),[8] [but] Lü Hou was jealous; she was not willing to explain [the situation to the Sovereign], and the Marquis of Pi-yang was not forcefully arguing [for the mother of King Li]. When it came that[9] the mother of King Li had already born King Li, she was in rage,[10] and then killed herself. When the officials held King Li up and presented him to the Sovereign,[11] the Sovereign had regrets[12]; he ordered Lü Hou to be a mother to him, and had the mother of King Li buried at Chen-ting 真定.[13] As for Chen-ting, the family of the mother of King Li was located there, and it had been the county of [her] fathers for generations.[14]

In the seventh month of the eleventh year of Kao-tsu [196 BC],[15] when Ch'ing Pu 黥布,[16] the King of Huai-nan, revolted, [Kao-tsu] enthroned his son [Liu] Ch'ang

---

[8] Lü Hou 呂后 (Empress Lü) was determined to take power after the death of Kao-tsu and the accession of her weak son Hsiao Hui-ti. Her wrath against the former favorites of her husband is well represented in the tragedy of the "human pig," a nickname given to Beauty Ch'i 戚, who was maimed by the Empress in the most barbarous way and made to live like a pig in the privy (Shih chi, 9.397, Grand Scribe's Records, 2:109–11). See Shih chi chapter 9 [Grand Scribe's Records, 2:105–44] and Loewe, Dictionary, pp. 426–29.

[9] As Takigawa (118.2) notes, Han shu (14.2135) has deleted the conjunction "when it came that" (chi 及), thus removing the original stress on the fact that she had not only been pregnant but actually had born him a healthy child.

[10] "Rage" (hui 恚) and "rancor" (yüan 怨) seem to be the traits of character that led to drastic consequences in this line of the Liu Clan.

[11] Wang Shu-min (118.3200) notes, that the Han chi (7.8a, SPTK) reads: 趙廉奉厲王詣長安 "Chao Lien [i.e., her younger brother who is called Chao Chien in the Shi chi] held King Li up and presented him at Ch'ang-an."

[12] According to "Cheng-yi," this indicates that the Emperor: 悔不理厲王母 "regretted that he had not paid attention to King Li's mother."

[13] Chen-ting 真定 was the later name of Tung-yüan mentioned above.

[14] "So-yin" refers the reader to the Han shu parallel (44.2135) that substituted the last part of the sentence reading: 厲王母家縣也 "it was the county of King Li's mother's family," and then explains the Shih chi wording by paraphrasing: 父祖代居真定 "[her] ancestors had dwelled for generations at Chen-ting." Considering the cognomen of her brother, this information could be an indirect hint that Liu Ch'ang's mother came for the Tung-yüan branch of the Chao family.

[15] The Chung-hua editors have emendated the original "tenth month" against the date given on Shih chi, 8.389–in accordance to Ch'en Jen-hsi's 陳仁錫 suggestion (cited in Takigawa, 118.3) and Wang Shu-min (118.3200), who reminds the reader of the similarity between the old characters for "seven" and "ten."

[16] Ch'ing Pu 黥布 (Pu, the Tattooed) was another name for Ying Pu 英布. Once a convict-laborer at Mount Li, he rose from a band of robbers into the service of Hsiang Yü. Possessing considerable military ability, he became a powerful supporter of Hsiang Yü's cause and his later defection to Liu Pang was a crucial blow to Hsiang Yü's campaign. In the year

[劉]長 as King of Huai-nan, to rule over Ching Pu's former territory, altogether four commanderies.[17] The Sovereign [*3076*] personally led troops to attack and wipe out [Ch'ing] Pu, after all this, King Li succeeded to the throne.[18] As King Li had early lost his mother, he always attached himself to Lü Hou, and for this reason, in the time of Hsiao Hui 孝惠 [The Filial and Kind (Emperor), 210–188 BC, r. 195–188][19] and Lü Hou, he gained [her] favor, did not have any worries and did not suffer any harm; and yet in his heart he always harbored resentment toward the Marquis of Pi-yang 辟陽, [but] he did not dare to vent [his feelings]. When it came that Hsiao Wen-ti 孝文帝 [The Filial and Cultured Emperor, Liu Heng 劉恆, r. 180–157][20] first acceded to the throne, the King of Huai-nan considered himself to be the relative that was closest to him,[21] became arrogant and obstinate, and did several times not follow the law.[22] The Sovereign, since he was his relative, often tolerated and pardoned him.

In the third year (177 BC), he entered the court [to pay respects]. He behaved extremely overbearingly. Following the Sovereign he entered the preserves and enclosures[23] and hunted, sharing a carriage with the Sovereign,[24] and always calling

---

203 BC he was made King of Huai-nan and supported Liu Pang to become the new emperor. How long, if ever, he had been harboring disloyal thoughts before he was accused of "plotting a rebellion" in 196 BC is difficult to tell. In the end, Ying Pu was slandered by one of his own Palace Attendants who feared for his life, after being accused of having an affair with the King's favorite consort. When Ying Pu and Liu Pang finally met in battle and Ying was asked for his reason to rebel, he replied: "It is just that I want to be Emperor"–which probably was merely a laconic answer to taunt the Emperor. See also his biography on *Shih chi* chapter 91 and Loewe, *Dictionary*, pp. 651–52.

[17] According to Hsü Kuang (cited in "Chi-chieh"), Huai-nan comprised Chiu-chiang 九江, Lu-chiang 廬江, Heng-shan 衡山, and Yü-chang 豫章 at that time.

[18] For a detailed account of the events of his campaign see *Shih chi*, 91.2604–2606 (*Grand Scribe's Records*, 8.56–61).

[19] Liu Ying 劉盈, the only son of Kao-tsu and his principal consort Empress Lü, became Heir in 205 and succeeded Kao-tsu after his death as emperor. He never escaped the domination of his mother. For further biographical information see *Shih chi* chapter 9 and his entry in Loewe, *Dictionary*, pp. 397–79.

[20] For further biographical information see *Shih chi* chapter 8 and his entry in Loewe, *Dictionary*, pp. 306–11.

[21] As Yen Shih-ku (cited in Takigawa, 118.3) observes, Liu Ch'ang and Wen-ti were by 180 BC the only survivors of Liu Pang's eight sons.

[22] The "Cheng-yi" Commentary (cited only in Takigawa, 118.3118) to this line glosses *chiao chien* 驕蹇 as *pu hsün shun* 不巽順 ("not obedient").

[23] The near-synonym characters of the compound *yüan-yu* 苑囿 (previously translated as "(royal) gardens and menageries") are glossed in contradicting ways, although there is a general agreement that both refer to sometimes large areas belonging exclusively to the ruler or his feudal lords (*chin yüan* 禁苑), used for raising animals, often serving as a hunting

the Sovereign "Big Brother." King Li had abilities and strengths, and only when [his] strength was sufficient to lift a tripod,[25] did he go to pay the Marquis of Pi-yang 辟陽 a visit. When the Marquis of Pi-yang appeared to received him, he immediately took a metal hammer from his sleeve, hammered down the Marquis of Pi-yang,[26] and had his follower, Wei Ching 魏敬,[27] cut [the Marquis of Pi-yang's] throat.[28] Then King Li hastened to flee to the palace gate, bared his torso and offered apologies [for his offenses] saying: "Your servant's mother did not deserve to be tried before the law for the incident at Chao 趙, at that time Marquis of Pi-yang had the power to have gotten [her release][29] from Lü Hou, but he did not argue against it[30]—this was the first

reserve (*lieh yüan* 獵苑): Kao Yu 高誘 (3rd cent.) posits in his commentary to the *Huai-nan Tzu* 淮南子, 8.8b, *SPTK*, that a *yu* 囿, as opposed to a *yüan* 苑, is without walls, while Hsü Shen's 許慎 (58?–147?) *Shuo-wen chieh-tzu* 說文解字 (6a.4a, *SPTK*) and Ku Yeh-wang's 顧野王 (5l9–581) [*Ta-kuang yi-hui*] *Yü-p'ien* [大廣益會]玉篇 (29.3a, *SPTK*), claim the exact opposite. Taking a diachronic approach, Chia Ku-yen 賈公彦 (7th cent.) explains in his subcommentary to the *Chou li* 周禮 that *yu* simply was the ancient term for what the Han would call *yüan* (*Chou li chu shu* 周禮注疏 9.21b, *SKCS*). The different glosses transmitted in Huilin's 慧琳 (737–820) *Yi-ch'ieh ching yin yi* 一切經音義, *j.* 28 (*T.* 2128, vol. 54, p. 493a) add a further aspect suggesting that there might have been a difference in the animal population: Maybe *yu* 囿 were used for cattle and horses, *yüan* 苑 for birds and other quadrupeds (*shou* 獸), as referred by the *Ts'ang chieh p'ien* 倉頡篇; yet other sources hold that *yu* 囿 were either meant for elaphures (*milu* 麋鹿), or just (all kinds) of quadrupeds. There are twelve occurrences in the main text of the *Shih chi* where *yüan-yu*, as a compound term, is basically the object of enlargement (*ta* 大; *Shih chi*, 59.2095, 117.3002, 3015, 3016, and 126.3203) or of the abandonment to the good of the public (*shih* 弛; *Shih chi*, 5.219, 8.369, 10.433, and 32.1498). In this instance the term seems simply connected to the pleasures of hunting.

[24] *Han Shu*, 44.2136, reads *nien* 輦 (push carts) instead of *ch'e* 車. This emendation is repeated below in the passage about the forty great horse chariots of the so called Ku-k'ou rebellion (see *Shih chi*, 118.3076).

[25] This kind of physical strength puts Liu Ch'ang in a league with Hsiang Yü (*Shih chi*, 7:296; [*Grand Scribe's Records*, 2:180]) and probably suggests on a symbolic level that he would have been able to rule the whole Empire.

[26] The "So-yin" reminds the reader of Chu Hai 朱亥 hammering Chin Pi 晉鄙 to death with a forty-catty hammer hidden in his sleeve (see *Shih chi*, 77.2381 [*Grand Scribe's Records*, 7:218]).

[27] Otherwise unknown. See Loewe, *Dictionary*, p. 571.

[28] The parallel account on *Shih chi*, 10.425, dates this incident in the fourth month of 177 BC.

[29] Alternatively "gotten her."

[30] In all three instances of the short phrase *fu cheng* 弗爭 in this passage it is probably up to the reader to understand Shen Yi-chi's failure being either "not arguing against it" (*cheng*

offense. As for [the case of Liu] Ju-yi [劉]如意 (205–195 BC), the King of Chao 趙, child and mother were without offense,[31] Lü Hou killed them, [as] the Marquis of Pi-yang did not argue against it—this was the second offence. When Lü Hou made all the various Lüs kings, and thereby wished to endanger the Liu-Clan 劉氏, the Marquis of Pi-yang did not argue against it—this was the third offense. Your servant has respectfully executed the seditious minister, the Marquis of Pi-yang, for the world, I have taken revenge on my mother's adversary, and respectfully I lay myself down at the palace gate to ask for punishment." Hsiao Wen[-ti] bemoaned his resolve,[32] and, since he was his relative, he did not try him, and pardoned King Li.[33] Meanwhile, Po T'ai-hou 薄太后 (Empress Dowager Po),[34] the Heir, and the various great ministers all dreaded King Li; therefore, when King Li returned to [his] state, he became even more arrogant and dissolute, he did not apply the laws of the Han, on [his] way out and the way in [his attendants] called out "Make Way!" and "Stop and Pay

爭 understood as *cheng* 諍) or "not struggling for it" (*cheng* 爭 understood as *yin* 引), since the main text of the *Shih chi*– in contrast to the *Han shu*–does not use the character *cheng* 諍.

[31] Liu Ju-yi, King Yin 隱 of Chao, and former King of Tai 代 (200–198 B.C), was the son of Lady Ch'i 戚夫人, a favorite of Liu Pang. After the death of Liu Pang, Lü Hou summoned the Liu Ju-yi three times to Ch'ang-an, yet the loyal Chancellor of Chao, Chou Ch'ang 周昌, was able to keep the young boy in Chao. And only after Chou Ch'ang himself was recalled to Ch'ang-an, Liu Ju-yi was transported to the Capital, where even Hui-ti was not able to protect his young sibling from being poisoned. His mother Lady Ch'i was incarcerated and mutilated in the worst manner. See Loewe, *Dictionary*, pp. 252–53 and p. 452.

[32] The phrase "bemoaned his resolve," *shang ch'i chih* 傷其志, resembles the tone of Emperor Hsiao Ming's 孝明皇帝 (r. 57–75) words: 吾讀秦紀，至於子嬰車裂趙高，未嘗不健其決，憐其志. "Every time I read the 'Ch'in chi' 秦紀 and come to the point where Tzu Ying drew and quartered Chao Kao, I always admire Tzu Ying's decisiveness and sympathize with his resolution" (*Shih chi*, 6.294 [*Grand Scribe's Records*, 1:175]). Wu and Lu (118.3106b) change the sentence into passive voice and take *shang* 傷 as "to arouse heart-broken sympathy" (引起哀傷同情).

[33] Wang Shu-min (118.3200) refers to the strikingly different account in Kao Yu's 高誘 (3rd century) preface to the *Huai-nan Tzu* that reads: 上非之。肉袒北闕謝罪，奪四縣，還歸國。"The Sovereign considered him to be wrong. When [Liu Ch'ang] bared his torso, apologizing for his offence at the northern gate, he took four counties from him and let him return to [his] state" (*Huai-nan Hong-lieh chieh hsü* 淮南鴻烈解敘, 1.1a, *SPTK*).

[34] Po T'ai-hou was a lesser consort of Liu Pang and mother of Liu Heng 劉恆, the future Wen-ti. Escaping the wrath of Lü Hou, she followed her son to Tai, when he was king there, and was later given the title Tai T'ai-hou 代太后. She died in 155 BC, after the death of Wen-ti. For further biographical information see her biography on *Shih chi*, 49.1970–72, and her entry in Loewe, *Dictionary*, pp. 14–15.

Respect!,"[35] and he called [his orders] (imperial) decrees,[36] made laws and ordinances of his own, imitating the Son of Heaven.[37]

In the sixth year (174 BC), [the King] ordered the fellows[38] Tan 但[39] and others, [altogether] seventy men, to plot together with [Ch'ai] Ch'i [柴]奇, the Heir of Ch'ai Wu 柴武, the Marquis of Chi-p'u 棘蒲,[40] and with forty large horse chariots[41] to

[35] This description tragically is reminiscent of Liu Wu 劉武 (184?–144 BC), the younger brother of Ching-ti, born by the same mother, Empress Dowager Tou 竇, who adopted a similar behavior. (see, for example, Han An-kuo's 韓安國 defense on *Shih chi*, 108.2858 [*Grand Scribe's Records*, 9:176]). Due to his close relation to the Emperor and the strong protection of his influential mother, the later King of Liang liked to display the special privileges granted to him and on several occasions even to dangerously overstep the laws. Reportedly, Ching-ti himself hinted at him once that he would like him to become his successor. This hope turned him into a strong defender of the Han during the Rebellion of the Seven Kingdoms in 154 BC, but also encouraged him to entertain a flourishing court with famous scholars from many of the states, just as Liu An, the King of Huai-nan, would do. After the dismissal of the former Heir, Liu Jung 劉榮 (170–148 BC), in 150 BC it was the strong intervention of Yüan Ang 爰盎 and other ministers that prohibited the nomination of Liu Wu. For further biographical information see his entry in Loewe, *Dictionary*, pp. 367–9.

[36] For the term *ch'eng chih* 稱制 see *Shih chi*, 9.400 (*Grand Scribe's Records*, 2:115)

[37] Takigawa (118.4) remarks that in the extra 840 characters (or 841 according to the modern Chung-hua edition) that follow in the *Han shu* parallel (44.2136–40), a section which basically introduces a long reply by Po Chao 薄昭 to the disobedient letters of Liu Ch'ang, the reasons for Huai-nan's arrogance become even more clear. Po Chao was the younger brother of Wen-ti's mother, Po T'ai-hou, and had acted as intermediary between Liu Heng and Ch'en P'ing 陳平 and Chou Po 周勃, persuading the former to accept the throne. It should to be noted that this happened at a time when Liu Heng and Liu Ch'ang were the only surviving sons of Liu Pang. Luckily, the "Basic Annals of Emperor Wen" tell of a portentous omen that quieted any doubt, whether the senior or the stronger son should succeed his father. (*Shih chi*, 10:413-4). After Liu Heng's accession, he was enfeoffed as the Marquis of Chih 軹. See also Loewe, *Dictionary*, pp. 14–15.

[38] Ch'en Chih 陳直 (*Shih chi hsin cheng* 史記新證 [Peking: Chung-hua Shu-chü, 2006], p. 176) suggests that the term *nan-tzu* 男子 ("fellow") refers to persons without an official position, pointing out that Tan in the following memorial by Chang T'sang is called *tai-fu* 大夫 ("Grandee") as he held that position by then.

[39] Otherwise unknown.

[40] Ch'ai Wu 柴武 (d. 163 BC) probably fought with Liu Pang against Hsiang Yü and was sent as a General to attack Han Hsin in 196 BC. Failing to persuade him into submission, he killed him in battle (*Shih chi*, 93.2635 [*Grand Scribe's Records*, 8.117–18]). For a discussion of the problems identifying the names of father and son, see Loewe, *Dictionary*, p. 24, and *Grand Scribe's Records*, 8:118, n. 59.

[41] Wang Shu-min (118.3201) surmises that the *Han shu* parallel (44.2140) mistakenly replaced *chü* 轝 ("great horse chariots" as Hsü Kuang [cited in "Chi-chieh"] explains) with

revolt[42] at Ku-k'ou 谷口 [Mouth of the Valley][43]; and he ordered men to go as envoys to the Min Yüeh 閩越 and the Hsiung-nu. When this incident was discovered, [the Emperor] had them tried, and sent an envoy to summon the King of Huai-nan. The King of Huai-nan came to Ch'ang'an 長安.

[3077] "Your servant, the Chancellor Chang Ts'ang 張倉,[44] your servant, the Director of Guests Feng Ching 馮敬,[45] your servant, the acting Grandee Secretary and the Director of the Imperial Clan Yi 逸,[46] your servant, the Commandant of Justice Ho 賀,[47] and your servant, the Guard against Rebels and Commandant of the Capital Fu 福,[48] risk at the pain of death saying: [Liu] Ch'ang, the King of Huai-nan, has abandoned the laws of the previous Emperors, he does not obey the edicts of the Son

---

nien 輦 ("push carts" that were pulled by men in order to transport weapons, as Yen Shih-ku comments in the *Han shu* [ibid.]), since people rarely saw those vehicles.

[42] Alternatively, *fan* 反 could also be read as "to return to."

[43] According to "Chi-chieh," the old county Ku-k'ou 谷口 was a place north of Ch'ang-an with many dangerous and difficult roads. "Cheng-yi" situates the old town itself forty miles east of Li-ch'üan 醴泉 county. The *T'ai-p'ing huan-yü chi* 太平寰宇記 (Peking: Chung-hua Shu-chü, 2007), 26.563–64, records that Ku-k'ou, "Mouth of the Valley," received its name because the Ching 涇 River came out of the mountains at this place. It furthermore explains, that Li-ch'üan county was established by the Sui Emperor K'ai 開皇 (r. 588–600) in the year 598 on the grounds of the old Ku-k'ou county. He named it after an eponymous palace from the Northern Chou 北周 (557–581), that some claim was built by Hsüan-ti 宣帝 (r. 74–49 BC) of the Han, after drinking from a well that tasted sweet like wine. Li-ch'üan county then became Li-ch'üan 禮泉 county in 1964 and is located about thirty miles northwest of modern Sian (see Tan Ch'i-hsiang, 2:15).

[44] Chang Ts'ang, written Chang Ts'ang 張蒼 in *Han shu* (see Wang Shu-min, 118.3201), was an important figure in establishing the imperial calendar of the Han Dynasty. He had previously been the Chancellor of Liu Ch'ang, King of Huai-nan, from his nomination in 195 BC until 184 BC. For further bibliographical information see also his biography on *Shih chi*, 96.2675–82 (*Grand Scribe's Records*, 8:205–10), and his entry in Loewe, *Dictionary*, pp. 675–76.

[45] Feng Ching is also known to have opposed the promotion of the scholar Chia Yi 賈誼 along with other influential officials (*Shih chi*, 84.2492 and *Grand Scribe's Records*, 7:302]). In 171 BC, he became Grandee Secretary (*Shih chi*, 22.1127). Wang Shu-min (118.3201) hence argues in the line of the *Han shu* (44.2141) parsing–against Takigawa (118.5) and the Chung-hua editors–that "the acting Grandee Secretary" 行御史大夫事 should refer to Feng Ching, who had at that time not officially assumed his later position. See also his entry in Loewe, *Dictionary*, p. 99.

[46] Otherwise unknown. Han Chao-ch'i (118.5845) notes Liu Yi 劉逸 as his full name without further explanation.

[47] Otherwise unknown.

[48] Otherwise unknown.

of Heaven, his daily life defies the proper standards, he made yellow silk to cover his chariot, in his comings and goings he imitates the Son of Heaven, and, arrogating to himself [the authority] to make laws and ordinances, he does not apply the laws of the Han. As for the officials he established: he made Ch'un 春,[49] his Gentleman-of-the-Palace, Chancellor; he gathers and receives men from the various feudal lords of the Han and fugitives that have committed offenses, hides them, giving them a place to stay, builds housing for them,[50] bestows them with his wealth, titles, salaries, fields and houses, and in giving titles in some cases he goes to the point of Marquis of the Land within the Passes, providing them with [a salary of] two thousand *shih*, [all honors] they do not deserve to receive;[51] thereby he desires to use them for his doings. Grandee Tan 但,[52] the common soldier[53] K'ai-chang 開章,[54] and others, [altogether] seventy men, have plotted rebellion with [Ch'ai] Ch'i, the Heir of the Marquis of Chi-p'u,[55] they thereby wish to endanger the ancestral temple and the altars of soil and

---

[49] Otherwise unknown.

[50] The above translation follows Wu and Lu's (118.3107) technical reading, understanding *wei chih chia shih* 為治家室 in the sense of "constructing houses for them." Since Wang Li-ch'i (118.2498) interprets the phrase as "arranging a good household for them" 為他料理好家屬 and Han Chao-ch'i (118.5846) even more specifically, as "giving them wives, building a family" 為其娶妻，組成家庭, the sentence might also be translated as "he procures households for them."

[51] As opposed to Takigawa (118.5), Wang Hsien-ch'ien 王先謙 (*Han shu pu chu*, 44.5a) is convinced that the negation *pu* 不 (not) was a later addition to the *Shih chi* text, since it is not featured in any of the *Han shu* editions; both comments cited in "Chi-chieh" seem to support that reading. Yet, as Wang Shu-min (118.3202) points out, keeping the negation is not in conflict with their content, as Ju Ch'un and Hsüeh Tsan are only paraphrasing that the King of Huai-nan provided fugitives with a salary of two thousand *shih* that equaled the income of a class of Han officials. Furthermore, "So-yin," although not present in all editions, actually refers to the fact, that criminals in general should not have been given such high positions as "Marquis of the Land within the Passes," a meritorious title, second only to the feudal lords that were bestowed with an actual fief.

[52] "So-yin" and Hsüeh Tsan (cited in "Chi-chieh") both refute Chang Yen 張晏 who suggests that *Tai-fu* 大夫 in this instance refers to Tan's *cognomen*.

[53] The Chung-hua edition does not follow Takigawa (118.6) or Wang Shu-min (118.3202) who prefer *shih wu* 士伍 over *shih wu* 士五. While Takigawa (*ibid.*) considers the term to be a general designation of a common soldier, Ju Ch'un (cited in "Chi-chieh") treats it as a legal term, referring to an offender who has lost his rank and position.

[54] Kai-chang's *cognomen* is unknown; see also his entry in Loewe, *Dictionary*, pp. 205–6.

[55] Hsü Kuang (cited in "Chi-chieh") notes at this second mentioning of Chai Wu and his son Chai Ch'i that Chai Wu was given the posthumous name Kang 剛 [The Toughened], which, according to the "Shih fa chieh," is given to those who "strive to mend previous

grain. [Ch'i] sent K'ai-chang to covertly inform [Liu] Ch'ang that they were plotting together to have the Min Yüeh and the Hsiung-nu send out their troops. When K'ai-chang went to Huai-nan and saw [Liu] Ch'ang, [Liu] Ch'ang sat, spoke, ate and drank several times together with him; he constructed housing for him, gave him a wife, and provided him with a salary of two thousand *shih*. K'ai-chang dispatched a man to inform Tan that he had already spoken about it [i.e., their plans] to the King. Ch'un dispatched an envoy to report to Tan and the others. When the officials discovered and knew about [their plans], they dispatched Ch'i 奇, the Commandant of Ch'ang-an, and others to go and arrest K'ai-chang. [Liu] Ch'ang hid him and did not give [him to them], and he plotted together with Chien Chi 蕳忌,[56] the former Commandant of the Capital, to kill him in order to shut [his] mouth.[57] He had an inner and an outer coffin, clothes and a quilt for the dead made, had him buried in the Town of Fei-ling 肥陵 [Fat Tomb],[58] and deceiving the officials he said: 'I don't know where he is.'[59] Furthermore, he fabricated a [grave] mound, planted a tablet on top of it,[60] reading:

mistakes" 追補前過 (see *Shih chi*, "Shih fa chieh," p. 27), and that their feoffdom was finally abolished after the alleged plotting of a rebellion by his son.

[56] For an overview of the scarce information on this aide of the King of Huai-nan see Loewe, *Dictionary*, p. 190.

[57] The "Cheng-yi" leaves no doubt, that the purpose of the planned murder was "to shut forever the mouth of a plotter of rebellion" 以閉絕謀反之口也.

[58] According to the "So-yin," the town of Fei-ling is located on the banks of the River Fei 肥 (also written Fei 淝) that joins the River Huai 淮 from the south, close to the capital of Huai-nan, Shou-ch'un 壽春, about ten miles northwest of modern Huai-nan Shih 淮南市 in Anhwei (see T'an Ch'i-hsiang, 2:24). The description in "Cheng-yi" points to a similar area. Ch'en Chih 陳直 (*Shih chi hsin cheng* 史記新證, p. 177) remarks that the addition of "town," *yi* 邑, to the place name reminds the reader of the "bathing towns" (*t'ang-mu yi* 湯沐邑) bestowed upon Empresses and Princesses. He thus takes this name as an indication that the King of Huai-nan had himself followed the early customs of the Han Imperial House, when establishing this place. It comes as no surprise that Pan Ku corrected this undue misnomer by dropping the "town" (*Han shu*, 44.2141).

[59] Takigawa (118.7) disagrees with the view of the "So-yin" that suggests the King's answers were given in order to lie about the place of K'ai-chang's grave. He argues that Ssu-ma Ch'ien intentionally presents the two answers of the King only after the narration of the events. First, the King denies to know his whereabouts, while he was still hiding him. Only when it became obvious, that giving K'ai-chang shelter would not stop the investigation, did the King have him killed and ostentatiously marked his grave mound.

[60] For further burial customs see Yang Shu-ta's 楊樹達 (1885–1956) *Han-tai hung sang li su k'ao* 漢代婚喪禮俗考 (Shanghai: Shang-hai Ku-chi Ch'u-pan-she, 2000), especially pp. 97–128.

'K'ai-chang has died and was covered over[61] beneath this.' As for those whom [Liu] Ch'ang himself personally murdered without having committed an offense, there is one person; as for those whom he had sentenced and executed by his officials without having committed an offense, there are six persons. On behalf of a man who escaped the sentence of his offense[62] to be executed and his corpse exposed in the marketplace, he on his own authority found another man guilty. Of guilty men whom who were not reported or exposed [to the Emperor] and whom he detained and sentenced to serve as daily wall-builder,[63] grain pounder or worse—there were fourteen persons; as for those who were pardoned and exempted from their offense, there were eighteen offenders sentenced to death, and fifty-eight persons [sentenced to serve as] daily wall builders, grain pounders, or less; as for those who were bestowed with the title of Marquis of the Land within the Passes or lower, there were ninety-four persons. Previously, when [Liu] Ch'ang was ill, Your Majesty was worried and felt miserable

[61] While the account of his formal burial at the town of Fei-ling uses the term *tsang* 葬, "to bury," the inscription on the tablet uses the word *mai* 埋, "to put away" or "covered over" that according to the *Shih ming* 釋名, 8.6a, *SPTK*, denotes "to bury somebody not according to the rites" (*tsang pu ju li* 葬不如禮). The *Han shu* (44.2141) features a repetition of the term *tsang* 葬, obliterating this subtle difference.

[62] Chin Cho's (cited in "Chi-chieh") equally dark paraphrase of this difficult sentence reads: 亡命者當棄市，而王藏之，詐捕不命者而言命，以脫命者之罪; "Those escaping their sentences deserved execution displaying the corpse in the marketplace, but the King hid them; he arrested those who had no sentences and called them 'sentenced [persons]' on false pretenses, in order to clear those [originally] sentenced from their offenses." In our translation of his comment we understood *wang ming* 亡命 as an acronym for "escaping the sentence of their offenses" (*wang tsui ming* 亡罪名). For further discussion of this key term see the exhaustive discussion by William H. Nienhauser, Jr. on *Grand Scribe's Records*, 8:1, n. 5.

[63] The legal terms "daily wall-builder" (*ch'eng tan* 城旦) and "grain pounders" (*ch'ung* 舂) refer respectively to men that had to build walls at night and watch prisoners at day and to women that had to pound grain (see the "Chi-chieh" explanation of *ch'eng tan* 城旦 on *Shih chi*, 6.255 [*Grand Scribe's Records*, 1:138, especially n. 239]). At least during the times of the Ch'in and Former Han dynasty these hard labor sentences seem to have often comprised corporal punishment, e.g. tattooing and cutting off a foot, tattooing and cutting off the nose (usually only applied to male convicts), or just tattooing (also applied to women). This severe sentence for theft, arson, attempted murder and other crimes short of deserving the death penalty, could be mitigated against a four year "complete wall-builder or grain pounder" (*wan ch'eng tan ch'ung* 完城旦舂) sentence that would imply no tattooing or mutilations, thus leaving the body "complete." Some scholars claim that only with Emperor Wen's reform of the penal law in 167 BC, and the depreciation of corporal mutilations these sentences started to be limited to a fixed period of five, or four years of labor service. See Ch'eng Wei-jung 程維榮, "Lun Ch'in Han ch'eng-tan ch'ung hsing te pien-ch'ien chi ch'i ying-hsiang" 論秦漢城旦舂刑的變遷及其影響, *Cheng-chih yü fa-lü*, 11 (2012): 128–36.

for him, you dispatched an envoy do bestow him with a letter and dried jujubes. [Liu] Ch'ang did not wish to formally receive the envoy.[64] When the people from Nan-hai 南海 that were dwelling on the border to Lu-chiang 廬江 revolted,[65] the officers and men from Huai-nan attacked them.[66] Your Majesty, because of the poverty and

[64] Shen Ch'in-han (cited in Takigawa, 118.7, and Wang Hs'ien-ch'ien, 44.6a) observes that the incident and the officials referred to in these lines is also mentioned Chia Yi's *Hsin shu* 新書 (4.10b, *SPTK*): 日接持怨言，以誹謗陛下之為．皇太后之餽賜，逆[{耳+卬}](拒)而不受．天子使者奉詔而弗得見，僵臥以發詔書．天下孰不知？ "Daily [the King of Huai-nan] invites and upholds words of resentment in order to slander and defame the deeds of our Majesty. The gift of foods bestowed upon him by the August Empress Dowager he refused and did not accept. The envoys of the Son of Heaven presented edicts but were not allowed to see [the King]; lying down motionless, he sent off the imperial edict. Who in the world does not know of this?!"

[65] The area of Lu-chiang 廬江 is located between the Huai 淮 and the Yangtze, southeast of modern Hofei City 合肥市 in Anhwei (see T'an Ch'i-hsiang, 2:24). It was part of the Ch'in Commandery of Chiu-chiang 九江 and Hsiang Yü's Kingdom of Chiu-chiang, before the Han incorporated it into the Kingdom of Huai-nan. In the year 165 BC it was separated as the Kingdom of Lu-chiang under the rule of Liu Tz'u 劉賜, a son of Liu Ch'ang, only to become a commandery under central government in 153 BC, when Liu Tz'u was moved to become King of Heng-shan 衡山 (see *Shih chi*, 17.834–42).

The area of the former Ch'in commandery Nan-hai 南海, situated around the modern city of Canton (see T'an Ch'i-hsiang, 2:11–12), became at the beginning of the Han dynasty part of Chao T'o's 趙佗 (d. 137 BC) Kingdom of Nan Yüeh 南越. See also "Nan Yüeh lieh-chuan," *Shih chi*, chapter 113 and the translation of that chapter in this volume.

[66] Wang Hsien-ch'ien (cited in Takigawa, 118.8) refers the reader in his *Han shu pu chu* (44.6a) to the memoir of Yen Chu 嚴助 (*Han shu*, 64A.2780), where a memorial of Liu An, the later King of Huai-nan, warns against a military expedition against the Yüeh. In his argument he also reminds of the catastrophic outcome of Chien Chi's earlier campaign: 前時南海王反，陛下先臣使將軍間忌將兵擊之，以其軍降，處之上淦．後復反，會天暑多雨，樓舩卒水居擊櫂，未戰而疾死者過半．親老涕泣，孤子謕號，破家散業，迎尸千里之外，裹骸骨而歸．悲哀之氣數年不息，長老至今以為記．曾未入其地而禍已至此矣; "When in former times, the King of Nan-hai revolted, your Majesty's former servant [i.e., his father, Liu Ch'ang] sent General Chien Chi to lead the troops and attack him. But since his troops surrendered, he had them dwell at the upper reaches of the Kan 淦 [River; situated in Yü-chang 豫章 Commandery, joining the Kan 贛 River near modern Chang-shu shih 樟樹市, fifty miles south of Nan-ch'ang 南昌 in Kiangsi (see *Tzu-chih t'ung-chien*, 17.571)]. When they later rebelled again, it happened that the weather was mostly rainy; the soldiers of the towering boats stayed on the waters, striking the oars hard, and, without having battled, those that died of diseases were more than half. The old people of their families cried, the orphans wailed; with [their] families destroyed and [their] enterprises fallen apart, they collected the corpses a thousand miles afar, bagged the bones, and returned. The air of sorrow and grieve did not settle for several years, and the elders

hardships of the people of Huai-nan, sent envoys to bestow [Liu] Ch'ang with five thousand rolls of silk, in order to bestow it on those who toiled and suffered among the officers and men. [Liu] Ch'ang did not [*3078*] wish to accept the bestowal, and deceiving [the envoys] he said: 'There is nobody who toiled and suffered here.' When King Chih 織 from the people of Nan-hai[67] submitted a memorial [to the court],

remember it until today. We had not yet invaded their territory but the disaster had already reached these [dimensions]."

[67] Ch'en Jen-hsi 陳仁錫 (1581–1636; cited in Takigawa, 118.8) and Liang Yü-sheng (118.1426) both believe in accordance with the *Han shu* (44.2141) parallel, that the character *min* 民 (people) is redundant and that Chih is the name of the King of Nan-hai. Chou Shou-ch'ang 周壽昌 (1814–1884; cited in Wang Hsien-ch'ien, *Han shu pu chu*, 44.6b) concurs and challenges the view of the Chung-hua edition by asking, if Wang Chih was just a commoner, how could he submit a memorial and offer *pi*-jade? Although no King Chih can be found in the text of the *Shih chi*, the *Han shu* (1B.77–78) presents the following memorial from the twelfth year (195 BC) of Kao-tsu's reign: 南武侯織亦粵之世也，立以為南海王 "The Marquis of Nan-wu is also a contemporary from Yüeh 粵, he is to be enthroned as King of Nan-hai." Wen Ying 文穎 (fl. 196–200; cited by Yen Shih-ku, *ibid.*) comments on this decision as follows: 高祖五年，以象郡、桂林、南海、長沙立吳芮為長沙王。象郡、桂林、南海屬尉佗，佗未降，遙虛奪以封芮耳。後佗降漢，十一年，更立佗為南越王，自此王三郡。芮唯得長沙、桂林、零陵耳。今復封織為南海王，復遙奪佗一郡，織未得王之。 "In the fifth year of Kao-tsu (202 BC), [Kao-tsu] took [the territory of] Hsiang-chün 象郡, Kuei-lin 桂林, Nan-hai 南海, and Ch'ang-sha 長沙 and enthroned Wu Jui 吳芮 (d. 202) as King of Ch'ang-sha 長沙. Hslang-chün, Kuei-lin, and Nan-hai belonged to Commandant [Chao] T'o, and as [Chao] T'o had not yet surrendered, he took [these commanderies only] from afar and virtually from [Chao T'o] and enfeoffed [Wu] Jui. Later [Chao] T'o surrendered to the Han, and in the eleventh year (196 B.C) he enthroned [Chao] T'o in his stead as King of Nan-hai. From this time on, [Chao T'o] ruled over three Commanderies. [Wu] Jui only got Ch'ang-sha, Kuei-lin, and Ling-ling 零陵. Now that [Kao-tsu] had again enfeoffed Chih as King of Nan-hai, he again took one commandery from a far and virtually from [Chao] T'o but Chih never got to rule over it." (For further context of the events mentioned in Wen Ying's comment see also *Shih chi* chapter 113). In light of this *Han shu* material, Han Chao-ch'i (118.5848) deduces that the King Chih of Nan-hai mentioned above stemmed probably from some minority of the northern part of Nan-hai, close to the borders of Yü-chang Commandery, that Chao T'o had not yet pacified at that time. According to him, Ssu-ma Ch'ien might even have misplaced the above mentioned rebellion of the people of Nan-hai. But even if their revolt actually took place in Lu-chiang 廬江 (and not, as Han Chao-ch'i prefers, further south in Yü-chang), it could well be that King Chih belonged to those people that were later defeated twice by Liu Ch'ang according to *Han shu*, 64A.2780 (see note above for a translation of the relevant passage). Unfortunately, the Chung-hua edition gives no absolute certainty: Although its marking of proper names seems to suggest, that the editors could have believed that the person in question was a certain "Wang Chih from the people of Nan-hai," the intriguing–and in the Chung-hua edition unmarked–character *min* 民 (people) could have had the sole

offering a *pi*-jade to the Emperor, [Chien] Chi[68] arrogated to himself [the authority] to burn his memorial, and did not make it known [at court]. When the officials requested to summon and try [Chien] Chi, [Liu] Ch'ang did not send him, and deceiving [the officials] he said: '[Chien] Chi is ill.' Furthermore, when Ch'un requested [instructions] from [Liu] Ch'ang, since he hoped to enter [court] for an audience [with the Emperor], [Liu] Ch'ang got angry and said: 'You wish to leave me and attach yourself personally to the Han.' [Liu] Ch'ang deserves to be executed dispaying his corpse in the marketplace, your servants request to have him sentenced according to the law."

[3079] The [Emperor's] decree read: "We cannot bear to apply the law to the King, let it be deliberated with the feudal lords and those [officials with a salary of] two thousand *shih*."

"Your servant, [Chang] Ts'ang, your servant, [Feng] Ching, your servant Yi, your servant Fu, and your servant Ho, risk at the pain of death to say: Your servants have respectfully discussed the matter with the feudal lords and those [officials with a salary] of two thousand *shih* like your servant, Ying 嬰,[69] and others, [altogether] forty-three men, all said: '[Liu] Ch'ang did not respect the law and standards, he did not obey the edicts of the Son of Heaven, and then he covertly gathered a party of followers and those plotting rebellion, he generously provided for fugitives, and thereby he desired to use them for his doings.' Your servants and the others have deliberated to sentence him according to the law."

The [Emperor's] decree read: "We cannot not bear to apply the law to the King, [Liu] Ch'ang shall be pardoned from his offense meriting death, he shall be dismissed so that he is not to be treated King."

"Your servant, [Chang] Ts'ang [張]倉, and others risk at the pain of death saying: [Liu] Ch'ang has committed a great offense [deserving] the death penalty, Your Majesty does not bear to apply the law, [you] favored [him] with a pardon, and dismissed him so that he is not to be treated as a King. Your servants request to have

intention to point out the problems of several concurrent claims at the title of "King of Nan-hai," hence our tentative translation as "King Chih from the people of Nan-hai."

[68] Wen Ying 文穎 (fl. 196–200; cited in "Chi-chieh") states that "Chi" refers to above mentioned "Chien Chi" 萠忌.

[69] Wang Hsien-ch'ien (*Han shu pu chu*, 44.6b) cites Ch'ien Ta-chao 錢大昭 (1744–1813) who excludes Kuan Ying 灌嬰 (d. 176 BC) and Ch'en Ying 陳嬰 as possible candidates for the person in question on grounds of their earlier passing and concludes that it must have been Hsia-hou Ying 夏侯嬰 (d. 172), the Marquis of Ju-yang 汝陽, who held the post of Grand Coachman at that time. For further biographical information see his entry in Loewe, *Dictionary*, pp. 596–97.

him stay at Ch'iung 邛 Postal Station in Yen 嚴 Shire in the Shu 蜀 Commandery,[70] and send his mothers [who bore him] children[71] to follow him and reside [there], the county shall construct a house for him, feeding them all from the official granary, giving them firewood, vegetables, salt, beans, cooking utensils, mats and cushions. Your servant and others risk at the pain of death requesting this, and we request to disseminate [these measures] and inform the world [about them]."

The [Emperor's] decree read: "Let it be calculated to give [Liu] Ch'ang daily five *chin* of meat and two *tou* of wine as nurture. Let ten of his former Beautiful Ladies and Talented Ladies who gained favor with him follow [him] to reside [there]. The other [measures suggested] are permissible."[72]

[The Emperor] had every one of those who joined in plotting executed. Only after this did he sent off the King of Huai-nan, conveyed in a covered cart,[73] and order the

---

[70] Shu was an old Ch'in Commandery under central administration, expanding around modern Ch'eng-tu in Szechwan. According to 'So-yin,' "Shire" (*tao* 道) was a barbarian term for "county" (*hsien* 縣). According to the *T'ai-p'ing huan-yü chi* 太平寰宇記, (Peking: Chung-hua Shu-chü, 2007), 77.1551), Yen Shire was named after the relocated descendants of King Yen 嚴 [i.e., Chuang 莊] (d. 591 BC) of Ch'u 楚 after Ch'u's defeat by the First Emperor of Ch'in in 222 BC. According to Hsü Kuang (cited in "Chi-chieh"), the Ch'iung 邛 postal station was established at Chiu-che-pan 九折阪 [Ninefold Winding Slopes], east of Ch'iung-po 邛僰 Mountain in Yen Shire. Ch'iung 邛 Postal Station is located ninety miles southwest of modern Ch'eng-tu (T'an Ch'i-hsiang, 2:29). "So-yin" takes the better known Ch'iung-lai 邛萊 Mountain as its point of reference, that is also called Lai 崍 or Ch'iung-tso 邛莋 Mountain (*T'ai-p'ing huan-yü chi* 太平寰宇記, 77.1554). On the base of archeological findings that indicate the frequent communication with the capital, Ch'en Chih 陳直 (*Shih chi hsin cheng* 史記新證 [Peking: Chung-hua Shu-chü, 2006], p. 147 and 177) concurs with Wang Li-ch'i (118.2499, n. 2) that Yen Shire was a common place to exile offenders.
According to the parallel account on *Shih chi*, 10.426 [*Grand Scribe's Records*, 2:169] Liu Ch'ang was to be sent to Ch'iung-tu 邛都, located one hundred miles southwest of modern Ch'eng-tu (Tan Ch'i-hsiang, 2:29).

[71] According to Yüeh Ch'an 樂產 (cited in "So-yin")—or, as Wang Shu-min (118.3203) points out, rather Yüeh Yen 樂彥 (a question which is to Yü Sheng-ch'un 余勝椿 ["'Shih chi·Hsiung-nu lieh-chuan' yü 'Han shu 'Hsiung-nu lieh-chuan'chi ch'i chu-wen hsin chiao cha chi " 《史記·匈奴列傳》與《漢書·匈奴傳》及其注文新校札記, *Min-tsu yen-chiu*, vol 1 (1985), p. 43] still a matter that awaits further investigation)–the term *tzu-mu* 子母 expresses the notion of: 妾媵之有子者 "those concubines who had a child."

[72] According to "So-yin," the short sentence *t'a k'o* 他可 means 他事可其制也 "The other conditions [of his punishment] could be regulated by them [the accusing ministers]."

[73] Wang Shu-min (118.3204) directs the reader's attention to the harsh difference between the "covered cart" (*tzu ch'e* 輜車) of this memoir and the "barred prison cart" (*chien ch'e* 轞車 or *chien ch'e* 檻車 [*Han shu*, 49.2268]) in the parallel account in *Shih chi*, 101.2738

[respective] counties [along the way] to have [the prisoner] transported in turn. At this time, Yüan Ang 袁盎[74] admonished the Sovereign saying: "Your Highness has always allowed the King of Huai-nan to be arrogant, you did not establish for him severe Tutors or Chancellors, and for this reason it has come to this. Moreover, the King of Huai-nan as a person is hard, and if you now briskly break him down, your servant is afraid that he might suddenly encounter fog and dew[75] and die of illness. If Your Majesty would because of this[76] have the reputation of someone who killed [his own] younger brother, what then!" The Sovereign said: "I just want him to suffer, I will now have him returned." Those counties transporting the King of Huai-nan dared not to open the seal of the cart.[77] [*3080*] Only then did the King of Huai-nan speak

(*Grand Scribe's Records*, 8:329). According to Li Shan's 李善 addition to the old *Shih ming* 釋名 (8.6a, *SBTK*) gloss, those barred prison carts were not only used to confine wild beasts, but also to lock away criminals (see *Wen hsüan* 文選, 9.1b, *SPTK*).

[74] Yüan Ang was an outspoken advisor of Wen-ti, who previously had suggested to punish the arrogance of Liu Ch'ang by reducing the size of his territory (*Shih chi*, 101.2738 [*Grand Scribe's Records*, 8:329]). He is furthermore known for bringing down his opponent Ch'ao Ts'o 鼂錯 at the outbreak of the Rebellion of the Seven Kingdoms and prohibiting the nomination of Liu Wu, King of Liang, as Heir to Ching-ti. For further biographical information see his biography in *Shih chi*, chapter 101, and his entry in Loewe, *Dictionary*, pp. 661–3.

[75] The term *yü wu lu* 遇霧露 ("to encounter fog and dew") refers to an unspecific disease that a person might catch due to the general hardships of such a journey in a prison cart.

[76] Wang Shu-min (118.3204) undertakes the effort to cite Wu Ch'ang-ying's 吳昌瑩 (19th cent.) *Ching tz'u yen shih* 經詞衍釋 in order to suggest that the character *wei* 為, that was deleted in the *Han shu* parallel (44.2143), should indicate a future aspect of the main verb, "to be about to have."

[77] "Chi-chieh" cites a seemingly slightly corrupted version of Meng K'ang's commentary from the *Han shu* parallel (44.2143), stating that barred prison carts (*chien ch'e* 檻車) had seals. Wang Shu-min (118.3204) thus speculates in his long note–against Shi Chih-mien's 施 之勉 (1891–1990; cited ibid.) argument–that the above mentioned transport vehicle was probably a barred prison cart after all. According to Wang Shu-min, the text was only later changed to "covered cart" (*tzu ch'e* 轀車) out of consideration for Wen-ti. Completely in line with this emendation, Wang Shu-min even concludes his comment by stating that transporting Liu Ch'ang in a barred prison cart must have been the doings of the various ministers, as this was never Wen-ti's intention.

Nakai Sekitoku (cited in Takigawa 118.10) points out that the *Han shu* parallel shifts its version of this sentence (縣傳者不敢發車封 "Those counties transporting him dared not to open the seal of the cart.") after the following account of his last words and death by starvation, creating the impression that the responsible counties were intentionally hiding their knowledge of his death.

to the attendants: "Who said that your master is brave?[78] How could I be brave! Because of my arrogance I did not hear that my transgressions have lead to this [grave situation].[79] In the span of one man's single lifetime,[80] how could I ever become heavyhearted[81] like this!" Only then did he die of starvation. When they arrived at Yung 雍,[82] the Prefect of Yung opened the seal, and made his death known. The Sovereign cried most sorrowfully, and said to Yüan Ang: "We did not listen to your words, Sir, and in the end [we] have lost the King of Huai-nan." [Yüan] Ang said: "There is nothing that could be done about it, I wish Your Majesty would go easy on yourself." The Sovereign said: "What can be done about this?" [Yüan] Ang said: "In order to apologize to the world only decapitating the Chancellor and Secretaries is permissible." The Sovereign then ordered the Chancellor and Secretaries to capture and examine all the various attendants that were in the counties transporting and

[78] Wang Hsien-ch'ien (*Han shu bu chu*, 44.7a) surmises that the county officials did not dare to open the seal of the cart, as they were afraid of Liu Ch'ang's bravery. Therefore, the King asks his attendants intentionally a rhetoric question, addressing himself as their master (see "So-yin").

[79] Assuming his words were not as remorseful as some commentators would have it, this sentence could also read: "I have for the reason of arrogance and without learning of my transgression arrived at this."

[80] The brevity of man's life is proverbial: 一生一世間，如白駒過隙耳。"Man's single lifetime simply resembles a white colt running past a crack in the wall" (see *Shih chi*, 90.2590 [*Grand Scribe's Records*, 8:35]).

[81] In accordance with most commentators, the expression *yi yi* 邑邑 was translated in the sense of *yi yi* 悒悒. However, Liu Ch'ang's outrage about his deportation might be compared to the following, quite similar words of the impatient ruler that Shang Yang 商鞅 tried to persuade (see *Shih chi*, 68.2228 [*Grand Scribe's Records*, 7:88]): 久遠，吾不能待。且賢君者，各及其身顯名天下，安能邑邑待數十百年以成帝王乎? "These [ways of the emperors and Kings] take too long. I cannot wait. Moreover, worthy rulers all spread their fame across the world within their own lifetime. How could I bear to stew for decades or a hundred years waiting to become an Emperor or King?" A resonant translation like "How could I bear to stew like this?!" might be thus in line with the temper of Liu Ch'ang and his mother—which, according to Han Chao-ch'i (118.5850), might have been Ssu-ma Ch'ien's focus in the depiction of this event. Furthermore, acknowledging the given form of the expression might also enable the reader to discover a possible pun in his words: "How can [I bear a transport] form town to town [*yi yi* 邑邑] like this?!"

[82] Yung County is located in modern Shansi about fifteen miles northeast of modern Pao-chi 寶鷄 and about ninety miles west of former Ch'ang-an (Tan Ch'i-hsiang, 2:15). Liu Ch'ang had probably not covered more than one sixth of his way into exile, when his dead body was discovered. Although one can only speculate how fast the younger brother of the emperor and his entourage could have been moved, assuming that the roads so close to the capital should have been in fairly good condition, Liu Ch'ang would, at any rate, not have had too much time to actually starve himself to death.

accompanying the King of Huai-nan without opening the seal and offering him food, they were all executed and their corpses displayed in the marketplace. Only then did he bury the King of Huai-nan as a ranking marquis at Yung, with thirty households to maintain the grave.[83]

In the eighth year of Hsiao Wen[-ti] (172 BC), the Sovereign felt pity for the King of Huai-nan. The King of Huai-nan had four sons, all of them being seven or eight years old. Only then did he enfeoff the son [Liu] An [劉]安 (179–122 BC) as Marquis of Fu-ling 阜陵,[84] the son [Liu] Po [劉]勃 (d. 152 BC) as Marquis of An-yang 安陽,[85] the son [Liu] Tz'u [劉]賜 (178–122 BC) as Marquis of Yang-chou 陽周,[86] and the son [Liu] Liang [劉]良 (d. 165 BC) as Marquis of Tung-ch'eng 東成.[87]

In the twelfth year of Hsiao Wen[-ti] (168 BC),[88] among the people a song was made to sing of King Li of Huai-nan, which went:[89]

[83] As a point of reference one might recall that Kao-tsu decreed in 195 BC, shortly before his own passing, to confer ten families for the maintenance of the graves of the First Emperor of Ch'in (d. 210 BC), Ch'en She 陳涉, King Yin 隱 of Ch'u (d. 208 B.C), King An-hsi 安釐 of Wei (d. 243 BC), King Min 緡 of Ch'i (d. 284 B.C), and King Tao Hsiang 悼襄 of Chao (d. 236 B.C; see *Shih chi*, 8.391[*Grand Scribe's Records*, 2:85]). According to a parallel account, even thirty families were to maintain Ch'en She's grave at Tang 碭 (see *Shih chi*, 48.1961). In 195 BC. Kao-tsu also established five families to maintain the grave of the Noble Scion of Wei (d. 243 BC; see *Shih chi*, 77.2385 [*Grand Scribe's Records*, 7:221].

However, as Nakai Setikoku (cited in Takigawa, 118.12) observes below, it is noteworthy that the *Shih chi* spells out the fact that the Emperor treated his dead brother at first only as a "ranking marquis" (*lieh hou* 列侯) and not–as he would have deserved–as a "feudal lord" (*chu hou* 諸侯). Six years had to pass, before he granted him the proper honor of a tomb garden (see below *Shih chi*, 118.3081).

[84] For further biographical information on Liu An, the later King of Huai-nan, see the second part of this memoir and his entry in Loewe, *Dictionary*, pp. 242–44.

[85] For further biographical information on Liu Po, who would first become King of Heng–shan 衡山, before he was promoted to become King of Chi-pei 濟北 in appreciation of his loyalty during the Rebellion of the Seven Kingdoms, see his entry in Loewe, *Dictionary*, pp. 267.

[86] For further biographical information on Liu Tz'u, who would first become King of Lu-chiang 廬江, before he would be moved to become the next King of Heng-shan 衡山, see the third part of this memoir and his entry in Loewe, *Dictionary*, pp. 284–86.

[87] For further biographical information on Liu Liang, who did not live long enough to be made a king, see his entry in Loewe, *Dictionary*, pp. 329–30.

Shih Chih-mien (cited in Wang Shu-min, 118.3205) points out that Tung-ch'eng 東成 should be written 東城, as in the second occurence in this memoir.

[88] Wang Shu-min (118.3205) remarks that the *Tzu-chih t'ung-chien* (14.480) records this event in the seventh year of his reign (173 BC).

> One *chih* of cloth can still be sewn,
> One *tou* of grain can still be hewn,
> Yet two men, each a brother,
> could not make space for each other.

The Sovereign heard it, then sighed and said: "Yao 堯 and Shun 舜 exiled their own flesh and blood, the Duke of Chou 周 killed Kuan 管 and Ts'ai 蔡,[90] and the world called them sages. Why? They did not, for private interests, damage public

---

[89] In the Chinese original of this song, all three verses share one rhyme (**tooŋ* 東). "Chi-chieh" quotes two interpretations from the *Han shu* (44.2144) commentary: Meng Kang's interpretation, that Takigawa (118.12) considers to be the most solid, runs: 尺布斗粟猶尚不棄，況於兄弟而更相逐乎; "If even a *chih* of cloth and a *tou* of grain is not wasted, even [two] brothers would rather exile each other!" In our translation we followed Yen Shih-ku's assertion (cited in *Han shu, ibid.*) that the reading of Hsüeh Tsan is right: 一尺布尚可縫而共衣，一斗粟尚可舂而共食也，況以天下之廣而不能相容; "If even one *chih* of cloth can still be sewn and shared for clothing, and even one *tou* of grain can still be hewn and shared for eating, how come that given the vastness of the world [two brothers] could not make space for each other?"

Nakai Sekitoku (cited in Takigawa, 118.12) feels that the song is about the unique relation between two brothers. While a *chih* of cloth may, as a fragment, not be enough to produce a clothing, one can still mend it with other cloths and stitch them together. The same holds true of a *tou* of grain that may, as a fraction, be not enough for hewing, yet could always be joined with any other grain. Only a brother is irreplaceable.

Wang Shu-min (118.3205–3206) refers to Kao Yu's preface to the *Huai-nan Tzu* that features a remarkably different version of the song, using the same rhyme as above three times: 一尺繒，好童童。一升粟，飽蓬蓬。兄弟二人，不能相容; "Even one *chih* of silk gives you luxuriant beauty, and even a *sheng* of grain leaves you abundantly full; yet, two men, each a brother, could not make space for each other." (*Huai-nan Hong-lieh chieh hsü* 淮南鴻烈解敘, 1.1b, *SPTK*).

[90] While the "Cheng-yi" refers the first part of the sentences to the exile of the four ancient evildoers by Yao and Shun, most commentators–apart from Nakai Setikoku (cited in Takigawa, 118.12)–accept that it recalls Yao sending his son Tan-chu 丹朱 into exile, and Shun exiling his younger brother Hsiang 象 (for various references see Wang Shu-min, 118.3206).

The second part of the Wen-ti's utterance is far more troublesome, since only few passages like *Shih chi*, 3.109 (*Grand Scribe's Record*, 1:52) can be found that tell how the Duke of Chou received the order to put his older brother, Kuan 管, together with his younger brother, Ts'ai, to death, when they both rose in rebellion after the demise of their oldest brother, King Wu of Chou. The majority of the references to this incident, differentiates between the execution of Kuan and the exilement of Ts'ai (see e.g. *Shih chi* 4.132, 30.1518, 35.1565, 37.1589, 38.1621, and 130.3308). Wang Shu-min (118.3206–3207) thus presents different approaches to come to terms with this literally untenable statement of Wen-ti that in the end can only be taken as a generalizing figure of speech.

interests. How could the world think that I coveted the territory of the King of Huai-nan?" Only then did he move the King of Ch'eng-yang 城陽 [Liu Hsi 劉喜 (d. 143 B.C)][91] to be King of the former territory of Huai-nan, and he retroactively honored[92] the King of Huai-nan with the posthumous title **[*3081*]** King Li 厲 [The Pungent King],[93] and established a [tomb] garden, [treating him] again according to the rites of the various feudal lords.[94]

[91] As Hsü Kuang (cited in "Chi-chieh") reminds the reader, Liu Hsi is the Son of Liu Chang 劉章 (d. 176 BC), King Ching 景 of Ch'eng-yang 城陽. Liu Chang distinguished himself in eliminating the Lü Clan in the aftermath of Lü Hou's reign. After any hope that his older brother Liu Hsiang 劉襄 (d. 179 B.C), a grandson of Kao-tsu like himself, would accede to the throne were destroyed, he supported Liu Heng 劉恆 emerging as the new Emperor. He was finally, despite his initial support for his brother, enfeoffed as King of Ch'eng-yang 城陽 in 178 B.C, on the former grounds of Ch'i 齊 (see his entry in Loewe, *Dictionary*, pp. 405–406). Liu Hsi resumed his father's reign as King of Ch'eng-yang. After becoming King of Huai-nan from 168 to 164 B.C, he was once more restored as King of Ch'eng-yang until the end of his days (see his entry in Loewe, *Dictionary*, p. 370).

Hsü Fu-yüan 徐孚遠 (1599–1665; cited in Arii Shinsai 有井進斋 (1830–1889) *Hohyō Shiki hyōrin* 補標史記評林 [Tōkyō: Hōkokusha, 1885], 118.4a) comments on this decision: 淮南王死未置後，故移城陽王，王其故地為之後，因得置園如諸侯; "Since [the Emperor] had after the death of the King of Huain-nan not yet established a successor, he moved the King of Ch'eng-yang, to rule over his former territory and be his successor; therefore he could establish a [tomb] garden in the manner of a feudal lord."

[92] The *Shih chi* makes sure that nobody misses the truly "honorific" aspect of his title by choosing the rare formula: 追尊 sb. 謚 sth. that occurs only one more time on *Shih chi*, in the parallel account of this event, on 10.426 (*Grand Scribe's Records*, 2:169): 追尊淮南王長謚為 厲王 "He posthumously honored Liu Ch'ang the King of Huai-nan, with the posthumous title of King Li."

[93] "Cheng yi" cites the *Shih fa* 謚法 with the following explanation of his title: 暴慢無親 曰厲 "[Someone, who is] brutal, arrogant, and without affection [for his closest], is called 'pungent.'" Alternatively, the *Shih fa chieh* (*Shih chi*, "Shih fa chieh," p. 29) offers an equally devaluating definition: 殺戮無辜曰厲 "[Someone, who] kills and displays the corpses of the innocent, is called 'pungent.'"

[94] In the given context "garden" (*yüan* 園) is a reference to a "tomb garden"(*ch'in yüan* 寢園 or *ling yüan* 陵園), a compound, enclosed by a wall, situated next to or on top of the barrow. These remnants of Ch'in funeral culture adopted by the Han (see *Hou han shu*, 9.3199–200) would usually provide one or more buildings as their center, i.e., a "repose hall" (*ch'in tien* 寢殿), equipped with an altar, garment and other everyday objects from the live of the deceased, and a "resting hall" (*pien tien* 便殿), imitating the structure of their former residence halls–maybe even an "ancestral temple" (*miao* 廟), so that the living could perform their frequent services to the dead. See *Han shu*, 43.3115–6 (as well as Yen Shih-ku's comment on *Han shu*, 6.159). For an overview of the tomb culture of Han feudal kings,

In the sixteenth year of Hsiao Wen[-ti] (164 BC), [the Emperor] moved [Liu] Hsi [劉]喜, the King of Huai-nan 淮南,[95] back to the former Ch'eng-yang 城陽. Only when the Sovereign was feeling pity for the fact that King Li of Huai-nan, by abolishing the laws and being undisciplined, had caused himself to lose his state and meet an early death, did [the Emperor] enthrone his three sons:[96] [Liu] An, the Marquis of Fu-ling, became the King of Huai-nan, [Liu] Po, the Marquis of An-yang, became King of Heng-shan 衡山, and [Liu] Tz'u, the Marquis of Yang-chou, became the King of Lu-chiang 廬江, they obtained again all the territory of King Li's 厲 time, divided into three parts.[97] [Liu] Liang, the Marquis of Tung-ch'eng 東城, had passed on earlier, and had no descendants.

In the third year (154 BC) of Hsiao Ching[-ti; The Filial and Luminous (Emperor), Liu Ch'i 劉啓, r. 157–141 BC)],[98] the seven Kingdoms including Wu 吳 and Ch'u 楚 revolted, and when the envoys from Wu arrived in Huai-nan 淮南, the King of Huai-nan [Liu An 劉安] wished to sent out his troops in response to them.[99] His

including references to archeological findings, see Cheng Shao-tsung 鄭紹宗 and Cheng Luan-ming 鄭灤明, "Han chu-hou wang ling te ying-chien ho tsang-chih" 漢諸侯王陵的營建和葬制, *Wen wu ch'un-ch'iu*, 2.2001, pp. 1–14. The translator would like to thank Armin Selbitschka for his generous references for this note.

As a further point of reference, it may be interesting to note, that the father of Empress Po 薄 (d. 147 BC) was bestowed with a tomb garden of three hundred households (see *Shih chi*, 49.1971), while the father of Empress Tou 竇 (d. 135 BC; see *Shih chi*, 49.1973) and the father and mother of Empress Wang 王 (173–112 BC; see *Shih chi*, 49.1978) were each granted a tomb garden with two hundred families.

[95] At this point, "So-yin" reminds the reader that Liu Hsi is the Son of Liu Chang 劉章 (d. 176 BC), King Ching 景 of Ch'eng-yang 城陽. For further information on father and son see note above.

[96] According to *Shih chi*, 101.2739 (*Grand Scribe's Records*, 8:328), this late enfeoffment happened only upon a suggestion of his adviser Yüan Ang.

[97] According to Ch'en Jen-hsi (cited in *Hohyō Shiki hyōrin*, 118.4a), the King of Huai-nan obtained Chiu-chiang Commandery, the King of Heng-shan Lu'an Commandery, and the King of Lu-chiang Lu-chiang and Yü-chang Commandery.

[98] Liu Ch'i (188–141 BC) was the eldest son born to Wen-ti by his Empress Tou. For further biographical information see his entry in Loewe, *Dictionary*, pp. 338–44.

[99] As Liu P'i, the King of Wu, expressed openly in his letter to revolt, he expected all three sons of Liu Ch'ang to join him in rebellion and revenge their father's death: "The Son of King Yüan of Ch'u and the three Kings of Huai-nan may not have bathed and washed themselves for more than ten years, [their] rancor has entered the marrow of [their] bones, and it surely has been a long time that they wish to once have an opportunity to vent it, [but since] We have not yet obtained the intentions of the various kings, [We] have not ventured to heed them. Now if the various kings could bear it to restore fallen [states] and continue severed [successions], aid the weak and attack the violent, in order to secure the Liu Clan, it would be

Chancellor[100] said: "If you, Great King, are determined to send out your troops in response to Wu, then your servant would hope to be made [their] commander." Only then did the King entrust the troops to the Chancellor. When the Chancellor of Huai-nan was already commanding the troops, he took advantage of it, and defended [the city] from its walls [against the rebels]. He did not obey the King and acted on behalf of the Han. The Han in turn dispatched the Marquis of Ch'ü-ch'eng 曲城[101] to lead troops to rescue Huai-nan: Huai-nan for this reason was able to remain intact. When the envoys from Wu 吳 arrived at Lu-chiang 廬江, the King of Lu-chiang [Liu Tz'u 劉賜] did not respond to them, but had envoys sent back and forth to Yüeh 越. When the envoys from Wu arrived at Heng-shan, the King of Heng-shan [Liu Po 劉勃] resolutely defended [his city] and [acted] with undivided loyalty.

in hope of the altars of soil and grain" 楚元王子、淮南三王或不沐洗十餘年，怨入骨髓，欲一有所出 之久矣，寡人未得諸王之意，未敢聽。今諸王苟能存亡繼絕，振弱伐暴，以安劉氏，社稷之 所願也 (see *Shih chi*, 106.2828 [*Grand Scribe's Records*, 9:109]).

For further information on the background of the Rebellion of the Seven Kingdoms see the parallel accounts on *Shih chi*, chapter 101 and 106, as well as Reinhold Emmerich, "Die Rebellion der Sieben Könige, 154 v.Chr.," in Reinhard Emmerich and Hans Stumpfeldt, eds., *Und folge nun dem, was mein Herz begehrt: Festschrift für Ulrich Unger zum 70. Geburtstag* (Hamburg: Hamburger Sinologische Gesellschaft, 2002), pp. 397–497.

[100] Chou Shou-ch'ang (cited in *Han shu pu chu*, 44.8a), believes that since, according to *Han-shu* (50.2312), Chang Shih-chih 張釋之 became Chancellor in Huai-nan at the beginning of Ching-ti's reign, he might have been still serving on this post three years later, at the outbreak of the rebellion. The reason for the demotion of this upright and impartial official to Huai-nan might be found in an incident during Wen-ti's reign, that the *Shih chi* aptly refers to as his "former transgression," *ch'ien kuo* 前過 (see *Shih chi*, 102.2756 [*Grand Scribe's Records*, 8:364, furthermore p. 360, n. 17]). When Chang Shih-chih was still serving as Prefect of the Official Carriages, he stopped the Heir (i.e., the later Ching-ti) and his younger brother, the King of Liang, from entering the palace gates, after they had not descended at the Gate of the Marshals, and had them impeached for disrespectfulness. They were only spared from punishment by the intervention of their Mother, Empress Tou. For further information on Chang Shih-chih see also his entry on Loewe, *Dictionary*, pp. 690–91.

[101] According to Hsü Kuang (cited in "Chi-chieh"), his *cognomen* was Ch'ung 蟲 and his *praenomen Chieh* 捷, and his father's *praenomen* was Feng 逢. Ch'ung Chieh's father was one of Kao-tsu's meritorious Commandants, who rose to the position of a general fighting Yen 燕 and Tai 代. *Shih chi*, 18.911 bears his record under the name of Ch'ung Ta 蟲達 as Marquis Yu 圉 of Ch'ü-ch'eng, while his son appears at his various enfeoffments and demotions as Marquis Kung 恭. Shih Chih-mien (cited in Wang Shu-min, 118.3207) believes that Feng 逢 might be a mistake for Ta 達 and also reaffirms the doubt that their last name might have been Ku 蠱 instead of Ch'ung. For further biographical information on father and son see Loewe, *Dictionary*, p. 47 and p. 48.

In the fourth year of Hsiao Ching[-ti] (153), when Wu 吳 and Ch'u 楚 were already defeated, and the King of Heng-shan [Liu Po] paid respects at the court; the Sovereign believed him to be honest and trustworthy, and only then did he consider him to have toiled and suffered, saying: "The South is low lying [*3082*] and damp."[102] He had the King of Heng-shan moved to become King of Chi-pei 濟北,[103] this is how he rewarded him. When it came that he passed on, he finally granted him the posthumous title of King Chen 貞 [The Honest King].[104] As the King of Lu-chiang 盧江 [Liu Tz'u 劉賜] shared a border with Yüeh 越 and as he had several times dispatched envoys in order to make contacts with [Yüeh], [the Sovereign] had him therefore moved to become King of Heng-shan 衡山, to be King over [the territory] North of the Chiang 江.[105] The King of Huai-nan 淮南 [Liu An 劉安] remained as of old.[106]

Liu An

[Liu] An [劉]安, the King of Huai-nan 淮南, as a man was fond of reading books and playing the zither, he did not enjoy shooting and hunting, dogs and horses, or racing; he also wished by secretly [practicing] good deeds[107] to attach the people [to

---

[102] A common image of the South (see e.g. *Shih chi*, 101.2741, 113.2970, 129.3268.) and the reason why it was thus detested and feared by the officials of the capital as a dangerous place for banishment. Famous are Chia Yi's 賈誼 worries about his own health, when he could not avert his demotion to Ch'ang-sha 長沙, that was known to be "low lying and damp." His sorrows found artistic expression in two rhapsodies: "Condoling Ch'ü Yüan" (*Tiao Ch'ü Yüan fu* 弔屈原屈原賦) and the "Owl" (*Fu-niao fu* 鵬鳥賦) (*Shih chi*, 84.2492–2500 [*Grand Scribe's Records*, 7:303–307]).

[103] Chi-pei was a kingdom located in modern Shantung within the territory of the old Kingdom of Ch'i 齊.

[104] *Chen* 貞 was apparently an immaculate title, as all three explanations of the *Shih fa* (see *Shih chi*, "Shih fa chieh," p. 21) are full of praise: 清白守節 "innocent and principled," 大慮克就 "greatly anxious about his accomplishment in service," and 不隱無屈 "unconcealing and unbending."

[105] By stripping Liu Tz'u 劉賜 of his territory south of the Chiang, his new kingdom would no longer share a border with the barbarian kingdoms of the southeast.

[106] Remarkably the *Han shu* does not contain this sentence.

[107] The term *yin te* 陰德, might refer in the context of the ritual literature to the "virtue of concealed [nature]" that is preserved in the proper relation between a man and a women (that avoids the harms of licentiousness to one's virtue), or the secret virtue of the wife of a ruler who secretly governs the inner quarters by her deeds and instructions, while the ruler orders the outside world. On each of the six times the term occurs in the *Shih chi* it denotes a different idea that seems to be better captured by the tentative translation as "secretly

[practicing / practiced] good deeds": Chao Tun 趙盾 (d. 601 BC), who controlled the politics at Chin 晉 for a long time, is saved by Shih-mi Ming 示眯明, whom he once rescued from starving and now, in turn, aids his savior to escape the assassination attempts of Duke Ling 靈 of Chin. Without revealing his name, Shih-mi Ming did this to repay the "the secretly practiced good deed" of Chao Tun (See *Shih chi*, 39.1674 [*Grand Scribe's Records*, 5:351]). His Honor the Grand Scribe's words at the end of chapter 45 focus on the story of the orphan of the Chao 趙 familiy: 韓厥之感晉景公，紹趙孤之子武，以成程嬰、公孫杵臼之義，此天下之陰德也。 "When Han Chüeh moved Duke Ching of Chin and had the orphaned son of the Chao's, [Chao] Wu, continue [their family line], in order to fulfill the righteous intentions of Ch'eng Ying and Kung-sun Ch'u-chiu, it was all about secretly practiced goods in this world" (see *Shih chi*, 49.1878). This appraisal of Chao Tun's help in the restoration of the Chao Clan is repeated with a further reference to his "secretly practiced good deed" on *Shih chi*, 130.3310. It is interesting to note that the rescued orphan is the grandchild of Chao Tun. *Shih chi* chapter 46 tells of yet a further family's rise to power: Tien Ch'i 田乞 (d. 485 B.C), who served three subsequent Dukes of Ch'i 齊 and controlled its court politics, made his name by "secretly practicing good deeds" (*hsing yin te* 行陰德) amongst the people: 其收賦稅於民以小斗受 之，其稟予民以大斗 "collecting the taxes he used a small *tou* as measure to receive them but giving out grain to the people he used a large *tou*" (see *Shih chi*, 46.1881). This kind of generosity made sure that the Tien clan soon controlled everything in the state of Chin. Chao Kao's 趙高 words towards the newly enthroned Second Emperor of Ch'in clearly demonstrate how kindness was implemented as a soft power instrument in court politics: 嚴法而刻刑，令有罪 者相坐誅，至收族，滅大臣而遠骨肉；貧者富之，賤者貴之。盡除去先帝之故臣，更置陛下之所親信者近之。此則陰德歸陛下，害除而姦謀塞，羣臣莫不被潤澤，蒙厚德，陛下則高枕 肆志寵樂矣。計莫出於此。 "Make the laws more severe and the penalties harsher, have those who have committed crimes implicate each other in their punishment and include their entire clans. Exterminate the great vassals and distance yourself from your flesh and blood. Enrich the poor and honor the humble. Do away with all the old ministers of the Late Emperor and appoint in their place those whom you trust or feel close to. If you can do this, then they will turn to Your Majesty by the virtue of secretly practiced good deeds, your worries will be removed and treacherous plots cut short. All the officials will be blessed by your kindness, covered with your lavish favors, and Your Majesty can recline peacefully on a high pillow, giving free rein to your desires and favoring whatever you enjoy. No plan could be more outstanding." (see *Shih chi*, 87.2552 [*Grand Scribe's Records*, 7:346; translation of the key phrase adapted]). Finally, the term *yin te* is also the name of a constellation of two stars (*Shih chi*, 27.1290), that according to "So-yin" (cited *ibid.*) are the "guidelines of the world" (*t'ien-hsia wang* 天下綱). As Sung Chün 宋均 (cited by "So-yin") believes, if secretly good deeds are practiced, the "way will last" (*tao ch'ang* 道常). For our context, the most interesting commentary stems from a classic about stars cited in "Cheng-yi" (*ibid.*): 明，新君踐極也。 "If [this constellation] shines brightly, a new ruler will step on the top [i.e., accede to the throne]."

Whatever concrete expectations Liu An had, when he secretly practiced good deeds in his state, he could rely on a deeply rooted belief that his efforts were not made in vain. As it is

himself] and to spread his good name throughout the world.[108] He time and time again harbored rancor that King Li 厲 had died, and at times wished to turn in rebellion, although he did not yet have an excuse.

recorded in the *Kuei-ku Tzu* 鬼谷子 (1.17b, *SPTK*): 遠而親者，有陰德也. "Those who can make close [friends] of those who are far away have [the virtue of] secretly practicing good deeds"; or as Chia Yi 賈誼 has phrased it in his *Hsin shu* 新書 (6.17b, *SPTK*): 有陰德者，天報以福。 "Those who have secretly practiced good deeds, will be rewarded by Heaven with good fortune." We can even find this concept of retribution present in the *Huai-nan Tzu* (18.5a, *SPTK*): 夫有陰德者，必有陽報；有陰行者，必有昭名。 "Now, those who secretly practice good deeds are determined to openly receive rewards [for them]; those who acts secretly are determined to have bright names [for themselves]."

For a brief overview of the impact of the belief in good deeds in the *Han shu*, see Tsan Feng-hua 昝風華, "'Han shu' jen-wu hsing shen ch'i chia mo-shih yü Han-tai feng-su"《漢書》人物興身起家模式與漢代風俗 , *Kan-su she-hui k'o-hsüeh*, 5.2012, p. 166–69.

[108] The peculiar expression *liu yü t'ien hsia* 流譽天下, that the *Han shu* (44.2145) felt compelled to reproduce as *liu ming yü* 流名譽, "spread his name and reputation," might recall the following *Hsün Tzu* 荀子 passage (9.10b, *SPTK*; John Knoblock, *Xunzi* [Stanford: Stanford University Press, 1988], 2:206): 凡流言、流說、流事、流謀、流譽、流愬、不官而衡至者，君子慎之 "As a general principle, the gentleman will be cautious in dealing with wayward doctrines, wayward theories, wayward undertakings, wayward plans, wayward praises, wayward complaints, or anything that comes to him by irregular means or through unofficial channels."

The *Han shu* (44.2145) adds after this sentence a 136 character passage, elaborating on Liu An's literary skills and the Liu An's initially good relations with the young Wu-ti, that as a whole tries hard to mediate the following events: 招致賓客方術之士數千人，作為內書二十一篇，外書甚眾，又有中篇八卷，言神仙黃白之術，亦二十餘萬言。時武帝方好藝文，以安屬為諸父，辯博善為文辭，甚尊重之。每為報書及賜，常召司馬相如等視草乃遣。初，安入朝，獻所作內篇，新出，上愛祕之。使為離騷傳，且受詔，日食時上。又獻頌德及長安都國頌。每宴見，談說得失及方技賦頌，昏莫然後罷。 "He summoned several thousand guests and retainers, and practitioners of [magic] arts. He wrote 21 inner writings, a great many outer writings, and the 'Chung p'ien' 中篇 in 8 *chüan*, telling about the arts of [the inner alchemy] of gold and silver of the divine immortals, which comprised also more than 200.000 words. Just at that time, Wu-ti was fond of the arts and literature, and he made [Liu] An and his like [his] uncles. Since they were distinguished in many fields and good at composing literary texts, he deeply exalted and respected them. Every time he composed a reply or a letter of bestowment, he would often summon Ssu-ma Hsiang-ju and his like to look at the draft and only then dispatch it. Earlier, when [Liu] An had entered court, he presented the inner pieces he had composed. They had just recently appeared, when the Sovereign kept them secret out of appreciation [or: avarice]. The [Sovereign] had [Liu] An compose a 'Li sao chuan' 離騷傳 [Commentary to 'Encountering Sorrow'], [Liu An] received the order in the order in the morning and handed it

When it came to the second year (139 BC) of the Chien-yüan 建元 reign, the King of Huai-nan 淮南 entered the court [to pay respects]. He had always had good relations with the Marquis of Wu-an 武安 [T'ien Fen 田蚡], and since the Marquis of Wu-an was at this time acting as Grand Commandant, he then received the King at Pa-shang 霸上 (Pa Heights),[109] and recounted to the King: "Just now the Sovereign has no Heir, and you, Great King, are a close relative to him,[110] being the grandson of Kao Huang-ti (The Exalted August Emperor);[111] you practice benevolence and righteousness, no one in the world has not heard of [you]. If the palace chariot were to be hitched late one day [i.e., if the present Emperor passes away], who, if not you, Great King, would deserve to be the one to be enthroned!" The King of Huai-nan was greatly happy, and lavishly presented the Marquis of Wu-an with wealth and goods. He covertly attracted guests and retainers,[112] attached the people [to himself], [all] for [his] undertaking to rebel and disobey.

in at meal time during the day. Furthermore, he presented the 'Sung Te' 頌德 [Praising Virtue] and the 'Ch'ang-an tu-kuo sung' 長安都國頌 [Hymn on Ch'ang-an, Capital of the State]. He was received [by the Emperor] at every banquet, talking about gains and losses [in history], and when it came to the poetical pieces about the techniques of [magic] arts, they would only stop late after dusk."

In the light of the praise of Liu An's literary output in the *Han shu*, it is astonishing that the *Shih chi* does not concretize Liu An's writing activities. For a study on works attributed to Liu An see Yü Ta-ch'eng 于大成 (1934–2001), "Huai-nan wang shu k'ao" 淮南王書考, in *Huai-nan wang Hung-lieh lun-wen chi* 淮南鴻烈論文集 [Taipei: Li-jen, 2005], pp. 1–70, and further Ch'i Tzu-yang 漆子揚, "Liu An chi pin-k'o chu shu k'ao lüeh" 劉安及賓客著述考略, *Ku-chi cheng-li yen-chiu hsüeh-k'an*, vol. 1 (2006), pp. 38–41.

[109] According to Ying Shao (cited in "Chi-chieh, *Shih chi*, 6.275), the Pa Heights were located at the River Pa roughly thirty miles east of Ch'ang-an (T'an Ch'i-hsiang, 2:15).

[110] Wang Shu-min (118.3209) refers to the parallel passages in the *Shih chi* (107.2855) and the *Ch'ien Han chi* 前漢紀 (11.11b, *SPTK*) that both read: 大王最賢，高帝孫... "you, the Great King, are the most able, and being the grandson of Kao Huang-ti ..."

[111] The "Cheng-yi" cites the long inserted *Han shu* passage (44.2145), translated in note 109 above, relating that Wu-ti treated Liu An and his like as "uncles" (*chu fu* 諸父).

[112] The "So-yin" quotes a passage from the "Yao-lüeh" 要略 chapter of the *Huai-nan Tzu* 淮南子, reading: 安養士數千，高才者八人，蘇非、李尚、左吳、陳由、伍被、毛周、雷被、晉昌，號曰「八公」也。 "[Liu] An raised several thousand scholars, eight [amongst them] were highly talented: Su Fei 蘇非, Li Shang 李尚, Tso Wu 左吳, Ch'en Yu 陳由, Wu P'i 伍被, Mao Chou 毛周, Lei P'i 雷被, Chin Ch'ang 晉昌; they were called the "Pa Kung" 八公 [The Eight Masters]." This quote is not part of the transmitted editions and is treated as a fragment, see Ho Ning 何寧, *Huai-nan Tzu chi shih* 淮南子集釋 (Peking: Chung-hua Shu-chü, 1998), p. 1495. Almost the same list of names–Su Fei 蘇非 being written Su Fei 蘇飛–appears in Kao Yu's 高誘 (3rd century) preface to the *Huai-nan Tzu* (*Huai-nan Hung-lieh chieh hsü* 淮

In the sixth year (135 BC) of the Chien-yüan reign, a comet was seen, the King of Huai-nan 淮南王 in his heart marveled at it. Somebody advised the King, saying: "At the time when the previous armies of Wu 吳 rose,[113] a comet appeared over a length of several *chih*, but still blood flowed [over a distance of] thousand *li*. Now, since a comet stretches over the whole sky, the troops in the world should rise in great numbers." Since the King in his heart believed that the Sovereign had no heir and that the various feudal Lords in case of an emergency in the world would all struggle to annex [territory], he even more than before prepared weapons and intruments for offensive warfare, and he accumulated money to bribe and present to the various feudal lords of the Commanderies and States,[114] the gentlemen who wandered about [seeking a position], and extraordinary talents. The various rhetoricians and strategists recklessly created wild rumors, they flattered the King, and since the King was happy, he bestowed them with inordinate amounts of money, and the plotting of the revolt became ever more extreme.

The King of Huai-nan 淮南 had a daughter named [Liu] Ling [劉]陵; she was intelligent and possessed rhetorical gifts. The King loved [Liu] Ling, he always gave her inordinate amounts of money, and she became an inside agent[115] in Ch'ang-an, to ensnare the courtiers of the Sovereign.[116]

南鴻烈解敘, 1.1b, *SPTK*), which leads Wang Shu-min (118.3209) to the conclusion that Ssu-ma Chen mistook the words from the preface as the text proper. For further information on these legendary figures see Ch'en Yüeh-ch'in 陳月琴, "Huai-nan Pa-kung chih pien-che" 淮南八公之辨析, *Chung-kuo tao-chiao*, 2 (1991): 32–33.

[113]As Wang Shu-min (118.3210) points out, this refers to the rebellion of Liu P'i 劉濞, King of Wu, in the year 154 BC.

[114] Wang Shu-min (118.3210) is–like the *Han shu* (44.2146)–troubled by the fact, that technically the rulers of a Commandery would not be called *chu-hou* 諸侯 (various feudal lords), which is reserved for the royal rulers of the states–opts to delete these two characters.

[115] Meng K'ang (cited in "So-yin"), reads *hsiung* 詗 as homophonous to (rhyming with?) *chen* 偵, a word of the people of the West for a counter-spy (*fan chien* 反閒), which is, according to Wang Shu-min (118.3210), the best explanation for this passage.

[116] Chou Shou-ch'ang 周壽昌 (1814–1884; cited by Wang Hsien-ch'ien [*Han shu pu chu*, 44.9b]) refers to O Po 鄂伯, the great-great-grandson of O Ch'ien-ch'iu 鄂千秋, Marquis of An-p'ing 安平侯, who was executed, displaying his corpse in the marketplace, for having an affair with her and dispatching a letter to the King of Huai-nan referring to himself as *ch'en chin li* 臣盡力 "Your servant exerts all his powers to…," as well as Chang Tz'u-kung 張次公, the Marquis of An-t'ou 岸頭, who was tried and finally removed from office for having an illicit affair with her and receiving bribes in the first year of the Yüan-shuo 元朔 reign (128 BC).

In the third year of the Yüan-shuo 元朔 reign (126 BC),[117] [*3083*] the Sovereign bestowed the King of Huai-nan with an armrest and a cane and he did not go to the court [to pay respects]. As for T'u 荼, the Queen of the King of Huai-nan, the King loved and favored her. The Queen bore [Liu] Ch'ien [劉]遷,[118] the Heir, and [Liu] Ch'ien took the daughter of Hsiu-ch'eng Chün 修成君, a descendent of the female line of Wang Huang T'ai-hou 王皇太后 (Queen August Dowager) as his consort.[119] When the King was plotting to prepare the instruments for a revolt, he feared that the consort of the Heir would learn of it and from within leak [his] undertakings, and only then did he plot together with the Heir, making him pretend that he did not love [his consort] and for three months not share a mat with her. Only then did the King feign to be angry with the Heir because of her, confined the Heir, and made him spend three months with [his] consort in the same room; but until the end the Heir never approached [his] consort. The consort requested to leave, and thus the King submitted a memorial to send her back home with an apology. T'u, the Queen, [Liu] Ch'ien, the Heir, and [Liu] Ling, the daughter, gained the love and favor of the King, they arrogated the power in the state, invaded and seized the fields and houses of the people, and recklessly caused people to be detained.[120]

In the fifth year (124 BC) of the Yüan-shuo reign, the Heir learned to use a sword, he himself believing that no other man was up to him; he heard that Lei P'i 靁被,[121] the Gentleman-of-the-Palace, was skillful,[122] and only then did he summon him to sport with him. [Lei] P'i modestly yielded the first and second time,[123] [but then] he accidently touched the Heir. The Heir was angry, [Lei] P'i afraid. At this time, if somebody wished to join the army, he would at once go to the capital city; [Lei] P'i

---

[117] Liang Yü-sheng (118.1427) refers to the *Han shu* (6.170 and 44.2146) that records this event consistently in the second year of the Yüan-shuo reign (127 BC).

[118] The story of Queen T'u and her son Liu Ch'ien is told in the following passage of this memoir. See also Loewe, *Dictionary,* p. 514 and 345.

[119] According to Ying Shao (cited in "Chi-chieh"), Hsiu-ch'eng Chün 修成君 was the daughter from a previous marriage to the Chin 金 clan. Chou Shou-ch'ang 周壽昌 (1814–1884; cited by Wang Hsien-ch'ien [*Han shu pu chu*, 44.10a]) and Wang Shu-min (118.3211) both refer to the anecdote, e.g. recorded on *Shih chi*, 52.2007, when her daughter, named O 娥, failed–probably after her return from Huai-an–to marry the King of Ch'i 齊.

[120] According to Hsü Kuang (cited in Chi-chieh), one edition reads "beat up" (*ou chi* 毆擊) instead of "caused to be detained."

[121] Lei P'i's following flight to Ch'ang-an and report to the court played a major role in the case against Huai-nan. See also Loewe, *Dictionary*, p. 216.

[122] According to "So-yin," *ch'iao* 巧 means that he was good at using his sword.

[123] Although Yüeh Ch'an 樂產 (cited in "So-yin") explains that Lei P'i yielded to the heir the first and the second time, it is still up to the reader whether Lei P'i just let him win twice or chose to not engage at all.

then wished to fervently attack the Hsiung-nu. [Liu] Ch'ien 遷, the Heir, several times
maligned him to the King and the King ordered the Prefect of the Gentlemen-of-the-
Palace to expel and dismiss him, thereby wishing to prohibit later [imitators].[124] [Lei]
P'i fled after all and arrived at Ch'ang-an, he submitted a memorial explaining
himself. [The Emperor] decreed to hand down his case upon the Commandant of
Justice and Ho-nan 河南.[125] Ho-nan tried [the case and wanted to] capture the Heir of
Huai-nan.[126] [But] the King and the Queen laid plans, not wishing to send off the Heir,
they would after all sent out troops to revolt; but [their] planning was hesitative, after
more than ten days they had not yet decided upon it. Just then, there was a decree, to
immediately proceed [to Huai-nan] in order to interrogate the Heir.[127] Meanwhile, the
Chancellor of Huai-nan was angry about the Assistant of Shou-ch'un 壽春[128] for
keeping the Heir in custody and not sending him off,[129] he impeached him for being
disrespectful. In this matter the King begged the Chancellor [for him], but the
Chancellor did not listen to him. The King sent a man to submit a memorial accusing
the Chancellor; the case was handed down upon the Commandant of Justice to be
tried. Since the traces incriminated the King, the King had a man spy on the
Excellencies and Ministers of the Han; the Excellencies and Ministers requested to
capture and try the King. The King was afraid that his undertakings would be exposed,
thus [Liu] Ch'ien, the Heir, [*3084*] plotted [with him]: "The Han envoys will
immediately capture you, My King; My King should have men put on the clothes of
the Guards and bearing halberds be stationed in the court hall; and if next to you, My

---

[124] According to "Cheng-yi," the first part of the sentence refers to the dismissal of the
whole office of the Gentleman-of-the-Palace (lang-chung ling kuan 郎中令官), reading: "the
King ordered the Gentlemen-of-the-Palace [and their] Prefect to be expelled and dismissed".
However, Wang Shu-min (118.3211) and Takigawa (118.17) both cite Yü Yu-ting 余有丁
(1527–1584) who argues that it was Lei P'i who was dismissed by his superior, the Prefect of
Gentlemen-of-the-Palace.

[125] As "Cheng-yi" stresses, the matter was originally handed down to the Commandant of
Justice and Ho-nan to try it jointly.

[126] According to "Cheng-yi," tai 逮 means "to pursue and make him go to Ho-nan" (chui
fu Ho-nan 追赴河南).

[127] According to Yüeh Ch'an 樂產 (cited in "Cheng-yi"), chi 即 means chiu 就, "to go
to" Huai-nan and question him there.

[128] According to Ju Ch'un (cited in "Chi-chieh"), the Assistant (Ch'eng 丞) of Shou-
ch'un, the Captial of Huain-nan, was in charge of the corporal punishment cases and the
prisoners. He was chosen by the King himself, while the Chancellor of Huai-nan was sent by
the court, which becomes apparent by their respective loyalties in this matter.

[129] Alternatively reading: "…was angry about the Assistant of Shou-ch'un for delaying
the capture of the Heir and not sending him off."

King, there is someone challenging your rightful actions,[130] have [your men] stab and kill them; your servant would also send a man to stab and kill the Commandant of the Capital of Huai-nan 淮南, if you would only then raise the troops, it would not yet be too late." At this time, the Sovereign did not grant the request of the Excellencies and Ministers, but sent Hung 宏, the Commandant of the Capital of the Han,[131] to proceed [to Huai-nan] and interrogate and investigate [the King]. When the King heard that the Han envoys had come, he then acted in accordance to the plan of the Heir. When the Commandant of the Capital of the Han arrived, the King observed that his countenance was amicable, he interrogated the King only in regard to the case concerning the expelling of Lei P'i, and the King himself assessed that this meant nothing,[132] and did not set [his plan] in motion. When the Commandant of the Capital returned, he made [this] known to [the court]. The Excellencies and Ministers that were trying [the case] said: "[Liu] An, the King of Huai-nan, holds back and restrains those who would fervently attack the Hsiung-nu, like Lei P'i and that sort, putting aside and not complying with a radiant decree.[133] He deserves [to be executed and] have his corpse displayed in the marketplace." By decree this was not allowed. When the Excellencies and Ministers requested to abolish him and not treat him like a King, by decree this was not allowed. When the Excellencies and Ministers requested to reduce [the size of his territory] by five counties, by decree [the size of his territory] was decreased by two counties. [The Sovereign] ordered Hung 宏, the Commandant

---

[130] The expression *yu fei shih* 有非是 could also be understood as "if there is someone against our course" or "if there is something not right."

[131] The "So-yin" reference to the "Pai-kuan piao" 百官表, relating that the last name of Hung 宏 should be Yin 殷, is only partially helpful, since then, as Liang Yü-sheng (118.1427) already pointed out, his full name should rather be Yin Jung 殷容 (*Han shu*, 19B.772), who held the post of Commandant of the Capital in the year 124 BC–at least according to the Chung-hua edition and also Mizusawa's note (118.7). However, Takigawa (118.18), Wang Hsien-ch'ien (*Han shu pu chu*, 44.10b) and Wang Shu-min (118.3211) all apparently refer to a *Han shu* edition that reproduces the name in the table as Yin K'o 殷客. The second passage adduced in the quest for the real name of the Commandant of the Capital is located in the "Chi Cheng lieh-chuan" 汲鄭列傳 on *Shih chi*, 120.3111, where a certain Tuan Hung 段宏 (likewise *Han shu*, 50.2323, only "So-yin" refers to his name as Tuan K'o 段客) from P'u-yang 濮陽, who at first served Wang Hsin 王信, the elder brother of Ching-ti's Empress Wang, before he reached the rank of the nine ministers twice, is mentioned. While all those variants could be reduced to one proper form, e.g. Tuan Hung 段宏, as Michael Loewe (*Dictionary*, p. 86) does, Wang Shu-min's warning should not be forgotten: these different forms might actually be references to two distinct persons.

[132] According to Ju Ch'un (cited in "Chi-chieh") this meant "there was nothing to find him guilty of" (*wu ho ts'ui* 無何罪).

[133] For further occurrences of the technical term "putting aside and not complying with" a decree (*fei ko* 廢格) see *Shih chi*, 30.1453 and 122.4165.

of the Capital, to pardon the King of Huai-nan of his offense, and to punish him by reducing [his] territory. When the Commandant of the Capital entered the borders of Huai-nan, he announced [that the Emperor] had pardoned the King. At first, the King had heard that the Excellencies and Ministers of the Han had requested to execute him, he had not yet known that he had got [the punishment of] reducing [his] territory. When he heard that the Han envoys had arrived, he was afraid that they would arrest him, and only then did he plot with the Heir to stab them according to the previous plan. When it came that the Commandant of the Capital arrived, he then congratulated the King, and for this reason the King did not set [his plan] in motion. After this, he bemoaned himself and said: "Practicing benevolence and righteousness [my territory] has been reduced; I am deeply insulted by this."[134] But after the King of Huai-nan had been reduced in territory, his plotting to revolt increased dramatically. The various envoys came by road from Ch'ang-an,[135] they recklessly created wild rumors; when they told that the Sovereign had no male [offspring] and that the Han would not try [him], [the King] was then happy; but when they then told that the Han court would try [him], and that the [Sovereign] had a male [offspring], the King would become angry, believed it to be wild rumors and not true.

[3085] Day and night, the King explored the geographical maps[136] together with Wu P'i 伍被[137] and Tso Wu 左吳, laying out from which points the troops should

---

[134] As Wang Shu-min (118.3212) points out, Liu An should call himself lucky that he merely lost some of his territory "practicing benevolence and righteousness," and not his whole state, as happened to Hsü Yen Wang 徐偃王 (see *Han Fei Tzu* 韓非子, 19.2a, *SPTK*).

[135] As Ju Ch'un (cited in "So-yin") clarifies, *tao* 道 is to be taken as *lu* 路, i.e., "by road."

[136] The functional translation "geographical maps" for *yü-ti t'u* 輿地圖 (literally: "earth-as-carriage plans") obscures its relation to the concept of the *tao* 道 (the way) as exemplified in the first lines of the received text of the *Huai-nan Tzu*: 夫道者，覆天載地，廓四方，柝八極，高不可際，深不可測，包裹天地，稟授無形。 "As for the way, it covers Heaven and upholds Earth. It extends the four directions and divides the eight end points. So high, it cannot be reached. So deep, it cannot be fathomed. It embraces and enfolds Heaven and Earth, it endows and bestows the Formless" (see *Huai-nan Hung-lieh chieh* 淮南鴻烈解, 1.2b-3a, *SPTK*; John S. *Major* et al., trans., *The Huainanzi: A Guide to the Theory and Practice of Government in Early Han China* [New York: Columbia University Press, 2010], p. 48). As Su Lin (cited in "Chih-chieh") asserts, *yü* 輿 in the context of *yü-ti t'u* means to "fully carry" (*chi tsai* 盡載). Remarkably, to "take the earth as carriage" (*yü ti* 輿地) is an important part of the ideal of the Great Man that the first chapter of the *Huai-nan Tzu* propagates: 是故大丈夫恬然無思，澹然無慮；以天為蓋，以地為輿；四時為馬，陰陽為御；乘雲陵霄，與造化者俱; "Therefore, the Great Man calmly has no worries and placidly has no anxieties. He takes Heaven as his canopy; Earth as his carriage; the four seasons as his steeds, and yin and yang as his charioteers. He rides the clouds and soars through the sky to become a companion of the power that fashions and transforms us" (*Huai-nan Hung-lieh chieh* 淮南鴻烈解, 1.4b , *SPTK*;

invade. The King said: "The Sovereign has no Heir, if the palace chariot were be hitched late, the ministers at court would be sure to summon the King of Chiao-tung 膠東 [Liu Chi 劉寄 (d. 121 BC)], if not the King of Ch'ang-shan 常山 [Liu Shun 劉舜 (d. 114 BC),[138] and the various feudal lords would struggle to annex [territory], how could We remain unprepared! Furthermore, We are a grandson of Kao-tsu, and personally We have practiced benevolence and righteousness; since His Majesty has treated Us generously, We could tolerate this [situation]; but if ever after ten thousand

John S. Major, *ibid.*, pp. 52–53). Heaven and Earth are both conceptualized as part of an ancient carriage, i.e., the round canopy top and the actual square body of the carriage, that resembles with its rectangular struts a lidless cubic basket.

The question, whether *yü-ti t'u* were first drawn by the Han scholars, whether the name as such existed since antiquity, as "So-yin" (118.3085 and 60.2110) believes, or whether they were already used much earlier, awaits further investigation. The first surviving map that actually bears the title *yü-ti t'u* dates back to the mid 13th century (see Ts'ao Wan-ju 曹婉如 et al., *Chung-kuo ku-tai ti-t'u chi* 中國古代地圖集 [Peking: Wen-wu Ch'u-pan-she, 1990],vol. 1, map 82). Maps which contain "carriage" (*yü* 輿) as part of their title became current from the Yuan dynasty on, starting with the innovative *Yü t'u* 輿圖 ([Earth-as-]Carriage Map; ca. 1315, lost) by Chu Ssu-pen 朱思本 (1273–1337) that survived in the form of the *Kuang yü t'u* 廣輿圖 (Enlarged [Earth-as-]Carriage Map, 1555) by Lo Hung-hsien 羅洪先 (1504–1564). Since then, *kuang yü t'u* 廣輿圖 became a standard title for global maps in late imperial China.

The variety of maps found at Ma-wang-tui, i.e., a topographic map, a county map, and a military garrison map, dating from before 168 BC, attest at least to the level of cartography in the second century BC As Hsu and Martin-Montgomery have shown in their analysis of the military garrison map, the mapmaker's aim was not necessarily cartographic accuracy, they rather visualized temporal-tactical information that would have helped to simulate several attack and defense scenarios (see Agnes Hsin-Mei Hsu and Anne Martin-Montgomery, "An Emic Perspective of the Mapmaker's Art in Western Han China," *Journal of the Royal Asiatic Society*, 17 [2007]: 444–57).

The translator is grateful to Vera Dorofeeva-Lichtmann for all the materials and references she provided for this footnote that could not have been written without her help.

[137] "Chi-chieh" quotes from his *Han shu* biography (45.2167), noting that Wu P'i was a native of Ch'u and probably a descendant of Wu Tzu-hsü 伍子胥. According to Yen Shih-ku (*Han shu*, 45.2167), the pronounciation of his first name should be: initial 皮 and rime 義, suggesting a modern reading as *p'i*–or even *pi* (same as 髮). For further biographical information see also Loewe, *Dictionary*, pp. 585–86.

[138] As Hsü Kuang (cited in "Chi-chieh") reminds the reader, both kings were children of Ching-ti. Liu Chi 劉寄 was a younger brother of Wu-ti, born by the lesser consort Lady Wang 王, who succeeded the later Wu-ti as King of Chiao-tung in 148 BC, ruling until his death in 120 BC (see Loewe, *Dictionary*, p. 314). Liu Shun 劉舜, the youngest of Ching-ti' sons, also born by the lesser consort Lady Wang 王 and infamous for his arrogance and licentiousness, was established as King of Chang-shan in 145 BC and ruled until his death in 114 BC.

generations [his life came to an end], how could We face north and serve as a subject to theses chaps?"

The King was seated in the Eastern Palace, when he summoned Wu P'i to plot with him, saying:[139] "Come up here, General!"[140] [Wu] P'i was upset and said: "The Sovereign has tolerantly pardoned you, Great King, so where, My King, do you again get these words that will cause a state to perish? Your servant has heard that [Wu] Tzu-hsü [伍]子胥[141] admonished the King of Wu, but the King of Wu did not use [his advice]; only then did [Wu Tzu-hsü] say [to him]: 'Now, your servant sees how the elaphures will wander about the Ku-su 姑蘇 Terrace.'[142] Now, your servant also sees how thistles and thorns will grow in the palace and dew will moisten [their] clothes." The King was angry, detained Wu P'i's father and mother, incarcerating them for three months. He summoned him again and said: "Will the General agree with Us, the lonely one?" [Wu] P'i said: "No, I just came to draw it up for you, Great King. Your servant has heard that a sharp-eared man will hear the soundless and a keen-eyed man will see the yet formless,[143] and therefore a sage will in ten thousand endeavors meet ten thousand times with complete success. In former times, once King Wen 文王 made his move, his merit shone [*3086*] a thousand generations and [his dynasty] was ranked within the Three Eras; this is someone who took advantage of the heart of

---

[139] In the *Han shu* the whole following passage featuring Wu P'i's eloquent manoeuvers (*Shih chi*, 118.3085–3087) is moved into Wu P'i's newly created biography (45.2168–2172)–which, according to Wang Ao 王鏊 (1450–1524; cited in *Shih chi p'ing-lin*, 118.10a), was a grave mistake.

[140] Chou Shou-ch'ang 周壽昌 (1814–1884; cited by Takigawa, 118.20) believes that the title "general" is reserved for the officials of the Emperor, and thus directly relates Wu P'i's irritation to Liu An's misuse of this reserved address. However, Wang Shu-min (118.3213) demonstrates by examples from Shih Chih-mien and Ch'ien Ta-hsin that "general" was also used as an expression of appreciation–without the notion of arrogation of an imperial privilege. Hence, Wu P'i's reaction might have been caused by the plotting itself rather than this particular address.

[141] Wu Tzu-hsü (d. 484), *praenomen* Yün 員, is remembered as the loyal servant who could not persuade Fu-ch'ai 夫差, the King of Wu, to protect his kingdom against the dangers of an imminent attack by Yüeh in the South, and was forced into suicide, while, in the end, history would proof him tragically right. See also his "Wu Tzu-hsü lieh-chuan" (*Shih chi*, chapter 66; *Grand Scribe's Records*, 7:49–59) and the "Wu T'ai-po shih-chia" 吳太伯世家 (*Shih chi*, 31.1461–1475; Grand *Scribe's Records*, 5:16–24)

[142] Despite several parallel accounts of Wu Tzu-hsü's story, this verse is only to be found in the words of Wu P'i. Ku-su Terrace refers to the structure that Ho-lü 闔閭 (d. 496 BC), King of Wu, built on the Mount Ku-su (modern Mount Ling-yen 靈岩山) on the southern edge of modern Soochow 蘇州 in Kiangsu.

[143] As Wang Shu-min (118.3213) recalls, this ideal of foresight is also mentioned in the preceding "Ssu-ma Hsiang-ju lieh-chuan" 司馬相如列傳 (*Shih chi*, 117.3054).

heaven in order to make his move and establish [a dynasty], therefore all within the seas followed him without prior concertation. This has been a conspicuous case from a thousand years ago. [The case of] Ch'in from a hundred years ago, or Wu and Ch'u from a generation ago, also suffice to tell whether a state will survive or perish. Your servant does not dare to avoid the punishment of [Wu] Tzu-hsü, he only wishes that you, Great King, do not become a [poor] listener like the King of Wu. In former times, the Ch'in cut off the way of the sages,[144] killed the learned specialists, burnt the *Songs* and *Documents*, abandoned propriety and righteousness, honored deceit and force, indulged in corporal punishments and fines, and had the grain from the regions close to the sea transported up to the territory west of the Ho. All the while, although the men worked hard on the fields, they could not even provide dregs and chaffs, and although the women weaved silk and hemp, they had not enough to cover their bodies.[145] [The Emperor] dispatched Meng T'ien 蒙恬[146] to build the Long Walls, stretching several thousand *li* from east to west; exposed to the harsh elements, the troops counted constantly several ten thousands, the dead were innumerable, the stiff corpses lined up to a thousand *li*, the shed blood covered vast fields, the strength of the common people was exhausted, and those who wished to revolt were five out of ten households. Then, [the Emperor] sent Hsü Fu 徐福[147] to enter the sea and request from the gods rare goods; when he returned he made up a beautiful story and said: 'Your servant has met a great god amidst the sea, he said to him: 'Are you the envoy of the Emperor of the West?' Your servant replied: 'So it is.' 'What are your requests?' He said: 'We wish to ask for a medicine to prolong one's years and extend one's longevity.' The god said: 'The gifts of your King of Ch'in are meager, you get to look at it, but you cannot take any with you.' Then he made your servant follow [him] southeast until we reached the P'eng-lai Islands 蓬萊山;[148] I saw palaces and towers made of divine mushrooms; there was an envoy with a copper-colored body of a dragon, and a light arose illuminating the sky. At this, your servant bowed twice

---

[144] Wang Shu-min (118.3213) refers to the notes of Takigawa (118.22) to document the emendation of "sages" (*sheng jen* 聖人) in favor of "former kings" (*hsien wang* 先王) that is featured in various editions (see Mizusawa, 118.9).

[145] Wang Shu-min (118.32149 refers to two passages in the *Shih chi* (30.1464 and 112.2954) that paint an almost identical image of distress.

[146] Meng T'ien was the general responsible for building the defense systems in the North, known as the Long Walls. After the sudden death of the First Emperor, he became the victim of court intrigues and was asked to commit suicide. See his biography in *Shih chi* chapter 88 and on *Grand Scribe's Records*, 7:361–66.

[147] According to Liang Yü-sheng (118.1428), Hsü Fu 徐福 refers to the same voyager that appears on *Shih chi*, 6.247, as Hsü Fu 徐巿, a native of Ch'i 齊, who requested to send an expedition to the immortals of the Eastern Sea. See also Loewe, *Dictionary*, p. 618.

[148] P'eng-lai, Fang-chang 方丈, and Ying-chou 瀛洲 were the three islands of immortals that Hsü Fu had requested to search for (see *Shih chi*, 6.247; *Grand Scribe's Records*, 1:142).

before him and asked: 'What should we provide as tribute to you?' The sea god said: 'Take men of a sounding reputation, and young[149] women, and products of the various craftsmen, then you will obtain it.'' The August Emperor of the Ch'in was greatly pleased, he dispatched three thousand young men and women, provided them with the five grains and honest craftsmen, and let them go on [their journey]. When Hsü Fu reached plains and broad pools,[150] he stopped there, made himself king, and did not come back. At this point, the common people were grieving and yearning, and those who wished to revolt were six out of ten households. Then, [the Emperor] sent Commandant [Chao] T'o [趙]佗[151] to cross the Wu-ling 五嶺 (Five Mountain Ranges)[152] and attack the hundred [tribes of] Yüeh 越. Commandant [Chao] T'o knew that the central states toiled under extreme hardship, so he stopped there, made himself king, and did not come back;[153] he sent a man to submit a memorial requesting thirty thousand unmarried women in order to mend the clothes of the officers and men. The August Emperor of the Ch'in allowed him fifteen thousand. At this point, the hearts of the common people were drifting apart, dissolving like tiles, and those who wished to revolt were seven out of ten households. A retainer said to the August Emperor Kao 高皇帝: 'The time is right now.' But the August Emperor Kao said: 'Wait for it, a Sage is about to rise from the Southeast.' Before one year had passed, Ch'en Sheng 陳勝 and Wu Kuang 吳廣 had already set [their plan] in

[149] According to Hsüeh Tsung 薛綜 (cited in "Chi-chieh"), chen 振 (vibrant?) refers to young men and women. Liang Yü-sheng (118.1428) and Oka Hakku 岡白駒 (1692–1767; cited in Takigawa 118.23) take chen 振 as a miswriting or variant of chen 侲 (young child).

[150] P'ing-yüan 平原 ("plains") and kuang tse 廣澤 ("broad pools") are not treated as toponyms in the Chung-hua edition which leaves it to the reader to speculate about the legends of Hsü Fu reaching certain places in Japan or other islands in the Pacific Ocean.

[151] Chao T'o was first sent to the south of the Ch'in Empire and established the Kuei-lin 桂林, Hsiang 象 and Nan-hai 南海 commanderies, where he served as Prefect of Lung-ch'uan 龍川. Later on, he severed his ties to the Ch'in and started setting up his own Kingdom of Nan Yüeh 南越. See also Shih chi chapter 113 and the translation of that chapter in this volume.

[152] The Five Mountain Ranges stretching from Kiangsi to Kwangsi in the West roughly demarcate the watershed between the drainage area oft he Yangtze and the Chu-chiang 珠江 (Pearl River), they specifically refer to the Ta-yü Mountain Range 大庾嶺, the Yüeh-ch'eng Mountain Range 越城嶺, the Ch'i-t'ien Mountain Range 騎田嶺, the Meng-chu Mountain Range 萌渚嶺, and the Tu-p'ang Mountain Range 都龐嶺.

[153] Liang Yü-sheng (118.1428) notices the slightly distorted timeline of Wu P'i's account, since according to the parallel account in the "Nan Yüeh lieh-chuan" 南越列傳 (Shih chi, 113.2967) Chao T'o made himself King only after the end of the Ch'in. This twist might be excused by the extemporaneous nature of his speech, as Yen Shih-ku (cited by Liang Yü-sheng) pleads.

motion.[154] The August Kao started at Feng 豐 and P'ei 沛,[155] but once he raised his voice, those in the world who followed him in response without prior concertation were innumerable. This is someone who is characterized as profiting from [other people's] mistakes and waiting for the opening [of an opportunity], taking advantage of the destruction of the Ch'in and making his move. The common people were wishing for it, like the grass is hoping for rain,[156] and therefore he was made the Son of Heaven, although he rose from the ranks of a foot-soldier; his merits are higher than the Three Kings, and his virtuous deeds are passed down inexhaustibly. Now, you, Great King, [*3087*] see the ease with which the August Emperor Kao has obtained the world, why only won't you look at [the case of] Wu and Ch'u one generation ago? The King of Wu was granted the title 'Libationer of the Liu Clan,' he did not again go to the court [to pay respects], he was king over a host of four provinces, his territory stretched over several thousand *li*; in the interior he melted away the copper to mint cash, in the East he boiled the sea water to produce salt; high up [in the North] he took the trees of Chiang-ling 江陵[157] to make boats, the load volume of a single boat being several dozen chariots of the central states; the state was rich and the people were numerous. He spread pearls, jades, gold, and silk to bribe the various feudal lords, the imperial family, and the great ministers, only the Tou 竇 Clan[158] did not partake. When the plans were set and the plotting was complete, he raised his troops and marched west. He was crushed at Ta-liang 大梁,[159]

[154] Ch'en Sheng and Wu Kuang are the two famous leaders who initiated the revolt against the Ch'in in 209 BC. The *Shih chi* dedicated Ch'en Sheng with the "Ch'en She shih-chia" 陳涉世家 even its own chapter. See also Loewe, *Dictionary*, pp. 38–39 and p. 585.

[155] Feng refers at that time still to a village inside of P'ei County. Only after Liu Pang's rise, Feng would be elevated to county status. P'ei is located on the western banks of the modern Wei-shan Lake 微山湖, thirty miles southeast of modern Chi-ning 濟寧 in Kiangsu; Feng lies twenty miles to the west of it (T'an Ch'i-hsiang, 2:19).

[156] Wang Shu-min (118.3216) refers to the parallel use of this image in *Meng Tzu* 1B.16.

[157] Chiang-ling County is located on the northern banks of the Yangtze, five miles east of modern Ching-chou 荊州 in Hupeh (T'an Ch'i-hsiang, 2:22).

[158] The Tou clan refers to the mother of Ching-ti, Empress Dowager Tou 竇 (d. 135 BC) and her relatives, e.g. her brother Tou Kuang-kuo 竇廣國 (d. 150), *agnomen* Shao-chün 少君, her nephews Tou P'eng-tsu 竇彭祖 (d. 136 B.C) and Tou Ying 竇嬰 (d. 131?), who would rise to some importance during Wu-ti's reign. See Loewe, *Dictionary*, pp. 78–89, p. 76, p. 76, and pp. 79–80.

[159] According to Han Chao-ch'i (118.5872), Ta-liang refers to the capital of the Kingdom of Liang 梁, Sui-yang 睢陽, located at the southern edge of modern Shang-chiu 商丘 in Honan (T'an Ch'i-hsiang, 2:19)

and defeated at Hu-fu 狐父[160]; he fled in a rush and went east; when he reached Tan-t'u 丹徒,[161] the Yüeh caught him, with the death of his person ended the sacrifices [to his ancestors], and he was laughed at by the whole world. What was the reason that with the hosts of Wu and Yüeh[162] he was not able to accomplish merit? Honestly, it was because they went against the way of Heaven and were not aware of the right point in time. Nowadays, the Great King's troops do not account for even one tenth of those of Wu and Ch'u, and the world's state of peaceful serenity is ten thousand times higher than that of the time of the Ch'in,[163] thus I wish that you, Great King, would follow your servant's plan. If you, Great King, will not follow your servant's plan, I can now already see, how inevitably word about the Great King's undertakings will first leak out, before they are even completed. Your servant has heard that when the Viscount Wei 微 passed his former state, he felt sorrow; at this, he composed the 'Mai hsiu chih ko' 麥秀之歌 (Song of the Ears of the Wheat),[164] it is a piece about his grief that Chow 紂 did not make use of Prince Pi-kan 比干. Therefore the *Meng Tzu* reads: 'Chow 紂 was valued as a Son of Heaven, once dead, however, he did not even equal an ordinary man.' This was because Chow himself had cut himself off from the world already a long time ago, not because the world discarded him the day he

[160] According to Hsü Kuang (cited in "Chi-chieh"), the village of Hu-fu belongs to Tang 碭 County in Liang. Hu-fu is located about forty miles east of modern Shang-ch'iu 商丘 in Honan (T'an Ch'i-hsiang, 2:19). Wu P'i probably refers with this toponym to the decisive battle of Hsia-yi 下邑 ten miles north of Hu-fu (see *Shih chi*, 106.2834; *Grand Scribe's Records*, 9:121).

[161] Tan-t'u is located on the south bank of the estuary of the Yangtze River a few miles east of modern Chen-chiang-shih 鎮江市 in Soochow (T'an Ch'i-hsiang, 2:24).

[162] Wang Shu-min (118.3216) follows Takigawa (118.25) comments and doubts whether the text confused Yüeh 越 with Chu 楚, the eponymous ally of Wu during the rebellion of the seven kingdoms. The *Han shu* parallel (45.2922) eliminated the problematic "Yüeh."

[163] Wang Shu-min (118.3217) argues in line with previous commentators who preferred the current comparison to the times of the Ch'in over the alternative of some editions that read "[of the time] of Wu and Ch'u" (*yü Wu Ch'u* 於吳楚). Cf. also Mizusawa, 118.10.

[164] According to the "Sung Wei-tzu shih chia" 宋微子世家, it was not the Viscount Wei, the half-brother of Emperor Chow 紂, who wrote the "Song of the Ears of Wheat," but the Viscount Chi 箕, relative of Chow (possibly his uncle). He composed the song, when he passed by the ruins of the capital of the former Yin Dynasty on his way to pay homage to the ruling Chou. It ran: 麥秀漸漸兮，禾黍油油. 彼狡童兮，不我好仇. " Wheat sprouting up ears, how sharp are their awns; millet and sticky millet grows, how green and lush they are! The mischievous boy, why are not you dear to me" (see *Shih chi*, 38.1620–21; *Grand Scribe's Records*, 5:276–77). For sources that quote Viscount Wei as the author of this song see Wang Shu-min (118.3217).

died.[165] Now, your servant ventures to feel sorrow that you, Great King, will discard [your] princedom of a thousand chariots, and, furthermore, are sure to bestow me with a document to end my life, so I can be the first of the assembled subjects, and die in the eastern palace." At this moment, although his temper and resentment were tied up in a knot, [the King][166] did not vent [his emotions], tears filled the rims of his eyes and fell like a curtain; he then rose, ascended the stairs one by one, and walked away.

[3088] The King had a son of a concubine [named Liu] Pu-hai [劉]不害;[167] he was his eldest, but the King did not love him, thus the King, the Queen and the Heir did all not treat him as their son or elder brother. [Liu] Pu-hai had a son [named Liu] Chien [劉]建.[168] He was highly talented and energetic, [but] he constantly harbored resentment and hatred against the Heir for not treating his father right;[169] he also resented that, although at this time all the various feudal lords hat obtained [the right] to make their sons marquises and Huai-nan had only two sons, only one was made Heir, and only [Liu] Chien's father did not get to be a marquis. [Liu] Chien secretly made friends, wishing to destroy the Heir by accusations, in order that his father would replace him. When the Heir learned of this, he several times detained and flogged [Liu] Chien with a stick. Once [Liu] Chien knew all about the plotting of the Heir, and how he wished to kill the Han Commandant of the Capital, he sent his

---

[165] Prince Pi-kan was also a relative of Chow, who served the Emperor as a loyal servant. After upsetting Chow with his direct admonishments, the Emperor had him cut open to check if the heart of a sage really has seven holes as legend has it (see *Shih chi*, 38.1610; *Grand Scribe's Records*, 5:270).

[166] Wang Nien-sun (cited in Wang Shu-min, 118.3217) argues with regard to the *Han shu* parallel (45.2172) that reduced the concluding twenty-one characters of this passage to a mere: 被因流涕而起 "Thereupon, [Wu] P'i, while dropping tears, rose," that the subject of the first sentence should also be Wu P'i and not the King, Liu An. Wang Shumin (*ibid.*) concurs with his assessment and dismisses Takigawa's approach (118.26) that aims to preserve "King," a character that is marked as superfluous by the Chung-hua edition, by suggesting that he is supposed to be the subject in the first part of the sentence. However, as Han Chao-ch'i (118.5873) clarifies with reference to parallel occurrences of the term *li chieh* 歷階, i.e., ascending a flight of stairs (by putting two feet onto the same stair before taking the next one), in the *Shih chi* (32.1568, 33.1641, 47.2398, and 76.3162), the King is actually the subject of the whole passage that is deliberately used to describe his emotions and sudden departure into the inner quarters.

[167] Liu Pu-hai was the neglected first son of Liu An, see Loewe, *Dictionary*, p. 269.

[168] Liu Chien, looking for justice for his father, tried to cause the downfall of the appointed Heir, Liu Ch'ien, the second son of Liu An. See Loewe, *Dictionary*, p. 317.

[169] Fu Ch'ien (cited in "Chi-chieh") chooses, at least according to Wang Shu-min (118.3218), a rather winding way to report that the Heir: 不省錄著兄弟數中 "did not care to count [his father] amongst the ranks of [his] elder and younger brothers."

friend Chuang Chih 莊芷[170] from Shou-ch'un 壽春,[171] in the sixth year (123 B.C) of the Yüan-shuo reign, to submit a memorial to the Son of Heaven, that read: "Strong medicine tastes bitter in the mouth, but cures the disease, loyal words go against the ears, but benefit one's actions.[172] Now, Liu Chien, the Grandson of the King of Huai-nan, is highly talented and able, but T'u, the King of Huai-nan's Queen, and [Liu] Ch'ien, T'u's Heir, are constantly jealous of [Liu] Chien and harm him. Although [Liu] Bu-hai, Ch'ien's father, was innocent, [he] arrogated to himself [the authority] to detain him several times, and wished to kill him. Now, [Liu] Chien is alive, he could be summoned and questioned, in order to know all about Huai-nan's secret undertakings." When the memorial was made known [at court], the Sovereign handed down his case upon the Commandant of Justice, and the Commandant of Justice handed it down to [the officials of] Ho-nan 河南 to try. At this time, Shen Ch'ing 審卿, the grandson of the former Marquis of Pi-yang [Shen Yi-chi],[173] was on good terms with Kung-sun Hung 公孫弘,[174] the Chancellor, and harbored resentment against King Li of Huai-nan [Liu Ch'ang] for killing his grandfather [i.e., Shen Yi-chi]; thus did his best to have [Kung-sun] Hung investigate the Huai-nan affair to [Kung-sun] Hung sparing no expense; only then did [Kung-sun] Hung suspect Huai-nan of planning a revolt, and most thoroughly tried its criminal case. When Ho-nan tried [Liu] Chien, his elaborate statement implicated the Heir of Huai-nan and his party. The King of Huai-nan was worried about this, wished to set [his plan] in motion, and asked Wu P'i: "Is the Han court in order or in disarray?" Wu P'i said: "The world is in order." The King did not feel pleased, and said to Wu P'i: "My Lord,

[170] Liang Yü-sheng (118.2429) believes the *Han shu* is correct in giving his first name as Cheng 正, while Wang Shu-min (118.32189) favors Chih 芷. Otherwise unknown.

[171] Shou-ch'un, the capital of Huai-nan, is located ten miles southeast of modern Huai-nan-shih 淮南市 in Anhwei (see T'an Ch'i-hsiang, 2:24).

[172] Wang Shu-min (118.3218) traces this apparently popular saying (and its variations) through several ancient texts, and one parallel on *Shih chi*, 55.2623.

[173] Mao Tsan 茅瓚 (b. 1499; cited in *Shih chi p'ing-lin* 118.13a) marvels at this odd coincidence that brought together Liu Ch'ien, who wanted for his father to reveal the secret doings of Huai-nan, and Shen Ch'ing, who wanted to take revenge for the death of his grandfather Shen Yi-chi, the Marquis of Pi-yang. Shen Ch'ing is otherwise unknown. See Loewe, *Dictionary*, p. 470.

[174] Kung-sun Hung, the Marquis of P'ing-chin 平津侯, had become Chancellor in 124 BC and would continue to hold this position until his death in 121 BC. He was infamous for his application of the justice of the *Ch'un chiu* 春秋 and, although outwardly friendly to his enemies, would always repay any wrongs that had been done to him. He was responsible for the downfall of Tung Chung-shu 董仲舒 and Chu-fu Yen 主父偃. As Han Chao-ch'i (118.5874) remarks, he is one of Ssu-ma Ch'ien's most hated persons, see also his biography in the "P'ing-chin hou Chu-fu lieh-chuan" 平津侯主父列傳 (*Shih chi*, chapter 112.2946-53; *Grand Scribe's Records*, 9:363-72) and also Loewe, *Dictionary*, pp. 125-28.

why do you say the world is in order?" [Wu] P'i said: "P'i ventures to observe that the government of the court, the righteousness between the Lord and his vassals, the close relation between fathers and sons, the distinction between husbands and wives, and the order between seniors and juniors all achieved their proper order, because the Sovereign promotes the honored way of antiquity, and customs and practices and the guiding principles have never been faulty. Heavy loaded wealthy merchants travel all around the world; there is no place that roads have not been made accessible, and therefore trade routes run throughout [the world]. The Southern Yüeh serve and obey [the Han], the Ch'iang 羌 and Po 僰[175] come to court to present tributes, the Eastern Ou 東甌 come to court to offer submission, [the world] stretches as far as Ch'ang-yü 長榆,[176] [the regions of] Shuo-fang 朔方[177] are open to us, and the Hsiung-nu, with broken and damaged wings, have lost their allies, and are not rising. Although this does not come close to the times of greatest peace in antiquity, but it still could be taken as [an age of] order." The King became angry and [Wu] P'i apologized for his offence deserving death. The King then said to [Wu] P'i: "If there were troops [rising] in Shan-tung 山東 (East of the Mount), the Han would be sure to send the General-in-chief [Wei Ch'ing 衛青][178] [*3089*] to lead [their forces] and control Shan-tung. Master, what kind of man do you believe the General-in-chief is?" [Wu] P'i said: "Amongst P'i's friends is a certain Huang Yi 黃義,[179] he followed the General-in-chief in his assault on the Hsiung-nu; when he returned, he reported to P'i: 'The General-in-Chief treats the higher ups with courtesy, and the officers and men with kindness, all the troops are happy to be employed by him.[180] He rides up and down the

---

[175] According to Han Chao-ch'i (118.5875), the Ch'iang and the Po people had their homeland in modern the southern part of Szechwan, Shansi, and Kansu.

[176] Ju Ch'un (cited in "Chi-chieh") argues that Ch'ang-yü refers to the name of a pass, that according to Han Chao-ch'i was called Yü-mu sai 榆木塞 [Elm Tree Pass?], located north of Sheng-chou 勝州 (modern Tung-sheng 東勝, Inner Mongolia; T'an Ch'i-hsiang, 2:17).

[177] Shuo-fang refers to a Commandery established in the northern region of the Ordos loop, with its seat close to modern Urat Front Banner (Wu-la-t'e Ch'ien-ch'i 烏拉特前旗), Inner Mongolia (T'an Ch'i-hsiang, 2:17).

[178] Wei Ch'ing (d. 106 BC) was probably the foremost General of the Han-Dynasty, famous for his large scale expeditions against the Hsiung-nu. Under Wu-ti's reign his military carrier started with a first successful attack on the northern neighbors in 129 BC. He helped lead the great offensive in 119 BC that, although successful, was not crowned by the capture of the Shan-yü and finally resulted in Wei's loss of imperial favor. See his biography on *Shih chi*, 111.2921–29, *Grand Scribe's Records*, 9:311–28, and Loewe, *Dictionary*, pp. 574–75.

[179] Otherwise unknown; see Loewe, *Dictionary*, p. 166.

[180] As Wang Shu-min (118.3218) observes, this characterization presents Wei Ch'ing as comparable to the famous general Li Kuang 李廣 (Cf. "Li Chiang-chün lieh-chuan" 李將軍列傳, especially *Shih chi*, 109.2872, see also Loewe, *Dictionary*, p. 220–21.) who fought many battles against the Hsiung-nu. Late in his life, Li Kuang would be granted to join Wei Ch'ing

mountains on horseback like flying [on the wind], his skills and capabilities excel that of other men.' P'i believes that with skills and abilities like this, having several times led experienced troops [into battle], it would not be easy to resist him." When it came that Ts'ao Liang 曹梁,[181] the Internuncio, came on his mission to Ch'ang-an, he said that the General-in-chief's verbal orders were clear, he resisted the enemy with bravery, often [fighting] at the front line of his officers and men. When resting,[182] as long as the wells that are dug had not reached [the ground water], he would wait until all officers and men had gotten water, only then would he dare to drink.[183] When [his] troops were retreating, only when all his soldiers had crossed the river, would he cross. All the gold and silk that the August Empress Dowager had bestowed upon him, he completely took and bestowed upon [his] military officers. Even the famous generals of antiquity do not surpass him." The King was silent.[184]

When the King of Huai-nan saw that [Liu] Chien had been already summoned to be tried, he was afraid that the secret undertakings of [his] state were about to be discovered; he wished to send out [his troops], but when [Wu] P'i again believed [this move] to be difficult, only then did [the King] ask [Wu] P'i again: "Master, do you believe that it was right or wrong for Wu to levy his troops?" [Wu] P'i said: "I believe it was wrong. The King of Wu [Liu P'i] was most rich and noble, yet starting a rebellion was inappropriate, he himself died at Tan-t'u 丹徒, [his] head and feet were put to rest at a different place, and none of his children or grandchildren are counted among the living.[185] Your servant has heard that the King of Wu regretted [his] decision] enormously. I wish that the King would thoroughly consider this and not do

in 119 BC on his campaign, but only to see himself forced to take his own life due to the failure of reaching an appointed rendezvous after getting lost.

[181] Ts'ao Liang is otherwise unknown; see Loewe, *Dictionary*, p. 20.

[182] Wang Shu-min (118.3219) and Liang Yü-sheng (118.1429) are seduced by the *Han shu* parallel (45.2921), that reads 須士卒休，乃舍 "when the officers and men needed to rest, he set up camp," to speculate whether this *Shih chi* passage could be possibly corrupt, missing some characters.

[183] This behavior is again reminiscent of the way General Li Kuang 李廣 was depicted on *Shih chi*, 109.2872.

[184] Instead of the King's silence, the *Han shu* knows to report a rather different ending of this dialogue: 王曰：「夫蓼太子知略不世出，非常人也，以為漢廷公卿列侯皆如沐猴而冠耳。」被曰：「獨先刺大將軍，乃可舉事。」The King said: "This Heir of Liao [reference probably to his son by a concubine name Liao] knows strategies that are not from this world, he is not an ordinary man, and he believes all the Excellencies, Ministers, and various feudal Lords of the Han court are just like monkeys with an [official] hat on top." [Wu] P'i said: "If we could only first assassinate the Genearl-in-chief, then we could start a rebellion."

[185] According to Hsü Kuang (cited in "Chi-chieh"), one edition reads *chiao lei* 噍類 (living being) instead of *yi lei* 遺類 (surviving being).

something that [even] the King of Wu did regret." The King said: "It is a single word that men will die for.[186] Furthermore, what could Wu have known about a rebellion,[187] when more than forty Han Generals passed Ch'eng-kao 成皋 in a single day.[188] Now, I have ordered Lou Huan 樓緩[189] first to intercept [the Han] at the gorge of Ch'eng-kao, Chou P'i 周被[190] to lead down the troops from Ying-ch'uan 潁川[191] to block the roads of the Huan-yüan 轘轅 and the Yi Pass 伊闕,[192] and Ch'en Ting 陳定[193] to send out the troops of Nan-yang 南陽[194] to defend the Wu Pass 武關.[195] The Grand Administrator of Ho-nan 河南 will have only Lo-yang 雒陽[196] in his possession, how

[186] According to Hsüeh Tsan (cited in "Chi-chieh"), this meant that an accord sealed with one word would be fulfilled at the pain of death, or as a "Cheng-yi" fragment (cited in Chang Yen-t'ien 張衍田, ed., *Shih chi cheng-yi yi-wen chi chiao* 史記正義佚文輯校 [Peking: Chung-hua Shu-chü, 1985)], p. 415) states: 言男子出一言，至死不改，言反也; "By this is meant, if men utter one single word, till death they won't change [their minds]—that is they say 'Rebellion'."

[187] According to Hsüeh Tsan (cited in "Chi-chieh"), The King of Wu did not know how to start a rebellion.

[188] According to "Cheng-yi," the old town of Ch'eng-kao was situated just southeast of Ssu-shui 汜水 county (located between modern Loyang and Chengchow; T'an Ch'i-hsiang 2:16) in Honan. It controlled the strategic passage from the capital area within the passes toward the area east of the Mount, granted access to the Ao Grainery 敖倉 and Loyang, and thus witnessed many famous battles, e.g. between Liu Pang and Hsiang Yü. The King of Wu's negligence of its importance despite the advice of his General Huan 桓 (see *Shih chi*, 106.2832) is seen as one of the decisive reasons why the rebellion of the seven kingdoms failed.

[189] Lou Huan 樓緩 is otherwise unknown, and since the *Han shu* refers to him only by his first name, the "Chi-chieh" suspects this to be a later addition to the text.

[190] Otherwise unknown.

[191] Ying-ch'uan Commandery had its seat near modern Yu-chou 禹州, thirty miles south of Chengchow 鄭州 in Honan (T'an Ch'i-hsiang, 2:16)

[192] The Huan-yüan Pass (not located in T'an Ch'i-hsiang) was located twenty miles southeast of Loyang and northwest of modern Teng-feng 登封. The Yi Pass was south of Loyang on the eponymous Yi-ch'üeh Mountain 伊闕山, that today is better known as Lung-men 龍門 (T'an Ch'i-hsiang, 2:16).

[193] Otherwise unknown.

[194] Nan-yang Commandery had its seat at modern Nan-yang in Honan (T'an Ch'i-hsiang, 2:16).

[195] According to "Cheng-yi," the Wu Pass was located ninety miles east of Shang-lo 商洛 county in Shang-chou 商州. T'an Ch'i-hsiang (2:16) locates the pass five miles south of modern Shang-nan 商南 County in Shensi, roughly in equidistant between modern Sian and Nan-yang, controlling the access from southern Honan to the capital area.

[196] Lo-yang is located in modern Honan about fifteen miles east of modern Loyang (T'an Ch'i-hsiang, 2:16).

could this be enough to worry. In this way there will be still in the North the Lin-chin Pass 臨晉關, Ho-tung 河東, Shang-tang 上黨, and Ho-nei 河內, and the state of Chao 趙.[197] The people say: 'Cut off the gorge of Ch'eng-kao, and the world will be disconnected.' If we occupy the critical point at San-ch'uan 三川,[198] **[*3090*]** summon the troops of Shan-tung, and start a rebellion like this, Master, what would you think of this?" [Wu] P'i said: "Your servant sees how it is disastrous, but he has not yet seen how it could be fortunate." The King said: "Tso Wu 左吳, Chao Hsien 趙賢, and Chu Chiao-ju 朱驕如[199] all believe that there will be a fortunate outcome, with nine chances out of ten to succeed; Master, why do only you believe there will be a disastrous and no fortunate outcome?" [Wu] P'i said: "All those assembled vassals and favorites of the Great King who were ever able to make use of [our] hosts have been detained before in the imperial decretory trials,[200] among those left none is

---

[197] Liu An is basically describing the administrative divisions north of the Ho, moving from the eastern side of the Ordos loop on to the east of the T'ai-hang 太行 mountain range. The Lin-chin Pass is located close to the bend of the Ho, ten miles east of modern Dali 大荔 County in Shensi, controlling the access to the capital (T'an Ch'i-hsiang, 2:15). Ho-tung Commandery had its seat at An-yi 安邑, located five miles northeast of modern Yün-ch'eng 運城 in Shansi (T'an Ch'i-hsiang, 2:16). Shang-tang Commandery, bordering to the east on Ho-Tung Commandery had its seat at Ch'ang-tzu 長子, located ten miles west of modern Ch'ang-chih 長治 in Shansi (T'an Ch'i-hsiang, 2:16). Ho-nei Commandery stretched on the northern side of the Ho, eastwards of Lo-yang, and had its seat at Huai 懷 County, located at mondern Wu-chI 武陟 County, twenty miles northeast of Chengchow 鄭州 in Honan (T'an Ch'i-hsiang, 2:16). The Kingdom of Chao, bordering to the northeast on Ho-nei Commandery, was enfeoffed in 155 BC to Liu P'eng-tsu 劉彭祖 (d. 92 BC), a younger brother of Wu-ti from a different mother. Han-Tan 邯鄲 in Hopeh was its capital.

[198] According to "Cheng-yi," this refers to the Ch'eng-ao Pass 成皋關. San-ch'uan Commandery (T'an Ch'i-hsiang, 2:7) was the Ch'in name for what would roughly become the Ho-nan 河南 Commandery (T'an Ch'i-hsiang, 2:16) in Han times, named after the "three streams" (*san ch'uan* 三川): the Ho, the Lo 洛, and the Yi 伊.

[199] Liu An's three warrantors are otherwise unknown.

[200] The term *chao-yü* 詔獄 refers in this instance to an imperial decretory trial, i.e., a kind of "federal case" with a special protocol: Initiated by the decree of the Emperor himself (or powerful officials in place of him), be it in reaction to accusations by a third party or not, these cases usually tried high officials and feudal lords for capital crimes, like plotting a rebellion (for a brief overview over the crimal records of the members of the imperial familiy see P'eng Hai-t'ao 彭海濤, *Han-tai tsung-shih wang hou fan-tsui yen-chiu* 漢代宗室王侯犯罪研究 [Unpublished dissertation, Shou-tu Shih-fan Ta-hsüeh, 2012]). The accused would then be summoned, arrested, questioned and finally put to justice. For a list of accused persons see Kung Chia-wang 弓家旺, *Hsi Han chao-yü yen-chiu* 西漢詔獄研究 (Unpublished master thesis, Ch'ing-tao Ta-hsüeh, 2010), pp. 4–13. Remarkably, Kung Chia-wang also counts Han

of any use." The King said: "Ch'en Sheng and Wu Kuang did not have the territory to put [the point of] an awl [into it]; they were a group of thousand men, rose at Ta-tse 大澤,[201] and, when they raised [their] arms and cried out loud, the world answered in response. Thus when they marched west and reached Hsi 戲,[202] [their] troops counted 1,200,000 men. Now, although Our state is small, one could count on more than 100,000 elite troops, and they would not be a host of banished frontier guards, with sickles, chisels, and halberd handles; thus, Master, why do you say that there will be a disastrous and no fortunate outcome?" [Wu] P'i said: "Formerly, the Ch'in were devoid of moral principles and cruelly devastated the world. They mobilized 10,000 chariots, built palaces like the O-p'ang 阿房,[203] collected taxes amounting to the greater part [of the people's yield], sent off frontier guards [that where regardless picked] from the left side of the villages[204]; fathers did not give their children security, elder brothers did not grant their younger brothers any advantage, the government was harsh and the punishments severe, the world was drying out as if being scorched, and all the people stretched [their] necks to look out, and inclined [their] ears to listen

Hsin 韓信 and Chou Po 周勃 among the victims of this powerful imperial institution. According to Yü Hsing-mai 余行邁 ("Hsi Han chao-yü t'an-hsi" 西漢詔獄探析, *Yün-nan shih-fan ta-hsüeh hsüeh-pao*, 80 [1986]): 31–38) the "imperial decretory trials" of the Western Han dynasty were a product of the ongoing struggle between the emperor and the feudal lords, the central and the local government. It should therefore come as no surprise that this phenomenon reached a early peak during the reign of Wu-ti, when Tu Chou 杜周 became Commandant of Justice and large number of senior officials were brought to trial (*Shih chi*, 122.3153).

Furthermore, *chao-yü* as a term could also be a general reference to actual "decretorial prisons," maintained at various locations across the empire, usually located at the palaces and reserved for persons with a special status, e.g. members of the imperial clan.

[201] Ta-tse is located five miles southeast of modern Soochow 宿州 in Anhwei (T'an Ch'i-hsiang, 2:19).

[202] Hsi was located at the banks of the eponymous River Hsi at Hsin-feng 新豐 (Wang Shu-min, 118:3220), twenty miles northeast of Ch'ang-an, close to modern Lin-tung 臨潼 in Shansi (Tan Ch'i-hsiang, 2:15).

[203] The O-p'ang front hall was built by the First Emperor as he deemed his old palace in the capital as too small. It is described in its overwhelming dimensions on *Shih chi*, 6.256 (*Grand Scribe's Records*, 1:148), for a reconciliation with the archaeological findings see also Yang Tung-yü 楊東宇 and Tuan Ch'ing-po 段清波 "O-p'ang kung kai-nien yü O-p'ang kung k'ao-ku 阿房宮概念與阿房宮考古, *K'ao-ku yü wen-wu*, vol. 2 (2006), pp. 51–56.

[204] According to "Cheng-yi," the term *lü tso* 閭左 refers to those who dwelled on the left side of the village. According to "So-yin" (*Shih chi*, 48.1950), this expression might refer to a more general way of speaking: the "left ones" of a village were the poor and weak (*p'in jo* 貧弱) usually not sent awayas frontier guards, unless all the "right ones," i.e., the rich and strong (*fu ch'iang* 富強), were already conscripted.

hard, crying out sorrowfully and looking up to the heaven, they beat their hearts and resented the Sovereign. Therefore, when Ch'en Sheng cried out loud, the world answered in response. Right now, His Majesty is overlooking and controlling the world, he has unified all within the seas in harmony, he overflows in love to the common people, he distributes [his] virtue deeds and gives away [his] favor. Even though [his] mouth has not yet formed a word, [his] voice reaches out with the swiftness of thunder, even though [his] commands have not yet been issued, the changes spread along with the speed of the gods, whatever he harbors in his heart, by his authority it will shake everything within 10,000 *li*, as the subjects respond to the Sovereign like shadows or echoes. Moreover, the General-in-chief's skills and abilities are not just like [those of] Chang Han 章邯 and Yang Hsiung 楊熊.[205] If you, Great King, compare [the present situation to that of] Ch'en Sheng and Wu Kuang, then P'i believes that this is an error." The King said: "Even if it is like you say, Master, couldn't we get lucky by chance?" [Wu] P'i said: "P'i has a stupid plan." The King said: "What about it?" [Wu] P'i said: "Right now, the various feudal lords have no divergent hearts and the common people have no air of resentment. The farmlands of the Commandery of Shuo-fang are vast, its waters and meadows are fine, but those relocated as population are not enough to occupy the territory. According to your servant's stupid plan, you could forge a request letter from the Chancellor and the Imperial Scribe [to the following extent:] relocate the outstanding men, vigilante knights and [convicts] that were punished with more than a temporary shaving [of their heads] from the various states[206] and clear them of their crimes by pardon; in case of those whose wealth exceeds 500,000, relocate all the members of their households to the Commandery of Shuo-fang; additionally, dispatch [a host of] armored infantry and hasten the date of their gathering. [You could] also forge letters [requesting for] imperial decretory trials from the Left, Right, and Chief Director of Convict Labor and all the administrative departments of the Shang-lin Park, [to the following extent:] capture the Heirs and favorite ministers of the various feudal lords. In this way the people would harbor resentment and the various feudal lords would be

---

[205] Chang Han and Yang Hsiung were both famous Ch'in generals: While Chang Han was responsible for the defeat of several of Ch'en Sheng's confederates in his rebellion against the Ch'in, Yang Hsiung was two times defeated by Han Generals and finally executed as a warning by the Second Emperor. See Loewe, *Dictionary*, pp. 681–82 and p. 637.

[206] Ying Shao (cited in "Chi-chieh") claims that the term *nai* 耐 is a later substitution for *erh* 耏, a light form of punishment that did not go so far as to shave the whole head bald (*k'un* 髡) but preserved the convict's "beards and temples" (*erh pin* 耏鬢), hence its name. According to *Han shu* (23.1099), the *erh* punishment replaced the more severe form of *k'un* as a consequence of Wen-ti's reform of the corporal punishments. Su Lin (cited *ibid.*), however, believes that *nai* 耐 refers to sentences of two years and above that had to be "endured" (*nai* 耐).

frightened, if you would then send warriors skilled in debate[207] as follow up, and have them advise [the feudal lords], might we not get lucky and have one chance in ten [of success]?" The King said: "This would be permissible. Although, I believe it will not come to a situation like this." It was only after this that the King **[*3091*]** ordered the government slaves to enter the palace and produce an imperial seal for the August Emperor, seals for the Chancellor, the Imperial Scribe, the General-in-Chief, the military officials, the [officials with a salary of a] full two thousand *shih*, and the Prefects and Assistants of the Bureau of the Officials at the Capital, even seals for the Grand Administrators and Chief Commandants of the adjacent commanderies, and the caducei and law hats[208] of Han envoys, intending to follow the plan of Wu P'i. He sent men, pretending to have committed offences, westward, in order to serve the General-in-chief and the Chancellor; if one day he sent out [his] troops,[209] [these] agents were then to assassinate the General-in-chief [Wei] Ch'ing, and to persuade the Chancellor[210] to submit to him; it would be as easy as opening a lid.

[3092] The King wished to send out the troops from his state, but he was afraid that his Chancellor and the [officials with a salary of] two thousand *shih* would not obey. Only then did the King plot with Wu P'i first to kill the Chancellor and the [officials with a salary of] two thousand *shih*; they would fabricate a fire in the palace and, when the Chancellor and the [officials with a salary of] two thousand *shih* came to fight the fire, they would kill them on arrival. The plan had not yet been decided on, when he again wished to have men put on the clothes of thief-catchers, grasp a feathered proclamation [of war], and, come in from the east, shouting: "Troops of the Southern Yüeh have invaded the border"–as he wished to take advantage of this and

[207] According to Hsü Kuang (cited in "Chi-chieh"), the people from Huai-nan called "scholars" (*shih* 士) "warriors" (*wu* 武)—which might explain the *Han shu* (45.2924) phrasing: *pien shih* 辯士. A "Cheng-yi" fragment (cited in Chang Yen-t'ien 張衍田, ed., *Shih chi cheng-yi yi-wen chi chiao* 史記正義佚文輯校 [Peking, Chung-hua Shu-chü, 1985], p. 416) states: 辯武，謂辯口而武，所說必行也；"'Warriors skilled in debate' denotes warriors with eloquence in debates; whatever they advised, they would inevitably carry out."

[208] According to Ts'ai Yung 蔡邕 (133–192; cited in "Chi-chieh"), these "law hats" (*fa kuan* 法冠) were styled after the hat of the King of Chu. When Ch'in destroyed Ch'u, the hat of its ruler was given to the Imperial Scribe (*yü shih* 御史). According to Ts'ui Hao 崔浩 (d. 450; cited in "So-yin"), these hats were also called "*hsieh-chih* hats" after the mystical sheep (or cow) like animal with one horn, called *hsieh-chih* 獬豸 (alternatively written 獬㣇), that would ram the party at fault as an ordeal in difficult law cases, as for example remembered in the old form of the character for "law": *fa* 灋.

[209] As Ts'ui Hao 崔浩 (cited in "So-yin") emphasizes: 一日猶一朝，卒然無定時也。"'one day' is like 'one morning'; it means suddenly, not at some fixed point in time."

[210] As Wang Shu-min (118.3222) notes, the *Han shu* (44.2900) and later sources spell out that this refers to [Kung-sun] Hung [公孫]弘.

send out [his] troops. Only then did he order men to go to Lu-chiang and K'uai-chi 會 稽[211] as thief-catchers, but they had not yet been sent out. The King asked Wu P'i: "When We raise our troops and march west, there are sure to be some of the various feudal lords to respond to Our [call]; but if there will be none to respond, what then?" [Wu] P'i said: "In the south take Heng-shan in order to assault Lu-chiang; once you possess the boats of Hsün-yang 尋陽,[212] guard the walled city of Hsia-chih 下雉,[213] bind [your forces] at the banks of Chiu-chiang 九江 (Nine Rivers) ,[214] cut off the mouth [of the Yangtze] at Yü-chang 豫章[215] with your mighty crossbows overlooking the river and guarding it, in order to prohibit that [the troops of] Nan 南 Commandery[216] move down on you; to the east take Chiang-tu 江都 and K'uai-chi;[217] in the south join the powerful [*3093*] Yüeh; if you hold out firmly between the Huai and the Yangtze, you might even prolong your life for a short while.[218] The King said: "Well said, I have no reason to change this [plan]. If [the situation] should turn critical, I would flee to the Yüeh.

At this, the Commandant of Justice made it known that the oral statement of [Liu] Chien, the grandson of the King, implicated [Liu] Ch'ien, the Heir of the King of Huai-nan. The Sovereign dispatched the Inspector of the Commandant of Justice, and, taking advantage of [this situation], he appointed him as Commandant of the Capital of Huai-nan, in order to capture the Heir and take him into custody. When he arrived in Huai-nan, the King of Huai-nan heard of this, and together with the Heir he

[211] Lu-chiang Commandery roughly refers to a territory north of the Yangtze and south of the Huai; K'uai-chi Commandery with its eponymous seat at modern Soochow 蘇州 in Kiangsu refers to a territory south of the Yangtze delta (T'an Ch'i-hsiang, 2:24).

[212] Hsün-yang is located twenty miles northwest of modern Chiu-chiang 九江 in Hupei (T'an Ch'i-hsiang, 2:24) on the northern side of the Yangtze.

[213] Hsia-chih is located twenty-five miles west of modern Chiu-chiang 九江 in Hupei (T'an Ch'i-hsiang, 2:24) on the southern side of the Yangtze.

[214] Wang Li-ch'i (118.2512–3), Wu and Lu (118:3101) and Han Chao-ch'i (118.5881) all deduct that Chiu-chiang should refer to the area around the above mentioned Hsün-yang.

[215] According to "Cheng-yi," this refers to the mouth of P'eng-li lake 彭蠡湖 that debouches to the North into the Yangtze, owing its name probably from former Yü-chang Commandery (T'an Ch'i-hsiang, 2:24).

[216] Nan Commandery had its eponymous seat five miles northwest of modern Ching-chou 荊州 in Hupeh (T'an Ch'i-hsiang, 2: 22).

[217] As "Cheng-yi" explains, Chiang-tu refers to Yang-chou 揚州 in Kiangsu and K'uai-chi to Su-chou 蘇州. In this case Chiang-tu probably rather referred the Kingdom of Chiang-tu that had its seat at Kuang-ling 廣陵 five miles north of modern Yang-chou (T'an Ch'i-hsiang, 2:24) and was enfeoffed to Liu Chien 劉建, a son of Wu-ti's elder brother Liu Fei 劉非 (169–127 B.C), who followed his father, the first King of Chiang-tu, in 127 BC on this position.

[218] Literally: 延歲月之壽 "to prolong [your] long life of years and months."

planned to summon the Chancellor and the [officials with a salary of] two thousand *shih*, as he wished to kill them and sent out [his] troops. He summoned the Chancellor, and the Chancellor arrived; the Clerk of the Capital used an errand as apology. The Commandant of the Capital said: "Your servant has received an imperial mission, he cannot see the King." Since the King, thinking that killing only the Chancellor, while the Clerk of the Capital and the Command of the Capital had not come, would be of no use, he then dismissed the Chancellor. The King hesitated, and the plan had not yet decided on. The Heir thought he was tried for the plotting to assassinate the Commandant of the Capital of the Han, but since all those he had plotted with had already died, he believed that all mouths were silenced. Only then did he say to the King: "All those amongst the assembled vassals that could have been made use of have already been detained [by the law officials], now there are not enough to start a rebellion. If the King should set [his plan] in motion at the wrong time, I am afraid that there will be no merit, thus your servant wishes to meet his capture." Since the King also secretly wished to put [his plans] to rest,[219] he then granted the Heir [his request]. The Heir then cut his own throat, but did not die.[220] Wu P'i went himself to the [law] officials; and taking advantage of this, he informed them who had joined the King of Huai-nan plotting a rebellion, in this way the traces of the rebellion were furnished [them].

The [law] officials took advantage of [his statement] and took the Heir and the Queen in custody; they surrounded the King's palaces. They searched for every single guest and retainer within the state with whom the King had plotted rebellion, and took them into custody; they searched and found the instruments for a revolt and made them known [at court]. The Emperor handed down [the case] to the Excellencies and Ministers to try, the ranking marquises, [officials with a salary of] two thousand *shih*, and outstanding men that were implicated to have plotted rebellion with the King of Huai-nan counted several thousand men, they all received their punishments according to the gravity of the offenses. [Liu] Tz'u, the King of Heng-shan, since he was the King of Huai-nan's **[*3094*]** younger brother, deserved to be tried and imprisoned for liability of kin, and the official in charge requested to capture and arrest the King of Heng-shan. The Son of Heaven said: "Since each of the various feudal lords considers his state as [his] basic responsibility, they don't deserve to be tried for mutual liability. Meet with the various feudal lords, Kings and ranking marquises and examine the discussion [of this case] by the Chancellor and the various

---

[219] According to Hsü Kuang (cited in "Chi-chieh"), *t'ou* 偷, "secretly," should be understood as *kou-ch'ieh* 苟且, reading the sentence as "Since the King also sought merely temporary ease and wished to rest his plans…"

[220] According to Chin Cho (cited in "Chi chieh"), *pu shu* 不殊 means *pu ssu* 不死, "not to die."

feudal lords."[221] [Liu] P'eng-tsu [劉]彭祖, the King of Chao 趙,[222] Jang 讓,[223] the vassal[224] in the position of a ranking marquis, and others, altogether forty-three men, discussed [the case], and all said: "[Liu] An, the King of Huai-nan, acted most treasonous and unprincipled, it has been made very clear that he plotted rebellion, he deserves to be submitted for execution." [Liu] Tuan [劉]端,[225] the vassal in the position of King of Chiao-hsi 膠西, discussed [the case] and said: "[Liu] An, the King of Huai-nan, abolished the laws and practiced evil; he harbors a deceitful and deceptive heart, thereby he caused the world to be in disorder, confused the common people, turned his back on the ancestral temple, and recklessly created wild rumors. The *Ch'un chiu* says: 'A vassal should not have the intention [of revolting]; having the intention, he will be executed.'[226] [Liu] An's offence is graver than 'having the

---

[221] According to Hsü Kuang (cited in "Chi-chieh"), this sentence means that the Emperor had them: 詣都座就丞相共議也 "visit the hall for political affairs, so that they would yield to the Chancellor and discuss the case together." Takigawa (118.39) emendates the text on the base of variant editions (see Mizusawa, 118.16), believing the second *chu hou* 諸侯 is superfluous, reading: 與諸侯王列侯會肆丞者議 "Meet with the various feudal lords, Kings and ranking marquises and examine the discussion [of this case] by the Chancellor."

[222] The Kingdom of Chao was enfeoffed in 155 BC to Liu P'eng-tsu (d. 92 BC), a younger brother of Wu-ti from a different mother.

[223] Wang Hsien-ch'ien (*Han shu pu-chu*, 44.13b) suggests that *jang* 讓 might be a common miswriting of *hsiang* 襄, since at this point of time no feudal lord by the name of Jang is known. Thus the reference would then probably be to Ts'ao Hsiang 曹襄 (d. 115 BC), the Marquis of P'ing-yang 平陽, a great-great-grandson of Ts'ao Shen 曹參, who was married to a daughter of Wu-ti and the Empress Wei 衛. Ts'ao Hsiang later joined the offensive against the Hsiung-nu in 119 BC as General of the Rear. See Loewe, *Dictionary*, p. 23.

[224] *Ch'en* 臣 here seems to be used here as it is in court documents following an official title to indicate "servant (or vassal) in the position of [official title] as on *Shih chi*, 60.2107: 三月丙子，奏未央宮。「丞相臣青翟、御史大夫臣湯昧死言.

[225] Liu Tuan (d. 108) was an elder brother of Wu-ti by a different mother. He was enfeoffed as the King of Chiao-hsi 膠西 after the rebellion of the seven kingdoms in 154 BC. Liu Tuan is remembered as a cruel and evil man who suffered from a sexual dysfunction and brought countless officials to death. His transgressions against the law were well known but tolerated by Wu-ti. See Loewe, *Dictionary*, pp. 293–94. The small Kingdom of Chiao-hsi had its seat at Kao-mi 高密, located twenty-five miles east of modern Tsingtao in Shantung (T'an Ch'i-hsiang, 2:20).

[226] The reference to the *Kung-yang chuan* 公羊傳 is truly well chosen: When Duke Chuang (r. 693–662 BC) was about to die, he wanted to appoint his son from a concubine Pan 般 (or: 班) as his heir. His younger half-brother Shu-ya 叔牙 (d. 662 BC), however, suggested, when asked, to install the eldest younger half-brother of Duke Chuang, Ch'ing-fu 慶父 (d. 660 BC), while the youngest brother by the same mother of Duke Chuang, Chi-yu 季友 (d. 644 BC), indicated support the Duke's candidate, Pan. Thereupon, Chi-yu presented poison to

intention [of revolting],' his plotting of a revolt has been already established in its outlines. According to what your servant Tuan has seen, his letters, caducei, seals and maps, as well as his other treasonous and unprincipled undertakings have been made very clear; his acts were most treasonous and unprincipled and he deserves to be submitted to the laws that apply in this case. Furthermore, with regard to the sentencing of the state officials with [a salary of] more than two hundred *shih* as well as those comparable to them, and of the favorites of the royal household that are not subject of the law, since they could not mutually instruct him better, they deserve to be released from office, stripped of their noble titles and made common soldiers. They should not be given the opportunity to serve as officials. With regard to those who are not officials, all others should pay a ransom of two *chin* eight *liang* [to avoid] death. By exposing the offenses of the subject [Liu] An, we let the world clearly understand the proper way of a subject, so no one will dare to have again the intention to behave perniciously and wickedly and turn his back [on the ancestral temple]." Chancellor [Kung-sun] Hung and [Chang] T'ang [張] 湯,[227] the Commandant of Justice, made this known [at court], and the Son of Heaven sent the Director of the Imperial Clan with the credentials and the caduceus to take the King to court. He had not yet arrived, when [Liu] An, the King of Huai-nan killed himself by cutting his throat.[228] T'u, the Queen, [Liu] Ch'ien, the Heir, and all those that had joined plotting a rebellion were entirely wiped out with their clans. The Son of Heaven wished that Wu P'i, since he had many times invoked the splendor of the Han with elegant words, should not be executed. [Chang] T'ang, the Commandant of Justice, said: "[Wu] P'i was the first to draw up a rebellion plot for the King, thus [Wu] P'i's offense cannot be pardoned." In the end he had [Wu] P'i executed. The state was abolished becoming Jiu-chiang 九江 Commandery.

Shu-ya, offering him the choice to die quietly in return for having his posterity preserved, or become the laughing stock of the empire. The Commentary fully supports Chi-yu's action: 君親無將，將而誅焉 "The close relatives of a ruler must not have the intention [of revolting], if they have the intention, they are executed for this" (Duke Chuang 莊公, year 32.3). The quoted passage is thus in essence sanctioning the act of a younger brother killing an elder brother, who allegedly had the intention to become the next ruler of the kingdom. It praises the way of serving him poison in order to grant the victim the appearance of a natural death so that his intended evil would never come to light, as an example of: *ch'in ch'in chih tao* 親親之道 "the way close relatives treat each other with affection" (*ibid.*). Liu An's prosecutors obviously forgot that they were supposed to grant their victim a graceful escape.

[227] Chang T'ang was one of the infamous cruel officials of Wu-ti's reign. He had held the post of Commandant of Justice since 126 BC, when the case was brought against Huai-nan. See Loewe, *Dictionary*, pp. 692–94.

[228] As Hsü Kuang (cited in "Chi-chieh") notes, Liu An took his life in the tenth month of the first year of the Yüan-shou era (122 BC), after reigning forty-two years.

Liu Tz'u

[3095] The Queen of [Liu] Tz'u, the King of Heng-shan, Sheng-shu 乘舒[229] bore three children to him, [Liu] Shuang 爽, the eldest, became the Heir, the next boy was [Liu] Hsiao 孝, and the next daughter was [Liu] Wu-ts'ai 無采.[230] Furthermore, Beauty Hsü-lai 徐來[231] bore him four sons and daughters, the Beautiful Lady Chüeh-chi 厥姬[232] bore him two children. The King of Heng-shan and the King of Huai-nan were brothers, they blamed and hated each other for [denying the other] the proper etiquette, and had not been on good terms with each other for a while. When the King of Heng-shan heard that the King of Huai-nan was preparing instruments for a revolt in order to rebel, he also wholeheartedly bound guests and retainers to him in order to respond to him, since he was afraid that he would be annexed [by him].

In the sixth year of the Yüan-kuang 元光 reign (129 BC), the King of Heng-shan entered court [to pay his respects to the Emperor]; Wei Ch'ing 衛慶,[233] his Internun-cio, possessing magical techniques, wished to submit a memorial [requesting to] serve the Son of Heaven; the King got angry, and therefore he charged [Wei] Ch'ing with an offense deserving death, and forced him by beating to admit to it. Heng-shan's Clerk of the Capital believed that this was not right and dismissed his case. The King had a man submit a memorial accusing the Clerk of the Capital, but when the Clerk of the Capital was tried, he said the King had not been upright. Furthermore, that the King had several times invaded and seized other people's fields, and that he had destroyed other people's burial mounds and made them into fields. The authorities concerned requested to arrest the King of Heng-shan and have him tried. The Son of Heaven would not allow it, [but] he installed for [the King even those] officials [with a salary of] more than two hundred *shih*.[234] The King of Heng-shan was enraged about this, and plotted together with Hsi Tz'u 奚慈 and Chang Kuang-ch'ang 張廣

---

[229] Liu Tz'u's first queen, see Loewe, *Dictionary*, p. 471.

[230] The story of the three intriguing children of Liu Tz'u is told in the following passage. For Liu Shuang, Liu Hsiao, and Liu Wu-ts'ai, see Loewe, *Dictionary*, p. 362, pp. 375–6, and p. 369.

[231] The second Queen of Liu Tz'u, who allegedly killed her predecessor by means of poisonous sorcery (*ku* 蠱), see Loewe, *Dictionary*, p. 621.

[232] A jealous lesser consort of Liu Tz'u, who spread the accusations against her rival Hsü-lai see Loewe, *Dictionary*, p. 204.

[233] Otherwise unknown.

[234] As Ju Ch'un (cited in "Chi-chieh") notes, according to Han customs, officials with a salary of four hundred *shih* and below were supposed to have been appointed by the local Kings. Having all officials with a salary of two hundred *shih* and above installed by the central court meant a further curtailment of Liu Tz'u's royal powers.

昌;[235] he searched for men that were able to practice the art of war and watch the stars and ethers, and [those men] incited[236] the King to secretly[237] plot day and night the act of rebellion.

When the Queen Ch'eng-shu died, [the King] invested Hsü-lai as Queen. But since Chüeh-chi enjoyed all his favor, the two women were jealous of each other, and only then did Chüeh-chi malign Hsü-lai, the Queen, to the Heir saying: "Hsü-lai ordered a female slave to kill the Heir's mother by ways of poisonous sorcery."[238] The Heir in his heart harbored resentment against Hsü-lai. When the elder brother of Hsü-lai arrived at Heng-shan, the Heir drank with him, and with his blade stabbed and wounded the elder brother of the Queen. The Queen [*3096*], resentful and angry, several times defamed and maligned the Heir to the King. [Liu] Wu-ts'ai, the younger sister of the Heir, was rejected and returned [to her family] after her marriage, had illicit intercourse with a slave, and had illicit intercourse again with a retainer. When the Heir reproached [Liu] Wu-ts'ai several times, [Liu] Wu-tsai was angry, and had no more relations with the Heir. When the Queen heard of this, she then treated [Liu]

[235] Liu Tz'u's two conspirators are otherwise unknown.

[236] Wang Shu-min (118.3223) adduces several related passages and glosses to enforce his reading of *ts'ung-jung* 從容 in the sense of *sung-yung* 慫慂, "to incite."

[237] As Hsü Kuang (cited in "Chi-chieh") elaborates, "secretly" (*mi* 密) means that he *yü tso chi hsiao* 豫作計校 "made plans in advance."

[238] A prior "case of poisonous sorcery" (*ku yü* 蠱獄) concerned with Wu-ti's Empress Ch'en 陳, who desperately tried to win back the favor of the Emperor. She was finally tried by the cruel official Chang T'ang 張湯 (*Shih chi*, 122.3138). It is not clear what *ku* precisely referred to at this time. Later accounts suggest a practice of breeding poisonous "mutants" by placing several lethal animals together into a vessel until there is a survivor. The deadly poison is then secured from this *ku* and administered to the victim in various ways. If no antidote was given, death was imminent. The *ku* was sometimes regarded as some kind of spirit and its victims would have to serve the master of the *ku* after their deaths. For a general overview of the diffferent historical notions of the term *ku* 蠱 and the related customs see also H. Y. Feng and J. K. Shryock, "The Black Magic in China Known as ku," *JAOS* 55.1 (1935): 1–30.

According to *Han shu* accounts that deal with the far more prominent cases of the first decade of the last century BC, those practices seemed, at least in part, to have involved some kind of burried "voodoo dolls," "nocturnal sacrificers," and the lethal *ku* themselves (*Han shu*, 45/2178). At least, those "items" were part of the evidence Chiang Ch'ung 江充 produced in order to bring the downfall of the Heir Apparent Liu Chü 劉據 (128–91 B.C), his mother Empress Wei 衛 (d. 91 BC) and probably many others. These incidents indirectly suggest that by the time of Wu-ti the charge of practising *ku* sorcery had become an equally lethal tool in the struggle for imperial power and influence. For the historical background of these cases see Michael Loewe's "The Case of Witchcraft in 91 BC. Its Historical Setting and Effect on Han Dynastic History," *Asia Major* (New Series) 15.2 (1970): 159–196.

Wu-ts'ai well. Since 7[Liu] Wu-ts'ai as well as [Liu] Hsiao, her second elder brother, in their youths had lost their mother, they had attached themselves to the Queen, and the Queen calculatingly took good care of them, so they could jointly defame the Heir. For this reason the King had the Heir beaten and whipped several times.

In the midst of the fourth year of the Yüan-shuo reign (125 BC), some one had the stepmother of the Queen wounded in an assassination [attempt]; the King suspected that the Heir had sent a man to do her injury, and thus had the Heir whipped. Later, when the King was ill, the Heir claimed that he was ill at that time, and did not attend upon him. [Liu] Hsiao, the Queen, and [Liu] Wu-ts'ai maligned the Heir: "The Heir is not really ill; he says of himself that he is ill, but he looks cheerful." The King was enraged, wished to abolish the Heir, and install [Liu] Hsiao, his younger brother. When the Queen learned that the King had decided to abolish the Heir, she also wished to have [Liu] Hsiao abolished together with him. The Queen had an attendant who was good at dancing and the King had favored her; thus the Queen intended to order the attendant to have a illicit affair with [Liu] Hsiao in order to sully [his reputation]. She intended to have the elder and younger brother abolished together and have [Liu] Kuang, her own son, installed as a replacement for the Heir. When [Liu] Shuang, the Heir, learned of this, he thought that the Queen's numerous maligning of his person would have no end, thus he wished to have an illicit affair with her to stop her mouth. When the Queen was drinking, the Heir advanced in front of her and toasted to her longevity; he took advantage of the situation, rested on the thighs of the Queen, and sought to lie down with the Queen. The Queen got angry, and informed the King about it. Only then did the King summon him, intending to have him tied up and whipped. The Heir knew that the King had always wished to abolish himself and install [Liu] Hsiao, his younger brother, and only then did he tell the King: "[Liu] Hsiao is having illicit intercourse with a royal servant, [Liu] Wu-tsai is having illicit intercourse with a slave; eat well, My King, I request to submit a memorial." He then turned his back on the King and left. The King send men to stop him, but none could prohibit [his departure]. Only then did the King himself drive his chariot in pursuit and arrest the Heir. The Heir was reckless in his maligning, thus the King had the Heir put in a cangue and detained in the palace. [Liu] Hsiao was daily more close to the King and received his favor. The King marveled at [Liu] Hsiao's skills and abilities, and only then did he allow him to wear a royal seal on his belt, calling him: "General," letting him reside in an exterior residency, and giving him abundant sums of money, in order to recruit guests and retainers. Those guests and retainers that arrived knew through secret channels that Huai-nan and Heng-shan had a plan to rebel, thus they incited and urged them on, day and night. Only then did the

King order Chiu Ho 救赫[239] and Ch'en Hsi 陳喜,[240] natives from Chiang-tu and retainers of [Liu] Hsiao, to produce towered war chariots and metal-head arrows, to cut an imperial seal for the Son of Heaven and the seals for generals, ministers, and military officials. The King was searching day and night for stalwart warriors like Chou Ch'iu 周丘,[241] several times quoting the strategies of the time of the rebellion of Wu and Ch'u, in order to reach agreements and oaths. The King of Heng-shan did not dare to imitate the King of Huai-nan in his quest to accede to the throne of the Son of Heaven, since he feared that Huai-nan would rise and annex his state; he believed once Huai-nan had already marched west, he would send out his troops, stabilize the region between the Yangtze and the Huai, and take it into his possession; he hoped, it would be like this.

[*3097*] In the autumn of the fifth year of the Yüan-shuo reign (124 BC), the King of Heng-shan was supposed to go to the court [to pay respects];[242] he passed through Huai-nan, and only then did the King of Huai-nan talk to him like a brother, putting an end to the previous rift, and coming to an agreement regarding the instruments for the rebellion. The King of Heng-shan then submitted a memorial pleading illness, the Sovereign bestowed him with a letter [allowing him] not to go to court [to pay his respects].

In the midst of the sixth year of the Yüan-shuo reign (123 BC), the King of Heng-shan sent a man to submit a memorial requesting to abolish [Liu] Shuang, the Heir, and to install [Liu] Hsiao as the Heir. When [Liu] Shuang heard of it, he then sent his friend Po Ying 白贏,[243] to go to Ch'ang-an and submit a memorial stating that [Liu] Hsiao had produced towered war chariots and metal head arrows, had illicit intercourse with a royal palace woman,[244] intending to ruin [Liu] Hsiao this way. Po

---

[239] The "So-yin" notes that the *Han shu* parallel (44.2906) gives Mei 枚 as his surname, yet it also quotes the *Liu Hsiang pieh lu* 劉向別錄 telling of a commentator of the *Yi ching* called Chiu 救.

[240] The two collaborators are otherwise unknown.

[241] Chou Ch'iu was a leader under Liu P'i, King of Wu, during the rebellion of the seven kingdoms, who by the help of one credential, subdued his hometown Hsia-p'ei 下邳, gathered a host of thirty thousand men, that grew to over a hundred thousand upon reaching Ch'eng-yang 城陽, where he defeated the Commandant of the Capital. Learning of the King of Wu's defeat he withdrew his troops. Returning to Hsia-p'ei he died from an ulcer on his back.

[242] The Chung-hua editors have emendated the following two characters, *liu nien* 六年, "in the sixth year." They are thus following Shen Chia-pen's suggestion (cited in Wang Shu-min, 118.3224). Mizusawa has no note on this.

[243] Otherwise unknown.

[244] The vague term *yü* 御, "palace women" (*kung-nü* 宮女) is specified in the text below as *yü-pi* 御婢, "a palace maid" (see *Shih chi*, 118.3097). Hsia-hou P'o 夏侯頗 (d. 115 BC),

Ying reached Ch'ang-an [but] he had not yet come to submit a memorial, when officers arrested [Po] Ying and had him detained because of the undertakings of Huai-nan. As the King heard that [Liu] Shuang had sent Po Ying to submit a memorial, he was afraid that he had talked about the secret undertakings of [his] state, and then submitted a memorial to counter-accuse [Liu] Shuang, the Heir, of the unprincipled undertakings that he had committed, amounting to offenses [deserving to have] his corpse displayed in the marketplace. The case was handed down to [the officials of] P'ei 沛 Commandery[245] to be tried.

In the winter of the first year of the Yüan-shou 元狩 reign (122 BC),[246] the Ministers and Excellencies of the office in charge referred [the case] to the [officials of] P'ei Commandery in order to search and arrest all those that had joined Huai-nan in plotting a rebellion, but had not yet been captured; they captured Ch'en Hsi 陳喜 in the household of [Liu] Hsiao, the son of the King of Heng-shan. The officials charged [Liu] Hsiao with having been the first to hide [Ch'en] Hsi. [Liu] Hsiao believed that Ch'en Hsi had so many times joined the King in making plans and plotting a rebellion, and he was afraid that he would expose this, but since he had heard of the statute that those who first accuse themselves would be cleared of their offenses, and since he also suspected that the Heir had sent Po Ying to submit a memorial exposing his undertakings, he then accused himself first, thus accusing those that had joined him in plotting a rebellion like Chiu Ho and Ch'en Hsi. When the Commandant of Justice tried and examined [the case], the Ministers and Excellencies requested to capture and arrest the King of Heng-shan in order to try him. The Son of Heaven said: "Don't arrest him." He dispatched [Ssu-ma] An [司馬]安,[247] the Commandant of the Capital, and [Li] Hsi [李]息,[248] the Grand Usher, to then question the King; while the King

Hsia-hou Ying's 夏侯嬰 (d. 172 BC) great grandson, was convicted of a similar (if not the same) transgression, see *Shih chi*, 95:3586; *Grand Scribe's Records*, 8.186, especially n. 260.

[245] P'ei Commandery was reestablished by Ching-ti, with Hsiang 相 County, located five miles east of modern Huai-pei shi 淮北市 in Anhwei (T'an Ch'i-hsiang, 2: 19) as its seat.

[246] Facing the impossibility of a seventh year in the Yüan-shuo reign, the Chung-hua editors followed Liang Yü-sheng (118.1430) and Takigawa (118.45) who both prefer the *Han shu* (44.2154) dating as basis for their emendation.

[247] According to "So-yin," this refers to Ssu-ma An 司馬安, a nephew of the righteous official Chi An 汲黯 (see his biography in "Chi Cheng lieh-chuan" 汲鄭列傳 (*Shih chi* chapter 120), with whom he served in his early days as Forerunner of the Heir Apparent (probably Emperor Wu; see *Shih chi*, 120.3111). He is remembered as having reached a position among the Nine Ministers four times. His legal writings were known to be crafty (*ibid.*), if not outright evil (*Shih chi*, 122.3135). See also Loewe, *Dictionary*, p. 484.

[248] Li Hsi 李息 started his career at the court of Emperor Ching and was sent as general on campaigns against the Hsiung-nu in 133, 128, 127, and 124 BC, without obtaining notable merit. Later on, he was made Grand Usher (see *Shih chi*, 111.2942; *Grand Scribe's Records*, 9:349). See also Loewe, *Dictionary*, p. 231.

replied to him with the whole truth about the situation. The officers had all surrounded the palace of the King and were guarding it. When the Commandant of the Capital and the Grand Usher had returned to make [this] known [at court], the Ministers and Excellencies requested to dispatch the Director of the Imperial Clan and the Grand Usher, together with [officials of] P'ei Commandery, to jointly try the King. When the King heard of it, he then killed himself by cutting his throat. Since [Liu] Hsiao had accused himself of rebellion first, he was cleared of his offenses [regarding the rebellion]; he was convicted of illicit intercourse with a royal palace maid, executed, and his corpse was displayed in the marketplace. Hsü-lai, the Queen, was also tried for killing Ch'eng-shu, the former Queen, by poisonous sorcery, and [Liu] Shuang was as well tried for the fact that the King had him accused of non-filial behavior, all their corpses were displayed in the marketplace. All those that had joined the King of Heng-shan in plotting rebellion were entirely wiped out with their clans. The state was abolished; it became Heng-shan Commandery.

[3098] His Honor the Grand Scribe says: "When the *Book of Odes* says "He smote the barbarians of the west and the north; he punished Ching and Shu,"[249] how true are these words! Huai-nan and Heng-shan were as close as bones and flesh [to the Son of Heaven], [their] territory covered a thousand *li*, and they ranked as feudal lords. They did not strive to comply with their duties as shielding vassals in order to assist the Son of Heaven, but they arrogated to themselves the right to harbor pernicious and wicked plans, and were plotting to rebel, and thus[250] father and son twice caused [their] state to perish, neither of them living out his days, and becoming the laughing stock of the world. This was not a failure of the Kings alone; it was also because the customs of their [territories] were base, and [their] ministers and

---

[249] The lines are taken from the fifth stanza of "Pi Kung" 閟宮 of the Odes of Lu 魯 (*Mao* #300, Legge, 4:626). According to the "Little Preface" (see Legge, 4:80–81), the "Pi Kung" celebrates the praise of Duke Hsi 僖 (659–627 BC) from Lu, as he was able to recover all the territory of the Duke of Chou 周公, whose son Po Ch'in 伯禽 became the first of the feudal lords of Lu in his stead (see *Shih chi* 33.1515–22 [*Grand Scribe's Records*, 5:132–39, especially n. 18]). The chosen lines seem to be a prominent quote, featured twice in *Meng Tzu* (3A.4 and 3B.14), and one more time in the *Shih chi*, 20.1127. It might be noteworthy, that at least to Mencius any (positive) influence of the barbarians of the South upon people from the Middle Kingdoms was unimaginable: 吾聞用夏變夷者, 未聞變於夷者也; "I have heard of men using the doctrines of our great land to change barbarians but I have never yet heard of any being changed by barbarians" (*Meng Tzu*, 3A.4; Legge, 2:253–54). Apparently, there was only one way to deal with those southern people unmoved by the superiority of the north: *hen hen ta chi* 狠狠打擊 "hit them hard," as Han Chao-ch'i (118.5891) puts it.

[250] Alternatively, *jeng* 仍 could be rendered as "following [each other]," or "time and again."

subordinates gradually wore them down, and made them become like this. That the men from Ching and Ch'u are swift and brave, fickle and ferocious,[251] and have a fondness of making rebellion has been recorded since antiquity!

*   *   *   *   *

Ch'ing Pu 黥布 rebelled [there], [Kao-tsu's] son, [Liu] Ch'ang ruled as King over it, in order to guard the South of the Yangtze and the Huai, and to pacify the agile commoners of Ch'u.[252] [Thus] I composed the "Memoir of Huai-nan and Heng-shan, Number 58.[253]

[251] "Fickle and ferocious" (*ch'ing han* 輕悍) was already used twice to describe the men from Wu and Ch'u in the "Wu P'i Wang lieh-chuan" (*Shih chi*, 106.2821 and 2823; *Grand Scribe's Records*, 9:91 and 96). Looking back at the second instance, it seems rather conspicous how the presumed bad influence of the masters and mentors of the Heir of Wu who were all men from Ch'u is adduced, when the memoir is supposed to explain how it came about that the Imperial Heir killed the son of Liu P'i, King of Wu, over a game of *liu-po* 六博. As in the cases of the later Kings of Huai-nan, the reader may ask who were the actual victims of barbarity.

[252] Cf. Chang Liang's admonition to Kao-tsu when the emperor was about to undertake an expedition against Ch'u in 196 BC: "I should go with you but my illness is too severe. The men of Ch'u are agile and quick, I would that you not cross swords with the men of Ch'u" 臣宜從，病甚。楚人剽疾，願上無與楚人爭鋒 (*Shih chi*, 55.2045).

[253] This is Ssu-ma Ch'ien's account of why he wrote this chapter as found in his postface (see *Shih chi*, 130.3317: 黥布叛逆，子長國之，以填江淮之南，安剝楚庶民。作淮南衡山列傳第五十八).

Translator's Note

"The Memoir of Huai-nan and Heng-shan" is the chapter of the *Shih chi* in which the events centered on Liu Ch'ang, King of Huai-nan, and his sons, Liu An and Liu Tz'u, unfold. All three become finally victims of "rumors of revolt," and, if we may believe later sources, countless numbers of their "followers" were executed in the bloody aftermath.[254]

Ssu-ma Ch'ien's depictions of these cases of "plotting a revolt" (*mou fan* 謀反) have puzzled his readers over centuries. The main account of the memoir is time and time again somehow contradicted by little details[255] and crowned by a long dialogue between Liu An and his counselor Wu P'i, that is given so much weight that Pan Ku could not help elevating his notably elaborated statements even more by creating a separate biography for Wu P'i, in a memoir dedicated to political schemers, turning him into a half-loyal servant of the Han who ended up head of the plot. However, as Kuo Sung-tao 郭嵩燾 (1818–1891) has correctly observed:[256] "The whole memoir is just describing [Liu An's] exchange of words with Wu P'i, and when he was finally accused, [claiming] that the traces of the rebellion were completed, it was just [the testimony of] Wu P'i; there was never one soldier sent out, not one general dispatched. Therefore, one knows that in both cases of Huai-nan [the kings] could in the end not escape false accusations" 全傳僅敘與伍被往復之辭，終告反跡具者伍被也，未嘗發一兵、遣一將，故知兩淮南獄之終不免於誣也.

The following closer look at some key passages of the memoir shall therefore reveal some of the underlying patterns, since it seems that just those often bemoaned

---

[254] See A. F. P. Hulsewé, "Royal Rebels," p. 317.

[255] Griet Vankeerberghen, for example, speaks of two parts of the biographies in *Shih chi* and *Han shu* that are carefully interwoven: a base text, derived from court records describing the relations between Ch'ang-an and Huai-nan, and insertions from the evidence the prosecutors assembled in order to neutralize, if not subvert, the message of the base account (*The* Huainanzi *and Liu An's Claim to Moral Authority,* pp. 67–69).

[256] Cited in Han Chao-ch'i, 118.5892.

narrative peculiarities might suggest some of Ssu-ma Ch'ien's personal views on these events.

After the introduction of the precarious circumstances of his birth, and a reference to the "rebellion" of Ching Pu, the former King of Huai-nan, we are told that Liu Ch'ang waited until he was a strong young man around the age of twenty, on less than close terms with Emperor Wen, his older brother, before he took revenge for his mother and hammered down Shen Yi-chi, the Marquis of Pi-yang, in his own residence in the year 177 BC. In his eyes, Shen Yi-chi had not used his influence on Lü Hou to save his mother's life. Afterwards, Liu Ch'ang immediately offered apologies, skillfully listing the three occasions where Shen Yi-chi had clearly not acted in the interest of the Liu Clan. Emperor Wen ostentatiously pardoned his own brother, while the Empress Dowager Po,[257] the Heir Liu Ch'i (i.e., the later Emperor Ching), and the various great ministers all dreaded Liu Ch'ang–who retreated to his fief and became more arrogant by the day, his actions imitating the Son of Heaven.

The memoir then reports suddenly of a curious plot of seventy strong men, the Heir of Ch'ai Wu, Marquis of Chi-p'u, and the King of Huai-nan. This incident clearly has also startled Ch'en Tzu-lung 陳子龍 (1608–1647):[258]

> Seventy men, how could they have been able to revolt?! Maybe they were sent on a secret mission to assassinate the Han [ruler], to go there and burn down [his] amassments, and set the masses in terror.

七十人何能反。或遣刺漢陰事，及焚積聚，驚動眾也.

Although the suggested explanation appeals to the modern mind, it misses a point that becomes even more obvious, when we continue to read the following well designed request by the Chancellor Chang Ts'ang and various other officials to execute Liu Ch'ang. Despite their very best efforts, they can hardly account for more than the–not unusual–hospitality the King of Huai-nan offered talented fugitives and something like a long bill of legal cases decided arbitrarily. The only link to the aforementioned "plotting of a revolt" is a certain common soldier, named K'ai-chang 開章, who supposedly acted as a messenger between the Heir Ch'ai Ch'i and the King of Huai-nan. When the prosecutors eventually came to Liu Ch'ang's court to arrest him, the King somewhat laconically refused to hand him over and had even a fake grave erected to bury the case.

---

[257] The *Han shu* (44.2137–40) has preserved her younger brother Po Chao's 薄昭 well put letter to the overbearing Liu Ch'ang that, according to Pan Ku's presentation, prompted the alleged rebellion of the seventy men.

[258] Cited in Shinsai Arii (1830–1889), *Hohyō Shiki hyōrin* 補標史記評林, 118.1b.

Nonetheless, the involved officials were determined to have the King executed. According to the cited exchange of documents, the Emperor only slowly met the requests of the various Excellences. First, agreeing to have Liu Ch'ang deposed as a King; then, to have him exiled to the far West–but under the explicit condition that he be given his daily ration of "five *chin* of meat and two *tou* of wine."[259] All the admonishments by Yüan Ang did not appeal to the Emperor, who admittedly just wanted to make him "suffer" for a while. When Liu Ch'ang died of starvation on the way to his exile, his last words sound like he could not believe that he had been thrown in a lethal trap–for nothing. How could he find such a cruel end under the reign of his own brother, Hsiao Wen-ti, "the Filial and Cultured Emperor," who had explicitly ordered that he be fed well on this journey? And why does the memoir tell us that none of the local officials dared to open his cart, until they reached Yung 雍, where the local Prefect finally opened the seal and made his death known?

When he learned of the death of his brother, the Emperor cried out loudly. What now? Yüan Ang again gave him a true piece of advice that basically said everything about the powers in action behind the incident: "Could anything short of decapitating the Chancellor and Secretaries in order to apologize to the Empire be permissible?"[260] Of course, the Emperor, who had finally earned the reputation of fratricide, again did not follow Yüan's frank words.

Then, the narrative moves by jumps and starts, relating the various stages of Emperor Wen's "pity": In 172 BC, the Sovereign enfeoffed the four young sons of Liu Ch'ang as marquises to relieve his conscience; in 168 BC, a song circulating among the people reveals that someone had perceived quite clearly what actually had happened under the cover of many crocodile tears. Filled with indignation that the empire could come to think that he coveted the territory of Huai-nan, he finally moved Liu Hsi, King of Ch'eng-yang to be King of the former territory of Huai-nan, and retroactively honored his brother with the truly exalted posthumous title "The Pungent" (Li 厲), a title reserved for "a violent and arrogant person, without affection for his relatives." Only in 164 BC, did the Emperor enthrone the three still living sons as kings, elegantly splitting up former Huai-nan–as if to ensure that they would never have a real base of power again.

Ssu-ma Ch'ien brilliantly manages to display the almost incredible hypocrisy of the involved persons simply by juxtaposing the repeatedly demonstrated remorse of the Emperor with the bare essence of his actions. Why say more?

---

[259] *Shih chi*, 118.3079.
[260] *Shih chi*, 118.3080.

While his father was gifted with the physical strength to lift a tripod with his bare hands, his eldest son, Liu An, is characterized as a refined, cultivated person, with a strong affinity for literature and the Taoist arts. While the *Han shu* in its rather diffusives style elaborates on this aspect by mentioning the good old times, when the King of Huai-nan was sharing his passion for the arts with the young Emperor Wu, the *Shih chi* oddly loses after only twenty-seven characters–all interest in the famous cultural achievements of "Master Huai-nan," who according to later legends even attained immortality, and continues with his endless pondering of the right moment to start a rebellion. The Grand Scribe created a true masterpiece, as Li Ching-hsing 李景星 (1876–1934) readily admits in his praise:

> His [Liu An's] hesitations are completely confined to [his] heart, this is a unique strength of his Honor the Grand Scribe, others do not possess this kind of literary skill. Therefore, he uses the words 'he wanted,' the words 'he was afraid,' the words 'he feared,' the words 'he thought,' even 'at that time he wished,' 'he secretly wished,' and 'he laid plans wishing…' and the like–[his] description enters into the subtlest aspects.
> 其猶豫處全在心上，是太史公獨擅，他人無此手筆也．故用欲字、畏字、恐字，念字、及亦欲、時欲、偷欲、計欲等字，摹寫入微．

A first attempt by the court to simultaneously try his brother, the King of Heng-shan, was denied by the Emperor, claiming that each of the kings is responsible for his own fief and hence should not be held mutually liable for their actions. Luckily for the prosecutors, they also found a "rat" in the household of Liu Tzu, who was under the naive impression that his last minute collaboration (purely out of spite) would save him. After the incredible net of envy and malevolence that unfolded around the King of Heng-shan in the first part of his memoir, the reader is left without doubt, that even if the entanglement in the King of Huai-nan's plans to revolt once more was circumstantial at best, this kingdom could have been easily taken down for any other reason at any other time–under Emperor Wu's newly established administrative machinery.

It is also noteworthy, that Wu P'i, the principal witness in the case against Liu An, was executed despite his praise of the Han. The same holds true for Liu Hsiao, the other important witness in the case of Heng-shan, who was also executed quite arbitrarily despite his crucial testimony. He initially thought himself safe, relying on a proclaimed impunity in case of self-indictment, but in the end, the prosecutors simply executed him for another crime. Judging from the force and extent the "plotting" parties were extinguished, one can only deduce that the imperial court wanted to set an example and–at the same time–leave behind not even remote witnesses who might question the official narrative of these events.

Lastly, one should keep in mind, that all these events were collateral results of the feared "imperial decretory cases" (*chao yü* 詔獄), initiated directly by the Emperor and enforced by his new breed of rapidly risen petty officials having their way with the "justice of the *Ch'un-ch'iu*."[261] A topic that will be consequently developed in the following memoirs about officials and scholars.

Whatever really happened in Huai-nan–whether Liu An was on the verge of a rebellion or whether he was merely preparing to defend his life as one of the last powerful Kings of the Han, whether he was led on by the heretic talks of his advisers, or whether he was determined to avenge his strong but naïve father Liu Ch'ang right from the beginning, is hard to tell. But as Ssu-ma Ch'ien reminds us in his concluding words: "This was not a failure of the Kings alone." The rest of his rather hollow assessment that plays on old prejudices against the South is oddly contradicted by the way he arranged this memoir as a chapter of some 'traitors' and kings being framed.[262]

[261] Even the otherwise utterly cruel and perverse Liu Chien 劉建 (r. 127–121 BC),[261] King of Chiang-tu 江都, who bought his way out of the investigations into the plottings of Huai-nan and Heng-shan (despite tangible preparations of his own), apparently dreaded the *chao yü* 詔獄, as the *Han shu* (53.2417) relates in the following words addressed at his close servants: 我為王，詔獄歲至，生又無驩怡日，壯士不坐死，欲為人所不能為耳; "Me being a king, year by year I face the advent of imperial decretory cases; but when in life there are no more days of joy and pleasure, a stalwart man does not die sitting [on his bottom], I wish to do, what other men are [were?] not able to do."

[262] Hans van Ess introduces an intriguing perspective on the Grand Scribe's assessment: Apparently, two members of the imperial family became barbarians under the influence of the bad customs of the region of Ch'u. Yet Ch'u was also the homeland of the Han themselves, who once had risen to overturn the rule of the Ch'in. Is Liu An's rebellion against Emperor Wu hence to be seen on the same level as the rebellion of the Han against the Ch'in? (cf, van Ess, *Politik und Geschichtsschreibung im alten China*, pp. 185–86).

Bibliography

Translations
Aoki, *Shiki*, 12:376–461.
Watson, 2:361–392.

Studies
Arima Takuya 有馬卓也. "Wainan ōkoku no hachijū nen–Ei Fu yori Ryū Chō、Ryū An he" 淮南王国の八十年–英布より劉長、劉安へ, *Chūgoku kenkyū shūkan*, 25 (1999.12): 2565–2586.

Ch'en Kuang-chung 陳廣忠. "'Huai-nan Tzu' te ch'ing-hsiang-hsing ho huai-nan wang chih ssu" 《淮南子》的傾向性和淮南王之死, *Chiang Huai lun-t'an* 1 (1981): 82–87.

Ch'en Ligui 臣麗桂. "Huai-nan wang liang shih mou-fan yen-yi" 淮南王兩世謀反研議, *Chung-kuo shu-mu chi-k'an*, 18.2 (1984): 54–70.

Cheng Liang-shu 鄭良樹. "Liu An yü Huai-nan Tzu" 劉安與淮南子, *Shu ho jen*, 101 (1969): 793–800, 102 (1969): 801–808.

Hulsewé, A. F. P. "Royal Rebels," *Bulletin de l'Ecole française d'Extrême-Orient*, 69 (1981): 315–325.

Kandel, Barbara. "Der Versuch einer politischen Restauration–Liu An, der König von Huai-nan," *Nachrichten der Gesellschaft für Natur und Völkerkunde Ostasiens* 113 (1973): 33–96.

Hsü Fu-kuan 徐復觀. "Liu An te shih-tai yü Huai-nan Tzu" 劉安的時代與淮南子, *Ta-lu tsa-chih*, 47.6 (1973): 1–38.

Van Ess, Hans. *Politik der Geschichtsschreibung im alten China. Pan-Ma i-t'ung* 班馬異同, Harrassowitz: Wiesbaden, 2014.

Vankeerberghen, Griet. *The* Huainanzi *and Liu An's Claim to Moral Authority*, Albany: State University of New York Press, 2001.

Wallacker, Benjamin E. "Liu An, Second King of Huai-nan (180?-122 B. C.)," *Journal of the American Oriental Society*, 92 (1972): 36–49.

Wang Ch'i-ts'ai 王啟才. "Lun Liu An te ming-yün pei-chü—chien chi Huai-nan Tzu hung-lieh te huo-huan yi-shih ch'eng-yin" 論劉安的命運悲劇—兼及淮南子鴻烈的禍患意識成因, *Fu-yang Shih-fan Hsüeh-yüan hsüeh-pao*, 2 (2009): 1–4.

Yen Meng-lien 閆孟蓮. "Hsi Han cheng-chih yü wen-hua pei-ching hsia te Huai-nan wang mou-fan an" 西漢政治與文化背景下的淮南王謀反案, *Yi-bin hsüeh-yüan-pao*, 12.3 (2012): 38–41.

Yao Chih-chung 姚治中. "'Huai-nan Tzu' tui chuan-chih chu-yi huang-ch'üan ssu-hsiang te fan-ni—tsai lun 'Huai-nan Tzu' te shih-tai t'e-hsing" 《淮南子》對專制主義皇權思想的叛逆—再論《淮南子》的時代特征, *Wan-hsi Hsüeh-yüan pao*, 27.1 (2011): 38–43.

[The Officials Who] Follow Reason,[1] Memoir 59

translated by William H. Nienhauser, Jr.

[119.3099] His Honor the Grand Scribe says, "Laws and orders are that by which one guides the common people, punishments and penalties are that by which one prohibits villainy.[2] When the civil [laws and orders] and martial [punishments and penalties] are not at hand, the good people are afraid. But among those [officials] who cultivate themselves, there have not been any who caused disorder.[3] By carrying out the duties of their positions and following reason, they can still effect good government. What need is there to threaten severity?[4]

---

[1] *Hsün-li* 循理 is actually an abbreviation for *hsün-li li* 循理吏, "officials who follow reason" (see "So-yin"). as in the historian's comments in chapter 130 cited below: "Those officials who upheld the law and followed reasonable methods, did not boast of their merits nor brag about their abilities" 奉法循理之吏，不伐功矜能.

[2] Compare the opening lines of "The Memoir of the Harsh Officials" (*Shih chi*, 122.3131) which begins with a citation of Confucius from the *Analects* (*Lunyü*, 2.3; Legge, 1:146): "If you lead them [the people] with administrative rules and bring them to unison with punishments, the people will avoid [the punishments], but will have no sense of shame. If you lead them with virtue and bring them to unison with rites, they will have a sense of shame and moreover will be corrected" 孔子曰：「導之以政，齊之以刑，民免而無恥。導之以德，齊之以禮，有恥且格」. A few lines later in the same chapter (ibid.) Ssu-ma Ch'ien himself comments: "Laws and orders are only the tools of government but not the source to regulate whether the government is pure or polluted" 法令者治之具，而非制治清濁之源也. Indeed, as Watson (2:373, n. 1) observes, this chapter is intended to be read in tandem with that of the harsh officials.

[3] Following the punctuation in Takigawa (119.2): 文武不備，良民懼然。身修者，官未曾亂也.

[4] Another reminder to readers that this chapter is a bookend for that of the severity of the "harsh officials" in chapter 122.

Sun Shu-ao 孫叔敖

Sun Shu-ao 孫叔敖[5] was a private gentleman[6] of Ch'u. The Prime Minister of Yü-ch'iu 虞丘 (Yü Hillock)[7] recommended him to King Chuang 莊 of Ch'u (r. 613–591)[8] to replace himself. After three months, Sun was made Prime Minister of Ch'u,[9]

[5] His *cognomen* was the Ch'u royal Mi 芈, his *nomen* was Wei 蒍, his *praenomen* Ao 敖, and his *agnomen* Sun 孫, and his sibling rank 叔 (the Younger; see also Fang Hsüan-ch'en, p. 616, #2174). There are a number of anecdotes related to him in early literature. Sun Shu-ao also appears in the story of how performer Meng 蒙 imitated the recently deceased prime minister in leading King Chuang to reward Sun's son (*Shih chi*, 126.3201). See also the notes which follow, the article by William H. Nienhauser, Jr., listed in the bibliography below, and the translator's note.

[6] *Ch'u-shih* 處士. Much discussed in our annotation in previous volumes, this expression is parallel to *ch'u-nü* 處女 and indicates a member of the *shih* 士 (lower nobility class; serviceman) who, although qualified to serve in an official position, is still living a private life at home.

Sun Shu-ao's father, known as Wei Chia 蒍賈, and his grandfather Wei Lü-ch'en 蒍呂臣, opposed the powerful Tou 鬥 clan in Ch'u for years. In 605 BC Wei Chia was imprisoned and killed by his enemies (*Tso chuan*, Hsüan 4, pp. 680–82). Thus it is possible that Sun Shu-ao became a "private gentleman in Ch'u" for his own safety. Following the defeat and annihilation of the Tou clan shortly thereafter (ibid.), he would have been able to take a high position.

[7] Precisely what *xiang* 相 means in this context is speculative, perhaps just "minister." The Prime Minister of Ch'u was called *ling-yin* 令尹 in Ch'u but *zai* 宰 from without (see n. 9 below).

Given the syntax (虞丘相進之於楚莊王), Yü-ch'iu 虞丘 does not seem to be a personal name but rather a toponym (Wu and Lu, 119.3117n.). Liang Yü-sheng (3:35.1431-2) pointed out that there is no Yü-ch'iu recorded in the *Tso chuan* or other early texts. From a number of variant names in parallel passages, Liang prefers Shen Yin 沈尹 (Governor of Shen). He is also known as Ch'in Yin 寢尹, possibly from his service at Ch'in-ch'iu 寢丘 (= Ch'i-ssu 期思 [modern Huai-pin 淮濱 in Honan] where Sun Shu-ao was living in reclusion). Liang suggests that Shen Yin may have served as an official at Yü-ch'iu where he met and was impressed by Sun Shu-ao. Wang Shu-min (119.3227–28) is equally speculative but concludes that the reference to Yü-ch'iu is correct, referring to a hillock named Yü in Shen 沈 County. He believes Sun Shu-ao's predecessor's *praenomen* was Shih 筮 and all other references are to his place of origin. His *praenomen* was Hsü 戌 and he was said to have been an opponent of the Ch'u Premier, Nang Wa 囊瓦 (d. 506 BC) and have died ca. 505 BC.

[8] See the note on "bandits and robbers" just below.

[9] In 597 BC, see *Tso chuan* (Yang, Hsüan 12, p. 723): 蒍敖為宰.

promulgating teachings [10] so that the common people were guided [properly], [11] superiors and subordinates were in harmony, and current behavior and customs rose to an excellent [level]; once an administrative policy was relaxed, prohibitions would come to an end. [12] Among the petty officials there was no villainy, [13] and bandits and robbers did not rise up. [14] In autumn and winter he exhorted the people to go into the mountains to gather [bamboo and wood], in the spring and summer to make use of the waters [to transport the bamboo and wood], [15] so that everyone was able to obtain that

[10] Mizusawa (8:1) notes that an early printed version of this chapter omitted *shih chiao* 施教 "promulgated teachings."

[11] Just above it was "laws and commands" (*fa ling* 法令) which guided the common people (*tao min* 導民). The repetition of *tao min* may be intended to emphasize Sun Shu-ao's ability to "follow reasonable methods" to achieve the same ends.

[12] An example can be seen in the anecdote about the low-slung carriages that follows in the text. Sun Shu-ao was able to demonstrate that issuing orders could be circumvented by clever use of administrative policy.

[13] This echoes the Grand Scribe's own commentary to the "K'u-li lieh-chuan" 酷吏列傳 (*Shih chi*, 122.3154) which reads "Yet among these ten men, those who were honest may serve as a model of dutiful conduct, and those who were corrupt may serve as an admonition. By their methods and strategies, their teaching and leadership, restricted villainy and curtailed evil" 然此十人中，其廉者足以為儀表，其污者足以為戒，其污者足以為戒，方略教導，禁姦止邪．

[14] Chang Wen-hu (2:701) cites Liang Yü-sheng's note that following *tao tsei pu ch'i* 盜賊不起 one citation of this text reads *sui pa chu-hou* 遂罷諸侯, "and finally became hegemon of the feudal lords." Indeed, the history of King Chuang's rule has often been portrayed as an attempt to gain hegemony for Ch'u (see for example the title of *chüan* 57, "Ch'u Chuang-wang cheng-pa" 楚莊王爭霸, in the *Yi shih* 繹史). King Chuang has also been the subject of numerous similar anecdotes stressing his profligacy and the need for a series of ministers to rectify his behavior.

This passage recalls references to Sun in two early texts: (1) "Sun Shu-ao reclined contentedly holding a feather-fan and the men of Ying [the Ch'u capital] threw away their arms" 孫叔敖甘寢秉羽而郢人投兵 (*Chuang Tzu* 莊子, *SPPY* 8:18a); (2) "In antiquity Sun Shu-ao lay peacefully and the men of Ying had nothing on which to damage their spears" 昔孫叔敖恬臥，而郢人無所害其鋒 (*Huai-nan Tzu* 淮南子, *SPPY*, 9:3a). The *Lieh-nü chuan* 列女傳 (*SPPY*, 6:2a) has a similar passage: "In antiquity when Sun Shu-ao was made prime minister, no one picked up articles that had been left along the roadside, doors were not locked, and the bandit groups ceased to exist on their own" 昔孫叔敖之為令尹也，道不拾遺，門不閉關，而盜賊自息．

[15] Following Hsü Kuang's note cited in "Chi-chieh." This reading does not transition well into what follows. If it was only bamboo and wood that were gathered and transported, how were the people able "to obtain that which was easy for them"? A literal reading is just "in

which was convenient for them and the people all delighted in their lives.

[3100] King Chuang considered that the coins were too light and had the small ones changed for larger ones. The families of the hundred *cognomens* [16] found this inconvenient and they all left their occupations. The Master of the Market spoke of this to the Prime Minister: "The market is in chaos! The people are not secure in their places and the order [of their stalls] is not set."[17] The Prime Minister said, "How long a time has it been like this, is it recent?" The Master of the Market said, "The most recent three months." The Prime Minister said, "Say no more! I will now cause things to be restored."[18] Five days later, when he went to the morning court session, the Prime Minister spoke of this to the King: "On a recent day the coins were changed because they were considered too light. Now the Master of the Market came to me and said that 'The market is in chaos! The people have not settled into their places and the order [of their stalls] is not set.' I request that thereupon you order [the coins] restored as they were of old." The king allowed this, issued the order, and after three days the market was again was it was of old.[19]

The people of Ch'u were by custom fond of low-slung carriages, but the King did not think low carriages were convenient for the horses and wanted to issue an order to

autumn and winter to go into the mountains to gather and to make use of the waters in spring and summer." Watson, 2:374 renders: "In autumn and winter Sunshu Ao encouraged the people to gather wood in the mountains, and in spring and summer to make use of the resources of the rivers and lakes." Mizusawa (8:1) points out that four traditional editions read *ch'un hsia hsia yi shui* 春夏下以水, "in the spring and summer they sent them down by means of the streams," and this variant at the very least suggests the difficulties traditional readers seem to have had with this passage. Alternate suggestions argue that this passage refers to hunting in the autumn and winter and fishing in the spring and summer (see, for example, the comments of the modern scholar Li Li's 李笠 [1894–1962] cited by Takigawa, 119.3) or refer to hunting and irrigation (i.e., "using water" [to irrigate fields]).

[16] At this time the term *pai hsing* 百姓, [families of] the hundred *cognomens*, was not yet an equivalent for "common people" as it became later, but referred to the families among the *kuo jen* 國人 who had originally been artisans (*pai kung* 百工; see the discussion in "A Note on Terms: The Chou Socio-political Structure as Seen in *Shih chi* chapters 31–40," *Grand Scribe's Records*, 5.1:xxx–xxxi).

[17] *Tz'u-hang* 次行 refers to the normal order and location of each merchant's stall or shop (Takigawa, 119.3).Wu and Lu (119.3121) read this compound as *tz'u-hsing*, "to stay or leave" the market. Perhaps the chaos in the market and was due to customers who tried to pay for things with older, small coins.

[18] The *chih* 之 here might refer either to the market or to the coins.

[19] This anecdote cannot be found in any other Han or pre-Han text. It could be intended to satirize Emperor Wu's implementation of the new "white-metal coins" 白金錢 and "five-*chu* cash" 五銖錢 (mentioned in the "Memoir of the Harsh Officials," *Shih chi,* 122.3140 and 3146).

make [carriages] higher.[20] The Prime Minister said, "If orders are issued too often, the people won't know which to follow, and this would not be acceptable. If Your Majesty would raise the carriages, your subject requests that you instruct [the common people in] the wards and alleyways[21] to raise their doorsills. Those who ride in carriages are all gentlemen and a gentleman cannot be getting down from his carriage too often." The king consented and, within half a year, the people all had of their own accord raised their carriages.

In this way, without instructing them, the people followed his [Sun Shu-ao's] influence, those who were near observing and imitating [Sun], those who were distant looking up to him from the four directions and taking him as their model. Therefore, he was able to become prime minister three times and did not rejoice,[22] because he understood it was through his talents that he naturally obtained it; and three times he was dismissed from the position and did not show regret, because he understood it was not due to his own faults.[23]

[20] In *Han Fei Tzu* 韓非子 ("Wai-ch'u shuo, tso-hsia san-shih-san" 外儲説左下第三十三, *Han Fei Tzu chin-chu chin-yi* 韓非子今註今譯 [Taipei: Kuo-li Pien-yi Kuan 國立編譯館, 1982], 5.636), Sun Shu-ao is said to have driven a carriage made of plaited bamboo and wood driven by a mare (棧車牝馬, i.e., a simple, inexpensive rig).

[21] The duties of the Minor Minister, according to the *Chou li* 周禮, included listening to legal cases in the wards and neighborhoods according to maps of population registers ("T'ien-kuan, Hsiao-tsai" 天官, 小宰: 以官府之八成經邦治：一曰聽政役以比居，二曰聽師田以簡稽，三曰聽閭里以版圖 ... [*Chou li chin-chu chin-yi* 周禮今注今譯 (Taipei: Shang-wu Yin-shu Kuan, 1983), p. 20]; compare the translation by Edouard Biot, *Le Tcheou-li ou Rites des Tcheou* [Paris: L'Imprimerie Nationale, 1851], v. 1, p. 51).

[22] Wang Shu-min (119.3229) believes that Ssu-ma Ch'ien took the account of Sun Shu-ao winning and losing the position three times from *Chuang Tzu* and *Lü-shih ch'un-ch'iu*. In a memorial Tsou Yang 鄒陽 submitted from prison recorded on *Shih chi*, 83.2475 (*Grand Scribe's Records*, 7:290), Tsou argues that Sun Shu-ao was willing to abandon the post of Prime Minister three times because other prime ministers of other states had been executed (*Grand Scribe's Records*, 7:290).

[23] In the *Kuo yü* 國語 (Shanghai: Ku-chi Ch'u-pan-she, 1978, 2:573) the same story is told about another Ch'u Prime Minister, Tou Tzu-wen 鬥子文 (see also *Lun-yü*, 5.19; Legge, *Chinese Classics*, 1:290).

Tzu-ch'an 子産

[3101] Tzu-ch'an 子産 (d. 522 BC)[24] was a Ranking Grand Master of Cheng.[25] During the reign of Lord Chao of Cheng 鄭昭君 (r. 696–695 BC)[26] because his favorite, Hsü Chih 徐摯,[27] became Prime Minister, the country became chaotic. Superiors were not close to their subordinates, and fathers were not on good terms with sons.

Ta-kung Tzu-ch'i 大宮子期[28] spoke of him to the lord and he made Tzu-ch'an Prime Minister. After he had been Prime Minister for a year, frivolous fellows stopped idling about and being disrespectful, gray-haired elders were no longer seen carrying heavy burdens,[29] and servant boys did not plow fields beyond the boundary markers.

---

[24] Also known as Kung-sun Ch'iao 公孫僑; Kung-sun, Noble Scion was his noble status, Ch'iao 僑 was his *praenomen*, and his *cognomens* were Ch'an and Mei 美 (the *tzu* 子 is an honorific). Fang Hsüan-ch'en (pp. 192-3, #383) notes that his *nomen* was Wei 韋. Tzu-ch'an was the son of Tzu-kuo 子國 and the grandson of Duke Mu 穆 of Cheng (r. 617-606 BC; see Wu and Lu, 119:3118n.). He was a prominent statesman in Cheng from 563 BC until his death, a period in which the political and economic status of Cheng was elevated (Pines, p. 313). There are a number of references to Tzu-ch'an in the "Hereditary House of Cheng" (see especially *Shih chi*, 42.1771ff.). See also the translator's note.

[25] Lu Zongli (p. 349) explains this position as a Middle-level Grand Master (*Chung Tai-fu* 中大夫).

[26] Tzu-ch'an served dukes Chien 簡 and Ting 定 (r. respectively 564-530 and 529-514 BC; "So-yin"). Thus this entire passage seems suspect. See also the translator's note. On Tzu-ch'an's life as reconstructed from early sources, see E. R. Eichler, "The Life of Tsze-ch'an," *The China Review,* 1886–87: 12–23 and 65–78; V. A. Rubin, "Tzu-ch'an and the City State of Ancient China," *TP,* 52(1965–66): 8–34; Burton Watson's discussion of "Tzu-ch'an's Government Policies" in Watson's *The Tso Chuan* (New York: Columbia University Press, 1989), pp. 154–63; and Jen Fang-ch'iu 任訪秋, *Tzu-ch'an p'ing chuan* 子產評傳 (Chengchow: Chung-chou Ku-chi, 1987).

[27] *Terrae filius.*

[28] Although the exact meaning of Ta-kung 大宮 is unclear, since it refers to the Cheng ancestral temple it may be used here as a *nomen.*

Ssu-ma Chen ("So-yin") notes that there is no record of Tzu-ch'i recommending Tzu-ch'an in either the *Tso chuan* or the *Kuo yü* but speculates that Tzu-ch'i and Tzu-ch'an were brothers. Takigawa (119.5a) cites the Shen Family 沈家本 edition to the effect that there was no Tzu-ch'i in Cheng and Ssu-ma Chen was mistaken. Wu and Lu (119.3118n.) argue that nothing is known of Tzu-ch'i outside this text. Wang Shu-min (119.3230) notes that numerous other texts record that Tzu-p'i 子皮 (Han Hu 罕虎) while serving as Prime Minister of Cheng recommended Tzu-ch'an to succeed him in the position.

[29] Cf. *Meng Tzu,* "Liang Hui Wang, shang" 梁惠王: "Let careful attention be paid to education in schools–

the inculcation of it, especially of the filial and fraternal duties, and grey-haired men will not

After two years, no one arbitrarily raised prices beforehand in the markets.[30] After three years, doors were not locked at night and what was left along the road was not picked up.[31] After four years, farm tools were not taken home [but left in the fields]. After five years, for gentlemen there were no foot[-long] [conscription] tablets[32] and the people observed periods of mourning without being ordered to follow the rules.[33] He ruled

be seen upon the roads carrying burdens on their backs or on their heads" 謹庠序之教，申之以孝梯之義，頒白者不負戴于道路矣 (*Meng Tzu cheng-yi* 孟子正義, 1.58; translation is that of Legge, 2:149).

[30] Our translation follows "Cheng-yi" cited in Takigawa, 119.5. In other words, prices would not be pre-set at a higher level to allow for haggling (see also the examples given by Wang Shu-min, 119.3230).

[31] *Pu shih yi* 不拾遺 is an expression that is found in a number of classical texts (several referring to Confucius's tenure as minister in Lu such as that on *Shih chi*, 47.1917: After three months of K'ung Tzu's administration, lamb and pork vendors ceased raising their prices, men and women walked on different sides of the street, no one picked up anything lost on the road" 國政三月，粥羔豚者弗飾賈；男女行者別於塗；塗不拾遺). It is used both to depict rulers who ruled by virtue or reason such as the passage on *Shih chi*, 68.2231 depicting the results of Shang Yang's issues strict ordinances in Ch'in: "After they had been in effect for ten years, the commoners of Ch'in were all delighted; no one picked up articles lost on the road and there were no bandits or thieves in the mountains" 行之十年，秦民大說，道不拾遺，山無盜賊 (*Grand Scribe's Records*, 7:90). But perhaps most significantly, the expression ironically appears three times in the "K'u-li lieh-chuan" 酷吏列傳. First to depict Chih Tu's 郅都 harsh rule of a commandery: "no one in the commandery would pick up anything left [along the roads]" 郡中不拾遺 (*Shih chi*, 122.3133); the second passage describes the fear the people of Ho-nei Commandery had for Yi Tsung 義縱 (*Shih chi*, 122.3144): "When he reached [Ho-nei] he wiped out all adherents of the powerful Jang Clan and in Ho-nei no one picked up anything left [along the roads]" 至則族滅其豪穰氏之屬，河內道不拾遺; the final passage (*Shih chi*, 122.3147) describes how Wang Wen-shu 王溫舒 used local criminals from powerful families in Kuang-p'ing to round up bandits: "For this reason the robbers and bandits from the outlying areas of Ch'i and Chao did not dare to come near to Kuang-p'ing and Kuang-p'ing gained a reputation for people not picking up anything left [along the roads]" 以其故齊趙之郊盜賊不敢近廣平，廣平聲為道不拾遺.

[32] As Aoki (119.469n.) points out, gentlemen (or perhaps better "servicemen," *shih* 士) did not need to be drafted to serve, they joined the army voluntarily.

[33] The orders would have designated the proper mourning period for each type of relative.
V. A Rubin's translation of this passage differs (*op. cit.*, p. 22): "After one year of Tzu-ch'an's government, young people ceased to joke independently, older people lifted (loads) no more, and slaves no more ploughed up the boundaries. After two years, prices on the markets rose no more. After three years, the doors at night were locked no more, and nobody lifted (the things) lost on the roads. After four years, agricultural tools could be left on the fields. After

Cheng for twenty-six years[34] and when he died the able-bodied men wailed and wept, the old cried like children, saying "Tzu-ch'an has left us and died! To whom will the common people turn to [now]!?"[35]

Kung-yi Hsiu 公義休

Kung-yi Hsiu 公義休[36] was an academician of Lu.[37] Because of his high estate, he was made Prime Minister of Lu. In carrying out the laws he followed reasonable methods, not making changes in them, so that all the officials under him were naturally upright. He caused those on government salaries not to be able to contend for profit with the common people, and those who had [already] received large [benefits] not to be able to [further] derive small [benefits].[38]

[3102] A retainer once sent him a fish but the Prime Minister did not accept it. The retainer said, "I heard that you have a craving for fish,[39] so I sent you this. Why didn't you accept it?" Kung-yi Hsiu replied, "It is just because I am partial to fish that I didn't accept it. Now as Prime Minister I can provide fish for myself. If I were to lose my position by accepting this fish, who would ever give me fish again?

five years, the officials took no more census and at times of mourning they governed without orders." Wang Shu-min (119.3230) cites other sources which relate the success of Tzu-ch'an's administration in terms of progress year by year

[34] As Wu and Lu note (119.3119n.), according to the records in the *Tso chuan* Tzu-ch'an was Prime Minister of Cheng for twenty-two years (from 543 until his death in 522 BC). Both the "Cheng shih-chia" 鄭世家 and the chronological tables in the *Shih chi* (14.670) claim Tzu-ch'an died in 496 BC, but that would mean he was Prime Minister for forty-seven years.

[35] For a number of other recorded reactions to Tzu-ch'an's death, see Wang Shu-min, 119:3230–31).

[36] Kung-yi Hsiu does not appear in the *Tso chuan*. Scholars believe that this is the same person as Kung-yi Tzu 公義子 whom the "Kao Tzu, hsia" 高子下 chapter of *Meng Tzu* (compare Chiao Hsün 焦循 [1703–1760], *Meng Tzu cheng-yi* 孟子正義 [Peking: Chung-hua, 1982], 2:830–31, and Legge, 2:433) says held control of the administration in Lu under Duke Mu 穆 (r. 407–377 BC). The records for Lu in this period are scant. Chiao Hsün also notes that in the *Yen-t'ieh lun* 鹽鐵論 Kung-yi Hsiu is said to have been Prime Minister of Lu under Duke Mu.

[37] There has been some doubt expressed by scholars as to whether the position of *po-shih* 博士 (academician) existed prior to the Ch'in (see the discussion in Wang Shu-min, 119.3231).

[38] This is illustrated by the anecdote which follows in which Kung-yi Hsiu, who has received the large benefit of becoming Prime Minister, gives up the smaller benefit of the gift of a fish.

[39] Cf. the homily in *Meng Tzu* (6a.10 *SPPY*; Legge, *Chinese Classics*, 2:411) which begins "I like fish and I also like bear paws" 我所欲也，熊掌，亦我所欲也.

Therefore, I have not accepted it."[40]

When he ate vegetables and found them delicious, he pulled up all the mallow[41] in his garden and threw it away. When he saw that the cloth woven in his home was of good quality, he quickly sent away his wife and burned her looms, saying, "Where would you have the farmers and weaver-women sell their goods?"[42]

Shih She 石奢

Shih She 石奢[43] was Prime Minister to King Chao of Ch'u 楚昭王 (r. 515–490 BC).[44] He was steady and straightforward, honest and upright, and there was no one he

[40] A similar account is recorded in the "Wai-ch'u" 外儲 chapter of the *Han Fei Tzu* 韓非子 (*Han Fei Tzi chi-chieh teng chiu-chung* 韓非子集解等九種, Wang Hsien-ch'ien 王先謙, ed. Taipei: Shih-chieh, 1988)], 14:255): "While Kung-yi Hsiu was Prime Minister of Lu he craved fish. The entire state strove to buy fish to present to him. [But] Master Kung-yi would not accept them. His younger brother admonished him saying: 'You have a craving for fish and yet you haven't accepted any. Why is this?' He replied, 'It is solely because I have a craving for fish that I still haven't accepted any. If I were to accept the fish, I would certainly take on the appearance of an underling. If I took on the appearance of an underling, I would be bending the law. If I bent the law, then I would be dismissed from my position as prime minister. Although I have a craving for fish, in this I certainly cannot allow others to provide fish for me. . . . Although I have a craving for fish, I am able to always provide my own fish.' This makes clear that relying on others is not as good as relying on oneself, and clear that others doing things for oneself are not as good as doing things oneself." 公儀休相魯而嗜魚，一國盡爭買魚而獻之，公儀子不受，其弟諫曰：「夫子嗜魚而不受者何也？」對曰：「夫唯嗜魚，故不受也。夫即受魚，必有下人之色，有下人之色，將枉於法，枉於法則免於相，雖嗜魚，此不必能自給致我魚 . . . 即無受魚而不免於相，雖嗜魚，我能長自給魚。」此明夫恃人不如自恃也，明於人之為己者不如己自為也.

[41] *K'uei* 葵 or *malva verticillata*, "Chinese mallow." This was a stable vegetable in ancient China as well as in ancient Rome. Horace mentions it in reference to his own diet, which he describes as very simple: "Me pascunt olivae, me cichorea, me malvae" ("As for me, olives, endives, and mallows provide sustenance"; Horace, *Odes* 31, vers. 15, ca. 30 BC).

[42] This passage may originally have come from an early *Han Fei Tzu* edition since a similar anecdote is cited in the *T'ai-p'ing yü-lan* 太平御覽 as originating from the *Han Tzu* 韓子 (see Wang Shu-min, 119.3232).

[43] Although there is no record of Shih She serving as Prime Minister under King Chao, the *Lü-shih ch'un-ch'iu* 呂氏春秋, the *Han Shih wai-chuan* 韓詩外傳, and the *Hsin hsü* 新序 all record the King asking Shih She to take over the administration of Ch'u (see Liang Yü-sheng, 3:1433).

[44] Liang Yü-sheng (ibid.) notes that the Prime Minister of Ch'u was referred to as *Ling-*

flattered, no one he shunned [to investigate]. When he was on an inspection tour of the counties [of Ch'u], someone killed a man along the road. When the Prime Minister gave chase, it was none other than his father. He let his father escape, turned about, and bound himself up. He sent someone to report this to the king, "The one who killed a man was your servant's father. Now if I use my father to establish good government, it will be unfilial. But if I abandon the law and let someone escape his punishment, I will be disloyal [to you]. Your servant is guilty and deserves death. The king said, "To pursued him and not catch[45] does not deserve to submit punishment. You, sir, should just attend to administrative matters!" Shih She said, "If one were not partial to his own father, he would not be a filial son. But if one does not uphold the laws of his ruler, he would not be a loyal subject. If Your Majesty pardons his offense, it is by the grace of the Sovereign. For him to submit to execution and die would be the duty of a minister."[46] In the end he would not accept the [king's] order, slit his own throat and died.

Li Li 李離

Li Li 李離[47] was a judge[48] under Duke Wen of Chin 晉文公 (r. 636–628 BC).[49] As he made a mistake in hearing a legal case and had someone put to death, he bound himself and sentenced himself to die.[50] Duke Wen said to him, "As there are honored and mean official positions, so there are light and heavy punishments. If one of your subordinate officials made a mistake, it is not your offense." Li Li replied, "Your servant occupies the position as head of the officials and has not yielded his position to any of his officers. His salary and benefits are numerous, and he does not share my profit with his subordinates. Now **[*3103*]** he have made a mistake in hearing a legal

yin 令尹 (a term we translate as "Premier").

[45] The King presumably knows that Shih She did in fact catch the criminal but pretends that he did not in order to allow Shih She an honorable way out of his dilemma.

[46] This entire passage could be read specifically to refer to Shih She himself rather than a hypothetical "he."

[47] There are parallel accounts of this story in *Han-shih wai-chuan* (*Han-shih wai-chuan chin-chu chin-yi* 漢詩外傳今注今譯, Lai Yen-yüan 賴炎元, ed. [rpt. Taipei: Shang-wu, 1981], 2.65–66) and *Hsin hsü* (*Hsin hsü chin-chu chin-yi* 新序今注今譯, Lu Yüan-chün 盧元駿, ed. [Taipei: Shang-wu, 1984], 7.243–47. Both of these parallels are more detailed and more detailed than this narrative (see also Takigawa, 119.7).

[48] Cf. Lü Zongli, p. 719.

[49] The famous noble scion, *praenomen* Ch'ung-erh 重耳, who wandered for nineteen years before claiming power in Chin and becoming a hegemon of the feudal lords (see his biography on *Shih chi*, 39.1656–69, and *Grand Scribe's Records*, 5.1:321–44.

[50] Or "bound himself deserving to die."

case and had a man killed. To transfer this offense to a subordinate officer is something he has never heard of." [Thus] he declined to accept the duke's command.[51] Duke Wen then said, "If you feel you have committed an offense, has this lonely one not also committed an offense [as your superior]?" Li Li said, "A judge has his laws. If one errs in carrying out a punishment, then one must be punished [in the same fashion]; if one errs in causing a death, then one must die. Milord considered your servant was able to attend to details in hearing cases and resolve all doubt and for that reason made me a judge. Now that I have made a mistake in hearing a legal case and had a man killed, my offense makes me deserve to die.

In the end he was unwilling to accept the [duke's] order, fell on his sword, and died.

His Honor the Grand Scribe says: Sun Shu-ao uttered one word and the market of Ying[52] was restored. When Tzu-ch'an died of an illness, the people of Cheng wailed and wept. Master Kung-yi saw the cloth was of good quality and drove his wife away from his home. Shih She let his father escape and died, establishing the fame of King Chao of Ch'u. Li Li erred in executing a man and fell on his sword, enabling Duke Wen of Chin to regularize his state's laws.

*   *   *   *   *

Those officials who upheld the law and followed reasonable methods, did not boast of their merits nor brag about their abilities. Though the families of the hundred *cognomens* did not praise them, neither did they err in their actions. [Thus] I composed the "Memoir of the Reasonable Officials."[53]

---

[51] Much as Shih She would not accept his ruler's command in the previous section.

[52] The Ch'u capital.

[53] These are the Grand Scribe's reasons for compiling this chapter as given in his postface (*Shih chi*, 130.3317: 奉法循理之吏，不伐功矜能，百姓無稱，亦無過行。作循吏列傳第五十九).

Translator's Note

This chapter leaves careful readers with two impressions. First that the information and, indeed, some of the narratives are unique in ancient Chinese literature or differ from other early sources. Second, that the reasonable officials all antedate the Han dynasty. For example, the two anecdotes that depict Sun Shu-ao have no parallels in early literature. The brief, formulaic account of Tzu-ch'an, a figure for whom there are rich materials in early sources, contains major errors.[54] Li Li's narrative seems to be a summary of other versions of the same story. Moreover, secondary figures in these biographies such as Ta-kung Tzu-ch'i 大宮子期 and Hsü Chih 徐摯 appear in no other early work. This has led traditional scholars to the conclusion that this chapter is based on an unknown source or sources.[55] The present author has speculated in an earlier publication that the materials in this chapter were taken from the Han archives and thus in part served as the source of the parallel narratives in the *Hsin hsü* and other Han miscellanea.[56] That possibility remains.

The claim in the Grand Scribe's comments at the end of this chapter that "the families of the hundred *cognomens* did not praise them" 百姓無稱, contradicts the lamentations of the able-bodied men of Cheng at Tzu-ch'an's death as well as the claims that the people far and wide took Sun Shu-ao as their model.[57] Hans van Ess has

[54] According to all other sources, including the "Cheng shih-chia" 鄭世家 in the *Shih chi* itself (*Shih chi*, 42.1771-5), Tzu-ch'an played an important role in Cheng politics in the second half of the sixth century BC, serving dukes Chien 簡 (r. 565–530 BC) and Ting 定 (r. 529–514 BC), not Lord Chao (who reigned briefly early in the seventh century BC) as this chapter claims. Moreover, the *Kuo yü* and *Tso chuan* accounts of Tzu-ch'an (which also differ from the material in the "Cheng shih-chia") report his death in 522 BC (Yang, *Tso*, Chao 28, p. 1490), whereas on *Shih chi*, 42.1775 he is said to have expired in 496 BC. Ssu-ma Chen attempts to explain this "biography" as Ssu-ma Ch'ien's choice to record the strange using another unknown source ("So-yin" on *Shih chi*, 119.3101: 蓋別有所出，太史記異耳).

[55] Although Liang Yü-sheng believes that the Shih She biography is based on the *Lü shih ch'un-ch'iu* (35.1433).

[56] Nienhauser, "A Reexamination of 'The Biographies of the Reasonable Officials' in the *Records of the Grand Historian*," *Early China*, 16 (1991): 209–33 (see esp. pp. 230–34).

[57] Ts'ui Shih 崔適 (1852–1924; *Shih chi t'an-yüan* 史記探原, p. 212) lists seven reasons why he believes the chapter is a forgery but his argument is tautological and fits his overall conclusion that much of the current *Shih chi* text was based on other texts, primarily the *Han*

recently pointed out this contradiction.[58] Van Ess has further argued that the chapter biographies, especially those of Shih She and Li Li who both committed suicide, are meant to be read not only as foils for the harsh officials (in "K'u-li lieh-chuan" 酷吏列傳), but also as an indirect critique of Liu An's 劉安 minister Wu P'i 伍被 who advised him to rebel as recorded in the preceding chapter 118, "Huai-nan, Heng-shan lieh-chuan" (Memoir of [the Kings of] Huai-nan and Heng-shan). Indeed, the assessment of Liu An's crimes uses language that suggests this comparison: "Liu An, the King of Huai-nan, abolished the laws and practiced evil; he harbors a deceitful and deceptive heart, thereby causing the world to be in disorder and confusing the common people" 南王安廢法行邪, 懷詐偽心, 以亂天下, 熒惑百姓 (*Shih chi*, 118.3094).

Yet as Liang Yü-sheng points out, there are significant differences between the biographies of the first three men here, all prime ministers whose service fits that of "reasonable officials," and the final two, Shih She and Li Li, men whom Liang claims acted rather as "worthy men" *hsien* 賢. Moreover, there is a second set of the Grand Scribe's comments at the beginning of the chapter which explains in detail what it means to be a reasonable official. This opening section resonates clearly with the introduction to the "K'u-li lieh-chuan" (Memoirs of the Harsh Officials, chapter 122). It also contains language that is reflected in the subsequent biographies. The phrase *tao min* 導民, for example, also appears in Sun Shu-ao's biography, where Sun was said to have guided the people of Ch'u by promulgating teachings (施教導民, *Shih chi*, 119.3099).[59] The final line of Tzu-ch'an's biography also implies the dependence of the common people on him: "To whom will the common people turn to [now]?!" (民將安歸, *Shih chi*, 119.3101). Kung-yi Hsiu is said to have "followed reasonable methods in carrying out the law" (奉法循理, *Shih chi*, 119.3101), thus benefitting the common people by removing competition with "those on government salaries" (使食祿者不得與下民爭利, *Shih chi*, 119.3101). Shih She "upheld the laws of his ruler (奉主法, *Shih chi*, 119.3102). Li Li is said to have been a *li* 理, a term glossed as "judge" but graphically identical to "reasonable," and to have had his own particular laws (理有法, *Shih chi*, 119.3103). Yet the Grand Scribe's prefatory comments argue for guidance through the use of standardized "laws and orders" 法令. If this preface is to guide the reader, then the theme of this chapter may be to govern. Other collective biographies (*lei chuan* 類傳) have shown that such themes reverberate in the language

shu.

[58] Van Ess, *Politik*, 1:186–90.

[59] Note *Lun yü*, 5.16: "The Master said of Tzu-ch'an, 'He has four of the characteristics of a gentleman: in his conduct of himself, he was humble; in serving his superior, he was respectful, in nourishing the people, he was kind; in employing the people, he was just'" 子謂子產, 「有君子之道四焉: 其行己也恭, 其事上也敬, 其養民也惠, 其使民也義」.

of the biographies themselves: thus *chih* 知 "to recognize" occurs almost thirty times in the "Tz'u-k'o lieh-chuan" 刺客列傳 where recognition is so vital to the actions of the five assassins it depicts. The reader searches in vain for that sort of repetition here. Neither *li* 理 nor any other abstract term occur with any pattern.

Perhaps this introduction was aimed at a different set of biographies, a set now lost or even never written. The closing comments are merely a summary of the biographies and could have been written by the author of the biographies, if that is someone other than one of the Ssu-mas. In attempting to read the text and its framed comments from the Grand Scribe as a whole, however, the only feasible scenario is that proposed by van Ess.

Bibliography

Translations
Aoki, *Shiki*, 12:462–77.
Watson, *Han*, 2:373–7.

Studies
Nienhauser, William H., Jr. "A Reexamination of 'The Biographies of the Reasonable Officials' in the *Records of the Grand Historian*," *Early China*, 16 (1991): 209–33.
van Ess, *Politik*, 1:186–90.

Chi [An] and Cheng [Tang-shih], Memoir 60

translated by Jakob Pöllath and Andreas Siegl

Chi An

[3105] Chi An 汲黯 had the *agnomen* Chang-ju 長孺; he was a man from P'u-yang 濮陽.[1] His ancestors were favored by the former Lord of Wey 衛.[2] Down to [Chi] An there were seven generations,[3] in each of them one served as minister or great official. [Chi] An was employed because of his father's privilege[4] and at the time of [Emperor] Hsiao Ching 孝景 (r. 157–141 BC) served as Forerunner of the Heir Apparent.[5] He was feared for his sternness. [After] Hsiao Ching-ti passed away and the heir ascended to the throne (141 BC), [Chi] An was made Internuncio. [At the time when the people of] Tung Yüeh 東越 attacked one another, the Sovereign sent [Chi] An to go there and inspect this.[6] He did not arrive [there but instead,] when he

---

[1] P'u-yang is a city in Yen-chou 兗州, about five miles southeast of modern P'u-yang, Honan (T'an Ch'i-hsiang, 2:19).

[2] The "Hereditary House of Wey" records that after 320 BC P'u-yang was the last remaining possession of Wey and that its ruler was reduced to the rank of "lord" (*chün* 君) the same year (see *Shih chi*, 37.1604).

[3] The *Han shu* (50.2316) speaks of ten generations.

[4] This so called *jen* 任 privilege provided for officials ranking two thousand *shih* or above and serving for at least three years to appoint a close relative without having to go through the normal recruitment process. The thus appointed usually had to pass through a probationary peroid as an attendent (*lang* 郎) (see Bielenstein, *Bureaucracy*, pp. 132-3).

[5] The later Emperor Hsiao Wu 孝武 (r. 141–87 BC).

[6] These are the kingdoms of Min Yüeh 閩越 and Tung-hai 東海 (generally known as Tung-Ou 東甌). In 138 BC Min Yüeh led an army against Tung-hai, at which point Grand Commandant T'ien Fen 田蚡 made a remark to the same effect as the one Chi An is about to make (see *Shih chi*, 114.2980). It is possible that Chi An's commission was in the same context, although the memoir on the Tung-Yüeh contains no mention of it. For the location of

arrived in Wu, he returned and reported saying: "That the people of Yüeh are attacking each other is certainly [due to] their custom being that way. It is not worth to disgrace an envoy of the Son of Heaven on account of this." There was a conflagration in Ho-nei 河內[7] that spread to burn down more than a thousand households. The Sovereign sent [Chi] An to go there and inspect this. He returned and reported, saying: "[Whenever] a conflagration happens among the commoners, spreading over a neighborhood and burning [it] down, it is not worth worrying [about it]. [But when] your servant passed through Ho-nan 河南,[8] amongst the poor people in Ho-nan there were more than ten thousand households which were suffering from flood or drought, in some fathers and sons fed on one another.[9] Your servant has cautiously, according to what was expedient and appropriate, [used] the [imperial] caduceus he carried to distribute millet from the Ho-nan 河南 granary, so as to relieve the poor. Your servant asks to return the caduceus and lies prostrate [to await the punishment for] the crime of forging an imperial order." The Sovereign thought him worthy and therefore set him free. He transferred him to become Prefect of Hsing-yang 滎陽.[10] [Chi] An felt humiliated to be made prefect and returned to his home town on account of illness. The Sovereign heard of this and only then appointed him Palace Grandee. Because he sharply remonstrated [with the emperor] several times, he could not remain long at court, and was transferred to serve as Grand Administrator of Tung-hai 東海.[11] As [Chi] An had studied the teachings of Huang-Lao 黃老, in his managing the officials and ordering the people he valued peace and calm. He chose assistants and scribes and left things to them. In his way of governing he supervised only the most important things and did not get lost in the details. [Chi] An was often ill, he lay in his inner quarters and did not go out. [Still,] after [a little] more than a year, Tung-hai was well governed, and he was praised [for it]. The Sovereign heard of this and summoned him to make him Chief Commandant over the

their capitals Tung-chih 東治 and Tung-Ou see T'an Ch'i-hsiang's map for the Ch'in dynasty (2:12) and the map preceding the translation of chapter 114 in this volume.

[7] Ho-nei is a commandery roughly 250 miles west-northwest of Ch'ang-an, in modern northwestern Honan, on the northern bank of the Yellow River (T'an Ch'i-hsiang 2:16).

[8] Ho-nan is just south of Ho-nei and the Yellow River, around present-day Chengchow (*ibid.*).

[9] The fire can be seen as purely accidental, while in Chi An's mind the latter situation must be seen as a result of a failure to govern correctly.

[10] Hsing-yang is a county within the commandery of Ho-nan, about ten miles northeast of modern Hsing-yang city (*ibid.*). It was an important site in the struggle for the empire between Liu Pang and Hsiang Yü in the years ca. 205 BC (see the basic annals for Hsiang Yü on *Shih chi* 7.324–26).

[11] This Tung-hai is not identical with the aforementioned kingdom but a commandery on the Yellow Sea, straddling the border of modern Shantung and Kiangsu, reaching as far west as Wei-shan 微山 Lake (T'an Ch'i-hsiang 2:19–20).

Nobility, ranking him among the nine ministers. [His way of] governing lay simply in quiescence, he expanded [his actions to fit] the general political situation [and] did not restrict himself to the articles of the law.[12]

[3106] In his conduct, [Chi] An was proud by nature, short on propriety, openly critical [of others], and could not tolerate other people's mistakes. Those who conformed to him he treated well, those who did not conform to him he could not suffer to see. Gentlemen did not attach to him also for this reason. Yet he liked to learn from the knights-errant,[13] recommended for office those of the highest moral standards, was of utmost purity in his private dealings, liked to remonstrate with direct words, and several times slighted his ruler. He invariably admired the conduct of Fu Po 傅柏 and Yüan Ang 袁盎.[14] He was on good terms with Kuan Fu 灌夫, Cheng Tang-shih 鄭當時 and Liu Ch'i 劉弃, the Director of the Imperial Clan.[15] Again, because he candidly remonstrated several times, he could not retain his post for long.

Just at that time the younger brother of the Empress Dowager, [T'ien] Fen 田蚡, the Marquis of Wu-an 武安, had become chancellor.[16] [Whenever] officials ranking

---

[12] *Han shu* (50.2316) has *yin* 引 instead of *hung* 弘, resulting in "he took into account the general political situation."

[13] This translation follows the punctuation given in Takigawa (120.4). The punctuation used in the Chung-hua Shu-chü edition would result in "he liked to study, let the knights roam."

For the knights-errant in Chinese history see James J. Y. Liu, *The Chinese Knight-Errant* (Chicago: The University of Chicago Press 1967).

[14] Ying Shao 應劭 ("Chi-chieh") identifies Fu Po as a man from Liang 梁, general to King Hsiao 孝 (i.e., Liu Wu 劉武), and firmly upright. Some editions, as well as the *Han shu* (50.2317), have 伯 instead of 柏.

Yüan Ang was an outspoken and upright official (see his biography on *Shih chi*, 101). He was murdered at Liu Wu's behest. The *Han shu* (50.2317) has Yüan 爰 instead of Yüan 袁 (see also Loewe, *Dictionary*, pp. 661–63).

[15] These three men all held views close to those of Chi An. Kuan Fu was yet another outspoken and upright official (see his biography in *Shih chi*, 107.2845–54). He, too, was fond of knight-errantry (*Shih chi*, 107.2847). For Cheng Tang-shih see his biography below. Not much is known about Liu Ch'i. The parallel *Han shu* paragraph (50.2317) calls him Liu Ch'i-chi 劉棄疾, and its tables record him—under Liu Ch'i—as Director of the Imperial Clan from 125 to 122 (*Han shu*, 19B.772–73).

[16] T'ien Fen was a high official who rose to power mainly because of his family relationship to Emperor Hsiao Ching, whose empress was T'ien Fen's half-sister. He was described as arrogant and was principally responsible for the death of Kuan Fu, mentioned above, as well as Tou Ying's 竇嬰. In that matter Chi An and Cheng Tang-shih were the only officials at court speaking up against T'ien (see *Shih chi*, 107 and Loewe, *Dictionary* pp. 505–

fully two thousand *shih* came to have an audience [with him], [T'ien] Fen behaved contrary to propriety. But [Chi] An came to see him without kneeling and bowing his head, always [only] saluting him by cupping [one hand in the other].[17] The Son of Heaven had just summoned the classical scholars of textual learning.[18] [When] the Sovereign said: "I desire this and that,"[19] An countered by saying: "Your Majesty, while having many desires within, is displaying benevolence and righteousness without, how can you [thus] desire to imitate the reign of Yao and Shun?" The Sovereign fell silent, became angry, changed color, and dismissed the court. The high officials all feared for [Chi] An. The Sovereign withdrew and spoke to his courtiers saying: "Great indeed is the stubbornness of Chi An!" Among the assembled ministers some reproved [Chi] An. [Chi] An said: "The Son of Heaven established the high officials as assisting ministers, would you rather have me fawn and follow every whim, [thereby] causing [our] Lord to fall into unrighteousness? Now [that] I am already in this position, even though I cherish myself, how can I bring shame over this court!"

[3107] [Chi] An was often ill. When his illness was about to last for a full three months, the Sovereign regularly granted him respite time and again, [yet] to the end he did not get better. [When it came to] the last of these illnesses, Chuang Chu 莊助 asked for a respite in his name.[20] The Sovereign said: "What kind of man is Chi An?" Chu said: "If you make An take office and hold a position, there is nothing in which he will surpass others, but if it comes to assisting a young ruler, he will protect the

---

6 for T'ien Fen; for Chi An's and Cheng Tang-shih's involvement, see also the latter's biography, *infra*).

[17] The Chinese expression *chi* 揖 describes a simple form of greeting by cupping one hand in the other before one's chest while making a small bow. The expression appears again below, on *Shih chi*, 120.3108, in connection with Chi An greeting Wei Ch'ing.

[18] The only other occurrence of the term *wen-hsüeh ju-che* 文學儒者 "classical scholars of textual learning" is on *Shih chi,* 121.3118, in the description of the same event: after the death of Empress Dowager Tou, several hundred such scholars are called to court, marking an end to the dominance of the teachings of Huang-Lao and the school of dispositions and designations (*hsing-ming* 刑名).

[19] Wang Shu-min (*Shih chi chiao-cheng*, 9.120:3237) draws on Hsün Yüeh's 荀悅 *Han chi* 漢紀 to reconstruct the words of the emperor as: 吾欲興政治，法堯舜，何如？ "I desire to give rise to [the true way of] governing, to emulate Yao and Shun, how to go about it?" This clearly would tally with Chi An's response recorded here.

[20] Chuang Chu was an official executed for involvement in the rebellion of Liu An. Earlier, he successfully advocated Han intervention in the war between Min Yüeh and Tung-Ou, thus disagreeing with T'ien Fen and Chi An (see his biography in *Han shu*, 64A.2775–90 and Loewe, *Dictionary* pp. 748–49).

fortress and firmly hold steadfast.[21] If one summons him, he will not come, if one waves him away, he will not leave. Even if you call yourself [Meng] Pen 孟賁 or [Hsia] Yü 夏育,[22] you still will not be able to contend with him!" The Sovereign said: "Right. In olden times there were the servants of the altars of soil and grain:[23] as far as An is concerned, he comes close to them."

[When] Commander-in-Chief [Wei] Ch'ing 衛青 attended at the palace, the Sovereign received him while sitting on his privy.[24] [When] Chancellor [Kung-sun] Hung 公孫弘 was received outside of regular audience, the Sovereign sometimes wore no cap[25]; [yet] when it came to receiving [Chi] An, if the Sovereign was wearing no cap, he [the emperor] would not receive him. Once [when] the Sovereign was sitting behind curtains, [Chi] An came forward reporting on affairs. The Sovereign wore no cap and observed [Chi] An from a distance, hiding within his curtains. He sent people to approve [Chi An's] memorial. When it came to [Chi An], so much did he respect [him] and act according to propriety.

Chang T'ang 張湯 had at that time just become Commandant of Justice because he had revised the statutes and laws.[26] An reproved him several times in front of the

---

[21] *Han shu* (50.2317) has *ch'eng* 成 instead of *ch'eng* 城, resulting in "he will protect what has been accomplished." Cf. also the opinion of Li Li 李笠 (Takigawa, 120.5), who agrees with the *Han shu* reading and thinks the received text of the *Shih chi* is corrupted here.

[22] These were two men from pre-Ch'in times famous for their physical strength.

[23] For a discussion of the term *she chi chih ch'en* 社稷之臣 "servants of the altars of soil and grain," denoting loyal servants to one dynasty, see note 11 to Memoir 41 on *Grand Scribe's Records*, 8:325.

[24] Wei Ch'ing was Emperor Wu's brother-in-law through Empress Wei, as well as one of the foremost generals of the time, famous especially for his exploits in the northwest. See (*Shih chi,* 111.2921–46 and Loewe, *Dictionary* pp. 573–75).

The commentaries are undecided what is meant by the word *ts'e* 厠 here. "Chi-chieh" and Takigawa (120.5) both think it means "side", thus being identical to 側, while "Chi-chieh" gives "privy" as an alternative explanation. Ch'ien Chung-shu 錢鍾書 (*Kuan chui pien* 管錐 編, 4 vol. [Peking: Chung-hua Shu-chü, 1979], vol. 1, pp. 368–69) first cites several other authors throughout the ages who considered its several meanings, then concludes that here it indeed means privy, discarding other explanations as incongruous. He compares it to the later European custom of monarchs conducting state business while seated on their privy, yet he does not believe this was customary in ancient China.

[25] Kung-sun Hung was one of the foremost officials espousing Confucian thought under Emperor Wu (see his biography in *Shih chi* chapter 112 and Loewe, *Dictionary*, pp. 125–28).

[26] Chang T'ang was an official famous for his ruthless application of the laws. His biography is included in the memoir on harsh officials (*Shih chi,* 122.3137–44). As opposed to others like Chao Yü 趙禹, he is much criticized for using severe punishments not out of a sense of integrity but in order to ingratiate himself with the emperor (see also Loewe, *Dictionary* pp. 692–94).

Sovereign, saying: "You, Sir, are a principal excellency. [Yet] above you cannot acclaim the meritorious achievement of the former emperors, below you cannot keep in check the evil thoughts [within] the world. To pacify the realm and enrich the people, and to cause the prisons to empty, of these two you have not done one. To do away with causing suffering, that would be the [correct] behavior; to cast aside the hair-splitting, that would be meritorious.[27] Why then are you taking measures to complicate and alter the covenant of Emperor Kao?[28] You, Sir, will have no progeny because of this." At times [Chi] An had discussions with [Chang] T'ang; [Chang] T'ang argued often by a severe [interpretation of] the laws and going into the tiniest details.[29] [Chi] An directly and sternly defended [*3108*] the high [principles] but could not make him yield. He would get angry and scold him, saying: "In the world it is said a knife-and-brush official should not be made one of the excellencies and ministers, this is true.[30] If [you], T'ang, [would have your way], you would cause the empire to stand with one foot on the other and look only with sideway glances [i.e. to be too afraid to look directly]!"[31]

At this time the Han had just launched the attack on the Hsiung-nu 匈奴 and they called and placated the four barbarians.[32] [Chi] An endeavored to reduce [the number of] engagements. He took advantage of the Sovereign's spare time and often talked of

---

[27] This sentence could also be translated as "slanderously causing suffering constitutes [your] behavior; willful hair-splitting constitutes [your] achievement."

[28] Emperor Kao is said to have instituted a legal code in 207 BC, simplifying previous models to just three articles: 殺人者死，傷人及盜抵罪 "those who kill another person shall die, those who injure another person or steal shall be given [their appropriate] punishment" (*Shih chi*, 8.362; cf. also notes 236 and 237 on *Grand Scribe's Records*, 2:38–39).

[29] This is the direct opposite of Chi An, about whom it is said above that "he supervised only the most important things and *did not get lost in the details*" (120.3105).

[30] The term knife-and-brush official (*tao-pi chih li* 刀筆之吏), denoting a petty clerk, likened by Enno Giele to modern day "pencil pushers," appears twice in the *Shih chi* (see note 118 to memoir 49 on *Grand Scribe's Records,* 9:224).

[31] *Ch'ung tsu* 重足, "to layer one foot above the other", appears once in the *Mo-tzu* (Sun Yi-jang 孫詒讓, *Mo-tzu chien-ku* 墨子閒詁 [Peking: Chung-hua Shu-chü, 1986], vol. 1, p. 89), where it simply means to stand still, to come to rest. Later on it seems to have acquired the connotation of not daring to move. Cf. also the similar use of *ch'ung tsu yi-chi* 重足一迹, "to layer one foot[step] above the other, [thus leaving] a single track," in the memoir on harsh officials (*Shih chi,* 122.3146), equally describing the fear the officials and people of Nan-yang 南陽 feel when facing the prosecutions of Yi Tsung 義縱.

[32] For a political history of the Hsiung-nu see Yü Ying-shih, "The Hsiung-nu" (in *Cambridge History of Early Inner Asia: From Earliest Times to the Rise of the Mongols*, Denis Sinor, ed. [Cambridge: Cambridge University Press, 1990], pp. 118–49. See also the memoir on the Hsiung-nu in *Shih chi* chapter 110.

forming marital alliances with the Hu 胡, not raising troops.[33] The Sovereign at that time was partial towards the Confucian techniques and revered Kung-sun Hung. As the [number of] lawsuits increased,[34] the officials and the people became adroit at manipulating [the law]. The Sovereign reinterpreted the laws, and [Chang] T'ang and others repeatedly memorialized the throne to have cases decided, thereby gaining favor. Yet [Chi] An often defamed the Confucianists. He clashed face to face with [Kung-sun] Hung and his people, [accusing them of] only harboring deceit and affecting wisdom in order to pander to their lord and curry favor,[35] while the [common] knife-and-brush officials specialize in making up charges and slander people in order to entrap them in crime, so that they cannot revert to the truth. [Thus] to be successful in [entrapping the innocent] counted as an achievement. The Sovereign increasingly cherished [Kung-sun] Hung and [Chang] T'ang. [Kung-sun] Hung and [Chang] T'ang wholeheartedly detested [Chi] An. As the Son of Heaven did not like [him] as well, they desired to have him executed for something. When Hung became chancellor, he finally spoke to the Sovereign: "Within the territory under the Scribe of the Capital to the Right there are many noble men and members of the imperial clan. They are hard to govern, one cannot appoint any but a long serving minister. We ask you to transfer [Chi] An to [the post of] Scribe of the Capital to the Right." [Chi An] was made Scribe of the Capital to the Right for several years, [yet] there were no missteps [during that time].[36]

Commander-in-Chief [Wei] Ch'ing had already risen in esteem, and his elder sister was empress,[37] but as far as etiquette was concerned, [Chi] An was on the same level with him. Someone tried to persuade [Chi] An: "Since the Son of Heaven wishes for the collected ministers to subordinate themselves to the Commander-in-

[33] Hu here clearly refers to the Hsiung-nu, as is often the case. For a discussion of this term see note 10 on *Grand Scribe's Records,* 9:203.

[34] The term *shih* 事, rendered here as "lawsuits" and just above as "engagements," is a fairly encompassing term that at its most basic might be translated simply as "affairs" or "incidences." However, here it most likely refers specifically to legal matters. Compare the very similar expression 好興事舞文法, "[He] likes to give rise to lawsuits and toy with the articles of the law," Chi An uses when talking about Chang T'ang further down in this chapter (*Shih chi,* 120.3110), as well as the end of the biographies of Ning Ch'eng 寧成 and Chou-yang Yu 周陽由 on *Shih chi,* 122.3136, where it is said that after their time 事益多民巧法 "the lawsuits increased [and] the people became adroit with the law."

[35] For an account of these clashes see *Shih chi,* 112.2950–51.

[36] The idea was that Chi An was bound to commit some indictable mistake on this post but, despite the sensitive nature of his position, he did nothing which his enemies could pin on him.

[37] His sister was Wei Tzu-fu 衛子夫, with whom he shared the same mother. She became empress in 128 BC after the former Empress Ch'en 陳 had failed to bear an heir (see *Shih chi,* 49.1978–86, *Han shu,* 97A.3949–50 and Loewe, *Dictionary,* p. 581).

Chief, the Commander-in-Chief is held in high esteem and increasingly noble. You, Sir, cannot but kneel and bow your head." [Chi] An said: "If the Commander-in-Chief has a guest who [just] salutes him by cupping [one hand in the other], does that not make him all the more important?" The Commander-in-Chief heard [of this] and held [Chi] An to be even worthier. [Wei Ch'ing] called on him several times to ask about matters of state which were in doubt at court, he [thus] treated An beyond the ordinary.

[3109] When [Liu An 劉安], the King of Huai-nan 淮南, plotted his rebellion,[38] he feared [Chi] An, saying: "One who likes to remonstrate candidly, protects integrity and [is willing to] die for righteousness, [will be] hard to be misled with falsehood. When it comes to convincing Chancellor [Kung-sun] Hung, it is nothing more than popping a lid or shaking [down] falling [leaves]."[39]

[Since] the Son of Heaven had later on successfully led several campaigns against the Hsiung-nu, the words of [Chi] An were heeded less and less.

In the beginning [Chi] An ranked amongst the Nine Ministers while Kung-sun Hung and Chang T'ang served [only] as petty officials. When [Kung-sun] Hung and [Chang] T'ang little by little became increasingly noble and achieved the same rank as [Chi] An, [Chi] An still censured and defamed [Kung-sun] Hung, [Chang] T'ang, and their lot. Soon after, [Kung-sun] Hung reached [the post of] chancellor and was enfeoffed as a marquis;[40] [Chang] T'ang reached [the post of] Grandee Secretary. Thus, [among] those who had at certain points been assistants or scribes of [Chi] An, all now had the same rank as he, some [even] outranked him in esteem and employment. As [Chi] An was narrow-minded,[41] he could not be without some grudge. [When] he was received by the Sovereign, he stepped forth and spoke, saying: "Your majesty's [method of] using your servants is just like [that of] collecting firewood, those who come later sit on top." The Sovereign fell silent. After some time [Chi] An was dismissed from office, the Sovereign said: "Indeed, it is not permissible that a man should have no learning:[42] observe the words of [Chi] An, they become more outrageous by the day."

---

[38] For an account of this see Liu An's biography on *Shih chi*, 118.3082–94 and Loewe, *Dictionary*, pp. 242–44.

[39] This translation follows "Cheng-yi." Takigawa (120.8) contradicts this and understands *meng* 蒙 not as "lid" but as "sprout", changing the meaning to: "[...] nothing more than growing sprouts or shaking [down] falling [leaves]."

[40] He was made the Marquis of P'ing-chin 平津 (Peaceful Ford). His marquisate was probably located in modern Hupei, south of Yen-shan County 鹽山 (cf. n. 35 on *Grand Scribe's Records*, 9:370).

[41] The term *pien hsin* 褊心, here rendered as "narrow-minded," appears in the *Shih ching* ode "Ko-chü," Mao #107 (Legge, 4:163–64), where it equally seems to denote an overly narrow, unforgiving disposition.

[42] That is to say, Confucian learning.

Shortly thereafter, the Hun-yeh 渾邪 King of the Hsiung-nu led his throngs to come and surrender.[43] The Han sent out twenty thousand carriages. The authorities had no money, [so] they requisitioned horses from the people. Some people hid their horses, and [thus] the horses were not sufficient. The Sovereign grew angry and wished to have the prefect of Ch'ang-an beheaded. [Chi] An said: "The prefect of Ch'ang-an committed no crime. Just behead [me,] An, only then the people will be willing to bring forth their horses. Furthermore these Hsiung-nu have rebelled against their leader and submitted to the Han, and the Han transport them slowly from county to county. How can it come so far that we let the empire be in turmoil, tiring and exhausting the Central States and thereby serving the people of the Yi 夷- and Ti 狄-barbarians?"[44] The Sovereign fell silent. When the Hun-yeh [King] arrived, more than five hundred merchants who had traded with [the Hsiung-nu] were tried for a capital crime.[45] An asked [to meet the emperor in the latter's] spare time and met him at the High Gate.[46] [He] said: "When the Hsiung-nu attack the passes and sever the marital alliance, [and when] the Central States raise troops to punish them, the dead and wounded are uncountable and the expenses number in the hundreds of myriads. Your servant foolishly believes that [when] Your Majesty captures Hu, they should all be made into slaves and bestowed upon the households of those who, while on campaign, died in service; if all that has been taken in plunder is subsequently given to them, this will compensate for the hardship of the empire and mend the hearts of the people. Now, if we are not able to do this, [but instead] the Hun-yeh is leading several ten thousands of [his] throng to come and submit, [and] if [one then] empties the treasuries and warehouses to reward and bestow [everything upon them] and send out good people to wait on and provide for [them], this is like serving a spoiled son. How [could] the ignorant people know that when they trade things within Ch'ang-an [with the Hsiung-nu], the law officials will judge it to be the same as transporting contraband across the border? Even if Your Majesty cannot obtain the resources of

[43] For the circumstances of this submission see *Shih chi*, 51.2933–34.

[44] The Yi and the Ti were thought of as the barbarians of the East and West, respectively. For a work on Chinese-steppe relations in pre-Han times and the conception of the various steppe groups as the Other, see Nicola Di Cosmo, *Ancient China and Its Enemies: The Rise of Nomadic Power in East Asian History* (Cambridge: Cambridge University Press, 2002; see especially pp. 93–127 and, on the thoughts on "barbarians" in the *Shih chi*, pp. 255–312). Ssu-ma Ch'ien's famous memoir of the Hsiung-nu and their subgroups can be found in *Shih chi* chapter 110 (see also the translation in *Grand Scribe's Records*, 9:237–310).

[45] It seems these merchants were seen as running foul of some sort of anti-smuggling statute, forbidding them to engage in cross-border trading. Through legal analogy, this was judged to be the same as the mere trading with any foreigners, even if taking place within the capital.

[46] Ju Ch'un 如淳 ("Chi-chieh") states that in the geographic work *[San-fu] Huang-t'u* [三輔]黃圖, the High Gate [*Kao men* 高門] was a hall in the imperial palace in Ch'ang-an.

the Hsiung-nu to compensate the empire, moreover to use intricate laws to kill more than five hundred ignorant men, that is what is called [*3110*] 'to hurt the branch by protecting the leaves.' That is an option that your servant thinks your Majesty will not select."[47] The Sovereign fell silent, did not approve [this], and said: "I had not heard the words of Chi An for a long time, now again he has had one of his outrageous outbursts!" Some months later [Chi] An was put on trial for belittling the law. There happened to be an amnesty. [He] was dismissed from his post and upon that An withdrew to his fields and gardens.

After several years passed it so happened that the five-*chu* 銖 coin was introduced.[48] Many of the people counterfeited money, in the lands of Ch'u 楚 this was especially severe.[49] The Sovereign considered Huai-yang 淮陽 to just be on the outskirts of the lands of Ch'u, only then did he summon and appoint [Chi] An to become Grand Administrator of Huai-yang. [Chi] An prostrated himself and declined, refusing to accept the seal. [The emperor] issued edicts several times to force it upon him. After that he accepted the edict. [Again] an edict was issued summoning [Chi] An to an audience. [Chi] An, weeping before the emperor, said: "Your servant himself assumed [his remains] would fill in some ditch or gully, never to see Your Majesty again. It did not come to [your servant's] mind that Your Majesty would again receive and have use for him. Your servant constantly has the illness of dogs and horses,[50] his strength is not sufficient to take on the duties of a commandery.

---

[47] Compare the use of the identical phrase, 臣竊為陛下不取也 "that is an option that your servant would in the place of Your Majesty not take," by Ssu-ma Hsiang-ju on *Shih chi*, 117.3054, in order to dissuade the emperor from taking part in the perils of the hunt.

[48] One *chu* was a measure of weight equivalent to one hundred grains of millet, or one twenty-fourth of a *liang* 兩.

This coin was introduced in 118 BC (*Shih chi*, 30.1429; cf. Sung Hsü-wu 宋叙五, *Hsi-Han huo-pi shi* 西漢貨幣史 [Hong Kong: Chinese University Press, 2002] p. 100). For Ssu-ma Ch'ien's treatise on commerce and money, see *Shih chi*, 30. See also *Grand Scribe's Records*, 8:xlv for more information on currency in Han times.

[49] Meant here is probably the old state of Ch'u of the Warring States Period, which at its height encompassed modern Hupei and Hunan, as well as parts of Honan and Anhwei, or even more generally "the South." Huai-yang was situated on the river Huai, about ten miles northeast of modern Hung-tse Lake 洪澤湖, and thus indeed at the border of this vast region (T'an Ch'i-hsiang 2:20).

The Han dynasty Kingdom of Ch'u was lying approximately sixty miles northwest of Huai-yang, south of the Wei-shan lake 微山湖, around the modern city of Hsuchow 徐州 (T'an Ch'i-hsiang 2:19–20).

[50] It is not entirely clear what is meant by *kou ma chih ping* 狗馬之病, "illness of dogs and horses." *Han shu* reads this passage slightly different as 狗馬之心今病 "[I have] the heart of dogs and horses, now I am sick" (*Han shu*, 50.2321). If understood this way, the "illness of dogs and horses" in the *Shih chi* may be understood as a metaphor for the unwavering loyalty

Your servant would rather serve as a Gentleman-of-the-Household, going in and out the forbidden quarters to correct mistakes and mend oversights. [This] is your servant's hope." The Sovereign said: "You take Huai-yang lightly? I summoned you today!⁵¹ Seeing that the officials and the [common] people in Huai-yang do not get along, I merely want to make use of your gravitas. [Just] govern them while lying down." [Chi] An then took his leave to start his journey. When he came across the Grand Usher Li Hsi 李息,⁵² he said: "[I,] An, have been cast away to reside in a commandery and cannot participate in the discussions at court. But the intelligence of the Grandee Secretary Chang T'ang is enough to reject all censure, [his] deceit is enough to cover up his wrongs, [he] pursues crafty and flattering speech and argumentative and involute rhetoric. He is not acknowledging what is right in speaking for the empire, solely pandering to the ruler's mind. What the ruler's mind does not desire he accordingly slanders, what the ruler's mind desires he accordingly praises. [He] likes to give rise to lawsuits and toy with the articles of the law. Within [he] harbors deceit, thereby to ingratiate himself with the heart of the ruler, without he relies on rogue officials, thereby to create authority and gravitas. Your Honor ranks among the nine ministers. [If] you do not speak of this early on, Your Honor will together with him suffer his humiliation!" [Li] Hsi feared [Chang] T'ang [and] to the end did not dare to speak of this. [Chi] An administered the commandery like he had governed before [and] the administrative affairs of Huai-yang cleared up. Later Chang T'ang indeed fell, the Sovereign heard of [Chi] An having spoken to [Li] Hsi [and he] held [Li] Hsi responsible for his crime. He had [Chi] An reside in Huai-yang with the salary of a chancellor to a feudal lord.⁵³ After seven years [*3111*] [he] expired.⁵⁴

of Chi An. Yet in another part of the *Han shu*, Pan Ku uses the same formulation as the one used by Ssu-ma Ch'ien here as an official's excuse to be relieved of his duty to take up a position (*Han shu*, 64.2788).

⁵¹ "So-yin" understands this as "I will summon you back shortly."

⁵² Li Hsi started his career as an official under Emperor Ching 景. Under Emperor Wu he was thrice made general against the Hsiung-nu, apparently without distinguishing himself. He became Grand Usher in 124 (see his brief biography on *Shih chi*, 111.2942 and Loewe, *Dictionary*, p. 231).

⁵³ According to the *Chung-kuo li-tai kuan-chih ta tz'u-tien* 中國歷代官制大辭典 this would have been two thousand *shih* (Lü Tsung-li 呂宗力, ed., *Chung-kuo li-tai kuan-chih ta tz'u-tien*, [Peking: Pei-ching Ch'u-pan she, 1994], p. 581).

Older printings of the Chung-hua Shu-chü editions had *chin* 今, "now, presently," instead of *ling* 令, "to order" (rendered here simply as "had") at the beginning of this sentence. This has now been corrected.

⁵⁴ Hsü Kuang 徐廣 ("Chi-chieh") dates this to the fifth year of the Yüan-ting 元鼎 period, thus to the year 112 BC.

Like with the number of generations preceding Chi An (see the beginning of this chapter), the *Han shu* here has ten years instead of seven (*Han shu* 50.2322).

After he had expired, the emperor on account of An employed his younger brother Chi Jen 汲仁 as an official [serving] up to [the rank of one of] the nine ministers, [his] son Chi Yen 汲偃 up to [the post of] a chancellor to a feudal lord. Ssu-ma An 司馬安, the son of [his] father's elder sister,[55] [while] young also served as Forerunner of the Heir Apparent together with [Chi] An. [Ssu-ma] An was severe [in the application of] the law,[56] was skillful and talented in being an official. His official rank four [times] reached [the rank of one of] the nine ministers [and] he expired as Grand Administrator of Ho-nan 河南. Among his brothers there were ten who, on account of [Ssu-ma] An, [all] reached [an official salary of] two thousand *shih* at the same time. Tuan Hung 段宏 from P'u-yang at first served [Wang] Hsin 王信, the Marquis of Ko 蓋.[57] [Wang] Hsin recommended [Tuan] Hung for office. [Tuan] Hung, too, twice reached [positions among] the nine ministers. Still, those of the people of Wey 衛 who served as officials all respectfully shrunk from Chi An [and] came out below his [rank].[58]

[55] *Han shu* (50.2323) omits the character *ku* 姑, thus making Ssu-ma An not a cousin but a nephew of Chi An by the latter's elder sister. In chapter 122, Ssu-ma An, together with Li Hsi, was charged with interrogating Liu Tz'u 劉賜, King of Heng-shan 衡山, in connection to his alleged rebellion (*Shih chi*, 118.3097). See also his involvement in the downfall of Cheng Tang-shih in this chapter below and Loewe, *Dictionary*, p. 484.

[56] *Grand Scribe's Records*, 8:382, n. 67, understands the phrase *wen-shen* 文深, here rendered as "severe [in the application of] the law," thus as a negative attribute used to describe cruel officials in the *Shih chi* and mentions three passages where this occurs: First, on *Shih chi*, 103.2768, characterizing Shih Ch'ing 石慶. Second, in chapter 122, referring to Chao Yü 趙禹 (*Shih chi*, 122.3136; there is one more occurrence in that chapter not mentioned in the note, on 122.3139, in connection with Chang T'ang). And finally, further above in the present chapter, also referring to Chang T'ang (120.3107). To this, one can add the occurrence to describe Ssu-ma An here.

[57] Ko County 蓋縣 lies in the eastern part of Ch'in-shan 秦山 Commandery of Shantung Province, fifteen miles southeast of modern Yi-yüan 沂源 (T'an Ch'i-hsiang 2:20). Wang Hsin was the elder brother of Hsiao Ching's Empress Wang. See the story of his contested enfeoffment as Marquis of Ko, pursued by Empress Dowager Tou and strongly opposed by chancellor Chou Ya-fu 周亞夫, on *Shih chi*, 57.2077–80.

[58] Wey was an old name for the area of Chi An's hometown (see the beginning of this chapter).

Cheng Tang-shih

Cheng Tang-shih 鄭當時 had the *agnomen* Chuang 莊; he was a man from Ch'en 陳.[59] His ancestor Lord Cheng[60] was once a commander of Hsiang Chi 項籍.[61] Shortly after [Hsiang] Chi died, he attached [himself] to the Han. [Emperor] Kao-tsu 高祖 ordered all former ministers of Hsiang [*3112*] Chi to put their names on a register.[62] Lord Cheng alone refused this edict. An edict conferred on all those who registered their names [the title of] Grandee[63] and banished Lord Cheng. Lord Cheng died at the time of [Emperor] Hsiao Wen 孝文 (r. 180–157 BC).

Cheng Chuang delighted himself in playing the role of a knight-errant, [he once] freed Chang Yü 張羽 from distress,[64] [and his] reputation became known in Liang 梁 and Ch'u.[65] At the time of [Emperor] Hsiao Ching 孝景 he served as Member of the Suite of the Heir Apparent. On the bathing and hair washing [i.e. free] day every five days, he often arranged for post-horses in all the areas near Ch'ang-an in order to look

---

[59] Ch'en was a county in the Kingdom of Huai-yang 淮陽, on the site of the modern city of Huai-yang, Honan (T'an Ch'i-hsiang 2:19).

[60] "Chi-chieh" quotes *Han shu yin-yi* 漢書音義 that Lord Cheng was Cheng Tang-shih's father. But compare Wang Shu-min, 120.3243, who considers the "Chi-chieh" interpretation to be at fault, and maintains that the Lord Cheng mentioned here is indeed an ancestor of Cheng Tang-shih further removed.

[61] The famous erstwhile rival of Liu Pang for control of the empire, also known under his *agnomen* Hsiang Yü 羽 (see his own basic annals in *Shih chi* chapter 7 and Loewe, *Dictionary*, pp. 599–602).

[62] This translation is suggested by the absence of a name-marking bar in the Chung-hua Shu-chü edition and quoted by the *Han-yü ta tz'u-tien*. Alternatively: ". . . to name Chi directly" (that is, use his real *praenomen* as a sign of disrespect), following Ku Yen-wu cited by Takigawa (120.14).

For a more thorough discussion of registration in Han times, citing copious further literature, see *Grand Scribe's Records*, 8:1–2, n. 5.

[63] This is *Ta-fu* 大夫, the fifth-lowest of the twenty aristocratic ranks of the Han (see Michael Loewe "The Orders of Aristocratic Rank of Han China," *TP Second Series*, 48 [1960]: 97–174).

[64] Chang Yü was a general of Liu Wu 劉武, King of Liang 梁, during the Rebellion of the Seven Kings together with Hu An-kuo 胡安國 (see the latter's biography on *Shih chi*, 108.2857, as well as *Shih chi*, 58.2082, *Han shu*, 47.2208 and his entry in Loewe, *Dictionary*, p. 698).

To save others from distress (*o* 厄) is given as a characteristic of knights-errant on *Shih chi*, 130.3318.

[65] Liang, nowadays usually known under its alternative name Wei 魏, was a state during the Warring States period with its last capital in Ta-liang 大梁 south of the Yellow River, about five miles northwest of modern Kaifeng (T'an Ch'i-hsiang, 1:36).

after old friends, invite[66] and see off guests and retainers, [all] night and continuing [the next] day up to dawn, constantly afraid [he could not] reach everyone. Chuang liked the teachings of Huang-Lao. He admired worthy men[67] so [much] that he was afraid not to be recognized by them. He was young in years and his official position was low, yet all those he befriended were of his grandfather's generation [and] scholars renowned throughout the empire. [After Emperor] Wu-ti was installed, [Cheng] Chuang was gradually promoted to serve as Commandant of the Capital in Lu 魯,[68] Grand Protector of Chi-nan 濟南,[69] Chancellor in Chiang-tu 江都,[70] up to [a position among] the nine ministers [where he] served as Clerk of the Capital to the Right. Because of the discussions at the time of the Marquis of Wu-an and [the Marquis of] Wei-chi 魏其,[71] he was demoted to be Supervisor of the Household, and promoted [again] to serve as Grand Prefect of Agriculture.

[When] Chuang served as Grand Scribe,[72] he admonished a gate-keeper: "When guests arrive, no matter whether noble or disdained, do not have them wait at the gate." He upheld the [proper] etiquette [between] guest and host, [even] in his position of high esteem he lowered himself before others. [Cheng] Chuang was upright; moreover he did not administer his own estate, relying on his salary and gratuities given to the various lords. Yet in serving food to others, he did not go beyond a dish in a bamboo-container. Each time he appeared at court, he waited for the Sovereign to have spare time, [and when he] spoke, he never failed to mention the worthy men of the empire. In recommending scholars for [the post of] subordinate assistants and scribes, he described them in truly savory words, often expressing that

[66] Takigawa (120.15) quotes Nakai Sekitoku 中井積德 (1732–1817) who understands *ch'ing* 請 "invite" as *hou* 候 "to call on."

[67] On the term *ch'ang-che* 長者 see note 165 on *Grand Scribe's Records*, 2:30.

[68] The Kingdom of Lu lay to the northwest of modern Nan-yang Lake 南陽 (T'an Ch'i-hsiang, 2:19).

[69] The Kingdom of Chi-nan was situated about forty-five miles inland from the estuary of the Huang-ho on its Southern bank (T'an Ch'i-hsiang, 2:19–20).

[70] The town of Chiang-tu lay about fifteen miles southwest of modern Yangchow (T'an Ch'i-hsiang, 2:20).

[71] These were T'ien Fen and Tou Ying. Tou Ying was a high official and cousin of the Empress Dowager Tou, wife of Emperor Wen 文. His rival T'ien Fen in turn was related to the empress of Emperor Ching 景. Thus this episode can be interpreted as a struggle between two different families both by marriage related to the imperial house (see Tou Ying's biography in *Shih chi* chapter 107 and Loewe, *Dictionary*, pp. 79–80).

For the discussions mentioned here, see *Shih chi* 107.2851–52 (*Grand Scribe's Records*, 9:157f).

[72] Takigawa (120:15) quotes Chang Wen-hu 張文虎, who suspects that this was a mistake. In his view, it should read *Nei-shih* 內史 "Clerk of the Capital" instead of *T'ai-shih* 太史 "Grand Scribe." The *Han shu* (50.2324) has *ta-li* 大吏, meaning just "high official."

he thought they were more worthy than him. He never called petty officials by their *praenomen*.[73] He talked to his subordinates as if he were afraid to injure them. When he heard other people's worthy words, he brought them before the Sovereign, only fearing to be too late. The various lords east of the Mount unanimously praised him for that.[74]

[3113] [When] Cheng Chuang was sent to inspect a breach of the Yellow River, he personally asked for five days to prepare his voyage. The Sovereign said: "I have heard: '[Whenever] Cheng Chuang travels, [even] for a thousand miles he does not take provisions along.' What is the meaning of now asking to prepare the voyage?" Thus when Cheng Chuang [afterwards] was present at court, he constantly pursued harmony and [readily] accepted the ideas [of others], not daring to express much arguments for or against. When it came to his latter years, the Han led attacks on the Hsiung-nu and called upon the four barbarians. The empire's expenses were great and the wealth was more and more exhausted. The people who [Cheng] Chuang had recommended for office and his guests and retainers were the ones who raised income for the Grand Prefect of Agriculture. Many [people] were driven into debts. When Ssu-ma An became Grand Administrator of Huai-yang and brought this affair to light, Chuang because of this became involved in a crime. [He] paid compensation [and] was [reduced to the status] of a commoner. After a short time he was made temporary Chief Clerk. [As] the Sovereign took [him] to be too old, he appointed Chuang as Grand Administrator of Ju-nan 汝南.[75] After a few years, he expired in office.

Cheng Chuang and Chi An originally ranked amongst the nine ministers, were upright, and in their private dealings of utmost purity. These two men were dismissed in the middle [of their careers], their families [left] poor, their guests and retainers increasingly scattered. [Although] they came to govern commanderies, after they expired their families had no resources or wealth left. Among Chuang's brothers, sons and grandsons there were six or seven who, on his account, reached [an official salary of] two thousand *shih*.

His Honor the Grand Scribe said: "Take the worthiness of Chi [An] and Cheng [Tang-shih], [when they] held positions of power, then the guests and retainers [increased] ten-fold, [when they] did not hold positions of power, then it was not like this; how much more so would it be for a man of the masses? Of Honorable Chai 翟

---

[73] This was seen as a sign of respect.

[74] "The Mount" is Mount Hsiao 崤, located about fifteen miles southeast of modern San-men-hsia 三門峽 in western Honan. See T'an Ch'i-hsiang's map for the Autumn and Spring period (1:23).

[75] The commandery of Ju-nan was situated north of the Huai, straddling the border between modern Anhwei and Honan (T'an Ch'i-hsiang, 2:19).

from Hsia-kuei 下邽 [*3114*] it is said:[76] 'In the beginning, when Honorable Chai served as Commandant of Justice, the guests and retainers filled his gate. When he was dismissed, outside of his gate one could set up bird nets. When he became Commandant of Justice once more, the guests and retainers wished to flock to him [again]. Only then did Honorable Chai inscribe upon his gate in bold letters: "Once dead, once alive, only then does one know one's friends' affection. Once poor, once rich, only then does one know one's friends' attitude. Once ennobled, once disdained, one's friends' affection can only then be seen."' [These words] can also be said of Chi [An] and Cheng [Tang-shih], how sad!"

*   *   *   *   *

With correct garb and cap he stood at court, so among the officials no one dared to speak frivolously, in this [Chi] Chang-ju held firm. He liked to recommend men and was praised as a worthy, [Cheng] Chuang[77] made fertile[78] [the empire]. [Thus] I composed "The Memoir of Chi [An] and Cheng [Tang-shih], Number 60."[79]

[76] Not much is known about Master Chai above what is stated here. According to the tables of the *Han shu* (19B.770–72) he was Commandant of Justice from 130 to 127 (see also Loewe, *Dictionary*, p. 671).

The town of Hsia-kuei was located about forty miles northeast of Ch'ang-an, modern Sian (T'an Ch'i-hsiang 2:15).

[77] Here Cheng Chuang's *agnomen* is written with the character Chuang 壯, instead of Chuang 莊 (used throughout chapter 120), omitting the radical *ts'ao* 艹.

[78] Literally this reads "irrigated" (*kai* 溉).

[79] This is the explanation, given on *Shih chi*, 120.3318, of the reasons this chapter was composed: 正衣冠立於朝廷，而群臣莫敢言浮說，長孺矜焉；好薦人，稱長者，壯有溉。作汲鄭列傳第六十.

Translator's Note

> "Both [Chi An and Cheng Tang-shih] are what His Honor the Grand Scribe praised and liked to talk about. Therefore he made one and the same memoir [for them] [...]. Chi [An] and Cheng [Tang-shih] are the people with whom His Honor the Grand Scribe is the most content, therefore he goes all out in writing about them."[80]

Our chapter deals with two exponents of the teachings of Huang-Lao 黃老–a school opposed to the rise of Confucianism at the court of Emperor Wu–at a time when Huang-Lao was already in steep decline. Ssu-ma Ch'ien was probably close to this school, and one can see this in his predominantly positive description of Chi An and Cheng Tang-shih as upright and competent officials.

This is constantly contrasted with, and might very well serve as a foil to, the deceit and pandering of other officials who feature prominently in this chapter. The distinction can best be seen in Ssu-ma Ch'ien's portrayal of Chi An's and Kung-sun Hung's respective demeanors at court. Where Chi An is righteous and direct, Kung-sun Hung, one of the foremost advocates of Confucianist thought of the times, is opportunist and deceitful. About Chi An this chapter says–on this point not without some criticism:

> [Chi] An was proud by nature, was short on propriety, openly critical [of others] and could not tolerate other people's mistakes. Those who conformed to him he treated well, those who did not conform to him he could not suffer to see (*Shih chi*, 120.3106).

As opposed to this, Ssu-ma Ch'ien depicts Kung-sun Hung:

> He appeared to be tolerant but inside he was hiding intentions. To all those with whom [Kung-sun] Hung once had a rift, he pretended to be friendly but secretly he repaid all wrongs (*Shih chi*, 112.2951).

---

[80] 皆太史公所嘉予樂道者也，故同爲列傳 (...) 汲鄭乃太史公最得意人，故特出色寫之; Niu Yün-chen 牛運震 (1706–1758), *Shih chi p'ing-chu* 史記評注, ch. 11, quoted in: Yang, *Li-tai*, pp. 818–819.

Perhaps not by accident, these words in Kung-sun Hung's memoir directly follow an episode featuring Chi An (ibid.). Before the emperor, the latter had criticized Kung-sun Hung's humble clothing as mere posturing.

> Chi An said: "[Kung-sun] Hung holds one of the positions of the Three Excellencies and his salary is extremely high but he is always dressed in plain cloth. This is [nothing but] deception." The sovereign asked [Kung-sun] Hung. Hung apologized, saying: "This is true. Among the Nine Ministers none knows your servant as well as [Chi] An. But on this day he has rebuked me at court. He really has hit my weakest point. [...] Really, it is as Chi An said. However, if not for Chi An's loyalty, how could Your Majesty have heard these words?" The Son of Heaven took this as a humble way of yielding to [Chi An] and treated [Hung] all the more generously.

But despite his laudable uprightness and candor, this passage also shows that Chi An is no match for the craftiness of Kung-sun Hung. The latter's superior mastery of court politics can also be seen when Chi An reprimands the emperor for ordering the composition of a song to celebrate the acquisition of "Thousand Mile Horses" from Ferghana (*Shih chi*, 24.1178). Kung-sun Hung then turns the tables on Chi An, claiming that Chi "defamed imperial orders" and recommending the extermination of the entire Chi clan.

Chi An's inability to compromise and gain favor with others, and thus to attract a following, is not shared by Cheng Tang-shih. He delights in socializing and maintains a host of clients.[81] Yet in the end, he lacks the backbone of Chi An: once criticized by the emperor, we learn, he henceforth "pursued harmony and [readily] accepted the ideas [of others], not daring to express arguments for or against" (*Shih chi*, 120.3113). Again, in the final struggle between T'ian Fen and Tou Ying, Chi An and Cheng Tang-shih were the only two officials siding with the latter. Yet Cheng Tang-shih shrank away and did not speak at all (*Shih chi*, 120.3112; *Shih chi*, 107.2851-2). Indeed, it seems almost as if Ssu-ma Ch'ien, by including these two officials in the same chapter, tried to present the picture of an ideal official that would combine the attributes of both. But, alas, neither of them alone could stem the tide. And it was turning against their faction.

One can already see an example of these changes in the last case mentioned above. Tou Ying was a scion of the Tou family, related to the wife of Emperor Ching. As Empress Dowager, she was the main support for the Huang-Lao school at court but after her death in 135 BC this protection disappeared, making possible the

---

[81] The importance of these clients, or "guest-retainers," *pin-k'o* 賓客, is another important theme of this chapter. While Chi An is unable to get them in the first place, Cheng Tang-shih is unwilling to use them to advance his cause. For the significance of these guest-retainers for Ssu-ma Ch'ien, compare William H. Nienhauser's translator's note to Memoir 47 on *Grand Scribe's Records*, 9:167–68.

execution of her cousin Tou Ying in 132 BC and opening the gates for an upswing of officials with Confucianist leanings at court, officials such as Kung-sun Hung.[82]

[82] This is a simplification of course. In fact, Tou Ying himself is seen as a supporter of the Confucian methods (*Shih chi*, 107.2843). Nevertheless it is his family network and Empress Dowager Tou that he depends on, and after her death he loses not only the support of the court but also a great part of his clients (*Shih chi*, 107.2845).

Bibliography

Translations
Aoki, *Shiki*, 12:478–516.
Watson, *Han*, 2:307–18.

Studies
Hsing Hsüeh-min 邢學敏, "Hsi-Han ming-ch'en Cheng Tang-shih sheng-p'ing schih-chi shu-lun" 西漢名臣鄭當時生平事跡述論, *Ch'i-Lu hsüeh-kan* 齊魯學刊 2006.1, pp.103–105.
Nitta Kōji 新田幸治, "Yomu 'Kyū-Tei retsuden'" 読「汲鄭列伝」, *Tōyō Daigaku Chūgoku Tetsugaku-bungakuka kiyō* 東洋大學中國哲學文學科紀要 11 (2003), pp. 1–15.
Tanaka Masami 田中麻紗巳, "Kan Wu ki no Kō-Rōha Kyū An o megutte" 漢武期の黄老派汲黯をめぐって, *Kyōto Joshi Daigaku jinbun ronsō* 京都女子大學人文論叢 29 (1981), pp. 93–113.
Tseng Wei-hua 曾維華 and Tsou Wei-yi 鄒維一, "Hsi-Han ming-ch'en Chi An tsu-nien k'ao" 西漢名臣汲黯卒年考, *Chung-hua wen-shih lun-ts'ung* 中華文史論叢 2010.1, pp. 381–88.
van Ess, *Politik*, 1:313–316 and 465–67.

The Confucian Scholars,[1] Memoir 61[2]

translated by William H. Nienhauser, Jr. et al.[3]

[121.3115] His Honor the Grand Scribe says: Whenever I read over the regulations [for assessing scholars'] merits,[4] and reach the [part about] broadening and encouraging

---

[1] The discussion of how to translate the term *ju* 儒 has been energetic of late. Although we render it "Confucian scholar," many readers would prefer to refer to these men as "classical scholars" or even *ju/ru*. Yao Ch'eng's 姚承 comment on the chapter title cited in "Cheng-yi" seems to support the second reading: "*Ju* means erudite, those who formed a forest of culture, put in order ancient writings, promulgated the old arts, completely encouraging classical scholarship, in order to complete the civilizing influence of the king" 儒謂博士，為儒雅之林，綜理古文，宣明舊藝，咸勸儒者，以成王化者也. But other uses of *ju* in the *Shih chi* argue for our translation; for example, *Shih chi*, 74.2348: "[Hsün Ch'ing] was contemptuous of scholars arguing over minutiae, like Chuang Chou and the like disordering convention with smooth talk. Thus he discoursed on the advantages and disadvantages of the Confucian, Mohist, and Taoist ways of conduct, writing several tens of thousands of characters, and expired" 鄙儒小拘，如莊周等又猾稽亂俗，於是推儒、墨、道德之行事興壞，序列著數萬言而卒 (*Grand Scribe's Records*, 7:184). See also the translator's note and Hans van Ess's n. 245 on p. 236 above.

[2] "So-yin" refers several times to this chapter as the "Ju-lin chuan" 儒林傳 (e.g., *Shih chi* 67.2211), perhaps indicating that the chapter was originally so titled.

Takigawa (121.1–2) in a head-note points out that the *Shih chi* and *Han shu* rank the classics differently, the *Shih chi* giving the first place to the *Shih* 詩, followed by the *Shang shu* 尚書, *Li* 禮, *Yi* 易, and *Ch'un ch'iu* 春秋, the *Han shu* ranking the *Yi* first, then the *Shang shu*, *Shi*, *Li*, and *Ch'un ch'iu*.

[3] A draft of this chapter was translated by the members of a seminar taught by Nienhauser in fall 2011: Yang Gu, Masha Kobzeva, Lu Lu, Thomas D. Noel, Dewei Shen, Yiwen Shen, Chen Wu, Lianlian Wu and Xin Zou. The chapter and the notes have been thoroughly revised by Nienhauser with the help of Hans van Ess's *Shih chi* group in Munich as well as Yaping Cai, Anthony Wu, and Noel.

[4] "So-yin" glosses the term *kung-ling* 功令 as "[to assess scholars'] achievements and [record] them in the ordinances, which are the same as the ordinances for scholars today" 學者

267

the road of education officials and their staff,[5] I never fail to cast aside the documents and sigh,[6] saying: "Alas! When the house of Chou declined, 'Kuan chü' 關雎 (The Ospreys Cry) was composed.[7] When [King] Yu 幽王 (r. 781–771 BC) and [King] Li 厲 王 (r. 878–841 BC) [caused their dynasty to] wane, rites and music were ruined[8]; the feudal lords acted without restraint, and the administrative decisions came from the

課功著之於令，即今之學令是也. The term occurs only one other time in the *Shih chi* later in this chapter (*Shih chi*, 121.3119).

Yen Shih-ku claims that *kung-ling* is the title of a text (see *Han shu*, 88.3596).

[5] Lu Zongli (p. 558) glosses *hsüeh-kuan* 學官 as "officials in charge of government schools and education," including, in the central government Po-shih 博士 (Erudites) and Po-shih chi-chiu 博士祭酒 (Libationer of the Erudites). From the time of Emperor Wu such officials were appointed in every commandery and state designated as, among other titles, *Wen-hsüeh yüan-shih* 文學掾史 (Head of the Division of Study of Texts [or just "of Education"]), Ching-shih 經 師 (Tutor of a Classic). In a personal note Lu Zongli points out that *hsüeh-kuan* "has multiple meanings and can refer to (1) the educational bureaus and schools managed by the bureaus, (2) the buildings of the bureaus and schools, and (3) heads, officers and teaching staff of the bureaus and schools at both imperial and regional levels."

On the overall role of education officials in the early Han, Bielenstein (p. 138) comments: "The Erudites informally taught students, and collectively formed what amounted to an academy [which eventually was formally titled the T'ai-hsüeh (太學) or Academy] . . . The chairs were limited to give, one each for the *Book of Changes*, the *Book of Documents*, the *Book of Songs*, the *Book of Rites*, and the *Spring and Autumn Annals* with the *Kung-yang Commentary*. In 124 BC, 50 disciples were for the first time formally attached to the Erudites, i.e., 10 for each classic. The disciples had to be at least eighteen years old, and were annually selected and examined by the administrators of the commanderies and kingdoms. . . they were enrolled with the appropriate Erudite. The term of study was one year, followed by an examination . . . Emperor Wu . . . had the first campus constructed. It was located seven *li* (about two miles) northwest of Ch'ang-an."

[6] This passage reminds the reader of the opening comments in the "Meng Tzu, Hsün Ch'ing lieh-chuan" 孟子荀卿列傳 (*Shih chi* chapter 74).

[7] "Kuan-chü" 關雎 (The Ospreys Cry, Legge, 4:59-60) is the first song in the *Shih ching* 詩經. As Takigawa (1.2) observes this sentence is modeled on *Meng Tzu* 4B.21.1: "Mencius said, 'When the traces of real [Chou] kings ceased to be, the [practice of the] *Songs* was lost. When the *Songs* were lost, then the *Spring and Autumn* was composed" 孟子曰：王者之迹熄 而詩亡，詩亡然後春秋作 (translation revised from Legge, 2:327). Both this passage and that of *Meng Tzu* refer to the power of the *Songs* to modify behavior.

[8] King Yu 幽王 (r. 781–771 BC), the last ruler of Western Chou who was notorious for his depraved governance and dissolute personal life, put an end to his dynasty. King Li 厲王 (r. 878–841 BC), the tenth ruler of the Western Chou, by levying exorbitant taxes and ceaselessly launching wars aroused public indignation and was expelled from the capital by his people. Cf. "Chou pen-chi" (*Shih chi*, 4.144).

powerful states.[9] For this reason Chung-ni 仲尼 (i.e., Confucius) grieved that the path of the [ancient] kings had been abandoned and that evil ways had arisen; thereupon he put in order and arranged the *Shih* 詩 (Songs) and the *Shu* 書 (Documents), and revised and revived the rites and music.[10] When he went to Ch'i 齊 and heard the "Shao" 韶 music,[11] he did not know the taste of meat for three months.[12] He returned to Lu 魯 from Wey 衛 and thereafter the music was rectified, and the *Ya* 雅 (Elegantiae) and the *Sung* 頌 (Hymns) [of the *Shih* 詩] each obtained their [proper] places.[13] Because that era was confused and chaotic,[14] no one was able to employ him [Confucius]. For this

[9] Two parallels to this passage can be found in the Grand Scribes' comments elsewhere in the *Shih chi*: "Chou pen-chi" 周本紀 reads (*Shih chi*, 4.149; slightly revised from *Grand Scribes' Records*, 1:75: After King P'ing was enthroned, he moved the capital east to Lo City to avoid the Jung invasions. During the time of King P'ing, the Chou House fell into decline. Among the feudal lords the mighty annexed the weak; Ch'i, Ch'u, Ch'in and Chin first became grand and the administration [of each state] obeyed the local lords" 平王立，東遷于雒邑，辟戎寇。平王之時，周室衰微，諸侯彊并弱，齊、楚、秦、晉始大，政由方伯；also *Shih chi*, 7.338–39: 三年，遂將五諸侯滅秦，分裂天下，而封王侯，政由羽出，號為「霸王」; *Grand Scribes' Records*, 1:208: ". . . within three years Hsiang Yü finally led the five feudal lords to subjugate Ch'in divide up the world, and enfeoff kings and marquises. All power came from by Hsiang Yü, who proclaimed himself 'Hegemon King'" (slightly revised from the original).

[10] A more detailed account of Confucius's editing the *Book of Songs* and the *Book of Documents* as well as his revival of rites and music can be found in the "K'ung-tzu shih-chia" 孔子世家 (Hereditary House of Confucius; *Shih chi*, 47.1936–37).

[11] Although most of Pan Ku's introductory paragraph (*Han shu*, 88.3589–90) presents a similar historical background, it has been recast to express Pan's point of view. This sentence and that following are, however, identical in both the *Shih chi* and *Han shu*.

[12] This sentence is adapted from Confucius's *Lun yü*, 7.14. The original line reads: "When the Master heard the "Shao" music in Ch'i, he could not recognize the taste of meat for three months, saying: 'I did not expect that music-making reached such perfection'" 子在齊聞韶，三月不知肉味，曰：「不圖爲樂之至於斯也。」See also Yang Po-chün 楊伯峻 (1909–1992), annot. and trans., *Lun-yü yi-chu* 論語譯註 (Peking: Chung-hua Shu-chü, 1980), p. 70, *Shih chi*, 47.1910, and *Lun yü*, 9.14.

[13] This complete sentence is quoted from *Analects*, 9.15. See *Lun-yü yi-chu*, p. 92 and also *Shih chi*, 47.1936–37.

[14] Cf. "Po Yi lieh-chuan" 伯夷列傳 (*Shih chi*, 61.2126), an "introduction" of sorts to all the memoirs, where Confucius is quoted to have said: "When a whole age is muddy, the pure knight stands out 舉世混濁，清士乃見 (*Grand Scribe's Records*, 7:5); and also Ch'ü Yüan's comment to the fisherman (*Shih chi*, 84.2486: "The whole world is muddied, only I am pure. All men or drunk, only I am sober. For this reason I was exiled" 何故而至此？」屈原曰：「舉世混濁而我獨清，眾人皆醉而我獨醒，是以見放 (*Grand Scribe's Records*, 7:299).

reason, though Confucius sought a position with over seventy rulers,[15] there was none with whom he was well met.[16] He said: "If someone would employ me, within but a year [I could make a difference]."[17] When a unicorn was captured at the western hunt, he said, "My way has come to an end."[18] Therefore, based on scribal records,[19] he composed the *Ch'un ch'iu* (Spring and Autumn [Annals]), in order to be taken as a

[15] Cf. the "T'ien-yün" chapter of *Chuang Tzu* (*Chuang Tzu chi-shih* 莊子集釋 [Peking: Chung-hua, 1987], 4.130–31; as pointed out by Takigawa, 121.2–3): "Confucius said to Lao Tan, 'I have been studying the Six Classics, the *Songs, Documents, Ritual, Music, Changes and the Spring and Autumn* for what I would call a long time, and know their contents through and through But I been around to seventy-two rulers with them, expounding the ways of the former kings and making clear the path trod by [the dukes of] Chou and Shao, and yet not a single ruler has found anything to put to use. How very difficult it was been. Men are difficult to persuade, the Way is difficult to make clear!'" 孔子謂老聃曰：「丘治《詩》，《書》，《禮》，《樂》，《易》，《春秋》六經，自以為久矣，孰知其故矣，以奸者七十二君，論先王之道而明周、召之跡，一君無所鉤用。甚矣夫！人之難說也，道之難明邪！」(translation modified from Watson, *Chuang Tzu*, pp. 165–66).

[16] Confucius's difficulty in finding a position is not mention in the *Han shu* parallel. On the line 是以仲尼干七十餘君無所遇, although *kan* 干 may mean "touch" in several senses (perhaps even "go against, offend"), it another very common meaning should be considered here, namely "to seek, pursue." So the sentence may also be read "For this reason Confucius sought [positions from] more than seventy lords, there was none with whom he was well met."

The "So-yin" points out that the figure of "more than seventy" seems to be an exaggeration.

[17] Confucius's words are adapted from *Analects*, 13.10. The original line reads: "If someone would employ me, within a full year things would become acceptable, and after three years there would be accomplishment" 苟有用我者，期月而已可也，三年有成. See *Lun-yü yi-chu*, p. 137, and also *Shih chi*, 47.1924.

[18] According to the *Ch'un ch'iu Kung-yang chuan* 春秋公羊傳 (Kung-yang Commentary on the *Spring and Autumn Annals*), this happened in the fourteenth year (481 BC) of Duke Ai's reign (r. 494–468 BC). "K'ung-tzu shih-chia" (*Shih chi*, 47.1942) has a similar line and the "Chi-chieh" comments: "The unicorn is the beast of great peace and an analogy for the sage. At that time it was captured and died, this was Heaven also announcing proof that the Master was about to die" 麟者，太平之獸，聖人之類也。時得而死，此天亦告夫子將歿之證.

[19] Other scribes have also read texts which foretell events (compare *Shih chi*, 4.147: "The Grand Scribe of Chou, Po Yang, as he was reading the historical records [of Queen Shen being removed in favor of Lady Ssu of Pao] said, 'Chou will perish!'"; 周太史伯陽讀史記曰「周亡矣。」(translation revised from *Grand Scribe's Records*, 1:73).

model by the kings.[20] Since its language is subtle and its implications are profound,[21] men of learning[22] in later generations often copied [passages] from it.[23]

[20] On the Grand Scribes' detailed ideas on Confucius's composition of the *Spring and Autumn Annals* see *Shih chi*, 130.3319–20 and Burton Watson's translation (*Ssu-ma Ch'ien*, pp. 50–54).

[21] Cf. *Han shu* 30.1701: "Long ago Chung-ni died and subtle words ended; the seventy gentlemen [Confucius's disciples] passed on and the expanded meanings [of the Master's subtle words] became [point of] disaccord" 昔仲尼沒而微言絕，七十子終而大義乖.

"K'ung-tzu shih-chia" (*Shih chi*, 47.1943) describes the composition of the *Ch'un ch'iu* 春秋 (Spring and Autumn Annals) in more detail: 因史記作春秋，上至隱公，下訖哀公十四年，十二公。據魯，親周，故殷，運之三代。約其文辭而指博。故吳楚之君自稱王，而春秋貶之曰「子」；踐土之會實召周天子，而春秋諱之曰「天王狩於河陽」：推此類以繩當世。貶損之義，後有王者舉而開之。春秋之義行，則天下亂臣賊子懼焉. "[Confucius] on the basis of historical records composed the *Spring and Autumn Annals*, which go back to Duke Yin and come down to finish in the fourteenth year of Duke Ai [481 BC], [covering] twelve dukes. He based [his composition] on Lu, familiarized himself with Chou, modeled it on the old [accounts] of Yin, connected it to [the records of] the Three Dynasties. He abbreviated trope and diction but broadened the implications. Therefore, when the lords of Wu and Ch'u declared themselves kings, the *Ch'un ch'iu* concealed this by calling them 'viscounts'; whereas the meeting in Chien-t'u actually summoned the son of Heaven of Chou, the *Ch'un ch'iu* concealed that and said 'the Heavenly King toured at Ho-yang.' [Confucius] extended this kind [of principle; or "these analogies"] to restrain his contempor-aries. The principle of denouncement and depreciation awaited the later true kings to raise and decipher. When the principle of the *Ch'un chiu* was practiced, then the rebellious subjects and undutiful sons were fearful of it."

Cf. also *Shih chi*, 47.1944 (Chavannes, 5:422–23): "When Confucius was in his official position [as *Ssu-k'ou* 司寇 "Bandit Catcher"] in Lu] and heard legal cases, the language [of his decisions] contained that which could be shared with other [judges] and was not something he uniquely possessed. When it came to the Spring and Autumn, he wrote what he wanted to write and excised what he wanted to excise, [so that even] the followers of Tzu-hsia were not able to comment on a single phrase" 孔子在位聽訟，文辭有可與人共者，弗獨有也。至於為春秋，筆則筆，削則削，子夏之徒不能贊一辭.

[22] *Hsüeh-che* 學者; distinguish from *Hsüeh-shih* 學士, scholars who were studying in the Han educational system.

[23] On the reading of *lu* 錄 as "copied from" see Han Chao-ch'i, 121.5944, n. 13. The variant *miao* 繆 for *lu* seen by Hsü Kuang in an early manuscript ("Chi-chieh") would lead to a translation "scholars in later generations were confused by it," which also makes sense in this context.

[3116] After Confucius expired (479 BC), his seventy disciples[24] dispersed and traveled among the feudal lords.[25] The major ones became tutors, mentors, excellencies and ministers,[26] the minor ones acted as friends to teach the servicemen and grand masters, and some others went into seclusion and were never seen again.[27] Thus Tzu-lu 子路 lived in Wey,[28] Tzu-chang 子張 lived in Ch'en,[29] T'an-t'ai Tzu-yü 澹臺子羽 lived in Ch'u,[30] Tzu-hsia 子夏 lived in Hsi-ho 西河,[31] and Tzu-kung 子貢 died in

[24] For the number of Confucius's disciples, *Meng-tzu* 孟子, *Lü-shih Ch'un ch'iu* 呂氏春秋 (The Annals of of Lü Pu-wei), *Huai-nan Tzu* 淮南子 and "Yi-wen chih" 藝文志 in the *Han shu* 漢書 all claim that there were seventy disciples; "Kung-tzu shih-chia" in the *Shih chi*, "Tsai Yung chuan" 蔡邕傳 in the *Hou Han shu* 後漢書, *Shui-ching chu* 水經註 *juan* eight, "Li P'ing chuan" 李平傳 in the *Wei shu* 魏書, and "Chieh-ping p'ien" 誡兵篇 in the *Yen-shih chia-hsün* 顏氏家訓 all record seventy-two; while "Chung-ni ti-tzu lieh-chuan" 仲尼弟子列傳 (Memoir of Confucius's Disciples) in the *Shih chi* and *Kung-tzu chia-yü* 孔子家語 both give the number seventy-seven.

[25] Cf. also the account on in the "Li shu" 禮書, *Shih chi*, 23.1159 (Chavannes, 3:208–209): "After Confucius died, those followers who had received his instruction sunk into oblivion and were not raised up [by employment or preferment]. Some went to Ch'i, some to Ch'u, some to the [Yellow] River and the seas [compare *Lun yü*, 18.9]"; 仲尼沒後，受業之徒沈湮而不舉，或適齊、楚，或入河海. According to the *Han Fei Tzu* 韓非子, after Confucius's death his followers split into eight sects (cited by D. C. Lau, *Confucius, the Analects* [London: Penguin, 1979], p. 213, n. 10).

[26] The *Han shu* parallel reverses the order to read "excellencies, ministers, tutors and mentors."

[27] "So-yin" reads: "Tzu-hsia became the teacher of Marquis Wen of Wei. Tzu-kung paid a visit to Wu and Yüeh on behalf of Ch'i and Lu. Probably he was also a minister. But as for Tsai Yü also serving Ch'i as a minister, this I have never heard" 子夏為魏文侯師。子貢為齊、魯聘吳、越，蓋亦卿也。而宰予亦仕齊為卿，餘未聞也. Takigawa (121.3) quotes Nakai Sekitoku 中井積德 (1732–1817) that: "Tzu-kung was traveling and persuading, rather than [serving as] an excellency in Ch'i, the excellency of Ch'i [from Confucius's disciples] was named Tzu-wo, not Tsai Yü."

[28] Tzu-lu is the *agnomen* of Chung Yu 仲由 (542–480 BC), one of the major disciples of Confucius. Tzu-lu's biography in "Chung-ni ti-tzu lieh-chuan" on *Shih chi*, 67.2191-3 (*Grand Scribe's Records*, 7:67-69) relates how he died loyally defending his patron K'ung K'uei 孔悝.
    Tzu-lu is not mentioned in the *Han shu* parallel passage (88.3591).

[29] Tzu-chang is the *agnomen* of Chuan-sun Shih 顓孫師 (503–447 BC). See his biography on *Shih chi*, 67.2203–2204 (*Grand Scribe's Records*, 7:75–76). He was a native of Ch'en.

[30] Tzu-yü is the *agnomen* of T'an-t'ai Mieh-ming 澹臺滅明 (b. 512 BC) He was born in Wu-ch'eng 武城, but later went south to the Yangtze region and had three hundred followers there (see his biography on *Shih chi*, 67.2205–06; *Grand Scribe's Records*, 7:76).

[31] Tzu-hsia is the *agnomen* of Pu Shang 卜商 (507–425 BC). After Confucius died, Tzu-hsia resided at Hsi-ho and lived by teaching. He became the teacher of Marquis Wen of Wei 魏

Ch'i.[32] T'ien Tzu-fang 田子方, Tuan-kan Mu 段干木, Wu Ch'i 吳起 (ca. 440-ca. 381 BC), Ch'in-ku Hsi 禽滑釐 and the like, all received instruction from Tzu-hsia's peers,[33] and became the tutors of those who were kings.[34] At that time, only Marquis Wen of

文侯 (r. 445–396 BC), see *Shih chi*, 24.1221–22, 44.1839–40 and his biography on *Shih chi*, 67.2202–2203 (*Grand Scribe's Records*, 7:74–75). "So-yin" notes that he was also a specialist in the *Li* 禮 and *Yi* 易; "Cheng-yi" (67.2203) says that after Confucius's death Tzu-hsia went to An-yi 安邑 where he taught and advised Marquis Wen. However, it seems possible that he may have *first* become the teacher of Marquis Wen and *then* retired to Hsi-ho; compare the "T'an-kung" 檀弓, *Li chi* 禮記, passage cited by Takigawa [2.3]: 退而老於西河之上; this seems to also suggest that the Hsi-ho referred to here is not that suggested by the "Cheng-yi" commentary (Fen-chou 汾州), but more likely the location Cheng Hsüan 鄭玄 gives in his *Li chi* comments: 西河龍門至華陰之地), which Han Chao-ch'i (121.5945, n. 19) points out was on the western side of the Yellow River, an area that at that time was held by Wei. In the *Lun yü* (11.2; Legge, p. 238) Confucius praised Tzu-hsia as one of two men (the other was Tzu-yu) who were versed in *wen-hsüeh* 文學 (textual studies?).

[32] Tzu-kung is the *agnomen* of Tuan-mu Tz'u 端木賜 (b. 520 BC), who is portrayed at some length in the "Chung-ni ti-tzu lieh-chuan" as a wise and eloquent advisor to several rulers. He was a minister in both Lu and Wey and his family property amounted to thousands of *chin*; he died in Ch'i. See his biography on *Shih chi*, 67.2195–2201 (*Grand Scribe's Records*, 7:70–75).

[33] Or "from Tzu-hsia and his sort"; Wu and Lu translate *lun* 倫 as 等人的學生, Watson 2:356 as "companions."

[34] T'ien Tzu-fang 田子方 (fifth century BC) and Tuan-kan Mu 段干木 (fifth century BC) were both teachers of Marquis Wen of Wei. The "Wei Shih-chia" 魏世家 (Hereditary House of Wei) reads: "[Marquis Wen of Wei] obtained Pu Tzu-hsia, Tien Tzu-fang and Tuan-kan Mu from the east. The lord considered all these three men his teachers" 東得卜子夏、田子方、段干木。此三人者，君皆師之 (*Shih chi*, 44.1840). Takigawa (121.4) cites Shen Ch'in-han 沈欽韓 who notes that the *Lü-shih Ch'un ch'iu* says T'ien studied with Tzu-kung and Tuan studied with Tzu-hsia and was an important figure (*ta tsang* 大駔) in the state of Chin 晉. Yen Shih-ku points out that these four were all natives of Wei (*Han shu*, 88.3591n.).

Wu Ch'i also served Marquis Wen of Wei as a general. His biography (*Shih chi*, 65.2165–70; *Grand Scribe's Records*, 7:41–45) relates that he once studied under Tseng Tzu 曾子 (Tseng Shen 曾參, 505–436 BC). Wu at first served in Lu but was denounced and then went to serve Marquis Wen of Wei and his son Marquis Wu 武 (r. 395–370 BC).

According to the "Chi-chieh" in "Meng Tzu, Hsün Ch'ing lieh-chuan" 孟子荀卿列傳 (Memoirs of Mencius and Excellency Hsün, *Shih chi*, 74.2350), Ch'in-ku Li 禽滑釐 (fourth century BC) was a student of Mo Tzu 墨子 (Mo Ti 墨翟, ca. 480–ca. 390 BC). The *Lü-shih Ch'un ch'iu* reads: "T'ien Tzu-fang studied under Tzu-kung; Tuan Kan-mu studied under Tzu-hsia; Wu Ch'i studied under Tseng Tzu; and Ch'in-ku Hsi studied under Mo Tzu" 田子方學於子貢，段干木學於子夏，吳起學於曾子。禽滑釐學於墨子. See Ch'en Ch'i-yu 陳奇猷

Wei 魏文侯 (r. 424–396 BC) was fond of learning.[35] Later, [learning] waned until it reached [the time] of the First Emperor [of Ch'in],[36] the empire being struggled for by warring states and the methods of the Confucian [scholars] having already been dismissed in them; but within Ch'i and Lu alone, men of learning had not discarded them.[37] Within [the reigns] of [Kings] Wei 威 (r. *378–343 BC) and Hsüan 宣 (r. *342–329 BC) [of Ch'i],[38] Mencius 孟子 and Hsün Ch'ing 荀卿 and company all followed the legacy[39] of the Master and embellished it, distinguishing themselves in that age by their learning.[40]

(1917–2006), annot., *Lü-shih Ch'un ch'iu hsin chiao-shih* 呂氏春秋新校釋 (Shanghai: Shanghai Ku-chi Ch'u-pan-she, 2002), 2.96.

[35] The "Wei Shih-chia" (*Shih chi*, 44.1839) reads: "Marquis Wen learned classics and literature from Tzu-hsia, and treated Tuan Kan-mu as a retainer. Whenever [Marquis Wen] passed by his village, he would lean on the crossbar in the carriage front [to show respect]. Once [the Lord of] Ch'in wanted to attack Wei, someone said: 'The Lord of Wei respected the worthies, and people of the state claim him as benevolent. [Wei is] harmonious from the top down, so it is not yet feasible to scheme it" 文侯受子夏經藝，客段干木，過其間，未嘗不軾也。秦嘗欲伐魏，或曰：「魏君賢人是禮，國人稱仁，上下和合，未可圖也。」文侯由此得譽於諸侯.

[36] The First Emperor of the Ch'in was Ying Cheng 嬴政 (r. 246–210 B.C). See "Ch'in Shih-huang pen-chi" 秦始皇本紀 (Basic Annals of the First Emperor of the Ch'in) in *Shih chi*, 6.223–64. This sentence is omitted from the *Han shu* parallel (88.3591).

[37] The Chung-hua text here reads: 然齊魯之閒，學者獨不廢也. Chang Wen-hu (2:704) points out that many editions (e.g., Po-na, 121.2a) read *men* 門 for *hsien* 閒 (i.e.,"Those disciples who studied in Ch'i and Lu alone had not discarded them"; see also *Shih chi*, 121.3117 just below where a similar wording occurs: 夫齊魯之閒於文學，自古以來，其天性也).

[38] That is, T'ien Yin-ch'i 田因齊, the fourth ruler of Ch'i, and T'ien P'i-chiang 田辟疆, the fifth. The dates given in the *Shih chi* for their reigns differ from those in other texts: 356–320 BC and 319–301 BC. See also Robert Reynolds' discussion of these problems in "A Note on Chronology," *Grand Scribe's Records*, 1:xxvii–xxx. Both rulers were famous for recruiting worthy men.

[39] *Yeh* 業 here is more than just Confucius's enterprise, since it is said in the following paragraph that the K'ung Family *yeh* had been burned by Ch'in. We read it as including Confucius's teaching in both oral and written form.

[40] See the biographies of Mencius (i.e., Meng K'o 孟軻, 372–289 BC) and Hsün Ch'ing (i.e., Hsün K'uang 荀況, ca. 313–238 BC) biographies in "Meng Tzu Hsün Ch'ing lieh-chuan" in *Shih chi*, 74.2343–50.

On *jun* 潤, see *Lun yü*, 14.9 (revised from Legge, 1:178) "Tzu-ch'an of Tung-li gave them [government notifications] the proper elegance and finish" 東里子產潤色之 .

When it came to the last generation of the Ch'in,[41] the *Shih* 詩 (*Songs*) and the *Shu* 書 (*Documents*) were burned and those scholars [who followed the 孟子 Scholarly] methods were buried alive, and the Six Classics[42] following this had gaps in them.[43] When Ch'en She 陳涉[44] declared himself a king, the Confucian scholars of Lu carried the ritual vessels from the K'ung Clan and went to give their allegiance to King Ch'en. At this time K'ung Chia 孔甲 became an erudite for Ch'en She and in the end he died together with She.[45] Ch'en She rose from an ordinary man; by spurring on a banded together ragtag group of garrison troops,[46] in less than a month he became the King of

[41] The rather disjointed structure of this chapter (see translator's note) is suggested by the sectional breaks indicated by an extra space before next sections (as here).

[42] *Liu yi* 六藝 can also refer to the Six Arts (Rites 禮, Music 樂, Archery 射, Charioteering 禦, Writing 書, and Mathematics 數, but here seems to refer to the Six Classics, *Shi* (Songs), *Shu* (Documents), *Li* (Ritual), *Yüeh* (Music), and *Yi* (Changes), as on *Shih chi*, 61.2121: "The scholars [possess] books and records that are extremely catholic, they still rely upon the Six Classics. Although the *Songs* and Documents have gaps, yet [through them] the texts of Yü and Hsia [i.e., Shun 舜 and Yü 禹] can be known" 夫學者載籍極博，猶考信於六蓺。詩書雖缺，然虞夏之文可知也, as well as *Shih chi*, 126.3197: "Confucius said, 'The Six Classics with regard to regulating [the state] are one and the same. The *Rites* are to give humans a standard, the *Music* to enhance their harmony, the *Documents* to provide a guide for their affairs, the *Songs* to allow them to express their ideas, the *Changes* to afford mystical transformation, and the *Spring and Autumn* to express their meaning'" 孔子曰：「六蓺於治一也。禮以節人，樂以發和，書以道事，詩以達意，易以神化，春秋以義」. See also Loewe, *Dong Zhongshu* (pp. 38 and 177) who renders the term as "Six Choice Works" (or "Texts").

[43] On the burning of the books, a proposition raised by Li Ssu 李斯 (280–208 BC), see *Shih chi*, 6.254–55 and *Grand Scribe's Records*, 1:147-48.

The *Han shu* (88.3592) version is more cautious in its depiction of these events: "When it came to the First Emperor of the Ch'in, he united the empire, burned the *Shih* and the *Shu*, and killed the scholars of [traditional] methods, the *Six Classics* as a result of this were all incomplete" 及至秦始皇兼天下，燔詩書，殺術士，六學從此缺矣.

[44] See his biography in *Shih chi* chapter 48.

[45] The "Chi-chieh" says: "[Kung Chia] was an eighth-generation descendant of Confucius. His *praenomen* was Fu and *agnomen* was Chia" 孔子八世孫，名鮒字甲也. "K'ung-tzu shih-chia" in the *Shih-chi* (*Shih chi*, 47.1947) adds: "[K'ung] Shen begot Fu. When Fu was fifty-seven years old, he became the erudite of King Ch'en She and died under Ch'en" 慎生鮒，年五十七，為陳王涉博士，死於陳下. K'ung Chia was the reputed author of the *K'ung ts'ung-tzu* 孔叢子 (see Yoav Ariel, *K'ung-ts'ung-tzu, The K'ung Family Masters' Anthology* [Princeton: Princeton University Press, pp. 13–14).

[46] The *Han shu* (88.3592) says simply "he drove troops garrisoned at the border to establish his title" 毆適戍以立號.

Ch'u and in not even half a year he [and his men] were wiped out.[47] This affair being extremely trivial, why did these sort of officials bear Confucius's ritual vessels and go to submit themselves to him as subjects? **[*3117*]** Because Ch'in had burned their legacy, they vented their accumulated resentments through King Ch'en.

When August Emperor Kao 高皇帝 put Hsiang Chi 項籍 to death, and raised troops to besiege Lu,[48] the Confucians in Lu went on lecturing on, reciting, and practicing ritual and music, and the sounds of singing accompanied by string music did not cease.[49] Was this not the bequeathed influence of the sage, a state that was fond of rites and music?[50] Therefore, when Confucius was in Ch'en,[51] he said: "Let us return! Let us return! The young ones in my school are wild and impractical, brilliant in completing writing but I do not know that by what means I can shape them."[52] Thus refinement in studies of [Confucian] texts[53] within Ch'i and Lu has since ancient times been a part of people's nature. For this reason, only when the Han arose were the Confucians able to begin to be able to revise their classics and traditions, and to teach and practice the rituals of grand archery matches and community banquets.[54] Shu-sun T'ung 叔孫通 composed the rituals and ceremonies for the Han and accordingly was

---

[47] According to "Ch'in Ch'u chih chi yüeh-piao" 秦楚之際月表, Ch'en She rose up in the seventh month of the first year of the Second Emperor of Ch'in (209 BC) and died in the twelfth month of the same year (see *Shih chi*, 16.763).

[48] The *Han shu* parallel (88.3592) reads "led troops" (*yin ping* 引兵), perhaps referring to the fact that these were not actually troops raised for the siege of Lu.

[49] These scholars were imitating Confucius who when besieged in the wilds between Ch'en and Ts'ai "lectured, recited and sang to the accompaniment of stringed instruments without flagging" 孔子講誦弦歌不衰 (*Shih chi*, 47.1930).

[50] The *Han shu* (88.3592) reads "a state that was fond of ritual studies" 好禮學之國哉, wherein *hsüeh* 學 is probably a scribal variant for *yüeh* 樂.

[51] The *Han shu* omits the next forty-eight characters, returning to the *Shih chi* text with the line "at this the Confucian were first able to begin to revise their classics and arts." It would seem that Pan Ku did not mention the rise of the Han (*ku Han hsing* 故漢興), because the paragraph opens by noting the time frame.

[52] See the parallels in *Lun yü*, 5.21/22 (*Lun-yü yi-chu* 論語譯註, p. 51) and on *Shih chi*, 47.1927: 孔子曰：「歸與歸與！吾黨之小子狂簡，進取不忘其初。」於是孔子去陳.

On *fei ran* 斐然 compare *Shih chi*, 130.3315: 結子楚親，使諸侯之士斐然爭入事秦. 作呂不韋列傳第二十五. Our translation is based on the "Chi-chieh" reading, attributed to K'ung An-kuo, in *Lun-yü chi-shih* 論語集釋, p. 344.

[53] Or "texts and study" for *wen-hsüeh* 文學.

[54] On these rituals see the "Ta-she" and "Hsing-yin" chapters in the *Yi li* 儀禮.

made the Grand Master of Ceremonies. [55] Those masters and disciples [56] who participated in determining these rituals and ceremonies were selected as the top [candidates for official positions]. At this [people] sighed with deep feeling and were themselves aroused to study. However, the weapons of war were still pacifying [the lands within] the four seas, [57] and there was still not yet time to waste with the matter of establishing local schools. [58] During the time of [Emperor] Hsiao Hui 孝惠 (r. 195–188 BC) and Empress Lü 呂 (r. 188–180 BC), the highest officials were all subjects who had gained merit through military force. In the time of [Emperor] Hsiao Wen 孝文 (r. 179–157 BC), [Confucian scholars] were sometimes recruited and employed, [59] but Emperor Hsiao Wen was basically fond of theories of dispositions and designations. [60] When it came to [Emperor] Hsiao Ching 孝景, (r. 156–141 BC), he did not appoint

[55] See Shu-sun T'ung's biography in *Shih chi* chapter 99. *Han shu* gives his position as Feng-ch'ang 奉常 (Upholder of Ceremonies); Han Chao-ch'i (121.5948, n. 35) points out that this was another name for this high position (one of the Chiu-ch'ing 九卿 or Nine Ministers); the duties included being in charge of the royal ancestral temple and court ritual. See also *Shih chi*, 130.3319: "When Shu-sun T'ung determined the rituals and ceremonies, the study of literature flourished and [Confucians] were gradually promoted, [so that] the [texts of] the *Songs* and the *Documents* steadily began to appear" 叔孫通定禮儀，則文學彬彬稍進，詩書往往閒出矣.

[56] *Han shu* (88.3592) reads only "disciples who determined" here. Cf. *Shih chi*, 99.2721–2722 (*Grand Scribe's Records*, 8:291–92): "When Shu-sun T'ung surrendered to the Han, the Confucian masters and disciples who followed him were more than one hundred . . . [after convincing Han Kao-tsu that he needed Confucians to rule] he was sent as an envoy to summon a group of more than thirty scholars from Lu" 叔孫通之降漢，從儒生弟子百餘人 . . . 叔孫通使徵魯諸生三十餘人.

[57] The "Cheng-yi" quotes Yen Shih-ku: "When Ch'en Hsi, Lu Wan, Han Hsin, Ch'ing Pu and the like rebelled one after another, there were punitive expeditions" 陳豨，廬綰，韓信，黥布之徒相次反叛，征討也.

[58] The text in Takigawa (121.6) reads "During the period of Emperor Hsiao Hui and Emperor Dowager Lü, there was not yet time to care about the affairs of establishing schools 孝惠呂后時，亦未暇遑庠序之事也," but the Chung-hua Shu-chü 中華書局 edition, as well as the Po-na (121.3a and *Shih chi p'ing-lin* (121.2a) editions, all read 亦未暇遑庠序之事也 preceding 孝惠呂后時, as we have translated.

[59] The *Han shu* parallel reads *teng yung* 登用 ("ascended and were employed") for *cheng yung* 徵用 here.

[60] *Hsing ming* 刑名, "dispositions and designations," were Legalist concepts espoused by Shen Pu-hai (fourth century BC) and Shang Yang (d. 338 BC) which were often the focus of court discussions under Emperor Wen (see *Shih chi*, 101.2745 and especially 103.2773 as well as *Grand Scribe's Records*, 8:390).

Confucians. Moreover, Empress Dowager Tou 竇 (ca. 209–135 BC)[61] was fond of the methods of Huang-Lao; for this reason the various erudites only occupied official posts[62] awaiting to consulted [by the emperor] but there had not yet been one who had been presented [to him].

[3118] When the Present Sovereign ascended the throne,[63] Chao Wan 趙綰 and Wang Tsang 王臧[64] and their sort thoroughly understood Confucian learning, and the Sovereign was also bent towards it,[65] so he summoned upright and worthy scholars as well as those versed in textual learning. From this time on, in Lu 魯[66] it was the Master

[61] Empress Tou had been taken into the harem under Emperor Hui (r. 195–188 BC) and continued to serve under Empress Lü. Later she was sent with four other women as a gift from Empress Lü to the King of Tai, Liu Heng 劉恒 (202–157 BC). She found favor with the King of Tai and when he was enthroned (Emperor Wen, r. 179–156 BC) she became empress. Her son, Liu Ch'i 劉啟 succeeded Emperor Wen and became known as Emperor Ching (r. 155–141 BC). She was a strong supporter of Huang-Lao thought and thus her death eased the way for Emperor Wu to bring Confucian scholars into his government. See also notes 145 and 146 below.

[62] Yen Shih-ku (*Han shu*, 88.3593n.) glosses *chü kuan* 具官 as *pei yüan erh yi* 被員而已 "merely staffed official positions."

[63] Here the *Han shu* parallel (88.3593) differs considerably. It begins with "when the Han arose, the explaining of the *Changes* all derived from Scholar T'ien of Tzu-ch'uan . . ." 漢興, 言易自淄川田生, then treats the teaching of the *Shu* 言書自濟南伏生, *Shih*, *Li* and *Ch'un ch'iu* in order with only minor variations from the *Shih chi* text.

[64] Chao Wan and Wang Tsang are the two most prominent Confucian scholars promoted in the first year of Emperor Wu's reign (140 BC; see *Shih chi*, 12.452 and *Grand Scribe's Records*, 2:220). Chao was a native of Tai and Wang from Lan-ling 蘭陵 (formerly territory of Ch'i). Both men were scholars of the *Shih* 詩. According to the biography of Wei Chi 魏其 (*Shih chi*, 107.2843; *Grand Scribe's Records*, 9:144; also in *Han shu* annals, 6.157), Wei Chi favored Confucian scholars and promoted Chao Wan 趙綰. Once the latter was Grandee Secretary, he asked permission to submit memorials without sending a copy to Empress Dowager Tou. This angered her and led to the imprisonment of Chao Wan and the subsequent suicides of both Chao and Wang.

[65] Takigawa (121.7) notes that Chao Wan 趙綰, the Grand Master of Imperial Scribes, and Wang Tsang 王臧, the Perfect of the Palace Attendants, both studied with Master Shen P'ei 申培.

[66] Although Lu was a commandery during the reign of Emperor Wu, it probably is used anachronistically for the region centered around Ch'ü-fu 曲阜 that was one of the two states mentioned just above in the text (along with Ch'i 齊) as those which kept alive the Confucian tradition during the Warring States era. The reference to Ch'i just below is similar, used as a general term for that area associated with Confucian scholarship (centered on Lin-tzu 臨淄).

Shen P'ei 申培[67] who settled [the meaning of][68] the *Shih* 詩, in Ch'i 齊 it was Scholar Yüan Ku 轅固, and in Yen 燕[69] it was Grand Mentor Han [Ying] 韓[嬰]. Settling [the meaning of] the *Shang shu* 尚書 began from Scholar Fu 伏 from Chi-nan 濟南,[70] explaining the *Li* [*ching*] 禮[經] ([The Classic of] Rites)[71] began from Scholar Kao-t'ang 高堂[72] from Lu, explaining the *Yi* 易 (Changes) from Scholar T'ien 田 from Tzu-ch'uan 菑川.[73] Explaining the *Ch'un ch'iu* 春秋 (Spring and Autumn [Annals]) in Ch'i and Lu began from Scholar Hu-wu 胡毋[74] and in Chao 趙[75] from Tung Chung-shu 董仲舒.[76] After Empress Dowager Tou passed away (135 BC), when T'ien Fen 田蚡,

[67] Shen is his *cognomen*, P'ei his *praenomen* (see alternative pronunciations for P'ei in the "Chi-chieh" and "So-yin"). Brief biographical accounts for all these scholars follow in the text and translation below (*Shih chi*, 121.3020ff.).

[68] Our understanding of *chih* 治 is "to settle on the meaning of" still partially in the sense of oral transmission. We considered other readings such "put in order" but felt this overly emphasized a textual tradition that was only evolving at the time.

[69] Yen also refers here to the area (centered on Chi 薊 [near modern Peking]) that was one of the Warring States.

[70] Chi-nan was a Han commandery with its seat at Tung-p'ing Ling 東平陵 west of Chang-ch'iu 章丘 in modern Shantung (Wang Li-ch'i, 121.2552n.).

[71] Wu and Lu (121.3142n.) point out that *Li* here refers to the *Li ching* 禮經, a Han Confucian text that has been transmitted under the title *Yi li* 儀禮.

[72] His *agnomen* was Po 伯 (Wang Li-ch'i, 121.2552n.) from "So-yin."

[73] Tzu-ch'uan was one of the Han feudal kingdoms with its capital at Chü 劇 (south of modern Shou-kuang 壽光 in Shantung).

[74] "So-yin" notes Hu-wu 胡毋 was his *cognomen* and his *agnomen* was Tzu-tu 子都.

[75] Once again Chao probably refers not to the Han kingdom, but to the broader area that was encompassed by the Warring States entity (see Wu and Lu's notes on these places, 121.3142). Takigawa (121.8) points out that Ch'ien Ta-hsin 錢大昕 comments on the places names mentioned in this passage: "Chung-shu 仲舒 is from Kuang-ch'uan 廣川, but [this text] claims he was a native of Chao. Kuang-ch'uan used to belong in Chao. Kung-sun Hung 公孫弘 was from Tzu-ch'uan 菑川, but is said to have been a native of Ch'i. Chu Mai-ch'en 朱買臣 was from K'uai-chi 會稽, but is said to have been a native of Ch'u. These claims are of the same sort [as that for Tung Chung-shu]."

[76] Here there is a lengthy (over 250 words) "Cheng-yi" entry in Takigawa (121.8) which is not in the Chung-hua edition of the *Shih chi*—i.e., one of those lost "Cheng-yi" notes that Takigawa rediscovered in old Japanese manuscripts. This entry makes no mention of Tung Chung-shu but rather treats in a fascinating manner the history of *Ch'un ch'iu* exegesis through the end of the Han dynasty, with considerable focus on Tso Ch'iu-ming's 左丘明 role and the reception of his *chuan* 傳 ("commentary" or "account of the tradition"). Tung Chung-shu's contribution to this scholarship was traditionally thought to be the *Ch'un ch'iu fan-lu* 春秋繁露, although the received text is not from his hand (see Loewe, *Early Chinese Texts*, pp. 77–87).

Marquis of Wu-an 武安,[77] became chancellor, he dismissed the theories of the hundred schools of Huang-Lao and of dispositions and designations,[78] and of the hundred schools, and invited several hundred Confucians of textual learning; but, Kung-sun Hung 公孫弘 (200–121 BC)[79] through his proficiency in the *Ch'un ch'iu* went from a commoner to become one of the Three Most Honorable Officials[80] of the Son of Heaven,[81] and was enfeoffed with the title of Marquis of P'ing-chin 平津侯.[82] The scholars of the empire were bent by these winds of change [towards studying Confucian texts].

Only when Kung-sun Hung became an education official,[83] lamenting that the Way [of Confucian scholarship] had been obstructed,[84] did he request [in a memorial]:
Your Chancellor and Imperial Scribe report that an [Imperial] Decree read:

We have heard that the people are led through rites and influenced through [*3119*] music; as for marriage, that is the primary relationship within the

---

[77] See T'ien Fen's biography in *Shih chi* chapter 107.

[78] We read *pai-chia* 百家 as referring to the many schools of Huang-Lao and Hsing-ming popular in the early Han, not to the Chu-tzu pai-chia 諸子百家.

[79] See Kung-sun Hung's biography in *Shih chi* chapter 112 and the translator's note below.

[80] Enno Giele (*Imperial Decision-Making and Communication in Early China* [Wiesbaden: Harrassowitz, 2006], p. 330) calls the San-kung 三公 the "Executive Council" of the Han government which included the Ch'eng-hsiang 丞相 (Chancellor), Yü-shih Ta-fu 御史大夫 (Grand Master of the Imperial Scribes) and the T'ai-wei 太尉 (Grand Commandant).

[81] There is likely some textual corruption here. The *Shih chi* text reads: 白衣為天子三公. Hsü Kuang 徐廣 ("Chi-chieh") notes that another manuscript he saw read: "[Kung-sun Hung] came from Ch'i to become one of the Three Most Honorable Officials of the Son of Heaven 自齊為天子三公 wherein *tzu Ch'i* 自齊 and *pai-yi* 白衣 may easily have been confused in handwritten texts of the Han. The *Han shu* (88.3593) perhaps reflects the Pan's recognition of this problem and reads simply "[Kung-sun Hung] by means of settling [the meaning of] the *Spring and Autumn Annals* became Chancellor" 公孫弘以治春秋為丞相.

[82] Kung-sun Hung was enfeoffed in 128 BC.
According to Wang Li-ch'i (112.2375n.) P'ing-chin was located in modern Hupei south of Yen-shan 鹽山 County. T'an Ch'i-hsiang has no reference. "So-yin" (*Shih chi*, 112.2951) says that it was a fief of only 650 families and notes that Kung-sun Hung was the first chancellor to be made a marquis. "Cheng-yi" (*Shih chi*, 6.264) speculates that P'ing-chin may have been what was formerly called P'ing-yüan Chin 平原津 (Flat Plain Ford) in modern Shantung. See also the long entry on P'ing-chin in Wang Hui 王恢, *Han wang-kuo yü hou-kuo chih yen-pien* 漢王國與侯國之演變 (Taipei: Kuo-li Pien-yi-kuan 國立編譯館, 1984), pp. 338–39.

[83] Between 134 and 130 BC (see Han Chao-ch'i, 121.5952, n. 51).

[84] This line might also be read as "The way [for promotion of Confucian scholars] being blocked" 悼道之鬱滯.

household.[85] Now rites have been abandoned and music has perished, and We deeply grieve for this. For this reason We have thoroughly summoned all those gentlemen who are morally upright and of wide learning from throughout the world and raised them all to court.[86] Let it be ordered that the ritual officials' study [of ritual], debate it, expand knowledge of it, and revive ritual,[87] and that this be considered the first priority under heaven.[88] [Let the] Grand Master of Ceremonies debate this [before Us] and with the erudites and [their] disciples, celebrate education in village and hamlet, and thereby expand the worthy and talented in these [places]." I have carefully discussed this with the Grand Master of Ceremonies [K'ung] Tsang 孔臧,[89] the Erudite Ping 平,[90] and others, and we have said: "We have heard that the Way of the Three Eras [of Hsia, Yin and Chou] was that there was instruction in the villages and hamlets, the Hsia called it hsiao 校, the Yin called it hsü 序, and the Chou called it hsiang 庠.[91] To exhort goodness, they manifested it at court; to punish wickedness, they applied bodily punishments and fines. For this reason, to put into effect transformation through teaching, to establish the primacy of goodness, originates from the capital city, from the inner to the outer.[92] Now Your Majesty displaying supreme virtue and showing great lucidity, matches Heaven and

[85] This line is not in the *Han shu* parallel.

[86] Pan Ku's *Han shu* (88.3593) account omits *cheng* 正 and *po* 博 from this phrase, thus reading: 故詳延天下方聞之士, "For this reason I have recruited all those gentlemen who are of wide learning from throughout the world."

[87] *Han shu* (88.3593) omits *hsing li* 興禮, "revive ritual."

[88] Watson (1:399) understands the phrase 以為天下先 as: "in order to act as leaders of the empire."

[89] The T'ai-ch'ang 太常 was one of the Nine Ministers, charged with oversight of sacrifices at the Ancestral Temple of the Imperial Household, as well as the examination of candidates nominated by officials in territorial administration units. See Hucker, p. 476, and Loewe, *Dictionary,* p. 211. K'ung Tsang appears to have ascended to this position in 127 BC (*Shih chi,* 18.900). See also *Shih chi,* 18.899–900, and *Han shu,* 16. 551–52.

[90] Little can be found among traditional sources concerning Erudite Ping, who appears only in this chapter of the *Shih chi* and the corresponding parallel account in *Han shu* (88.3593).

[91] "Cheng-yi" glosses these three terms as follows: 校，教也. 可教道蓺也. 序，舒也. 言舒禮教. 庠，詳也。言詳審經典. "*Hsiao* 校 means *chiao* 教 (teaching); that able to teach the Way and the Arts. *Hsü* 序 means *shu* 舒 (unfolding); this speaks of the unfolding of the teaching of the rites. *Hsiang* 庠 means *hsiang* 詳; this speaks to being thorough and meticulous in the study of the classics." Yen Shih-ku (*Han shu,* 88.3595) only glosses the first of these terms, but his gloss is identical to that of "Cheng-yi" discussed above.

[92] *Han shu* (88.3594) replaces the graph *yu* 由 (from) with a synonym *yao* 繇 (from), another example of standardization.

Earth, takes human relationships as basic, exhorts study and cultivates ritual,[93] esteems those who transform and encourages the worthy, to [positively] influence the four regions; this is the source of Great Peace. In former times, governance and teaching were not yet wide spread and the ritual system was not complete. We request that you take advantage of the old official system to give rise to [a complete ritual system]. For each erudite there should be officially established fifty men as disciples,[94] exempting these persons [from tax and corvée labor]. The Grand Master of Ceremonies should select common people eighteen years and older, whose bearing and appearance are proper and upright, to fill the ranks of the erudites' pupils. As for the commanderies, kingdoms, counties, march counties,[95] and manors that have those fond of texts and study, who respect their elders and superiors and revere governance and teaching, who observe [the customs] of villages and hamlets, and who in their coming and going will not go against what they have learned,[96] the magistrates, assistants, small county magistrates, and deputy magistrates [should recommend them] to those two thousand *shih* officials to whom they are subordinated.[97] Those who the two thousand *shih* officials carefully examine and find capable should with the officials in charge of accounts be sent to the Grand Master of Ceremonies and receive instruction as disciples. After one year all should then be examined, those able to master one of the classics or more should fill vacancies among the literary scholars[98] and Authorities on Ancient Matters or Precedents.   Those highest ranking pupils could be taken as Gentlemen of the Palace, and the Grand Master of Ceremonies would make a roster and present it to the court. If there are flourishing talents or those of an exceptional sort, they should be made known by name [to the emperor]. Those who do not work at their studies or those of lower capabilities unable to master

---

[93] Here the *Han shu*. 88.3595 parallel reads *hsing* 興 for the *hsiu* 修, rendering the phrase "revive ritual propriety," a phrase used earlier in a simplification of the text.

[94] During the Han period the erudites occupied positions under the oversight of the Grand Master of Ceremonies and were often engaged in the carrying of state rituals. However, during the Han, the distinction between these officials and those simply referred to as "erudite" is not always clear, and in the case of this passage, it appears that either is possible. See Hucker, p. 389.

[95] Takigawa notes (121.10) that these would have been counties with high minority populations.

[96] *Ch'u ju* 出入, literally, "going out and entering" refers here to one's conduct in daily affairs (i.e., in "coming and going"). The *Han shu* (88.3594) omits the particle *che* 者, resulting in a different rendering of this clause: 出入不悖，所聞，令相長丞上屬所二千石. "Who in going out and entering are not [thereby] discredited, those who are heard [to meet these criteria] …"

[97] The translation of this sentence is tentative. Compare Watson (2:359) who adds "in order to supply candidates for the selection . . . ."

[98] Or "scholars of textual study."

one classic are then to be dismissed; moreover we request that those who do not bespeak [expectations] should be punished.[99] Your subjects have carefully examined the edict[100] and the statutes and ordinances that have been issued, clarifying the differing realms of Heaven and man and comprehending the meaning of the ideas of ancient and modern times. Their language and composition approach ancient elegance, their teachings and diction deep and profound, their grace and kindness extremely beautiful. The petty officials of shallow learning, unable to examine and promulgate them, have no means to clearly disseminate and explain them to the people. Those who regulate ritual are ranked below those who regulate matters of ancient precedence; because of their textual studies and [their understanding of] the meaning of ritual, they became officials [and yet] their advancement is delayed and impeded. I request that those whose salaries are two hundred *shih* and above, and those functionaries whose salaries are one hundred *shih* and above, and who have mastered one of the classics or more, be selected to fill positions of the Left and Right Scribe of the Capital and the Secretariat of Grand Usher; those below one hundred *shih*, should fill the offices in the commanderies of the Grand Administrators, two men for each [of the central provinces], and one for the march commanderies. The first to be used [should be] those who can recite most; only if they are insufficient,[101] should [selections] from those [who regulate] matters of ancient precedence, supplemented by the subordinates of those with a salary of two-thousand *shih*, and those who study texts and are masters of ancient precedence be added to the subordinates of the commanderies to complete the [required number of] positions. We request to display the ordinances for [assessing] merit and that all else follow the [existing] statutes and ordinances.[102]

The [response in the form of Imperial] Decree read: "This is indeed permissible." From then onward, among the excellencies, [*3120*] ministers, grand masters, gentlemen and minor officials were many scholars of textual study.[103]

[99] *Han shu* (88.3595) reads *neng* 能 for *pu* 不 (not/do not) and omits the final graph *fa* 罰 (punish), thus rendering the final clause of this sentence as: "And request [the services of] all those who are able to be named" 而請諸能稱者. Yen Shih-ku (*Han shu*, 88.3595) annotates the *Han shu* account as meaning: "To rank all those able to master a classic, to declare their responsibilities, and to request in a memorial that they be allowed to fill postions" 謂列其能通藝業而稱其任者，奏請補用之也.

[100] *Chao-shu* 昭書, see also Giele, *Imperial-Decision Making*, p. 232.

[101] *Han shu* (88.3594) again simplifies its text, removing the graphs *juo* 若 (if) and *nai* 乃 (only then) which appear at the beginning of these two clauses in the *Shih chi* account.

[102] On *lü* 律 and *ling* 令 see Hulsewé, *Han Law*, pp. 30–31.

[103] The *Han shu* (88.3595) reads *pin-pin* 彬彬 (refined and courteous) for *pin-pin* 斌斌 (increasingly).

Honorable Shen 申公
[Lu 魯 Tradition of the *Shih* 詩]

Honorable Shen [P'ei] 申公[培]¹⁰⁴ was a native of Lu 魯.¹⁰⁵ When Kao-tsu 高祖 (r. 202–195 BC) stopped by in Lu,¹⁰⁶ Honorable Shen as a disciple followed his tutor to go in and have an audience with Kao-tsu in the Nan-kung 南宮 (Southern Palace) in Lu.¹⁰⁷ During the time of Empress Dowager Lü 呂 (ca. 241–180 BC),¹⁰⁸ [*3121*] Honorable Shen traveled to Ch'ang-an, studied [there], and shared the same tutor [Fu-ch'iu Po 浮丘伯] with Liu Ying[-k'o] 劉郢[客].¹⁰⁹ Before long, [Liu] Ying[-k'o] became the King of Ch'u (r. 179–174 BC) and ordered Honorable Shen to tutor [Liu] Wu 戊, his Heir. Wu was not fond of learning and loathed Honorable Shen. When [Liu] Ying, the King, expired, Wu was enthroned as King of Ch'u (r. 174–154 BC).¹¹⁰ He had Honorable Shen castrated.¹¹¹ Honorable Shen was ashamed of this and returned to Lu;

---

¹⁰⁴ Compare James R. Hightower's translation of the much longer *Han shu* biography of Shen P'ei, "The *Han-shih wai-chuan* and the *San-chia Shih*," *HJAS* 11 (1948): 268–72.

¹⁰⁵ At this point the *Han shu* (88.3595) parallel begins a much more detailed account of the lines of classical scholars from Confucius down to Han times. Pan Ku's sketch of Honorable Shen begins some pages later (88.3608) following short biographies of a number of Han scholars (including only Scholar Fu from the *Shih chi*).

¹⁰⁶ The only record in the *Shih chi* of Kao-tsu "stopping by in Lu" (*kuo Lu* 過魯) is in Confucius's biography (*Shih chi*, 47.1945–6). The must have occurred after Kao-tzu had gone east in 196 BC and then stopped by his hometown, P'ei, in 195 on his way back to the capital (compare *Shih chi*, 8.389 and *Grand Scribe's Records*, 2:81–82).

¹⁰⁷ The *Han shu* 漢書 (88.3608) says that when he was young, Honorable Shen studied the *Shih* together with Liu Chiao 劉交 (d. 179 BC), King Yüan 元 of Chu 楚, under the instruction of Fu Ch'iu-po 浮丘伯, a native of Ch'i, himself supposedly a student of Hsün Ch'ing 荀卿 (see Wu and Lu, 121.3145n. and Loewe, *Dictionary*, p. 111). It adds that when King Yüan sent his son Liu Ying-k'o 劉郢客 to study with Honorable Shen it was under the instruction of his old teacher Fu-ch'iu Po who was then in Ch'ang-an.

The Nan-kung 南宮 was located near modern Ssu-shui 泗水 in Shantung province (T'an Ch'i-hsiang, 2:19).

¹⁰⁸ Empress Dowager Lü 呂 (241–180 BC) was the wife of Emperor Kao-tsu and the mother of Emperor Hui 惠 (210–188 BC; r. 195–188 BC). During Emperor Hui's reign and after his death, Empress Lü was ruled for almost fifteen years (see *Shih chi*, 9.395–412 and *Grand Scribe's Records*, 2:105–44).

¹⁰⁹ The *Shih chi* here and on 50.1988 gives his *praenomen* as simply Ying. *Han shu* (4.108) is the same. But Liang Yü-sheng (7.251) and Wang Nien-sun (1.21a) both support the name Liu Ying-k'o. See also Loewe, *Dictionary*, p. 399 and *Han shu*, 14.397 and 36.1922.

¹¹⁰ Liu Wu was posthumously titled King Yi 夷王 (see Loewe, *Dictionary*, pp. 366–67).

¹¹¹ Hsü Kuang, cited in "Chi-chieh," argues that *hsü-mi* 胥靡 meant "to castrate." Yen Shih-ku's 顏師古 (581–645) gloss on the *Han shu* parallel (88.3609) claims it referred to tying

he retired and gave private lessons from his home. For the rest of his life he did not go out of his gate, again and again severing relationships with his clients and retainers.[112] Only when the king summoned him by royal command, did he go.[113] Those disciples who came to him from distant places to receive instruction were more than one hundred persons. [114] Honorable Shen taught the classic, *Shih* 詩, [115] only through oral explanations without a written commentary.[116] If he was doubtful [about something], then he omitted it [from his teaching] and did not pass it on [to his students].

Wang Tsang 王臧

Wang Tsang 王臧 (d. 139 BC) of Lan-ling 蘭陵,[117] having received [instruction in] the *Shih*, used this [this knowledge] in serving Emperor Hsiao-ching 孝景 (r. 157–141 BC) as the Lesser Mentor of the Heir [the future Emperor Wu]. He was dismissed

a prisoner to a labor gang, i.e., putting him on a chain gang. Most modern scholars have followed Yen's explanation (see additional comments on Takigawa, 121.13). Hightower (p. 268) translates "put Honorable Shen into fetters." However, these readings do not fit with the text that follows (why would he be embarrassed for merely being imprisoned?) and we therefore have adopted Hsü Kuang's understanding of the term.

[112] Or "declining guests of all stations" 謝絕賓客.

[113] Hsü Kuang, cited in "Chi-chieh," says it was King Kung 恭 of Lu (Liu Fei 劉非, d. 127 BC; Loewe, *Dictionary*, p. 296) who summoned Honorable Shen. Wu and Lu (121.3145n.) argue that this was Liu Yü 劉餘 (Loewe, *Dictionary*, p. 402), Emperor Ching's son, who became King of Lu (transferred from ruling Huai-yang 淮陽) when Lu was created out of northern Ch'u in 155 BC.

[114] The *Han shu* (88.3608) parallel reads "more than one thousand persons" 千餘人 came to study with him. Takigawa (121.13) cites Ch'i Shao-nan 齊召南 who pointed out that later in this paragraph it is said that more than one hundred of Shen's disciples reached various positions, thus the *Han shu* reading should be preferred.

[115] Neither the 1959 edition nor the newly edited Chung-hua version (121.3765) include *ching* 經 as part of the title; thus our translation. The *Han shu* (88.3608) parallel reads the *ching* 經 (in *Shih ching*) as part of the title and then adds *ku* 故 [i.e., 詁] to *hsün* 訓, resulting in "Honorable Shen only taught the *Classic of Poetry* by means of oral explanations of words" 申公獨以詩經為訓故以教.

[116] *Wu chuan* 無傳, could also be read "these explanations have not been passed on" (or "transmitted"), reading 傳 as *ch'uan* as in the following line (see also the lengthy discussion of this section in Hightower, "*Han-shih wai-chuan*," p. 269, n. 9). Wu and Lu (121.3145n.) read the two occurrences of 傳 as we do: the first as *chuan* "commentary" and second as *ch'uan* "to transmit."

[117] Located to the southeast of modern Tsao-chuang 棗莊 county in Shantung province (T'an Ch'i-hsiang, 2:20).

and left [Ch'ang-an]. Only when the present Sovereign [Emperor Wu, r. 141–87 BC] had just ascended the throne, did Ts'ang submit a memorial to the Palace Bodyguard.[118] He was promoted several times and within a year became the Prefect of the Palace Attendants. When Chao Wan 趙綰[119] from Tai 代 [Commandery] had received [instructions in] the Shih from Honorable Shen, Wan became Grandee Secretary. Only when Wan and Ts'ang made a plea to the Son of Heaven, intending to establish a Ming-t'ang 明堂 (Hall of Light) to cause the feudal lords to pay homage [at court],[120] [but] were not able to accomplish this task, did they accordingly mention their tutor Honorable Shen [to the emperor]. At this point, the Son of Heaven sent envoys with a bundle of silk, a jade disc, and a comfortable carriage [drawn by] four horses to welcome Honorable Shen.[121] Two disciples accompanied him in a post-station carriage [with two horses]. When [Honorable Shen] arrived, he had an audience with the Son of Heaven. The Son of Heaven asked about some matters relating to governing well and handling chaos. At the time, Honorable Shen was already more than eighty and, being too old, he replied[122]: "The way to achieve good government does not lie in talking excessively about [such matters], [*3122*] but only making efforts to put things into practice."[123] Just at this time, the Son of Heaven was fond of rhetorical flourish and,

[118] Su-wei shang 宿衛上.

[119] See Loewe, Dictionary, pp. 711–12. The appointment came in 139 BC, presumably before Wang Tsang's death that same year.

[120] On discussions of the Ming-t'ang in some key Han-dynasty texts, see Hans van Ess, "The Apocryphal Texts of the Han Dynasty and the Old Text/New Text Controversy," TP 85 (1999): 52ff. See also Loewe, Dong Zhongshu, pp. 33 and esp. p. 79, where there is a good summary of how Emperor Dowager Tou's opposition to the Ming-t'ang led to the imprisonment and suicide of both Wang Tsang and Chao Wan. These events are also portrayed in this chapter below (Shih chi, 121.3122).

[121] Shu-po 束帛 consisted of five bolts of silk, each about ten meters in length. Similar gifts were provided Ch'un-yü K'un 淳于髡 after he spoke for three days before King Hui of Liang (Shih chi, 74.2347).

An-chü 安車 "comfortable carriage," was a special carriage designed for honored guests, especially women and the elderly, in which you could sit rather than stand. The wheels were covered by cattails which made the ride more comfortable (see Han shu, 88.3608). An-chü were also used to convey Ch'un-yü K'un (Shih chi, 74.2347) and Lu Chia 陸賈 (Shih chi, 97.2699; see also "Chin-chü" 巾車 in the chapter "Ch'un-kuan" 春官 in Chou Li 周禮, 27:1b, SPPY, and Bielenstein, p. 132.

[122] Compare the passage below where Yüan Ku is dismissed because he is too old.

[123] Honorable Shen's comments were perhaps intended to resonante with a Li chi passage (Li chi 禮記, "Chung yung" 中庸: "The Master said, "To be fond of learning is to approach knowledge, to make efforts to put it into practice is to approach goodness" 子曰：「好學近乎知，力行近乎仁」", Han Chao-ch'i (121.5963, n. 17) argues that Shen's response fits the Huang-Lao tradition.

faced with Honorable Shen's reply, he fell silent. However, having already summoned [Honorable Shen] to come [to court], [the Son of Heaven] then appointed him as Grand Master of the Palace, housed him in the Lu Residence,[124] and had him discuss the matter of the Ming-t'ang. Grand Empress Dowager Tou 竇 (135 BC) was fond of Lao Tzu's 老子 opinions and did not like the Confucian methods. She seized on Chao Wan and Wang Tsang's errors and reprimanded the Sovereign.[125] The Sovereign took advantage to abandon the matter of the Ming-t'ang and sent both Chao Wan and Wang Tsang down to the [judicial] officials. Later they both committed suicide. Pleading illness, Honorable Shen was able to return again [to Lu] and be dismissed [from office]. After several years, he expired.

More than ten of [Shen's] disciples became erudites: K'ung An-kuo 孔安國 (ca. 154–174 BC)[126] reached [the position of] Grand Administrator of Lin-huai 臨淮[127]; Chou Pa 周霸 reached [the position of] Clerk of the Capital of Chiao-hsi 膠西[128]; Hsia K'uan 夏寬 reached [the position of] Clerk of the Capital of Ch'eng-yang 城陽[129]; Lu Tz'u 魯賜 of Tang 碭[130] reached [the position of] Grand Administrator of Tung-hai 東海[131]; Mu Sheng 繆生 from Lan-ling reached [the position of] Clerk of the Capital of Ch'ang-sha 長沙[132]; Hsü Yen 徐偃 became the Commandant of the Capital of Chiao-

---

[124] The residence in which the Duke of Lu resided when he came to court to pay homage to the Emperor.

[125] In the *Han shu* parallel (88.3608), the Grand Empress Dowager warned Emperor Wu that Wang Tsang and Chao Wan were charlatans much like Hsin-yüan P'ing 新垣平 who had deceived Emperor Hsiao-wen with several schemes (including a jade cup from the immortals that predicted a long life for the emperor, see *Shih chi*, 10.430 and *Grand Scribe's Records*, 2:175-6); see also more details of Hsin-yüan P'ing's activities on *Shih chi*, 28.1382–83.

[126] Traditionally considered to be a descendant of Confucius in the eleventh generation. He held position of erudite during the reign of Emperor Wu. See Loewe, *Dictionary*, p. 206, and *Shih chi*, 47.1947.

[127] Its seat was located south of modern Ssu-hung 泗洪 county in Shantung province (T'an Ch'i-hsiang, 2:20).

[128] Chou Pa was an *Yi* 易 specialist (Loewe, *Dictionary*, p. 729).

[129] Located near modern Chü-hsien 莒縣 county in Shantung province (T'an Ch'i-hsiang, 2:20).

[130] Lu Tz'u is otherwise unknown. Tang was located northwest of modern Huai-pei 淮北 city in Anhwei 安徽 province (T'an Ch'i-hsiang, 2:19).

[131] Located near modern T'an-ch'eng 郯城 city in Shantung province (T'an Ch'i-hsiang, 2:20).

[132] Mu Sheng (Scholar Mu), also known as Scholar Po 白生, studied the *Shih* with Master Shen P'ei under Fu-ch'iu Po 浮丘伯 (see Loewe, *Dictionary*, p. 3). Ch'ang-sha was located the modern city of the same name in Hunan province (T'an Ch'i-hsiang, 2:23).

hsi[133]; Ch'üeh-men Ch'ing-chi 闕門慶忌, a native of Tsou 鄒, became the Clerk of the Capital of Chiao-tung 膠東.[134] In governing officials and the common people they all had an honesty and integrity which bespoke their fondness of learning. Though the conduct of the disciples of the officials in charge of education was not perfected, those reaching the positions of Grand Master, Gentlemen-of-the-Palace, and Authority on Ancient Matters could be counted in the hundreds. In explaining the *Shih*, although they differed, for the most part they based [their explanations] on Honorable Shen.

Scholar Yüan Ku 轅固
[Ch'i 齊 Tradition of the *Shih* 詩]

Scholar Yüan Ku 轅固,[135] Grand Tutor[136] of the King of Ch'ing-ho 清河,[137] was a native of Ch'i. Because he settled [the meaning of] the *Shih* [Songs], he became an Erudite during the time of [Emperor] Hsiao-ching. He [once] disputed Master Huang 黃子 before Emperor Ching.[138] Master Huang said, "[King] T'ang 湯 and [King] Wu 武 did not receive the mandate of Heaven, they simply murdered [(the kings) Chieh 桀 and Chow 紂]."[139] Scholar Yüan Ku said, "Not so. Thus the tyranny of [kings] Chieh 桀 and Chow 紂 led to chaos, the hearts and minds of all under Heaven turning to T'ang and Wu. T'ang and Wu, in accordance with [*3123*] the hearts and minds of all under Heaven, executed Chieh and Chow. Chieh and Chow's people [were no longer willing] to be used by them, and gave their allegiance to T'ang and Wu; T'ang and Wu had no choice but to be enthroned. If this was not 'receiving the mandate of Heaven,' what was

[133] Loewe, *Dictionary*, p. 624， notes he was a *li* 禮 specialist (see also *Shih chi*, 12.473 and 30.1433).

[134] A Han kingdom with its capital near modern Chi-mo 即墨 in Shantung (Wu and Lu, 212.3146n.).

[135] See Hightower's translation of this biography ("*Han-shih wai-chuan*," pp. 274–77).

[136] This biography is noteworthy as the only one in this chapter that begins with the identification of the subject's position.

[137] Liu Chia 劉嘉 (see Wu and Lu, 121.3146n.).

[138] Takigawa (121.16) notes that in his autobiography Ssu-ma Ch'ien mentioned that "the Grand Scribe (here refers to Ssu-ma Ch'ien's father Ssu-ma T'an) studied the theories of Taoism with Master Huang" 太史公習道論於黃子. See *Shih chi*, 130.8233. Master Huang is otherwise unknown.

[139] On T'ang's overthrow of Chieh, the final, tryannic ruler of the Hsia, see *Shih chi*, 2.88 (*Grand Scribe's Records*, 1:38) and *Shih chi*, 3.95 (*Grand Scribe's Records*, 1:43–44). But in the *Shih chi* accounts Chieh is not murdered, but dies in exile. King Wu of Chou 周武王 cut off the head of King Chow 紂, the notoriously evil last Shang ruler (*Shih chi*, 3.105–108 and 4.120–24; *Grand Scribe's Records*, 1:49–52 and 59–61).

it then?" Master Huang said, "Hats, even if they are dilapidated, must be set on the head; sandals, even if they are new, must be worn on the feet.[140] Why? [It is due to] the differences between what is above and what is below. Now although Chieh and Chow lost the Way, [they were] still lords above; although T'ang and Wu were sages, they were [still] vassals below. Thus when rulers have lost proper conduct and vassals are unable to rectify their words and correct their errors in order to honor [the position of] the Son of Heaven but instead take advantage of their errors and execute them, replacing them and ascending the throne to face south—if this was not murdering [the rulers], what was it then?" Scholar Yüan Ku said "If what you say is indeed so, [then] in this way was it not wrong for Emperor Kao to replace [the ruler of] Ch'in and ascend the throne of the Son of Heaven?" At this, Emperor Ching said "[Those who] eat meat but do not eat horse liver, do not do so because they don't appreciate its taste; those who speak of learning but do not talk about T'ang and Wu's receiving of the mandate of Heaven, are not being foolish."[141] In the end he dismissed them. After this, among those who men of learning no one dared to explicate matters concerning receiving the mandate, exiling, or killing.[142]

Empress Dowager Tou was fond of the writings[143] of *Lao Tzu*.[144] [She once] summoned Scholar Yüan Ku and asked him about the writings of *Lao Tzu*. Ku said: "These are just the words of for commoners."[145] The Empress Dowager was furious

[140] This seems to be an old saying that occurs in various wordings in a number of texts including the *Huai-nan Tzu*, *Han Fei Tzu*, and *Hsin shu*.

[141] Horse liver was believed to be poisonous. Emperor Wu attributed the necromancer Shao-weng's death to eating it (*Shih chi*, 12.462 and *Grand Scribes' Records*, 2:232 and n. 91). Duke Mu of Ch'in also believed that eating horse flesh was harmful (see *Shih chi*, 5.189). Here Emperor Ching is indirectly but clearly cautioning Master Huang, Yüan Ku, and anyone else privy to their discussion that the question of who has the right to overthrow his sovereign could be as deadly as eating horse liver. See also the description of Pien Ch'üeh's treatment of a man who had eaten horse liver (*Shih chi*, 105.2809 and *Grand Scribe's Records*, 9:63, especially n. 323).

[142] Chieh was exiled, Chow was killed. See n. 139 above. See also the discussion in *Meng Tzu* 1B.8 (Legge, 2:167) of the actions of kings T'ang and Wu.

[143] Or "documents" (*shu* 書).

[144] *Shih chi*, 63.2141 (*Grand Scribe's Records*, 7:22 reports that when Lao Tzu left Chou he wrote out a "book" in two sections which e the meaning of *tao* 道 and *te* 德. This has led some modern scholars to conclude that a Lao Tzu text was current in Western Han times. Han texts of the *Lao Tzu* have been discovered at Ma-wang-tui (see Robert G. Henricks, "Examining the Mai-wang-tui Silk Texts of the *Lao-tzu*," *TP* 65 [1979]: 166–99); see also Liu Hsiao-kan 劉笑敢, *Lao Tzu ku-chin* 老子古今 (Peking: Chung-kuo She-hui K'o-hsüeh, 2006) which includes a discussion of the Peking University bamboo-slip *Lao Tzu* mss. among other texts.

[145] Yü Cheng-hsieh 俞正燮 (1775–1840, cited by Takigawa, 121.17) argues that *chia-jen* 家人 here means an official without a formal position, referring indirectly in this instance to a palace woman without rank such as a maid or attendant. If Yü was correct, this reference could

and said, "How could I have [Confucian] books by which the Minister of Public Works sentences people to wall-building?"[146] Then she made [Yüan] Ku enter a pen to [try to] stab a wild boar. Only when Emperor Ching found out that the Empress Dowager was angry and that Ku had spoken too straightforwardly without committing a crime, did he hand Ku a sharp weapon. Ku went down into the pen to stab the boar and hit it right in the heart; with a single thrust, the boar fell in one motion. The Empress Dowager fell silent. Having no other means to find him guilty of an offense, she dismissed him. After a short time, Emperor Ching, taking into consideration Ku's honesty and straightforwardness, appointed Ku as Grand Tutor to the King of Ch'ing-ho 清河.[147] After a long while, [Ku] was allowed to leave [office] because of illness.

When the current sovereign first ascended the throne, he again recruited [Ku] as a "worthy and excellent man." Many of the fawning Confucian scholars[148] jealously slandered Ku saying that "Ku is too old," [the sovereign then] dismissed him and sent

have particularly offended Empress Dowager Tou since, although she was from a prominent family (Loewe, *Dictionary*, p. 78), she had entered the palace as a maid with no formal rank. But the distinction Yuan Ku was trying to make might also be between Lao Tzu resembling the words of *chia jen* as "members of the family" and the Confucian texts which could guide the emperor in governing.

[146] Empress Tou 竇后 (d. 135) played a leading role in court politics from the time her husband, Emperor Wen 文 took the throne in 179 BC until her death in 135 BC. Under her influence Emperor Ching 景 and Emperor Wu 武 both studied the texts of the Huang-ti and *Lao Tzu* (see *Shih chi*, 49.1975).

Although there are at various interpretations of the Empress's comments, our reading is that is that she replys to Yüan Ku's claim that Huang-Lao texts are for commoners by saying that Confucian texts have been used in a political context to sentence people to forced labor (following Takigawa's point that the culture background to this statement was *yi ching tuan yü* 以經斷獄, especially the use of the *Ch'un ch'iu* and *Shang shu* by men such as Ch'ao Ts'o and Tung Chung-shu, and the close reading of this passage by Feng Yu-lan 馮友蘭 [1895–1990] in his *Ch'an-chiu pang yi fu hsin-ming* 闡舊邦以輔新命 [Shanghai: Shang-hai Yüan-tung Ch'u-pan-she, 1996], p 354). Watson (2:364) understands the passage differently, but provides a useful note which reads in part: "Some of the Confucian works such as the 'Institutes of Zhou' dealt with the bureaucratic system of the Zhou dynasty and its officials, such as the Director of Public Works, etc. The empress dowager is here deriding this attention to bureaucratic and legal details which seems to have absorbed much of the time of Han Confucian scholars."

On *ch'eng-tan* 城旦, a form on punitive forced labor, see n. 63 to chapter 118 above.

[147] This was Liu Sheng 劉乘 (153–135 BC), King Ai 哀 of Ch'ing-ho (r. 147–135 BC), who was the thirteenth son of Emperor Ching ("Chi-chieh").

[148] Presumably Kung-sun Hung and his like (compare Tung Chung-shu's assessment of Kung-sun below on *Shih chi* 121.3128).

him home.[149] At that time, Ku was already more than ninety. **[*3124*]** When Ku was recruited, a native of Hsüeh 薛 [County] named Kung-sun Hung was also recruited.[150] He averted his eyes but stole a glance at Ku.[151] Ku said, "Honorable Kung-sun, you must endeavor to use correct learning in explaining, not twisted learning in order to cater to the world." From this time on those who explain the *Shih* in Ch'i all based [their readings] on Scholar Yüan Ku. Those men of Ch'i who achieved distinction and honor through the *Shih* were all Ku's disciples.

<h2 style="text-align:center">Scholar Han 韓生
[Han 韓 Tradition of the Shih 詩]</h2>

Scholar Han [Ying] 韓生[嬰][152] was a native of Yen 燕. During the time of Emperor Hsiao Wen 孝文 (r. 179–157 B.C.) he became an erudite 博士, and during the time of Emperor Ching 景 (r. 156–144 B.C.), he became Grand Mentor to the King of Ch'ang-shan 常山.[153] Han expanded the meaning of the *Shih* 詩 (Songs) and composed a *Nei*

---

[149] Our translation follows the Chung-hua punctuation which reads: 曰『固老』罷歸之, but it would make more sense to include the last five characters as part of what the toadying scholars said: "Ku is old, dismiss him and send him home" 曰『固老，罷歸之』.

[150] In his biography Kung-sun Hung is simply said to have come from Tzu-ch'uan 淄川 Commandery (*Shih chi*, 112.2949).

[151] Hightower ("*Han-shih wai-chuan*," p. 276 and n. 45) believes this look indicated Kung-sun Hung respected Yüan Ku. The same expression on *Shih chi*, 120.3108 (see the translation above), however, suggests fear. Yen Shih-ku (*Han shu*, 88.3614n.) concurs. The *Han shu* parallel reads *shih* 事 for *shih* 視, yielding "watched him out of the corner of his eye and served Ku." A passage in Su Ch'in's biography, however, supports Hightower's reading (*Shih chi*, 69.2262; *Grand Scribe's Records*, 7:108): "Su Ch'in's older and younger brothers and their wives averted their eyes and did not dare look up at him, but with their heads lowered, bowed down and served him food. Su Ch'in laughed and said to his older brother's wife, 'Why were you so arrogant before and so respectful now.'" 蘇秦之昆弟妻嫂側目不敢仰視，俯伏侍取食。蘇秦笑謂其嫂曰：「何前倨而後恭也？」

[152] Hightower, op. cit., pp. 277-8, gives an annotated translation of this biography.

[153] Hsü Kuang 徐廣 points out ("Chi-chieh") that the King of Ch'ang-shan 常山 was Liu Shun 劉舜, the fourteenth and youngest son of Emperor Ching 景, who as the favorite child became notorious for his licentious behavior. He was posthumously titled King Hsien 憲 (ca. 155–114 BC, r. 145–114 BC). See the short note on Liu Shun on *Shih chi*, 59.2102–2103. Does this mean that Emperor Ching respected Han Ying's influence enough to hope that he could sway the young Liu Shun, or that he wanted to remove Han from court and place him in a difficult position.

Ch'ang-shan 常山, which was set up as a kingdom explicitly for Liu Shun to rule, was located to the south of modern Shih-chia-chuang City, Hopei (Tan Ch'i-hsiang, 2:26).

Wai Chuan 內外傳 (Inner and Outer Tradition)[154] in tens of thousands of words. His discourses were rather different from those of the Ch'i and Lu [traditions], but they revert to one and the same [principle].[155] Scholar Fei 賈生[156] of Huai-nan 淮南 received instruction [from him]. From this time on those who explained the *Shih* in Yen 燕 and Chao 趙 all originated from Scholar Han. Scholar Han's grandson, Shang 商, became an Erudite of the present sovereign.

Scholar Fu 伏生
[*Shang shu* 尚書 Transmission]

Scholar Fu 伏生[157] was a native of Chi-nan 濟南.[158] Formerly he had been an erudite in Ch'in. During the time of Emperor Hsiao Wen, [the Emperor] intended to find those who could put in order the *Shang shu* 尚書 (Exalted Documents) but there was no one under Heaven [who could]. Only when he heard that Scholar Fu could put it in order did he wish to summon him. At that time Scholar Fu was more than ninety and, as he was too old, and was not able to travel. Only at this point was an edict issued to the Grand Master of Ceremonies[159] to dispatch the Authority on Ancient Affairs,

---

[154] The surviving text is known as the *Han Shih wai-chuan* (韓詩外傳; cf. the translation and study by James R. Hightower, *Han Shih Wai Chuan: Han Ying's Illustration of the Didactic Application of the Classic of Songs* [Cambridge: Harvard University Press, 1952]). Wang Li-ch'i (121.2556) notes that after the Southern Song Dynasty the *Nei chuan* 外傳 was lost, although fragments have been reconstructed by Ch'ing scholars.

[155] Compare the opening line to *Shih chi* chapter 126 (126.3197): "Confucius said, 'With regard to administering [a state] the Six Classics are one and the same" 孔子曰：六藝於治一也.

[156] "So-yin" notes that 賈 should be pronounced "*Fei*." Watson (2:305) reads Pi.

[157] "Chi-chieh" notes that his *praenomen* was Sheng 勝. Takigawa (121.7) quotes Ch'ien Ta-chao 錢大昭 (1744–1812) giving his *agnomen* as Tzu-chien 子賤. The *Shang shu ta-chuan* 尚書大傳 [Grand Commentary of Book of Documents of High Antiquity] is considered to be his work. See also his biography in Loewe, *Dictionary*, p. 107.

[158] See also the parallel passage in Ch'ao Ts'o's biography (*Shih chi*, 101.2746; *Grand Scribe's Records*, 8:344). Scholar Fu is said to have concealed a copy of the *Shang shu* when Ch'in proscribed "books." The "Chi-chieh" (ibid.) points out that Ch'ao Ts'o could not understand the aged Fu Sheng who spoke the Ch'i dialect and, after trying to have his daughter explain his ideas, finally just read the *Shang shu* according to his own ideas.

The seat of Chi-nan [Commandery] was located about twenty miles northeast of modern Tsinan, the capital of Shantung province.

[159] The position of *T'ai-ch'ang* 太常 (Grand Master of Ceremonies) was established in the Ch'in dynasty and its original designation was *Feng-ch'ang* 奉常 (Chamberlain of Ceremonies).

Ch'ao Ts'o 朝錯 (ca. 200–154 B.C.),[160] to go to [Scholar Fu] and receive [his teachings on the *Shang shu*]. When the books were burned in Ch'in times,[161] Scholar Fu hid [the *Shu ching* documents] inside the walls. After this, when warfare rose up on a grand scale, he fled to escape it. After the Han stabilized [the world], Scholar Fu searched for his documents. Several dozen chapters having been lost, he only obtained twenty-nine chapters. Then with these [chapters] [*3125*] he taught within Ch'i and Lu. Because of this men of learning[162] were somewhat able to explain the *Shang shu*. There were none among all of the Grand Tutors (or just "Great Teachers") east of the Mount[163] who did not include the *Shang shu* in teaching.

Scholar Fu taught Scholar Chang 張生 and Scholar Ou-yang 歐陽生 of Chi-nan.[164] Scholar Ou-yang taught Ni K'uan 兒寬 (d. 103 B.C.) of Ch'ien-ch'eng 千乘 [Commandery].[165] When Ni K'uan had already mastered the *Shang shu*, by means of his refined learning he was recommended by his commandery, and sent to the erudite to receive instruction, and he received instruction from K'ung An-kuo. [Although] Ni

The position was among the *Chiu-ch'ing* 九卿 (Nine Ministers). One responsibility of this position involved selecting the erudites (Wang Li-ch'i, 121.2556).

[160] Ch'ao Ts'o 朝錯 (also 晁錯 and, according to Loewe, *Dictionary*, p. 27, correctly 鼂) was a native of Ying-ch'uan 潁川 [Commandery] (surrounding modern Yü-hsien 禹縣 in the middle of Honan). Ch'ao had difficulty understanding Scholar Fu's dialect and may just have used the Shang shu to foster his own political ideas ("Chi-chieh," *Shih chi*, 101.2746). Whatever the case, upon his return from Scholar Fu, Ch'ao Ts'o gained the emperor's recognition and was assigned to the position of *T'ai-tzu Chia-ling* 太子家令 (The Director of the Household of the Heir Apparent). At that time, the Heir Apparent was the future Emperor Ching. Ch'ao's positions continued to improve with the accession to the throne of Emperor Ching (156 BC), until he was promoted to be Imperial Counselor. The measures and policies that he pursued were not in much favor at the court. Court intrigues could be part of the reason for his execution in 154 BC. Loewe also points out that *Shih chi* and *Han shu* had different assessments of Ch'ao Ts'o. For more details biography see Ch'ao's biography on *Shih chi* 101.2745–47 (*Grand Scribe's Records*, 8:343–350), in *Han shu* chapter 49, and Loewe, *Dictionary*, pp. 27–29.

[161] The *Shih chi* dates the infamous burning of canons and books of the "hundreds schools" as well as execution of Confucian scholars, to 213 BC (see *Shih chi* 6.255 and *Grand Scribe's Records*, 1:147).

[162] Or "those who studied it [*Shang shu*]."

[163] During the Han dynasty Shan-tung 山東 referred to the region located to the east of either the Mount Hsiao 崤山 (to the north of modern Lo-ning 洛寧 in Honan province) or the Mount Hua 華山 (to the south of modern Hua-yang 華陽 in Shenxi province). See also notes on *Grand Scribes' Records*, 1:158 and *Shih chi*, 6.269.

[164] According to "Chi-chieh" and the parallel account in *Han shu* (88.3603), Scholar Ou-yang's *agnomen* was Ho-po 和伯. His *praenomen* is unknown.

[165] Ch'ien-ch'eng was the name of a Han commandery, located to the northeast of modern Kao-ch'ing 高青 county in Shantung (Wu and Lu, 121.3148n.).

K'uan was so poor he had no resources for bare necessities, he would often cook for all [his disciples][166]; he would also sometimes steal away to work as a hired laborer to provide for [their] food and clothes. When he went out, he would always take a classical text and, when he stopped to rest, he would recite and practice it. According to the ranking [he attained] in the examination, he filled the position of Scribe for the Commandant of Justice.[167] At that time Chang T'ang 張湯 (d. 115 B.C.)[168] had just become inclined towards [Confucian] learning and because of that he made [Ni K'uan] Assistant in the Bureau of Memorials Requesting Judicial Decisions. [Ni K'uan] by means of the ancient laws[169] discussed and presented judgments on questionable and major cases, and [Chang T'ang] thought highly of and favored [Ni] K'uan. As a man [Ni] K'uan was mild-mannered and good, possessed honesty and wisdom, restrained himself, and was skilled at composing [official] documents and writing memorials. He was clever at writing but could not express himself clearly in speech. Chang T'ang regarded him as an honorable man, and repeatedly praised him. When [Chang] T'ang became Grandee Secretary,[170] he made Ni K'uan his assistant and recommended him to the Son of Heaven. The Son of Heaven questioned him during the audience and was delighted with him. Six years after Chang T'ang's death (110 B.C.), Ni K'uan became the head of the Imperial Scribes. After nine years he passed away in this office.[171] When Ni K'uan occupied the position of one of the Three Most Honorable Officials, because he was docile and good and accepted [imperial] opinions it was easy for him to [stay in

---

[166] "So-yin" explains *tu-yang* 都養 as "to cook for his disciples.

[167] *T'ing-wei* 廷尉 [Commandant of Justice] was the highest juridical position, and was one of the Nine Ministers. This Commandant of Justice was Chang T'ang 張湯.

[168] Chang T'ang was a native of Tu-ling 杜陵 (southeast of the modern city of Sian in Shensi province). Throughout his governmental career he occupied many high-ranking positions. In the third year of the Yüan-shuo reign 元朔 of the Emperor Wu (126 BC) he became a Commandant of Justice. In the second year of Yüan-ting 元鼎 (115 BC) he was charged with crimes and was forced to commit suicide. His biography can be found in "K'u-li lieh-chuan" 酷吏列傳 (*Shih chi*, 122.3137; see also Loewe, *Dictionary*, pp. 692–94).

[169] *Ku-fa* 古法 "ancient laws" are mentioned only on *Shih chi*, 106.2825 where the context makes clear they were a very strict code. They may refer to the Ch'in code, which Kao-tsu simplified in 207 BC to three articles (*Shih chi*, 8.362). Emperor Wen further mitigated the code (see his annals, *Shih chi* chapter 10 and especially 10.423ff. and also the comments on abandoning corporal punishment on 130.3303).

[170] This happened in the third year of the Yüan-shou 元狩 reign (120 BC). Grandee Secretary (*Yü-shih ta-fu* 御史大夫) was the second-highest position to that of the Chancellor (*Ch'eng-xiang* 丞相) and one of the *San-kung* 三公 (Three Honorable Officials).

[171] The "Pai-kuan kung-ch'ing piao" 百官公卿表 (The Table of Hundred Officials and Ministers) in the *Han shu* records that Ni K'uan served eight years (not nine), dying in that post in 102 BC (see Wu and Lu, 121.3148n).

office] for a long time, but as there was nothing he would revise or criticize [in these opinions], he would not rectify or criticize any of [the emperor's decisions], in official business his subordinates treated without respect and did not exert themselves on his behalf.[172] Scholar Chang also became an erudite. The grandson of scholar Fu was recruited to help put the *Shang shu* in order, but he could not clarify it.[173]

From this time on Chou Pa 周霸 of Lu and K'ung An-kuo and Chia Chia 賈嘉[174] of Lo-yang were sometimes able to explain matters in the *Shang shu*. The K'ung Clan had the old-script [version] of the *Shang shu*, which [K'ung] An-kuo read together with the modern-script [version], accordingly starting his own school [of the *Shang shu*] with this.[175] Those lost [sections of the] *Shu* he obtained were more than ten chapters, and it was surely from this that the [number of] *Shang shu* chapters increased.

Scholar Kao-t'ang 高堂生
[*Li* 禮 Transmission]

[3126] Among the [Confucian] men of learning many explained the *Li* 禮 (The Rites) but Scholar Kao-t'ang 高堂生[176] of Lu's [explanations] were fundamental. The text of the *Li*, certainly from the time of Confucius, was incomplete and when it came to the Ch'in burning the books, the books that were scattered and lost were even more. At the present we only have the "Shih-li" 士禮 (The Rites of Servicemen)[177] and Scholar Kao-t'ang was able to explain it.[178]

---

[172] As Loewe (*Dictionary*, p. 442) points out, this kind of characterization usually appears in the historian's comment, but not in the main text. The viewpoint contrasts the one about Ni K'uan in *Han shu*, where he is not only assigned a separate biography (*Han shu* chapter 58), but also regarded as a man of outstanding ability.

[173] Perhaps like his grandfather, Scholar Fu, he was not an eloquent speaker.

[174] One of the grandsons of Chia Yi 賈誼 (200–168 BC; Wu and Lu, 121.3148n.) who later rose to be a grand administrator of a commandery and one of the Nine Ministers.

[175] For a thorough discussion of the *ku-wen/chin-wen* controversy, see Hans van Ess, "The Apocryphal Texts of the Han Dynasty and the Old Text/New Text Controversy," *TP* 85 (1999): 29–64, esp. 39–47.

[176] Little else is known about Scholar Kao-t'ang. The *Han shu* (30.1710 and 88.3614) notes he was an erudite specializing on the *Li* in the early Han and transmitted a text titled *Shi li* 士禮 in seventeen *p'ien* 篇 that is thought to be the *chin-wen* 今文 version of the text we know as the *Yi li* 儀禮 (see Loewe, *Dictionary*, p. 115).

[177] See the preceding note.

[178] Takigawa (121.23–24) has added a lengthy "Cheng-yi" note (not in the 1959 Chung-hua edition nor noted in the 2013 edition) which traces the history of the ritual texts from Confucius's time; it also cites Hsieh Ch'eng 謝丞 who explains that Scholar Kao-t'ang 高堂生 was the Ch'in dynasty scholar Kao-t'ang Po-jen 高堂伯人 of Lu.

Scholar Hsü 徐生 of Lu was skilled in proper demeanor.[179] During the time of Emperor Hsiao Wen, due to his proper demeanor, Scholar Hsü became the Grand Master of the Office of Ritual.[180] [Scholar Hsü] passed on [his learning] to his son Hsü Yen 徐延[181] and even on to his grandson Hsü Hsiang 徐襄. As for Hsiang, though he was naturally endowed with skill in acting with proper demeanor, he was unable to master the *Li ching*; [Hsü] Yen was able to master more [of the *Li ching*], [but] was not skilled in it.[182] Due to his proper demeanor, Hsiang became Grand Master of the Office of Ritual of the Han and [his rank] reached Scribe of the Capital 內史 in Kuang-ling 廣陵.[183] Yen and the disciples of the Hsü Clan, Kung-hu Man-yi 公戶滿意,[184] Huan Sheng 桓生 and Shan Tz'u 單次,[185] had all been Grand Masters of the Office of Ritual. Moreover, Hsiao Fen 蕭奮[186] of Hsia-ch'iu 瑕丘,[187] through [his knowledge or the *Li*], became Grand Administrator of Huai-yang 淮陽 [Commandery]. After this, those who could explain the *Li* and show proper demeanor all came from the Hsü Clan.

Shang Ch'ü 商瞿
[*Shang shu* 尚書 Transmission]

[3127] Since Shang Ch'ü 商瞿[188] received [instruction] in the Yi 易(Changes) from Confucius,[189] when Confucius expired, Shang Ch'ü passed down the *Yi*

---

[179] On *Han shu* (88.3614) the text reads *sung* 頌 for *jung* 容.

[180] That is, *Li-kuan ta-fu* 禮官大夫 (not in Bielenstein).

[181] See the entry in Loewe, *Dictionary*, p. 624.

[182] Or "was not skilled in acting with proper demeanor."

[183] The kingdom of Kuang-ling 廣陵 was located on the north bank of Yangtze River in modern Kiangsu Province with its capital northwest of modern Yangchow (Wang Li-ch'i, 121.2557).

[184] He reached the rank of *T'ai-chung Ta-fu* 太中大夫 (Grand Palace Grandee) under Emperor Chao 漢昭帝 (r. 94-74 BC; see also Loewe, *Dictionary*, p. 123).

[185] For Huan Sheng and Shan Tz'u see the entry in Loewe, *Dictionary*, p. 624 (under Hsü Yen).

[186] See the entry in Loewe, *Dictionary*, p. 603.

[187] A Han county near modern Yen-chou 兗州 in Shantung (Wang Li-ch'i, 121.2557n.).

[188] His *agnomen* was Tzu-mu 子木 ("So-yin"). He has a short biography focusing on his transmission of the *Yi* in the "Chung-ni Ti-tzu lieh-chuan" 仲尼弟子列傳 (Memoir of the Disciples of Confucius), *Shih chi*, 67.2211 (*Grand Scribe's Records*, 7:79).

[189] The syntax of the original text is awkward. The *Han shu* formulation is much clearer (compare *Han shu*, 88.3597 and "So-yin"). The renderings by Wu and Lu (121.3157) and Wang Li-ch'i (121.2563) are similarly awkward.

[tradition],[190] in the sixth generation reaching, T'ien Ho 田何,[191] a native of Ch'i, *agnomen* Tzu-chuang 子莊. When the Han arose, T'ien Ho passed down the *Yi* [tradition] to Wang T'ung 王同,[192] a native of Tung-wu 東武,[193] *agnomen* Tzu-ch'ung 子仲.[194] Tzu-ch'ung passed down the *Yi* [tradition] to Yang Ho 楊何,[195] a native Tzu-ch'uan 菑川.[196] [Yang] Ho, due to [his mastery of] the *Yi* [tradition], was recruited [by the education officials] in the first year of the Yüan-kuang 元光 Era (134 B.C.), his official position reaching that of Palace Grandee. Chi-mo Ch'eng 即墨成,[197] a native of Ch'i, due to [his mastery of] the *Yi* [tradition] reached the position of Minister of Ch'eng-yang 城陽.[198] Meng Tan 孟但,[199] a native of Kuang-ch'uan 廣川,[200] due to [his mastery of] the *Yi* [tradition], became the Grandee at the Gate of the Heir-apparent. Chou Pa,[201] a native of Lu, Hung Hu 衡胡,[202] a native of Chü 莒,[203] Chu-fu Yen 主父偃,[204] a native of Lin-tzu 臨菑,[205] all due to [their mastery of] the *Yi* [tradition] reached positions with [an emolument of] two thousand *shih*. However, in essence those who explained the *Yi* all originated from the school of Yang Ho.

[190] All these references to "passing down the Yi" refer to what was learned from their teachers, perhaps including an oral version of the text and its commentary as well some documentary material.

[191] See also *Shih chi*, 67.2211 and Loewe, *Dictionary*, p. 507.

[192] See also *Shih chi*, 67.2211.

[193] A Han county near modern Chu-ch'eng 諸城 County in Shantung (Wang Li-ch'i, 121.2558n).

[194] Takigawa (121.25) points out that the *Han shu* parallel here mentions three other scholars who transmitted the *Yi*: Chou Wang-sun 周王孫 and Ting K'uan 丁寬 from Lo-yang and Scholar Fu 服生 from Ch'i.

[195] See also *Shih chi*, 67.2211.

[196] A Han kingdom created in 164 BC located in modern Shantung (see n. 2 on *Grand Scribe's Records*, 9:363 and Wang Li-ch'i, 112.2373).

[197] Otherwise unknown.

[198] Ch'eng-yang was a kingdom in modern Shantung with its capital at Chü 莒 (Wang Li-ch'i, 121.2558n.).

[199] Otherwise unknown.

[200] On Kuang-ch'uan see n. 207 on Tung Chung-shu's birthplace just below.

[201] Chou Pa is said to have been a *Shang shu* scholar (see text above).

[202] Otherwise unknown.

[203] The capital of the kingdom of Ch'eng-yang (see n. 201 above).

[204] See his biography in *Shih chi* chapter 112 (*Grand Scribe's Records*, 9373–89).

[205] Lin-tzu is located in modern Shantung province about forty miles northwest of the modern city of Tzu-po 淄博; it had been a capital of Ch'i during the Warring States era (T'an Ch'i-hsiang, 2:20).

Tung Chung-shu 董仲舒
[*Ch'un ch'iu* 春秋 Transmission]

Tung Chung-shu 董仲舒[206] was a native of Kuang-ch'uan 廣川.[207] Because he applied himself to settling [the meaning of] the *Ch'un ch'iu* 春秋 (Spring and Autumn Annals), he became an erudite in the reign of Emperor Hsiao-ching. He lectured and intoned [the text] having lowered the curtains [in the room].[208] His disciples transmitted [his teachings] by receiving instruction from each other according to their length of study [with him]. Some had never seen his face.[209] It seems that Tung Chung-shu did not view his courtyard garden for three years, such was his focused concentration.[210] In advancing, withdrawing, maintaining a presentable appearance, and bearing,[211] he did

---

[206] Tung Chung-shu has an independent biography in *Han shu* (56.2495–2526). The most extensive study of Tung is Michael Loewe's *Dong Zhongshu, A 'Confucian' Heritage and the Chunqiu fanlu* (Leiden and Boston: Brill, 2011; hereafter Loewe, *Dong Zhongshu*); Loewe provides a translation of this biography (on pp. 45–47), followed by a rendition of the *Han shu* biography (pp. 47–50) and an analysis of these texts (pp. 50–81). Compare Van Ess, *Politik*, 1:274–83.

[207] Kuang-ch'uan was a county thirty miles east of modern Tsao-ch'iang 棗強 County, some eighty miles southeast of Shih-chia-chuang, in Hopei (T'an Ch'i-hsiang, 2:26). Loewe (*Dong Zhongshu*, p. 50) points out that Tung would have been born in the Han state of Chao. Takigawa (121.26) further locates Tung's birthplace in Wen-ch'eng 溫城 in Kuang-ch'uan county (see also the lengthy note in Wang Hsien-ch'ien 王先謙 [1842–1917] *Han shu pu-chu* 漢書補注, 56.4017, which locates Wen-ch'eng in the early Han state of Hsin-tu 新都). The *Yi* 易 scholar Meng Tan (text just above) was also born in Kuang-ch'uan.

Meng T'an, introduced just above, was also a scholar from Kuang-ch'uan.

[208] The sense of *hsia wei* 下帷 may be to divide teacher from students as occurred in some classical classrooms and as Burton Watson (2:368) understands the passage. But we read it as closing off both teacher and students from outside diversions (see Loewe, *Dong Zhongshu*, p. 45: "read his books in seclusion"). Thus "he did not view his courtyard garden for three years." The fact that some students had never seen his face was due to his practice of having his students who had been with him for a longer period of time teach the newer arrivals.

[209] Yen Shih-ku's *Han shu* note to the *Han shu* parallel (56.2495) reads: "This means that new students would receive instruction from his older disciples and did not necessarily meet [Tung] Chung-shu in person" 師古曰：言新學者但就其舊弟子受業，不必親見仲舒.

[210] Loewe reads (p. 45) "was never seen in the garden of his residence." Both readings emphasize Tung's lucubration. Wang Shu-min (121.3269) cites a number of *lei-shu* that read "for ten years" and also note that he rode a horse for three years without realizing whether it was a mare or a stallion.

[211] In the "Sheng chih" 聖治 chapter of the *Hsiao ching* 孝經 Confucius is said to have depicted a gentleman as one whose "deportment is worthy of contemplation; his movements in advancing or retiring are all according to the proper rule"; 容止可觀，進退可度.

nothing that went against social norms.[212] The scholars[213] all honored him as "Tutor."[214] When the present sovereign [*3128*] ascended the throne,[215] [Tung] became [Prime] Minister of Chiang-tu 江都.[216] He used the disasters and abnormal celestial phenolmenon [recorded in] the *Ch'un ch'iu* to infer that by which *yin* and *yang* move in alteration.[217] For this reason, in seeking when seeking rain, he shut off the various *yang*

[212] Or "did not act against ritual practice" 非禮不行.

[213] *Hsüeh-shih* 學士, referring to men of learning who were part of the Han educational system. See also the Glossary at the end of this volume (compare *hsüeh-che* 學者, a general term for "men of learning").

[214] Compare *Shih chi*, 7.315: "Only then did [Hsiang Yü] honor King Huai as Emperor Yi" 乃尊懷王為義帝 (translation revised slightly from *Grand Scribes' Records*, 1:194).

[215] In the *Han shu* parallel (56.2495–2522) there three imperial edicts and Tung's replies to them just before this line (not translated in Loewe, *Dong Zhongshu*).

[216] After the suppression of the Rebellion of the Seven Kings in 154 BC, the rebellious state of Wu was renamed Chiang-tu 江都 with its capital in Kuang-ling 廣陵 (located near modern Yangchow in Kiangsu). Liu Fei 劉非 (168–127 BC), Emperor Wu's elder brother, was moved from King of Ju-nan 汝南 (r. 155–154 BC) to become Chiang-tu's first king. He had distinguished himself in subduing Wu. But he was seen to be too warlike and given to luxury. Thus after Tung Chung-shu presented his third memorial to the newly enthroned Emperor Wu (ca. 140 BC), Tung was appointed [Prime?] Minister of Chiang-tu to curb Liu Fei's excesses (perhaps this was done by one of the Emperor's advisors, since Liu Fei could have been seen as a threat to Emperor Wu's rule; Michael Loewe believes Tung served in Chiang-tu from about 124-120 BC [*Dong Zhongshu*, p. 53]). The *Han shu* (56.2523) parallel reads: "When his responses [three memorials in response to the emperor's summons for talented men] were completed, the Emperor appointed Chung-shu as the Prime Minister of Chiang-tu to serve King Yi. King Yi was the Emperor's elder brother. He had always been arrogant and too fond of acts of bravery. Chung-shu rectified [the King's behavior] through ritual and righteousness. The King respected [Tung] for this." 對既畢，天子以仲舒為江都相，事易王。易王，帝兄，素驕，好勇。仲舒以禮誼匡正，王敬重焉. See also the entry for Liu Fei in Loewe, *Dictionary*, p. 296.

This demotion represented a reduction in salary from two thousand *shih* to one thousand *shih* (Han Chao-ch'i, 121.5972n.).

[217] This presumably refers to the *Ch'un ch'iu fan-lu* 春秋繁露 that is traditionally attributed to Tung. Loewe argues that it is a composite text collecting the writings of several authors, but reflecting some of Tung's ideas (Loewe, *Dong Zhongshu*, p. 212).

We read *pien* 變 as *t'ien-pien* 天變, "celestial phenomenon" (see "Wu-hsing chih" 五行志中 on *Han shu*, 27.1425: 災異俞甚，天變成形). Another possible reading is *shih pien* 事變 (exigency, emergency). Loewe (*Dong Zhong shu*, p. 48) translates: "In administering the kingdom, by noting the changes wrought by way of disaster and abnormality, as recorded in the *Chunqiu*, [Dong] Zhongshu predicted how aberrations come about thanks to Yin and Yang." Loewe seems to have mistakenly included a translation of the phrase "Chung-shu chih kuo" 仲

[forces] of *yang* and let loose the various *yin* [forces]; should he want to stop the rain,[218] he reversed this.[219] When he practiced this throughout the state [i.e., Chiang-tu], he never failed to obtain that which he desired. In the midst [of his service], [Tung] was removed [from the position of Prime Minister] and made a Palace Grandee. He lived at home [220] and wrote *Tsai-yi chih chi* 災異之記 [A Record of Disasters and Abnormalities].[221] At this time, there was a disastrous [fire] in Kao[-tsu's] temple in Liao-tung 遼東 [Commandery].[222] Chu-fu Yen 主父偃 [223] was distressed by [the fire], took Tung's book, and presented it to the Emperor. When the Emperor summoned the

舒治國 "in administering the kingdom" here (it occurs only in the *Han shu* biography, not in the *Shih chi*).

[218] Takigawa (121.26) quotes Yen Shih-ku 顏師古 (581–645) that "shutting off all the *yang* elements" 閉諸陽 refers to shutting the southern gates and forbidding raising fires; "letting loose all the *yin* elements" 縱諸陰 refers to opening the northern gates and spraying water about (Takigawa, 121.26). The details of Tung Chung-shu's method of praying for rain and stopping the rain can be found in his *Ch'un ch'iu fan-lu* 春秋繁露.

[219] On various texts that record Tung's system of rainmaking see Loewe, *Dong Zhongshu*, pp. 168–173.

[220] *Chü-she* 居舍. Loewe (*Dong Zhongshu*, p. 46) has "in the residence of his office"; Watson (2:368): "lived in the dormitory for officials"; but see *Han-yü ta tz'u-tien*, 4:23a.

[221] Although the Chung-hua edition reads 災異之記 as a book title, it is possible it simply refers to "recording of disasters and abnormalities"; the *Han shu* parallel does not include this sentence. See also the description of Liu Hsiang appealing to the emperor by "bringing together the records of portents, omens, disasters and abnormalities from highest antiquity on down through the Spring and Autumn and Six Kingdoms to the Ch'in and Han, to deduce guides to behavior"; 集合上古以來歷春秋六國至秦漢符瑞災異之記，推跡行事 (*Han shu*, 36.1950) where *tsai-yi chih chi* clearly does not refer to a book title (nor does "Ch'un ch'iu" 春秋). In the *Han shu* account Tung Chung-shu's deductions from such events are shifted to after the disastrous fire depicted just below (see text and notes following).

[222] The fire occurred in the sixth year of Chien-yüan 建元 (135 BC; Wang Li-ch'i, 121.3150n). Tung's biography in the *Han shu* (56.2524) gives details as follows: "Previously fires had broken out in the Kao-tsu's shrine in Liao-tung and in the main hall in the grounds of Kao-tsu's [tomb] at Ch'ang-ling. Living at home, Chung-shu had propounded his opinions [in writing], but had not yet submitted the draft to the emperor. Chu-fu Yen had been keeping an eye on Chung-shu and had stolen a glance [at the draft]. Envious of Tung, he stole the document and presented it to him [the emperor]"; 先是遼東高廟、長陵高園殿災，仲舒居家推說其意，槁未上，主父偃候仲舒，私見，嫉之，竊其書而奏焉. Takigawa (121.27) argues that the fires took place before Tung was sent to Chiang-tu; he also cites Ch'ien Ta-hsin 錢大昕 (1728–1804) and Wang Hsien-ch'ien, both of whom believe that there is probably no connection between the fires and Chu-fu Yen's submitting Tung's draft to the emperor.

[223] See his biography in *Shih chi* chapter 112 (*Grand Scribe's Records*, 9:373-89).

various scholars[224] and showed them his book, there were attacks and criticism [of the book].[225] Lü Pu-shu 呂步舒,[226] a disciple of Tung Chung-shu's, not knowing it was his tutor's book, took it to be the lowest stupidity.[227] At this point, Tung Chung-shu was handed over to the legal officials and deemed deserving the death penalty. An imperial decree pardoned him. From then on Tung Chung-shu did not dare to speak of disasters and abnormalities again.

[224] Here we use "various scholars" for *chu sheng* 諸生, although we have used scholars for *hsüeh shih* 學士 above. English does not have a good alternative for either expression. For the passage on *Shih chi*, 12.473: 太常諸生行禮不如魯善, our translation (*Grand Scribes' Records*, 2:242) read: "The performance of the rites by the various scholars under the Grand Master of Ceremonies is not as good as that of [the state of] Lu." Bielenstein (pp. 20-21) notes that the Grand Master of Ceremonies oversaw the T'ai-hsüeh 太學 (Grand Academy) and it is possible that *chu sheng* here refers to the "various students" then in the Academy. This possibility is enhanced by the following sentence in which a disciple of Tung Chung-shu criticizes the book.

[225] The "Wu-hsing chih" 五行志 (Treatise on the Five Phases) in the *Han shu* records Tung Chung-shu's analysis about the fire in detail (27A.1332). Tung believes the incident was a warning from Heaven, therefore the unjust nobles and courtiers should be killed to restore the righteousness. This is why the book was censured for "containing a slanderous attack" 有刺譏. Interestingly, these three graphs are missing in *Han shu* "Tung Chung-shu chuan." Pan Ku 班固 may have altered the text to avoid mentioning Tung's having criticized the imperial court as a means to maintain Tung's image as "the head of Confucian scholars" 群儒首. See *Han shu*, 56.2524 and 2526.

[226] Lü Pu-shu was a native of Wen 溫, Tung Chung-shu's hometown. His name was also written 呂步荼 ("Chi-chieh" citing Hsü Kuang 徐廣). Loewe (*Dong Zhongshu*, p. 46, n. 14) points out that the *Yen-t'ieh lun* claims Lü was put to death for loose talk (*nung-k'ou* 弄口).

[227] Compare *Lun yü*, 17.3: "The Master said, 'There are only the wise of the highest class and the stupid of the lowest which cannot be changed'" 子曰：唯上知與下愚不移.

Tung Chung-shu as a man acted honestly and straightforwardly.[228] At this time, [the Han] had just expelled the Four Barbarians beyond its borders.[229] Kung-sun Hung 公孫弘, [although] in settling [the meaning of] the *Ch'un ch'iu* could not compare with Tung Chung-shu,[230] yet Hung catered to [the customs] of the age[231] and was employed

[228] Compare *Shih chi*, 121.3123: "After a short time, Emperor Ching, taking into consideration [Yüan] Ku's honesty and straightforwardness, appointed Ku as Grand Tutor of King of Ch'ing-ho 居頃之，景帝以[轅]固為廉直，拜為清河王太傅; see also *Shih chi*, 63.2147. Han Fei "mourned for the upright who were no tolerated by wicked and perverse vassals" 悲廉直不容於邪枉之臣; *Shih chi*, 96.2683: [申屠]嘉為人廉直，門不受私謁 [*Grand Scribes' Records*, 8:223: "[Shen-t'u] Chia as a man was pure and straightforward; he would not receive those who came to his gate on private matters"].

Compare the assessment of Kung-sun Hung's character: "Hung was a man who was out of the ordinary and well informed" 弘為人恢奇多聞 (*Shih chi*, 112.2950) and again "Hung was a man who dwelt on jealousy, appearing to be tolerant, but with [harmful thoughts] deep inside him" 弘為人意忌，外寬內深 (*Shih chi*, 112.2951).

[229] Although there are references in both "Ch'in-shih-huang pen-chi" 秦始皇本紀 (*Shih chi*, 6.271; *Grand Scribe's Records*, 1:160) and "T'ien-kuan shu" 天官書 (Treatise on the Governors of the Heavens; *Shih chi*, 27.1348) to Ch'in expelling the Four Barbarians beyond its borders, the *locus classicus* is the *Ku-liang chuan* 穀梁傳 (Duke Hsi 僖公, 4) which credits Duke Huan of Ch'i with saving the empire by expelling the Four Barbarians 桓公救中國，而攘夷狄.

Although the Four Barbarians (*Ssu-yi* 四夷) became a standard designation for the foreign tribes on the Chinese borders and is used a number of times in the *Shih chi*, it is not defined. It generally refers to the Eastern Yi 東夷, the Southern Man 南蠻, the Western Jung 西戎, and the Northern Ti 北狄. Here it may well refer to the expeditions against the Hsiung-nu 匈奴, Nan Yüeh 南越, Min Yüeh 閩越, Ch'ao-hsien 朝鮮, and Hsi-nan Yi 西南夷 during the reign of Emperor Wu (see also *Shih chi* chapters 110, 113, 114, 115 and 116).

[230] Kung-sun Hung's biography says he only began to study the various schools of *Ch'un ch'iu* when he was over forty (*Shih chi*, 112.2949 and *Grand Scribe's Records*, 9:364–65).

[231] See also the comments on Shu-sun T'ung's biography (*Shih chi*, 99.2726: "Shu-sun T'ung adapted himself to the customs of the times and considered what was needed, regulating the rituals and his behavior according to the times, in the end becoming the ancestor of the Confucian School. 'The great upright one seems to be crouching, the way is indeed serpentine [from *Lao Zi*, 45],' this may well be said about him" (modified from *Grand Scribes' Records*, 8:301); 叔孫通希世度務，制禮進退，與時變化，卒為漢家儒宗.「大直若詘，道固委蛇」，蓋謂是乎?

See also the "Jang-wang" 讓王 chapter of the *Chuang Tzu* (Wang Hsien-ch'ien, *Chuang Tzu chi-chieh* 莊子集解 [Peking: Chung-hua, 1987], 8.255), where Yüan Hsien 原憲 is said to have been living in poverty when he was visited by Tzu-kung 子貢, then a wealthy official. Tzu-kung lamented Yüan Hsien's apparent distress, and Yüan replied: "'To act catering to the customs of the age [or "of the world"]; to pretend to be public-spirited and yet be a partisan; to learn in order to please men; to teach for the sake of one's own gain; to conceal one's wickedness

[in government] matters, his position reaching that of a high official. Tung Chung-shu considered Hung a fawning flatterer. Only when [Kung-sun] Hung was distressed by this did he speak of him to the sovereign, "Tung Chung-shu is the only one who can be appointed as the Prime Minister of the King of Chiao-hsi 膠西."[232] The King of Chiao-hsi had always heard that Tung Chung-shu had acted virtuously [like Po Yi and Shu Ch'i][233] and treated him charitably. Tung Chung-shu was afraid that if he stayed long [in Chiao-hsi] he would incur offense, so he claimed illness to resign from his position and live at home. Until he died he never managed his property,[234] giving full service to

under the garb of benevolence and righteousness; and to be fond of the show of chariots and horses: these are things which I, Hsien, cannot bear to do"; 夫希世而行，比周而友，學以為人，教以為己，仁義之慝，輿馬之飾，憲不忍為也.

[232] The King of Chiao-hsi was Liu Tuan 劉端 (born in 165 BC; r. 154–108 BC), King Yü 于 of Chiao-hsi. He was the eighth son of Emperor Ching. According to "Wu-tsung shih-chia" 五宗世家 (Hereditary House of the Five Lineages [referring to the five mothers of Emperor Ching's thirteen sons]; *Shih chi*, 59.2097) Liu Tuan was extremely excessive in his behavior, fond of executing anyone who went against his wishes. Since to go along with Liu Tuan often meant violating Han law, many officials in Chiao-hsi were also condemned by the central government. Thus Kung-sun Hung hoped that by having Tung Chung-shu assigned to Chiao-hsi he would bring about his downfall (see also Wang Li-ch'i, 121.3150n; Takigawa, 121.28; and Loewe, *Dictionary*, pp. 293–94). The *Han shu* parallel (56.2525) has an additional sentence here explaining the king's depravity and the danger to high officials in his state.

[233] Reading *yu hsing* 有行 as in *Meng Tzu.* "Kung-sun Ch'ou, shang" 公孫丑，上: "'Their [Po Yi 伯夷 and Yi Yin's 伊尹] ways were different from mine,' said Mencius. 'Not to serve a prince whom he did not esteem, nor command a people whom he did not approve; in a time of good government to take office, and on the occurrence of confusion to retire–this was the way of Po Yi. To say "Whom may I not serve? My serving him makes him my ruler. What people may I not command? My commanding them makes them my people." In a time of good government to take office, and when disorder prevailed, also to take office–that was the way of Yi Yin. When it was proper to go into office, then to go into it; when it was proper to keep retired from office, then to keep retired from it; when it was proper to continue in it long, then to continue in it long–when it was proper to withdraw from it quickly, then to withdraw quickly–that was the way of Confucius. These were all sages of antiquity, and I have not attained *to act virtuously* [as they did]. But what I wish to do is to learn to be like Confucius" (revised slightly from Legge, 2:193-4); 不同道。非其君不事，非其民不使；治則進，亂則退，伯夷也。何事非君，何使非民；治亦進，亂亦進，伊尹也。可以仕則仕，可以止則止，可以久則久，可以速則速，孔子也。皆古聖人也，吾未能有行焉；乃所願，則學孔子也. See also the *locus classicus* of the expression in the "Sheng-te"盛德 chapter of the *Ta Tai li chi* 大戴禮記 "Those who are able to enact virtuous laws are [those who] have virtuous 能行德法者為有行 (8.7a, *SPTK*).

[234] The *Han shu* parallel (56.2525) reads "until he died he never asked about his family property" (reading 終不問家產業 for 終不治產業). Shen Ch'in-han 沈欽韓 (1735–1831; cited in *Han shu pu-chu*, 56.4055n.) notes that the "Tsan-hsüeh p'ien" 讚學篇 of the *Ch'ien-fu lun*

honing his scholarship and writing books. For this reason,[235] in the period from the rise of the Han until its fifth generation,[236] only Tung Chung-shu gained fame for having gained an understanding of the *Ch'un ch'iu*. His explications were [based on the text] by Mr. Kung-yang 公羊.[237]

Scholar Hu-wu 胡毋生

Scholar Hu-wu 胡毋生[238] was a native of Ch'i. He became an erudite in the time of Emperor Hsiao-ching, [but] because he was too old, he returned home to teach. Of the scholars who explicated the *Ch'un ch'iu* in Ch'i, most received [instruction] from Scholar Hu-wu. Kung-sun Hung also received some [instruction] from him.

潛夫論 reads: "Tung Chung-shu till the end of his life did not inquire about his family's affairs" 董仲舒終身不問家事, which Wang Hsien-ch'ien argues is similar to the *Shih chi* account. My thanks to Hans van Ess for pointing this out.

[235] These two sentences do not occur in the *Han shu* parallel (56.2525).

[236] That is, *Wu shih* 五世 "Five *Royal* Generations" or eras refer to the reigns of Kao-tsu, Emperor Hui, Emperor Wen, Emperor Ching, and the reigning Emperor Wu.

[237] Reading *chuan* 傳 as "explication" (compare *Kung-yang chuan*, Duke Ting, 1: 主人習 其讀而問其傳).

The *Kung-yang Chuan* 公羊傳 was a commentarial tradition on the *Ch'un ch'iu* that originated with Tzu Hsia 子夏 and was orally transmitted until Kung-yang Kao 公羊高 (otherwise unknown) wrote it down during Emperor Ching's reign (see Loewe, *Early Chinese Texts*, p. 68).

Tung Chung-shu's biography in the *Han shu* (56.2525-26; Loewe, *Dong Zhongshu*, pp. 49-50) contains two more paragraphs tracing his career in more detail, recording his death of natural causes at an advanced age, and briefly introducing his writings.

[238] Hu-wu is a double surname (see "So-yin," *Shih chi*, 121.3118). His *agnomen* was Tzu-tu 子都 (Takigawa, 121.28) and he was a native of T'ai-shan 泰山 in Ch'i (compare Huang Ch'ing-hsüan 黃慶萱, *Shih chi, Han shu, "Ju-lin lieh-chuan shu-cheng"* 史記，漢書 "儒林列 傳"疏證. [Taipei: Chia-hsin Shui-ni Kung-ssu Wen-hua Chi-chin-hui, 1966], p. 93, n. 21). The Po-na edition (121.12a) reads Hu-mu 胡母. He has a slightly more detailed biography on *Han shu*, 88:3615, where it is pointed out that he shared Tung Chung-shu's "enterprise" (*yeh* 業) to established the Kung-yang Commentary and that he praised the virtue of Tung's writings. This section also notes that when Tung was a minister in Chiang-tu he composed his own written commentary (*chuan* 傳) on the *Ch'un ch'iu* which other of his followers (listed in the *Shih chi* after the biography of Scholar Chiang) adhered to. For more details see Huang Ch'ing-hsüan, op. cit., p. 230, n. 3).

Scholar Chiang 江生

[3129] Scholar Chiang 江生[239] of Hsia-ch'iu 瑕丘[240] worked on the *Ku-liang Ch'un ch'iu*.[241] From the time Kung-sun Hung obtained employment [in the government], he used to gather and compare their [the various *Ch'un ch'iu* scholars'] ideas but in the end he employed Tung Chung-shu's.[242]

Those of Chung-shu's disciples who achieved success[243] were Ch'u Ta 褚大 of Lan-ling 蘭陵,[244] Yin Chung 殷忠[245] of Kuang-ch'uan, [and] Lü Pu-shu of Wen 溫.[246] Ch'u Ta reached [the position of] Minister of Liang,[247] Pu-shu reached [the position of] Chief Clerk.[248] He was sent carrying a caduceus to adjudicate the sentence of [the King of] Huai-nan.[249] As for the feudal lords who had made arbitrary decisions without

---

[239] In the *Han shu* parallel (88.3617) Scholar Chiang 江公 is said to have received instruction in the *Ku-liang Ch'un ch'iu* and the *Shih* from Master Shen P'ei 申培公 of Lu 魯 and to have passed this on to his son and grandson, both erudites. The emperor had him compete with Tung Chung-shu in discussing the *Ch'un ch'iu*, but Chiang could match Tung's arguments and thus for a time the *Kung-yang Ch'un ch'iu* that Tung advocated was dominant at court. On this

[240] Hsia-ch'iu was a Han county just north of modern Yen-chou 兗州, about twenty miles northeast of Tsining in Shantung (T'an Ch'i-hsiang, 2:19).

[241] Ku-liang refers to Ku-liang Ch'ih 穀梁赤, the founder of Ku-liang Commentary of *Ch'un ch'iu* (Wang Li-ch'i, 121.3151n). The Ku-liang Commentary seems to have been first written down only during Emperor Wu's reign (Loewe, *Early Chinese Texts*, p. 68).

[242] Which were those based on the Kung-yang School.

[243] *Ti-tzu sui-che* 弟子遂者; several editions read *t'ung-che* 通者 (those who found their way through [government ranks]), an expression which occurs just below in the text. The text here could also be read "among those who were accomplished [in the *Ch'un ch'iu*].

[244] According to "So-yin" (*Shih chi*, 12.451), Ch'u was the grand-uncle of Ch'u Shao-sun 褚少孫 and was also an erudite (*Shih chi*, 30.1433).

Lan-ling was a Han county about fifty miles northeast of modern Hsü-chou in Shantung (T'an Ch'i-hsiang, 2:20). Hsün Tzu served as an assistant magistrate (*ling* 令) there and his traditions continued into the Han (Huang Ch'ing-hsüan, op. cit., p. 95, n. 27)

[245] Otherwise unknown. The "Chi-chieh" cites Hsü Kuang that one variant of Yin Chung's surname was 段, and another was 瑕 (Takigawa, 121.29).

[246] Wen was a Han county about ten miles west of modern Wen County, some thirty-five miles east of Loyang in Honan (T'an Ch'i-hsiang, 2:16).

[247] Liang was a vassal state of Han, with its capital located near Sui-yang 睢陽 (south of modern Shang-ch'iu in Honan; Wang Li-ch'i, 121.3151n).

[248] *Chang-shih* 長史. The *Han shu* parallel reads *Ch'eng-hsiang Chang-shih* 丞相長史.

[249] Liu An 劉安 (r. 164–122 BC), the King of Huai-nan, was the son of Liu Ch'ang 劉長 (King Li 厲王 of Huai-nan; 198–174 BC), grandson of Liu Pang. In the first year of Yüan-shou

[imperial] authority, he did not report them [to the Emperor], [but] corrected them according to the principles of the *Ch'un ch'iu*. The Son of Heaven considered all [these things that Lü Pu-shu did] to be right. [Tung Chung-shu's] disciples who best found their way through [government ranks][250] reached the position of Grandees at Imperial Command[251]; those who Palace Attendants, Internuncios, [and] Authorities on Ancient Matters could be counted by the hundreds. Moreover, Tung Chung-shu's sons and grandsons because of their study all reached [the positions of] high officials.

*   *   *   *   *

From the time K'ung Tzu expired, scholars of the capital did not venerate the country schools; only during the Chien-yüan (140-135 B.C.) and Yüan-shou (122–117 B.C.) eras, did literary writings exhibit brilliance. [Thus] I composed the "Memoir of the Confucian Scholars, Number Sixty-one."[252]

元狩 (122 BC) his conspiracy to rebel was unmasked and he committed suicide. The trial also involved other vassals, such as Liu Tz'u 劉賜 (d. 122 BC), the King of Heng-shan 衡山, Liu Fei 劉非, the King of Chiang-tu, and Liu Chi 劉寄 (?–121 BC), the King of Chiao-tung 膠東 (Wang Li-ch'i, 121.3151n). On Lü Pu-shu's role see also *Han shu*, 27A.1333 and Loewe, *Dictionary*, p. 420). See also the translation of *Shih chi* chapter 118 in this volume.

[250] The text here could also be read "those who mastered [the *Ch'un ch'iu*]" 弟子通者.

[251] The reading of *ming ta-fu* 命大夫 as "command counselor" is tentative. This passage might also be read "those who reached by imperial command [the positions of] Counselor (or "Grandee"), Palace Attendant, etc."

[252] These are the reasons, given on *Shih chi*, 130.3318, for the composition of this chapter: 自孔子卒，京師莫崇庠序，唯建元元狩之間，文辭粲如也。作儒林列傳第六十一。

Translator's Note

Although there is no template for *Shih chi* chapters, this memoir stands out structurally. Wu Chien-ssu notes some of the vagaries:

Every piece of writing [in the *Shih chi*] has a head and a tail. This memoir alone has a head but no tail. As a start it goes from the Chou to the Wei, to the Ch'in, Ch'en She, Hsiang Chi, to the rise of the Han. First exalting Confucius, it then comes to [his disciples] Tzu-lu, Tzu-chang, Tzu-yü, Tzu-hsia, Tzu-kung, then comes to Tzu-fang, Tuan-kan Mu, Wu Ch'i, Ch'in-ku Hsi, then comes to Excellency Hsün, Meng Tzu, K'ung Chia, on down to Shun-shu T'ung, Wang Tsang and Chao Wan, first stringing them together to compose a section, then afterwards moving in and out of biographical accounts in the midst of which are inserted reflections on Kung-sun Hung. In the front part it is loose, in the back it is tight, at the front it summarizes [what a Confucian scholar is], in the back is treats them separately, a unique form of composition. 凡文各有首尾，獨此傳有首無尾，以前由周而魏，而秦，而陳涉，項藉，以致漢興。首崇孔子，而及子路，子張，子羽，子夏，子貢，而及田子方，段干木，吳起，禽滑釐,而及荀卿，孟子，孔甲，以致叔孫通，王臧，趙綰，先穿挽作一篇，乃後又出入傳，中間處處以公孫弘插映，前散後整，前合後分，另一體格. Cited from Wu Chien-ssu (fl. 1686), *Shih chi lun-wen* 史記論文 (Shanghai: Shang-hai Ku-chi, 2008), p. 72.

Although Wu goes on to praise the compositional skill found in these juxtapositions, the chapter seems to the modern reader to lack coherence as it moves from the Grand Scribe's disappointment with current methods of picking educational officials, to a survey of Confucian text transmission, to Kung-sun's Hung's memorial, then through the Six Classics and finally to a biography of Tung Chung-shu. Wu Chien-ssu notes that not only Kung-sun Hung's memorial but various references to him are inserted throughout the text, including Tung Chung-shu's contempt for him as "a fawning flatterer" (*song yü* 從諛).[253] Takigawa (121.1–2) also speculates that this

---

[253] "*Shih chi*, 120.3106: "The Son of Heaven established the high officials as assisting ministers, would you rather have me fawn and flatter every whim, [thereby] causing [our] Lord to fall into unrighteousness? Now [that] I am already in this position, even though I cherish myself, how can I bring shame over this court!" 天子置公卿輔弼之臣，寧令從諛承意，陷主於不義乎？且已在其位，縱愛身，奈辱朝廷何！.

chapter originally was "a unified piece" (*yi p'ien* 一篇), not broken into "sections that each begin with a new line" (*mei tuan t'i-hang* 每段提行) but this seems to refer simply to the *Shih chi p'ing-lin* 史記評林 (Takigawa's base edition, see Introduction to this volume) practice of breaking the text into sections.

One way to make sense of this confusion of Confucianism can be found in the comments of T'ang Hsieh 湯諧 (fl. 1700) argues that this chapter is intended to censure (*pien* 貶) Kung-sun Hung and exalt (*tsun* 尊) Tung Chung-shu:

> In composing the "Memoir on the Confucian scholars, aside from a joint account of the Confucian scholars of the Six Classics, His Honor the [Grand] Scribe had yet another hidden meaning, to censure Kung-sun [Hung] and to exalt Master Tung [Chung-shu], to belittle Kung-sun's conforming to the world to obtain honor and face/fame, and to lament Master Tung's suffering distress because of following the upright way.
>
> 傳儒林自是并敘六經諸儒，然史公卻另有微意，則以貶公孫而尊董子，薄公孫之希世取榮容，而悲董子之直道見疾也.[254]

Thus although Ssu-ma Ch'ien's biography of Kung-sun Hung (chapter 112) already makes clear the kind of reprehensible man Kung-sun is, this chapter adds further condemnation put in words of Tung Chung-shu and Yüan Ku. This technique of criticizing a person in a chapter other than his biography is found throughout the *Shih chi*. In the preceding chapter (chapter 120) Chi An also berates Kung-sun.

Moreover, Kung-sun Hung seems to be representative of one of the two types of Confucians that Ssu-ma Ch'ien recognizes. These types can best be seen in the Grand Scribe's opening remarks to the "Yu hsia lieh-chuan" 游俠列傳 (Memoir on the Knight-errants):

> Master Han says: "The Confucians with their learning pervert the law, the knights with their contentiousness violate the prohibitions."[255] Both are to be ridiculed, yet the [Confucian] scholars are much praised by the world. At one extreme they used their methods to become chancellors, excellencies and grand masters, aiding the rulers of their times. Their meritorious names are all recorded in the historical annals and there is certainly no reason to speak of them [here]. When it comes to Chi Tz'u and Yüan Hsien, [however,] they were simple commoners living in their villages, reading books and cherishing their independent action and the virtue of the superior man. In their righteousness they did not compromise themselves with their age and therefore their age even laughed at them. For this reason Chi Tz'u and Yüan Hsien spent their whole lives in empty houses with vine-women doors, wearing coarse clothing and eating a bit of unpolished rice. They died already over four hundred years ago

---

[254] *Shih chi pan-chieh* 史記半解 cited from *Shih chi yen-chiu tzu-liao ts'ui-pien* 史記研究資料萃編, Chang Hsin-k'o 張新科 et al., eds. (Sian: San-ch'in, 2001), p. 660.

[255] *Han Fei Tzu, chuan* 19, "Wudu" 五蠹.

yet their disciples remain tireless in recording [their lives] (revised from Watson, 2:409); 韓子曰：「儒以文亂法，而俠以武犯禁。」二者皆譏，而學士多稱於世云。至如以術取宰相卿大夫，輔翼其世主，功名俱著於春秋，固無可言者。及若季次、原憲，閭巷人也，讀書懷獨行君子之德，義不苟合當世，當世亦笑之。故季次、原憲終身空室蓬戶，褐衣疏食不厭。死而已四百餘年，而弟子志之不倦.[256]

Kung-sun Hung is said to have aimed at the world's praise (*Shih chi*, 121.3128). He used his methods to aid his rulers. Tung Chung-shu on the other hand was someone who "read books and cherished his independent action." These two men, Tung Chung-shu and Kung-sun Hung, represent in Ssu-ma Ch'ien's eyes the two types of *ju* that Confucius distinguished in the "Chung-ni ti-tzu lieh-chuan" 仲尼弟子列傳 (*Shih chi*, 67.2203): "The Master said to Tzu-hsia, 'You should be a gentleman ritualist, not a petty ritualist'" 子謂子夏曰:「汝為君子儒, 無為小人儒」 (*Grand Scribe's Records*, 7:75; original in *Lun yü*, 6.13 [Liu Pao-nan, *Lun yü cheng-yi*, 7.10b, *SPPY*]).

[256] *Shih chi*, 124.3181.

Bibliography

Translations
Aoki, *Shiki*, 12:517–36.
Watson, *Han*, 2:355–72.

Studies
Cai, Liang. *Witchcraft and the Rise of the First Confucian Empire*. Albany: SUNY Press, 2014.
Cheng, Anne. "What Did It Mean to Be a "*Ru*" in Han Times?" *Asia Major* 14 (2001): 101–18.
Huang Ch'ing-hsüan 黃慶萱. *Shih chi, Han shu, "Ju-lin lieh-chuan shu-cheng"* 史記，漢書 "儒林列傳"疏證. Taipei: Chia-hsin Shui-ni Kung-ssu Wen-hua Chi-chin-hui, 1966.
van Ess, *Politik*, 1:284–89; II:622–24.
Zufferey, Nicolas. *To the Origins of Confucianism, the* Ru *in pre-Qing Times and during the Early Han Dynasty*. Bern: Peter Lang, 2003.

Frequently Mentioned Commentators

Chang Shou-chieh 張守節 (fl. 725)
Chang Yen 張晏 (fl. 250)
Ch'en Jen-hsi 陳仁錫 (1581-1636)
Ch'en Tzu-lung 陳子龍 (1608-1645)
Cheng Hsüan 鄭玄 (127-200)
Ch'i Shao-nan 齊召南 (1706-1768)
Chia K'uei 賈逵 (30-101)
Chia Shan 賈善
Ch'iao Chou 譙周 (ca. 200-270)
Ch'ien Ta-chao 錢大昭 (1744-1813
Ch'ien Ta-hsin 錢大昕 (1728-1804)
Chin Cho 晉灼 (fl. 275)
Ching Fang 京方 (77-37 BC)
Ch'in Chia-mo 秦嘉謨 (*fl.* 1814)
Chou Shou-ch'ang 周壽昌 (1814-1884)
Chung Wen-cheng 鐘文烝 (1818-1877)
Fang Pao 方苞 (1668-1749)
Fu Ch'ien 服虔 (fl. 188)
Fu Yen 伏儼 (end of the later Han)
Ho Cho 何焯 (1661-1722)
Hsü Fu-yüan 徐孚遠 (1599-1665)
Hsü Kuang 徐廣 (352-425)
Hsü Shen 許慎 (ca. 58-147)
Hu An-kuo 胡安國 (1074-1138)
Hu Kuang 胡廣 (91-172)
Hung Liang-chi 洪亮吉 (1746-1809)
Ju Ch'un 如淳 (fl. 230)
Kao Shih-ch'i 高士奇 (1645-1703)
Kao Yu 高誘 (fl. 205-212)
Ku Chieh-kang 顧頡剛 (1893-1980)
Ku Tung-kao 顧棟高 (1679-1759)
Ku Yen-wu 顧炎武 (1613-1682)

Kuei Yu-kuang 歸有光 (1506-1571)
K'ung An-kuo 孔安國 (ca. 156-ca. 74 B.C.)
Kuo P'u 郭璞 (276-324)
Lei Hsüeh-ch'i 雷學淇 (fl. 1814)
Li Ch'i 李奇 (fl. ca. 200)
Li Hsien 李賢 (654-684)
Li Li 李笠 (1894-1962)
Li Shan 李善 (d. 689)
Li Tz'u-ming 李慈銘 (1830-1894)
Liang Yü-sheng 梁玉繩 (1745-1819)
Ling Chih-lung 凌稚隆 (fl. 1576-1587)
Liu Feng-shih 劉奉世 (1041-1113)
Liu Wen-ch'i 劉文淇 (1789-1854)
Lo Pi 羅泌 (fl. 1165)
Meng K'ang 孟康 (ca. 180-260)
Nakai Sekitoku 中井積德 (1732-1817)
P'ei Yin 裴駰 (fl. 438)
Shen Chia-pen 沈家本 (1840-1913)
Shen Ch'in-han 沈欽韓 (1775-1832)
Shih Chih-mien 施之勉 (1891-1990)
Ssu-ma Chen 司馬貞 (fl. 745)
Ssu-ma Piao 司馬彪 (243-306)
Sun Yi-jang 孫詒讓 (1848-1908)
Tsou Tan-sheng 鄒誕生 (fl. 479)
Ts'ui Hao 崔浩 (d. 450)
Ts'ui Shih 崔適 (1852-1932)
Ts'ui Shu 崔述 (1740-1816)
Tu Yü 杜預 (222-284)
Wang Chung 汪中 (1745-1794)
Wang Hsien-ch'ien 王先謙 (1842-1918)
Wang Nien-sun 王念孫 (1744-1832)
Wang Su 王肅 (195-256)
Wang Wei-chen 王維楨 (1507-1556)
Wang Yi 王逸 (ca. 89-158)
Wei Chao 韋昭 (204-273)
Wen Ying 文穎 (fl. 196-200)
Wu Chien-ssu 吳見思 (*fl.* 1680-90)
Wu Ju-lun 吳汝綸 (1840-1903)
Yang Po-chün 楊伯峻 (1909-1992)
Yao Tsu-en 姚祖恩 (fl. 1784)

Yen Shih-ku 顏師古 (581-645)
Ying Shao 應劭 (ca. 140-203/204)
Yü Fan 虞翻 (164-233)
Yü Yüeh 俞樾 (1821-1907)
Yüeh Ch'an 樂產 (8th c. or earlier)

Selected Recent Works on the *Shih chi*

An P'ing-ch'iu 安平秋 et al., ed., *Shih chi lun–ts'ung: Ch'u-Han jen-wu yen-chiu hsüeh-shu t'ao-lun-hui chi Chung-kuo Shih chi Yen-chiu-hui ti-ch'i-chieh nien-hui lun-wen* 史記論叢：楚漢人物研究學術研討會暨中國史記研究會第七屆年會論文. Lanchow: Kan-su Jen-min Ch'u-pan-she, 2008.

Brooks, E. Bruce. "Dual Authorship in Shǐ Jì 63," *Warring States Papers* 1 (2010): 164-7.

Chang Hsin-k'o 張新科. *Shih chi hsüeh kai-lun* 史記學概論. Peking: Shang-wu Yin-shu-kuan, 2003.

___, Kao Yi-jung 高一榮, and Kao Yi-nung 高一農, eds. *Shih chi yen-chiu tzu-liao cui-pien* 史記研究資料萃編. 2v. Xian: San Ch'in Ch'u-pan-she, 2011.

Chao Sheng-chün 趙生群, ed. *Shih chi* 史記. 10v. Peking: Chung-hua Shu-chü, 2013.

Chin, Tamara. "Defamiliarizing the Foreigner," *HJAS* 70 (2010): 311-54.

Ch'ü Ying-chieh 曲英杰. *Shih chi tu-ch'eng k'ao* 史記都城考. Peking: Shang-wu Yin-shu-kuan, 2007.

Fujita Katsuhisa 藤田勝久. *Shih chi Chan-kuo shih-liao yen-chiu* 史記戰國史料研究. Ts'ao Feng 曹峰 and Hirose Kunio 廣瀨薫雄, translators. Shanghai: Ku-chi Ch'u-pan-she, 2008.

____. *Shiki Shin Kan shi no kenkyū* 史記秦漢史の研究. Tokyo: Kyoko Shoin, 2015.

Galer, Scott W. "Toward Better *Shiji* Reading: Two Scholars' Efforts to Elucidate the Text," *CLEAR* 30 (2008): 31-42.

Han Chao-ch'i 韓兆琦. *Shih chi chiang tso* 史記講座. Kweilin: Kuang-hsi Shih-fan Ta-hsüeh Ch'u-pan-she, 2008.

Han Chao-ch'i 韓兆琦 and Chen Chin-hsia 陳金霞. "Ssu-ma Ch'ien tui Huang-lao ssu-hsiang te chieh-shou yü fa-chan" 司馬遷對黃老思想的接受與發展, *Pei-ching Shih-fan Ta-hsüeh hsüeh-pao* 北京師範大學學報, 214.4 (2009): 27-35.

Klein, Esther Sunkyung. "The History of a Historian: Perspectives on the Authorial Roles of Sima Qian." Unpublished Ph. D. dissertation, Princeton University, 2010.

Knechtges, David R. "'Key Words,' Authorial Intent, and Interpretation: Sima Qian's Letter to Ren An," *CLEAR* 30 (2008): 75-84.

Kroll, Juri L. "*Shih chi, Han shu* and the Han Culture," *Archiv Orientalni* 74 (2006), 299-348.

Li Fu-lun 李鍑倫. Review of *Grand Scribe's Records*, v. 8. *Han-hsüeh yen-chiu t'ung-hsün* 漢學研究通訊, 28.3 (August 2009): 57-58.

Lin Fu-shih 林富士. *Han-tai te wu-che* 漢代的巫者. Second edition, Pan-ch'iao 板橋, Taiwan: Tao-hsien 稻鄉 Ch'u-pan-she, 2004 [1988].

Liu Ning 劉寧. *Shih chi hsü-shih-hsüeh yen-chiu* 史記敍事學研究. Peking: Chung-kuo She-hui K'o-hsüeh Ch'u-pan-she, 2008.

Lü Shih-hao 呂世浩. "Ts'ung *Shih chi* tao Han shu: chuan-che kuo-ch'eng yü li-shih yi-yi" 從史記到漢書: 轉折過程與歷史意義. Unpublished Ph. D. dissertation, National Taiwan University, 2008.

Lü Tsu-ch'ien 呂祖謙 (1137-1181). *Shih chi hsiang chieh* 史記詳節. Chou T'ien-yu 周天游 and Wan Yen Chao-yüan 完顏紹元, eds. Shanghai: Ku-chi Ch'u-pan-she, 2007.

Ni Hao-shih 倪豪士 (William H. Nienhauser, Jr.). "Shih-kung ho shih-shih—lun *Shih chi* tui Wu-ti shih-cheng te wei-ch'ü p'i-p'ing" 史公和時勢—論史記對武帝時政的委曲批評, *Pei-ching Ta-hsüeh hsüeh-pao* 北京大學學報 *(Che-hsüeh she-hui k'o-hsüeh pan* 哲學社會科學版*)*, 45.4 (July 2008): 111-119.

Nienhauser, William H., Jr. "For Want of a Hand: A Note on the 'Hereditary House of the Jin' and Sima Qian's '*Chunqiu*,'" *Journal of the American Oriental Society* 127.3: 229-48.

___. "Qing Feng, Duke Xian of Wey and the *Shijing* in the Sixth Century B.C.; Some Preliminary Remarks on the *Shi* in the *Zuo zhuan*," forthcoming in *OE* 50 (2012): 75-98.

"Sima Qian and the *Shiji*," *Oxford History of Historical Writing, Volume I: Beginnings to AD 600*. Grant Hardy and Andrew Feldherr, eds. Oxford: Oxford University Press, pp. 463-484.

"Takigawa Kametarō and His Contributions to the Study of the *Shiji*," forthcoming in *Han-dynasty History* to be published by Harrassowitz, Olga Lomova and Hans van Ess, eds.

Schaab-Hanke, Dorothee. "Der Fall Ziying: Ein Beispiel für Ban Gus Kritik am *Shiji* und ihr ideologischer Hintergrund," *OE* 46 (2007): 101-16.

___. "Schreiber (*shi* 史) als Autoritäten in der Rezeption des *Shiji*," *ZDMG* 157.1 (2007): 169-96; 157.2 (2007): 427-56

Takamura Takeyuki 高村武幸. *Kandai no chiho kanri to chiiki shakai* 漢代の地方官史と地域社會. Tokyo: Kyuko Shogen 汲古書院, 2008.

van Ess, Hans. "Cosmological Speculations and the Notions of the Power of Heaven and the Cyclical Movements of History in the Historiography of the *Shiji*," in *BMFEA* 78 (2007): 79-107.

___. "The Ethos of the Envoy and his Treatment by the Enemy in Han History," *Crossroads* 5 (2012): 27-43.

___. "Einige Anmerkungen zur Biographie des Konfuzius im *Shih-chi* und vergleichbaren Stellen im K'ung-tzu chia-yü," *OE* 50 (2011): 157-180.

___. "Emperor Wu of the Han and the First August Emperor of Qin in Sima Qian's *Shiji*," in Yuri Pines et al., eds., *Birth of an Empire. The State of Qin Revisited*. Berkeley: University of California Press, 2013, pp. 238-258.

___, Olga Lomová, and Dorothee Schaab-Hanke, eds. *Views from Within, Views from Beyond: Approaches to the Shiji as an Early Work of Historiography*. Wiesbaden: Harrassowitz, 2015.

Wang, John C. Y. "English Translations of the Shiji: A Preliminary Study," in Tao Tao Liu et al., eds. *Style, Wit and Word-Play: Essays in Translation Studies in Memory of David Hawkes*. Newcastle upon Tyne: Cambridge Scholars, 2012, pp. 173-186.

Wu Ch'ing-feng 吳慶峰. *Shih chi hsü-tz'u t'ung-shih* 史記虛詞通釋. Tsinan: Ch'i Lu Shu-she, 2006.

Wu Fei 吳飛. "Tzu-hsia tso-wei Chung-kuo wen-t'i: 'li-chieh tzu-hsia' cha-chi chih san" 自殺作為中國問題: 理解自殺札記之三, *Tu-shu* 讀書, 2005.9: 87-94.

Yang Chao-ming 楊朝明. "*Shih chi* 'Chou pen-chi' chien yü Chou Hsien-wang shih-hsi te chi-shu" 史記周本紀間於周先王世系的記述, *Wen shih* 84 (2008.3): 239-44.

Yang Shu-tseng 楊樹增. *Shih chi yi-shu yen-chiu* 史記藝術研究. 2nd printing, Peking: Hsüeh-yüan Ch'u-pan-she, 2006 (2004).

Yang Yen-ch'i 楊燕起, Ch'en K'o-ch'ing 陳可青, and Lai Chang-yang 賴長揚, eds. *Shih chi yen-chiu chi-ch'eng* 史記研究集成. 14v. Peking: Hua-wen Ch'u-pan-she, 2005.

Yates, Robin. "Soldiers, Scribes, and Women: Literacy among the Lower Orders in Early China," in *Writing and Literacy in Early China*, Li Feng and David Prager Branner, eds. Seattle: University of Washington Press, 2011, pp. 339-69.

Ying San-yü 應三玉. *Shih chi San-chia chu yen-chiu* 史記三家注研究. Nanking: Feng-huang 鳳凰 Ch'u-pan-she, 2008.

Index

CPSIA information can be obtained
at www.ICGtesting.com
Printed in the USA
BVHW030857030320
573941BV00005B/34